DORDOGNE
BERRY
LIMOUSIN

S. Sauvignier/MICHELIN

Executive Editorial Director	David Brabis
Chief Editor	Cynthia Clayton Ochterbeck

THE GREEN GUIDE DORDOGNE BERRY LIMOUSIN

Editor	Gwen Cannon
Principal Writers	Helen Isaacs and Jeremy Kerrison
Production Coordinator	Allison Michelle Simpson
Cartography	Alain Baldet, Michèle Cana, Peter Wrenn
Photo Editor	Brigitta L. House
Proofreader	Anne Marie Scott
Layout	Allison Michelle Simpson, Nicole D. Jordan, Susan Young
Cover Design	Laurent Muller
Interior Design	Agence Rampazzo
Production	Pierre Ballochard, Renaud Leblanc

Contact Us :

The Green Guide
Michelin Travel Publications
One Parkway South
Greenville, SC 29615
USA
☎ 1-800-423-0485
www.michelintravel.com
michelin.guides@us.michelin.com

Hannay House, 39 Clarendon Road
Watford, Herts WD17 1JA, UK
☎ 01923 205 240 - Fax 01923 205 241
www.ViaMichelin.com
TheGreenGuide-uk@uk.michelin.com

Special Sales :

For information regarding bulk sales, customized editions and premium sales, please contact our Customer Service Departments:

USA	1-800-423-0485
UK	(01923) 205 240
Canada	1-800-361-8236

Note to the reader

One Team...
A Commitment to Quality

There's just one reason our team is dedicated to producing quality travel publications—you, our reader. We want you to get the maximum benefit from your trip—and from your money. In today's multiple-choice world of travel, the options are many, perhaps overwhelming.

In our guidebooks, we try to minimize the guesswork involved with travel. We scout out the attractions, prioritize them with star ratings, and describe what you'll discover when you visit them.

To help you orient yourself, we provide colorful and detailed, but easy-to-follow maps. Floor plans of some of the major museums help you plan your tour.

Throughout the guides, we offer practical information, touring tips and suggestions for finding the best views, good places for a break and interesting shops.

Lodging and dining are always a big part of travel, so we compile a selection of hotels and restaurants that we think convey the feel of the destination, and organize them by geographic area and price. We also highlight shopping, recreational and entertainment venues, especially the popular spots.

If you're short on time, driving tours are included so you can hit the highlights and quickly absorb the best of the region.

For those who love to experience a destination on foot, we add walking tours, often with a map. And we list other companies who offer boat, bus or guided walking tours of the city, some with culinary, historical or other themes.

In short, we test and retest, check and recheck to make sure that our guidebooks are truly just that: a personalized guide to help you make the most of your visit. After all, we want you to enjoy traveling as much as we do.

The Michelin Green Guide Team
michelin.guides@us.michelin.com

PLANNING YOUR TRIP

INTRODUCTION TO THE REGION

SYMBOLS

⊘	**Tips to help improve your experience**
⊘	**Details to consider**
⊙⊙	**Entry fees**
⊶	**Walking tours**
⊶	**Closed to the public**
⊙	**Hours of operation**
⊙	**Periods of closure**
⊳	**See also, Time permitting**

CONTENTS

DISCOVERING THE REGION

How to Use this Guide

Orientation

To help you grasp the "lay of the land" quickly and easily, so you'll feel confident and comfortable finding your way around, we offer the following tools in this guide:

- Detailed table of contents for an overview of what'll you find in the guide, and how it is organized.
- Map of Principal Sights showing the starred places of interest at a glance.
- Detailed maps of city centres, regions and towns.
- Floor and site plans of museums and cathedrals.
- Principal Sights ordered alphabetically for easy reference.

Practicalities

At the front of the guide, you'll see a section called "Planning Your Trip" that contains information about planning your trip, the best time to go, getting there and getting around, basic facts, tips for making the most of your visit, and more. You'll find themed tours and suggestions for outdoor fun. There's also a calendar of popular annual events in the region. Information on shopping, sightseeing, kids' activities, and sports and recreational opportunities is included as well.

LODGINGS

We've made a selection of hotels and arranged them within the cities, categorized by price to fit all budgets *(see the Legend at the back of the guide for an explanation of price ranges)*. For the most part, we selected accommodations based on their unique regional character. So, unless the individual hotel embodies local ambience, it's rare that we include chain properties, which typically have their own imprint. If you want a more comprehensive selection of lodgings in Dordogne Berry Limosin, see the red-cover *Michelin Guide France*.

RESTAURANTS

We thought you'd like to know popular eating spots in the cities and towns described in this guide. So we selected restaurants that capture the flavour of the region. Many of them feature regional specialties, though we're not rating the quality of the food per se. As we did with the hotels, we organized the restaurants within the Principal Sights and categorized them by price to appeal to all wallets *(see the Legend at the back of the guide for an explanation of price ranges)*. If you want a more comprehensive selection of eateries in the region, see the red-cover *Michelin Guide France*.

Attractions

Contact information, admission charges and hours of operation are given for the majority of attractions. Unless otherwise noted, admission prices shown are for a single adult only. Discounts for seniors, students, military personnel, etc. may be available; be sure to ask. If no admission charge is shown, entrance to the attraction is free.

Within each Principal Sight, attractions within a town or city are described first, sometimes in the form of a walking tour. Then come the outlying sights and Excursions. If you are pressed for time, we recommend you visit the three-and two-star sights first—the stars are your guide.

STAR RATINGS

Michelin has used stars as a rating tool for more than 100 years:

★★★	Highly recommended
★★	Recommended
★	Interesting

SYMBOLS IN THE TEXT

Besides the stars, other symbols in the text indicate tourist information ⓘ; wheelchair access ♿; camping facilities ⚠; on-site parking 🅿; sights of interest to children Kids; and hiking trails 🚶.

See the box appearing on the Contents page for other symbols used in the text.

See the Maps explanation below for symbols appearing on the maps.

Throughout the guide you will find peach-colored text boxes or sidebars containing anecdotal or background information. Green-colored boxes contain information to help you save time or money.

Maps

Unless otherwise indicated by a directional arrow, all maps in this guide are oriented north.

See the map Legend at the back of the guide for an explanation of map symbols.

A complete list of the maps found in the guide appears at the back of this book.

Addresses, phone numbers, opening hours and prices published in this guide are accurate at press time. We welcome corrections and suggestions that may assist us in preparing the next edition. Please send your comments to:

Michelin Travel Publications
Editorial Department
P.O. Box 19001
Greenville, SC   29602-9001
Email: michelin.guides@us.michelin.com
Web site: www.michelintravel.com

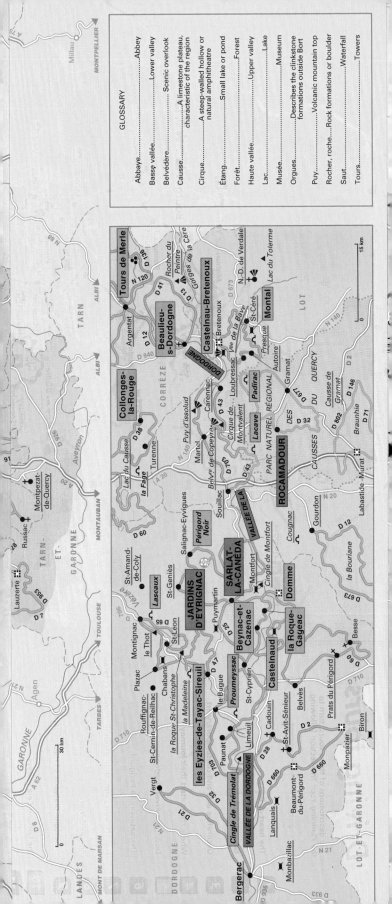

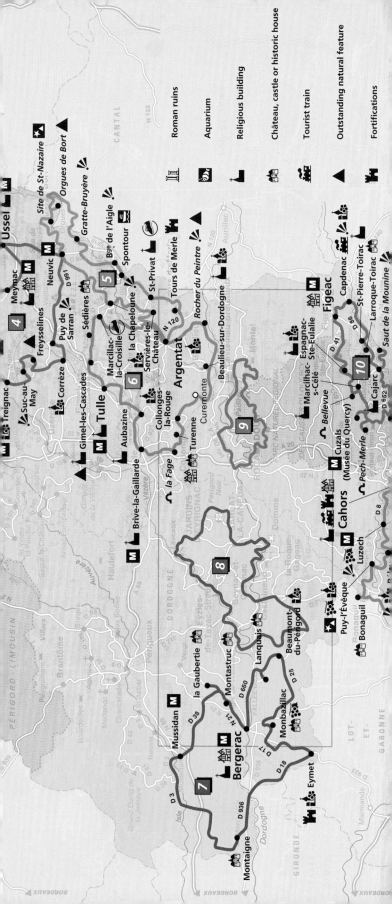

Roman ruins

Aquarium

Religious building

Château, castle or historic house

Tourist train

Outstanding natural feature

Fortifications

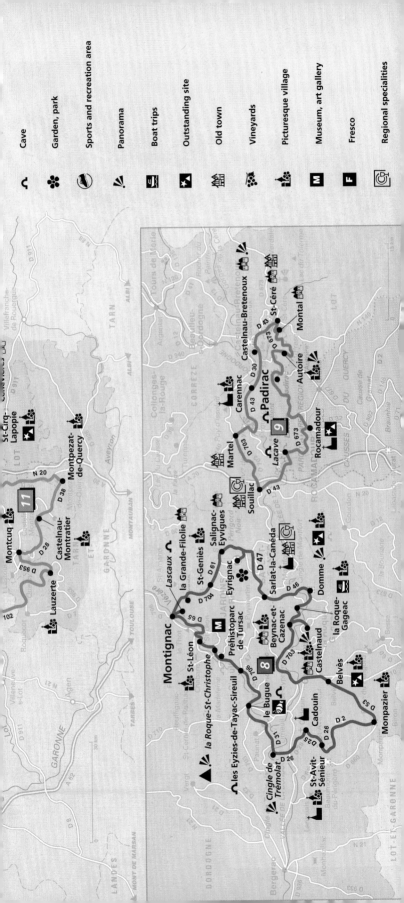

Cave

Garden, park

Sports and recreation area

Panorama

Boat trips

Outstanding site

Old town

Vineyards

Picturesque village

Museum, art gallery

Fresco

Regional specialities

Canoeing on the River Lot

S. Sauvignier/MICHELIN

WHEN AND WHERE TO GO

Driving Tours

The following is a brief description of each of the driving tours shown on the map on page 12.

☐ THE HEART OF BERRY

235km/146mi starting from Bourges

If you like variety, this itinerary is made for you. From Bourges and its magnificent cathedral drive to Mehun-sur-Yèvre at the heart of porcelain country, then on to Reuilly, Quincy and, further on, to Châteaumeillant, where local wines will delight wine-lovers. Stop to contemplate the medieval gardens at Notre-Dame d'Orsan, then continue to the feudal castle of Culan. The Renaissance château of Ainay-le-Vieil is less austere, as are the richly decorated Château de Meillant and the elegant Château de Jussy-Champagne. Also on the tour: the vast and inspiring Noirlac Abbey and the more humble but very interesting abbey church of Plaimpied.

☐ GEORGE SAND COUNTRY

210km/130mi starting from La Châtre

Journey through the landscapes which inspired George Sand's novels from the Vallée Noire to the Creuse Valley, from Nohant Château to Gargilesse, from the Crozant ruins to La Motte-Feuilly.

☐ DECORATIVE ARTS AND CONTEMPORARY ART

250km/155mi starting from Limoges

This itinerary offers an insight into the artistic wealth and variety of the Limousin region. The Creuse Valley inspired two Impressionist painters, Claude Monet and Armand Guillaumin (some of their works are on display in Limoges and Guéret). The other fine arts and crafts to see on this tour include: the famous Aubusson tapestries, woodcarving (stalls in Moutier-d'Ahun) and stone carving (in the village of Masgot), contemporary art on the island of Vassivière and, of course, Limoges porcelain and enamel work.

☐ WHERE RIVERS START THEIR JOURNEY

230km/143mi starting from Ussel

Several rivers start their journey in the Limousin mountains. From Ussel, it is only a short way up the Monédières massif (splendid panorama from the Suc-au-May viewpoint); then up again onto the Plateau de Millevaches, the rooftop of Limousin. Rugged winters and plenty of rain have turned it into a reservoir feeding the many rivers that run from it, including the Creuse, the Vézère and the Corrèze. The pastoral Site du Rat, the remote Tourbière du Longéroux and the enigmatic Site des Cars are ideal for rambling. A stroll through the old town of Meymac will offer a welcome contrast.

☐ DOWN THE RIVER DORDOGNE

210km/130mi starting from Argentat

In bygone days, traditional gabares were moored along the River Dordogne. Today, you can take a trip aboard one of these boats, once intended for cargo, from Pont-de-Chambon or Spontour. Dams (Chastang and l'Aigle) bar the Dordogne below the spectacular Orgues de Bort and the route is dotted with viewpoints.

☐ THE GATEWAY TO PÉRIGORD

195km/121mi starting from Brive-la-Gaillarde

Brive and its foie gras market, Aubazine and its monastery, Tulle and its lace, Gimel and its waterfalls, Sédières and its castle and the leisure park in Marcillac…and that is just the beginning of the region the French know as Périgord! Follow the Gorges de la Cère then drive on to Beaulieu-sur-Dordogne and admire the proud outline of Curemonte castles before reaching the red-sandstone village of Collonges-la-Rouge and the nearby Château de Turenne.

☐ FORESTS, VINEYARDS AND BASTIDES AROUND BERGERAC

230km/143mi starting from Bergerac

Montaigne and his legendary wisdom, Cyrano de Bergerac and his sharp wit form the historic background of this itinerary, which meanders through picturesque vineyards producing wines with enchanting names like Pécharmant, Rosette, Montravel and above all Monbazillac (the cellars are open to visitors). Picturesque castles can be seen along the way and the itinerary goes through the former bastide (fortified town) of Beaumont-du-Périgord.

8 PÉRIGORD NOIR

185km/115mi starting from Montignac
The Vézère and Dordogne valleys have revealed 30 000 years of mankind's history… Drive from Lascaux to Le Bugue via Les Eyzies, the European capital of prehistory. Continue your journey forward into medieval times from Monpazier to Domme: fortresses, bastides and abbeys tell the terrible story of the Hundred Years War. Leave the Dordogne Valley to reach the heart of Périgord Noir in Sarlat-la-Canéda which has retained the charm of a fine Renaissance city and upholds the region's gastronomic traditions (foie gras and Bergerac wines).

9 LIMESTONE PLATEAUX OF HAUT-QUERCY

125km/78mi starting from Padirac
This amazing journey starts more than 100m/110yd underground, inside the fascinating Gouffre de Padirac; next comes the extraordinary site of Rocamadour with its sheer cliff crowned by ramparts. The route then leads you to the borders of Périgord Noir, through the towns of Souillac and Martel, along the Dordogne Valley hemmed in by high cliffs and on to St-Céré among green hills overlooked by the castles of Castelnau and Montal.

10 THE LOT AND CÉLÉ VALLEYS

120km/75mi starting from Figeac
The two rivers have carved their way through the limestone plateau between St-Cirq-Lapopie and Figeac, meandering across a varied and picturesque landscape of sheer cliffs alternating with undulating meadows. Of particular interest are the Pech-Merle cave, the hilltop village of St-Cirq-Lapopie, the castles of Cénevières and Laroque-Toirac and the churches of St-Pierre-Toirac and Marcilhac.

11 THE LOT VINEYARDS AND QUERCY BLANC

185km/115mi starting from Cahors

The wide and imposing River Lot meanders through the Cahors vineyards, lined with picturesque towns and villages such as Luzech, Belaye (perched on top of a cliff) and Puy-l'Évêque, leading you straight to Bonaguil, an amazing fortress standing on the border of Périgord and Quercy. Beyond the Lot Valley and its vineyards lies an area known as Quercy Blanc dotted with bastides and windmills, with a definite southern flavour.

Themed Tours

Travel itineraries on specific themes have been mapped out to help you discover the regional architecture and the traditions that make up the cultural heritage of the region. As you drive through the region, you are likely to see signs posted for the following routes: walk into the nearest tourist office or make a detour and follow along!

Jacass/MICHELIN

Vineyards of Sancerre

PREHISTORY, HISTORY

Prehistoric Périgord-Quercy

Below is a list of the main prehistoric caves of the Périgord and Quercy areas mentioned in this guide; they all contain paintings or engravings:

Bara-Bahau (Périgord), **Bernifal** (Périgord), **Combarelles** (Périgord), **Cougnac** (Quercy), **Font-de-Gaume** (Périgord), **Lascaux II** (Périgord), **Pech-Merle** (Quercy), **Rouffignac** (Périgord) and **St-Cirq** (Périgord).

Historic Routes

Routes historiques are signposted local itineraries following an architectural and historical theme, accompanied by an explanatory booklet, available from local tourist offices.

- **Berry** – *La route des Dames de Touraine, la route François I, la route Jacques Cœur.*

- **Limousin** – *La route des Plantagenêts, la route Richard Cœur de Lion, la route de St-Jacques.*

- **Dordogne** – *La route des mille et un châteaux en Périgord, la route des Marches du Quercy.*

TRADITIONS AND CULTURAL HERITAGE

These thematic routes have been created by regional associations; contact the local tourist offices for details and maps.

Berry

- **Chemin des Lavoirs dans le Cher** – 15 waterside wash-houses to discover in the Germigny Valley, maintained by the association Nos villages en Berry.

- **Ronde des Champs d'Amour** – fields of love in the Champagne Berrichonne region around Issoudun.

- **Route des vignobles du Cœur de France** – a tour of the vineyards of the Berry region, Quincy, Reuilly, Menetou-Salon, Sancerre, Coteaux du Giennois and Châteaumeillant, producing fine AOC wines; information on www.vins-centre-loire.com.

- **Route de la porcelaine** – factories, museums, workshops and shops devoted to porcelain between Vierzon and St-Amand-Montrond.

- **Vallée des peintres** – in the footsteps of Guillaumin, Monet and other artists along the Creuse Valley from Argenton to Glénic.

Limousin

- **Circuit du Châtaignier** – a day trip in chestnut country, where the crafting of hoop-wood strips for barrel-making is traditional.

- **Parcs et jardins du Limousin** – the tour includes over 30 parks and gardens selected by the association Découverte du Patrimoine Paysager et Botanique.

Dordogne

- **Sentiers romans en Quercy Blanc** – Romanesque churches in the Quercy Blanc area.

- **Route des métiers d'art en Périgord** – the itinerary includes 60 workshops of traditional craftsmen; www.cm-perigueux.fr.

- **Route des metiers d'art dans le Lot** – 45 workshops of traditional craftsmen; www.rm-art46.org.

- **Vallée de la Dordogne** – 8 short itineraries from Souillac across the Périgord Noir and Quercy areas; www.tourisme-souillac.com.

- **Route des vins** – discovering local wines in the Bergerac area; www.vins-bergerac.com.

WINE TOURS

See the chapter Food and Wine in the Introduction.

COOKERY COURSES

If your favourite recreation takes place with pots and pans for equipment, why not spend 2 or 3 days in a French kitchen for a holiday? In Dordogne, the season for preparing foie gras is generally from October to mid-December and from mid-January to April. A number of farmhouse-inns offer sessions which include lessons on preparing foie gras, confits, cou farci and other delights, as well as lodging and board. Generally, you must buy your own duck or goose.

For information, contact:

- **Loisirs-Accueil Corrèze** – *Quai Aristide Briand, 19000 Tulle,* ☎ *05 55 29 98 70. From 320€ per person on full board.*

- **Loisirs-Accueil Dordogne** – *25 rue du Président-Wilson, BP 2063, 24002 Périgueux,* ☎ *05 53 35 50 24 or 05 53 35 50 00.*

- **Loisirs-Accueil Lot** – *Place François-Mitterrand, 46000 Cahors,* ☎ *05 65 53 20 90; www.reservation-lot.com.*

Two family-run operations, specialising in goose and duck, respectively, are more than learning experiences, but take the visitor right into the heart of local matters. Excellent cooking and facilities and a warm welcome await at:

🍲 **Ferme du fort de la Rhonie**
– Coustaty Family, Boyer, 24220 Meyrals, ☎ 05 53 29 29 07.

🍲 **La Maurinie** *– Alard Family, Eyliac, 24330 St-Pierre-de-Chignac, ☎ 05 53 07 57 18.*

Sessions open when enough participants have enrolled. You are also welcome to stay and eat as a regular guest, without cooking, and just enjoy the food, the company, and life on the farm.

When to Go

CLIMATE

This inland region is open to oceanic influences from the Atlantic. The climate on the whole is mild, winter frosts are limited, spring is early and warm and summer is hot. Rainfall is evenly distributed throughout the year. In Berry, however, several micro-climates make for small, distinct weather systems within the region. For example, the Champagne Berrichonne, with its vast fields of grain crops, is often dry and gets very hot in the summer, while the humidity keeps things cooler in the Boischaut, the Brenne wetlands and the high forests of the Motte d'Humbligny. The climate in Limousin is also variable, in particular with regard to altitude. The prevailing south-west winds blow hard against the foothills of the Massif Central mountain range, provoking significant rainfall (1 200-1 700mm/ 47-67in per year) – although summer droughts are not unusual. Winter on the high plateaux (Millevaches, Gentioux, Monédières, Combraille) is long and harsh, with low temperatures and chill,

stiff winds. Elsewhere in the region, winters are milder, with less rain, but crops are often damaged by freezing temperatures in the spring and fall.

The Dordogne is more clement on the whole, beginning with the Brive basin. While the climate is nearly Mediterranean, there is enough water to keep the landscape green and crops prosperous throughout the summer. A blanket of flowers soon covers the countryside, as the region quickly warms to the new season.

SEASONS

The **summer** holidays bring many tourists to enjoy the delights of the beautiful natural settings, towns and monuments and the many festivals and activities organised for visitors.

In Dordogne in the summer, rain often falls in torrential storms, in the wake of a hot wind blowing steadily from the west. In the **winter**, snow is infrequent; frosty nights and foggy mornings come with the spring.

Autumn is quieter and a lovely time to appreciate the flowering heather, the browns and golds of the changing leaves, the colourful markets with an abundance of harvest produce, or the delights of wild mushrooms served with game from the forest.

WHAT TO PACK

As little as possible! Cleaning and laundry services are available everywhere. Most personal items can be replaced at reasonable cost. Try to pack everything into one suitcase and a tote bag. Porter help may be in short supply, and new purchases will add to the original weight. Take an extra tote bag for packing new purchases, shopping at the open-air market, carrying a picnic etc. Be sure luggage is clearly labelled and old travel tags removed. Do not pack medication in checked luggage, but keep it with you.

KNOW BEFORE YOU GO

Useful Web Sites

www.ambafrance-us.org

The French Embassy in the USA has a Web site providing basic information (geography, demographics, history), a news digest and business-related information. It offers special pages for children, and pages devoted to culture, language study and travel, and you can reach other selected French sites (regions, cities, ministries) with a hypertext link.

www.franceguide.com

The French Government Tourist Office / Maison de la France site is packed with practical information and tips for those travelling to France. The home page has a number of links to more specific guidance, for American or Canadian travellers for example, or to the FGTO's London pages.

www.FranceKeys.com

This sight has plenty of practical information for visiting France. It covers all the regions, with links to tourist offices and related sites. Very useful for planning the details of your tour in France!

www.fr-holidaystore.co.uk

The French Travel Centre in London has gone on-line with this service, providing information on all of the regions of France, including updated special travel offers and details on available accommodation.

www.visiteurope.com

The European Travel Commission provides useful information on travelling to and around 27 European countries, and includes links to some commercial booking services (ie vehicle hire), rail schedules, weather reports and more.

Tourist Offices

FRENCH TOURIST OFFICES ABROAD

For information, brochures, maps and assistance in planning a trip to France travellers should apply to the official French Tourist Office or Maison de France in their own country:

Australia – New Zealand

Sydney – Level 13, 25 Bligh St, Sydney, New South Wales 2000

☎ (02) 9231 5244;
Fax (02) 9221 8682;
info@au.franceguide.com

Canada

Montreal – 1981 Avenue McGill College, Suite 490, Montreal PQ H3A 2W9
☎ (514) 288-2026; Fax (514) 845 4868; canada@franceguide.com

Toronto – 30 St Patrick's Street, Suite 700, Toronto, Ontario
☎ (416) 979 7587.

Ireland

Dublin – 10 Suffolk Street, Dublin 2
☎ (01) 679 0813 or 1560 235 235 (€0.95/minute); Fax (01) 679 0814; info.ie@franceguide.com

South Africa

P.O. Box 41022, Craig Hall 2024,
☎ (011) 880 8062;
mdfsa@frenchdoor.ca.za

United Kingdom

London Maison de France – 178 Piccadilly, London WIJ 9AL
☎ (09068) 244 123 (60p/minute);
Fax 020 793 6594;
info.uk@franceguide.com

United States

East Coast – New York – 444 Madison Avenue, 16th Floor, NY 10022-6903,
☎ (514) 288-1904;
Fax (212) 838-7855;
info.us@franceguide.com

West Coast – Los Angeles – 9454 Wilshire Boulevard, Suite 715, Beverly Hills, CA 90212-2967.
☎ (514) 288-1904;
Fax (310) 276-2835;
info.losangeles@franceguide.com

Information can also be requested from:
France on Call ☎ (202) 659-7779.

LOCAL TOURIST OFFICES

Visitors may also contact local tourist offices for more precise information, to receive brochures and maps. The addresses and telephone numbers of tourist offices in the larger towns are listed after the symbol 🛈, in the *Discovering the Region* section of the guide. Opposite, the addresses are given for local tourist offices of the départements and régions covered in this guide.

Four regional tourist offices are concerned with the area covered by this guide; address inquiries to the Comité Régional de Tourisme (C.R.T.):

Aquitaine: Cité Mondiale, 23 parvis des Chartrons, 33074 Bordeaux Cedex, ☎ 05 56 01 70 00; www.tourisme-aquitaine.info

Limousin: 27 boulevard de la Corderie, 87031 Limoges Cedex, ☎ 05 55 45 18 80; www.tourismelimousin.com

Midi-Pyrénées: 54 boulevard de l'Embouchure, 31022 Toulouse Cedex, ☎ 05 61 13 55 55; www.tourisme-midi-pyrenees.org

Centre-Val de Loire: 37 avenue de Paris, 45000 Orléans, ☎ 02 38 79 95 00; www.visaloire.com

For each département within the region, address inquiries to the Comité Départemental de Tourisme (C.D.T.), unless otherwise stated:

Dordogne

25 rue du Président-Wilson, BP 2063 24002 Périgueux ☎ 05 53 35 50 24 www.perigord.tm.fr/tourisme/cdt

Cher

Maison Départementale du Tourisme 5 rue de Séraucourt, 18000 Bourges ☎ 02 48 48 00 10 www.berrylecher.com

Haute-Vienne

Maison du Tourisme 4 place Denis-Dussoubs, 87031 Limoges ☎ 05 55 79 04 04 www.tourisme-hautevienne.com

Corrèze

Maison du Tourisme 45, quai Aristide Briand, 19000 Tulle ☎ 05 55 29 98 78 www.vacances-en-correze.net

Indre

1 rue Saint-Martin BP 141, 36003 Châteauroux Cedex ☎ 02 54 07 36 36 www.berrylindre.com

Creuse

43 place Bonnyaud 23005 Guéret ☎ 05 55 51 93 23 www.tourisme-creuse.com

Lot

107 quai Eugène-Cavaignac, BP 7 46001 Cahors Cedex 9

☎ 05 65 35 07 09 www.tourisme-lot.com

Tarn-et-Garonne

7 boulevard Midi-Pyrénées, BP 534 82005 Montauban Cedex ☎ 05 63 21 79 09 www.tourisme82.com

Maisons de Pays – These regional promotion centres provide a whole range of information including special events, mapped-out tours of the area and places to stay.

Maison Aquitaine: 21 rue des Pyramides, 75001 Paris, ☎ 01 55 35 31 42; www.maison-aquitaine.fr.

Maison du Limousin: 30 rue Caumartin, 75009 Paris, ☎ 01 40 07 04 67; www.maisonsregionales.com/limousin.htm.

Nine towns and areas, labelled **Villes et Pays d'Art et d'Histoire** by the Ministry of Culture, are mentioned in this guide (*Bourges, Cahors, Figeac, Pays Monts et Barrages, Pays de la Vézère et de l'Ardoise, Périgueux, Sarlat, Souillac and Vallée de la Dordogne*). They are particularly active in promoting their architectural and cultural heritage and offer guided tours by highly qualified guides as well as activities for 6 to 12-year-olds. More information is available from local tourist offices and from www.vpah.culture.fr.

International Visitors

EMBASSIES AND CONSULATES IN FRANCE

Australia   Embassy
4 rue Jean-Rey, 75015 Paris – ☎ 01 40 59 33 00 – Fax: 01 40 59 33 10 www.austgov.fr

Canada   Embassy
35 avenue Montaigne, 75008 Paris ☎ 01 44 43 29 00 Fax: 01 44 43 29 99 paris@international.gc.ca

Ireland   Embassy
4 rue Rude, 75016 Paris ☎ 01 44 17 67 00 Fax: 01 44 17 67 60 – paris@dfa.ie

New Zealand   Embassy
7 ter rue Léonard-de-Vinci, 75016 Paris ☎ 01 45 01 43 43 Fax: 01 45 01 43 44 nzembassy.paris@fr.oleane.com

South Africa   Embassy
59 quai d'Orsay, 75007 Paris

☏ 01 53 59 23 23
Fax: 01 53 59 23 68
info@afriquesud.net

UK   Embassy
35 rue du Faubourg St-Honoré,
75008 Paris – ☏ 01 44 51 31 00
Fax: 01 44 51 31 27
www.britishembassy.gov.uk

UK   Consulate
16 rue d'Anjou, 75008 Paris
☏ 01 44 51 31 02 (visas)

USA   Embassy
2 avenue Gabriel, 75008 Paris
☏ 01 43 12 22 22
Fax: 01 42 66 97 83
www.amb-usa.fr

USA   Consulate
2 rue St-Florentin, 75001 Paris
☏ 01 42 96 14 88

DOCUMENTS

Passport – Nationals of countries within the European Union entering France need only a national identity card. Nationals of other countries must be in possession of a valid national **passport**. In case of loss or theft, report to your embassy or consulate and the local police.

Visa – No **entry visa** is required for Canadian, US or Australian citizens travelling as tourists and staying less than 90 days, except for students planning to study in France. If you think you may need a visa, apply to your local French Consulate.

US citizens should obtain the booklet *Safe Trip Abroad* (US$1), which provides useful information on visa requirements, customs regulations, medical care etc for international travellers. Published by the Government Printing Office, it can be ordered by phone – ☏ (202) 512-1800 – or consulted on-line (www.access.gpo.gov). General passport information is available by phone toll-free from the Federal Information Center (item 5 on the automated menu), ☏ 800-688-9889. US passport application forms can be downloaded from http://travel.state.gov.

CUSTOMS

Apply to the Customs Office (UK) for a leaflet on customs regulations and the full range of duty-free allowances; available from HM Customs and Excise, Thomas Paine House, Angel Square, Torrens Street, London EC1V 1TA, ☏ 08450 109 000. The US Customs Service offers a publication *Know*

Before You Go for US citizens: for the office nearest you, consult the phone book, Federal Government, US Treasury (www.customs.ustreas.gov).

There are no customs formalities for holidaymakers bringing their caravans into France for a stay of less than six months. No customs document is necessary for pleasure boats and outboard motors for a stay of less than six months but the registration certificate should be kept on board.

Americans can take home, tax-free, up to US$ 400 worth of goods (limited quantities of alcohol and tobacco products); Canadians up to CND$ 300; Australians up to AUS$ 400 and New Zealanders up to NZ$ 700.

Residents from a member state of the European Union are not restricted with regard to purchasing goods for private use, but the recommended allowances for alcoholic beverages and tobacco are as follows:

Duty-Free Allowances	
Spirits (whisky, gin, vodka etc)	10 litres
Fortified wines (vermouth, port etc)	20 litres
Wine (not more than 60 sparkling)	90 litres
Beer	110 litres
Cigarettes	800
Cigarillos	400
Cigars	200
Smoking tobacco	1 kg

HEALTH

First aid, medical advice and chemists' night service rotas are available from chemists drugstores (pharmacie) identified by the green cross sign. All prescription drugs should be clearly labelled; it is recommended that you carry a copy of the prescription.

It is advisable to take out comprehensive insurance coverage as the recipient of medical treatment in French hospitals or clinics must pay the bill. **Nationals of non-EU countries** should check with your insurance companies about policy limitations. Reimbursement can then be negotiated with the insurance company according to the policy held.

✚ **British and Irish citizens** should apply to the Department of Health and Social Security before **travelling** for Form E 111, which entitles the holder to urgent treatment for accident or unexpected illness in EU countries. A refund of part of the costs of treatment can be obtained on application in person or by post to the local Social Security Offices (Caisse Primaire d'Assurance Maladie).

✚ **Americans** concerned about travel and health can contact the International Association for Medical Assistance to Travelers, which can also provide details of English-speaking doctors in different parts of France: ☎ (716) 754-4883; www.iamat.org

✚ The **American Hospital of Paris** is open 24hr for emergencies as well as consultations, with English-speaking staff, at 63 boulevard Victor-Hugo, 92200 Neuilly-sur-Seine, ☎ 01 46 41 25 25; www.american-hospital. org. Accredited by major insurance companies.

✚ **The British Hospital** is just outside Paris in Levallois-Perret, 3 rue Barbès, ☎ 01 46 39 22 22; www. british-hospital.org.

Accessibility

The sights described in this guide which are easily accessible to people of reduced mobility are indicated in the admission times and charges information by the symbol ♿ *(see individual sights in the Discovering the Region section).*

On TGV and Corail trains operated by the national railway (SNCF), there are special wheelchair slots in 1st class carriages available to holders of 2nd-class tickets. On Eurostar and Thalys, special rates are available for accompanying adults. All airports are equipped to receive physically disabled passengers. Web-surfers can find information for slow walkers, mature travellers and others with special needs at www. access-able.com. For information on museum access for the disabled contact La Direction, Les Musées de France, Service Accueil des Publics Spécifiques, 6 rue des Pyramides, 75041 Paris Cedex 1, ☎ 01 40 15 80 72.

The Michelin Guide France and the **Michelin Camping France** guide indicate hotels and camp sites with facilities suitable for physically handicapped people.

GETTING THERE

By Air

Choose between scheduled flights on national airlines (Air France, TAT) or commercial and package-tour flights with rail or coach link-ups or fly-drive schemes. The following airlines operate flights from the UK to the Dordogne and Limousin regions, as well as to neighbouring regions in south-west France:

- **Ryanair** – www.ryanair.com (flights to Limoges, Bergerac, Poitiers and Rodez);
- **EasyJet** – www.easyjet.com (flights to Toulouse);
- **Bmibaby** – www.bmibaby.com (flights to Bordeaux and Toulouse);
- **British Airways** – www.ba.com (flights to Bordeaux and Toulouse);
- **Air France** – www.airfrance.com (flights to Bordeaux and Toulouse).

It is very easy to arrange air travel to one of Paris' two airports (Roissy-Charles-de-Gaulle to the north, and Orly to the south). Contact airline companies and travel agents for details of package tour flights with a rail link-up or fly-drive schemes.

Visitors arriving in **Paris** who wish to reach the city centre or a train station may use public transportation or reserve space on the **Airport Shuttle** (for Roissy-Charles-de-Gaulle ☎ 01 45 38 55 72, for Orly ☎ 01 43 21 06 78). Air France operates a coach service into town with frequent departures (☎ 01 41 56 89 00). The cost and duration of a taxi ride from the airport to the city centre varies with traffic conditions. From Charles-de-Gaulle: about 1hr, 40€; from Orly about 30min, 30€. There is an extra charge (posted in the taxi) for baggage; the extra charge for airport pick-up is on the meter; drivers are usually given a tip of 10-15% of the fare.

There are daily flights between Paris (Orly Airport) and Bergerac, Brive, Périgueux; for information and reservations, ☎ 0 820 820 820. www.airlinair.com.

In addition, Brit'AirLimoges operates flights from Paris and Lyons to **Limoges**, ☎ 05 55 43 30 30, www.aeroportlimoges.com. Three daily connections with Paris-Orly, one daily connection with Paris-Charles-de-Gaulle) and three daily connections with Lyon-Saint-Exupéry. The other main airports in the region are:

- **Aéroport de Périgueux-Bassillac** (9km/5.6mi E of Périgueux) – 24330 Bassillac, ☎ 05 53 02 79 71;
- **Aéroport de Bergerac-Roumanière** (5km/3mi SE of Bergerac) – Route d'Agen, 24100 Bergerac, ☎ 05 53 22 25 25;
- **Aéroport de Brive-Laroche** – 19100 Brive, ☎ 05 55 86 88 36;
- **Aéroport de Bourges** (SW of Bourges) – 18000 Bourges, ☎ 02 48 50 37 11.

Contact airlines and travel agents for information. There are daily flights from Paris Orly to Périgueux and Bergerac (Air Littoral) and Brive (TATAir Liberté); private planes can land at the Bourges airfield. Limoges airport is linked daily to 18 French towns and 5 European ones. Daily flights are scheduled from Limoges-Bellegarde Airport to Paris, Clermont-Ferrand and Lyon.

By Sea

There are numerous **cross-Channel services** (passenger and car ferries, hovercraft) from the United Kingdom and Ireland, as well as the rail Shuttle through the Channel Tunnel (**Le Shuttle-Eurotunnel**, ☎ 08705 35 35 35 or 08000 969 992; www.eurotunnel.com). To choose the most suitable route between your port of arrival and your destination use the Michelin Tourist and Motoring Atlas France, Michelin map 726 (which gives travel times and mileages) or Michelin maps from the 1:200.000 series.

For details apply to travel agencies or to:

- **Stena Line Ferries** – Reservations for all UK routes: ☎ 08705 70 70 70; www.stenaline.ferries.org
- **Hoverspeed** – In the UK: ☎ 0870 240 8070; in France: ☎ 00800 1211 1211; www.hoverspeed.com
- **Brittany Ferries** – In the UK: ☎ 08703 665 333; in France: ☎ 0825 828 828; www.brittany-ferries.com
- **Irish Ferries** – In the UK: ☎ 08705 17 17 17; in Ireland: ☎ 0818 300 400; in France: ☎ 01 43 94 46 94; in the US: ☎ (772) 563 2856; www.irishferries.com

Seafrance — **Eastern Docks** – In the UK: ☎ 01304 205 108 or 08705 711 711; in France: ☎ 08 03 04 40 45 (Mon-Fri, 9am-6.30pm) or 03 21 46 80 00; www.seafrance.fr

By Rail

Eurostar runs via the Channel Tunnel between **London** (Waterloo) and **Paris** (Gare du Nord) in 3hr (bookings and information ☎ 08705 186 186 in the UK; ☎ -888-EUROSTAR in the US). Trains leave from Paris (Gare d'Austerlitz) for Bourges, Limoges, Brive and Cahors. You can take the high-speed TGV train to Bordeaux or Angoulême and change for Périgueux. The Paris-Rodez line serves Martel, Rocamadour, Gramat, Figeac and Capdenac.

Eurailpass, Flexipass, Eurailpass Youth, EurailDrive Pass and **Saverpass** are five of the travel passes which may be purchased by residents of countries outside the European Union. In the US, contact your travel agent or **Rail Europe** 2100 Central Ave. Boulder, CO, 80301, ☎ 1-800-4-EURAIL or **Europrail International** ☎ 1 888 667 9731. If you are a European resident, you can buy an individual country pass, if you are not a resident of the country where you plan to use it. In the UK, call Rail Europe at ☎ 08708 371 371. Information on schedules can be obtained on web sites for these agencies and the **SNCF**, respectively: www.raileurop.com.us, www.eurail.on.ca, www.sncf.fr. At the SNCF site, you can book ahead, pay with a credit card, and receive your ticket in the mail at home.

There are numerous **discounts** available when you purchase your tickets in France, from 25% to 50% below the regular rate. These include discounts for using senior or youth cards (the nominative cards with a photograph must be purchased – 44 and 41€, respectively), and for 2-9 people travelling together (no card required, advance purchase necessary). There are a limited number of discount seats available at peak travel times, and the best discounts are available for travel at off-peak periods.

Tickets must be validated (composter) by using the orange automatic date-stamping machines at the platform entrance (failure to do so may result in a fine).

The French railway company SNCF operates a telephone information, reservation and prepayment service in English from 7am to 10pm (French time). In France call ☎ 08 36 35 35 39 (☎ when calling from outside France, drop the initial 0).

By Bus

Eurolines (London), 4 Cardiff Road, Luton, Bedfordshire, LU1 1PP, ☎ 08705 143219, Fax 01582 400694.

Eurolines (Paris), 22 rue Malmaison, 93177 Bagnolet, ☎ 01 49 72 57 80, Fax 01 49 72 57 99.

www.eurolines.com is the international web site with information about travelling all over Europe by coach (bus).

Driving in France

PLANNING YOUR ROUTE

The area covered in this guide is easily reached by main motorways and national routes. **Michelin map 726** indicates the main itineraries as well as alternate routes for avoiding heavy traffic during busy holiday periods, and gives estimated travel times. **Michelin map 723** is a detailed atlas of French motorways, indicating tolls, rest areas and services along the route; it includes a table for calculating distances and times. The latest Michelin route-planning service is available on the Internet, **www.ViaMichelin.com**. Travellers can calculate a precise route using such options as shortest route, route avoiding toll roads, Michelin-recommended route and gain access to tourist information (hotels, restaurants, attractions). The service is available on a pay-per-route basis or by subscription.

The roads are very busy during the holiday period (particularly weekends in July and August) and, to avoid traffic congestion it is advisable to follow the recommended secondary routes (signposted as Bison Futé – itinéraires bis). The motorway network includes rest areas (aires de repos) and petrol stations (stations-service), usually with restaurant and shopping complexes attached, about every 40km/25mi, so that long-distance drivers have no excuse not to stop for a rest every now and then.

DOCUMENTS

Driving licence – Travellers from other European Union countries and North America can drive in France with a valid national or home-state **driving**

licence. An **international driving licence** is useful because the information on it appears in nine languages (keep in mind that traffic officers are empowered to fine motorists). A permit is available (US$10) from the **National Automobile Club**, 1151 East Hillsdale Blvd., Foster City, CA 94404 ☎ 650-294-7000 or www.nationalautoclub.com; or contact your local branch of the **American Automobile Association**.

Registration papers – For the vehicle, it is necessary to have the registration papers (logbook) and a nationality plate of the approved size.

INSURANCE

Certain motoring organisations (AAA, AA, RAC) offer accident insurance and breakdown service schemes for members. Check with your current insurance company in regard to coverage while abroad. If you plan to hire a car using your credit card, check with the company, which may provide liability insurance automatically (and thus save you having to pay the cost for optimum coverage).

ROAD REGULATIONS

The minimum driving age is 18. Traffic drives on the right. All passengers must wear **seat belts**. Children under the age of 10 must ride in the back seat. Headlights must be switched on in poor visibility and at night; use side-lights only when the vehicle is stationary.

In the case of a **breakdown**, a red warning triangle or hazard warning lights are obligatory. In the absence of stop signs at intersections, cars must **give way to the right**. Traffic on main roads outside built-up areas (priority indicated by a yellow diamond sign) and on roundabouts has right of way. Vehicles must stop when the lights turn red at road junctions and may filter to the right only when indicated by an amber arrow.

The regulations on **drinking and driving** (limited to 0.50g/l) and **speeding** are strictly enforced – usually by an on-the-spot fine and/or confiscation of the vehicle.

Speed limits – Although liable to modification, these are as follows:

- toll motorways (autoroutes) 130kph/80mph (110kph/68mph when raining);
- dual carriageways and motorways without tolls 110kph/68mph (100kph/62mph when raining);
- other roads 90kph/56mph (80kph/50mph when raining) and in towns 50kph/31mph;
- outside lane on motorways during daylight, on level ground and with good visibility – minimum speed limit of 80kph/50mph.

Parking regulations – In built-up areas there are zones where parking is either restricted or subject to a fee; tickets should be obtained from the ticket machines (horodateurs – small change necessary) and displayed inside the windscreen on the driver's side; failure to display may result in a fine, or towing and impoundment. Other parking areas in town may require you to take a ticket when passing through a barrier. To exit, you must pay the parking fee (usually there is a machine located by the exit – sortie) and insert the paid-up card in another machine which will lift the exit gate.

Tolls – In France, most motorway sections are subject to a toll (péage). You can pay in cash or with a credit card (Visa, Mastercard).

PETROL/GASOLINE

French service stations dispense:

- *sans plomb 98* (super unleaded 98)
- *sans plomb 95* (super unleaded 95)
- *diesel/gazole* (diesel)
- *GPL* (LPG).

Petrol is considerably more expensive in France than in the USA. Prices are listed on signboards on the motorways; it is usually cheaper to fill up after leaving the motorway; check the large hypermarkets on the outskirts of town.

CAR RENTAL

There are car rental agencies at airports, railway stations and in all large towns throughout France. European cars have manual transmission; automatic cars are available in larger cities only if an advance reservation is made. Drivers must be over 21; between ages 21-25, drivers are required to pay an extra daily fee; some companies allow drivers under 23 only if the reservation has been made through a travel agent. It is relatively expensive to hire a car in France; Americans in particular will notice the difference and should make arrangements before leaving; take advantage of fly-drive offers when you buy your ticket, or seek advice from a travel agent, specifying requirements. There are many on-line services that will look for the best prices on car rental around the globe. Nova can be contacted at www.rentacar-worldwide.com or ☎ 0800 018 6682 (freephone UK) or ☎ 44 28 4272 8189 (calling from outside the UK). All of the firms listed below have Internet sites for reservations and information. In France, you can call the numbers in the chart below.

MOTORHOME RENTAL

Worldwide Motorhome Rentals

Offers fully equipped camper vans for rent. You can view them on the company's web page.

☎ 888- 519-8969 *US toll-free*
☎ 530-389-8316 *outside the US*
Fax 530-389-8316.
www.mhrww.com

Overseas Motorhome Tours Inc.

Organises escorted tours and individual rental of recreational vehicles.

☎ 800-322-2127 *US*
☎ 1-310-543-2590 *outside the US*
www.omtinc.com.

Rental Cars – Central Reservation in France	
Avis:	☎ 08 20 05 05 05 www.avis.com
Europcar:	☎ 08 25 358 358 www.europcar.com
Budget France:	☎ 08 25 00 35 64 www.budget.com
Hertz France:	☎ 01 47 03 49 12 www.hertz.com
SIXT-Eurorent:	☎ 08 20 00 74 98 www.e-sixt.com
National-CITER	☎ 01 45 22 77 91 www.citer.fr
A Baron's Limousine:	☎ 01 45 30 21 21

WHERE TO STAY AND EAT

For specific Hotel and Restaurant listings, ☕ see the Address Books within the Principal Sights in *Discovering the Region*.

Finding a Hotel

Included in this guide are lists of selected hotels and restaurants for the region (☕ *see Address Books in the Discovering the Region section*). The Legend at the back of the guide explains the symbols and abbreviations used in these sections. We have reported the prices *(double occupancy)* and conditions as we observed them, but of course changes in management and other factors may mean that you will find some discrepancies. Please feel free to keep us informed of any major differences you might encounter.

Use the **map of Places to stay** (☕ *pp 32-33)* to identify recommended places for overnight stops. For an even greater selection, use **The Michelin Guide France**, with its famously reliable star-rating system and hundreds of establishments all over France. **The Michelin Charming Places to Stay** guide contains a selection of 1 000 hotels and guest houses at reasonable prices.

Be sure to book ahead to ensure that you get the accommodation you want, not only in tourist season, but year round, as many towns fill up during trade fairs, arts festivals etc. Some places require an advance deposit or a reconfirmation. Reconfirming is especially important if you plan to arrive after 6pm.

For further assistance, **Loisirs Accueil** is a booking service that has offices in some French départements – contact the local tourist offices for further information or log onto www.loisirsaccueilfranc.com

A guide to good-value, family-run hotels, **Logis et Auberges de France,** is available from the French Tourist Office, as are lists of other kinds of accommodation such as hotel-châteaux, bed-and-breakfasts etc.

Relais et châteaux provides information on booking in luxury hotels with character: 15 rue Galvani, 75017 Paris, ☎ 01 45 72 96 69; www.relaischateaux. com.

ECONOMY CHAIN HOTELS

If you need a place to stop en route, these can be useful, as they are inexpensive (30-45€ for a double room) and generally located near the main road. While breakfast is available, there may not be a restaurant; rooms are small, with a television and bathroom. Central reservation numbers:

🛏 **Akena** ☎ 01 69 84 85 17; www.hotels.akena.com

🛏 **B&B** ☎ 08 92 78 29 29 (11am-5pm); www.hotel-bb.com

🛏 **Etap Hôtel** ☎ 08 92 68 89 90; www.etaphotel.com

🛏 **Mister Bed** ☎ 01 46 14 38 00; www.misterbed.fr

🛏 **Villages Hôtel** ☎ 03 80 60 92 70; www.villages-hotel.com

The hotels listed below are slightly more expensive (from 45€), and offer a few more amenities and services. Central reservation numbers:

🛏 **Campanile, Climat de France, Kyriad** ☎ 0 825 003 003 (in France); 33 1 64 62 46 46; www. envergure.fr

🛏 **Ibis** ☎ 0 803 88 22 22; www. ibishotel.com

RURAL ACCOMMODATION

The **Maison des Gîtes de France** is an information service on self-catering accommodation in France. Gîtes usually take the form of a cottage or apartment decorated in the local style where visitors can make themselves at home, or bed and breakfast accommodation (chambres d'hôtes) which consists of a room and breakfast at a reasonable price.

Contact the **Gîtes de France** office at 59 rue St-Lazare, 75439 Paris Cedex 09, ☎ 01 49 70 75 75, or their representative in the UK, **Brittany Ferries** Millbay Docks; Plymouth, Devonshire. PL1 3EW, ☎ 0990 360 360, www.brittany-ferries. com. The Internet site, www.gites-de-france.fr, has a good English version. From the site, you can order catalogues for different regions illustrated with photographs of the properties, as well as specialised catalogues (bed and breakfasts, chalets in ski areas, farm stays etc). You can also contact the local tourist offices, which may have lists of available properties and local bed and breakfast establishments.

The **Fédération Française des Stations Vertes de Vacances,** 6 rue Ranfer-de-Bretenières, BP 71698, 21016 Dijon Cedex, ☎ 03 80 54 10 50, www.stationsvertes.com, is able to provide details of accommodation, leisure facilities and natural attractions in rural locations selected for their tranquillity.

The **Centre permanent d'initiation à l'environnement** (CPIE, Environment awareness centre), 35 rue Hersent-Luzarche, 36290 Azay-le-Ferron, ☎ 02 54 39 23 43, Fax 02 54 39 25 12, has been entirely renovated and now offers 76 beds (including 6 for disabled travellers) to those who wish to explore the Parc naturel regional de la Brenne. Entertainment for adults and children is organised at weekends. Equipment used for observation is available on location. There are various activities centred on nature and astronomy.

FARM HOLIDAYS

The guide *Bienvenue à la ferme* is published by and available from the Assemblée Permanente des Chambres d'Agriculture, Service "Agriculture et Tourisme", 9 avenue Georges-V, 75008 Paris, ☎ 01 53 57 11 44, www.bienvenue-a-la-ferme.com. It includes the addresses of farmers providing guest facilities who have signed a charter drawn up by the Chambers of Agriculture. *Bienvenue à la ferme* farms, vetted for quality and meeting official standards, can be identified by the yellow flower which serves as their logo.

HIKERS

Hikers can consult the guide entitled *Gîtes d'étapes, refuges* by A and S Mouraret *(Rando-Éditions, BP 24, 65421 Ibos, ☎ 05 62 90 09 90 – www.gites-refuges.com).* The guide and the Web site are intended mainly for those who enjoy hiking, cycling, climbing, skiing and canoeing-kayaking holidays.

HOSTELS, CAMPING

To obtain an International Youth Hostel Federation card (there is no age requirement, and there is a senior card available too), you should contact the IYHF in your own country for information and membership applications (US ☎ 202 783 6161; UK ☎ 01727 855215; Canada ☎ 613-273 7884; Australia ☎ 61-2-9565-1669).

There is a new booking service on the Internet (iyhf.org), which you may use to reserve rooms as far as six months in advance.

The main youth hostel association *(Auberges de Jeunesse)* in France is the **Ligue Française pour les Auberges de la Jeunesse** (67 rue Vergniaud, 75013 Paris, ☎ 01 44 16 78 78; www.auberges-de-jeunesse.com). Annual membership costs 15.25€ (10.70€ for under-26-year-olds).

There are numerous officially graded **camp sites** with varying standards of facilities throughout the Loire Valley. The **Michelin Camping Caravaning France** guide lists a selection of camp sites. The area is very popular with campers in the summer months, so it is wise to reserve in advance.

Finding a Restaurant

Included in this guide are descriptions of selected hotels and restaurants in the region (☾ *see Address Books in the Discovering the Region section).* The Legend at the back of the guide explains the symbols and abbreviations used in these sections. Use **The Michelin Guide France**, with its famously reliable star-rating system and hundreds of establishments all over France, for an even greater choice. If you would like to experience a meal in a highly rated restaurant from the Michelin Guide, be sure to book ahead! In the countryside, restaurants usually serve lunch between noon and 2pm and the evening meal between 7.30-10pm. It is not always easy to find something in-between those two meal times, as the non-stop restaurant is still a rarity in small towns in the provinces. However, a hungry traveller can usually get a sandwich in a café, and ordinary hot dishes may be available in a brasserie.

Another guide series to help you with your culinary quest is Michelin's **Les Guides Gourmands** for the various regions of France, including Dordogne.

L'assiette de pays – This simple menu option, initiated by the Fédération nationale des pays touristiques, consists of a reasonably priced single course (either savoury or sweet), prepared from local produce and accompanied by a glass of local drink. Restaurants taking part have a small sticker in their window (a plate with a knife and fork and the mention "l'assiette de pays". Regional guides are available from:

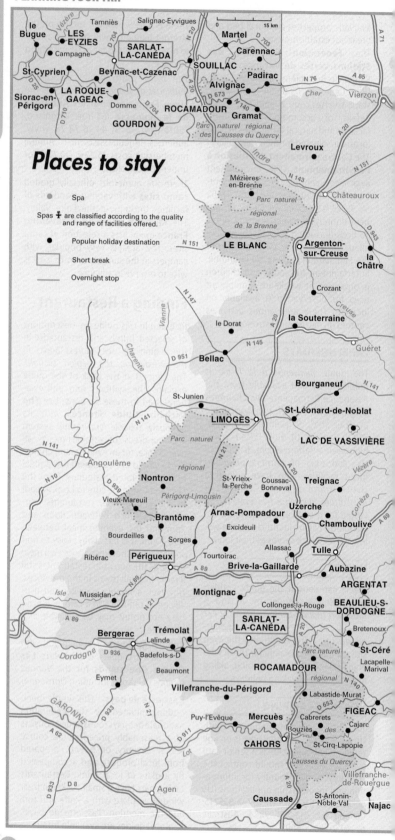

Places to stay

● Spa

Spas ✚ are classified according to the quality and range of facilities offered.

● Popular holiday destination

▢ Short break

— Overnight stop

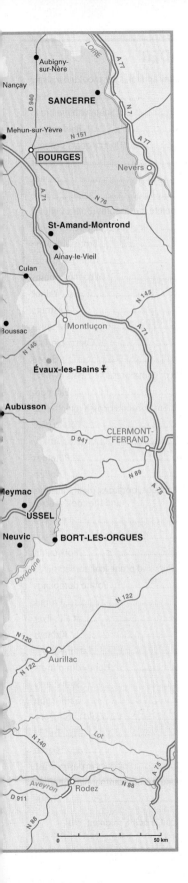

Fédération nationale des pays d'accueil touristiques, 31bis rue du Faubourg-Montmartre, 75009 Paris, ☎ 01 48 24 49 49.

In the region covered by this guide, Berry alone offers the "assiette de pays" option.

In French restaurants and cafés, a service charge is included. Tipping is not necessary, but French people often leave the small change from their bill on their table, or about 5% for the waiter in a nice restaurant.

Sites remarquables du goût – Among places in the Périgord-Quercy region that have been awarded the special distinction of *site remarquable du goût* (tempting moments for the palate) are Brive-la-Gaillarde (for its fairs and markets), Sarlat (for its foie gras and poultry market), Martel-en-Quercy (for its walnut oil) and Monbazillac (for its world-famous sweet white wine). You can find out more on the internet at www. sitesremarquablesdugout.com (French version only).

MENU READER

Ballottine	Turkey and foie gras moulded in aspic
Jambon	Ham
Bréjaude	Soup with rye bread
Langue de bœuf	Beef tongue
Cabecou	Quercy goats's cheese
Lapin	Rabbit
Canard	Duck
Lièvre	Hare
Cèpes	King bolete mushrooms (Boletus edulis)
Magret	Filet (cutlet) of duck or goose
Chabrol	Broth with wine
Marcassin	Young wild boar
Champignons des bois	Wild mushrooms
Noix	Walnut
Châtaignes	Chestnuts
Œufs au vin	Eggs in wine sauce
Clafoutis	Cherry pie/flan
Oie	Goose
Confit	Duck or goose preserved in its own fat
Petit salé	Salt pork
Crottin	Small, round goats's milk cheese
Picard	Potato pâté
Dinde	Turkey
Pommes de terre	Potatoes
Écrevisse	Crayfish
Potée	Boiled dinner with cabbage, potatoes, meat, sausage, and the cook's secret
En conserve	Preserved
Poulet en barbouille	Chicken in thick wine sauce
Enchaud or Anchaud	Pork confit
Pounti	Pork and prune loaf, served sliced
Farcidures	Potato dumplings
Pruneaux	Prunes
Foie de veau	Calf's liver
Rognons	Kidneys
Foie gras	Fattened liver
Sanciaux	Honey doughnuts
Fraise	Strawberry
Tourain blanchi	Garlic soup
Galantine	Cold cuts in jelly
Truffe	Truffle
Gibier	Game
Truffiat	Potatoes in pastry crust
Girole	Chanterelle mushroom (cantharellus cibarius)
Truite	Trout

well-done, medium, rare, raw = bien cuit, à point, saignant, cru

WHAT TO DO AND SEE

Outdoor Fun

WATER SPORTS

This inland region is awash with man-made lakes, many well-equipped for swimming and boating, and the rivers and streams are inviting, too. The region's leading water sports centre is the **Lac de Vassivière** (*970ha/2 397 acres*), which offers beaches suitable for youngsters as well as opportunities for sailing and wind-surfing. Contact the **Base Nautique de Vauveix** (*see Lac de VASSIVIÈRE*).

For general information on water-skiing, contact the **Fédération française de ski nautique**, 27 rue Athènes, 75009 Paris, ☎ 01 53 20 19 19; www.ffsn.asso.fr

The village of Trémolat, on the River Dordogne, also boasts an international water sports centre (☎ 05 53 22 81 18).

CANOEING AND KAYAKING

Canoeing is a popular family pastime on the peaceful waters of the region. In fact, on some weekends, in Dordogne, there seem to be more people on the water than on the road! **Kayaking** is practised on the lakes and, for more experienced paddlers, rapid sections of the rivers. For beginners, the River Dordogne and River Lot are not only ideally calm, but also offer splendid views. The Corrèze, Elle, Auvezère, Céou and the upper parts of the Dronne, Isle and Célé rivers are more of a challenge. In all cases, be sure to wear the buoyant life jacket the rental agent is obliged to provide.

For general information on these sports, contact:

- **Fédération française de canoë-kayak**, 87 quai de la Marne, BP 58 – 94344 Joinville-le-Pont, ☎ 01 45 11 08 50, www.ffcanoe-asso.fr, which publishes a map.

- **Ligue régionale de canoë-kayak du Val de Loire-Centre**, Maison des Sports, 1240 rue de la Bergeresse, 45160 Olivet, ☎ 02 38 49 88 80; www.canoe-regioncentre.org

- **Ligue régionale de canoë-kayak du Limousin**, Base de la Minoterie, 13 rue Jean-Moulin, 19140 Uzerche, ☎ 05 55 73 02 84.

- **Comité régional de canoë-kayak d'Aquitaine** – 119 boulevard du Président-Wilson, 33000 Bordeaux, ☎ 06 86 71 66 86.

- **Comité régional de canoë-kayak de Midi-Pyrénées** – Allées du Duc-de-Ventadour, 31810 Venerque, ☎ 05 61 08 74 40.

or the **Comité départemental de canoë-kayak** of the following départements:

- **Corrèze** – 23 bis Sajueix, 19130 Voutezac, ☎ 05 55 84 19 03 or 06 78 59 03 44.

- **Creuse** – La Chassagne, 23320 Gartempe, ☎ 05 55 81 30 22.

La Roque-Gageac

J. Damase/MICHELIN

- **Dordogne** – Philippe Vallaeys, 83 rue du 8-Mai-1945, 24430 Marsac-sur-l'Isle, ☎ 05 53 04 13 00.
- **Haute-Vienne** – 1bis rue de la Caraque, 87700 Aixe-sur-Vienne, ☎ 05 55 70 35 62.
- **Lot** – 314 route de Laroque, 46000 Cahors, ☎ 05 65 35 91 59.

Most canoeing/kayaking centres welcome all comers, experienced or not, renting boats and in some cases providing guides; a pick-up point downstream carries boaters and boats back to the base. Mountain bikes are sometimes available at the same sites.

FISHING

The rivers, lakes and streams are a joy for those who love to fish. A *Carte de Pêche* (fishing permit) is required; it may be purchased for a day or for the year in sports clubs, tourist information centres, and cafés where a sign so signifies. Local regulations are enforced; crayfish are protected in most areas, and anglers should seek information on which fish are in season. Frogs are a speciality of the Brenne wetlands.

For further details, contact the **Conseil supérieur de la pêche**, Immeuble "Le Péricentre", 16 avenue Louison-Bobet, 94132 Fontenay-sous-Bois Cedex, ☎ 01 45 14 36 00, or the **Fédération départementale de pêche** of the following départements:

- **Cher** – 103 rue de Mazières, 18000 Bourges, ☎ 02 48 66 68 90.
- **Corrèze** – Place Abbé-Tournet, 19000 Tulle, ☎ 05 55 26 11 55; www.peche-correze.com.
- **Creuse** – 60 avenue Louis-Laroche, 23000 Guéret, ☎ 05 55 52 24 70.
- **Dordogne** – Jacques Laguerre, 16 rue des Prés, 24000 Périgueux, ☎ 05 53 06 84 20.
- **Haute-Vienne** – 31 rue Jules-Noël, 87000 Limoges, ☎ 05 55 06 34 77.
- **Indre** – 17-19 rue des Etats-Unis, 36000 Châteauroux, ☎ 02 54 34 59 69; www.unpf.fr/36
- **Lot** – 182 quai Cavaignac, 46000 Cahors, ☎ 05 65 35 50 22; www.pechelot.com

HIKING

There is an extensive network of well-marked footpaths in France which make hiking a breeze. Several Grande Randonnée (GR) trails, recognisable by the red and white horizontal marks on trees, rocks and in town on walls, signposts etc, go through the region. Along with the GR exist the Petite Randonnée (PR) paths, which are usually blazed with blue (2hr walk), yellow (2hr 15min-3hr 45min) or green (4-6hr) marks. Of course, with appropriate maps, you can combine walks to suit your desires.

To use these trails, obtain the Topo-Guide for the area published by the **Fédération Française de la Randonnée Pédestre**, 14 rue Riquet, 75019 Paris, ☎ 01 44 89 93 90; www. ffrp.asso.fr. Some English-language editions are available as well as an annual guide (Rando Guide) which includes ideas for overnight itineraries and places to stay together with information on the difficulty and accessibility of trails.

Local tourist organisations also provide maps of itineraries. In Sarlat the tourist office publishes *Promenades et Randonnées en Périgord Noir*, a series of 73 itineraries ranging from 2km/1.2mi to 24km/15mi. The **Comité départemental du tourisme du Lot** publishes *Promenades et randonnées*, which contains over 50 hiking and mountain-biking routes.

Useful addresses

- **Comité régional de la randonnée pédestre en Aquitaine**, Mairie, 40180 Narosse, ☎ 05 58 90 12 84; www.rando-aquitaine@tiscali.fr

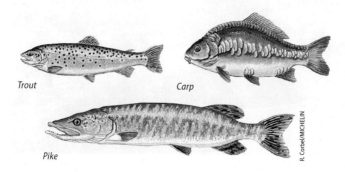

Trout

Carp

Pike

R. Corbel/MICHELIN

Guidelines for Hikers

Choosing the right equipment for a hiking expedition is essential: flexible hiking shoes with non-slip soles, a rain jacket or poncho, an extra sweater, sun protection (hat, glasses, lotion), drinking water (1-2l per person), high energy snacks (chocolate, cereal bars, banana...), and a first aid kit. Of course, you'll need a good map (and a compass if you plan to leave the main trails). Plan your itinerary well, keeping in mind that while the average walking speed for an adult is 4kph/2.5mph, you will need time to eat and rest, and children will not keep up the same pace. Leave your itinerary with someone before setting out (innkeeper or fellow camper).

Respect for nature is a cardinal rule and includes the following precautions: don't smoke or light fires in the forest, which are particularly susceptible in the dry summer months; always carry your rubbish out; leave wild flowers as they are; walk around, not through, farmers' fields; close gates behind you.

If you are caught in an electrical storm, avoid high ground, and do not move along a ridge top; do not seek shelter under overhanging rocks, isolated trees in otherwise open areas, at the entrance to caves or other openings in the rocks, or in the proximity of metal fences or gates. Do not use a metallic survival blanket. If possible, position yourself at least 15m/15yd from the highest point around you (rock or tree); crouch with your knees up and without touching the rock face with your hands or any exposed part of your body. An automobile is a good refuge as its rubber tyres ground it and provide protection for those inside.

Comité régional de la randonnée pédestre en Midi-Pyrénées, Maison des Sports, rue Buissonière, BP 81908, 31683 Labège Cedex, ☎ 05 62 24 18 77; www.randonnees-midi-pyrenees.com

Comité régional de la randonnée pédestre du Val de Loire-Centre, La Vilaise, 36370 Bélâbre, ☎ 02 54 37 61 73; www.rando-centre.com.fr.

Information is also available from the **Comité départemental de la randonnée pédestre** of the following départements:

Cher – 4 rue Didier-Daurat, 18000 Bourges, ☎ 0248 20 01 78.

Corrèze – La Chassagnite, 19200 Mestes, ☎ 05 55 72 53 90.

Dordogne – 46 rue Kléber, 24000 Périgueux, ☎ 05 53 54 51 21.

Haute-Vienne – Maison des Sports, Mme Texier, Présidente du CDRP 87, 35 rue Jean-Louis Paguenaud, 87100 Limoges, ☎ 05 55 10 93 87.

Indre – Maison départementale des Sports, 89/22 allée des Platanes, 36000 Châteauroux, ☎ 02 54 35 55 63.

Lot – BP 7, 46001 Cahors Cedex 9, ☎ 05 65 35 80 82.

CYCLING

For general information concerning cycling in France, write or call the **Fédération Française de Cyclotourisme** (12 rue Louis-Bertrand, 94200 Ivry-sur-Seine Cedex, ☎ 01 56 20 88 87; www.ffct.org). Off-road enthusiasts, contact the **Fédération Française de Cyclisme** (5 rue de Rome, 93561 Rosny-sous-Bois Cedex, ☎ 01 49 35 69 24; www.ffc.fr) and request the Guide des centres VTT.

Other useful addresses

Ligue régionale de cyclotourisme du Limousin, 6 rue Léon-Tolstoï, 87000 Limoges, ☎ 05 55 38 26 11.

Ligue régionale de cyclotourisme de Midi-Pyrénées, 7 rue André-Citroën, 31130 Balma, ☎ 05 61 99 86 46.

You can also contact the **Comité départemental de cyclotourisme** of the following départements:

Corrèze – 45 quai Aristide-Briand, 19000 Tulle, ☎ 05 55 20 71 46.

Creuse – M. Jean-Louis Jagot, Lycée professionnel Roussillat, 23320 St-Vaury, ☎ 05 55 80 13 69.

Dordogne – Hubert Prévost, 14 route de Montbreton, 24340 Mareuil, ☎ 05 53 60 70 13.

Haute-Vienne – 5 rue Georges-Bizet, 87170 Isle, ☎ 05 55 50 29 71.

Lot – Résidence Soulhol, A423, 46400 Saint-Céré, ☎ 05 65 10 98 90; www.randocyclovtt46.com.

Local tourist offices have a list of cycle hire firms, which include SNCF train stations in St-Amand-de-Montrond, Uzerche, Bergerac, Le Bugue, Cahors, Gourdon, Gramat, Rocamadour-Padirac, Sarlat and Souillac. Maps and suggested itineraries are provided.

LAKES AND PONDS	Dép.	Acreage	Swimming	Water sports	Fishing
Argentat (Lac de Feyt)	19	198	≈	–	🐟
Aubazine (Plan d'eau du Coiroux)	19	59	≈	–	Cat. 1
Bessais (Étang de Goule)	18	334	≈	⛵	🐟
Bort-les-Orgues (Lac de Val)	19	3459	≈	⛵	Cat. 2
Bourges (Lac du Val d'Auron)	18	203	–	⛵	Cat. 2
Bujaleuf	87	198	≈	⛵	🐟
Carsac-de-Gurson (Lac de Gurson)	24	27	≈	–	🐟
Compreignac (Lac de St-Pardoux)	87	815	≈	⛵	Cat. 2
Egletons (Lac du Deiro)	19	32	≈	–	Cat. 1
Éguzon (Lac de Chambon)	36	741	≈	⛵	–
Gimel (Étang de Ruffaud)	19	49	≈	⛵	🐟
Guéret (Étang de Courtille)	23	30	≈	⛵	–
Lissac-sur-Couze (Lac du Causse)	19	222	≈	⛵	Cat. 2
Luzech (Base de Caix)	46	371	≈	–	🐟
Marcillac (Barrage de la Valette)	19	568	≈	–	Cat. 2
Meymac (Lac de Sechemailles)	19	104	≈	–	Cat. 2
Mézières (Étang de Bellebouche)	36	247	≈	⛵	🐟
Neuvic (Lac de Triousoune)	19	1013	≈	⛵	🐟
Seilhac (Lac de Burnazel)	19	79	≈	–	–
Sénaillac-Latronquière (Lac du Tolerme)	46	17	≈	⛵	Cat. 1
Sidiailles (Lac de)	18	222	≈	⛵	🐟
St-Estèphe (Étang de)	24	74	≈	⛵	🐟
Trémolat (Barrage de Mauzac)	24	247	≈	⛵	🐟
Treignac (Lac de Bariousses)	19	247	≈	⛵	Cat. 2
Vassivière (Lac de)	23	2471	≈	⛵	Cat. 2
Viam (Lac de)	19	467	≈	–	Cat. 2
Videix (Plan d'eau de Lavaud)	87	99	≈	–	Cat. 1
Vigeois (Lac de Pontcharral)	19	35	≈	–	–

Dép means **département:** 18 Cher; 19 Corrèze; 23 Creuse; 24 Dordogne; 36 Indre; 46 Lot; 87 Haute-Vienne.

Lac means lake; *Étang* means pond or small lake; *Barrage* means dam; *Plan d'eau* means a flat body of water.

Category 1: Fish from the Salmonidae family (trout), usually the upper portion of major rivers.

Category 2: Cyprinidae (carp, barbels, tench, bream, chub, dace, shiners).

HORSEBACK RIDING

There are numerous itineraries suitable for horseback riding through forested areas, across the causses and along the main river valleys.

The **Comité National de Tourisme Équestre** (9 boulevard Macdonald 75019 Paris, ☎01 53 26 15 50; www. tourisme-equestre.fr) is a useful source of information if you would like to plan a riding holiday. It publishes the brochure *Cheval Nature, l'Officiel du tourisme équestre*, where you will find the addresses of riding centres (Centres de Tourisme Equestre) region-by-region, and practical tips on holidays for kids, insurance and more.

Other useful addresses

🐎 **Association régionale de tourisme équestre d'Aquitaine**, Hippodrome du Bouscat, BP 95, 33492 Le Bouscat Cedex, ☎ 05 53 48 02 28.

🐎 **Association régionale de tourisme équestre de Midi-Pyrénées**, Jean Bergraser, 31 chemin des Canalets, 31400 Toulouse, ☎ 05 61 14 04 58; www.artemip.com.

🐎 **Association régionale de tourisme équestre du Val de Loire-Centre,** A.R.T.E. Val de Loire-Centre, 34 rue de Villebrême, BP 50, 41914 Blois Cedex 9, ☎ 02 54 42 95 60 (Tue-Thu, 1.30-5.30pm).

Information on local conditions and opportunities is available from the **Comité départemental de tourisme équestre** of the following départements:

🐎 **Cher** – Chemin des Fondereaux, 18100 Vierzon, ☎ 02 48 71 05 51.

🐎 **Corrèze** – La Cassière, 19370 Soudaine-Lavinadière, ☎ 05 55 28 50 09 or 05 55 73 60 99.

🐎 **Creuse** – 52 avenue de la Gare, 23700 Auzance, ☎ 05 55 83 92 22 or 05 55 67 08 00.

🐎 **Dordogne** – 25 rue Wilson, 24002 Périgueux, ☎ 05 53 56 05 04. The Comité publishes the map *Sentiers et relais équestres du Périgord*.

🐎 **Haute-Vienne** – La Maurie, 87150 Oradour-sur-Vayres, ☎ 05 55 78 77 52.

🐎 **Indre** – L'Ébaupin, 36330 Velles, ☎ 02 54 36 38 48.

🐎 **Lot** – Denis Letartre, BP 103, 46002 Cahors Cedex 9, ☎ 05 65 35 80 82; www.cheval-lot.com. The map *Carte départementale de la randonnée*, showing GR footpaths and riding tracks is available at this address.

EXPLORING CAVES

The Dordogne attracts many speleologists; its limestone relief is pitted with caves and caverns. Contact any of the following organisations for further information:

♦ **Fédération française de Spéléologie** – 23 rue Delandine, 69002 Lyon, ☎ 04 72 56 09 63; www.ffspeleo.fr

♦ **Comité régional de spéléologie d'Aquitaine** – Maison des Comités, 46 rue Kléber, 24000 Périgueux, ☎ 06 81 96 89 26.

♦ **Comité régional de spéléologie de Midi-Pyrénées** – 7 rue André-Citroën, 31130 Balma, ☎ 05 61 11 71 60; http://comite.speleo.midipy.free.fr

♦ **Comité départemental de spéléologie de la Dordogne** – Les Crouzilles, 24250 Grolejac, ☎ 05 53 31 27 30.

♦ **Comité départemental de spéléologie du Lot** – 391 rue Anatole de Monzie, 46000 Cahors, ☎ 05 65 35 43 22 (M. Bonnet) or 05 65 38 79 97; www.ffspeleo.fr/cds/46.

GOLF

The Michelin map *Golf, les parcours français* (French golf courses) will help you locate golf courses in the region covered by this guide.

For further information, contact the **Fédération française de golf**, 68 rue Anatole-France, 92309 Levallois-Perret Cedex, ☎ 01 41 49 77 00; www.ffgolf.org. These events may be held at different dates, depending on the year. It is best to inquire at the tourist office for precise details.

Activities for Children

This region of France has a lot to offer children from boat trips aboard traditional gabarres to visiting caves, châteaux, museums and sights of special interest (👣 *see also Tourist trains, Rail-biking and Donkey Trekking in Sightseeing below*).

The towns and areas, labelled Villes et Pays d'Art et d'Histoire by the Ministry of Culture (Bourges, Cahors, Figeac, Pays Monts et Barrages, Pays de la Vézère et de l'Ardoise, Périgueux, Sarlat, Souillac and Vallée de la Dordogne), offer activities for 6 to 12-year-olds. More information is available from local tourist offices and from www.vpah.culture.fr

Throughout the Sights section of the guide, your attention is drawn to activities particularly suited to children by the symbol ⚹ .

Calendar of Events

Many Regional Tourist Offices publish brochures listing local fêtes, fairs and festivals. Most places hold festivities for France's National Day (14 July) and many organise events on 15 August, also a public holiday.

FESTIVALS

JANUARY-FEBRUARY
Limoges
Danse Emoi – Dance festival (even-numbered years), ☎ 05 55 45 94 00 (Jean-Gagnant cultural centre).

APRIL
Bourges
Printemps de Bourges – International festival of popular contemporary music and songs, ☎ 02 48 27 40 40; www.printemps-bourges.com

MAY-SEPTEMBER
La Borne
Rencontre internationale de la céramique – International ceramics festival, ☎ 02 48 64 06 43.

MAY-JUNE
Bourges
Synthèse – International festival of experimental music (first two weeks in June), ☎ 02 48 20 41 87; www.imeb.net

Nohant
Fêtes romantiques (3 weekends in June), ☎ 02 54 48 46 40; www.festival-george-sand.com

MID-JUNE TO MID-SEPTEMBER
Bourges
Un été à Bourges – Classical music and jazz in various venues, ☎ 02 48 24 93 32.

Bellac
Festival national de Bellac – Jean Giraudoux theatre and music festival, ☎ 05 55 68 10 44; www.festival-national-bellac.com

JULY TO SEPTEMBER
Coussac-Bonneval
Moments Musicaux – Music festival, ☎ 05 55 75 27 40.

JULY
Cahors
Blues Festival, ☎ 05 65 35 99 99; www.cahors.bluesfestival.free.fr

La Châtre
Rencontres internationales Frédéric-Chopin – Piano festival (third week of July), ☎ 02 54 48 22 64; www.festivals-chopin.com

Montignac
Danse et musique du Monde (last week of July), ☎ 05 53 50 14 00.

Périgord
Fête de la Félibrée – Regional folklore festival hosted by a different town every year. ☎ 05 53 09 57 64.

Souillac
Jazz festival (third week of July) ☎ 05 65 37 81 56; www.souillacenjazz.net

Argenton-sur-Creuse
Mercuria – European folklore festival (odd-numbered years, 4th week of the month), ☎ 02 54 24 05 30.

Gourdon
Chamber music festival (end July), ☎ 05 65 41 20 06.

JULY-AUGUST
Aubusson
Musique au cœur de la tapisserie – organ and chamber music concerts. ☎ 05 55 66 32 12.

Biron, Bergerac, Cadouin, Monpazier, Abbaye de St-Avit-Sénier
L'été musical en Bergerac, ☎ 05 53 74 30 94.

Bourges
Très Riches Heures de l'Orgue en Berry – Organ festival, ☎ 02 48 20 57 66; www.grandorguebourges.org

Brive-la-Gaillarde
Festival de la Vézère – Various cultural events in selected venues, ☎ 05 55 23 25 09; www.festival-vezere.com

Castelnau-Montratier, Lauzert, Montcuq
Festival de musique du Quercy Blanc (late July to mid-August), ☎ 05 65 31 83 12.

Domme
Festival de la chanson – Song festival (mid-July to early August), ☎ 05 53 28 67 00.

Sarlat
Festival des jeux de théâtre (mid-July to early August), ☎ 05 53 31 10 83; www.festival-theatre-sarlat.com

St-Léonard-de-Noblat
Été musical de St-Léonard: classical and traditional music concerts, ☎ 05 55 30 53 44.

St-Céré
Festival de Musique (late July to mid-August), ☎ 05 65 38 29 08; www.festival-saint-cere.com

Noirlac
Festival de Noirlac – International singing festival, ☎ 02 48 48 00 27; www.festivaldenoirlac.com

AUGUST

Belaye
Cello festival (early August), ☎ 05 65 29 18 75.

Audrix, Le Bugue, Les Eyzies, St-Cyprien
Musique en Périgord (1st two weeks of August), ☎ 06 07 97 01 23.

Bonaguil
Theatre festival, ☎ 05 53 71 17 17.

Brive-la-Gaillarde
Orchestrades universelles – Festival of youth orchestras (mid-Aug), ☎ 05 55 92 39 39; www.orchestrades.com

Gargilesse-Dampierre
Festival musical d'été – Harp workshops (second half of August), ☎ 02 54 47 83 11.

St-Léon-de-Vézère, Montignac and St-Amand-de-Coly
Festival musical du Périgord Noir, ☎ 05 53 51 95 17.

SEPTEMBER-OCTOBER

Brantôme, Chancelade, Périgueux
Sinfonia en Périgord – Baroque music festival (late August-early September), ☎ 05 53 04 78 78.

Solignac
Rencontres photographiques – Photography festival, ☎ 05 55 32 30 78.

Tulle
Festival Les Nuits de Nacre – Pearly nights festival (3rd weekend in September), ☎ 05 55 20 28 28; www.accordeon.org

OCTOBER-NOVEMBER

Châteauroux
Lisztomanias – International Franz Liszt Festival, ☎ 02 54 34 10 74.

SON ET LUMIÈRE

Sound and light shows are a great way to spend a summer night outdoors and give new perspectives on the monuments they highlight. There are a lot of variations on the theme, from living history plays through costumed pageantry and creative combinations of lighting effects and music which bring out the details of architecture. Check with the local tourist office for details; in some cases you may need to bring your own blanket and chairs; in others, visitors stand and walk around the site. These shows are held in July and August, and generally start at nightfall, which may mean after 10pm.

TRADITIONAL FESTIVALS, FAIRS AND MARKETS

JANUARY

Brive
Epiphany fair (early January).

Périgueux
Epiphany fair (first Wednesday after 6 January).

EASTER WEEKEND

Reuilly
Wine fair, ☎ 02 54 49 84 54; www.ot-reuilly.fr

APRIL

Aubazine
Goat fair, ☎ 05 55 25 79 93.

MAY

Beaulieu-sur-Dordogne
Strawberry fair (2nd or 3rd Sunday of the month), ☎ 05 55 91 11 31.

MAY-JUNE

Lignières
Donkey and mule fair (Whit Sunday), ☎ 02 48 60 22 14.

Rocamadour
Cheese fair (Whit Sunday – Pentecôte), ☎ 05 65 33 22 00.

Domme
Fête de la Saint-Clair – Folklore festival and concerts (1st weekend of June).

Sarlat
Fête de la Ringuetta – Traditional games (even-numbered years), ☎ 05 53 31 45 45.

JULY

Martel
Wool fair (late July).

Aubigny-sur-Nère
Franco-Scottish Festival – Historical tableaux, parades, folk dancing and music (mid-month), ☎ 02 48 81 50 07; www.aubigny-sur-nere.fr

Aubusson
Cheese and wine fair (penultimate Saturday of the month).

AUGUST

Argentat
International ceramics fair (1st weekend of the month), ☎ 05 55 28 16 05.

Gourdon
Medieval pageant in the old town (1st weekend and Monday of the month). ☎ 05 65 27 52 50.

Belfort-du-Quercy
Melon Fair (15 August).

Bué-en-Sancerre

Foire au sorciers – village fair and folk festival (1st Sunday of the month), ☎ 02 48 54 06 61.

Duravel

Wine and local-produce fair (14-15 August).

SEPTEMBER

Rocamadour

Annual pilgrimage (two Sundays before and after 8 September).

Issoudun

Foire du tout et de la curiosité – "A-bit-of-everything" fair: second-hand market, entertainment, tasting of local specialities (1st Sunday of the month), ☎ 02 54 21 13 53.

Arnac-Pompadour

Horse festival (late September), ☎ 05 55 98 55 47; www.pompadour.net

Brive-la-Gaillarde

Bird fair (mid-month), ☎ 05 55 23 73 37.

OCTOBER

Limoges

Frairie des petits ventres (3rd Friday of the month) – Regional festival for food and wine lovers.

NOVEMBER

Brive-la-Gaillarde

Book fair (early November).

Périgueux

Salon international du livre gourmand – Cookbook show (even-numbered years), ☎ 05 53 05 94 60.

SPORTS EVENTS

JUNE

Argentat

International de canoe-kayak rally (mid-June), ☎ 05 55 28 86 45.

AUGUST

Chambon-sur-Voueize

International de pétanque – International boules competition (1st weekend of the month). ☎ 05 55 82 15 89.

Aubusson

Creuse Valley rally – Swimming, running, kayaking, shooting and mountain biking (14-15 Aug), ☎ 06 08 47 92 84; www.raid23.org

NOVEMBER

St-Sétiers

International husky race across the Plateau de Millevaches (depending on snow cover), ☎ 05 55 95 61 51.

Shopping

OPENING HOURS

Most of the larger shops are open Mondays to Saturdays from 9am to 7 or 7.30pm. Smaller, individual shops may close during the lunch hour. Food shops – grocers, wine merchants and bakeries – are generally open from 7am to 7 or 7.30pm; some open on Sunday mornings. Many food shops close between noon and 2pm and on Mondays. Bakery and pastry shops sometimes close on Wednesdays. Hypermarkets usually stay open non-stop from 9am until 9pm or even later. People travelling to the USA cannot import plant products or fresh food, including fruit, cheeses and nuts. It is permitted to carry tinned products or preserves.

MARKETS

The souvenir of choice is edible, but remember that foie gras and truffles are expensive, even here at the source! Dordogne is also famous for its red fruit and nut liquors (especially in Villamblard and Brive), pork and duck preserves, and wines from Cahors and Bergerac. The wines of Sancerre in Berry deserve their fine reputation. Many of the specialities can be purchased directly from the producer – look out for signs along the road side (dégustation – vente for wines, produits de la ferme for preserves).

Fresh food and plants may not be carried home, and for Americans this includes non-pasteurised cheeses, nuts and fruit. It is acceptable to carry tinned products or preserves.

Main markets in the region:

Périgueux: livestock and flowers, Wednesday and Saturday.

Brive-la-Gaillarde: local farm produce, preserves and confits etc Tuesday, Thursday and Saturday.

Sarlat: chestnuts and walnuts, Saturday in October and November; foie gras and truffles, Saturday mornings from December to March; weekly markets on Wednesdays and Saturdays with a wide choice of local specialities.

Brantôme: chestnuts, walnuts and foie gras, Friday in the winter months; local farm produce, Tuesday mornings in July and August.

RECOVERING VALUE ADDED TAX

There is a Value Added Tax in France (TVA) ranging from 5.5% to 19.6% on almost every purchase. However, non-European visitors who spend more than 183€ (figure subject to change) in any one participating store can get the VAT amount refunded. Usually, you fill out a form at the store, showing your passport. Upon leaving the country, you submit all forms to customs for approval (they may want to see the goods, so if possible don't pack them in checked luggage). The refund is usually paid directly into your bank or credit card account, or it can be sent by mail. Big department stores that cater to tourists provide special services to help you; be sure to mention that you plan to seek a refund before you pay for goods (no refund is possible for tax on services). If you are visiting two or more countries within the European Union, you submit the forms only on departure from the last EU country. The refund is worth while for those visitors who would like to buy fashions, furniture or other fairly expensive items, but remember, the minimum amount must be spent in a single shop (though not necessarily on the same day).

PORCELAIN

See Decorative arts in the Introduction.

Limoges is synonymous with fine china, and there is no dearth of shops selling it, including factory outlets (vente directe d'usines) just outside of town. Many workshops (manufactures) and showrooms (magasins) are also open on the road between Vierzon and Bourges. The larger outlets often have interesting museums, video presentations and demonstrations.

Limoges is also a historical and contemporary centre for the production of enamelware (émaux). Look for shops around place Wilson in town, or stop in one of the many workshops scattered around the region.

Porcelaine à pâte dure
  True porcelain (hard-paste) or china: Resonant when struck, translucent, made from ground feldspathic rock and kaolin clay.

Porcelaine tendre
  Artificial porcelain (soft-paste): Softer than true porcelain, it can be cut with a file, whereas true porcelain cannot. Dirt accumulated on an unglazed base can only be removed with difficulty; on true porcelain it comes off easily.

Porcelaine phosphatique
  Bone china: A translucent ware, neither hard-paste or Porcelaine hybride nor soft-paste porcelain, that contains kaolin, petuntse and bone ash.

Faience fine
  White earthenware, opaque porcelain or creamware: A generic term for a fine, hard earthenware of high strength and durability.

Grès or Grès céramique
  Stoneware: Glassy in appearance, or semi-vitreous, with a fine texture, stoneware is always hard and is always fired in a high temperature kiln; the non-porous clay does not require a glaze.

Terre Cuite
  Terra Cotta, redware: This clay is fired at a low temperature to a rather soft and porous body ranging in colour from pinkish-buff to brick-reds and reddish browns. As a rule it is covered with a soft lead glaze.

Sightseeing

TOURIST TRAINS

In the **Limousin**, different routes are travelled by vintage, 1930s trains, with a steam engine leading the way. Visit the Haute Vallée de la Vienne (Limoges-Eymoutiers-Limoges); the Millevaches Plateau (Limoges-Meymac-Limoges); the Vienne Gorges (Eymoutiers-Châteauneuf-Bujaleuf-Eymoutiers) or the Realm of Ventadour (Meymac-Ussel-Meymac). Contact local tourist offices or the association **Vienne Vézère Vapeur** (☎ 05 55 69 57 62).

In the **Dordogne, Autorail Espérance** offers a guided tour and a taste of regional cooking, travelling from Sarlat to Bergerac in 1hr (reservation required: ☎ 05 53 59 55 39). **Quercyrail** runs trains from the 1950s along the old Cahors-Capdenac line, where passengers get a good look at the Lot Valley (for further information, call ☎ 05 65 23 94 72; reservations recommended ☎ 05 63 40 11 93).

The **Chemin de fer touristique du Haut-Quercy "Le Truffadou"** runs full steam ahead between Martel and St-Denis-près-Martel along the top of 80m/262ft cliffs overlooking the Dordogne Valley; ☎ 05 65 37 35 81. Trip with commentary (1hr). Steam engine: Apr-Sep Sun and public hols (also Wed in Jul and Aug) at 11am, 2.30pm and 4pm. Diesel engine: Apr-Jun and Sep Tue and Thu 2.30pm, Jul-Aug Mon, Tue, Thu and Fri at 11am, 2.30pm and 4pm.

TAKE TO THE SKIES

Several options are on offer for a bird's-eye view of **Périgord**: hot-air balloon, light aircraft, glider, microlight…

Montgolfière du Périgord – St-Donat, 24250 La Roque Gageac, ☎ 05 53 28 18 58; www.montgolfiere-du-perigord.com. Preparation and flight (3hr minimum) daily early morning and late afternoon in high season; the rest of the year by request (prices start at 180€).

The **Aéroclub de Brive**, Aéroport de Brive-Laroche, ☎ 05 55 86 88 37, offers introductory flights aboard a plane or a glider.

The **Aéroclub du Quercy**, Aérodrome de Cahors-Lalbenque, 46230 Cieurac, ☎ 05 65 21 05 96 offers flights over the area.

The **Aéroclub du Sarladais**, Aérodrome de Sarlat-Domme, 24250 Domme, ☎ 05 53 28 32 95 organises flying tours aboard a plane or a microlight.

The **Association Rocamadour Aérostat**, Hôtel de Ville, ☎ 05 65 33 71 50, proposes year-round 45min flights over Rocamadour. Reservation required. 150€ per person.

RAIL-BIKING

Pedal away along disused railtracks aboard specially adapted rail trucks:

Les cyclodraisines d'Aubigny, route de Clémont, 18700 Aubigny-sur-Nère, ☎ 02 48 81 50 07 (weekdays), 02 48 58 35 81 (weekends); 9am-7pm weekends and holidays from Easter to September, Fridays, weekends and holidays in July and August; 8€ per hour, 19€ per half-day, 30€ per day.

Vélo-rail de Bussière, Plan d'eau des Ribières, 87230 Bussière-Galant, ☎ 05 55 78 86 47, www.velo-rail.com; 10am-7pm weekends and public holidays from May to October, daily in July and August; 19€ (2hr 30min maximum).

RIVER CRUISING

Houseboats – For a weekend or a week, enjoy the pleasant pace of life as you cruise the River Lot, where new sections of locks have been opened for pleasure craft. No license is required; the captain must be an adult, and go through a brief course given on board before departure. The rental agent explains, in particular, the methods for going through a lock and for docking, which is about all you need to know to operate these holiday barges.

Babou Marine
Port St-Mary, 46000 Cahors, ☎ 05 65 30 08 99; www.baboulene-jean.fr

Crown Blue Line
Le Moulinat, 46140 Douelle, ☎ 05 65 20 08 79; www.crown-blueline.com

Lot Navigation Nicols
Le Bourg, 46330 Bouziès, ☎ 05 65 24 32 20. Central Reservation Service: route du Puy-St-Bonnet, 49300 Cholet, ☎ 02 41 56 46 56; www.nicols.com

Maps and guides are available from:

Éditions Grafocarte-Navicarte
125 rue Jean-Jacques-Rousseau, BP 40, 92132 Issy-les-Moulineaux Cedex, ☎ 01 41 09 19 00.

Éditions du Plaisancier
43 porte du Grand-Lyon, 01700 Neyron, ☎ 04 72 01 58 68.

Boat trips – For a shorter trip, and without the responsibility of the helm, take a cruise on the Lac de Vassivière, or the Lac de Val at Bort-les-Orgues, or enjoy a ride in a traditional gabarre on the Dordogne from Chalvignac, Spontour, Pont du Chambon, Barrage du Chastang, La Roque-Gageac, Vezac-Beynac, Bergerac.

Gabarres de Beynac – 24250 St-Martial-de-Nabirat, ☎ 05 53 28 51 15, www.

CDT Indre

gabarre-beynac.com. May-Jun and Sep, 10.30am-12.30pm and 2-6pm; Jul-Aug, every 30min 10am-12.30pm and 2-6pm; Mar-Apr and Oct, by request. 1hr trips. 6.50€ (children: 4€, no charge in the morning).

Gabarres Norbert – La Roque-Gageac, ☎ 05 53 29 40 44; www.norbert.fr. Apr-Oct: 1hr trips with commentary. Departures every hr. 7.50€ (children: 4.50€).

EQUESTRIAN TOURS

Horse-drawn caravans

Savour the countryside at a gentle pace aboard a horse-drawn caravan. At 4kph/2.5mph, you will have ample time to look around the back roads and lanes you are travelling. This nomadic life can last for 2-7 days, according to the itinerary.

Équitation et Roulottes du Périgord – Métairie du roc, 24560 Faux, ☎/Fax 05 53 24 32 57 or 06 83 30 83 63.

Les Roulottes du Quercy – 46700 Sérignac, ☎ 05 65 31 96 44; www.perso.wanadoo.fr/roulottes.du.quercy.

Château d'Aynac (Castel SARL) – Château d'Aynac, 46120 Aynac, ☎ 05 65 11 08 00; www.castel-aynac.fr.

Horse-drawn carriage rides

These last 1hr, half a day or a day (with picnic).

Calèche de Dordogne – Ferme de Charmonteil, 24350 Lisle, ☎ 05 53 03 58 35.

Les Attelages du Haut Repaire – Haut Repaire, 24390 Coubjours, ☎ 05 53 50 32 79.

Le Périgord en calèche – Le Bourg, 24550 Mazeyrolles, ☎ 05 53 29 98 99; www.perigord-en-caleche.com

Donkey-trekking

A donkey is a useful companion for carrying your luggage (up to 40kg/88lb) if you plan a long walking tour, and children usually feel motivated by its presence.

The **Fédération nationale ânes et randonnées (FNAR)**, 16 route de Canlers, 62310 Ruisseauville, ☎ 03 21 41 21 97, www.ane-et-rando.com, will provide general information.

You can rent a donkey for a day or a week with or without a guide from:

Arcâne – "Ravary", 24250 Cenac, ☎ 05 53 59 63 79 or 06 07 75 90 84;www.arc-ane.com.

Brahmâne – Cazillac, 82110 Cazes-Mondenard, ☎ 05 63 95 84 61.

Books

Eleanor of Aquitaine, queen of France and England, a 12C divorcée, patroness of poets, source of inspiration for chivalry and Courtly Love, ruler of a kingdom that spanned from Scotland to the Pyrenees, mother of 10 children (including Richard the Lion Heart), lived her 82 years as few women in history before or since. The story of her life is a good introduction to regional history, and a fascinating tale:

Eleanor of Aquitaine: The Mother Queen, Desmond Seward, N.Y., Dorset Press, 1986.

Eleanor of Aquitaine and the Four Kings, Amy Kelly, Cambridge MA, Harvard University Press, 1950.

Beloved Enemy: the Passions of Eleanor of Aquitaine: a Novel, Ellen Jones, N.Y., Simon and Schuster, 1994.

For young readers:

A Proud Taste for Scarlet and Miniver, EL Konigsburg, N.Y., Atheneum, 1974 (illustrated).

Queen Eleanor: Independent Spirit of the Medieval World, Polly S. Brooks, N.Y., Lippincott, 1983 (illustrated).

George Sand was a prolific novelist and correspondent, and many of her works have been translated *(see her biography under NOHANT).* Her rustic tales of country life are suitable for younger readers, too, in particular The Story of My Life and Tales of a Grandmother. Among the many biographies, the following are especially recommended:

Infamous Woman: the Life of George Sand, Joseph Barry, 1977.

The Double Life of George Sand, Woman and Writer, Renée Winegarten, 1978.

For an even closer view of the author's life:

The Intimate Journal of George Sand, Chicago, Cassandra Editions, 1988.

The George Sand – Gustave Flaubert Letters, Chicago, Academy Chicago LTD, 1979.

Alain-Fournier was the pen name of Henri-Alban Fournier (👈 see *ÉPINEUIL-LE-FLEURIEL*). His only completed novel has been published in English both under its French title, *Le Grand Meaulnes* and as *The Lost Domain.*

Josephine Baker's life of scantily clad artistry, wartime heroism, social idealism, bankruptcy and triumphant stage returns makes for good reading. There was more to this woman than a banana skirt, as you will learn in these excellent biographies:

Jazz Cleopatra: Josephine Baker in Her Time, Phyllis Rose, N.Y., Doubleday, 1989.

Naked at the Feast: A Biography of Josephine Baker, Lynn Haney, N.Y., Dodd-Mead, 1981.

Josephine, Josephine Baker and Jo Bouillon (Translated by Mariana Fitzpatrick), N.Y., Harper & Row, 1977.

To whet your appetite:

The Wine Regions of France, Michelin Travel Publications, 2005. An in-depth guide to the wine-producing regions of France.

The Wines of France, Alexis Lichine, N.Y., Knopf, 1963. A classic that ages well.

Enjoying Wine, Don Hewitson, London, Elm Tree Books, 1985. Friendly, no-nonsense approach to one of life's great pleasures, with useful explanations and illustrations.

The Wine Lover's Guide to France, Michael Busselle, London, Pavilion Books, 1986.

At Home in France, Ann Barry, N.Y., Ballantine, 1996. An American journalist explores happiness in Carennac.

USEFUL WORDS & PHRASES

For Architectural terms, see the section on architecture in Introduction to the Region.

SIGHTS

abbaye	abbey
beffroi	belfry
chapelle	chapel
château	castle
cimetière	cemetery
cloître	cloisters
cour	courtyard
couvent	convent
écluse	lock (canal)
église	church
fontaine	fountain
halle	covered market
jardin	garden
mairie	town hall
maison	house
marché	market
monastère	monastery
moulin	windmill
musée	museum
parc	park
place	square
pont	bridge
port	port/harbour
porte	gate/gateway
quai	quay
remparts	ramparts
rue	street
statue	statue
tour	tower

NATURAL SITES

abîme	chasm
aven	swallow-hole
barrage	dam
belvédère	viewpoint
cascade	waterfall
col	pass
corniche	ledge
côte	coast, hillside
forêt	forest
grotte	cave
lac	lake
plage	beach
rivière	river
ruisseau	stream
signal	beacon
source	spring
vallée	valley

ON THE ROAD

car park	parking
driving licence	permis de conduire
east	Est
garage (for repairs)	garage
left	gauche
motorway/highway	autoroute
north	Nord
parking meter	horodateur
petrol/gas	essence
petrol/gas station	station essence
right	droite
south	Sud
toll	péage

traffic lights	feu tricolore
tyre	pneu
west	Ouest
wheel clamp	sabot
zebra crossing	passage clouté

TIME

today	aujourd'hui
tomorrow	demain
yesterday	hier
winter	hiver
spring	printemps
summer	été
autumn/fall	automne
week	semaine
Monday	lundi
Tuesday	mardi
Wednesday	mercredi
Thursday	jeudi
Friday	vendredi
Saturday	samedi
Sunday	dimanche

NUMBERS

0	zéro
1	un
2	deux
3	trois
4	quatre
5	cinq
6	six
7	sept
8	huit
9	neuf
10	dix
11	onze
12	douze
13	treize
14	quatorze
15	quinze
16	seize
17	dix-sept
18	dix-huit
19	dix-neuf
20	vingt
30	trente
40	quarante
50	cinquante
60	soixante
70	soixante-dix
80	quatre-vingt
90	quatre-vingt-dix
100	cent
1000	mille

SHOPPING

bank	banque
baker's	boulangerie
big	grand
butcher's	boucherie
chemist's	pharmacie
closed	fermé
cough mixture	sirop pour la toux
cough sweets	cachets pour la gorge
entrance	entrée
exit	sortie
fishmonger's	poissonnerie
grocer's	épicerie
newsagent, bookshop	librairie
open	ouvert
post office	poste
push	pousser
pull	tirer
shop	magasin
small	petit
stamps	timbres

FOOD AND DRINK

beef	bœuf
beer	bière
butter	beurre
bread	pain
breakfast	petit-déjeuner
cheese	fromage
chicken	poulet
dessert	dessert
dinner	dîner
fish	poisson
fork	fourchette
fruit	fruits
glass	verre
ice cream	glace
ice cubes	glaçons
ham	jambon
knife	couteau
lamb	agneau
lunch	déjeuner
lettuce salad	salade
meat	viande
mineral water	eau minérale
mixed salad	salade composée
orange juice	jus d'orange
plate	assiette
pork	porc
restaurant	restaurant
red wine	vin rouge
salt	sel
spoon	cuillère

sugar	sucre
vegetables	légumes
water	de l'eau
white wine	vin blanc
yoghurt	yaourt

PERSONAL DOCUMENTS AND TRAVEL

airport	aéroport
credit card	carte de crédit
customs	douane
passport	passeport
platform	voie
railway station	gare
shuttle	navette
suitcase	valise
train/plane ticket	billet de train/d'avion
wallet	portefeuille

CLOTHING

coat	manteau
jumper	pull
raincoat	imperméable
shirt	chemise
shoes	chaussures
socks	chaussettes
stockings	bas
suit	costume
tights	collant
trousers	pantalon

COMMONLY USED WORDS

goodbye	au revoir
hello/good morning	bonjour
how	comment
excuse me	excusez-moi
thank you	merci
yes/no	oui/non
I am sorry	pardon

why	pourquoi
when	quand
please	s'il vous plaît

USEFUL PHRASES

Do you speak English?
Parlez-vous anglais?

I don't understand
Je ne comprends pas

Talk slowly
Parlez lentement

Where's...?
Où est...?

When does the... leave?
À quelle heure part...?

When does the... arrive?
À quelle heure arrive...?

When does the museum open?
À quelle heure ouvre le musée?

When is the show?
À quelle heure est la représentation?

When is breakfast served?
À quelle heure sert-on le petit-déjeuner?

What does it cost?
Combien cela coûte?

Where can I buy a newspaper in English?
Où puis-je acheter un journal en anglais?

Where is the nearest petrol/gas station?
Où se trouve la station essence la plus proche?

Where can I change traveller's cheques?
Où puis-je échanger des traveller's cheques?

Where are the toilets?
Où sont les toilettes?

Do you accept credit cards?
Acceptez-vous les cartes de crédit?

BASIC INFORMATION

Electricity

The electric current is 220 volts. Circular two-pin plugs are the rule. Adapters and converters (for hairdryers, for example) should be bought before you leave home; they are on sale in most airports. If you have a rechargeable device (video camera, portable computer, battery recharger), read the instructions carefully or contact the manufacturer or shop. Sometimes these items only require a plug adapter, in other cases you must use a voltage converter as well or risk ruining your device.

Public Holidays

Public services, museums and other monuments may be closed or may vary their hours of admission on the following public holidays:

1 January	New Year's Day (Jour de l'An)
	Easter Day and Easter Monday (Pâques)
1 May	May Day (Fête du Travail)
8 May	VE Day (Fête de la Libération)
Thurs 40 days after Easter	Ascension Day (Ascension)
7th Sun-Mon after Easter	Whit Sunday and Monday (Pentecôte)
14 July	France's National Day (Fête de la Bastille)
15 August	Assumption (Assomption)
1 November	All Saint's Day (Toussaint)
11 November	Armistice Day (Fête de la Victoire)
25 December	Christmas Day (Noël)

National museums and art galleries are closed on Tuesdays; municipal museums are generally closed on Mondays. In addition to the usual school holidays at Christmas and in the spring and summer, there are long mid-term breaks (10 days to a fortnight) in February and early November.

Mail/Post

Main post offices open Mondays to Fridays, 8am to 7pm, Saturdays, 8am to noon. Smaller branch post offices often close at lunchtime between noon and 2pm and in the afternoon at 4pm.

✉ UK: letter (20g) 0.55€
✉ North America: letter (20g) 0.90€
✉ Australia and NZ: letter (20g) 0.90€

Stamps are also available from newsagents and tobacconists.
Stamp collectors should ask for timbres de collection in any post office.
Poste Restante (General Delivery) mail should be addressed as follows: Name, Poste Restante, Poste Centrale, post code of the département followed by town name, France. The Michelin Guide France gives local post codes.

Metric System

👌 *See the Conversion Tables at the end of this chapter.* France operates on the metric system. Some equivalents:

1 gram = 0.04 ounces
1 metre = 1.09 yards
1 kilogram = 2.20 pounds
1 kilometre = 0.62 miles
1 litre = 1.06 quarts\

Money

CURRENCY

There are no restrictions on the amount of currency visitors can take into France. Visitors carrying a lot of cash are advised to complete a currency declaration form on arrival, because there are restrictions on currency export.

Notes and Coins

The European currency unit, the **euro**, went into circulation as of 1 January 2002, and since 17 February 2002, euros are the only currency accepted as a means of payment. Notes in francs will be accepted by the Banque de France until 2012; coins in francs were accepted until 2005. 👌 *See the illustrations of Notes and Coins at the end of this chapter.*

BANKS

Although business hours vary from branch to branch, banks are usually open from 9am to noon and 2pm to 5pm and are closed either on Mondays or Saturdays. Banks close early on the day before a bank holiday. A passport is necessary as identification when cashing travellers cheques in banks. Commission charges vary and hotels usually charge more than banks for cashing cheques.
One of the most economical ways to use your money in France is by using **ATM machines** to get cash directly

from your bank account (with a debit card) or to use your credit card to get a cash advance. Be sure to remember your PIN number, you will need it to use cash dispensers and to pay with your card in shops, restaurants etc. Code pads are numeric; use a telephone pad to translate a letter code into numbers. Pin numbers have 4 digits in France; inquire with the issuing company or bank if the code you usually use is longer. Visa is the most widely accepted credit card, followed by Mastercard; other cards, credit and debit (Diners Club, Plus, Cirrus etc) are also accepted in some cash machines. American Express is more often accepted in premium establishments. Most places post signs indicating which card they accept; if you don't see such a sign and want to pay with a card, ask before ordering or making a selection. Cards are widely accepted in shops, hypermarkets, hotels and restaurants, at tollbooths and in petrol stations.

⊘ Before you leave home, check with the bank that issued your card for emergency replacement procedures. Carry your card number and emergency phone numbers separate from your wallet and handbag; leave a copy of this information with someone you can easily reach. If your card is lost or stolen while you are in France, call one of the following 24-hour hotlines:

American Express ☏ 01 47 77 72 00

Visa ☏ 0 800 901 179

MasterCard/Eurocard ☏ 0 800 901 179

Diners Club ☏ 0 810 314 519

These numbers are also listed at most ATM machines.

You must report any loss or theft of credit cards or travellers cheques to the local police who will issue you with a certificate (useful proof to show the issuing company).

PRICES AND TIPS

Since a service charge is automatically included in the prices of meals and accommodation in France, it is not necessary to tip in restaurants and hotels. However, if the service in a restaurant is especially good or if you have enjoyed a fine meal, an extra tip (this is the *pourboire*, rather than the service)

will be appreciated. Usually 1.5 to 3.5 euros is enough, but if the bill is big (a large party or a luxury restaurant), it is not uncommon to leave 7 to 8 euros or more.

As a rule, the cost of staying in a hotel and eating in restaurants is significantly higher in Paris than in the French regions. Nevertheless, reserve a hotel room well in advance and take advantage of the choice of restaurants to make the most of your money.

Restaurants usually charge for meals in two ways: a menu, that is a fixed price menu with 2 or 3 courses, sometimes a small pitcher of wine, all for a stated price, or à la carte, the more expensive way, with each course ordered separately.

Cafés have very different prices, depending on where they are located. The price of a drink or a coffee is cheaper if you stand at the counter *(comptoir)* than if you sit down *(salle)* and sometimes it is even more expensive if you sit outdoors *(terrasse)*.

DISCOUNTS

Significant discounts are available for senior citizens, students, youth under age 25, teachers, and groups for public transportation, museums and monuments and for some leisure activities such as movies (at certain times of day). Bring student or senior cards with you, and bring along some extra passport-size photos for discount travel cards.

The **International Student Travel Conference** (www.istc.org), global administrator of the International Student and Teacher Identity Cards, is an association of student travel organizations around the world. ISTC members collectively negotiate benefits with airlines, governments, and providers of other goods and services for the student and teacher community, both in their own country and around the world. The non-profit association sells international ID cards for students, youth under age 25 and teachers (who may get discounts on museum entrances, for example). The ISTC is also active in a network of international education and work exchange programmes. The coorporate headquarters address is Herengracht 479, 1017 BS Amsterdam, The Netherlands ☏ 31 20 421 28 00; Fax 31 20 421 28 10.

⊙ *See Getting There: By Rail* for other discounts on transportation.

Telephone

Most public phones in France use pre-paid phone cards *(télécartes)*, rather than coins. Some telephone booths accept credit cards (Visa, Mastercard/Eurocard). *Télécartes* (50 or 120 units) can be bought in post offices, branches of France Télécom, *bureaux de tabac* (cafés that sell cigarettes) and newsagents and can be used to make calls in France and abroad. Calls can be received at phone boxes where the blue bell sign is shown; the phone will not ring, so keep your eye on the little message screen.

Emergency numbers	
Police:	17
SAMU (Paramedics):	15
Fire (Pompiers):	18

NATIONAL CALLS

French telephone numbers have 10 digits. Paris and Paris region numbers begin with 01; 02 in north-west France; 03 in north-east France; 04 in south-east France and Corsica; 05 in south-west France.

INTERNATIONAL CALLS

To call France from abroad, dial the country code (33) + 9-digit number (omit the initial 0). When calling abroad from France dial 00, then dial the country code followed by the area code and number of your correspondent.

International Dialling Codes (00 + code)			
Australia	☎ 61	New Zealand	☎ 64
Canada	☎ 1	United Kingdom	☎ 44
Ireland	☎ 353	United States	☎ 1

To use your personal calling card	
AT&T	☎ 0-800 99 00 11
Sprint	☎ 0-800 99 00 87
MCI	☎ 0-800 99 00 19
Canada Direct	☎ 0-800 99 00 16

International information (US/Canada): 00 33 12 11

International operator: 00 33 12 + country code

Local directory assistance: 12

Toll-free numbers in France begin with 0 800.

Minitel – France Télécom operates a system offering directory enquiries (free of charge up to 3min), travel and entertainment reservations, and other services (cost per minute varies). These small computer-like terminals can be found in some post offices, hotels and France Télécom agencies and in many French homes. 3614 PAGES E is the code for directory assistance in English (turn on the unit, dial 3614, hit the connexion button when you get the tone, type in PAGES E, and follow the instructions on the screen).

CELLULAR PHONES

In France these have numbers which begin with 06. Two-watt (lighter, shorter reach) and eight-watt models are on the market, using the Orange (France Télécom) or SFR networks. Mobicartes are prepaid phone cards that fit into mobile units. Mobile phone rentals (delivery or airport pickup provided):

🖉 **A.L.T. Rent A Phone**
  ☎ 01 48 00 06 06; altloc@jve.fr

🖉 **Rent a Cell Express**
  ☎ 01 53 93 78 00,
  Fax 01 53 93 78 09

🖉 **Ellinas Phone Rental**
  ☎ 01 47 20 70 00

Time

France is 1hr ahead of Greenwich Mean Time (GMT). France goes on daylight-saving time from the last Sunday in March to the last Sunday in October.

When it is **noon in France**, it is	
3am	in Los Angeles
6am	in New York
11am	in Dublin
11am	in London
7pm	in Perth
9pm	in Sydney
11pm	in Auckland

In France "am" and "pm" are not used but the 24-hour clock is widely applied.

Australia and New Zealand are not observing daylight saving time (DST) at the moment.

Conversion Tables

Weights and measures

1 kilogram (kg)	2.2 pounds (lb)	2.2 pounds
1 metric ton (tn)	1.1 tons	1.1 tons

to convert kilograms to pounds, multiply by 2.2

1 litre (l)	2.1 pints (pt)	1.8 pints
1 litre	0.3 gallon (gal)	0.2 gallon

to convert litres to gallons, multiply by 0.26 (US) or 0.22 (UK)

1 hectare (ha)	2.5 acres	2.5 acres
1 square kilometre (km²)	0.4 square miles (sq mi)	0.4 square miles

to convert hectares to acres, multiply by 2.4

1centimetre (cm)	0.4 inches (in)	0.4 inches
1 metre (m)	3.3 feet (ft) - 39.4 inches - 1.1 yards (yd)	
1 kilometre (km)	0.6 miles (mi)	0.6 miles

to convert metres to feet, multiply by 3.28 . kilometres to miles, multiply by 0.6

Clothing

Women							Men
	35	4	2½	40	7½	7	
	36	5	3½	41	8½	8	
	37	6	4½	42	9½	9	
Shoes	38	7	5½	43	10½	10	Shoes
	39	8	6½	44	11½	11	
	40	9	7½	45	12½	12	
	41	10	8½	46	13½	13	
	36	4	8	46	36	36	
	38	6	10	48	38	38	
Dresses &	40	8	12	50	40	40	Suits
Suits	42	12	14	52	42	42	
	44	14	16	54	44	44	
	46	16	18	56	46	48	
	36	08	30	37	14½	14,5	
	38	10	32	38	15	15	
Blouses &	40	12	14	39	15½	15½	Shirts
sweaters	42	14	36	40	15¾	15¾	
	44	16	38	41	16	16	
	46	18	40	42	16½	16½	

Sizes often vary depending on the designer. These equivalents are given for guidance only.

Speed

kph	10	30	50	70	80	90	100	110	120	130
mph	6	19	31	43	50	56	62	68	75	81

Temperature

Celsius (°C)	0°	5°	10°	15°	20°	25°	30°	40°	60°	80°	100°
Fahrenheit (°F)	32°	41°	50°	59°	68°	77°	86°	104°	140°	176°	212°

To convert Celsius into Fahrenheit, multiply °C by 9, divide by 5, and add 32.
To convert Fahrenheit into Celsius, subtract 32 from °F, multiply by 5, and divide by 9.

Notes and Coins

The euro banknotes were designed by Robert Kalinan, an Austrian artist. His designs were inspired by the theme "Ages and styles of European Architecture." Windows and gateways feature on the front of the banknotes, bridges feature on the reverse, symbolising the European spirit of openness and co-operation. The images are stylised representations of architecture typical of each period, rather than specific structures.

Classical

Baroque and Rococo

Romanesque

19C Iron and glass

Gothic

Renaissance

20C Modern

Euro coins have one face common to all 12 countries in the European single currency area or "Eurozone" (currently Austria, Belgium, Finland, France, Germany, Greece, Ireland, Italy, Luxembourg, The Netherlands, Portugal and Spain) and a reverse side specific to each country, created by their own national artists.

Euro banknotes look the same throughout the Eurozone. All Euro banknotes and coins can be used anywhere in this area.

Little Red Riding Hood

But Little Red Riding Hood had her local map with her, and so she did not fall into the trap. She did not take the path through the wood and she did not meet the big bad wolf. Instead, she chose the picturesque touring route straight to Grandmother's house, and arrived safely with her cake and her little pot of butter.

The End

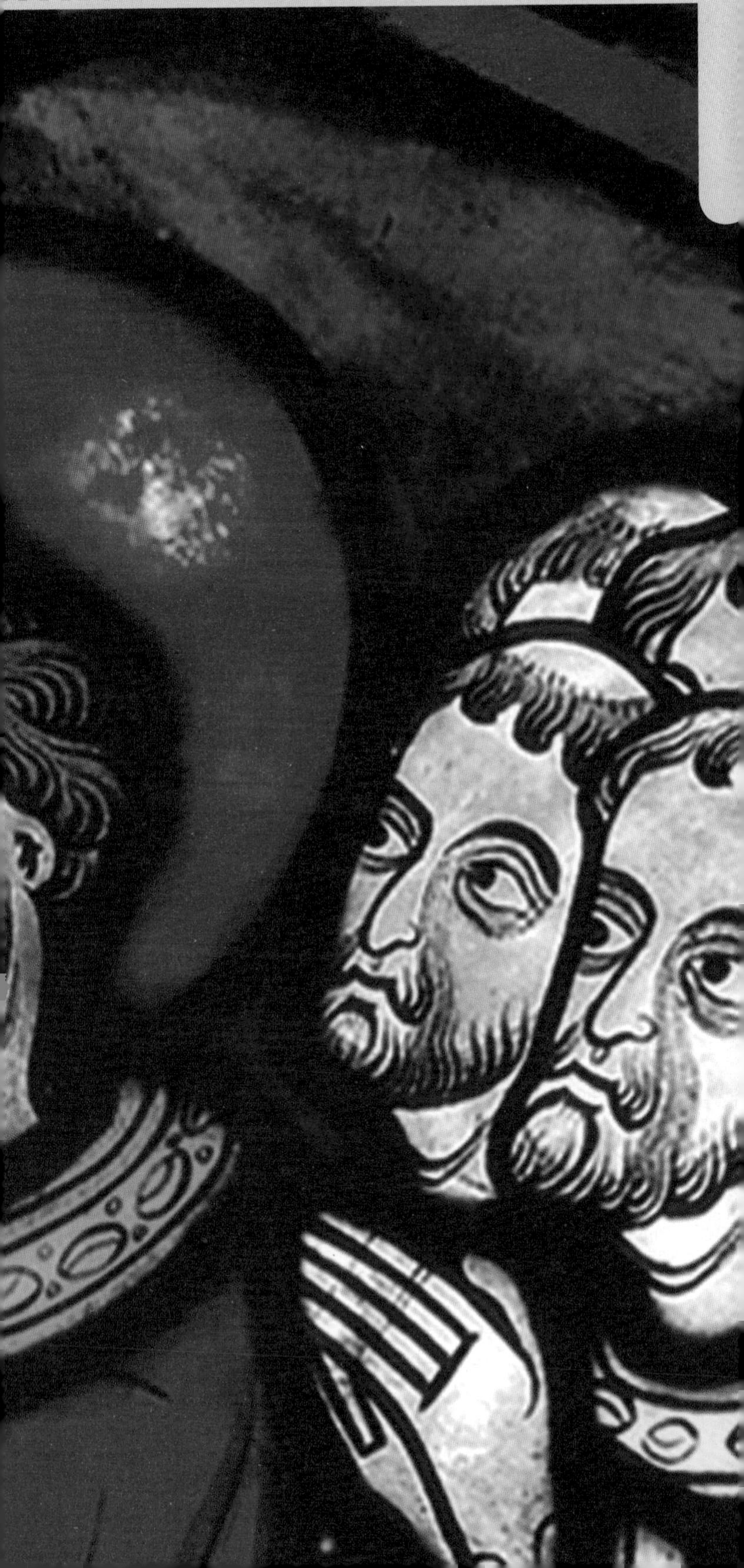

NATURE

The *région* (there are 22 in France) is the largest administrative division in the country, followed by the *département* (96, excluding overseas territories), which is sub-divided into communes run by an elected mayor. In total, there are 36 394 mayoral districts in France.

Berry (formerly Berri) is the name historically and popularly applied to the area south of the Paris basin, comprising the *départements* of Cher and Indre in the Centre *région*. This old county, later a duchy, came under the crown in the 13C.

Limousin is the name of an administrative *région* comprising three *départements*: Corrèze, Creuse and Haute-Vienne. For a long time an Anglo-Norman fief, it was united to the French throne by Henry IV, and later administered by appointed Intendants.

Dordogne is a *département* which is part of the larger *région* of Aquitaine. The French *départements* were created in 1790 and were generally given the name of the main river within the territory, hence the Dordogne, named after the two rivers (the Dore and the Dogne) which combine to form this famous waterway. Before that time, the same area was known as **Périgord** (named after the Petrocorii who occupied the area at the time of the Gauls), a free county dating back to the 11C, which fell into the possession of the Albret family. Henry IV, its last feudal lord, brought it under the authority of the French crown. Many French people still use the old appellation to refer to this popular holiday destination, especially when describing its culinary delights.

Land Formation

PRIMARY ERA

This began about 600 million years ago. It was towards the end of this era that an upheaval of the earth's crust took place. This upheaval or folding movement, known as the Hercynian fold, the V-shaped appearance of which is shown by dotted lines on the map, resulted in the emergence of a number of high mountains, notably the Massif Central, formed by crystalline rocks which were slowly worn down by erosion.

SECONDARY ERA

This began about 260 million years ago. Towards the middle of this era, there was a slow folding of the Hercynian base, resulting in the flooding of the area by the sea. Sedimentary deposits, mainly calcareous, accumulated on the edge of the Massif Central, forming the Quercy causses (limestone plateaux) during the Jurassic period and then the beds of Cretaceous limestone of the Périgord region. The same types of formations are also found in Champagne Berrichonne, Boischaut and Sancerre.

TERTIARY ERA

This began about 65 million years ago. During this period siderolithic deposits (clay and gravel, rich in iron) originating from the Massif Central covered some parts of the Quercy, such as the Bouriane region, whereas clay-rich sands accumulated to the west of Périgord, creating the heathlands of the Brenne, Sologne, Double and Landais regions, with their numerous lakes.

QUATERNARY ERA

This began about 2 million years ago. It was during this period that human evolution gathered pace. By this time, the effects of erosion had given the region its present-day appearance. Rivers with their source in the Massif Central created the Vézère, Dordogne and Lot valleys.

THE COUNTRYSIDE TODAY

Regions which are totally different in character lie side by side in the area between the Berry and the plains of the Agenais. This region of contrasting countrysides is one of great natural beauty: the wide horizons of the Berry succeeded by the green mountain country of the Limousin; the limestone plateaux of the Quercy stretching out in stark silhouette; and the wooded plateaux of the Périgord divided by picturesque valleys and bountiful orchards.

Rich in prehistoric sites, the area has many visible traces of its earliest settlers. Charming churches, the imposing religious sanctuaries of the Limousin and the hundreds of fortresses, castles, manors and mansions in a variety of architectural styles all bear witness to the region's rich historical past. In addition, it is renowned for its delicious traditional cuisine and excellent local wines, offering the perfect accompaniment to your voyage of discovery.

Berry

This province is one of the oldest agricultural regions in France, with a unity that is the result of its shared heritage, rather than of its geography. The geological position of the Berry lies at the contact point between the Paris Basin and the Massif Central. The area consists of a vast low-lying plateau, rising in the northeast to the Sancerre Hills (highest point: the Motte de Humbligny at an altitude of 434m/1 424ft), tilting westwards in a series of steps towards the Brenne depression. To the south, the countryside is more undulating with numerous isolated hills and escarpments. The River Cher and River Indre are part of the Loire drainage system, whereas the Creuse is a tributary of the Vienne.

NORTHERN BERRY

The **Pays Fort** and **Sancerrois** are transitional areas bordering the Pays de la Loire. The former, characterised by its marl and clayey soils, slopes towards the Sologne, whereas the vine-covered, chalky slopes of the Sancerrois rise above the river banks. This once-forested landscape has been remodelled as bocage (wooded farmland). The Forêt d'Allogny, the last remaining area of primitive forest cover, overlooks the vast orchards of St-Martin-d'Auxigny.

The **Northern Boischaut**, meanwhile, is an area of rich pasture.

The **Southern Berry – Champagne Berrichonne** is a region of plateaus and limestone soil extending between the Loire to the east and the Indre to the west, and is covered in the main by scattered woods and forests. Manure and rich fertilisers have transformed this light, sandy soil into excellent farm land. In addition to grain crops, sheep and Normandy dairy cows are bred indoors and fed on beetroot pulp; beekeeping is also an important economic activity around Châteauroux. Away to the east, the **Val de Germigny** is a long depression, formerly marshland, which runs along the foot of the escarpments crowned by the Bois de Meillant. The pastures here are grazed by Charolais cattle.

BOISCHAUT

This district lies between the Cher and the Creuse, its clay soils overlapping the neighbouring Marche province. This is an area of small farms where the emphasis is on livestock rearing, in particular the Charolais breed, and sheep.

The countryside, crisscrossed with many rivers, farms and gardens, is much the same as when described by the novelist George Sand (*see NOHANT*).

BRENNE

This vast sand and clay depression, characterised by its abundant marshes, is predominantly covered with heather, pine trees and broom. Once the exclusive haven of hunters and fishers, the Brenne is now a nature park, popular with visitors interested in observing its exceptional flora and fauna (*see La BRENNE*).

Limousin

This vast region of crystalline rocks forms the western bastion of the Massif Central. The area takes its name from the Lemovices, the large tribe which occupied the country at the time of the Gauls. The individuality of the region is emphasised by its wet winter climate and verdant countryside. Limousin has been aptly described by Jérôme and Jean Tharaud in their novel La Maîtresse Servante: "Before us unrolled a green and ever-changing countryside, silent and impenetrable, cut by thick hedges, filled with dark shadows and watered by running brooks. No rivers, only streams; no lakes, only pools; no ravines, only valleys."

LA MONTAGNE

This vast series of plateaus, at altitudes no higher than 977m/3 205ft, has been levelled by erosion. The "Mountain" is the source of many rivers and streams which filter across the rest of the region. The weather on these highlands is rugged, the rains heavy, the winds strong and snow has been known to lie on the ground for four months at a time. Farms are few and far between and stony wastes and moors are more common than ploughed land, particularly on the Plateau de Millevaches (*see MEYMAC*) and in the Massif des Monédières (*see TREIGNAC*). As you pass through this eerily quiet landscape, your eyes are drawn to a landscape of meadows, moors and woodlands of beech and pine, dotted with the ever-present sight of grazing sheep.

THE PLATEAUX OF HAUT-LIMOUSIN

The plateaux to the northwest are undulating in appearance – the **Monts d'Ambazac** and the **Monts de Blond** – with alternating escarpments and deeply incised valleys. The bocage is a patchwork of woods and fields. Trees thrive in this wet climate, with oak and beech on the uplands and chestnut trees at lower levels. Quickset hedges surround fields and meadows. The pastures enriched by manure and artificial fertilisers make good cattle-grazing country. Further north, the drier, less-wooded **Marche** area is a marshland between the Massif Central and the Pays de la Loire. The **Haute-Marche**, drained by the Creuse, is an area of stock-rearing, whereas arable farming is more prevalent in the **Basse-Marche**, particularly around Bellac.

To the west, the *Confolentais* is the name given to the green and forested foothills of the Massif Central, which are dissected by the River Vienne.

THE PLATEAUX OF BAS-LIMOUSIN

This area, where the influence of Périgord and Quercy is already evident, is characterised by its wonderful light, milder climate and fertile basins. The **Xaintrie** is an area dotted with woods of pine and silver birch – this granite plateau is deeply incised by the Dordogne, the Maronne and numerous smaller rivers.

The depression of the **Bassin de Brive** straddles the Lower Limousin and the northernmost part of the Périgord. The *Nontronnais* is also partly in the Limousin and takes on a similar appearance, with its grassy fields, chestnut trees, heather, gorse and isolated farmhouses.

BASSIN DE BRIVE

The depression of the Brive Basin is a sunken zone between the crystalline escarpments of the Uzerche plateau and the limestone ridges of the Causses du Quercy. It is an area of sandstone and schist, drained by the River Vézère and River Corrèze. In its green valleys demarcated by screens of poplar, the gentle south-facing slopes are given over to orchards. Today, Brive is an important centre for the fruit and vegetable canning industries.

South of Brive, the **Causse Corrèzien** is covered with large farms devoted to the rearing of geese and sheep, and truffle oak plantations.

Perigord

PÉRIGORD VERT

The Green Périgord, located between the Nontronnais and Excideuil, comprises fragments of the old massif, small basins scoured out of the soft Lias marl, and the occasional table of limestone. Its landscape of woodlands, well-tended farms and patches of bright sunflowers echoes the neighbouring Limousin. The handful of towns scattered across this lush borderland act as centres for light industry and the marketing of locally produced farm products.

Contrasting colours are provided by pastures grazed by dairy cattle and calves (for veal), especially around Ribérac, and fields of cereal crops. Numerous agricultural markets are held in local towns.

PÉRIGORD BLANC

The White Périgord takes its name from the frequent outcrops of chalky limestone which illuminate this open landscape.

The countryside of hills and slopes around Périgueux consists of meadows interspersed with coppices of oak and chestnut. This region is drained by the River Beauronne and River Vern, whose valleys are covered with pasture and arable land; the extensive **Vallée de l'Isle** is dotted with small industrial towns, its alluvial soil used as pasture, or for growing maize (corn), tobacco and walnuts.

South of Périgueux, around Vergt and Rouffignac, the iron-rich siderolithic deposits covering the limestone have proven to be ideal for the cultivation of strawberries, which are exported to all parts of France.

To the northeast of the town, Central Périgord meets the **Périgord Causse**. This block of Jurassic limestone, scored by the Isle, Auvézère and Loue valleys, is characterised by its sparse vegetation, although its stunted oak trees harbour the famed, yet elusive truffle.

The **Double,** lying to the west, between the River Dronne and the River Isle, is an area of forests where tall oak and chestnut trees predominate; the clay soil here favours the formation of ponds. The **Landais**, to the south of the Isle, is a less rugged region abundant in fruit orchards. The maritime pine is more common here than the chestnut; meadows are also more abundant than to the north of the river.

PÉRIGORD POURPRE

The Purple Périgord around Bergerac is divided into several areas, all of which share a mild climate favourable to the cultivation of crops more commonly associated with more southerly parts of the country. The Dordogne Valley, which is particularly wide here, is divided into plots of land where tobacco, maize (corn), sunflowers and cereals all flourish in the rich alluvial deposits.

Timber production predominates to the west of Bergerac, in an area whose slopes are covered with the vineyards of Bergerac and Monbazillac.

The town of Bergerac itself is an important centre for the tobacco and wine industries.

PÉRIGORD NOIR

Dissected by the Vézère and Dordogne valleys, the Black Périgord owes its name to the high density of trees growing in the sandy soil covering the limestone areas, and to the predominance of the holm oak, with its dark, dense foliage, particularly in the area around Sarlat. The alluvial soil of the valleys, whose river courses are lined with screens of poplar or willow, supports a variety of crops, including wheat, maize (corn), tobacco and walnuts. The bustling and colourful local markets all sell excellent nuts, mushrooms, truffles and foie gras. Springs, chasms and prehistoric caves and shelters with sculpted or painted walls offer further attractions for visitors to this area. Along the River Dordogne the landscape is gentle and harmonious, as can be seen from the viewpoints at Domme, and the castles of Beynac and Castelnaud. The former capital of Périgord Noir, Sarlat-la-Canéda, with its *lauze* roofs and medieval atmosphere, is a lively tourist centre and popular holiday base.

Vast stretches of gently undulating molassic hillside, with the occasional limestone outcrop and terrace extend beyond the wine-producing slopes of Monbazillac. Small farms interspersed with woodlands are planted with cereal crops, vineyards (AOC Bergerac) and plum trees. To the east, in an area of transition with the Bouriane region in the Quercy, the dense **Forêt de Bessède**, a forest which continues to flourish on the millstone or siderolithic sands, has hardly been disturbed by the foundation of *bastides* and abbeys during the Middle Ages.

Quercy

Quercy corresponds to a region which stretches from the Massif Central to the plains of Aquitaine and was occupied by the Cadurques who made Cahors their capital. The region has a strong historical unity: in the Middle Ages Quercy belonged to the province of Guyenne; under the Ancien Régime two regions were recognised – the Haut-Quercy, centred on Cahors and seat of the main administrative departments, and the Bas-Quercy, governed from Montauban. During the Revolution they were reunited as part of the Lot *département*. However, in 1808 Napoleon separated them once more, creating the *département* of the Tarn-et-Garonne, which covers most of the Bas-Quercy, and parts of Rouergue, Gascony and Languedoc.

THE CAUSSES

This dry land, dissected by dry valleys known locally as *combes*, forms a protected area known as the **Parc Naturel Regional des Causses du Quercy.** Flocks of sheep graze on the sparse grass of the pastures which are sub-divided by drystone dikes. Stunted oaks and maple are the only trees growing here. The more fertile valleys are a mix of pasture, vineyards and other crops.

The **Causse de Martel** is a vast, arid, stone-covered plain, dissected by a relatively fertile zone. The numerous drystone walls here were built by shepherds as they cleared stones from the ground to allow sheep to graze and marked out boundaries. The area takes its name from the nearby agricultural town of Martel.

The **Causse de Gramat**, an extensive limestone plateau at an average altitude of 350m/1 150ft is home to a number of sites of natural interest (♦ *see Gouffre de PADIRAC)* and unusual landscapes: to the north lie the Ouysse and Alzou canyons (the spectacular village of Rocamadour clings to the cliff face); to the south the much longer Célé Canyon. Between the narrow gashes of the Alzou and the Célé lies the waterless **Braunhie**, an arid region riddled with caves and ravines. Like many of their neighbours, the local towns of Gramat and Labastide-Murat have suffered from serious depopulation in recent decades.

The low-lying plateau of the **Causse de Carjac** is hemmed in by the banks of the River Célé and River Lot, the banks of which are particularly fertile.

The **Causse de Limogne**, with its drier climate, takes on a very different

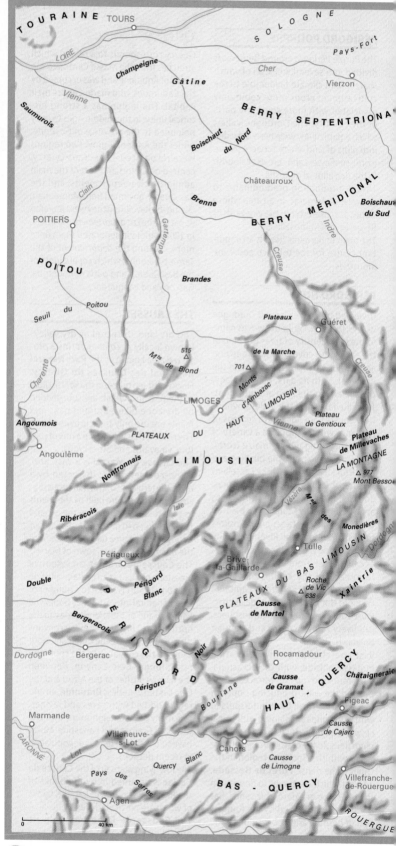

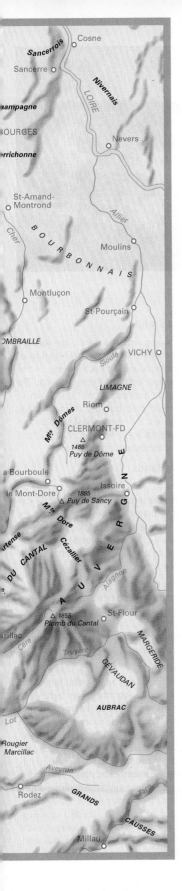

appearance. Bordered by the Lot Valley, the plateau is dotted with dolmens and megaliths which appear amid clusters of white truffle oak, juniper bushes and fields of lavender. Dotted around this landscape are unusual shepherds' shelters built of flat stone with strange conical roofs, known as *garriottes*, *cazelles*, or *bories* (see SARLAT: Cabanes de Breuil). There are few big towns in this area, although Limogne-en-Quercy and Lalbenque remain busy centres for the truffle trade.

THE VALLEYS

Cutting a wide swath through limestone, the region's rivers have carved out their valleys, shaping meanders which enlarge as the valley broadens, to the point that they become ever-widening loops *(cingles)* in the course of rivers.

The valleys of the Dordogne, Célé and Lot have been inhabited since prehistoric times. During the Roman era, settlers lived in fortified *oppidums*; castles and châteaux bear witness to the role of these valleys in the region's later history. Today, they are richly covered with crops, vineyards and orchards. The main centres of population in this area today are Souillac (Dordogne Valley), Figeac (Célé) and Cahors (Lot).

HAUT-QUERCY

The major part of the Haut-Quercy comprises limestone plateaux or *causses* with an average altitude of 300m/1 000ft. The fertile areas of the **Limargue** and **Terrefort** extend across flat basins and vast plains; the soils of the area favour the production of a variety of crops including greengage plums and strawberries *(between Carennac and St-Céré)*, grapes, walnuts and tobacco. The eastern part of the Haut-Quercy includes the **Châtaigneraie**, an area with a cold, damp climate and poor soil. This plateau, at an altitude of 700m/2 300ft, tilts eastwards and is cut by deep gorges. The widely cultivated chestnut tree has given the area its name; cereal crops are grown on lowering hilltops, while cattle are raised on small farms. The **Bouriane** is blanketed in heath, coppices and woods, and bears more resemblance to the Périgord than the Quercy. In this area, timber, chestnuts and walnuts are harvested, maritime pines are tapped for resin, and livestock is raised and sold. The capital of this area is the bustling town of Gourdon.

Landscape of the lower Lot Valley

E. Larribère/MICHELIN

QUERCY BLANC

Southwest of the Lot Valley and the town of Cahors, the Jurassic limestone disappears under tertiary limestone to create unusual landscapes known as *planhès* – vast undulating areas of white which have given the region its name (White Quercy). These plateaux are cut into narrow ridges *(serres)* by the rivers. The crests of the *serres* are levelled off into plains which are covered with pastures used for grazing sheep, oak forest and, occasionally, fertile fields of crops. Between the *serres*, the valleys are fertile corridors, spreading between the sandstone as they get closer to the Garonne. Pastures lined with poplars produce abundant crops of fruit, cereals and tobacco, in addition to wine from local vineyards. The lively market towns of Montcuq, Lauzerte, Castelnau-Montratier, and Montpezat-de-Quercy are all situated on rocky hilltops known as *puechs*.

Flora and Fauna

WATER

The region has a dense network of rivers and streams. In the Limousin, the rivers tumble through picturesque valleys, whereas in the Berry they tend to flow more peacefully. With a few exceptions (near urban areas), the waters are pure and clean, harbouring myriad species of fish. The region is home to numerous natural ponds and wetlands, man-made lakes, as well as an abundance of flora and fauna.

La Brenne

This nature park is part of the region's commitment to the preservation of wetlands and their ecosystems, and to the development of green tourism. The hundreds of ponds and the diversity of habitats make it an ideal refuge for many species, including a host of migrating birds. (♻ *See La BRENNE for further details and illustrations of local wildlife.)*

Wetlands

These ecosystems, characterised by the presence of slow-moving water or saturated soil, are vitally important in maintaining the region's ecological balance. The protection of these often fragile areas has led to a better understanding of their morphology.

Wet Meadows – The outer ring of the pond system, these meadows of variable size are often rich with wildflowers in springtime. The flora is diverse and in La Brenne includes as many as 50 species: marsh violets, gentian, orchids etc.

Swamps – The waterlogged banks of the region's ponds are invaded by willows which develop into groves extending from the water's edge to firmer ground. Trees provide nesting for green-winged teal; the branches dipping in the water protect paddling ducks; while the grey heron and the black-crowned night-heron gather beneath them. The muddy banks are teeming with mollusks which attract waders such as black-tailed godwits, curlews, crested lapwings and snipe. Partially submerged plant life includes perennial herbs, quillwort, clovers and ferns.

Marshes – Plant life in the mineral-rich soil is dominated by grasses in many forms, including sedge, reeds, cattails and bulrushes. Impenetrable and considered undesirable for fish hatcheries, these grassy areas are essential to the survival of certain rare species. Waders such as bitterns and other members of the heron family build their nests in these protected zones alongside marsh harriers, millerbirds, swamp sparrows, reed-buntings etc.

Ponds – Floating plants make good nests for crested grebes. Many species of duck are also found here (such as mallard, pintails (with their wide, spatula-shaped bills), canvas-backs and grey ducks). Osprey choose the region's ponds to rest during their annual migrations, while black and striped terns are a regular sight gliding over the water.

European pond turtles are shy creatures, living off water-lilies and sunbathing by the reeds. Insects are everywhere, with as many as 600 to 1 000 species identified. Snakes, frogs, toads, newts and some rare mammals have also been spotted, including a remarkable sighting of the European mink, at the Etang Ricot (*Réserve Naturelle de Chérine*) in 1982.

The abundant **lakes and rivers** of the Limousin are popular with fishing enthusiasts: the Creuse is a favourite for trout; the Gartempe is popular for carp; while the river's oxygen-rich rivers are the domain of trout, grayling and salmon. In still waters, look out for freshwater fish (carp, barbel, tench, bream, goldfish, chub, dace and shiner). Several species of fish, in particular pike and perch, can grow to a considerable size.

MOORS AND FORESTS

Moorland and Peatland

The Brenne is poor in pastureland and has been gradually abandoned by its rural population; as a result, the few tilled fields have mostly given way to idle, uncultivated land. The humid ground is covered with besom heather, a tall bushy plant with greenish-white flowers. On drier ground, gorse, Scotch broom and bracken grow beneath a few isolated trees. The skies here are populated with birds such as the kingfisher, harrier and hawk, while the undergrowth provides a natural habitat for hare, boar, deer, badger and genet.

In the Limousin, the high plateaux with their vast granite depressions (Millevaches, Gentioux) have highly acidic soil where sphagnum moss flourishes; consequently, parts of the countryside have developed into peat bogs. Near Meymac, a protected bog, the Tourbière du Longéroux, harbours the source of the Vézère.

Peat is made by the slow decomposition of organic materials (especially sphagnum) in cold, acidic water and is a process that takes centuries. In Longéroux, where the average thickness of the peat is 2m/6.5ft, the analysis of fossilised pollen shows that the deposits began forming 8 000 years ago. The bog's inhabitants include lizards, snakes, toads, frogs, newts and the birds who prey on them, as well as the elusive otter, whose presence can often only be deduced by its spoor.

The granite hills around the site are drier, and are covered with common heather, fuzzy broom and scattered bilberry bushes. Over the decades, however, indigenous deciduous trees such as birch and ash have been disappearing as a result of unchecked development.

FORESTS

In the 19C, state-owned forests began operating a coppice-with-standards system, whereby selected stems are retained, as standards, at each felling to form an unevenly aged canopy which is then harvested selectively. The forest is managed so that part of the growth is natural and part of seedling origin, together forming a composite forest. The Indre *département*, one of the first to use this method, has become a leading producer of oakwood for panelling. The **Forêt de Châteauroux** (5 204 ha/13 000 acres) and the **Forêt de Bommiers** (4 470 ha/11 000 acres) are remarkable examples of successful forestry. The dark, low-acidic soil has produced a seedling forest of English oak growing alongside plan-

Beech

M. Janvier / MICHELIN

Spruce

M. Janvier/ MICHELIN

tations of hornbeam and ash, with ferns growing low to the ground. Boar, deer, martens, skunks, squirrels and wild cats wander the reserve, where the bird population includes wood pigeons and woodpeckers.

To the north, the acidic, wet soil of the Boischaut is home to birch (*Forêt de Gâtine*); oak and beech are found in the Marche; while pubescent oak grow on the limestone plateaux in the southwest of the Indre *département*. On the highest plateaux of the Limousin, conifers have multiplied, with spruce, larch and pine replacing meadows of heather and fields of grain crops.

To the south, and on the borders of the Périgord, deciduous hardwood forests prevail on the sunny slopes, and chestnut trees, which are native to the region, are cultivated for their nuts.

At certain times of the year, the region's woods become the haunt of mushroom-hunters searching for varieties including king bolete (*Boletus edulis*), bay bolete (*Boletus badius*), chanterelle (*Cantharellus cibarius*) and yellow morel (*Morchella esculenta*). In rural France, pharmacists are able to identify edible mushrooms, so if you are unsure of what mushrooms you have picked, take them to the local *pharmacie* before taking them home.

Chestnut

M. Janvier/ MICHELIN

FIELDS AND BOCAGE

The **Champagne Berrichonne**, an open land of large, ploughed fields which attracts numerous birds, is the most northerly area covered in this guide. South of this area, the **Boischaut-Sud** and parts of **La Brenne** are completely different, with a more secretive feel. The *bocage* landscape here is one of hedges and hedgerows, groves of trees, small plots of land and protected pastures. This maze of vegetation is further marked by *chemins creux* – tunnel-like pathways laid out between high banks topped with vegetation. These deep-sided lanes, many now overgrown and too narrow for tractors, prevented erosion; prickly bushes held climbing vines tight together to keep the animals safely enclosed; trees provided wood for cooking and making tools; and the leaves of elm trees could be used as fodder. (⟲ *see ST-AMAND-MONTROND for details on excursions through this region.*)

CAVES AND CHASMS IN DORDOGNE

Although dispersed throughout the region, the arid *causse* slices through the otherwise luxuriant landscape of the Périgord. In the Quercy, the limestone plateaux roll away to the horizon, stony, grey and deserted. The dryness of the soil is due to the calcareous nature of the rock which absorbs rain like a sponge.

Water Infiltration

Rainwater containing carbonic acid dissolves the carbonate of lime found in the limestone. Depressions form, known as **cloups**, which are usually circular in shape and small in size. When the *cloups* increase in size, they form large, closed depressions known as **sotches**. Where rainwater infiltrates the countless fissures in the plateau more deeply, the hollowing out and dissolution of the calcareous layer produces wells or natural chasms which are called **igues**.

Underground Rivers and Resurgent Springs

Infiltrating water eventually reaches the impermeable layers (marl) of the earth, developing into rivers which sometimes flow for miles. The waters merge into more powerful streams, widening their beds and tumbling over falls. In zones where the impermeable marl comes close to the surface of a hillside, the water bubbles up to the surface, sometimes with great force, in the form of a **resurgent spring**.

The circulation of water underground through chasms and galleries follows an unpredictable course, for the cracks in the rock continually affect the underground drainage. There are many dry river beds underground, where waters have sought out deeper domains.

When water flows slowly, as at Padirac, small lakes are formed by natural dams called **gours**. The walls holding back the waters are built up by the deposit of lime carbonate. Dissolution of limestone continues above the water level, with blocks of stone falling from the roof, resulting in the creation of domes. As the dome pushes upwards and its roof grows thin, it may cave in, opening the chasm to the surface above. The *Gouffre de Padirac* is such a dome, with the top of its ceiling just a few feet beneath the surface of the earth.

Cave formations

As it circulates underground, water deposits the lime it carries, building up concretions of fantastic shapes which seem to defy the laws of gravity. The seeping waters deposit calcite (carbonate of lime) to form a series of stalactites, stalagmites, pendants, pyramids, draperies and features known as eccentrics.

Stalactites are formed on the roof by water dripping down. The concretion builds up slowly as drops deposit calcite on the surface before falling to the ground.

Stalagmites are a sort of mirror image, rising up from the deposits of dripping water from the ceiling above, eventually meeting the stalactite above to form a pillar.

Such concretions form very slowly: the rate of growth in temperate climates is about 1cm/0.5in every 100 years.

Eccentrics are very delicate protuberances, formed by crystallisation, which seldom exceed 20cm/8in in length. They emerge at odd angles, as slender spikes or in the shape of small translucent fans.

Modern exploration

The caves and chasms of the Dordogne were initially inhabited by animals and then by people, who abandoned these natural shelters about 10 000 years ago.

At the end of the 19C, the methodical and scientific exploration of the underground world led to the discovery of a number of caves and their subsequent conversion into tourist attractions. Yet, despite significant research, many mysteries still lie beneath the surface of the earth.

HISTORY

Prehistory in the Dordogne

The Quarternary Era is relatively young, since it only began about two million years ago. Nevertheless, it is during this short period that human evolution has taken place. There is no definitive evidence of life having existed on Earth in the Pre-Cambrian Age; reptiles, fish and tailless amphibians appeared in the course of the Primary Era, mammals and birds during the Secondary Era. Primates, the most ancient ancestors of mankind, appeared at the end of the Tertiary Era and were followed in the Quarternary Era by ever more advanced species.

The slow pace of human progress during the Palaeolithic Age is quite extraordinary: it took people nearly two million years to learn to polish stone. Yet, the few thousand years that followed saw in the Middle and Far East the development of brilliant civilisations which reached their zenith in the construction of the pyramids in Egypt. A few centuries later bronze was discovered, followed, in approximately 900 BC, by that of iron.

RESEARCHERS

The study of prehistory is a science essentially French in origin which began in the early 19C. Until that time only the occasional reference by a Greek or Latin author, a study by the Italian scholar Mercati (1541-93) in the 16C and a paper by Jussieu, published in 1723, gave any hint of the existence of ancient civilisations. In spite of the scepticism of most learned men – led by Cuvier (1769-1832) – researchers pursued their investigations in the Périgord, Lozère and the Somme Valley, and it was Boucher de Perthes (1788-1868) who had the honour of having **prehistory** (the science of human society prior to the invention of writing) recognised. His discoveries at St-Acheul and Abbeville were the catalyst for an important series of studies. Among the eminent pioneers who laid the foundations on which modern archaeology is based are:

Édouard Lartet (1801-71), who undertook many excavations in the Vézère Valley and established a preliminary classification for the various eras of prehistory; Gabriel de Mortillet (1821-98), who undertook and completed the classification, adding the names Chellean, Mousterian, Aurignacian, Solu-

trean and Magdalenian to correspond with the places where the most prolific or most characteristic deposits were found: Chelles in the Seine-et-Marne, Le Moustier in the Dordogne, Aurignac in the Haute-Garonne, Solutré in the Saône-et-Loire and La Madeleine in the Dordogne.

Excavations can only be performed by specialists with knowledge of the geological stratigraphy, the physics and chemistry of rock formations, the nature and form of stones and gravels, and the ability to analyse fossilised wood, coal and bone fragments.

In rock shelters and the entrances to caves, prehistorians have discovered hearths (accumulations of charcoal and kitchen debris), tools, weapons, stone and bone furnishings and bone fragments. These vestiges are collected in layers; during excavations each of these different layers is uncovered and the civilisation or period is then reconstructed.

PREHISTORY IN THE PÉRIGORD

The Périgord has been inhabited since Palaeolithic times. The names Tayacian (Les Eyzies-de-Tayac), Micoquean (La Micoque), Mousterian (Le Moustier), Perigordian and Magdalenian (La Madeleine) are evidence of the importance of these prehistoric sites. Nearly 200 deposits have been discovered, of which more than half are in the Vézère Valley near Les Eyzies-de-Tayac.

THE PALAEOLITHIC AGE

Our most distant ancestors (some three million years ago) were the early hominids (ie the family of man) of East Africa, who, unlike their instinctive predecessors, were rational thinkers. They evolved into *Homo habilis*, followed by *Homo erectus*, characterised by his upright walking (Java man or *Pithecanthropus erectus*, discovered by E Dubois in 1891, with a cranial capacity midway between that of the most highly developed ape and the least developed man): and Peking man or *Sinanthropus* (identified by D. Black in 1927), who made rough-hewn tools, tools for chopping from split pebbles and heavy bifaced implements.

Neanderthal man appeared c 150 000 years ago. In 1856, in the Düssel Valley (also known as the Neander Valley, east of Düsseldorf, Germany) portions of a human skeleton were discovered with the following characteristics: a cranial capacity of approximately 1 500cm³/ 91.5in³ an elongated cranium (dolicho-cephalus), a sharply receding forehead, prominently developed jawbones and a small stature (1.60m/5ft 3in).

Skeletons with similar characteristics were found in France at La Chapelle-aux-Saints (Corrèze) in 1908, at Le Moustier (Dordogne) in 1909, at La Ferrassie (Dordogne) in 1909 and 1911, and at Le Régourdou (Dordogne) in 1957. The Neanderthal group completely disap-peared without descendants 35 000 years ago; at the same time the first burial sites started to appear.

Homo sapiens were flourishing in France about 40 000 years ago. Their essential characteristics – perfect upright stance, raised forehead, slightly projecting eyebrows – showed them to be highly developed and comparable to people today (*sapiens* means intelligent). Several races have been traced as belonging to this same family. Cro-Magnon individuals must have been quite similar in appear-ance to the present *Homo sapiens*.

Cro-Magnon man (named after skel-etons found in the rock shelters of Cro-Magnon in the Dordogne and Solutré in the Saône-et-Loire) was tall – about 1.80m/5ft 11in – with long, robust limbs denoting considerable muscular strength; the skull was dolichocephalic in shape. These people lived from the Upper Palaeolithic to the Neolithic Ages.

Chancelade man (from a skeleton discovered in 1889 at Chancelade, near Périgueux) appeared in the Magdalenian Period; these people had a large cranium of dolichocephalic form, a long, wide face, pronounced cheekbones and a height of not more than 1.55m/5ft 1in.

Culture and Art in the Palaeolithic Age

The oldest skeletons belonging to Nean-derthals, found in the Périgord and the Quercy, date from the Mousterian Cul-ture (Middle Palaeolithic).

Later, during the Ice Age, tribes are thought to have come from Eastern Europe and settled in the Vézère and Beune valleys. Bordering these valleys were cliffs and slopes pitted with caves and shelters offering many natural advantages which flatter landscapes were unable to provide: protection from the cold, nearby springs and rivers abun-dant in fish, and narrow ravines used for intercepting game as it passed through. There were, however, several dwelling huts found in the Isle Valley, upstream from Périgueux.

The Palaeolithic Age (*palaeos* means ancient, *lithos* means stones) covers the period in which people knew only how to chip flints. An intermediate age, the Mesolithic (*mesos* means middle), separates it from the Neolithic Age (*neos* means new), when they learnt to polish stone. The first group were predators (hunting, fishing and gathering), whereas the last group were farmers and breed-ers. Skill in flint-knapping evolved very slowly and, therefore, the Palaeolithic Age is subdivided into three periods: the Lower, Middle and Upper.

LOWER PALAEOLITHIC

This began about two million years ago. People living in this period in the Péri-gord knew how to use fire and hunted big game. The earth suffered three suc-cessive ice ages known as the Günz, the Mindel and the Riss (after the tributary valleys of the Danube where they were studied). Between each ice age, France and Britain had a tropical climate.

Flint-knapping began with a cut made by striking two stones violently one against the other, or by striking one against a rock which served as an anvil.

MIDDLE PALAEOLITHIC

This began about 150 000 years ago. Neanderthal society brought with it bet-ter finished and more specialised tools. Mousterian industry used both bifaced implements and flakes. New methods enabled triangular points to be pro-duced, also scrapers, probably used for working skins, and flints adapted to take a wooden handle and serve as hunting clubs (bear skulls pierced by such weap-ons have been found).

During the Mousterian Culture some cave entrances were used as dwellings, others were used as burial places. More sophisticated weapons were developed and used to hunt big game and animal skins provided protection from the cold.

UPPER PALAEOLITHIC

This began about 35 000 years ago. Cro-Magnon and Chancelade individu-als replaced Neanderthals. During this period there was a constant improve-ment in the production of tools; living conditions were made easier with the perfecting of new hunting methods, resulting in more leisure time and, there-fore, artistic expression.

Perigordian and Aurignacian cultures

These two cultures, following the Mousterian and Levalloisian cultures and preceding the Solutrean culture, were contemporary but parallel.

The **Aurignacian** stone industry produced large blades, stone flake tools, burins (a sort of chisel) and points made from antlers (early ones have a split base). Cave decoration, applied to blocks of limestone (La Ferrassie near Le Bugue) and at times in tiny caves, consisted of engraved animals, painted or partially carved, or female figures.

At the end of the Perigordian culture, Gravettians made burins and points; these people decorated their shelter walls (Le Poisson, Laussel), and carved Venus figurines (small female statues with exaggerated curves evoking fertility).

Burial places contain some ornaments and jewellery, such as shells and bead necklaces. The first examples of wall decoration appear as hands placed flat against the rock and outlined in black or red; these can be found at Font-de-Gaume and Le Pech Merle, although the animals depicted are sketched in a rudimentary fashion. By the end of this period, people had truly discovered their artistic nature, as the sculptures at the Abri du Poisson (Fish Shelter) and the engravings and paintings found at Font-de-Gaume and Lascaux show. The Grève cave with its engraved bison in turned profile dates from between the late Perigordian and early Solutrean periods.

Solutrean Culture

Very well represented in the Dordogne, this period is distinguished by exquisite low-relief sculptures carved out of limestone slabs, such as the Devil's Oven, found near Bourdeilles and now exhibited in the National Museum of Prehistory at Les Eyzies.

The stone-cutting industry also underwent a brilliant period during the Solutrean culture. Flint blades, following a method of splitting under pressure, became much slimmer, forming blades in the shape of laurel or willow leaves. Shouldered points were used as weapons, after they had been fitted with wooden shafts. It was during this period that the first needles with eyes appeared.

Magdalenian Culture

It was in this period that bone and ivory craftsmanship reached its peak. The existence of herds of reindeer, which is accounted for by the very cold climate that occurred at the end of the Würm Glacial Period, encouraged carvers to work with bone and antler, producing perforated batons, sometimes engraved, which were used as armatures for points and harpoon heads; projectile tips, sometimes engraved, used as spears; and decorated flattened points.

This is also the period when cave wall art, depicting essentially animal subjects, reached its peak. To protect themselves from the cold, people of the Magdalenian culture lived in the shelter of overhanging rocks or at the mouths of caves; inside, these caves were underground sanctuaries, at times quite some distance from the cave entrance.

They used the shelter (as at the Cap-Blanc Shelter) and sanctuary walls to express their artistic or religious emotions by low-relief carving, engraving and painting. This period introduced a very sophisticated style compared to the more rudimentary outline drawings of the Perigordian and Aurignacian cultures. However, due to the juxtaposition or superimposition of the figures drawn and deterioration (only a few Magdalenian caves are open to the public due to the difficulty in preserving these works of art), the study of these paintings is not easy.

After Lascaux, numerous cave-sanctuaries appeared during the Middle and Upper Magdalenian periods. Portable art, manifested through smaller objects, is another form of expression developed in the shelters. Animals are much less stylised and increasingly realistic in the details of their anatomy and their movements, as well as the faithful and detailed rendering of their physical aspects: coat, tail, eyes, ears, hoofs, antlers and tusks. Nonetheless, the style is more ornamental. The perspective of the animals in profile, non-existent in the beginning, was pursued and even distorted during Lascaux's last period. New graphic techniques appeared: stencilling, areas left intentionally without colour, polychrome colours etc. Towards the end of the Magdalenian culture, art became more schematic and human figures made their appearance. Animal art then disappeared from France and Spain, as the herds of reindeer migrated northwards in search of the lichen which was disappearing during the climatic warming at the end of the Würm Glacial Period.

Time Line

PREHISTORY

As early as the Middle Palaeolithic Age, the region is inhabited.

GAULS AND ROMANS

BC The Périgord is inhabited by the Petrocorii and the Quercy by the Caduici.

6-5C The Bituriges Cubi people settle in the Berry.

59-51 Conquest of Gaul by Caesar. The last Gaulish resistance to Caesar is at Uxellodunum, which historians believe to be in the Quercy.

16 Emperor Augustus creates the province of Aquitaine. The capital of the land of the Petrocorii is Vesunna (Périgueux) and of that of the Caduici, Divona Cadurcorum (Cahors).

AD

1-3C Pax Romana. For three centuries towns develop and several public buildings are built. In the countryside around the towns new crops are introduced by the Romans: walnut, chestnut and cherry trees and above all vineyards.

late 3C The Berry and the Limousin are incorporated into primitive Aquitaine; Bourges is its capital.

235-284 Alemanni and Franks invade the region. In 276, several towns are razed. Vesunna defends itself behind fortifications hastily built from the stones taken from Roman public buildings.

313 Edict of Milan. Emperor Constantine grants Christians the freedom of worship.

476 End of the Roman Empire.

Merovingians and Carolingians

486-507 Clovis, king of the Franks, conquers Gaul and Aquitaine.

8C The Quercy and Périgord become counties under the kingdom of Aquitaine.

800 **Charlemagne** is crowned Emperor of the West in Rome.

9C The Dordogne and Isle valleys and Périgueux are laid waste by Vikings.

10C The four baronies of the Périgord – Mareuil, Bourdeilles, Beynac and Biron – are formed as well as the overlordships of Ans, Auberoche, Gurson etc.

The County of Périgord passes to the house of Talleyrand. Powerful families rule the Quercy.

c 950 Beginning of the pilgrimage to St James' shrine in Santiago de Compostela, Spain.

12C Many influential abbeys are founded in the region (Noirlac, Chancelade, Cadouin, Rocamadour etc). Construction started on the cathedral in Bourges.

WARS BETWEEN ENGLAND AND FRANCE

1152 Eleanor of Aquitaine marries Henry Plantagenet, bringing as her dowry all of southwest France (🕭 see below). In 1154 Henry Plantagenet becomes King Henry II.

1190 The Quercy is ceded to the English with the exception of the abbeys of Figeac and Souillac.

1191 Richard the Lionheart dies at Châlus.

early 13C Albigensian Crusade. Simon de Montfort raids the Quercy and Périgord.

1234 Louis IX purchases the Berry from the Count of Champagne.

1259 By the Treaty of Paris, St Louis cedes the Périgord and the Quercy to the English. The treaty puts an end to the constant fighting and enables the people of the region to live in peace until the Hundred Years War.

1273 Construction is started on the cathedral in Limoges.

1324 Bourges Cathedral is consecrated.

1337 French king Philip VI declares the English-held duchy of Guyenne confiscated.

1340 Edward III of England proclaims himself king of France.

1345 Beginning of the Hundred Years War in Aquitaine.

1346 Edward III defeats the French at Crécy.

1355-1370 Edward the Black Prince begins his campaign, ravaging the Berry and the Limousin. Edward defeats and captures King Jean II (Battle of Poitiers 1356).

1360 The Treaty of Brétigny cedes Aquitaine to the English as part of the ransom for Jean II's liberty.

1369 The Quercy and Périgord are won back by the king of France (Charles V). Du Guesclin, constable of France, is active in the liberation of the Périgord.

During the period that follows the lords of the north of Périgord owe allegiance to the king of France; the lords of the south of Périgord to the English. Many regularly swap sides in unabashed support of their own interests.

1415 Henry V defeats the French at Azincourt.

1420 Henry V of England is recognised as king of France under the Treaty of Troyes. France is divided into three parts controlled by Henry V (Normandy, Guyenne, Paris area); Philip the Good, duke of Burgundy (other parts of the area in and around Paris, Burgundy); and the Dauphin (Central France and the Languedoc).

1444 Truce of Tours (Charles VII and Henry V); the English retain Maine, the Bordelais region, parts of Artois and Picardy and most of Normandy.

1449 The French begin a campaign in Guyenne, but the people of the region are hostile to the French from years of loyalty to the English crown; Bergerac falls in 1450, Bordeaux in 1451.

1453 Defeat of John Talbot, earl of Shrewsbury, at the Battle of Castillon, which marks the end of the Hundred Years War.

1463 University of Bourges founded.

2nd half of 15-early 16C Towns and castles are rebuilt during this period of peace.

1558 England loses Calais to the French.

WARS OF RELIGION

1562 Massacre of Protestants at Cahors.

1572 St Bartholomew's Day massacre (20 000 Huguenots die).

1570-90 War is declared; Bergerac and Ste-Foy-la-Grande are Huguenot bastions whereas Périgueux and Cahors support the Catholic League.

Vivans, the Huguenot leader, scours the Périgord; Périgueux falls in 1575 and Domme in 1588.

1580 Cahors is taken by Henri de Navarre (Henri IV).

1589 Henri IV accedes to the throne, converts to Catholicism in 1593 and is crowned in 1594.

Under Henri IV, the County of Périgord becomes part of the royal domain.

1594-95 Croquant peasant revolt.

1598 Edict of Nantes grants Huguenots freedom of worship and places of refuge.

1607 The Viscounty of Limoges comes under the French crown.

1610 Henri IV is assassinated; Louis XIII's reign begins.

Lands held by the English

in 1253

at the beginning of the Hundred Years War (1338)

after the Treaty of Brétigny (1360)

after the reconquest by Charles V and Du Guesclin (1380)

1637	Croquants' revolt against Louis XIII's government and Richelieu's taxes.
1643-1715	Louis XIV's reign.
1685	Revocation of the Edict of Nantes. Huguenots flee France.

18C TO 20C

1743-57	Tourny, administrator of the Treasury of Bordeaux, instigates a number of town planning projects in the southwest (Allées de Tourny in Périgueux).
1763	Peace of Paris ends the French and Indian War (1754-63), marking the end of France's colonial empire in America.
1768	Kaolin is discovered in St-Yrieix-la-Perche.
1789	Storming of the Bastille and the beginning of the French Revolution.
1790	Creation of the Dordogne *département*.
1792	Proclamation of the French Republic after the Battle of Valmy.
1812-14	Périgord is a Bonapartist fief; several of Napoleon's generals and marshals (Murat, Fournier-Sarlovèze, Daumesnil) are natives of the region.
1868	Phylloxera destroys the vineyards of Cahors and Bergerac, causing a rural exodus.
	Discovery of Cro-Magnon cave skeletons.
1914-18	First World War.
1940	Discovery of Lascaux Cave.
1942-1944	The French Resistance movement intensifies in the Limousin during the Second World War.
1944	Massacres at Tulle and Oradour-sur-Glane.
20C	Marked by a continued rural exodus, the depopulated regions live essentially from agriculture and tourism.
1963	The first Maison de la Culture opens in Bourges, an initiative of André Malraux.
1964	The Limousin *Région* is created.
1977	Le Printemps de Bourges music festival holds its first concerts.

1989	The Parc Naturel Régional de la Brenne is established. A new motorway is opened from Paris to the centre of France, via Bourges.
2000	Construction begins on the A89 motorway linking Bordeaux to Clermont-Ferrand.
2003	Completion of the last section of the A20 motorway around Cahors, providing the region with a fast road link with northern and southern Europe.
2007	Scheduled completion date of A89 motorway between Bordeaux and Clermont-Ferrand.

Key Historical Figures

Over the centuries, three key figures have left an indelible mark on the region, sparking the imagination and bringing to life the history of this part of France.

ELEANOR OF AQUITAINE

In 1122, a daughter was born to William X, duke of Aquitaine and count of Poitiers, who was to become heiress to one of the largest domains in France (more extensive than that of the king's). In 1137, Eleanor wed Louis VII, who succeeded his father to the throne just one month later. The young queen of France was beautiful and influential, though some historians have criticised her juvenile frivolity. Eleanor accompanied her husband on the Second Crusade, where her capricious enthusiasm fired Louis' jealousy, and the marriage was annulled in 1152, shortly after their return to France. Thanks to feudal customs, she regained possession of Aquitaine, and two months later married Henry Plantagenet, count of Anjou and duke of Normandy. When her second husband became king of England (1154) as Henry II, England, Normandy and the west of France were united under one crown. In addition to her two daughters from her first marriage, Eleanor bore eight more children, including Richard the Lionheart, John Lackland, Eleanor (who married the king of Castille) and Joan (who married the king of Sicily and later the count of Toulouse). No wonder some have called her the grandmother of Europe!

Eleanor was both a political and cultural force to be reckoned with. She turned the court at Poitiers into a centre of courtly life and manners, celebrated by the troubadours; she also promoted the historical legends of Brittany, romantic songs in the Celtic tradition. She supported her sons in a failed revolt against their father; afterwards, Henry had her kept guarded under close watch in England until his death. Released at last, she became an invaluable advisor to her son Richard, keeping the kingdom intact and administering it during his long absences. She was 80 years old when she set off across the Pyrenees to fetch her granddaughter Blanche of Castille for marriage to the son of the French king, hoping thus to cement peace between the Plantagenets and the Capetians. Her influence was felt even after her death: following the loss of Normandy (1204), her ancestral lands, and not the old Norman territories, remained loyal to England.

She died in 1204 in the monastery at Fontevrault where she had retired. The nuns of Fontevrault described this exceptional queen as "beautiful and just, imposing and modest, humble and elegant".

JEAN DE BERRY

In the 14C, when its population was about 350 000, the Berry was plunged into the turmoil of the Hundred Years War following the Black Prince's raids. The region had strategic importance as a potential base for the conquest of Poitou and Aquitaine. King John the Good elevated the Berry and Auvergne to the rank of duchies, and granted them to his third son; thus, in 1360, Jean de Berry came into control of at least one-third of the territory of France.

After a period spent in captivity in England, the young duke was in urgent need of funds. He taxed his lands heavily for the defence of the kingdom, and also spent lavishly on the arts. His military career was marked by a triumphant march on Limoges, which brought the local bourgeoisie and clergy into the Valois camp, but also led to terrible English reprisals. Pursuing his campaign with Du Guesclin and the duke of Anjou, he took control of Poitou in 1373.

Meanwhile, his brother, by then King Charles V, passed away, and his nephew, the young Charles VI, took the throne. As a member of the regency council from 1380-88, Berry shared royal powers while Charles was too young to rule. He thus gained control of the Languedoc. In conflict with the royal family, Berry also struggled against the peasants' revolt (1381-84) which resulted from his oppressive fiscal policies and opulent lifestyle. The king, although beset by fits of insanity, announced his determination to rule alone, but soon earned the surname Charles the Mad.

Still bent on power, and always ready to take advantage, Berry handled negotiations between the conflicting factions of John the Fearless, duke of Burgundy, and his own brother Louis, duke of Orléans, and even promised the English to deliver the province of Guyenne (1412). The end result of his scheming was the siege of the city of Bourges by royal troops. Berry capitulated and died four years later, at the age of 76.

Throughout his life, he showered his fortune on the arts and artists, building palaces and fine residences in his cities, so much so that at his death there was not enough in the coffers to pay for his funeral. History has recognised his importance as a supporter of the arts, and the treasures he commissioned remain as his monument: paintings, tapestries, jewellery and illuminated manuscripts, including the world-famous Très Riches Heures du Duc de Berry.

JACQUES CŒUR

Born the son of a furrier in Bourges, Cœur's life is exemplary of the spirit of enterprise and the rise of the merchant classes in the period of prosperity that followed the Hundred Years War. His generation was perhaps the first in Europe to aspire to honours, noble rank, wealth and property, without being born into the aristocracy. If he may be said to have represented the rise of the merchant class, his downfall signifies how difficult it was for such social changes to take root.

Gifted with an uncanny flair for business opportunities, Cœur gained the confidence of Charles VII, and became his argentier, managing the royal funds like a modern-day investment tycoon. His power and fortune grew simultaneously as he became a member of the king's council, the tax collector for the Languedoc and the inspector general of the salt tax. He diversified his affairs, stocking all kinds of merchandise – cloth, spices, jewels, armour, wheat and salt – from around the world in his vast stores in Tours. He had a large staff of salesmen, shipowners (he himself owned seven ships) and negotiators, as well as 40 manor houses and a beautiful palace in Bourges, one of the finest examples of lay Gothic architecture in Europe. Cœur set up individual companies for each branch of trade, and sought political support from all quarters. His prosperity was held up by a delicately spun web of bills of exchange, credit, and fiscal receipts issued by the king. A creditor for many of France's aristocrats and the king himself, Cœur was the object of intense jealousy.

His skyrocketing career plummeted to the depths on 31 July 1451, when he was arrested on trumped-up charges of having poisoned Agnès Sorel, the king's mistress. His enemies came forth with more accusations: currency fraud, trading arms with the infidels, returning a Christian slave to a Muslim master, running ships with slave crews, and abuse of power. Found guilty on all counts except the poisoning, he was sentenced to banishment, and was also ordered to relinquish all of his goods and property, and pay an impossibly high fine for his release.

Meanwhile, French troops, paid with the confiscated funds, won the final battle of the Hundred Years War. And the fate of Cœur, financial adventurer and proto-bourgeois? Friends helped him escape from prison; he took refuge in Italy before setting out on a naval expedition organised by the Pope against the Turks. He is believed to have died on the Aegean island of Chios in 1456. The following year, in an attempt to make amends for his father's treatment of Cœur, King Louis XI returned his unsold property to his sons and revived some of his old companies.

ART AND CULTURE

Literature

THE COURTS OF LOVE

In the 12C an original type of lyric poetry appeared which developed and flowered in the feudal courts, where idle but educated nobles and their ladies enjoyed singing, music and poetry. **Troubadours** were inventors (tobar is the Occitan word for find) of musical airs – melodies for verses in the Oc language. Under the protection and encouragement of their lords, they created new poetic forms; love poems (songs and romances) in which lyrical homage to the lady of the castle illustrated the theme of courtly love; songs of war and satirical ballads. The courts of love each had several troubadours who would vie in wit with one another on a set subject. **Bernard de Ventadour**, **Bertrand de Born** (author of the political and moralist Sirventès), Bertrand de Gourdon, Aimeric de Sarlat, Girault de Borneil, a native of Excideuil, and Arnaut de Ribérac were the most famous of these. **Dormunda de Cahors** is the only female poet whose name has survived from this period. The social influence of the poets themselves was unprecedented in the history of poetry, and their work strongly influenced all European poetry that followed.

HUMANISTS

During the 15C, in the immediate aftermath of the Hundred Years War, intellectual life continued, centring on new universities – Cahors was founded in 1331 by Jacques Duèze, who became Pope John XXII. In the early 16C, printing houses were established in Périgueux, Cahors and Bergerac. But it was the Renaissance, and the intellectual movement known as humanism, which restored respect for classical languages and poetic forms. A native of Cahors, **Clément Marot** (1496-1544), one of the great poets of the French Renaissance, excelled in composing epigrams and sonnets. His brilliant life at court, where he rose from his initial station of valet to that of official court poet, was often interrupted by prison sentences, due to his penchant for the Reformation. In Limoges, **Jean Dorat** (1508-88) was a scholar of Greek and a poet in Latin, a teacher who inspired Ronsard and other French writers. He also influenced **Olivier de Magny** (1529-65), from Cahors, and **Etienne de la Boétie** (1530-63), a native of Sarlat who was a friend of the essayist Montaigne, and denounced tyranny in his Discourse on Voluntary Subjection and Against One. In addition, Pierre de Bourdeille (1535-1614), who wrote under the pseudonym of **Brantôme** (the name of the abbey of which he was abbot), was a talented chronicler who described the lives of great captains and soldiers as well as giving accounts of life in the French courts. **Jean Tarde** (1561-1636), born in La Roque-Gageac, one of the most learned men of his time, was a historian, cartographer, astronomer and mathematician.

AGE OF ENLIGHTENMENT

In the Limousin, the historians **Étienne Baluze** (1630-1718) and **Jean-François Marmontel** (1723-99) gained fame for works on the Middle Ages and as the king's historian, respectively. On the banks of the Dordogne, **Fénelon** (1631-1715) worked on Télémaque, a tract for the edification of his student the duke of Burgundy, dauphin of France. Philosophers **Joseph Joubert** (1754-1824) and **Maine de Biran** (1766-1824) wrote sensitive, precise treatises which heralded the movement of spiritualistic philosophy.

ROMANTIC AND CONTEMPORARY AUTHORS

Probably the most famous writer to emerge from the Berry was **George Sand** (1804-78). Born Aurore Dupin in Paris, she spent her youth in the countryside, and her many works are strongly imprinted with images of the region. **Eugène Le Roy** (1836-1907) is likewise the novelist of the Périgord; his Jacquou le Croquant, set in the Château de l'Herm, describes in very vivid style the peasant uprising which ravaged the region. Success came after death to **Alain-Fournier** (1886-1914), based on his sole novel, Le Grand Meaulnes, inspired by the school in his town of Épineuil-le-Fleuriel. The playwright **Jean Giraudoux** (1882-1944) has been influential on an international scale, and is also appreciated for his novels.

Art and Architecture

The Vézère Valley, the prehistoric sites of Les Eyzies and the caves of the Quercy contain some of the finest known examples of prehistoric art, the earliest manifestations of art in France. Since that time, art and architecture have evolved in close connection with the region's turbulent history. The significant periods of construction took place in periods of peace: the Pax Romana, the 12C (many monasteries date from this century) and the period spanning the end of the 14C to the 16C. During times of war – the Hundred Years War, the Wars of Religion – the main concern of the local population was its protection, hence the fortification of towns, castles and churches.

Gallo-Roman Art

Only a few buildings constructed by the Romans have withstood the test of time, although vestiges of the Gaulish period do still survive. Excavations undertaken at **Drevant**, near St-Amand-Montrond, have established that a large Gallo-Roman centre developed on the site of a small Gaulish market town; a theatre, baths and a vast walled area which may have been a Gallo-Roman forum or temple have been uncovered here.

In **Limoges**, an amphitheatre was built on the northwest outskirts of the old town; however, it was razed to the ground in the 16C and its ruins are now hidden beneath the Jardin d'Orsay.

In Périgueux, traces have been discovered of the ancient **Vesunna**, capital of the Petrocorii. The finds include the Vesunna tower, the arena and the perimeter wall. The Puy d'Issoulud near Vayrac is believed to be the site of the **Uxellodunum** encampment – this was the last bastion of the Gauls in their resistance against the all-conquering Caesar. At Luzech, traces of the Impernal encampment which commanded a bend in the River Lot have been unearthed; the ruins of the Murcens oppidum have also been discovered near the Vers Valley.

Romanesque Art and Religious Architecture

IN THE BERRY

Though characteristics of the Poitou School are widely represented across the region, most Romanesque churches in the Berry have a precise plan with certain features peculiar to the area: the chancel generally consists of two bays flanked by aisles which communicate with the choir through arches resting on columns adorned with historiated capitals; the apse is semicircular; the transept has a dome on squinches above the crossing and barrel vaulting above the arms; the nave is wider than the transept crossing and communicates with the arms of the transept by narrow passages known as **Berrichon** passages.

The abbey churches are based on the Benedictine design, for the Order of St-Benedict spread throughout Berry and built abbeys at Fontgombault, Chezal-Benoît and at Châteaumeillant, where the church of St-Genès has an unusual arrangement of the chevet with six parallel apsidal chapels. Noirlac was created by the Cistercians, Plaimpied and Puy-Ferrand by the Augustinian Canons Regular. One church in the Bourges diocese is designed quite differently: the basilica of Neuvy-St-Sépulcre was built in the form of a rotunda and was inspired by the church of the Holy Sepulchre in Jerusalem.

THE LIMOUSIN SCHOOL

The Limousin School combines many of the characteristics of its neighbours: the Auvergne School, whose chief feature is that the vaulting above the nave is buttressed by the semi-barrel vaulting of the aisles or the galleries (Beaulieu-sur-Dordogne); the Poitou School, whose influence can be seen in the collegiate church of St-Pierre in Le Dorat – a blind nave with broken-barrel vaulting and aisles with groined vaulting; and the Périgord School – the domes on the church at Solignac.

Nevertheless, certain elements can be considered as purely Limousin. Firstly, the use of granite, which is found throughout the region and whose colour, while usually grey, sometimes verges on a golden tone.

Secondly, in the peculiar design of some belfries: the octagonal spire which crowns them is joined to the square tiers that form the base of the tower by one or two octagonal storeys; and the gables that stand on the upper square tiers are not only ornamental but play a part in the overall construction, since they divide and balance the weight of the upper octagonal tiers. The best examples of this style are the **belfries** at St-Léonard, Collonges, Uzerche and Brantôme (in the Périgord). The belfry at St-Junien was probably planned to follow this pattern as the beginning of a steeply sloping gable can be seen above the second square tier.

Lastly, the façades present a more or less uniform style: massive belfry-porches adorned with blind arcades of various sizes and forms (Le Dorat, St-Junien); doorways with recessed elongated arcades on either side (St-Junien); a first storey flanked by bell turrets which are pierced at Le Dorat and encircled by a corbelled gallery at St-Junien; and doorways with twin doors framed by recessed covings, which in some cases are scalloped, showing the influence of Islamic art (Mozarabic style).

IN THE DORDOGNE

The plain, almost severe appearance of the area's many Romanesque churches was enhanced by the use of fine golden sandstone. The exteriors are startling for the extreme simplicity of their decoration: the doorways without tympana were embellished with recessed orders, and carved with rounded mouldings and festoons in a saw-tooth pattern. Inside, the churches are equally plain, with apsidal chapels opening off the chancel, which is usually flat. Only a few churches were built with side aisles; as a general rule the nave stands alone.

The originality of the **Périgord Romanesque** style is in its vaulting and dome. Some specialists believe that this shows eastern influence, others that it is a French invention. The **dome** offers several advantages over cradle vaulting, which requires the use of powerful buttresses. The dome on pendentives allows the support of the weight of the vault to be divided between the side walls and the transverse arches of the nave. Often set over the transept crossing, the domes also vault the nave when they follow one after another in a series (such as at St-Étienne-de-la-Cité, Périgueux). The nave is thus divided into several square bays vaulted with a dome on pendentives. The pendentives serve as a transition from a square base to the circular dome. The cathedral of St-Front in Périgueux (&see illustration: PÉRIGUEUX) is unique, with its five domes erected above a Greek-cross plan. However, some of the region's numerous Romanesque churches illustrate different designs: as an example, in St-Privat-des-Prés and Cadouin the naves have aisles with rounded and pointed barrel-vaulting. Some façades are adorned with rows of arcades; this reflects the influence of the Saintonge and Angoumois regions.

The neighbouring Quercy has a slightly different Romanesque style, characterised by richer sculptural embellishment (influence of the Moissac and Languedoc schools). Inspired by Byzantine art, illuminations and Antiquity, some of the carved doorways and tympana in this region are stunning: Cahors, Carennac, Martel, and Collonges-La-Rouge, on the border with the Limousin.

Civil and Military Architecture

THE BERRY AND LIMOUSIN

The fortresses of Turenne, Merle, Ventadour, Châlus, Montbrun and Chalusset all existed in the Limousin in the 13C. The ruins of Crozant overlooking the valley of the Creuse evoke what was once the powerful stronghold of the counts of Marche.

Numerous castles were built in the Berry during the Middle Ages: on Henry II's accession to the throne of England in 1154, the English controlled Aquitaine and threatened the neighbouring Berry. The local lords therefore improved the fortification of their castles to resist the enemy. The Château de Culan, taken by Philip Augustus in 1188, was rebuilt in the 13C but retained its severity of appearance emphasised by its three round towers topped by a wooden hoarding. Ainay-le-Vieil is protected by its perimeter wall with nine towers, while Meillant still possesses its seven haughty feudal towers.

THE DORDOGNE

There are few traces left of the civil architecture of the Romanesque period. The feudal fortresses erected in the 10C and 11C were greatly altered in later centuries and can scarcely be said to have

Château Culan

L. Lambière/ MICHELIN

withstood the warfare and destruction of the times. The only remaining buildings of this period are the square keeps – the last refuge of the defensive system. Castelnau-Bretenoux in the Quercy, with its strongly fortified keep, is a good example of feudal construction built on a hilltop site.

In the Périgord, parts of the castles of Biron and Beynac, Bourdeilles, Commarque and Castelnaud date back to the Romanesque period.

Decorative Arts

The Abbaye de St-Martial, in Limoges, with its many dependent priories, was the principal centre in the Limousin for the development of enamel, gold and silverwork. From the 10C onwards, the monks here produced shrines, episcopal rings and statues in gold and silver. The skill of the Limousin gold and silversmiths and their proven technique paved the way for the subsequent development of **enamelwork**.

Using methods practised from the 6C onwards by Byzantine enamellers, the Limousin workshops at first undertook cloisonné ware (in which the colours are kept apart by thin outline plates). But in the 12C they turned entirely to champlevé enamelware (in which a thick sheet of copper is hollowed out in certain areas and the cavities are filled in with enamel). Towards the end of the Romanesque period, colours became more subtle and often the cavities were filled with two or even four colours, placed one on top of the other. The folds of garments were rendered by the use of a highlight – white, light blue or yellow – around areas of dark blue and green.

Most of the work was inspired by the art of illuminators, by manuscripts, ivories and Byzantine and Oriental silks. From the beginning of the 12C, small enamelled figures were represented on a background of smooth gilded copper. From 1170 onwards this background was chiselled with decorative foliage motifs, with fantastic fauna intermingled with religious symbols. The compositions, although often naïve, show a very strong artistic sense. Of the many objects produced in this way, the most remarkable are the reliquary shrines of Ambazac, Gimel and Bellac. The municipal museums of Limoges and Guéret contain rich collections of enamelwork.

Gothic Art

RELIGIOUS ARCHITECTURE

The essential elements of Gothic art – quadripartite vaulting based on diagonal ribs and the systematic use of the pointed arch – underwent various regional modifications. Diagonal ribs revolutionised construction and architects became masters of the thrust and balance of a building. Through the use of pointed arches, piers and flying buttresses, they freed the inner space so that a church could be lofty and light, illuminated by stained-glass windows.

The Berry

The most important Gothic building in the region, recognised worldwide as an architectural masterpiece inscribed on UNESCO's World Heritage List, is **Bourges Cathedral**. It bears no resemblance to any of the other great cathedrals of France; its high nave covered with sexpartite vaulting, its double side aisles which extend round the chancel and the absence of a transept make it unique.

The Limousin

The simultaneous influences of the Languedoc School (southern Gothic) and the schools of northern France were in play in the region. The passion for building in the 13C and 14C is illustrated in the **cathedral of St-Étienne** and the churches of St-Pierre-du-Queyroix and St-Michel-des-Lions at Limoges, in the nave of the church of St-Martin at Brive, the collegiate church at St-Yrieix, and the belfry-porch of Tulle Cathedral.

The Dordogne

Sarlat Cathedral is an example of the influence of both southern and northern Gothic styles: the nave has wide side aisles and soaring flying buttresses typical of the north, whereas the side chapel shows southern influence. Another commonly found aspect of the Languedoc School is the nave's shape, almost as

F. Magnoux/Musée municipal de l'Evêché, Limoges

Vase, Henriette Marty, 1930

wide as it is high, with side chapels but no aisles (Gourdon, Martel, Montpezat-du-Quercy and St-Cirq-Lapopie).

In the Berry, Limousin and Dordogne, many **monasteries** were built during this period, although few have emerged intact from the ravages of time. In Cadouin and Cahors, there are still cloisters built in the Flamboyant style, and in Périgueux the cloisters were built between the 12C and the 16C.

During the 13C-14C, **fortified churches** were built in the region in response to unrest, in particular during the Hundred Years War. The sanctuaries provided villagers with a safe place of refuge from marauders and the churches and abbeys were like fortified castles in appearance, with crenellations, watch-paths, and sometimes even protective moats.

SCULPTURE AND PAINTING

The Berry

Art in stained glass reached its climax in Bourges with the completion in the 13C of a remarkable series of windows.

Around the middle of the 14C, under the guidance of Duke Jean de Berry, the Berry developed into a great intellectual and artistic centre. As an example, the stained-glass window known as the *Grand Housteau* in the cathedral at Bourges was a gift from the duke.

The duke assembled excellent artists but most of the masterpieces created in the studios and workshops in Bourges have unfortunately disappeared: only a few fragments of Berry's tomb remain in the cathedral crypt (originally placed in the Sainte-Chapelle in Bourges, since demolished). The greater part of the statuary, however, dates from this period and has survived. At Issoudun, in the chapel of the former Hôtel-Dieu, there is a fine carved Tree of Jesse.

The Limousin

In Limoges, two tombs executed in the purest 14C style can still be seen in the ambulatory around the chancel in the cathedral of St-Étienne; the village of Reygade in the Corrèze possesses an Entombment dating from the 15C which resembles the one at Carennac; and the church at Eymoutiers is ornamented with interesting 15C stained glass.

Limousin enamelwork which flourished in the Romanesque period was transformed in the 15C with the appearance of painted enamels produced under the direction of such famous mastercraftsmen as Monvaerni and Nardon Pénicaud.

The Dordogne

From the second half of the 13C until the 15C, several remarkable works were produced: the tomb of St Stephen at Aubazine, a magnificent shrine carved in limestone in the second half of the 13C; the Entombment (15C) at Carennac; the tomb of the Cardaillacs at Espagnac-Ste-Eulalie; and the recumbent figures of Cardinal Pierre des Prés and his nephew Jean in the church at Montpezat-du-Quercy.

Frescoes, mural paintings produced with water-based paint on fresh plaster (a technique which allows the colours to sink in), were used to decorate many chapels and churches. The west dome of Cahors Cathedral is entirely covered with 14C frescoes. Naïve 14C and 15C polychrome statuary and certain frescoes give a good idea of how peasants and nobility dressed at the time. In Rocamadour, the interiors of chapels are painted, with further embellishment on the façades.

Civil and Military Architecture

THE BERRY AND LIMOUSIN

A few Gothic residences remain in the region, the most noteworthy example of which is the **Palais Jacques Cœur** in Bourges, one of the finest Gothic palaces in Europe. Built on the vestiges of a Gallo-Roman wall, the building is a combination of massive, forbidding towers and a lively, sculpted façade. Inside, the architecture seems to hint at the approaching Renaissance in its graceful lines and fanciful motifs.

The Dordogne

Many of the **castles** in the Périgord and Quercy were constructed during the Gothic period, as is visible in their architectural detail; examples of these are at Bourdeilles, Beynac-et-Cazenac, Castelnaud and Castelnau-Bretenoux. Bonaguil is unique in that although it was built at the end of the 15C and in the early part of the 16C, it has all the features of a medieval fortress.

A considerable boom in town building occurred after the Hundred Years War with Sarlat, Périgueux, Bergerac, Cahors, Figeac, Gourdon and Martel all benefiting from this. The façades of town houses were decorated with large pointed arches on the ground floor (where small shops were set up), flattened arches or rose windows adorned the upper floors, with turrets crowning the roof. Among

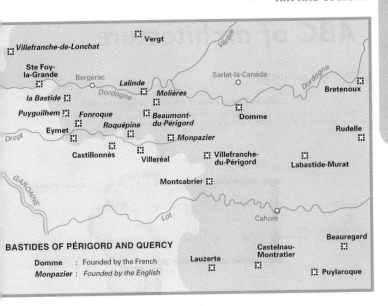

BASTIDES OF PÉRIGORD AND QUERCY

Domme : Founded by the French
Monpazier : Founded by the English

(Map labels:) Villefranche-de-Lonchat, Vergt, Vézère, Ste Foy-la-Grande, Bergerac, Lalinde, Sarlat-la-Canéda, Dordogne, Bretenoux, Dordogne, Molières, la Bastide, Puyguilhem, Fonroque, Beaumont-du-Périgord, Domme, Rudelle, Eymet, Roquépine, Drop, Monpazier, Castillonnès, Villeréal, Villefranche-du-Périgord, Labastide-Murat, GARONNE, Montcabrier, Lot, Cahors, Beauregard, Lauzerte, Castelnau-Montratier, Puylaroque

the finest examples of this period, note the Hôtel de la Raymondie in Martel, the Hôtel de la Monnaie in Figeac, the Hôtel Plamon in Sarlat and the famous Pont Valentré in Cahors.

Bastides

These new, fortified towns (in the *Oc* language: *bastidas*) appeared in the 13C; their fortified aspect was further developed during the course of the following century.

Foundation

The principal founders of *bastides* were Alphonse de Poitiers (1249-71), count of Toulouse and brother to St Louis and, from 1272 on, seneschal lords under Philip the Bold, Philip the Fair and King Edward I of England, who also held the title of duke of Aquitaine.

Development

Their construction satisfied economic, military and political needs, with founders taking advantage of the growth of the population and encouraging people to settle on their land, in turn rationalising its use and cultivation. In return, inhabitants were granted a charter, guaranteed protection, exempted from military service and given the right to inherit. The bailiff represented the king, dispensed justice and collected taxes, whereas the consuls, elected by the people, administered the town; towns flourished under this system. After the Albigensian Crusade, when the count of Toulouse, Raymond VII, built about 40 *bastides*, and with the outbreak of

hostilities between the French and the English over the Périgord, Quercy and the Agenais, the political and military advantages of the *bastides* were confirmed. Alphonse de Poitiers built Eymet, Catillonès and Villeréal along the River Dropt as well as Villefranche-du-Périgord and Ste-Foy-la-Grande. The king of England responded with the construction of Beaumont, Molières, Lalinde and Monpazier, while in 1281 Philip the Bold founded Domme.

All of the *bastides*, French and English, were built to the same plan – a square or rectangle – and yet they differed because of the terrain, the type of site, the potential for population growth, and their defensive plan. Occasionally, the *bastide* was built around a pre-existing building such as a fortified church (Beaumont) or a castle.

The design of Monpazier is most characteristic: it is built according to a quadrilateral plan with straight streets crossed at right angles by alleys known as **carreyrous**; narrow spaces, **androns**, stand between the houses and serve as fire breaks, drains or even latrines. In the centre of town, the main square is surrounded by covered arcades or **couverts** (also known as **cornières**). The covered market or **halle,** also stands in this square. The church and the cemetery stand nearby, and the outer walls are punctuated with towers and gateways. The best-preserved *bastides* are today found in Monpazier, Domme and Eymet.

ABC of architecture

Religious architecture

CADOUIN – Ground plan of the abbey church (1119-1154)

This ground plan is characteristic of the Aquitaine school of ecclesiastical architecture with aisles flanking the nave and chancel on both sides, forming a Latin cross with short arms.

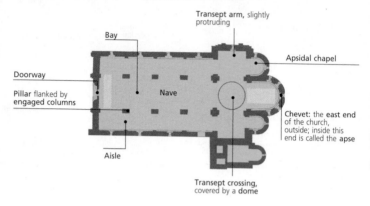

Bay

Transept arm, slightly protruding

Apsidal chapel

Doorway

Pillar flanked by engaged columns

Nave

Chevet: the east end of the church, outside; inside this end is called the **apse**

Aisle

Transept crossing, covered by a **dome**

CARSAC-AILLAC – Vaulting in Saint-Caprais (12-16C)

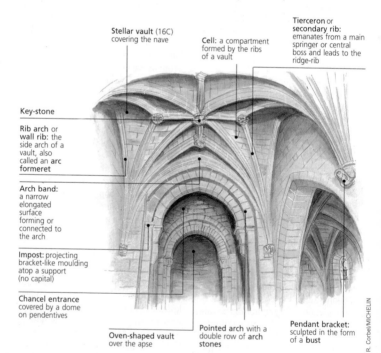

Stellar vault (16C) covering the nave

Cell: a compartment formed by the ribs of a vault

Tierceron or **secondary rib:** emanates from a main springer or central boss and leads to the ridge-rib

Key-stone

Rib arch or **wall rib:** the side arch of a vault, also called an **arc formeret**

Arch band: a narrow elongated surface forming or connected to the arch

Impost: projecting bracket-like moulding atop a support (no capital)

Chancel entrance covered by a dome on pendentives

Oven-shaped vault over the apse

Pointed arch with a double row of **arch** stones

Pendant bracket: sculpted in the form of a **bust**

R. Corbel/MICHELIN

ST-LÉONARD-DE-NOBLAT – Church belltower (12C)

Belltower with 4 storeys of square design surmounted by 2 receding storeys on an octagonal plan; characteristic of Romanesque gabled belfries in Limousin.

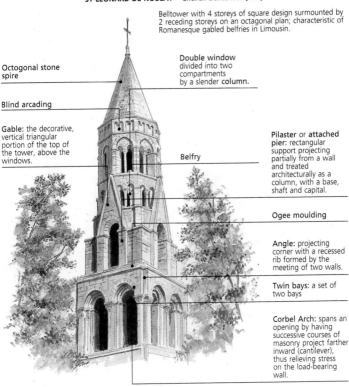

Octogonal stone spire

Double window divided into two compartments by a slender **column**.

Blind arcading

Gable: the decorative, vertical triangular portion of the top of the tower, above the windows.

Belfry

Pilaster or **attached pier:** rectangular support projecting partially from a wall and treated architecturally as a column, with a base, shaft and capital.

Ogee moulding

Angle: projecting corner with a recessed rib formed by the meeting of two walls.

Twin bays: a set of two bays

Corbel Arch: spans an opening by having successive courses of masonry project farther inward (cantilever), thus relieving stress on the load-bearing wall.

BEAULIEU-SUR-DORDOGNE – East end (chevet) of St-Pierre (early 12C)

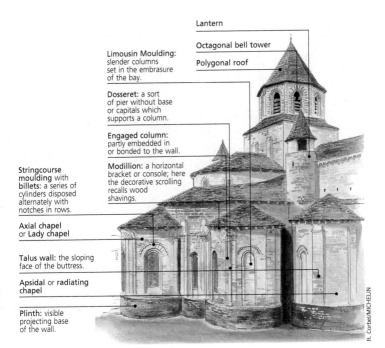

Lantern

Octagonal bell tower

Limousin Moulding: slender columns set in the embrasure of the bay.

Polygonal roof

Dosseret: a sort of pier without base or capitals which supports a column.

Engaged column: partly embedded in or bonded to the wall.

Stringcourse moulding with **billets:** a series of cylinders disposed alternately with notches in rows.

Modillion: a horizontal bracket or console; here the decorative scrolling recalls wood shavings.

Axial chapel or **Lady chapel**

Talus wall: the sloping face of the buttress.

Apsidal or **radiating chapel**

Plinth: visible projecting base of the wall.

R. Corbel/MICHELIN

Military and Civil Architecture

Château de MONTBRUN (12C and 15C)

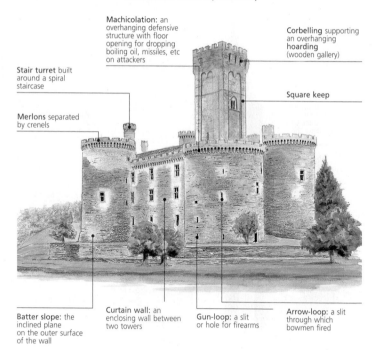

Machicolation: an overhanging defensive structure with floor opening for dropping boiling oil, missiles, etc on attackers

Corbelling supporting an overhanging **hoarding** (wooden gallery)

Stair turret built around a spiral staircase

Square keep

Merlons separated by crenels

Batter slope: the inclined plane on the outer surface of the wall

Curtain wall: an enclosing wall between two towers

Gun-loop: a slit or hole for firearms

Arrow-loop: a slit through which bowmen fired

Château de MEILLANT – Western side (early 14C)

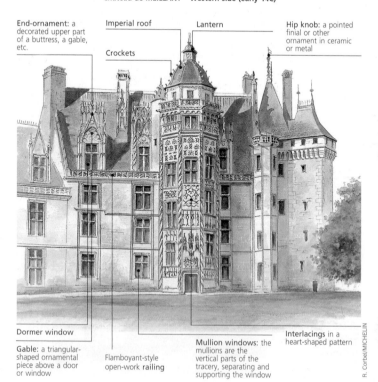

End-ornament: a decorated upper part of a buttress, a gable, etc.

Imperial roof

Lantern

Hip knob: a pointed finial or other ornament in ceramic or metal

Crockets

Dormer window

Gable: a triangular-shaped ornamental piece above a door or window

Flamboyant-style open-work **railing**

Mullion windows: the mullions are the vertical parts of the tracery, separating and supporting the window

Interlacings in a heart-shaped pattern

R. Corbel/MICHELIN

Architecture of the bastides

DOMME – Porte des Tours (late 13C)

In the 13C, the new towns known as bastides, often fortified, became common in Périgord and Quercy. This was the most important defensive gateway in the ramparts of Domme.

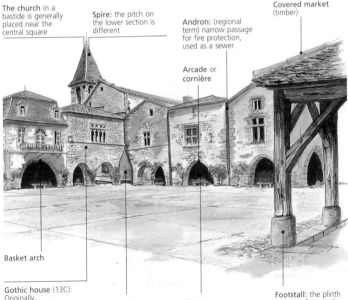

Crown of the tower, raised and fitted with loop-holes in the 14C

Two **circular towers**

Gable-wall

Curtain wall: an enclosing wall between two towers or bastions

Bartizan: a small overhanging turret with lookout holes and defensive loops

Balistraria: a cruciform loophole through which a crossbow could be fired.

Fortified gate: protected by two portcullis and a deadfall

Bossage: projecting, rough-finished stone; until the 15C, used only in military architecture

Arrow-loop

Moat (filled in)

MONPAZIER – Central square in the bastide (late 13C and 14C)

The most typical and best preserved of the Périgord bastides, it is designed around a central rectangular area, bordered by a covered market on the southern side.

The church in a bastide is generally placed near the central square

Spire: the pitch on the lower section is different

Andron: (regional term) narrow passage for fire protection, used as a sewer

Covered market (timber)

Arcade or **cornière**

Basket arch

Gothic house (13C): Originally, all of the residential buildings in the bastide were the same size

In the corner, an **opening** provides access to the square

Couverts: covered galleries

Footstall: the plinth or base of a wooden post, protecting it from ground water

Public building and civil engineering

FIGEAC – Hôtel de la monnaie (late 13C)

Probably a market place for money-changers, the "Oustal de lo Monédo" is representative of the urban architecture of Haut Quercy built during the Gothic period.

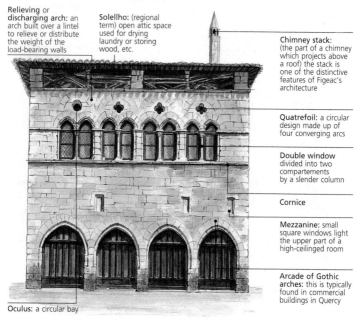

Relieving or discharging arch: an arch built over a lintel to relieve or distribute the weight of the load-bearing walls

Solellho: (regional term) open attic space used for drying laundry or storing wood, etc.

Chimney stack: (the part of a chimney which projects above a roof) the stack is one of the distinctive features of Figeac's architecture

Quatrefoil: a circular design made up of four converging arcs

Double window divided into two compartments by a slender column

Cornice

Mezzanine: small square windows light the upper part of a high-ceilinged room

Arcade of Gothic arches: this is typically found in commercial buildings in Quercy

Oculus: a circular bay

CAHORS – Pont Valentré (14C)

A remarkable example of Medieval military art, this fortified bridge has such an imposing air that it was never attacked.

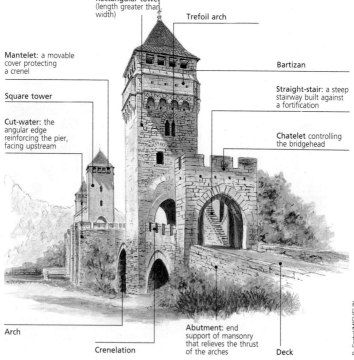

Rectangular tower (length greater than width)

Trefoil arch

Mantelet: a movable cover protecting a crenel

Bartizan

Square tower

Straight-stair: a steep stairway built against a fortification

Cut-water: the angular edge reinforcing the pier, facing upstream

Chatelet controlling the bridgehead

Arch

Crenelation

Abutment: end support of mansonry that relieves the thrust of the arches

Deck

R. Corbel/MICHELIN

The Renaissance

At the beginning of the 16C the artistic movement in France was revitalised by the influence of Italy. King François I and the aristocracy were moved by the desire to copy Italian architecture and sculpture and introduced new styles by employing Italian artists. In the space of a century, hundreds of châteaux were built or restored, as financial resources boomed with the end of the Hundred Years War. Other factors encouraging this artistic movement in the region included improved returns on farm estates (thanks to the development of share-cropping), increased freedom of trade, the mining of iron ore, low labour costs and the advent of ready credit.

ARCHITECTURE

The Berry

At least half of the châteaux in the Berry were rebuilt in the years between 1430 and 1550, and most of the urban centres were transformed. Yet it took a long time for the Italian influence to be felt in the Berry where Gothic art was so strongly implanted. Generally, the Italian styles were interpreted, rather than copied. In Bourges, which was ravaged by fire in 1487, the most notable examples of Renaissance architecture are the Hôtel Lallemant, the Hôtel Cujas and the Hôtel des Échevins. In the countryside, defensive castles became more comfortable residences, as was the case with Ainay-le-Vieil, Meillant, La Verrerie and Villegongis.

The Limousin

In Limoges, the Renaissance influence can be seen on the St John's doorway (Portail St-Jean) – the monumental entrance to the cathedral. In Tulle, the Maison de Loyac is a manor house dating from the 16C. Châteaux which were built or transformed in what is considered a transitional style include those at Rochechouart, Coussac-Bonneval, Pompadour and Sédières.

The Dordogne

The new style flourished in Montal and Puyguilhem, which are similar in appearance to the châteaux of the Loire Valley. Most of the other 16C châteaux incorporate significant defensive features besides the windows, dormers, chimneys and other purely Renaissance elements; this is particularly evident in Monbazillac. In Cénevières, Bourdeilles, Lanquais, Les Bories and Rouffignac (church), buildings were partially transformed; the Château de Biron is graced by a marvellous Renaissance chapel.

Civil architecture was also influenced by the Italian style, as witnessed in the Maison de Roaldès in Cahors, the Maison Cayla (or Maison des Consuls) in Périgueux, the Hôtel de Maleville in Sarlat, and the Hôtel Labenche in Brive.

SCULPTURE AND OTHER ARTS

The Berry and the Limousin

In the Marche, tapestry-making developed rapidly. Throughout the 16C the Aubusson, Bourganeuf and Felletin workshops profited from the growing demand for tapestries and hangings as part of contemporary furnishings.

Aubusson and Felletin continued to take pride in making tapestries and even as late as the Revolution produced *verdures* (greeneries) in which plants and fantastic animals appeared against a background of foliage.

Sculpture can be best admired in the cathedral in Limoges, where the magnificent rood screen, erected between 1533 and 1535, and the tomb of Jean de Langeac, are considered outstanding works of art.

Following the exceptional developments of the 12C to 14C, Limousin enamelwork found new favour in the 15C-16C through the Pénicaud, Nouailher and Limosin families. Léonard Limosin reached new artistic heights through the use of innovative techniques.

Leveau/CDT Cher

Château de Meillant

In Bourges, the art of making stained-glass windows was revived through the work of the artist Lescuyer.

The Dordogne

The inner court of the Château de Montal is an outstanding example of the Italian style, with its busts in high relief – superb works of art which are both realistic and refined. Inside, the remarkable staircase rivals those of the Loire Valley châteaux.

Stall in the chancel, Moutier-d'Ahun

B. Kaufmann/MICHELIN

In the chapel at Biron, the recumbent figures of the Gontaut-Biron family are decorated with figures influenced by the Italian Quattrocento (15C).

FROM THE 17C TO THE 20C

By copying the styles of Paris and Versailles, art lost all its regional character in the 17C.

In the Berry, François le Vau, brother of the architect who designed the Louvre, Vaux and Versailles, planned the Château de Lignières in the style of the *Grand Siècle*: the frontons are supported by pilasters, and the main buildings are reflected in sheets of water beyond which extend the French-style gardens.

The Château de Hautefort, on the border of the Limousin and Périgord, is a very good example of Classical architecture in its planning and unity of design; although it was ravaged by fire in 1968, it has since been completely restored. The Château de Rastignac was built at the end of the 18C: the purity of its lines and the harmony of its proportions place it among the most interesting buildings of that period.

In architecture, the 19C was largely devoted to the restoration and renovation of old buildings. Painting and tapestry, however, saw the introduction of numerous innovations. Auguste Renoir and Suzanne Valadon both heralded from the Limousin, although both left the province at a young age. Corot, on the other hand, was born in Paris and came to the region often to paint. His student, Berthe Morisot, a native of Bourges, was influenced by Renoir and Manet. Claude Monet was inspired by the ruins at Crozant, and painted 30 versions of the site in 1889. Ingres and Bourdelle, both from Montauban, are considered the most eminent representatives of the Quercy from this period.

The art of tapestry-making was revived in the 20C thanks to the new ideas and techniques introduced by Lurçat, Dufy, Marc Saint-Saëns, Gromaire and the Association of Tapestry Cartoon-Painters. Modern art is now displayed in many regional and municipal museums as well as at the Centre National d'Art et du Paysage at the Lac de Vassivière.

Traditional Rural Architecture

THE BERRY

Limestone, sandstone and cob are the traditional building materials of the Berry countryside, yet distinctive differences in style exist between one area and the next. For example, in the **Champagne Berrichonne**, large farm buildings are set around a courtyard. The low roof is covered in flat, brown tiles (or slate closer to the Loire); inside, where a big communal room is heated by a stone chimney, the floor is also tiled. The farms of the **Pays Fort** are more modest, with walls made from cob (clay and straw). Thatched roofs have gradually been replaced with tiles, with the extension of the eaves protecting the walls from wet weather. Around **Sancerre**, farms have a long façade of white limestone crowned with a roof punctuated with dormer windows; the living area is often flanked by a barn or stable. Other types of houses are found near the Sologne region and in La Brenne. Some features, however, are shared by all; these include ceramic finials, weathercocks or other ornaments placed on the ridge of the roof or at the apex of a gable, and plain interior furnishings.

THE LIMOUSIN

Most of the houses in the Limousin countryside date from the 19C and are made of local granite. In the area known as the **Montagne**, the low-built dwellings are attached to the barn and stable. The double-sloped roofs used to be predominantly thatch, but have been mostly replaced by slate. Many houses have lean-to additions next to the garden or orchard, and in the past each farm had its own well or spring.

In the **Xaintrie**, the barn dwellings are often built into a hillside and the rough-cast walls are biscuit-coloured. In the south of the area, half-timbering appears, along with upper storeys in the form of wooden terraces protected by overhanging *lauze* roofs.

The granite houses of the **Haute-Marche** are usually built with a door and a small window on the ground floor, two small windows on the floor above, and an attic used for storing grain on top.

In the **Bas-Pays Corrézien**, the ground floor is used for storage, whereas the dwelling rooms are located above. The sandstone houses are covered with a four-sided sloping roof; an outer stairway links the two storeys by way of a landing and the cellar entrance is at the bottom of the steps.

Higher up on the **plateau**, the box-shaped buildings in blue or ochre granite have small windows and round-tiled roofs. In addition to the stables, where the hay is stored above the animals, many farms have a special room for drying chestnuts, or a dovecot. Every farm is served by its own well.

THE DORDOGNE

The most typical type of house found in the **Périgord Noir** is a sturdy, block-like construction in golden limestone, topped with a steeply pitched roof covered with flat, brown tiles or *lauzes*. The *lauzes* are neither slate nor layered schist tiles, but small limestone slabs. Set horizontally, their weight is such (500kg per m^2/about 102lb per sq ft) that they require a strong, steeply pitched timberwork roof to distribute the weight. Towers or dovecots adjoin the houses of larger houses.

In the **Périgord Blanc**, low houses in grey or white limestone are lit through windows topped with bull's-eyes (*œils-de-bœuf*). The flat roof covered with Roman-style terracotta tiles already reflects the more southern style.

In the forested area known as the **Double**, houses were traditionally built of cob and half-timbering.

In the vineyards of **Bergerac**, the houses of wine-growers are understandably organised around the activities of pressing grapes and making wine; generally they form a U shape or else have two adjoining courtyards. The tumble-down cottages in the surrounding vineyards are used as dwellings for labourers etc.

The houses of the **Quercy** are built in blocks of white limestone mortared in lime, and display a range of shapes, additions, towers and windows. The lower level is partly below ground and called the *cave*; it was here that the stable, shed and storerooms were traditionally located. The floor above was reserved for the living quarters; the two levels are connected by an outside staircase above a terrace protected by a porch supported by stone or wood columns.

Dovecots

The region is dotted with numerous dovecots, many of which are particularly elegant. Some are no more than small towers attached to the main building; others stand alone, either resting on a porch or supported by columns. Before the French Revolution, the right to keep pigeons was generally reserved for large landowners, although the Quercy and Périgord (where the right could be purchased for a fee) were exceptions. Dovecots were built mainly for collecting pigeon droppings – the value of these droppings is evident in the fact that when a property was divided up after a death, they were shared out between heirs in the same way as the livestock. Not only was it excellent manure, but it was also prized by bakers (for the aroma it gave their bread) and by pharmacists as a relief for goitre – the swelling of the thyroid gland – among other conditions. The appearance of chemical fertilisers after 1850 led to a decline in production.

The oldest types of free-standing dovecots were arcaded (so-called hanging dovecots), built on small columns to protect them from the damp (🔊 *see illustration*). The stubby capitals (*capels*) created overhangs to deter would-be predators from climbing up the columns.

Drystone Huts

These small constructions are dotted around the region, and can be found either standing in isolation in a field or, more rarely, grouped together (🔊 *see SARLAT: Cabanes de Breuil*). They are built entirely of dry stones and crowned with conical roofs of stones supported by joggles (notches in each new layer are fitted into notches of the layer below to stop the roof from slipping, and the whole roof is fixed at the top by a sort of keystone). They are known as *gariottes*, *caselles* or *bories*, but it is not known precisely what their function used to be, nor exactly when they were built. Today's farmers may speculate about the mysterious origins of these surprisingly solid huts; meanwhile, they are happy to use them as tool sheds and storage space and proudly show them off to visitors.

THE REGION TODAY

The region's economy has long depended on its agricultural activities, as the scarcity of mineral wealth and raw materials prevented the development of major industrial centres as in northern and eastern France. More recently, investment in a wider range of sectors, including high-tech industries, tourism, and the development of high-quality culinary and craft products, have expanded the region's economic potential. The region's communication infrastructure has also improved, making the countryside less isolated. And of course, the region's trademark products continue to fly the region's flag, in particular Limoges porcelain, foie gras and truffles (see Food and Wine; and When and Where to Go: Wine tours).

The Economy

AGRICULTURE

Berry

Agriculture has long been the mainstay of the Berry's economy, although improvements to the road network have enabled industrial development. Mechanisation and the use of fertilisers reaped rewards in **Champagne Berrichonne**, which has become France's second-largest grain-producing region. However, there are few processing plants to handle the harvest, and this impedes growth. In the Indre *département*, another handicap is the ageing of the farming population (60% of working farmers are over the age of 55).

Limousin

As elsewhere, small farms have decreased in number over the years, to be replaced by larger, more modern operations. In the north, fields are planted with grain crops, whereas southern areas specialise in orchards, mostly apple.

Périgord-Quercy

Alongside the Lot-et-Garonne, the Dordogne *département* is the number one producer of **strawberries** in France, with almost 20 000t harvested annually. The protective plastic coverings visible in spring protect the young plants from bad weather and enable them to flower and grow in a controlled environment. The fruit ripens under these sheets before it is picked and packed off to the large markets of the Paris region and the north of France, where the Périgord strawberry is particularly appreciated.

Although on the decline, **walnuts** are another local speciality harvested in large quantity (5-7 000t per year). Several varieties are produced locally: Marbot walnuts ripen early and are often sold fresh; Grandjean are produced around Sarlat and Gourdon, accounting for most of the green walnuts; Corne is a small nut of good quality; while Franquette has increased in popularity in recent years. In 2002, the four varieties were awarded Appellation d'Origine Controlée (AOC) *Noix du Périgord* status.

Conditions in the Périgord and the Quercy, and southwest France as a whole, are favourable to the growing of **tobacco**, a hardy plant imported from America in the 16C and initially used for medicinal purposes (see BERGERAC: *Musée du Tabac*). The traditional dark tobacco that long gave French cigarettes their strong, distinctive flavour and aroma now grows side-by-side with lighter varieties such as Virginia tobacco, which have increased in popularity. Nowadays, there are around 3 000 planters in the region, mostly in family-run operations. The Dordogne is France's leading tobacco-producing *département* with 1 300 growers producing 15% of the country's crop.

Perhaps the most evocative of all the region's products, however, is the rare and secretive fungus known as the **truffle**, which grows underground, at the base of a tree, where it is sniffed out by specially trained pigs or dogs. Exchanged at market for fabulous sums which seem incongruous with their lumpy, dusty appearance, these subterranean "black diamonds" are not as plentiful as in the past and are threatened by imports from countries such as Italy, Poland and China. Whereas a century ago hundreds of tonnes would have been harvested every year, today this figure has dwindled to around 4t. To encourage production, oak trees continue to be planted in areas where conditions favour growth of these *diamants noirs.*

STOCK-RAISING

Each region has developed its stock-raising in line with the natural fertility of its soil, with rich pastureland given over to the grazing of cattle, and more arid plateaux set aside for the rearing of sheep.

SHEEP

In bygone days sheep-rearing was the only way of earning a living when a lack of money and materials were major obstacles on the plains of the Berry.

The Berry breed is declining in numbers and is being replaced by the Charmois and the English Southdown. Much prized for their meat, they are now reared in sheepfolds and no longer roam the open pastureland. Goat herds are also increasing, particularly as a result of the rise in popularity of goats' cheese.

The *causses* continue to play an important role in sheep-rearing: the plateau sheep or Gramat species is known as the spectacled breed, due to their white fleece and black rings around their eyes. These hardy, prolific animals bear fine wool, but are especially prized for their meat, which contains very little fat.

LIMOUSIN CATTLE

Limousin beef-cattle, with their short withers and distinctive russet hides, were already widely known in the 17C and 18C. Improved by culling and better feeding, the breed now produces some of the finest meat in the world. To supply market demands, Limousin farmers have turned to the production of young calves for white veal.

Natural features have transformed the Limousin into a leading area for the production and export of both the breed and its meat. Indigenous meadowland has been complemented by specially sown pastures where grass grows more profusely.

CRAFTS AND INDUSTRIES

The presence of metallic oxides which could be used in the production of enamelware resulted in the establishment of an **enamelling industry** in Limoges.

After three centuries of decline, the last 50 years have seen the re-establishment of Limoges' reputation, which is now as high as it was in the days of such master-enamellers as the Nardon Pénicauds, the Limosins and the Nouailhers.

The discovery of important deposits of kaolin near St-Yrieix at the end of the 18C was the catalyst for the development of the **china industry**. The first factories were scattered in the southern part of the Haute-Vienne, otherwise the wood needed for the kilns would have been liable to the payment of a toll upon entering the city of Limoges. By the end of the 19C, due to improvements in the production process, porcelain had become a major industry in the city.

Another traditional manufacturing activity is centred around Aubusson, famous for its **tapestries**.

The **leather** industry and its many ancillary sectors developed thanks to abundant water supplies, tanning resins from the forests and hides obtained from large-scale stock-raising. In the early 19C, some 50 tanneries were established in the region. Today, shoes are made at Limoges and St-Amand-Montrond, and St-Junien is famous for its gloves. While this industry seems to be past its heyday, the forest holds promise for the development of the **paper industry**, which is on the upswing.

The area around Limoges has seen a steady increase in new **high-tech** businesses as a result of the development of national institutes (industrial ceram-

Limousin cattle

S. Sauvignier/MICHELIN

ics, engineering, biotechnology, optical and microwave communication etc) and leading industries such as Ariane Espace and Airbus Industrie. Many smaller businesses have started up and experienced considerable international growth.

Prospection of the old Limousin granite massifs led to the discovery of the first uranium deposit near Crouzille in 1948, which became the largest processing centre in Western Europe. These mines are now closed, but a **gold** mine, the last of its kind in France, is still in operation in Bourneix.

Folklore and Traditions

The regions of the Berry, Limousin and Dordogne are home to age-old rural civilisations. Traditional costumes and time-honoured crafts have been preserved in all three areas and are actively on display and promoted in the many local festivals (see Calendar of Events). Legends, superstitions and folk tales have continued to flourish alongside religious events in which the lives and legends of saints play an important role. In addition, alchemists, sorcerers and werewolves, and creatures such as toads, owls, and wolves, to name but a few, have long fuelled the imagination of the region's inhabitants.

Local accents trace the boundaries of the different regions as clearly as a line drawn on a map. Regional patois (provincial dialects) are seldom heard nowadays, although interest in preserving the traditions of the langue d'Oc is reviving.

R. Corbel/MICHELIN

Feletin

LANTERNS OF THE DEAD

The earliest recorded reference to **lanterns** of the dead is found in a 12C text, *De Miraculis*, by Pierre le Vénérable, abbot of Cluny. The legend recounts how a young novice from the Abbaye de Charlieu (Loire) received a visit from his uncle Achard, the monastery's former prior, who had been dead for some years. The apparition led the youth to the cemetery where, wrapped in a glowing light which seemed to ring them in concentric circles, a group of holy persons had gathered. "In the middle of the cemetery, a stone edifice rose up; on the top, there was a small compartment for holding a lamp which, nightly and in honour of the faithful resting there, lights this sacred place. Steps lead to a platform where two or three people can stand or sit down." This definition is very similar

to one given in a study written in 1882 by a local abbot and scholar. Mostly built between the 11C and the 13C, in cemeteries near Romanesque churches, many of the lanterns were destroyed, moved or converted to other uses in later years. These structures, dubbed lanterns of the dead in the 19C, seem to be the expression of ancient ideals. Their form, with a height equal to six or eight times their diameter, complies with ancient Roman canon. The vertical design is symbolic of prestige, but also designates security, and indeed no reference to mourning or suffering seems apparent in the decoration or the exultant skyward movement. Experts still question the use made of the stone dais: perhaps a movable altar was placed upon it, or perhaps it was used to indicate the East, the direction of the Holy City of Jerusalem, thus serving to define the alignment of the graves in the cemetery. People have long believed that the spirits of those who have passed away seek out the light which death has extinguished for them. Although the early Christian church condemned the practice of lighting candles on tombs, the symbol of the eternal flame soon came to be totally assimilated.

THE LIMOUSIN OSTENSIONS

Every seven years the Haute-Vienne and Creuse *départements* honour their saints: St Martial, the apostle of the Limousin; St Valérie; the Good St Eligius, founder of the monastery at Solignac; St Stephen of Muret; hermits who lived in the forests of the Limousin and Marche; and St Junien, St Victurnien and St Leonard, founders of monasteries scattered in the region's valleys. The Virgin Mary is sometimes included under such invocations as Our Lady of the Relics (Aixe-sur-Vienne).

The *ostensions*, or solemn exhibition of relics to the faithful, date back to the 10C. One of the earliest of these festivals was held at Limoges when a terrible epidemic of ergotism, also known as St Anthony's fire, was raging. To combat the malady, the relics of St Martial were brought out. A visitation – whether in the form of a plague or an illustrious personage – became an occasion for holding these ceremonies, which later came to be repeated at regular intervals.

Each town has a traditional ceremony of its own, hosting religious festivals which are also based on local folklore. The blessing of the banner, which is solemnly hoisted to the belfry pinnacle, marks the opening of the *ostension*. Once the festival has been opened on the Sunday after Easter, the relics are presented to the faithful for veneration in their shrines or reliquaries which, in some cases, are masterpieces of the gold and silversmith's art. Colourful processions pass through bunting and flower-decked streets in towns and villages, accompanied by fanfares, drums and banners and escorted by guards of honour, representatives of different craft guilds, and other groups in rich finery. Neighbouring parishes often participate in these events; as an example, 50 parishes come together in Le Dorat for the closing ceremonies.

The next ceremony will take place in 2009.

THE FÉLIBRÉE

In July every year a different town in the Périgord hosts the Félibrée, a meeting of a society of poets and writers set up in the late 19C with the aim of preserving the Provençal language. The windows and doors of the chosen town are decorated with thousands of multicoloured paper flowers, and trees and shrubs are illuminated to form triumphal arches. The people of the Périgord flock from all corners of the *département* decked out in traditional costume: lace headdresses, embroidered shawls and long skirts for the women, and wide-brimmed black felt hats, full white shirts and waistcoats for the men.

The queen of the Félibrée, surrounded by a member of the Félibrige society committee and the guardians of local traditions, receives the keys of the town and makes a speech in the local dialect. The assembled gathering files off in procession to Mass, accompanied by the sound of hurdy-gurdies, before sitting down to a sumptuous feast. Traditionally, the meal begins with *chabrol*, a soup of wine and clear stock typical of the southwest, which is served in dishes made especially for the occasion, and bearing the year and the name of the host town. Everyone present keeps these soup dishes as a souvenir and they are displayed proudly in homes or even in regional museums (see NEUVIC: Mussidan).

Food and Wine

THE BERRY

The **cuisine** of the Berry is plain and simple and makes full use of farm produce. While vegetable, salt pork or bread soup blended with a little cream combine to produce the typical regional soup known as *mique*, the true Berry speciality is *poulet en barbouille*. This chicken dish is flambéed with brandy, cut into pieces and cooked with a blended sauce of blood and cream, an egg yolk and chopped liver. Dishes featuring a wine or cream sauce appear frequently on the tables of the Berry. Also look out for traditional staples such as pumpkin pâté, *truffiat* (potatoes covered in pastry), stuffed rabbit, eggs in wine, ox-tongue au gratin, kidneys, calf's liver, game and fish, often garnished with fresh mushrooms. For dessert, why not try local specialities such as plum flan, *sanciaux* (honey fritters) and *millats* (stewed black cherries).

Wines from the Berry are generally clean and crisp and of good quality. Sancerre is a well-known appellation known more readily for its white wines, although red and rosé are also produced here. Many small growers are scattered around outlying villages, with some of the best wines produced in Bué, Chavignol, Ménétréol and Fontenay - the expressive characteristics of these wines are best enjoyed young. A good companion for local dishes and cheeses is Menetou-Salon, a quality wine produced in limited quantities which is hard to come across elsewhere. Grown in the same chalky soil as Sancerre, many find it to be fuller and more rounded than its illustrative neighbour.

THE LIMOUSIN

The hearty **cuisine** of the Limousin is typified by the traditional dish known as *bréjaude*, a pork rind and cabbage soup garnished with rye bread.
Patés made from truffles or wrapped in pastry and garnished with a mixed veal and pork stuffing (especially the pâté de foies gras from Brive-la-Gaillarde), are deservedly famous.
Although the region is most renowned for its excellent beef, other delicious local dishes includes *lièvre en chabessal*, a dish made from hare stuffed with fresh pork and ham, and seasoned with salt, pepper, spices and condiments.
Cabbage is a traditional Limousin ingredient and is served with partridge, in heart-warming *potées* (country stews) or braised with chestnuts. For a long time, chestnuts (*châtaignes*) were a staple of the farmer's diet, and can still be found garnishing turkey, goose, black pudding, veal and pork stew, or served as a purée with venison.
Perhaps the dish most closely associated with Limousin is clafoutis, a creamy flan in pastry dotted with succulent, ruby red cherries.

THE PÉRIGORD AND QUERCY

Cuisine in the Dordogne (which the French invariably refer to as the Périgord when speaking of gastronomy) is one of France's culinary jewels. For centuries, the region has been synonymous with delicacies such as truffles, foie gras and confits. Sit down to a traditional meal here and you may never want to eat any other way again: perhaps start with *tourain blanchi* – a white soup made from garlic, goose fat and eggs, sometimes with sorrel or tomato added; next comes the foie gras or pâté de foie (a general term for liver pâté); the third course might perhaps be a delicious omelette made with cèpes (wild mushrooms) or delicately sliced truffles. For the main course, enjoy *confit d'oie aux pommes sarladaises* (goose preserved in its own fat, fried until brown, with potatoes fried in goose fat and garlic, and garnished with mushrooms). A refreshing salad drizzled in a light walnut oil dressing is then followed by the cheese platter. To round things off, why not indulge in a slice of walnut cake or a freshly baked plum pie?
The **truffe** (truffle) is the elegant name of a knobby, black fungus which weighs about 100g/3.5oz, and imbues all it touches with its unique aroma. A truffle must be fresh or very carefully preserved and their rarity and price make them a gourmet luxury. It is found in delicate black specks in foie gras, pâté, poultry dishes, *ballotines* (white turkey meat and liver moulded in aspic) and *galantines* (cold cuts); it is also sliced thinly into salads and omelettes. A truffle wrapped and cooked whole over an open fire – *à la cendre* – is a supreme extravagance.

FOIE GRAS

Foie gras is certainly the pride of the Périgord. Once their feathers have grown in (after approximately 1 month), ducks and geese are put outdoors. To prepare for force-feeding, they are nourished with grains and alfalfa, which help expand the digestive system. After three months in the open air, the birds are placed in individual cages for 15-18 days. Progres-

CLAFOUTIS

Clafoutis is derived from the old verb *clafir* and the Latin *clavo figere*, meaning "to fill up". First used as a name for a desert in the Limousin, it remains emblematic of the region's cuisine. The genius of the true Limousin clafoutis is the variety of cherries used, which are small and very dark, almost blue, without a lot of flesh around the pit. The cherries are baked whole in the batter, as the pits add flavour and a unique hint of bitterness.

French households commonly possess a clafoutis mould: a deep, round baking dish with a fluted rim. The basic recipe works well with summer fruits, especially apricots and plums, and in winter it can be used with apples, pears and raisins. Savoury clafoutis is a modern invention, a close cousin to the *tian* of Provence. The two recipes below, the first a traditional cherry clafoutis, the second a savoury vegetarian option best accompanied by a fresh green salad, highlight the versatility of this typical dish.

Clafoutis aux cerises

- Preheat the oven to 375°F (gas mark 5) and butter the clafoutis dish.

- Blend 1/4 cup (45g) of melted butter, 3 eggs, 1/2 cup (85g) of granulated sugar, 1/2 cup (100ml) of sour cream and 1/2 cup (85g) of flour in a large bowl until the mixture is smooth and homogenous.

- Pour the batter into the baking dish.

- Drop the cherries into the batter evenly (you may prefer to remove the pits, it is definitely easier to eat without them).

- Bake for 40 to 45min or until a toothpick stuck in the centre comes out clean.

- Sprinkle with powdered (icing) sugar and serve warm.

- If you use this recipe with very juicy fruit (such as plums), add a bit more flour; if the fruit is sour (early apricots), add sugar.

Vegetable clafoutis
(serves 6)

- Preheat the oven to 400°F (gas mark 6) and butter the clafoutis dish.

- Peel, seed and crush 4 ripe tomatoes.

- Chop up 2 large onions, 1 red and 1 yellow pepper, 2 small courgettes (zucchini) and two small aubergines (eggplant).

- Heat some olive oil in a deep frying pan and add the following ingredients in order: onions, peppers, courgettes, tomatoes and aubergine. Add oil as you go along as it gets absorbed by the vegetables.

- When the mixture begins to brown, remove from the heat and allow to cool.

- Crush 2 cloves of garlic. Spread the vegetables and garlic evenly around the baking dish, and season with herbs (thyme, basil, oregano etc).

- Beat 3 whole eggs with 4-5 tablespoons of cornstarch; add 1 cup (200ml) of thick cream, 4 ounces (100g) of farmhouse cheese and season with salt and pepper.

- The cheese should be fresh and unripened so that you can blend it in. Alternatively, use 1/2 cup (4oz/100g) of freshly grated Parmesan cheese, although the taste will be more Provençal.

- Pour the batter over the vegetables and cook for 35-40min.

- Enjoy either hot or cold.

sively over-fed, they are given ground meal then whole corn with a funnel-like feeding device known as the *gaveuse*. A duck thus absorbs 10-15kg/22-33lb, a goose up to 20kg/44lb of corn, tripling or even quadrupling the weight of its liver to achieve an ideal weight: 450-500g/1lb for a duck; 800-900g/2lb for a goose.

Preparation

Foies gras can be preserved with excellent results, and are labelled according to content; read the label or menu carefully to know what you are getting. **Foie gras entier** is sliced from a whole liver, the nerve fibres removed, seasoned and sterilised (*mi-cuit* livers must be kept refrigerated and eaten fresh). A **bloc de foie gras** is reconstituted, made from bits of liver chopped and mixed at high speed and emulsified with water. Other forms of foie gras are *parfait* (75% liver), *mousse, pâté, médaillon* and *galantine* (50% liver).

Savouring foie gras

Foie gras should be served chilled (allow 50grams/2oz per person), and cut with a knife rinsed in hot water. Enjoy a glass of cool, sweet Monbazillac wine with your foie gras.

CONFITS

Confits are the traditional base of the region's cuisine. Confit was first used as a method of preserving various parts of the goose, before the advent of the freezer. Now regarded as a gourmet dish, it is still prepared using traditional methods. The pieces of goose are cooked in their own fat for 3hr and then preserved in large earthenware pots (*tupins*). This procedure is also used to preserve duck, turkey and pork (pork confit is called *enchaud*). Goose grease is used instead of butter in local cooking, for example, when frying the delicious *pommes de terre sarladaises*.

STUFFINGS AND SAUCES

Stuffings and sauces, often comprising liver and truffles, are used frequently to garnish poultry, game, suckling pigs and in a favourite regional dish – *cou d'oie farci* – stuffed goose neck.

The most commonly used sauces are the *rouilleuse*, which is used to give colour and to accompany poultry fricassee, and *sauce Périgueux*, a Madeira sauce made from a base of chicken stock, to which fresh truffles are added.

WINES

The renown and popularity of **wines** from the region date way back to the Middle Ages. **Cahors** wine was transported by barges (*gabares*) to Bordeaux and from there by ship to the capitals of Europe. A deep-red colour, with a robust flavour to match, Cahors accompanies hearty foods including game, roast meats and strong-flavoured cheese. The bouquet only achieves subtlety and loses its rather harsh presence on the tongue after ageing two to three years in the cask and another dozen in the bottle.

The vineyards of **Bergerac**, largely planted with Sauvignon grapes, produce reds as well as whites. Among the latter, **Monbazillac** holds pride of place. Golden and smooth, and with a heady aroma, this syrupy wine is served as an aperitif, with foie gras or with dessert. Like other sweet, highly alcoholic wines (notably Sauternes), Monbazillac depends on the effects of the noble mould (*Botrytis cinerea*), a highly beneficent mould which forms on the skins of the ripening grapes, bringing about a concentration of sugar and flavour and a vast improvement in the quality of the resulting wine, without imparting any trace of this on the palate. The process has been employed since the Renaissance. The grapes are harvested in several batches as they reach the desired state. Monbazillac develops its full flavour after two to three years and will keep for up to 30 years.

Dry white wines such as Montravel and Bergerac, vigorous and fruity, go well with seafood and fish; sweeter wines like Côtes de Bergerac, Côtes de Montravel, Rosette and Saussignac are good as aperitif wines or with white meats.

Red Bergerac wines are firm, with a fruity bouquet, and can be enjoyed soon after bottling. **Pécharmant** is fuller-bodied, more complex, and must be left to mature before its charms can be fully appreciated.

Regional Wines

French wines are classified according to a system which provides a rough guide to price and quality, although there is plenty of room for overlapping, especially where small growers are concerned. The lowest category is simply labelled **Vin de table**. Such wines may have been elaborated using any variety of grape from any country in the EU (although this must be stated on the label). While generally to be avoided in shops and restaurants, you may buy satisfactory table wine from a local producer or cooperative (bring your own container). Next comes the **Vin de Pays**, which bears a label identifying the place of origin and possibly the grape variety (if not a blend) and the year. The category following is the **VDQS**, *Vin Délimité de Qualité Supérieure*, which also shows place of origin and may show variety and year. The superiority comes from the fact that the grape varieties are approved and the district of production clearly defined; in addition, these wines pass a yearly taste test to confirm their quality.

The top 20% of French wines are labelled **Appellation d'Origine Contrôlée** (abbreviated AOC or simply AC). These wines come from designated vineyards, use approved grape varieties and are vinified in a manner specific to each one. The system is controlled by the Institut National des Appellations d'Origine, and it is a serious business indeed. The AOC label is a reward for years of continuous merit and lobbying. Similar systems are now being put into use for other produce, notably meats and cheeses.

Sancerre

The wines of Sancerre are commonly classified as Eastern Loire Valley wines. The upper reaches of the Loire are mostly planted with the Sauvignon Blanc grape, which produces two of the finest wines in France: **Sancerre** and **Pouilly-Fumé**. These wines are produced within 8km/5mi of each other, on different sides of the river, and yet their taste is, to the connoisseur, leagues apart. Mostly white wines are produced; the term fumé is in reference to the smoky bloom that forms on the skin of the fruit rather than to the resulting flavour. Sancerre is reputed for its full, round finish, whereas Pouilly-Fumé is considered a more complex, flowery wine.

In addition to these famous labels, some of the other wines in the region are delightful discoveries for the traveller. Certain wines, produced in small quantity and difficult to find outside the region, make for a memorable and unique experience. It is worth a visit to the wine-growers of Bué, Chavignol, Ménétréol and Fontenay to savour the regional savoir-faire.

Mostly white, but also some rosé and red AOC wines are produced in the villages of Ménétou-Salon, Quincy, and Reuilly. Reds and rosés are drawn from Sauvignon Blanc, Pinot Noir, Pinot Gris and Meunier grapes.

Sancerre is a beautiful wine town, surrounded by hillside vineyards which sweep away from the town like striped skirts on a lovely lady. The signposted wine route meanders around back roads and through the village of Chavignol, famous for its crottin de Chavignol goat's milk cheese. The Sancerrois is not a very big region, but visitors will have plenty of temptation to stop and sample local wines and cheeses and to enjoy a slower pace of life.

Bergerac

Another leading wine-producing centre in the region covered in this guide is Bergerac, which has 12 different types of AOC wines. There is a well-marked wine route around the vineyards (information at the Maison des Vins, Cloître de Récollets, in Bergerac). The varieties grown are Cabernet Franc, Cabernet Sauvignon, Merlot, Cot, Semillon and Sauvignon Blanc. Bergerac, Côtes de Bergerac and Pécharmant are strong red wines; the rosés are less enticing, and the white wines are sweet (moëlleux) or if dry, bottled under a separate AOC, **Bergerac Sec. Ambrosial Monbazillac** white wines, very sweet, are often served with foie gras. The flavour is similar to Sauternes, and the wine keeps for about four years, although a good year may age better. **Rosette** is a less sweet white wine produced in small quantity and not found elsewhere; enjoy it as an apéritif wine. **Montravel** vineyards

A bit of local wine and cheese

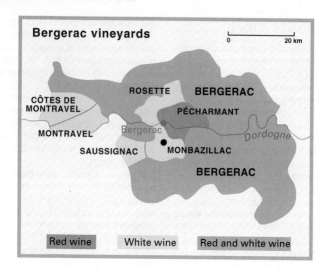

Bergerac vineyards

0   20 km

ROSETTE   **BERGERAC**

CÔTES DE
MONTRAVEL

PÉCHARMANT

MONTRAVEL   *Bergerac*   *Dordogne*

SAUSSIGNAC   MONBAZILLAC

BERGERAC

Red wine   White wine   Red and white wine

are in the Dordogne, but also on the far edge of Bordeaux territory. The white wines (from dry to sweet) are bottled as Montravel, whereas the reds are sold as Bergerac.

- **Maison des vins de Bergerac**, quai Salvette, 2 place Cayla, 24104 Bergerac Cedex, ☎ 05 53 63 57 57. Wine tasting, tour of selected vineyards and cellars listed in the Guide de la route des vins.

- **Cave cooperative de Monbazillac,** route de Mont-de-Marsan, 24240 Monbazillac, ☎ 05 53 63 65 06. Wine tasting.

Cahors

The deep-red wines of Cahors are made from Malbec, Merlot and Jurançon grapes, grown in ruddy soil scattered with limestone pebbles. Start a tour of the regional vineyard right at the famous Pont de Valentré across the River Lot. From here you can go to Pradines and Douelle, where wine was once loaded onto flat-bottomed boats for transportation. The wine road is a beautiful route through the countryside and along the river; many of the vineyards have been producing wine for centuries. During the Roman occupation, the Emperor Dolmitian ordered the vines uprooted as punishment for an uprising, thus temporarily (for 200 years) halting production, which is now back in full swing. The AOC label was awarded to regional wines in 1971.

To earn the name **Cahors**, the hearty red wines must have at least 70% Malbec, and at most 20% Merlot and Tannot; the remaining 10% is Jurançon. While they are known for their dark colour bordering on black, and their robust and tannic flavour, Cahors wines are evolving to suit modern tastes and now more subtle vintages are coming to light. Labelled vieux (old), it has aged three years or more in a wooden cask.

Locally made Coteaux de Quercy, red and rosé wines from the Lot Valley, are Vins de Pays.

- The **Union interprofessionnelle du vin de Cahors**, 430 avenue Jean-Jaurès, 46000 Cahors, ☎ 05 65 23 22 24, publishes a booklet listing winegrowers' addresses (also available from local tourist offices) but does not sell wine.

- **Maison du Vin des coteaux du Quercy,** 82270 Montpezat-de-Quercy, ☎ 05 63 02 03 50.

Château de Castelnaud

ARGENTAT★

POPULATION 3 125

MICHELIN LOCAL MAP 329: M-5

The name of the town has evolved from the Celtic *Argentoratum*, meaning "the passage of the river." In the 17C and 18C Argentat enjoyed great prosperity as a result of the transport of wood along the Dordogne by traditional, flat-bottomed "gabares" to Bergerac, where it was used in the barrel-making industry. Many of the elegant buildings in the centre of town and along the river bank, with their turrets and pepperbox towers, date from this period.

▶ **Orient Yourself:** If possible, try to approach Argentat from the south for a great view of the town.

Visit

Quai Lestourgie

Built in 1844, this riverside embankment is lined with fine houses crowned with turrets, gables and pepperbox towers. In olden days, it was here that the typical *gabares* were moored to load up their precious cargo.

Bridge

Walk onto the bridge for a pleasant view of the town, with its impressive houses fronted by wooden balconies jutting out over the river. Argentat's busy main street divides the town into two distinct districts. Note the unusual mix of **lauze** (roughly hewn slabs of stone of either schist or lava) and slate roofs.

La Cité

Beyond the bridge, continue along the riverside promenade as far as **rue des Conta-mines**, passing typical narrow streets along the way. Continue towards the centre via **place Delmas**, surrounded by old houses such as the Manoir de l'Eyrial and the Maison Filliol. From the church of **St-Pierre**, head down the steps towards **rue Ste-Claire** to the private mansion which was home to the Vicomtes de Turenne. Cross rue Henri IV to **rue des Goudous**, where the construction date on several impressive houses has been chiselled into the lintels. Beyond the **Chapelle Jeanne d'Arc**, rue Ledamp leads back to the car park.

Excursions

① La Xaintrie

Round trip of 55km/34mi – allow half a day

The name **Xaintrie** is a corruption of the word Saint-Trie. It consists of a granite plateau deeply cut by the gorges of the Dordogne, the Maronne and the Cère, where

Argentat – View of the town

Address Book

For coin ranges, see the Legend at the back of the guide.

WHERE TO EAT AND WHERE TO STAY

Crêperie des Quais – *2, rue du Port-Saulou -* ☎ *05 55 28 80 43 - creperiedes-quais@wanadoo.fr -* 🕘 *closed Wed except Jul-Aug.* The menu in this charming half-timbered house on the banks of the Dordogne includes salads and grilled meats, in addition to the good selection of crepes. Attractive nautical decor and a pleasant leafy terrace.

Camping Le Gibanel – *4.5/2.8mi NE of Argentat on the D 18 towards Égletons -* ☎ *05 55 28 10 11 - contact@camping-gibanel.com - www.camping-gibanel.com -* 🕘 *open Jun-14 Sep - reservation recommended - 250 pitches - mobile homes also available - restaurant and pizzeria.* One of the most pleasant campsites in France, located along the banks of the Dordogne and shaded by large trees in the grounds of the Château de Gibanel. Excellent facilities, including two swimming pools, sports activities, evening entertainment etc.

moorland and scrubland alternate with pine and silver birch woods. There is a marked contrast between the white Xaintrie in the north (St-Privat) and the black Xaintrie in the south (Mercœur).

▶ *Leave Argentat to the S towards St-Privat then turn left onto the D 129.*

Barrage d'Argentat

This is one of five dams with a hydroelectric power station on the Upper Dordogne. It was built 2km/1.2mi upstream from Argentat to maximise the use of the waters from the Le Chastang reservoir. It rises to a maximum height of 35m/115ft, with a crest spanning 190m/623ft long. Four sluices can empty 4 000m3/880 000 gallons per second. This power station has five hollow piles, three of which are equipped with hydroelectric generators.

🚶 Near the church of **St-Martial-Entraygues** on the west bank of the Dorgogne, a trail leads to the promontory of the **Roc Castel**, with its viewpoint over the river and dam.

Chapelle de Glény

The chapel, all that remains of the former church, has an attractive chevet and a bell gable (a high wall pierced with openings).

Barrage du Chastang★

🔑 *Visits are currently suspended for security reasons.* The power station at this dam is the largest producer of electricity in the whole valley.

🚶 Less than 1.6km/1mi beyond the dam, a narrow winding path (signposted) heads off to the right of the D 29, leading to a belvedere on the left bank of the Dordogne, from where there is an impressive view of the dam and reservoir.

Servières-le-Château

This former stronghold, owned in turn by the Turenne and Noailles families, enjoys a picturesque **setting**★ overlooking the deep gorges of the Glane. The stone *lauze* roofs of the village are encircled by jagged rocks and pine trees.

▶ *Head north out of Servières along the D 75.*

Lac de Feyt

Stop on the north side of the Barrage de la Glane to admire the splendid view of this 65ha/161-acre lake, a popular outdoor leisure and sailing centre.

▶ *Continue along the D 75 towards Darazac then turn right onto the D 75E1.*

St-Privat

The village's 13C and 16C church is crowned by an imposing square tower.

▶ *Leave St-Privat S along the D 13.*

Tours de Merle★★

👁 *See Tours de MERLE.*

▶ *Leave the D 13 and drive towards St-Bonnet-les-Tours.*

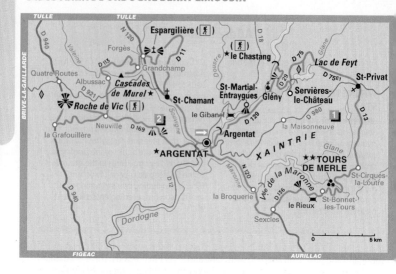

Vallée de la Maronne

The D 136 climbs through a wooded landscape to a plateau with fine views of the Tours de Merle. The road passes through St-Bonnet-les-Tours, before skirting the foot of the **Château du Rieux** (13C and 16C).

▶ *Beyond Sexcles, the N 120 follow the east bank of the Maronne back to Argentat.*

2 Vallée de la Souvigne★

Round-trip of 45km/28mi – allow 3hr

▶ *Head northwest out of Argentat along the N 120 towards Tulle.*

The road climbs through the wooded hills of the Souvigne Valley.

Église de St-Chamant

The doorway of the church, fronted by a belfry-porch and wooden gallery, is particularly interesting. Note the doorway capitals and the tympanum with its double register of carvings.

▶ *Drive north out of St-Chamant along the D 11 to St-Bonnet-Elvert, then turn left towards Forgès.*

Calvaire d'Espargilière

15min round trip on foot.

The view from the calvary extends over meadows to the wooded hillsides of the surrounding valleys.

▶ *Cross the N 120 to reach the west bank of the Souvigne. In Grandchamp, turn onto the D 113E.*

Cascades de Murel★

Walk along the banks of the crystal-clear Valeine to reach this waterfall, situated in a delightful setting of greenery and rocks.

▶ *Return to Grandchamp. Turn left onto the D 113, which flanks the hillside and provides fine views of the Souvigne Valley, then continue to Albussac along the D 87 before turning right on the D 176 towards Sirieix.*

Roche de Vic★

15min round trip on foot. Altitude 636m/2 087ft.

This bare-flanked hill of granite blocks is crowned by a small chapel and a statue of the Virgin Mary. The **view★** from here encompasses the Lower Limousin (*viewing table*). The hills roll northward as far as the Massif des Monédières, and south to the limestone plateaux of the Causse de Quercy.

▶ *Follow the D 940 as far as La Grafouillère, then turn left onto the D 169 leading back to Argentat.*

ARGENTON-SUR-CREUSE★

POPULATION 5 146

MICHELIN LOCAL MAP 323: F-7

Argenton is a pleasant provincial town with picturesque old houses lining the banks of the River Creuse. In the 19C, the town was a centre for the garment industry and still specialises in high-quality men's shirts today.

▶ **Orient Yourself**: The Vieux Pont spanning the Creuse provides a perfect vantage-point from which to admire the River Creuse, Argenton's old quarter and the upper part of the town. For a view of the town's rooftops, head for the terrace of the Chapelle Notre-Dames-des-Bancs.

☺ **Don't Miss**: The Musée de la Chemiserie, highlighting the history of the town's garment-making industry.

A Bit of History

The town of Argenton-sur-Creuse replaced the Gallo-Roman settlement of Argentomagnus which straddled a hill, the Colline de St-Marcel, 2km/1.2mi north of the town.

Visit

Église St-Sauveur

The foundations of the church probably date from the settlement of the lower town in the 13C. The neo-Gothic belfry-porch in front of the church is crowned by a pierced stone spire (50m/164ft). The nave, rebuilt in the 19C, has groined vaulting with emblazoned keystones.

▶ *Head out of the church and turn left onto rue Grande.*

Impasse de Villers

Note the Hôtel de Scévole, a fine 17C-18C manor.

▶ *Turn right at the end of rue Grande.*

Vieux Pont

The old bridge (17C, but rebuilt in the 19C) provides a good **view**★ of the River Creuse, the old quarter and the upper part of town. To the left you can admire a fine stretch of the Creuse, with twin overflows to provide water for the mills, and houses with balconies, balustrades, wooden galleries and slate roofs, either overlooking the river

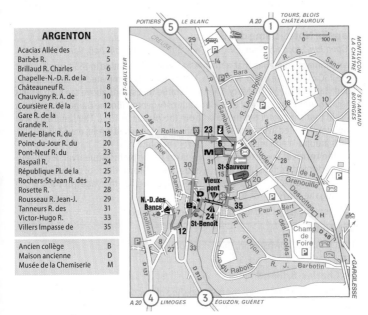

ARGENTON	
Acacias Allée des	2
Barbès R.	5
Brillaud R. Charles	6
Chapelle-N.-D. R. de la	7
Châteauneuf R.	8
Chauvigny R. A. de	10
Coursière R. de la	12
Gare R. de la	14
Grande R.	15
Merle-Blanc R. du	18
Point-du-Jour R. du	20
Pont-Neuf R. du	23
Raspail R.	24
République Pl. de la	25
Rochers-St-Jean R. des	27
Rosette R.	28
Rousseau R. Jean-J.	29
Tanneurs R. des	31
Victor-Hugo R.	33
Villers Impasse de	35

Ancien collège	B
Maison ancienne	D
Musée de la Chemiserie	M

or built into the now-overgrown cliff; to the right, the stone spire of St-Sauveur; and in the far distance the belfry of the Église St-Marcel. The imposing gilded statue of Notre-Dame of Argenton dominates the Chapelle Notre-Dame-des-Bancs.

Beyond the bridge, note the **old house** embellished with a small Renaissance door.

Rue Raspail

On the right, the **ancien collège**, now home to a regional archaeological restoration centre, was built in the late 15C in Renaissance style. It is crowned with a bell turret and adorned with a sculpted doorway. The building is also known locally as the old prison, for it served that purpose in 1782.

Chapelle St-Benoît

This former Gothic collegiate chapel (15C-16C) was restored and re-consecrated in 1873; the belfry was added in 1965. Outside, admire the fine doorway with wreathed columns; on the left stands a statue (1485) of the Virgin and Child.

▶ *Cross rue Victor-Hugo and follow the steep street.*

Rue de la Coursière

This picturesque street opposite the chapel leads uphill, providing a good view of the town.

Chapelle Notre-Dame des Bancs

🕑 *Open Jun-Sep, daily, 9am-7pm; Oct-May, Sat-Sun and public hols, 9am-7pm.*

This pilgrimage chapel, all that remains of a fortress dismantled in 1632, was erected in the 15C on the site of the ruins of a 2C sanctuary; is dominated by an enormous gilded statue of the Virgin Mary. The small statue that stands above the high altar is venerated under the name of the Good Lady of Argenton (Bonne Dame d'Argenton); it is said that she protected the town from the plague in 1632. The sanctuary was completely restored in the late 19C. The monumental, gilded Virgin, unveiled in 1899, weighs around 3t and measures 6.5m/21ft in height.

From the **terrace**, the extensive **view**★ takes in the picturesque riverside quays, houses adorned with gables, turrets, and slate or brown tile roofs, the belfries of the Église St-Sauveur and Chapelle St-Benoît, as well as the valley of the Creuse encircling the town.

▶ *Retrace your steps and turn left along rue Victor-Hugo.*

Pont-Neuf

Situated further downstream, this bridge provides another panoramic view of the town.

Rue Charles-Brillaud

At the end of the street stands the first workshop of machine-made garments founded in 1860 by Charles Brillaud, which now houses the Musée de la Chemiserie.

Musée de la Chemiserie

   Open Jul-Aug, Tue-Sun, 9.30am-12.30pm and 2-6pm, Mon, 2-6pm; Sep-Jun, daily except Mon, 9.30am-noon and 2-6pm. *Closed 23 Dec to mid-Feb.* 3€. 02 54 24 34 69.

This attractive museum, housed on several levels, provides an insight into the shirt (*chemise*) industry in Argenton and the local area. A production workshop exhibits several machines and accessories, with additional information provided by diagrams and plans explaining the various stages of manufacture. The museum also displays shirts worn by stars such as Richard Burton, Charlie Chaplin and Frank Sinatra, and includes a simulation cabin providing a virtual overview of men's fashion over the ages.

▶ *Return to Église St-Sauveur along rue Grande.*

Excursions

1 Hills and Castles

Round-trip of 50km/31mi – allow 3hr

St-Marcel★

  See ST-MARCEL.

▶ *Head along the D 927 and cross over the A 20 motorway.*

Le Pont-Chrétien-Chabenet

The 15C Château du Broutet now serves as the town hall. The Château de Chabenet, restored in the 19C, is visible on top of the limestone cliffs. The covered wooden bridge was built in 1847 when the Paris-Toulouse railway line was opened.

▶ *Continue along the D 927.*

St-Gaultier

This village is nestled amid white chalky hills dotted with wooded groves. The **priory** dates from the 12C. After admiring the Romanesque capitals inside, follow the steep path that leads down to the river, where you will be rewarded with a fine view of the River Creuse.

▶ *Continue along the N 151.*

Lanterne des Morts de Ciron

This funerary lantern, crowned by a conical roof, dates from the 12C.

▶ *Cross the River Creuse via the D 44.*

Château de Romefort

Although the château is not open to visitors, it is worth stopping to admire its superb position perched above the river. The main building dates from the 14C; the square keep to one side from the 12C. It was once surrounded by three protective walls punctuated with towers, which now form rows of jagged ruins.

▶ *Follow the D 3 to Oulches, then continue along the D 927.*

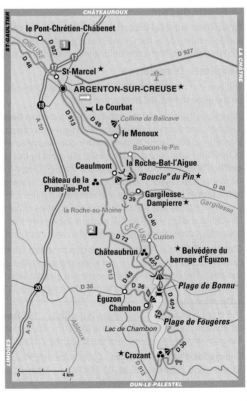

Between Rivarennes and Thenay, enjoy scenic views of St-Gaultier, rising in tiers above the river, which is spanned here by an attractive stone bridge.

▶ *The D 48 leads back to Argenton.*

② Vallée de la Creuse★

Round-trip of 80km/50mi – allow half a day

▶ *Drive southeast out of Argenton along the D 48 towards Gargilesse.*

Château du Courbat

This graceful manor is surrounded by a moat. The tower dates from the 13C, the building itself from the 17C. Restored in 1989, it now serves as the town hall.

▶ *Continue along the D 48.*

Le Menoux

This village overlooking the river (👁 for the best views head for the Coline de Bali-cave) was once famous for its wines, as can be seen in the wine-growers' houses and cellar entrances. The 19C church has been decorated by the Bolivian painter Jorge Carrasco. The artist's house, just a few doors away, is open to the public.

▶ *Return to the D 48.*

Barrage de la Roche-Bat-l'Aigue

Follow the road as it winds uphill and bear right onto a narrow road which runs close to the fast-flowing waters of the Creuse. A small dam *(barrage)*, a spillway and a leisure area are enclosed between rocks and high wooded slopes.

▶ *Turn around, return to Badecon-le-Pin, then take the D 40.*

Fresco, St-Menoux

La Boucle du Pin★

As you come out of Les Chocats, you get a good **view★** of the **Le Pin meander** *(boucle)* a wide bend made by the Creuse in a cirque of rocks and hills. On the opposite side of the river, above a high promontory, stands the Romanesque church of Ceaulmont.

Gargilesse-Dampierre★

This is one of the most attractive villages in the valley, with its pleasant leafy setting, picturesque streets, old houses and church.

The village itself has an interesting literary history as **George Sand** (👁 *see NOHANT*) lived here and chose it as the background for several of her novels and accounts of rural legends and life. Claude Monet and Théodore Rousseau were among several painters of their time who stayed in Gargilesse, attracted by the village's natural beauty. The **castle** (🕐*Open late-Apr to late-Sep, 2.30-7pm.* 🕐 *Closed Tue (except Jul-Aug).* 💶*2.50€ (children under 12 years, no charge).* ☎ *02 54 47 76 16. www.chateaudegargilesse.com)* of the former lords of Gargilesse houses an art gallery. The four bedrooms that can be visited on the first floor contain various styles of furniture (Louis XV, Louis XVI, Directoire and Empire). The 12C postern displays a collection of swords, including a heavy 12C blade which had to be wielded with both hands.

Church – The 11C-12C Romanesque church stands within the walls of a medieval castle rebuilt in the 18C. The old keep and a door flanked by two towers are still standing. The church is well proportioned and has interesting historiated capitals portraying the Twenty-four Old Men of the Apocalypse. A 12C Virgin and Child stands in the main chapel.

The crypt is enormous and decorated with 12C-15C **frescoes**: the Instruments of the Passion, St Gregory Celebrating Mass, the Apparition of Christ, Crucifixion, the Assumption, the Resurrection of the Dead, the Visitation and the Three Kings.

George Sand's Retreat, Aligra – 🕐*Open Apr-Sep;* 👁*guided tours (45min), 9.30am-12.30pm and 2-7pm.* 💶*4€.* ☎ *02 54 47 84 14.* Mementoes of the novelist, her son Maurice and her granddaughter Aurore are all on display in this small house.

▶ *Continue along the D 40. Beyond Cuzion, turn right onto the D 45 towards Éguzon. 2km/1.2mi further on, turn right to the Moulin de Châteaubrun.*

Châteaubrun

The massive towers of Châteaubrun, a 12C fortress built in a picturesque setting overlooking the valley by Hugues de Lusignan, inspired George Sand to describe this wild country in two of her novels, *Le Péché de Monsieur Antoine* and *Les Maupras*.

▶ *Turn right onto the D 45E just before Pont-des-Piles.*

Belvédère du Barrage d'Éguzon★

This belvedere above the dam provides a superb view of the reservoir (Lac de Chambon) blending into a landscape of hills and rocks and, downstream, the valley of the River Creuse.

▶ *Head to the D 40, then turn right onto the D 40A.*

Plage de Bonnu

Before heading down to the Lac de Chambon, take a moment to admire an elegant castle surrounded by a moat on the right-hand side.

Ruines de Crozant★

See Ruines de CROZANT.

▶ *A narrow road skirting the foot of the ruins runs down to the lake.*

Chambon

This resort, set in beautiful surroundings, makes full use of the stretch of water contained by the Barrage d'Éguzon dam, with a full range of water sports available here. In season there is a regular boat service to the **Plage de Fougères**.

Éguzon

Éguzon was formerly a fortified town. On rue Athanase-Bassinet, daily life and traditional crafts of the region are brought to life in the **Musée de la Vallée de la Creuse** (*Guided tours (45min), Apr-Sep, daily except Tue, 10am-noon and 2-6pm, Sat-Sun and public hols, 2-6pm; Mar and Oct-Nov, Sat-Sun and public hols, 2-6pm. 3€. ☎ 02 54 47 47 75.)*.

▶ *Continue along the D 45 to Pont-de-Piles, turn left onto the D 72, then follow the D 913.*

Ruins of the Château de la Prune-au-Pot

☛ *The ruins of the castle are closed to visitors*. It was here that Henri IV stayed during the siege of Argenton in 1589.

Ceaulmont

The name of this town derives from its dominant position. In a meadow to the right of the road, note the charming little Romanesque church on the edge of a spur. Skirt it to the south side to enjoy a fine **view**★ of a loop in the Creuse, with the plateaux of the Marche and Combraille in the distance.

▶ *Return to the D 913 which leads back to Argenton-sur-Creuse.*

ARNAC-POMPADOUR★

POPULATION 1 334

MICHELIN LOCAL MAP 329: J-3

These two villages in the Corrèze, just 2km/1.2mi apart, today form a single administrative area (commune). The château and title of Pompadour were given by King Louis XV to his favorite in 1745. In 1761, the king established a famous stud farm here which, in the 19C, saw the development of the Anglo-Arabian breed in France. A number of important horse races and other competitive events are held here regularly in summer.

Don't Miss: The National Stud Farm (Haras National) and Château de Pompadour.

Visit

Château

For information on visits, call ☎ 05 55 98 55 47. This imposing 15C castle with its magnificent façade stands in a delightfully verdant setting. The château is home to the stud farm's administrative offices.

Haras National (National Stud Farm)

For information on visits, call ☎ 05 55 98 51 10. The Puy-Marmont stallion farm, in a park opposite the château, is home to forty or so thoroughbreds, including pure-bred English, Arabian and Anglo-Arabian stallions. A number of other horses (draught horses from the French regions of the Ardennes, Brittany and Franche-Comté, Percherons etc) are also stabled here.

Façade of the château

E. Larribere/MICHELIN

Excursions

Upper Auvézère Valley

▷ *Head out of Pompadour along the D 126.*

Église d'Arnac

This church, with its severe appearance and imposing dimensions, was built in the 12C, and is an unusual mix of the Romanesque and Gothic styles.

The doorway, characteristic of the Limousin style, is decorated with capitals, medallions and pointed, hanging ornaments at the apexes of the vaults. Three statues are set into the façade above: from left to right, St Martial, the Virgin and St Pardoux – the two saints are patrons of the Limousin region.

Inside the nave, the keystones bear the arms of Pompadour, and the transept has preserved its Romanesque appearance. Interesting historiated capitals adorn the columns in the nave, including scenes of the Annunciation and Daniel in the Lion's Den.

▷ *Continue along the D 126, then turn left onto the D 127.*

Ségur-le-Château★

Nestled in a deep gorge carved out by the River Auvézère, the charming village of Ségur is a maze of old houses crowning two steep hills. On top of one of these hills stand the ruins of a 12C-13C castle with its double curtain walls. It is possible that Ségur's origins may go back as far as Gallo-Roman times; it certainly played an important role in the Middle Ages and under the Ancien Régime. Cradle of the first viscounts of Limoges, when feudalism was at its peak, this prosperous settlement was the birthplace, in 1470, of Jean d'Albret, first king of Navarre and grandfather of Jeanne d'Albret, herself mother of Henri IV. However, Ségur's main claim to fame derives from the time (15C to 1750) when it served as the seat of the high court of appeal for hundreds of feudal jurisdictions in the Limousin and the Périgord.

Ségur's charm lies in its beautiful residences built by the many court officials who lived here. These include the **Maison Febrer** (15C), with its Renaissance chimneys and turrets, and the **Maison Henri IV**, named in honour of the d'Albret family. Today the long robes and powdered wigs of magistrates are long gone, replaced by artists who paint the village's half-timbered houses embellished with turrets, crowned with characteristic pointed brown tiled roofs, and fronted by Gothic doorways opening onto narrow, winding lanes.

▷ *Head NE out of Ségur along the D 149.*

Lubersac

In the **Église St-Étienne** (*if the church is closed, contact the tourist office*) note the remarkable **historiated capitals**★ decorating the chancel and the delicately carved capitals adorning the north and south apsidal chapels. The village also boasts a fine arcaded house with Renaissance windows known as the **Maison des Archiprêtres.**

▷ *Leave Lubersac to the SE along the D 148. In St-Pardoux-Corbier, take the D 54E1 to Fargeas, and then the D 148 to Troche.*

Chartreuse de Glandier

For information, call ☎ 05 55 98 55 47. A **Carthusian monastery** (*chartreuse*) was established in the heart of the Loyre Valley in the 13C. Destroyed during the Revolution, the order repurchased it in 1860 and rebuilt it over a period of 10 years.

Nowadays the buildings serve as a medical centre, with an exhibition area devoted to its history, including a scale model of the site. One of the **monk's pavilions** has been reconstructed; its two floors show a workshop on the ground floor, with a bedroom and library (for meditation and spiritual needs) on the floor above.

Jumenterie Nationale de la Rivière

♿*For information, call ☎ 05 55 98 55 47.* The Domaine de la Rivière, covering an area of 88ha/217 acres, was created in the 18C on the site of a ruined 15C castle (only the towers and a Gothic chapel remain), and became a national centre for breeding mares in the 19C - nowadays, some 40 mares are permanently based here. In the months of May and June, proud mothers can be seen gambolling in the fields with their colts. The riding centre also owns a dozen stallions.

▷ *Take the D 7E3, then the D7 which will take you back to Pompadour.*

Les ARQUES★

POPULATION 158

MICHELIN LOCAL MAP 337: D-4 – LOCAL MAP SEE GOURDON

The tranquility of this Bouriane village is undoubtedly the reason the sculptor **Ossip Zadkine** (1890-1967) chose to live here. Russian by birth and French by adoption, he arrived in Paris in 1909, where he was first influenced by Cubism, a style which he subsequently abandoned. In 1934 he bought a house in Les Arques where he created his most important works (Diana, *Pietà*, Christ); their monumental expression and well-constructed forms give them a widespread and long-lasting appeal.

Visit

Musée Zadkine

🕐 *Open Apr-Sep and school hols, 10am-1pm and 2-7pm; Oct-Mar, 2-5pm.* 🕐 *Closed 1 Jan, 1 May, 1 and 11 Nov, and 25 Dec.* ✆2.50€. ☏ 05 65 22 83 37.

Three rooms display examples of the artist's work, including lithographs, tapestries, bronzes (Musical Trio, 1928) and monumental wood sculptures (Diana). An audio-visual presentation shows a lengthy interview with Zadkine.

Église St-Laurent★

Located in the centre of the village, this church is all that is left of a priory-deanery founded in the 11C by the Abbaye de Marcilhac. When the nave was restored in the 20C, it was narrowed and shortened; however the apse and apsidal chapels have retained the purity of the Romanesque style. Several old features have been preserved such as the oculus in the south transept, a characteristic of the Carolingean style, and the tori at the base of the columns supporting the transverse arches. The most original part of the interior is the shape of the arches.

Two moving works by Zadkine enhance the church's interior: the monumental **Christ**★ (on the back of the façade) and the **Pietà**★ (in the crypt).

S. Sauvignier/MICHELIN

Pietà by Ossip Zadkine
(crypt of St-Laurent)

Église St-André

By request at the Musée Zadkine,
☏ *05 65 22 83 37.*

▶ *Go down towards the River Masse, then cross the D 45.*

Set in a clearing, this church displays a remarkable series of **frescoes**★ from the late 15C, discovered in 1954 by Zadkine.

The chancel window is framed by the Annunciation and on either side by the Apostles with either the instruments of their punishment – St Andrew and the X-shaped cross and St Matthew and the halberd – or the instruments with which they are symbolised in art: St Peter with his keys, St James with his pilgrim's staff and St Thomas with his architect's set square. On the vault, spangled with red stars, is Christ in Majesty seated on a rainbow-shaped throne with one hand held up in blessing and the other holding the globe. He is surrounded by the symbols of the four Evangelists. On the pillars of the apse, which are holding up a triumphal arch, are St Christopher and, on the other side, the Infant Jesus waiting for Christopher to help him cross the river.

For coin ranges, see the Legend at the back of the guide.

EATING OUT

🍽 **La Récréation** – ☏ 05 65 22 88 08 - 🕐 open 1 Apr-30 Sep and weekends (except Jan-Feb) - 🕐 closed Wed and Thu. A pleasant restaurant housed in the old village school. Dine in the old classroom, or out in the playground when the weather is fine. Modern cuisine.

AUBAZINE★

POPULATION 732

MICHELIN LOCAL MAP 329: L-4

LOCAL MAP SEE BRIVE-LA-GAILLARDE AND TULLE: EXCURSIONS

The village of Aubazine and its Cistercian abbey are pleasantly situated between the River Corrèze and River Coiroux, on a promontory set back from the main road.

Don't Miss: The 12C Abbaye d'Aubazine, a superb example of a Cistercian abbey.

A Bit of History

At the beginning of the 12C a group of men and women, united by a common desire to lead a life of fasting and prayer, gathered together in the forest of Aubazine to join the hermit St Stephen who had come from the nearby Xaintrie area of the Corrèze Valley. Having adopted the rule of St Benedict, this small community built a monastery at Aubazine, and then a convent, just 600m/656yd away in the Coiroux Valley. In 1147, although the existence of a community of women proved to be a severe handicap, St Stephen nevertheless gained admittance for his communities into the Cistercian Order. This distinction of a dual monastery was preserved until the Revolution. The founder had decreed that the women take vows of complete enclosure, so they were totally dependent, both spiritually and materially, on the monastery. This no doubt gave rise to the local joke that anyone with a daughter at Coiroux gained a son-in-law at Aubazine.

Visit

Abbey★

The abbey was built in the second half of the 12C and dedicated to the Blessed Virgin, as were most Cistercian churches. In the 18C it was truncated, losing six of its nine bays, so it is easy to imagine how large the original must have been. The west façade was built during that period.

Bell tower★ – The bell tower crowning the transept crossing is of a very original design; the transition from a square shape to an octagonal one is made by a system of stone tiers, which form a geometrically regulated surface, a technical achievement unique to that time.

Interior – The central nave has a barrel vault and the huge square of the transept is crowned with an elegant dome on pendentives. Three radiating chapels, with flat

Address Book

For coin ranges, see the Legend at the back of the guide.

WHERE TO STAY AND EATING OUT

⊖⊖ **La Tour** – *Place de l'Église, 19190 Aubazine - ☎05 55 25 71 17 - Closed 2-24 Jan (restaurant also closed Mon lunchtime in winter and Sun eve)- 19 rooms (half board available) -* . This hotel, standing opposite the abbey, consists of two attractive houses, the oldest flanked by a tower. Traditional bedrooms decorated with coloured wallpaper. The restaurant specialises in regional cuisine served in rustic-style rooms adorned with copper and pewter pots. The hotel bar is popular with locals.

⊖⊖ **Le Saut de la Bergère** – *2km/1.2mi E of Aubazine on D 48 - ☎ 05 55 25 74 09 - closed 1 Jan-7 Mar, Sun evening and Mon Sep-Apr.* The name of this restaurant is also the name of a nearby escarpment that experienced climbers may tackle before settling down to enjoy regional specialities in this quiet country restaurant. A few simple rooms.

LEISURE ACTIVITIES

Parc du Coiroux – *4km/2.5mi E of Aubazine along the D 48 - ☎ 05 55 27 25 66 - www.golf-coiroux.com - open Jun to early Sep: daily 7am-7pm; Sep-May: daily 9am-5pm - golf course open all year - closed Christmas and New Year.* This 180ha/445-acre park offers a broad range of activities, including swimming in the lake, archery, tennis, volleyball, horse-riding and golf. The park also has a campsite and restaurant.

apses, open from each side of the choir which itself ends in a five-sided apse. The stained-glass windows in grisaille are the only ones to have been permitted in a Cistercian church.

Furnishings★ – In the south arm of the transept there is the remarkable **tomb of St Stephen**★★ made from limestone between 1250 and 1260, probably by artists from a studio in the Paris area. A blind arcade cuts across the height of the alcove in which the figure lies, and the canopy above has two sloping sides which are decorated with scenes in relief. On the side that can be seen, the Virgin holding the Child Jesus greets St Stephen and his communities on earth. The face of the recumbent figure has been disfigured by the faithful flock (who believed that the dust they obtained by scraping at the stone held miraculous powers).

The **liturgical cupboard**★ was made in the 12C from oak beams; its sides are decorated with blind arcades.

The **Coiroux Entombment** is a piece of originally polychrome stonework of an exceptional quality; it was rediscovered in 1985 during the excavation of the convent.

The choir stalls date from the 18C; the misericords are carved with very expressive figures.

Conventual buildings – ⏱ *Open Jul-Aug,* ⌒⌁ *guided tour (1hr 15min) daily except Mon at 10.30am, 3 and 4pm; Jun and Sep, daily except Mon at 10.30am and 3pm; Oct-Dec and Feb-May: daily except Mon at 3pm.* ⏱ *Closed Jan and during Holy Week.* ⌑*3.50€ (children under 10: 2.50€).* ☎ *05 55 84 61 12.* Once part of the men's monastery, the conventual buildings are home to a community of Catholic nuns. The visit includes the small library, the chapter house with its groined vaulting resting on two columns, the monks' common room and the large fish-breeding pond, its water sourced via the impressive **Canal des Moines** (Monks' Canal). Built in the 12C, this technical work of an exceptional standard for the time, starting from a capture on the River Coiroux, was partly hollowed out of the rock itself and partly cantilevered above a sheer drop of over 50m/164ft. It is possible to follow the whole of its course (*see route indicated to the right along the course of the River Coiroux; distance: 1.5km/1mi*).

Convent – *600m/656yd from Aubazine along the road to Palazinges.*

The church walls are all that remain of the convent, which was abandoned in 1791. However, recent excavation work has unearthed the irrigation system for drinking water and, beneath the embankment of the modern road, the arched doorway by which the monks and nuns communicated. This is designed like a lock chamber; one of the communities had the key to the outside door and the other the key to the inside door.

AUBETERRE-SUR-DRONNE★

POPULATION 365

MICHELIN LOCAL MAP 324: L-8

Located halfway between the Charente and the Aquitaine, the village of Aubeterre overlooks the Dronne Valley amid a landscape of verdant pastureland. With its picturesque steep, narrow streets fronted by houses adorned with wooden balconies, it is one of the prettiest villages in the whole region.

▶ **Orient Yourself**: The centre of the village is place Travieux. From here, you can either climb up towards the church of St Jacques, or walk down towards the monolithic church.

☺ **Don't Miss**: Aubeterre is famous, first and foremost, for its impressive churches, in particular its magnificent monolithic church, construction of which started in the 12C.

A Bit of History

The village takes its name from the local white chalk (*alba terra* in Latin, which translates as "white land"). It is centred around place Travieux, and the bust in honour of Ludovic Travieux, born in Aubeterre, who founded the League for the Defence of the Rights of Man.

Aubeterre-sur-Dronne – Monolithic church

Visit

Monolithic church★★

🕒 *Open mid-Jun to mid-Sep, 9.30am-noon and 2-7pm; mid-Sep to mid-Jun, 9.30am-noon and 2-6pm.* 🕒 *Closed 1 Jan and 25 Dec.* ⊗4€. ☎ *05 45 98 65 06.*

Dedicated to St John, this monolithic church is a rare example of a building hewn from a single block of rock. A corridor bordered with niches leads to a vast cavity cut into the rock; the inner surface is bare and rough.

A baptismal font from the 5C or 6C, sculpted in the shape of a Greek cross, testifies to the presence of a primitive church and evokes the practice of baptism by total immersion. The crypt must have hosted followers of Mithras, a god worshipped by members of a mystery cult which was one of early Christianity's most serious rivals. Mithraism excluded women, and was popular among Roman soldiers in Gaul. One of the seven rites of initiation they performed was slaying a bull (as Mithras killed the cosmic bull of creation, representing the conquest of evil and death).

The present church was probably started in the 12C to house relics brought back from the Holy Sepulchre in Jerusalem by the crusaders Pierre II de Castillon, who owned the castle here. Under the Revolution, the church was used as a saltpetre works, and later as the local cemetery (until 1865). The 20m/65ft-high nave, running parallel to the cliffs, is composed of three bays. It is flanked by a single aisle where a small spring venerated by early pilgrims still filters. The apse surrounds a monolithic Romanesque monument, carved from a block left in place when the church was hollowed out. In it, a shrine holds the relics of the Holy Sepulchre.

At the other end of the nave is a primitive 6C chapel, transformed into a necropolis in the 12C after work on the church was completed. Excavations have revealed a series of tombs hollowed out of the rock.

In the higher part of the nave, a gallery above the ambulatory overlooks this place of primitive worship.

Église St-Jacques

This church, situated in the upper part of the village, has a Romanesque façade, punctuated by arcades and decorated with finely sculpted geometric motifs based on Arabic designs. Left of the central doorway, a carved frieze depicts the Labours of the Months.

Below the church, the machicolated tower dates from the 16C.

AUBIGNY-SUR-NÈRE ★

POPULATION 5 907

MICHELIN LOCAL MAP 323: K-2

Situated on the borders of the Berry and the Sologne, Aubigny is a small yet bustling town on the banks of the River Nère, which flows partly underground here.

Don't Miss: A unique way of discovering the area is by cycle-rail (cyclodraisines) along old railway tracks. A fun activity for all the family!

A Bit of History

The City of the Stuarts – In 1423 Charles VII gave Aubigny to a Scotsman, John Stuart, his ally against the English. He was succeeded by Béraud Stuart - who effected a reconciliation between Louis XI and his cousin, the future Louis XII - and then by Robert Stuart, known as the Marshal of Aubigny, who fought in Italy under François I. Craftsmen from Scotland settled here, either working as weavers, using white wool from the Sologne, or glassmakers.

Sights

Old Houses★

A number of half-timbered houses have survived from the early 16C. The oak used in their construction was provided by Robert Stuart from the nearby Forêt d'Ivoy. Several of these houses are along rue du Prieuré and its continuation, rue des Dames, two charming streets hung with shop signs from the town hall to the church, as well

---

Address Book

For coin ranges, see the Legend at the back fo the guide.

WHERE TO EAT

Les Rives de l'Oizenotte – *Étang de Nohant - 18700 Oizon - 6km/3.6mi E of Aubigny along the D 923 -* ☎ *02 48 58 06 20 - oizenotte.g@infonie.fr -* 🕐 *closed Feb school hols, Nov half-term, Christmas, Mon eve, Tue and Wed - reserv. required.* This small lakeside restaurant serves simple, unpretentious and reasonably priced cuisine. Eat in the fishing-themed dining room or on the wood-floored terrace overlooking the water.

Le Lion d'Or – *41300 Pierrefitte-sur-Sauldre - 21km/13mi W of Aubigny along the D 13 -* ☎ *02 54 88 62 14 -* 🕐 *closed 3-19 Jan, 30 Aug-24 Sep, Wed eve and Thu eve in winter, Mon and Tue except for hols.* This charming traditional house stands opposite the church in the centre of the village. The exposed beams and dark wood in the dining room provide additional character, as does the small, flower-decked garden. Fixed-price menus featuring local specialities.

WHERE TO STAY

Le Domaine des Givrys – *18410 Clémont - 3 km/1.8mi SE of Clémont along the D 79 towards Ste-Montaine then 1.3km/1mi along a forest track to the left -* ☎ *02 48 58 80 74 -* 🛏 *- 5 rooms.* This typical Sologne farmhouse is a haven of peace and quiet in the middle of a forest bordered by a river and ponds (trout and black bass fishing). The rooms are spotlessly clean, with a mixture of country-style and modern furnishings. In the winter, enjoy dinner by the fire.

Les Aulnains – *Rte Presly - 18380 La Chapelle-d'Angillon - 14km/8mi S of Aubigny along the D 940 -* ☎ *02 48 73 40 09 -* 🕐 *closed in Mar -* 🛏 *- 2 rooms.* This 18C-19C manor house typical of the Sologne region is the perfect base for nature enthusiasts. Spacious rooms and a cosy, old-fashioned dining room. Animals roaming the grounds and plentiful fish in the nearby river and lakes.

Hôtel La Solognote – *18410 Brinon-sur-Sauldre -* ☎ *02 48 58 50 29 -* 🕐 *closed 15 Feb-15 Mar, 15-21 May and 9-17 Sep -* 🅿 *- 13 rooms -* 🍴*. Check into one of the neat and tidy bedrooms in this typically Solognot hotel, then reflect on your day's adventures over a drink by the cosy fireplace or over dinner in the renowned restaurant.

LEISURE ACTIVITIES

Les Cyclodraisines d'Aubigny (Cycle-railing) – *Rte de Clémont, lieu-dit "Gorgeot" -* ☎ *02 48 81 50 07 (weekdays) or 02 48 58 35 81 (weekends) -* 🕐 *open 1 May-20 Sep, Sat-Sun and public hols, 9am-7pm -* 🕐 *closed 21 Sep-30 Apr - 8€/hr; 19€/half day; 30€/full day.* Enjoy a day out cycle-railing through the countryside along old railway lines.

as in rue du Charbon and place Adrien-Arnoux. No 10 rue du Pont-Aux-Foulons is the only house to have survived the fire of 1512. In rue du Bourg-Coutant stands the **Maison du Bailli**★ with its carved beams, and almost opposite, at the corner of rue de l'Église, the pretty **Maison François I.**

Ancien Château des Stuarts

This 16C building was erected by Robert Stuart and modified by Louise de Kerouaille, duchess of Portsmouth; it now serves as Aubigny's town hall. The entrance gatehouse, dating from the time of Robert Stuart, is flanked with attractive brick bartizans; the keystone of the vault is emblazoned with the Stuart coat of arms. In the charming irregular courtyard, note the mullioned windows and round or polygonal turreted staircases.

Ramparts

The line of the old town wall, built originally by Philippe-Auguste, is marked by the streets enclosing the town centre and the two round towers overlooking the mall.

Église St-Martin

🕐 *Open Easter to 1 Nov, 2-6pm.* ☎ *02 48 58 40 20.*

The church is built in Gothic style, marking the arrival of Île-de-France influences in Berry. At the entrance of the chancel two 17C painted statues represent a charming Virgin and Child and a dramatic Christ Reviled, whereas in the chancel a 16C stained-glass window depicts the life of St Martin. In the third chapel to the right there is an admirable 17C wood *Pietà*.

St Martin is one of the missionaries who brought Christianity to Gaul in the 4C. He is famous for having shared his coat with a poor man when he was the bishop of Tours.

Musée Marguerite Audoux

This small museum is devoted to the life and work of **Marguerite Audoux** (1863-1937), a local writer whose novel about the shepherdess Marie-Claire, based on her own childhood, gave rise to the popular French magazine of the same name.

Excursions

Château de Blancafort★

9km/5.6mi NE along the D 30. 🕐 *Guided tour (45min), Jun-Sep, 10am-7pm; Apr-May and Oct, daily except Tue, 10am-noon and 2-6.30pm. Independent visit of the park and gardens 7€ (child: 4€).* ☎ *02 48 58 60 56.*

The 15C château is built of red brick and has a plain façade; the 17C courtyard is flanked by two pavilions. The visit includes the library, with its Regency panelling, and the dining room, with its walls covered in painted, gilded and embossed Flemish leather. The château also has a fine collection of pewter on display. After visiting the interior, enjoy a pleasant walk through the park with its attractive French-style flower beds, or along the woodland paths beside the river.

Musée de la Sorcellerie

▶ *From Blancafort, take the D 8 towards Vailly-sur-Sauldre.*

Kids ♿ 🕐 *Open 1 Apr to 1 Nov, 10am-6pm. 5.60€.* ☎ *02 48 73 86 11. www.museesorcellerie.fr.*

This Witchcraft Museum is housed in a 19C barn at La Jonchère, in the north of the Berry, a region known for its strong connections with sorcery. Around 20 scenes, some involving video animation and special effects (courtesy of the resident sorceress), and many explanatory panels delve into the mysterious world of superstition, myth and legend. The first floor, decorated and furnished in traditional Sologne style, highlights the tales of witchcraft that locals used to relate to each other during the long winter evenings, conjuring up *birettes* – the headless and handless local spirits with a penchant for haunting the Berry.

Domaine de la Jonchère – Musée de la Sorcellerie

Musée de la Sorcellerie

Witchcraft in the Berry Region

Ethnologists have an explanation for the prevalence of witchery and the supernatural in the Berry. They say that the flat landscape, often swathed in mist, and solitary trees, burned by lightning or twisted by the wind, create dark and menacing silhouettes in the lonely countryside.

Ask one of the Compagnons de Vin de Bué, a local wine-growers' association, and you may get a different answer. The members call themselves "birettes" and dress in appropriate costumes for festive occasions. A local "birette d'honneur" (who also works as a sommelier in a fine restaurant) has a word of advice: it is best to seek out spirits in the small hours, as in the daylight you can see right through them.

Château de la Verrerie★

11km/7mi SE along the D 89. 🦽 🕐 ●─ *Guided tour (45min, last entrance 1hr before closing), Jun to 3rd weekend in Sep, 10am-6pm; Easter to the end of May and late-Sep to 1 Nov, 10am-12.30pm and 1.30-5.30pm.* ●7€ *(child: 5€).* ☎ *02 48 81 51 60.*

The château stands in an isolated but beautiful **setting**★ near the Forêt d'Ivoy beside a lake formed by a broad stretch of the Nère. It is thought to have inspired Alain-Fournier for one of the episodes in his famous novel *Le Grand Meaulnes*.

The château originally consisted of four buildings around a courtyard; the oldest part was built by Charles VII who gave it to John Stuart at the same time as Aubigny-sur-Nère. At the end of the 15C Béraud Stuart built a château (house and chapel) which was completed during the Renaissance by his nephew Robert, Maréchal d'Aubigny. In 1672 the château reverted to the crown; in 1673 Louis XIV gave it to the Duchess of Portsmouth, the favourite mistress of Charles II of England.

The graceful **Renaissance gallery**★ was erected by Robert Stuart in 1525, the date when the frescoes were painted in the 15C chapel; the tabernacle in carved wood dates from the Renaissance. The 19C wing added behind the Renaissance gallery contains some fine furniture from the Renaissance to the Louis XVI period; two 18C Brussels tapestries hang in the dining room; the Renaissance cupboard in the salon contains four remarkable 15C alabaster **weeping figures**★ from the tomb of Jean de Berry. The boudoir displays a collection of 19C dolls together with their furniture as well as the library of **Melchior de Vogüë** (1829-1916), a member of the Académie Française, a diplomat and archaeologist who directed excavations in Palestine and Syria.

AUBUSSON★

POPULATION 4 662

MICHELIN LOCAL MAP 325: K-5

Aubusson, situated in the upper valley of the Creuse, still manufactures the tapestries and carpets that have been world-famous for the past five centuries. A College of Decorative Arts, opened in 1884, offers courses aimed at keeping up this tradition. The Centre Culturel et Artistique Jean Lurçat was established to promote this exceptional craft.

- ⊚ **Don't Miss**: The Musée Départemental de la Tapisserie; the Château de Villemonteix.
- 🅿 **Parking**: There are several car parks around the town (🦽 *see town plan*).
- 🕐 **Organising Your Time**: Allow half a day to visit the charming Haute Vallée de la Creuse.

A Bit of History

Tapestry-making – It would appear that tapestry weaving was imported from Flanders in the 14C by Marie de Hainault, who was to become Countess of Marche, although it was only in the 15C that the tapestry weavers of Aubusson started to receive wider acclaim. The Lady and the Unicorn, a 15C masterpiece now in the Cluny Museum in Paris, is believed to have been woven by the craftsmen of Aubusson. Their fame peaked in the 16C and 17C with verdures (flower and foliage designs in shades of green) as well as sacred, mythological and historical themes. Colbert granted them the title of royal tapestry-makers in the 17C.

Address Book

For coin ranges, see the Legend at the back fo the guide.

EATING OUT

🍽 **Le Viaduc** – *23150 Busseau-sur-Creuse* - ☎ *05 55 62 57 20* - *ch-cl-lemestre@wanadoo.fr* - 🕐 *closed Jan, Sun eve and Mon.* Not far from the railroad bridge that inspired Gustave Eiffel when he was designing his famous tower, this country inn is a good place to stop if you plan to explore the village. The dining room's large bay windows open onto a green landscape. Unpretentious cuisine.

WHERE TO STAY

🍽🛏 **Chambre d'hôte et Ferme-Auberge de la Vallée de la Creuse** – *23200 Ourdeaux - 6km/3.6mi N of Aubusson on the D 942A* - ☎ *05 55 66 29 65* - *patrice.dhiver@wanadoo.fr* - *reserv. required* - *6 rooms.* Regional cuisine, based on farm products, is served in the rustic dining room embellished with a large grandfather clock. The comfortable rooms all have a TV. Swimming pool and horse-riding. A charming property.

🍽🛏 **Chambre d'hôte M. et Mme. Dumontant** – *Les Vergnes* - *23200 Les Vergnes - 7km/4.2mi E of Aubusson on the N 141* - ☎ *05 55 66 23 74* - 🕐 *closed end Oct to early Apr* - 🍴 - *6 rooms.* Quiet and relaxation await guests at this 18C farm in the heart of the countryside. The spacious rooms have all been renovated. Facilities include a covered swimming pool and fishing lake. Three holiday cottages are available for longer stays.

🍽🛏 **Hôtel de France** – *6 r. des Déportés* – ☎ *05 55 66 10 22* - 🅿 - *23 rooms.* For a pleasant stay in this 18C home, choose one of the large rooms. Although they are a bit more expensive, they have been decorated with antique furniture and selected fabrics. In fine weather, enjoy dinner in the courtyard.

With the departure abroad of many of the weavers, particularly to Germany, following the Revocation of the Edict of Nantes in 1685, the industry faced ruin. It recovered only at the beginning of the 18C, thanks to the work of certain painters of that time, such as Watteau, Lancret and Boucher. The 19C was a period of decline, due in part to the aftermath of the Revolution but also to the development of a new source of competition: wallpaper. Nowadays the town takes pride in maintaining its old weaving methods and tools. The great speciality of Aubusson is *basse-lisse* (low-warp) tapestry using horizontal looms; the same technique is used in Beauvais and Gobelins.

A new beginning – At the beginning of the 20C inspiration was flagging. Although technically perfect, the tapestries were mere copies of paintings in a variety of colours.

In the 1930s fresh impetus came from a collector, Madame Cuttoli, who commissioned designs from the greatest contemporary painters. From 1937, **Jean Lurçat** (1892-1966), in collaboration with Gromaire, played a decisive role in the rebirth of the art of tapestry weaving. A new generation of cartoon designers emerged, including artists such as Prassinos, Tourlière, Saint-Saëns, Picart-le-Doux, Dom Robert and Wogensky.

Sights

Centre Culturel et Artistique Jean Lurçat

This austere, functional building on the banks of the River Creuse (avenue des Lissiers) was built in 1981 and has since been devoted to the art of tapestry weaving. The complex includes a theatre (*la Scène Nationale*), a library, a reference section and a museum.

Musée Départemental de la Tapisserie★

♿🕐 *Open Jul-Aug, 10am-6pm, Tue 2-6pm; Sep-Jun, daily except Tue, 9.30am-noon and 2-6pm.* 🎫*4€.* ☎ *05 55 83 08 30.*

The collection includes all types of tapestries and carpets from the 17C, 18C and 19C. The 20C is illustrated by various works by contemporary artists including Lurçat, Gromaire, Saint-Saëns, Picart le Doux, Tourlière and Julien. The modern works demonstrate the brilliance of the period of renewal inspired by Lurçat. A tour of the museum concludes with an exhibition on the history and technique of this art. Yearly exhibits are planned around themes linked to tapestry and textile arts; at certain times, demonstrations of the different production phases are given.

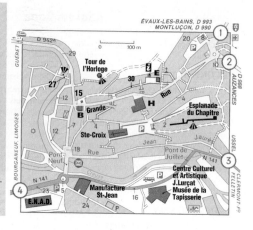

Manufacture de Tapis et de Tapisseries St-Jean

Open May-Oct, guided tour (1hr) by prior arrangement, 9am-noon and 2-5pm, Sat-Sun and public hols by prior arrangement; Nov-Apr, by prior arrangement. 7€ (child: 4€). ☎ 05 55 66 10 08.

The workshops in the former royal manufactory work on commissions only.

A tapestry begins to see the light of day in the design workshop. The artist creates a scale design (1:10), and once the client approves, the cartoon is painted life-size. Yarns are selected from the storage room accordingly and the different shades sorted out.

Carpets made by specialised weavers on high-warp looms are produced in the **savonnerie** workshop.

As an example, a linen warp 36m2/387sq ft in size requires two weeks to set up, and four weavers need 11 months to complete it.

Other carpets (**ras**), with a rougher finished feel, are woven on a low-warp loom, with a cotton warp. The weavers work on one section at a time.

The restoration workshop handles carpets which have been damaged over time. After finding the right colours and materials, the tapestry workers rebuild the warp and weft.

L'Exposition – Tapisseries d'Aubusson, Felletin

Open Jul-Aug, 10am-7pm, Sun and public hols, 10am-noon and 2.30-5.30pm (last entrance 45min before closing); Jun and Sep, 9.30am-12.30pm and 2-6pm, Sun and public hols, 10am-noon and 2.30-5.30pm. 4€ (under 12 years old: no charge). ☎ 05 55 66 32 12.

The exhibit in the Hôtel de Ville (town hall) comprises tapestries and carpets worked to traditional and modern designs.

École Nationale d'Art Décoratif d'Aubusson

Open Mon-Fri, 1-6pm. Closed Sat-Sun and public hols. No charge. ☎ 05 55 83 05 40.

This school offers a course leading to a nationally recognised diploma in textile design, and frequently puts on public exhibits.

Maison du Tapissier

Open Jul-Aug, 10am-7pm, Sun and public hols, 10am-noon and 2.30-5.30pm (last entrance 45min before closing); Easter to Jun and Sep: 9.30am-12.30 and 2-6pm, Sun 10am-noon and 2.30-5.30pm; Oct to Easter: daily except Sun and public hols, 10.30am-12.30pm and 3-5pm. 4€ (under 12 years old: no charge). ☎ 05 55 66 32 12.

In this lovely 16C house, which once belonged to the Corneille family of weavers, pieces of local furniture and other objects evoke life in Aubusson in bygone days. On the upper floor, an old-fashioned workshop displays a low-warp loom, reels, wheels for preparing shuttles and bobbin stands, as well as several tapestries, cartoons and embroidered pieces.

Old Town

Aubusson's old town straddles both sides of Grande-Rue.

Rue Vieille

This pedestrianised street is lined with old houses which have been completely renovated and turned into art galleries, craft and antique shops.

Tour de l'Horloge

This strategically located tower was once used as a watchtower.

Pont de la Terrade

From this old bridge, an interesting 16C construction with pointed cutwaters, there is a pleasant view of the houses rising in terraces on the left bank of the Creuse at the foot of some impressive rocks.

Place de la Libération

A 16C turreted house known as the **Maison des Vallenet** and a fountain dating from 1718, adorned with heraldic devices, are the main attractions in this square.

Église Ste-Croix

This sturdy church was built in the 13C and largely remodelled in the 19C. Only one of the four tapestries which once adorned its walls remains.

Esplanade du Chapitre

From the terrace near the church, a steep path climbs to the summit of the hill and the Esplanade du Chapitre, where the ruins (11C-13C) of the castle of the Counts of Aubusson still stand.

Excursions

Haute Vallée de la Creuse

Round trip of 90km/ 54mi – allow half a day

▶ *From Aubusson, drive N along the D 990A, then the D 990 towards Montluçon.*

St-Maixant

A charming church and a late-14C castle stand on the village square.

▶ *Return to the D 990.*

Église de Chénérailles

Built in the 13C, this church contains a handsome **haut-relief**★ in the third bay on the right which dates from the early 14C and was placed there in memory of Barthélemy de la Place, the church's founder. Sculpted in hard white limestone, this finely wrought, expressive commemorative stone has a lower section representing the funeral scene, a middle part showing the Virgin and Child in the company of St Aignan and St Barthélemy, and an upper panel illustrating the Crucifixion. The Virgin is a rendering of the 13C polychrome stone statue in the side chapel.

▶ *Follow the D 55 towards Ahun then turn right.*

Château de Villemonteix★

🕐 *Open Jul-Sep,* 👣 *guided tour (1hr) 10am-noon and 2-7pm; Easter to Jun and Oct, 2-7pm; Nov to Easter, by prior arrangement.* ⊚*6€ (8-15 years old: 3€).* ☎ *05 55 62 33 92.*

The entrance yard to this 15C feudal stronghold is preceded by two corner towers (the one on the right was converted

Château de Villemonteix

J. Malburet/MICHELIN

into a dovecote in the 17C). Strategically located, it was previously protected by a moat and drawbridge.

The watch-path, supported by corbels and two gargoyles, has a watchtower at each end. On the western side, two more towers fill out the defensive structure, safeguarding the rear of the central building.

Tastefully restored, the castle contains a fine collection of **period furniture**★★. On the ground floor, the visit includes the kitchen, followed by the drawing room, with 18C furnishings and woodwork, giving onto a small

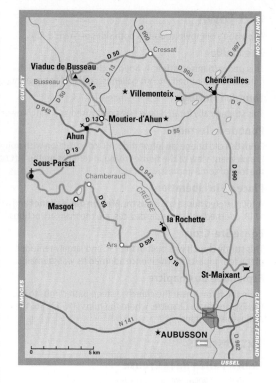

Gothic chapel and dining room (Berry porcelain and faience). A granite stairway in the tower leads to the upper floors. In the main room, three 17C Aubusson tapestries relate the tale of Achilles. The other rooms are occupied by various examples of period furniture and decorated with Aubusson, Felletin and Flemish **tapestries**★★ dating from the 16C to the 18C.

▶ *Leaving the château, turn left and go back to the D 53. Beyond Cressat, follow the D 50.*

Viaduc de Busseau

This 300m/328yd metallic viaduct spanning the Creuse blends in well with the pleasant landscape.

▶ *Once across the viaduct, turn left onto the D 16.*

Moutier-d'Ahun★

⌕ *See MOUTIER-D'AHUN.*

▶ *Take the D 13.*

Ahun

This small town on the banks of the Creuse was once the brilliant *Acitodunum*, a major city on the map of the Roman Empire, and probably one of the first places to be evangelised by St Martial.

Église St-Sylvain – On the outside, between the arched bays of the chevet, the capitals crowning the columns are carved with animals and palmettos. Inside, the remarkable **woodwork**★ panels and columns date from the late 17C. A gilded wood altarpiece, a 12C baptismal font hewn in granite and a 15C polychrome stone *Pietà* are also of particular interest.

The **crypt** (*use the stairway outside the church*) covers the area below the chevet and the far end of the chancel. There are two semicircular rooms: one has three naves with vaulted ceilings supported by monolithic pillars; the second is pre-Romanesque and shelters a reliquary tomb.

▶ *Take the D 13 towards Pontarion.*

Église de Sous-Parsat

The small church has some surprising **frescoes**⋆, the work of Gabriel Chabrat. Two main colour themes are employed in these energetic compositions: yellow (symbolising joy) and blue (dreams). The artist has used the walls to illustrate different biblical scenes with a personal interpretation. Genesis is found at the end of the chancel, facing a flamboyant Apocalypse. Light filters through the windows, also designed by Chabrat, accentuating the unique ambience of the church.

▶ *Drive to Le Sec via the D 45, and then onto Chamberaud. Turn right onto the D 16 towards St-Sulpice.*

Masgot

🕐 Guided tour (45min), Jul-Aug at 4pm, exhibition open in the afternoon. 2€.
☎ 05 55 66 98 88.

Frescoes in Sous-Parsat

S. Sauvignier/MICHELIN

The main attraction in Masgot are the stone sculptures by the artist François Michaud (1810-90), which are dotted around this sleepy hilltop village. Using local granite, Michaud brought a new dimension to this traditional local craft.

A **museum** has been opened in his home; in the summer, aspiring artists come here to work, taking inspiration from Masgot's buildings and history.

▶ *At the end of the path leading to the village, go back to Chamberaud and turn right onto the D 55 to reach La Rochette via Ars.*

Chapelle de la Rochette

Built in 1569 in Romanesque style and since restored, the chapel has a belfry topped with wooden shingles. The **setting** here is charming, enhanced by the background sound of the river running through rolling meadows.

▶ *Drive back to Aubusson along the D 18.*

BEAULIEU-SUR-DORDOGNE★★

POPULATION 1 286

MICHELIN LOCAL MAP 329: M-6

Built on the right bank of the Dordogne, Beaulieu is famous for its fine Romanesque church, once part of a Benedictine abbey. 🖪 *6 pl. Marbot, 19120 Beaulieu-sur-Dordogne, ☎ 05 55 91 09 94.*

🔎 **Don't Miss**: The Église St-Pierre and its south doorway; the old town.

A Bit of History

Foundation and growth of the abbey – Raoul, archbishop of Bourges, visited this part of the country in 855 and, enchanted by the beauty of this particular site which he christened *bellus locus – beau lieu (*beautiful place) – decided to found a community here. The monastery rose to significance despite the warlike struggles for control waged by the lords of Turenne and Castelnau. The abbots became the equals of city merchants and, as their special privileges increased, became virtually independent.

The Benedictine reform – The monks gradually came to interpret the order's rule of discipline more and more liberally. During the Wars of Religion (1562-98), they deserted their monastery. In 1663 the Abbot of La Tour d'Auvergne called on the austere Benedictine Congregation of Maurists to undertake the necessary reforms and to repair the buildings. The community prospered until the Revolution took hold, and drove them out again.

Address Book

For coin ranges, see the Legend at the back of the guide.

EATING OUT

🍽 **Au Beau-Lieu Breton** – *R. du Presbytère* - ☎ *05 55 91 20 46* - ⏰ *open Jul-Aug.* This crêpe and salad restaurant in the old town is a welcome stop for a simple yet pleasant meal. Take a table outdoors and tuck into house smoked magret or a buckwheat galette, complemented by a glass of Cahors wine or a bowl of cider.

🍽🍽 **Les Charmilles** – *20 blvd St-Rodolphe-de-Turenne* - ☎ *05 55 91 29 29* . The Dordogne flows just beyond the garden of this flowery inn situated in the village centre. Light, colourful dining room and terrace on the river. Attractive renovated bedrooms.

WHERE TO STAY

🛏🛏 **Charme d'hôte La Maison** – *11 r. de la Gendarmerie* - ☎ *05 55 91 24 97* - ⏰ *closed Oct to Mar* - 🍴 *- 6 rooms.* A friendly welcome awaits in this unexpected Mexican hacienda in the middle of Beaulieu. Arcades, a patio with flowers, walls in shades of red ochre and appealing rooms with original names. Hanging garden and pool. Charming.

🛏🛏 **Central Hôtel Fournié** – *4 pl. du Champs-de-Mars* - ☎ *05 55 91 01 34* - ⏰ *closed 2 Nov-31 Mar and Mon* - 🅿 *- 23 rooms.* This solid regional-style building enjoys a central location. Ask for one of the renovated rooms - the others are more sober. Dine on tasty local recipes served by the large fireplace in the dining room or on the terrace in the summer.

Old Town★

A maze of narrow streets and old houses is huddled around the church. Note the 16C tower, with its decorative shell motif, on rue Ste-Catherine, and the building known as the **Renaissance house** on place de la Bridolle, embellished with statues and medallions.

Église St-Pierre★★

⏰*Open Jul-Aug,* 👥*guided tour, 10am-noon and 2.30-6pm. No charge.*

The influence of both the Limousin and the Aquitaine are apparent in the architecture of this 12C abbey church, once an important place of pilgrimage.

Exterior – This sandstone building is typical of Benedictine establishments which served as places of pilgrimage. The choir, transept and eastern bay of the nave were the first to be completed, from about 1100 to 1140. In the middle of the 12C, works were continued from the southern end of the nave to the northern parallel walls. The project was finished in the 13C, with the western bay of the nave and the façade.

The **south doorway**★★ was carved in 1125 and is one of the great masterpieces of early Romanesque sculpture. The craftsmen who created it came from Toulouse and also worked on the carvings at Moissac, Collonges, Souillac and Carrennac.

The doorway is preceded by an open porch; the sculpture (which has been restored) is remarkable in its composition and execution. The theme on the tympanum is the Last Judgement. In the centre, Christ in Majesty dominates all by his height and extends his arm in welcome to the chosen. On either side two angels sound trumpets, whereas above, four angels hold the instruments of the Passion – the Cross, the Nails and the Crown of Thorns. The Apostles are grouped left and right and above them the dead rise from their graves. Monsters line the upper part of the lintel. The lower part, as at Moissac, is decorated with rosettes from which emerge chimera, serpents and monsters.

The style and proportions of the graceful **east end** of the church are highlighted by the window mouldings typical of the Limousin region, and cornices with sculpted modillions.

As you walk around the outside of the chevet, note the vestiges of the cloisters where they once extended from the northern side of the church (sacristy).

There is no tympanum above the wide doorway of the **west front**. The tower rising up to the right was added in the 14C during the Hundred Years War. Raised higher in 1556, it served as the town belfry.

Interior – The sanctuary was designed for pilgrimages and, like others so-dedicated, planned out to facilitate the movement of crowds, as evidenced in the wide aisles. The nave has barrel vaulting. The tall, asymmetrical dome on pendentives rises above the transept from recessed columns. The chancel is lit by five rounded bays.

Chapelle des Pénitents

The decorative aspect is rather rustic compared to the intricate beauty of the south doorway. There are just a few sculpted capitals, at the entrance to the ambulatory and the transept chapels; these are embellished with garlands and caryatids.

The other capitals bear geometrical designs typical of the Quercy region. In the northern arm of the transept, above the door to the stairway, an unsophisticated lintel carving represents two lions and a tree.

Trésor – ⊙ *Open Apr-Sep, 8am-8pm; Oct-Mar, 8am-7pm.* ☎ *05 55 91 18 78.* Housed in the north transept, the treasury includes a remarkable 12C **Virgin and Child**★ in silver-plated wood and a chased enamel shrine (chest) from the 13C.

Chapelle des Pénitents
For information, contact the tourist office, ☎ *05 55 91 09 94.*

This delightful Romanesque chapel is reflected in the waters of the Dordogne downstream from the town. Built originally in the 12C but since restored, it now hosts temporary exhibitions in summer.

 ⊙ **Gorges de la Cère** – The River Cère meets the Dordogne downstream of Bretenoux, at the foot of a promontory crowned by the Château de Castelnau. Along its course, it passes through wild gorges which can be best viewed from the **Rocher du Peintre**★ (*off the D 13, to the east of Beaulieu-sur-Dordogne*).

BEAUMONT-DU-PÉRIGORD

POPULATION 1 150

MICHELIN LOCAL MAP 329: F-7

Beaumont was built as a bastide in 1272 by the Seneschal of Guyenne in the name of Edward I, king of England. Today, it has preserved a few traces of its fortifications, such as the 13C fortified Porte de Luzier, a gateway which provides access to the town.

 ⊛ **Don't Miss**: The opportunity to explore this typical fortified *bastide*.

 ⊙ **Organising Your Time**: Allow a full day to visit the bastides and water mills of the area to the south of the River Dordogne.

Sights

Église St-Front
Built after 1272 in the Early Gothic style with four huge towers connected by a rampart walk, this church was the last place of refuge for the inhabitants of the town during periods of siege. The asymmetry of the towers on the main façade reflects their

The fortified church in Beaumont

different functions; the lower was a bell tower until 1789, and the higher a crenellated keep armed with machicolations. The towers frame a doorway, which has five archivolts and is supported by clustered columns, and a **gallery**★ with a beautifully decorated balustrade and an illuminated frieze underneath it. The elegant south porch has a trefoil arcade dominated by a lancet dais. It is protected by a brattice. Major restoration work during the 19C has significantly altered the church's originally military character.

Bastides

These fortified towns (in the *Oc* language: *bastidas*) first appeared in the 13C. They were usually built to the same plan (a square or rectangle) according to a grid sytem with streets built around a main square, often arcaded, and with a covered market hall at its centre. Depending on their location, bastides were often surrounded by walls to offer increased protection.

Interior – In the bell tower to the left, the enormous keystone (weighing 450kg/992lb) of the chancel vault can be seen. Decorated with carved figures of faces, it includes that of the church's patron, St Front. In the same side aisle towards the middle of the nave, note the chapel of St Joseph, almost certainly the remainder of a much older church.

Excursions

Dolmen de Blanc

3km/1.9mi S along the D 676.

According to a strange legend, a young girl lost during a storm stopped near the megaliths and prayed to be rescued. She then saw the stones move to show her the way.

Bastides and Mills★

110km/69mi round-trip – allow one day

▶ *Leave Beaumont travelling N along the D 660.*

Château de Bannes

Perched on a rocky spur, the château was built at the end of the 15C by the bishop of Sarlat, Armand de Gontaud-Biron. What is so incongruous in this château is that the military features – machicolated towers – are tempered by the carved doorway and richly decorated dormer windows surmounted by finials and pinnacles in the Early Renaissance style.

▶ *Continue along the D 660.*

For coin ranges, see the Legend at the back of the guide.

EATING OUT

🍽🍽🍽 **Côte-Rivage** – *24150 Badefols-sur-Dordogne* - ☎ *05 53 23 65 00* - *coterivage@online.fr* - 🕐 *closed mid-Oct to mid-Apr - 7 rooms. Closed Sun eve. This pretty house is near the banks of the River Dordogne. White walls, colourful curtains, a mix of furniture styles and air-conditioning make the rooms pleasant and comfortable. The contemporary dining room has wrought-iron furniture. Terrace. Fresh regional cuisine washed down with local wines.*

Couze-et-St-Front

Located at the mouth of the Couze Valley, this active small town has specialised since the 16C in the manufacture of Dutch paper, which was sold as far away as Russia. It was the most important paper-making centre in the Aquitaine, and, at its peak, 13 mills were in operation here.

Out of the three remaining mills, only two, the **Moulin de la Rouzique (Ecomusée du Papier)** (○ *Open*

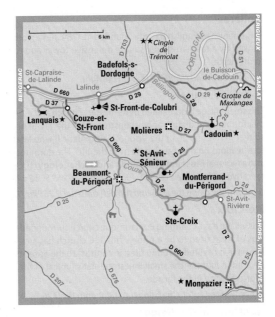

Jul-Aug, guided tour (1hr, last entrance 1hr before closing), 10am-7pm, Sat-Sun, 2-7pm; Apr-Jun and Sep, 2-6.30pm. 4.50€ (under 8 years old: no charge). ☎ 05 53 24 36 16) and the **Moulin de Larroque** (workshop open Mon-Fri, 9am-noon and 2-5pm; craft gallery open Mon-Fri, 9am-noon and 2-5pm, Sat 3-5pm. Guided tours only in summer. ○ Closed public hols and 24 Dec-1 Jan. 3€. ☎ 05 53 61 01 75) are still making filigreed paper using traditional methods.

▶ *Drive W out of Couze along the D 37.*

Château de Lanquais★

○ *Open Jul-Aug,* guided tour (1hr) 10am-7pm; May-Jun and Sep, daily except Tue, 10.30am-noon and 2.30-6.30pm; Apr and Oct-Nov, daily except Tue, 2.30-6pm. 7€ (child: 3.50€). ☎ 05 53 61 24 24.

The 14C and 15C main building, with all the defensive characteristics of a **fortified castle**, had a **Renaissance building** added to it during the Wars of Religion, and was extended further in the 19C. In the courtyard, the elegant **façades**★ are divided into vertical registers. Inside, the blue drawing room with its finely carved **chimney**★ and the reconstructed Renaissance kitchen are worth noting. Concerts and shows are staged here in summer.

▶ *Continue along the D 37 and cross the Dordogne 1.5km/0.9mi further on. Turn right onto the D 660 in St-Capraise-de-Lalinde, then right again in Lalinde, crossing the Dordogne once again.*

St-Front-de-Colubri

Built in the 12C on top of a cliff overlooking the Dordogne, the chapel sheltered sailors venturing along the Saut de la Gratusse rapids. This passage was the most difficult of the river's middle section; specialised river-hands were needed to guide sailors through it until the mid-19C, when the Canal de Lalinde canal was built.
There is a marvellous **view**★ of the valley and the rapids up-river.

▶ *The D 29 follows the river.*

Badefols-sur-Dordogne

The village occupies a pleasant site beside the Dordogne. The country church stands close to the foot of the castle ruins perched on the cliff. This fortress served as the hideout for local thieves and robbers who used to ransack *gabares* as they sailed downstream.

▶ *Continue along the D 29, then turn onto the D 28 4km/2.5mi further on.*

Cadouin★

↳ *See CADOUIN.*

▶ *Drive SE out of Cadouin along the D 25. After 2km/1.2mi, turn right onto the D 27.*

Molières

This unfinished English bastide, founded in 1284, has a Gothic church with a façade flanked by a tall two-storey square defensive tower and the ruins of an old castle to the north.

▶ *Turn back and rejoin the D 25 on the right.*

St-Avit-Sénieur★

This small village is dominated by its massive **church** and monastic buildings, vestiges of a former Benedictine abbey constructed in the 11C in honour of Avitus Senior, a soldier in the service of the Visogoth king Alaric II who later became a hermit. The fortifications on the church date from the 14C. The dormitory has been transformed into a regional **Museum of Geology and Archaeology** (🕐*Open Jul-Aug,* 👁️*guided tours available daily except Sat, 10am-6pm.* ☎ *05 53 57 52 64).*

▶ *Continue along the D 25 and turn left onto the D 26 2km/1.2mi further on.*

Ste-Croix

This village has a charming Romanesque church surrounded by the half-ruined build-ings of what used to be a priory. This 12C church has a clear, uncluttered outline. The nave is covered in round tiles, in contrast to the apse and side chapel which are covered in *lauzes* – the small limestone slabs typical of the region. A gabled belfry adorns the top of the façade.

▶ *Leave Ste-Croix to the E and turn right onto the D 26.*

Montferrand-du-Périgord

The main feature of this pretty terraced village above the Couze is the half-ruined château with its 12C keep.
The old houses, dovecotes and 16C covered market with its beautiful columns all add to Montferrand's charm.
🚶 In the cemetery above the village, the Romanesque chapel (accessible along a marked path starting from the foot of the castle) is decorated with a lovely collection of mural frescoes dating from between the 12C and the 15C.

▶ *Return to the D 26, then turn right onto the D 2.*

Monpazier★

👣 *See MONPAZIER.*

▶ *Drive W out of Monpazier along the D 660 which leads back to Beaumont-du-Périgord.*

BELLAC

POPULATION 4 576

MICHELIN LOCAL MAP 325: D-4

Bellac rises up on a spur overlooking the valley of the Vincou which flows into the Gartempe. This picturesque green and undulating setting is situated on the borders of the Limousin plateaus and the plains of the Poitou.

▶ **Orient Yourself**: For a good view of the church, river, bridge and viaduct, head for the terrace 100m/110yd up rue Lafayette.

🅿 **Parking**: Leave your car on place de la République near the 16C town hall.

😊 **Don't Miss**: The town's association with the novelist and playright, Jean Giraudoux.

🕐 **Organising Your Time**: Allow half a day to visit the sights and villages of the Basse-Marche area.

For coin ranges, see the Legend at the back of the guide.

EATING OUT

🍽️🍽️🍽️ **Bellevue** – *2 av. de Limoges - 87250 Bessines-sur-Gartempe -* ☎ *05 55 76 01 99 -* 🕐 *closed 10 Jan-10 Feb, Sat lunchtime and Fri from Oct-May - 12 rooms.* A typical regional house serving delicious traditional cuisine in a welcoming dining room. A dozen functional yet pleasant guest rooms.

The Town

Once you have enjoyed a view of the town, start your tour at no 29 rue Thiers, where a plaque commemorates La Fontaine's stay in the local inn, where he is said to have written one of his fables.

Église Notre-Dame

The church, built on a terrace overlooking the Vincou, is built in a mix of Romanesque and Gothic styles. A huge square belfry surmounts the two naves, one 12C and Romanesque, the other 14C and Gothic. The two naves lead to the chancel which ends in a flat east end. The south doorway is adorned with small, serpentine capitals.

Shrine★

To the left of the entrance, in a chest set in the wall, there is a beautiful 12C shrine (the oldest in Limousin), embellished with *cabochons* and medallions of *champlevé* enamel. Among the figurative decorations on the sacred receptacle are the symbols of the four Evangelists around the figure of Christ.

WHERE TO STAY

⊜⊜ **Auberge La Source** – *1 av. du Lac - 87250 Cieux - 7.5km/4.5mi S of Blond along the D 3 -* ☎*05 55 03 33 23 - awaldbauer@aol.com -* ◔ *closed 19 Jan-10 Feb, 4-11 Nov, Sun eve, Tue lunchtime and Mon - 8 rooms*. This former post house located in a village on the slopes of the Monts de Blond is a convenient stopover. The simply furnished rooms are reasonably spacious. Wooden beams crown the pleasant dining room located in the old stables.

Sights

In the Footsteps of Giraudoux

Châteauroux may claim the glory of having educated **Jean Giraudoux** at its *lycée*, but it was in Bellac that he was born, in 1882 (d 1944). The countryside he knew as a child is depicted in an early work of poetic fiction, *Suzanne et le Pacifique*. He describes Bellac with the following words: "a countryside of streams and hills, a patchwork of fields and chestnut woods for it was a land with a long history, it was the region of Limousin."

Author of five novels, numerous short stories and influential political and literary essays, Giraudoux is best-known for his 15 plays. He created a new type of drama for the theatre, containing irony, poetry and magic. *Siegfried et le Limousin, Amphytrion 38, Intermezzo, Tiger at the Gates, Electra, Ondine, The Madwoman of Chaillot* and *The Apollo of Bellac* have been performed to appreciative audiences around the world. His style is sparkling, full of twists and innovations.

As a young man, he travelled widely in Europe and North America, and spent a year (1906-07) as an instructor at Harvard. Returning to France, he served in the First World War, was twice wounded, and became the first writer ever to be awarded the wartime Legion of Honour. In 1939-40, he was Commissioner of Information in Daladier's short-lived government.

Every year in July, a festival (theatre, music, dance) commemorates this talented native son.

Giraudoux's childhood home (Maison Natale)

◔*Open mid-Jun to the end of Aug, daily except Tue, 2.30-6pm (5.30pm, Sat-Sun); rest of the year, Fri, 3.30-5.30pm or by prior arrangement.* ☎*2€.* ☎ *05 55 68 03 77.*

The author's birthplace is now home to an exhibition of letters, photographs, set models and posters for his plays. In his room, the library includes a priceless collection of his books and manuscripts.

In 1951, a **monument** commemorating the author, by the sculptor Chauvenet, was erected beneath the magnificent trees of the town hall garden. On either side of his portrait are cameos of six heroines from his works: Ondine, Alcmène, Judith and Bella, Isabelle and Suzanne.

Excursions

LA BASSE-MARCHE★

Round trip of 55km/33mi – allow 2hr 30min

▷　*Leave Bellac to the east along the D 1 towards Châteauponsac.*

Rancon

This peaceful hamlet in the Gartempe Valley is built into the hillside. The 12C Lantern of the Dead is surmounted by a cross with five foils (cusps).

The 13C **church**, built in the transitional Romanesque-Gothic style and fortified in the 14C, was formerly part of the town's defensive perimeter. Note the machicolations on the chevet and the openings for the archers; the belfry, a 16C square tower ends in an onion-shaped dome covered with shingles. In the chancel is a fine 13C wooden Christ.

Châteauponsac

The oldest part of this small town is huddled around the **church**, dating largely from the 12C, though the pointed vaulting was added in the narrow nave and aisles in the 15C. The tall transept is crowned with a dome on pendentives.

The chancel has fine round columns with carved capitals. Also of interest are the stone pulpit dating from 1642, a great 18C lectern and 16C-17C painted wooded statues.

Go around the church and walk to the promontory for a **view of the Gartempe**. From there the valley can be seen sloping steeply on the left bank. The Sous-le-Moutier quarter is in the foreground, with its busy pattern of old houses and terrace gardens.

Musée René-Baubérot – ⏱Open Jun-Sep and school hols, 2-6pm; Oct-May, Wed, Sat-Sun and public hols, 2-6pm. ⟿Guided tours possible by prior arrangement. ⏱Closed 25 Dec-1 Jan. 5€ (child: 2.50€). ☎ 05 55 76 39 52. Housed in a former Benedictine priory (1318), this museum recreates a dozen scenes of daily life, including a Limousin home, a young girls' bedroom, various workshops and a forge.

The impressive archaeological collections (prehistory, Gallo-Roman and medieval periods) include a quartz **polishing tool** used in the making of flint axes, Gallo-Roman chests, funerary urns, pottery and other items, most of which have been discovered in the local area.

The Maison du Terroir organises a number of annual exhibitions.

▶ *Follow the D 45 which wends its way through pleasant farmland.*

Magnac-Laval

This town is famous for a procession to St Maximus which travels more than 50km/32mi on Whit Monday (Pentecost). The pilgrims, wearing garlands of flowers around their necks, leave after midnight mass and return the following day after sunset.

The 12C **church** has a flat east end and a hexagonal belfry and contains the relics of St Maximus.

Collégiale St-Pierre du Dorat★★

♿ *See Collégiale St-Pierre du DORAT.*

▶ *Return to Bellac on the D 675, travelling through the Gartempe Valley.*

BELVÈS  ★

POPULATION 1 431

MICHELIN LOCAL MAP 329: H-7

Perched on a limestone promontory on the site of a Gallo-Roman castrum, Belvès enjoys a marvellous position overlooking the Nauze Valley. The surrounding rolling countryside is renowned for its wild mushrooms and chestnuts.

▶ **Orient Yourself**: Approach from the southwest along the D 53 (the Monpazier road) for a charming view of the town with its old turreted houses, bell towers and leafy garden terraces.

Visit

Plaques identify the town's major monuments (a town plan is available at the tourist office).

The 11C bell tower and 15C covered market (*halle*) with stone and wooden supports stand on **place d'Armes**, at the centre of the village. Take the covered passage to the right of the Archbishop's House, which leads to **rue Rubigan**. This attractive street leads to the Tour de l'Auditeur (Auditor's Tower), the former castrum keep. The Maison des Consuls (tourist office), is located along rue des Eiffols.

Along the high street, **rue Manchotte**, note the half-timbered houses at nos 27-29. Follow the street to the western edge of town, where you can admire the Gothic church of Notre-Dame-de-Montcuq (13C-15C), which used to be a Benedictine priory. Walk towards place Croix des Frères: the castle is on your right and a 14C octagonal keep, all that remains of a former convent, on your left.

Troglodyte Dwellings

🕐 *Open mid-Jun to mid-Sep,* ⟜ *guided tours (45min) at 10.30am, 11.15am, 3pm, 4.30pm and 5.15pm; mid-Sep to mid-Jun, by prior arrangement with the tourist office.* ⟜ *3.50€ (child: 1.50€).* ☎ *05 53 29 10 20.*

A complex of nine underground rooms situated in the medieval moat, beneath place d'Armes, gives an insight into the daily life of the families who lived here between the 12C and 18C.

Musée Organistrum et Vielles à Roues du Périgord Noir

14 rue J.-Manchotte. 🕐 *Open by prior arrangement.* ⟜ *No charge.* ☎ *05 53 29 10 93.*

This museum houses a small collection of reconstructed lutes, hurdy-gurdies and other medieval musical instruments.

Excursion

Land of Chestnuts and Wild Mushrooms

60km/37mi round tour – allow half a day

A view of Belvès

Address Book

For coin ranges, see the Legend at the back of the guide.

GUIDED TOURS

In season, guided tours of Belvès take place daily except Sun at 6pm. *For further information, contact the Tourist Office.*

Torchlight visits: 9pm Tue in Jul-Aug. Meet under the 15C *halle.*

Tours of local area: Guided tours on Tue and Thu in Jul-Aug. *For further information, contact the Tourist Office.*

EATING OUT

Auberge de la Nauze – *Fongouffier - 24170 Sagelat - 1km/0.6mi N of Belvès on the D 53 -* ☎ *05 53 28 44 81 -* ⏰ *closed Mon eve, Tue eve and Sat lunchtime.* This typical regional house stands above the picturesque town of Belvès. Large bay windows and warm colours brighten the dining room. The chef sets traditional dishes to simmer in the kitchen, where fresh local products hold pride of place.

Ferme-Auberge de la Caussine – *La Caussine - 24170 Doissat - 11km/6.6mi SE of Belvès on D 54 -* ☎ *05 53 29 94 84 -* ⏰ *closed late Sep to Easter -* ✍. A perfect place to retreat to the country, in the company of farm animals. Guests may choose from rooms in three outbuildings or chalets and mobile homes at the forest edge. Meals are served under the eaves of a former tobacco barn.

WHERE TO STAY

Le Branchat – Kids *- 24170 Sagelat - 3km/1.8mi S of Belvès on the D 710 towards Fumel and a secondary road to the left -* ☎ *05 53 28 98 80 - lebranchat@lebranchat. com -* ⏰ *closed Nov-Mar - 6 rooms.* A sheepfold, stable, barn and farmhouse have been wonderfully restored and turned into charming guestrooms. In the middle of a 5ha/12.5-acre park, you will be sure to have a quiet night's sleep. Relax in the pool, stroll around the grounds or ride on a pony.

Chambre d'Hôte La Grande Marque – *24220 Marnac - 9km/5.4mi NE of Belvès on the D 703 and to the right -* ☎ *05 53 31 61 63 -* ✍ *- 5 rooms.* The view from this 17C hill-top house will take your breath away. Under the eaves, three pretty rooms have recently been redecorated.

SHOPPING

Markets in Belvès – Traditional market in on Sat morning. Local growers' market Wed 4pm in Jul-Aug. Walnut market Wed morning Oct-Dec.

Markets in Villefranche-du-Périgord – *23km/13.8mi S of Belvès on the D 660.* Chestnut market Sat morning Oct-Dec. Mushroom market (cèpes) weekdays from 4pm and Sun all day (depending on the growing conditions).

▶ *Drive S out of Belvès along the D 710; turn left onto the D 54 after 1km/0.6mi, then right 2km/1.2mi further on.*

The road runs through fields and woodland dotted with charming small villages.

Orliac

This tiny village, buried in the hollow of a valley occupied by a pine forest, has a fortified church in which the nave served as a protective keep; the Renaissance doorway provides the only decorative touch.

Prats-du-Périgord

The Romanesque **Église St-Maurice**★, fortified in the 15C, has an unusual appearance, with its nave framed by a tall apse and a graceful belfry wall.

▶ *Leave Prats to the south along the D 60.*

Villefranche-du-Périgord

This *bastide* was founded in 1261 by **Alphonse de Poitiers**. An enormous covered market, with its heavy stone pillars, and part of the covered arcades are still standing. A chestnut market takes place here on Saturdays from late September to November.

Maison du Châtaignier, Marrons et Champignons – ⏰ *Open Jun-Sep, 9.30am-12.30pm and 3-6.30pm, Sun and Mon 3-6.30pm; Jan-May and Oct-Dec, daily except Sun and Wed, 9.30am-noon and 3-5pm, Mon 3-5pm.* ✍*3€.* ☎ *05 53 29 98 37.*

This ecological museum is devoted to mushrooms and the chestnut. The 1km/0.6mi nature trail (allow 30min) is particularly popular. A chestnut market is held here every Saturday morning during the harvest season.

▶ *Drive NE along the D 57.*

Église de Besse

This church is famous for its remarkable carved **doorway**★ in the west front, dating most probably from the 11C. Such features are rare in the architecture of the Périgord region, and this particular example is exceptional. The sculptures on the archivolt depict the Redemption, including images of Adam and Eve before and after the Original Sin, St Michael slaying the dragon and Isaiah being purified by a glowing coal.

▶ *Continue NE along the D 57.*

St-Pompon

This old village contains many houses typical of the Périgord region with its attractive dormer windows surmounted with shell ornamentation and framed with spiral scrolls. Cross the small bridge by the town hall to reach the **fortified doorway**★, all that remains of a fortress built here by the English in the 15C. Beyond the church, you will see the ruins of a castle dating from the same period. Farther east, on the road to Daglan, stands **Notre-Dame-de-Bedeau**, a chapel dating from the 13C and 17C and a place of pilgrimage for hunters at the start of the hunting season.

▶ *Drive NW out of St-Pompon along the D 60 towards Prats. After 1km/0.6mi, turn right onto the D 52 to St-Laurent then follow the D 51 back to Belvès.*

BERGERAC★

POPULATION 26 053

MICHELIN LOCAL MAP 329: D-6

Spread out on both banks of the Dordogne where the river tends to be calmer and the valley widens to form an alluvial plain, this distinctly southern town is surrounded by prestigious vineyards and fields of tobacco, cereals and maize. A project to restore the old quarter has seen the embellishment of a number of Bergerac's 15C and 16C houses. 🗐 97 r. Neuve-d'Argenson, 24100 Bergerac, ☎ 05 53 57 03 11. www.bergerac-tourisme.com.

🅿 **Parking**: There are several car parks dotted around the town (🐾 see town plan).

🐾 **Don't Miss**: The Old Town; Musée du Tabac; Musée Régional du Vin et de la Batellerie.

🄺🄸🄳🅂 **Especially for Kids**: Aqua Park Junior Land.

A Bit of History

An intellectual and commercial crossroads – The town's expansion began as early as the 12C. Benefiting from the town's situation as a port and bridging point, the local middle class developed rapidly, profiting from successful trade between the central provinces of Auvergne and Limousin and Bordeaux on the coast. In the 16C, this Navarre fief became one of the bastions of Protestantism. The city flourished. The town's printing presses published pamphlets which circulated throughout the Protestant world. In August 1577 the Peace of Bergerac was signed between the king of Navarre and the representatives of King Henri III; this was a preliminary to the Edict of Nantes (1598). But in 1620, Louis XIII's army took over the town and destroyed the ramparts. After the Revocation of the Edict of Nantes (1685), the Jesuits and Recollects tried to win back their Protestant disciples. A certain number of Bergerac citizens, faithful to their Calvinist beliefs, emigrated to Holland, a country where they had maintained commercial contacts.

Bergerac was the capital of Périgord until the Revolution, when the regional capital was transferred to Périgueux, which also became Préfecture of the Dordogne *département*.

In the 19C, wine-growing and shipping prospered until the onslaught of phylloxera and the arrival of the railway respectively.

Bergerac today – Essentially an agricultural centre, Bergerac is the capital of tobacco in France, and as a result the Experimental Institute of Tobacco and the Tobacco Planters Centre of Advanced and Refresher Training are located here.

In addition the 12 000ha/29 650 acres of vineyards surrounding the town produce wine with an *appellation d'origine contrôlée* (which means it is of an officially recognised vintage) including: Bergerac, Côtes de Bergerac, Monbazillac, Montravel and Pécharmant. The Regional Wine Council, which establishes the *appellation* of the wines, is located in the Recollects' Cloisters (🐾 see Old Bergerac below).

The main industrial enterprise of the town is the powder factory producing nitro-cellulose for use in such industries as film-making, paint, varnish and plastics.

Famous citizens – Oddly enough, the Cyrano of Edmond Rostand's play was inspired by the 17C philosopher **Cyrano de Bergerac** whose name had nothing to do with the Périgord town. Not discouraged in the slightest, the townspeople took it upon themselves to adopt this wayward son and erect a statue in his honour in place de la Myrpe.

Old Bergerac★★

Ancien port

Try to imagine the *gabares* of yesteryear mooring here to drop off goods and wood, which came from the upper valley, and load on the barrels of wine bound for England and Holland via Bordeaux.

▶ *Turn left at the end of quai Salvette.*

Rue du Château

An unusual balustraded balcony overhangs a sharp bend in the street.

Address Book

For coin ranges, see the Legend at the back of the guide.

EATING OUT

🍽 **Le Méli-Mélo de la Marquise** – *2 r. Ste-Catherine* - ☎ 05 53 57 10 86 - 🕐 *closed evenings, Sun lunchtime and Mon - reserv. recommended.* Big bay windows fill this cosy little place with light. Breakfast daily, brunch Wednesday and Saturday, market-fresh lunch-hour specials, tea in the afternoon. Lovely chocolates for sale. Treats for all!

🍽🍽 **Le Plat dans l'Assiette** – *18 r. du Mourrier* - ☎ 05 53 24 25 26 - 🕐 *closed 2 weeks in May, Sun (excluding lunchtime in season) and Mon. - reserv. recommended.* This Lyon-style bistro is a happy surprise in the land of foie gras and duck filet. The typical decor is a mix of bistro tables, knick-knacks, old advertising signs, paintings and a piano. Lyon meets Périgord on friendly ground here, on your plate and on the wine lists.

🍽🍽 **L'Enfance de Lard** – *Pl. Pélissière* - ☎ 05 53 57 52 88 - *lenfacedelard@yahoo.fr* - 🕐 *closed lunchtime and Tue - reserv. required.* This old house stands on a pretty square in old Bergerac. An intimate atmosphere prevails in the tiny, country-style dining room. The welcome is warm and the food is tasty. It is easy to see why this place is always crowded!.

🍽🍽🍽 **L'Imparfait** – *8 r. des Fontaines* - ☎ 05 53 57 47 92 - 🕐 *closed 14 Nov-14 Feb.* "The Imperfect" is a funny name for this restaurant in the heart of the old town. The medieval building has exposed beams in the dining room, local specialities, and an open fire for grilling meats.

WHERE TO STAY

🛏 **Europ Hôtel** – *20 r. du Petit-Sol* - ☎05 53 57 06 54 - 🅿 - *22 rooms* - ⚏ *5.50€.* This hotel away from the centre, close to the train station, has the feel of the countryside about it, especially if you happen to be relaxing under the trees around pool. The rooms are rather ordinary, with a 1970s decor, but they are well kept and the price is right.

🛏🛏 **La Flambée** – *153 av. Pasteur* - ☎05 53 57 52 33 - 🅿 - *21 rooms.* A recently renovated country house in an attractive leafy setting. Spacious bedrooms, some with their own terrace. An elegant restaurant where the emphasis is on regional cuisine.

🛏🛏🛏 **Château Lespinassat** – *Rte d'Agen - 3km/1.8mi SE of Bergerac along the N 21* - ☎ 05 53 74 84 11 - *5 rooms.* The fine lines of this 18C château are mirrored in the reflecting pool in the centre of the superb 5ha/12.5-acre park. Inside, you will see antique furniture, mouldings, silky draperies, impressive fireplaces and parquet floors. The rooms are very spacious and perfectly well fitted out. Pool.

BARS AND CAFES

La Désirade – *Pl. Pélissière* - ☎ 05 53 58 27 50 - 🕐 *Open Jun-Sep, daily, 10am-midnight; May, 9am-7pm* - 🕐 *closed Oct-Apr.* The terrace is just in front of a lovely fountain, making this café a cool and refreshing place to take a break. The friendly couple who run it offer old-fashioned ice cream and delicious alcohol-free cocktails.

La Treille – *12 Quai Salvette* - ☎ 05 53 57 60 11 - 🕐 *open daily in summer, 8am-2am; rest of the year, 9.30am-1am* - 🕐 *closed Tue eve and Wed.* Hard to believe, but this is the only café terrace that overlooks the River Dordogne. The arbour is a most inviting place to escape the heat and admire the natural surroundings, protected by environmental law. Or if you're a winter bird, you may prefer to sit indoors by the fire. A small nook with a vaulted ceiling is especially popular for romantic tête-à-têtes.

Victoria – *27 r. Boubarraud* - ☎ 05 53 58 48 36 - 🕐 *Open Tue-Sat, 10am-2pm and 3-6.30pm (boutique closes at 7pm)* - 🕐 *closed 2 weeks in Aug.* Here is a place to come and warm up on a chilly day. The tearoom above a card shop has red decor, embellished with doilies and embroidery and old engravings. More than 40 varieties of tea are available, served in pretty English cups along with home-made pastries.

SHOPPING

Markets – Farmers' market Wed and Sat morning in pl. du Marché Couvert, Fri morning in pl. de la Madeleine, Wed morning in pl. Doublet. *Marché au gras* (market selling duck and goose products) Sat from Oct-Feb.

Maison des Vins de Bergerac – *1 r. des Récollets* - ☎ 05 53 63 57 57. Bergerac wines for sale: Rosette, Pécharmant, Monbazillac, Saussignac, Montravel.

L'Art et le Vin – *17 Grand-Rue* - ☎ 05 53 57 07 42. 🕐 *Open Tue-Sat, 9am-12.30pm and 2-7pm.* The wine-coloured façade of this shop that has been operating next to the covered market for 30 years is a tip-off: inside a world of wine awaits. The selected products, attractively arranged in wooden cases, are mainly from small regional wine-growers well-known to the owners: Pécharmant, Bergerac, Monbazillac etc. The shop also carries a nice choice of eaux-de-vie and products from the Comtesse du Barry line.

Pâtisserie Rosier Castagna – *10 r. de la Résistance* - ☎ 05 53 57 04 42. 🕐 *Open Tue-Fri, 8am-7.15pm, Sat, 8am-7.30pm, Sun, 7.30am-12.30pm* - 🕐 *closed first week in Feb, one week in June and one week in Sept.* This shop has been selling pastries here since 1875. The period decor has been well preserved: gilded mouldings, big mirrors hanging from the wall and a pretty little tea room in the back. The merchandise is as attractive as it is tasty. Look for: truffles flavoured with Monbazillac wine, packaged in a bottle with a vintage label; le Succès, a meringue and almond confection with coffee or rum cream; le Noyer, garnished with a thin layer of walnut cream; l'Insolite, a chocolate cake with orange nougat. Ascetics abstain!

LEISURE ACTIVITIES

Aqua Park Junior' Land – *Rte de Bordeaux - ☎ 05 53 58 33 00 - www. bergerac-tourisme.com - ⏰ open 15 May-15 Sep - canoes: 10am-8pm; other times, depending on the weather - 5.70€ (children under 5: 2.80€).* Four floodlit swimming pools, a slide, a trampoline, bouncing games and other outdoor toys, archery, cross-country bikes, mini-motorcycles, evening events and above all wonderful guided canoe trips on the River Dordogne! In addition, you can count on a very warm welcome.

CALENDAR OF EVENTS

Les Mercredis du Jazz – Wednesday jazz sessions at the Cloître des Récollets and other venues around town. No charge.
Mai des Arts - During May, the town hosts a number of exhibitions, events and shows as part of this artistic festival.

▶ *Cross rue de l'Ancien-Port and turn left.*

The walls of the corbelled half-timbered houses lining **rue St-Clar** are a mixture of cob and small bricks.

▶ *Turn left onto rue des Rois de France then right onto rue de l'Ancien Port.*

Maison Peyrarède★

Also known as the French Kings' House, this elegant building dating from 1603 is ornamented with a corbelled turret.

Rue d'Albret

At the end of this street to the right is the town hall, the former convent of the Sisters of Faith.
On the left, on the corner of place du Feu, is a vast building with pointed arched doorways.

▶ *Walk to place du Docteur-Cayla.*

Place du Docteur-Cayla and place de la Myrpe

The 13C chapel adjacent to the former Couvent des Récollets became a **Protestant temple** (♿ ⏰*open mid-Jul to mid-Sep, 10am-noon and 3-7pm. ⬧No charge. ☎ 05 53 57 02 79*) in the 18C; it now houses exhibitions on local Protestantism. The charming shaded place de la Myrpe is lined with half-timbered houses. In the middle of the square stands the statue of Cyrano de Bergerac swathed in his cape.

▶ *Follow the narrow street leading off the square and turn right.*

Rue des Conférences

The name of this street calls to mind the conferences held before the Peace of Bergerac. It is bordered by half-timbered houses.

▶ *Turn left.*

Place Pélissière

This large square was opened up after the demolition of some run-down houses. Spread on different levels around a fountain it is overlooked by **Église St-Jacques** (⏰ *Open Jul-Aug, noon-7pm; Sep-Jun, 2-7pm, Wed 2-6pm, Sat 2-5pm*), once a centre for pilgrims on their way to Santiago de Compostela; it now houses contemporary works of art.

Rue St-Jâmes

There are 15C, 16C and 17C half-timbered houses with mullioned windows all along this street.

Bergerac old town

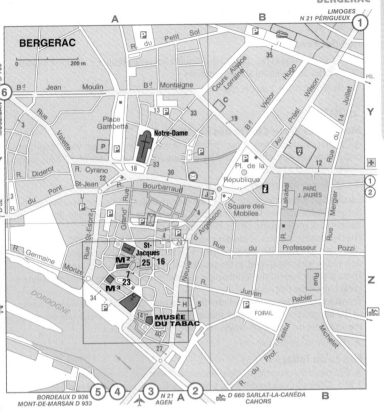

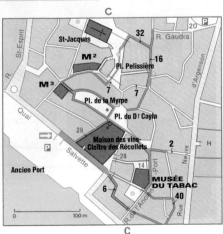

▶ *Turn right.*

Rue des Fontaines

The Vieille Auberge at the corner of rue Gaudra has well-preserved moulded arcades, 14C capitals, and pointed arched windows.

▶ *Walk back to place du Docteur-Cayla along rue des Fontaines.*

Sights

Maison des Vins – Cloître des Récollets

&.⊙*Open mid-Jun to Aug, 10am-7pm; May to mid-Jun, daily except Mon, 10am-1pm and 2-7pm; Sep-Apr, daily except Mon and Sun, 10.30am-12.30pm and 2-6pm.* ⊗*No charge.* ☎ *05 53 63 57 55.*

▶ *The former Couvent des Récollets is reached via quai Salvette.*

Go through the corridor into the vaulted wine cellar where the meetings of the Bergerac wine society, Conférence des Consuls de la Vinée, are held. There is an audio-visual presentation on the Bergerac vineyards.

The brick and stone cloister building was built between the 12C and 17C. The interior courtyard has a 16C Renaissance gallery beside an 18C gallery where exhibitions devoted to wine are staged. In the south-east corner is the monks' small oven.

There is a fine view of the Monbazillac vineyards from the sumptuously decorated great hall on the first floor.

The wine-testing laboratory includes the wine-tasting room (*open to visitors*), where all the Bergerac wines are tasted annually to determine whether they are worthy of the *appellation d'origine contrôlée* – the AOC mark on the label.

▶ *Walk to rue de l'Ancien-Port.*

Musée du Tabac★★

&. ⊙ *Open daily except Mon, 10am-noon and 2-6pm; Sat, 10am-noon and 2-5pm; Sun 2.30-6.30pm.* ⊙ *Closed public hols, Sat afternoon and Sun mid-Nov to mid-Mar.* ⊗*3€ (combined ticket with the Musée d'Histoire Urbaine below).* ☎ *05 53 63 08 12.*

This remarkable and beautifully presented collection, which includes satirical engravings, traces the history and evolution of tobacco through the centuries.

On the **second floor** works of art depicting tobacco and smokers are displayed. *Two Smokers* from the 17C Northern French School, *Three Smokers* by Meissonier and the charming *Interior of a smoke den* by David II Teniers, known as Teniers the Younger, are among the works exhibited.

Nearby is a pedestal table made by the Mexican Indians. It is fascinating to see how many cigar bands have been used to make the table's marquetry.

A section is devoted to the cultivation of tobacco (planting, harvesting, drying etc) with special reference to the Bergerac region.

Cloître des Récollets

The Tobacco Industry

Until the 15C tobacco was used only by the American Indians, who believed it possessed medicinal properties. After the discovery of the New World, tobacco was introduced to Europe. Jean Nicot brought it into France in c1560; he sent snuff to Catherine de' Medici to cure her migraines.

Use of tobacco was controversial from the very start: Pope Urbain VIII ordered the excommunication of nicotine fiends and Louis XIII forbade its sale (before hitting on the idea of taxing it). In those days, tobacco was sold as a carrot-shaped lump which was grated into powder. The familiar diamond-shaped orange sign, Tabac, which hangs outside of shops licensed to sell tobacco products, is still called a carotte today.

At the end of the 18C snuff was sold directly in powder form.

The next step in the art of smoking was the pipe. The pipe had been in use in Holland since the early 17C, but its use was considered vulgar and common. Officers of the First Empire started the fashion and were quickly followed by the Romantics, including George Sand.

Finally in the mid-19C, the cigarette arrived on the scene and with it its accessories, including the elegant ivory cigarette holders.

Musée d'Histoire Urbaine

&. Ⓒ ☻ 3€ (combined ticket with the Musée du Tabac). ☎ 05 53 63 04 13.

In a house adjoining the **Peyrarède Mansion** there is a display of various objects – maps, documents, architectural remains, furnishings – evoking Bergerac's history. Note, in particular, the collection of earthenware made in Bergerac during the 18C.

Musée Régional du Vin et de la Batellerie ★

Ⓒ Open mid-Mar to mid-Nov, 10am-noon and 2-5.30pm; Sat, 10am-noon; Sun, 2.30-6.30pm. ☻2€. ☎ 05 53 57 80 92.

Located in a lovely brick and half-timbered house at the end of place de la Myrpe, this museum is divided into three sections.

On the first floor, the importance of barrel-making to the Bergerac economy is explained. The coopers had to submit to strict control standards of barrel capacity, type of wood used and so on.

The section on wine shows the evolution of the Bergerac vineyards over the centuries and the type of houses the wine-growers lived in.

The second floor concerns river boats. There are models of the various kinds of river boats, *gabares*, flat-bottomed boats sometimes with sails, which transported different kinds of goods on the River Dordogne. They did not go above Bergerac, which was the port where the goods were transhipped. Photos show the bustling port of Bergerac in the 19C, as well as scenes of fishing with cast-nets strong enough to bring in enormous catches during the spawning season of fish such as salmon or shad.

▷ *From place de la Myrpe it is only a short walk to place Pelissière; the Musée d'Art Sacré is nearby.*

Église Notre-Dame

▷ *From the north end of place Pelissière, follow Grand'Rue then cross boulevard de la Résistance to reach place de Lattre-de-Tassigny.*

Built in the Gothic style, this 19C church has a slender bell tower. There are two fine paintings in the east chapel: an Adoration of the Magi attributed to Pordenone, a Venetian painter and student of Giorgione, and above all an Adoration of the Shepherds attributed to the Milanese, Ferrari, student of Leonardo da Vinci. In the west chapel is an immense **Aubusson tapestry** portraying the Bergerac coat of arms.

Excursions

Vallée du Caudau

60km/37mi – allow half a day

▷ *Leave Bergerac travelling NE along the N 21 to Les Pélissous then turn right onto the D 21E1.*

Lamonzie-Montastruc

Perched on a rock to the left of the road is Château de Montastruc, a handsome building in the Classical style. Its main building is 16C, flanked by 15C circular corner towers. There is a fine 12C Romanesque church in the village.

▶ *Continue along the D 21.*

Château de la Gaubertie

Built in the 15C, this castle was completely restored in the early 20C. The large main building, its façade overlooking the Caudau Valley, is flanked by a square tower on one side and a round corbelled tower on the other side. A watch-path runs right round it. The 17C chapel stands not far from the castle.

▶ *Turn back and continue along the D 21.*

Vergt

This large agricultural town has become one of the main strawberry centres. The sandy soil of the region is perfect for the cultivation of this fruit. At certain times during the year, big plastic sheets are spread over the strawberries to protect them. (*Daily market* 🕐 *Open mid-Apr to mid-Nov*).

Château de Montastruc

J. Damase/MICHELIN

▶ *Rejoin the D 8 and drive towards Bergerac taking the second road on the left 1.5km/0.9mi further on.*

Lac de Neufont

This is a pleasant recreational lake with swimming beaches and pedal boat rental. Go through **St-Amand-de-Vergt**, which has a pretty Romanesque church surmounted by a dome.

▶ *Continue S.*

Château de St-Maurice

The castle is partly hidden by the trees in its grounds, but its 14C and 15C buildings, pierced with Renaissance windows and crowned with machicolations, are nonetheless an attractive sight.

▶ *Drive onto St-Félix-de-Villadeix, then continue along the D 32 which leads back to Bergerac.*

BEYNAC et CAZENAC★★

POPULATION 506

MICHELIN LOCAL MAP 329: H-6

LOCAL MAP SEE VALLÉE DE LA DORDOGNE

The Château de Beynac stands on a remarkable **site**★★ crowning a rugged rockface. From this strategic position, it overlooks the beautiful Dordogne Valley as it winds its way between hills and castles. 🖹 *La Balme, 24220 Beynac-et-Cazenac, ☎ 05 53 29 43 08.*

▶ **Orient Yourself**: For a great view of the river and surrounding area, head up to the castle.

▶ **Don't Miss**: A visit of the castle; a boat trip on the Dordogne.

A Bit of History

A formidable stronghold – In the Middle Ages Beynac, Biron, Bourdeilles and Mareuil were the four baronies of Périgord. The castle was captured by Richard the Lion Heart and used as a base by the sinister **Mercadier**, master-at-arms, whose bands of men pillaged the countryside on behalf of the king of England. In 1214, during the Albigensian Crusade, Simon de Montfort seized the castle and demolished it. The castle was later rebuilt, as we see it today, by a lord of Beynac.

J. Damase/MICHELIN

The castle atop the cliffs, the village by the water

During the Hundred Years War, the Dordogne marked the front between the English and the French, and there were constant skirmishes and raids between Beynac under the English in 1360, then the French in 1368, and Castelnaud under the English (*see Château de CASTELNAUD*). Once peace had returned, Beynac Castle was left once more to watch over the village.

Village★

Rue Tibal Lo Garrel★, a steeply sloping footpath leads from the bottom of the village, through rows of houses dating from the 15C to the 17C, to the castle preceded by the former castle chapel, now the parish church (*open for services only*). All along the climb the architectural decor exudes elegance and the prosperity of Renaissance Beynac. There are gabled doorways, façades decorated with coats of arms or discs, ornate dormer windows, and small, beautifully laid out squares.

A *calvaire* (wayside cross) stands on the cliff edge, at the end of rue Tibal Lo Garrel. A **panorama**★★ as wide as the one from the castle watch-path can be seen from this point.

Château★★

Open Jun-Sep, 10am-6.30pm; Jan-Feb and Dec, noon to dusk; Mar-May, 10am-6pm; Oct-Nov, 10am to dusk. ☎ 05 53 29 50 40.

Address Book

For coin ranges, see the Legend at the back of the guide.

EATING OUT

La Petite Tonnelle – *La Balme - 24220 Beynac -* ☎ *05 53 29 95 18 -* closed Nov-Apr except school holidays at Christmas. This family restaurant offers a unique twist on traditional cuisine by spicing up dishes with an Asian flare (the chef is a native of Vietnam). In the winter, sit by the fireside; in the summer, sit beneath the arbour covered in Virginia creeper.

SHOPPING

Markets - A local producers' market is held every morning from mid-Jun-mid Sep in place de la Balme.

LEISURE ACTIVITIES

Gabares de Beynac – *24250 St-Martial-de-Nabirat -* ☎ *05 53 28 51 15 - www.gabarre-beynac.com -* Jul-Aug, 10am-12.30pm and 2-6pm, departures from the car park (1hr) - boats leave every 30min; May-Jun and Sep, 10.30am-12.30pm and 2-6pm; mid-Mar to Apr and Oct: by prior arrangement - 6.50€ (child under 12: 4€, no charge in the mornings). Boat trips along the Dordogne on traditional flat-bottomed *gabare* boats.

Aux Canoës Ròquegeoffre du Port d'Enveaux – *Enveaux Rive Droite - 24220 St-Vincent-de-Cosse -* ☎ *05 53 29 54 20 - www.canœ-roquegeoffre.com -* daily 9am-7pm - prices start at 8.50€. This recreation centre on the banks of the River Dordogne also offers guided canoe and kayak trips. Fishing boats can also be hired here.

The castle is in the form of an irregular quadrilateral extended on the south side to form a bastion. The austere crenellated keep dates from the 13C. A double curtain wall protected the castle from attack from the plateau; on all the other sides there is a sheer drop of 150m/492ft to the Dordogne. The main building, dating from the 13C and 14C, is extended by the 15C seigneurial manor house to which a bartizan was added in the 16C.

The castle was abandoned from 1798 until it changed hands in 1961. The present owner, who occupies the gatehouse has launched a vast renovation programme due to last a century. The kitchens, the drawbridge, the guard-room and the keep have already been restored.

Interior – Visitors enter the dark 13C guard-room, faintly lit by oil lamps, and proceed to the next floor where the 14C kitchen and its two fireplaces can be admired. There are latrines in the next room, as on all the floors.

Above the kitchen is the great Hall of State, where once the nobles of Périgord used to assemble; note the carvings decorating the fireplace from Italy. The oratory is adorned with Gothic frescoes, naïve in style, with lively draughtsmanship depicting biblical characters as well as members of the Beynac family.

The grand 17C staircase, denoting a Florentine influence, leads to a drawing room furnished in Louis XIII style; note the paintings on wood decorating the ceiling.

One last staircase leads to the watch-path and the south bastion, which overlook the Dordogne: there is a wonderful **panorama**★★ of the valley and from left to right, of the threshold to Domme and the castles of Marqueyssac, Castelnaud and Fayrac.

On the way down, visitors go through the 13C kitchen and across the drawbridge before leaving via the barbican.

Parc Archéologique

⏱*Open Jul to mid-Sep, daily except Sat, 10am-7pm.* ✑5€ *(child: 3.50€).* ☎ *05 53 29 51 28.*

This includes about 10 reconstitutions based on the discoveries of archaeological research, mainly living quarters from the end of the Neolithic period, a fortified gateway and a Gallic potter's oven. The display is further enhanced by demonstrations of flint-stone carving, the making and firing of earthenware and so forth.

Château de BIRON★

MICHELIN LOCAL MAP 329: G-8

From its strategic position on top of a rock, the massive bulk of the towers and walls of the Château de Biron commands this area on the borders of the Périgord and Agenais regions. The Dordogne *département* bought the castle in 1978 and began a massive restoration programme; an art centre was also established here, organising exhibitions every summer.

A Bit of History

From the Capitol to the Tarpeian Rock – Among the many celebrated men of the Biron family, **Charles de Gontaut** met with a particularly memorable fate. Friend of Henri IV and one of his first lieutenants, he was appointed first Admiral and then Marshal of France. In 1598 the Barony of Biron was created and conferred as a dukedom on Charles de Gontaut who was next promoted to Lieutenant-General of the French Army and then Governor of Burgundy. Even these honours did not satisfy him and, in league with the Duke of Savoy and the Spanish Governor of the state of Milan, he laid a plot which would have led to the breaking up of the kingdom of France. Biron, his treason exposed, was pardoned. But the mercy of

For coin ranges, see the Legend at the back of the guide.

WHERE TO STAY

⌲ **Camping Le Moulinal** – 24540 Biron - 4km/2.5mi S of Biron on the Lacapelle-Biron road - ☎ 05 53 40 84 60 - lemoulinal@perigord.com - www.lemoulinal.com - ⏱ open 5 Apr-13 Sep - reserv. recommended - 290 pitches: restaurant on-site. This campsite comes complete with a lake and swimming beach. There is also a nice pool, and a play area and organised activities for children. Canvas bungalows and mobiles homes available.

Henri IV did nothing to halt his ambitions. Once more he plotted against his lord. Once again he was exposed and was taken before the king, who agreed to pardon him if he would confess his crime. The proud Biron refused. He was beheaded in the courtyard of the Bastille prison on 31 July 1602.

From medieval fortress to the present building – This castle is made up of buildings of very different styles, the work of 24 generations of Gontaut-Birons, who owned the castle from the 12C to the 20C.

As early as the 11C a medieval fortress existed here. Razed by Simon de Montfort in the 13C, the castle was reconstructed. During the Hundred Years War, the castle changed hands constantly between the English and the French, getting badly damaged in the process.

In the late 15C and during the 16C, Pons de Gontaut-Biron, former chamberlain of Charles VIII, decided to transform his castle into a lovely Renaissance château like those he had seen in the Loire Valley. He altered the buildings east of the main courtyard and had the Renaissance chapel and colonnaded arcade built. Work was interrupted, however, and not resumed until the 18C.

Visit

Outer courtyard – Surrounding the castle's living quarters on three sides, the outer courtyard includes the caretaker's lodge, chapel, the receiving house and the bakery. The guards' tower, now the **conciergerie**, is an elegant building in which crenellations, a watch-path and Renaissance decoration are in felicitous juxtaposition.

The **chapel** was built in the Renaissance style in the 16C. A pierced balustrade runs round the base of the roof. The lower chamber once served as a parish church for the village; the upper chamber or seigneurial chapel has remarkable pointed vaulting. It shelters **two tombs with recumbent figures**, the sculptures showing the influence of the Italian Quattrocento (15C) period. The recumbent figure of Armand de Gontaut-Biron, bishop of Sarlat, is decorated with three seated figures of the virtues, whereas the recumbent figure of his brother Pons (d 1524) is carved in low relief and recounts the life of Christ in a macabre frieze. Both figures were damaged during the Revolution.

Cour d'honneur (main courtyard) – Access is by a staircase and a pointed vaulted corridor. On the right, the 16C seigneurial living quarters, with Renaissance windows, lead to the large 13C polygonal keep redesigned in the 15C. On the left, the 16C-18C main building has an elegant remodelled staircase, which goes up to the Great Hall of State.

In the basement, the kitchen, the former garrison's refectory, is a vast room (22x9m/72x30ft) with pointed barrel vaulting.

A portico leads to the castle terraces; from there, the **view**∗ extends over the rolling countryside and the Birons' other fief, the *bastide* of Monpazier.

Château de BONAGUIL★★

MICHELIN LOCAL MAP 336: I-2

LOCAL MAP SEE LUZECH: MEANDERS OF THE LOWER REACHES OF THE RIVER LOT

This majestic fortress, standing on the borders of the Périgord Noir and the Quercy, is one of the most perfect examples of military architecture from the late 15C and 16C. One of its unique features is that although it appears to be a typical medieval defensive stronghold, its design was adapted to the use of firearms. Such weapons were fairly common in Europe by the mid-14C, but not until the 15C did the invention of a firing mechanism make firearms accurate enough to have a significant impact on the conduct of warfare.

Address Book

For coin ranges, see the Legend at the back of the guide.

WHERE TO STAY

🛏 **Camping des Bastides** – *47150 Salles - 19km/12mi W via Fumel, then the D 710 and D 162 -* ☎ *05 53 40 83 09 - info@ campingdesbastides.com - www. campingdesbastides.com -* 🕐 *open Easter-Sep - reserv. recommended - 96 pitches - shop.* The view across the Lède Valley from this terraced campsite is charming, and in the summer months the landscape is bright with sunflowers. Facilities here include a swimming pool with slides,

volleyball court and children's play area. Mobile homes available.

🛏 **Camping Moulin du Périé** – *47500 Sauveterre-la-Lémance - 12km/7.5mi NW of Bonaguil on the D 440 and then the D 158 -* ☎ *05 53 40 67 26 - moulinduperie@ wanadoo.fr - www.camping-moulin-perie. com -* 🕐 *open 6 May-25 Sep - reserv. recommended - 125 pitches - restaurant.* This campsite, laid out around a restored mill, is spacious and well-maintained. Small lake and pool, bikes and bungalows for hire, plus a restaurant serving regional cuisine.

A Bit of History

A strange character – It was a strange quirk of character that made **Bérenger de Roquefeuil** enjoy proclaiming himself the "noble, magnificent and most powerful lord of the baronies of Roquefeuil, Blanquefort, Castelnau, Combret, Roquefère, Count of Naut." He belonged to one of the oldest families of Languedoc and was a brutal and vindictive man who, in his determination to be obeyed, did not hesitate to use force. But extortion and other outrages he perpetrated incited revolt. In order to crush this, Bérenger transformed Bonaguil Castle, which had been built in the 13C, into an impregnable fortress from which he would be able to observe and quell any

Château de Bonaguil

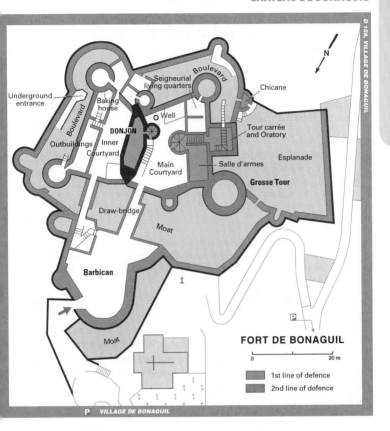

FORT DE BONAGUIL

0   20 m

▨ 1st line of defence

■ 2nd line of defence

P   *VILLAGE DE BONAGUIL*

signs of an uprising without delay. It took him nearly 40 years to build his fortified eagle's eyrie, which looked an anachronism when compared with the châteaux being erected by his contemporaries for a life of ease at Montal, Assier and along the Loire. However, his castle was never attacked and was intact until the eve of the Revolution. Although demolished during the Revolution in the prevailing urge to destroy all signs of the old feudal system, this colossus, notwithstanding its mutilations, still evokes the absolute power it once represented.

Visit

🕓 *Open Jun to Aug: 10am to 6pm; Apr to May: 10.30am to 1pm, 2.30 to 5.30pm; Sept: 10.30am to 1pm, 2.30 to 5pm ; Feb to Mar: 11am to 1pm, 2.30pm to 5.30; Oct: 11am to 1pm, 2.30 to 5pm; Nov: school vacations and public holidays 11am to 1pm, 2.30 to 5pm; Dec: school vacations 2.30 to 5pm.* 🕓 *Closed Jan, 25 Dec.* ⊛ *4,50€ (7-16 years old : 3€).* ☎ *05 53 71 90 33.*

To reach the castle stronghold, the visitor passes through the **barbican**. This was an enormous bastion on its own with an independent garrison, powder store, armouries and escape routes. The barbican formed part of the 350m/380yd-long first line of defence; its bastions, thanks to the embrasures, permitted cross-firing.

The second line of defence consisted of five towers of which one, known as the Grosse Tour, is among the strongest round towers ever to have been built in France. The tower is 35m/115ft high and is crowned with corbels; the upper storeys served as living quarters, the lower contained weapons, such as muskets, culverins and harquebuses etc.

The **keep** overlooked both lines of defence; it served, with its cant walls, not only as a watchtower but also as a command-post. Shaped like a vessel with its prow, the most vulnerable point, turned towards the north, it was the last bastion of defence. Inside, a room houses arms and objects found during the excavation of the moats.

With a well sunk through the rock, outbuildings (baking house) where provisions could be stored, monumental chimneys and drainage systems, dry internal ditches, and vaulted tunnels which enabled the troops to move about quickly, the castle garrison of about 100 men could easily withstand a siege provided they were not betrayed or starved out.

BORT-LES-ORGUES

POPULATION 3 534

MICHELIN LOCAL MAP 329: Q-3

The town of Bort, on a lovely site in the Dordogne Valley, is known for its huge dam (barrage) and for the cliffs rising above it. The cliffs are known as "les orgues", because the formation, seen from below, resembles the pipes of a massive organ.

Don't Miss: The Barrage de Bort and the Orgues de Bort.

Organising Your Time: Allow a couple of hours to visit Les Orgues de Bort and a full day to explore the Dordogne Valley.

Especially for Kids: The Insects of the World exhibition in Ydes.

Visit

Church

Dating from the 12C-15C, the plain architecture provides a frame for a 15C statue of St Anne, modern stained-glass windows and a bronze Christ sculpted by Chavignier. Outside, near the east end, traces of fortifications are still apparent. Next door, the former priory was built in the 17C.

Cascade du Saut de la Saule

2.5km/1.5mi SE, then 30min on foot there and back.

▸ *Take the road which climbs towards the Institut médico-pédagogique, continue along the alleyway crossing the Rhue then turn left and follow the river.*

The path reaches a small gorge dotted with picturesque potholes then continues to some rocks towering above the Saut de la Saule where the River Rhue flows over a 5-6m/17-20ft rocky shelf.

Barrage de Bort (Bort Dam)★★

Open May-Sep, 1hr boat trip taking in the Château de Val and the Dordogne Valley; Jul to mid-Sep, 1hr trip taking in the Barrage de Bort and the Château de Val, 11am and 2-5pm. 6€ (5 to 14 years old: 4€, 2 to 4 years old: 2€). Vedettes panoramiques. ☎ 04 71 40 30 14. There are car parks on either side of the dam, on the D 979 and D 922. 45min guided tours of the dam are also available by prior arrangement (24h in advance). Contact the tourist office for further information. ☎05 55 96 02 49. Passport/identity card required.

From the road across the top of the dam (390m/1 280ft long), the upstream view encompasses the vast reservoir, crisscrossed by the wakes of **pleasure cruisers** (downstream lie the main power plant and the spillway).
A **tour**, complete with video film and working model, starts at the base of the dam (between the small village of Les Granges and the Bort Tannery), illustrating the hydro-electric power system established along the River Dordogne and its tributaries.

Excursions

1 Les Orgues de Bort★

Round trip of 15km/9mi – allow 2hr

▸ *Leave Bort along the D 127 S, near the cemetery.*

The view to the left encompasses the Rhue Valley.

▸ *Just beyond the last houses in Chantery, take a stairway to the right, which leads directly to the stone columns. Follow signs to the Grottes des Orgues and the Site d'escalade des Orgues.*

The 80-100m/262-328ft high organ pipes, spread over a distance of 2km/1.2mi, are composed primarily of phonolite rock, known also as clinkstone or sound-stone.

For coin ranges, see the Legend at the back of the guide.

WHERE TO STAY

Camping Municipal de la Siauve – 15270 Lanobre - 3.5km/2mi N of Bort-les-Orgues via the D 922 and a side road - ☎ 04 71 40 31 85 - open 31 May-14 Sep - reserv. recommended - 220 pitches. Situated in a delightful lakeside setting, this campsite is the perfect base for a quiet and relaxing rural holiday. Activities on offer include swimming in the lake, fishing and exploring the local area on foot and by bike. Chalets and bungalows are available for rent here.

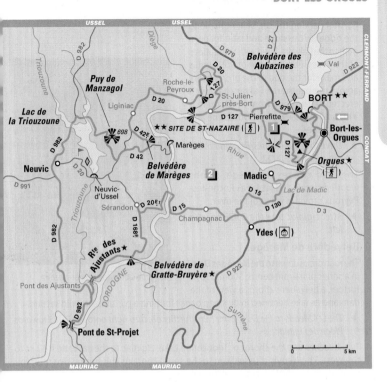

▶ *Go back to the D 127, continue for 2km/1mi until the right turn-off marked Point de vue des Orgues, and drive a short distance to the car park and picnic area on the plateau (alt 769m/2 523ft). From the parking area, there is a 15min walk there and back to the scenic overlook.*

There is a wide **panoramic view**★★ over the Dordogne Valley, the Cantal region and the Mont Dore range. To the southwest, Lake Madic lies on the former course of the Dordogne.

▶ *For the more adventurous, another path goes further along the cliff top (20min there and back; keep a close eye on children). A rock formation known as the Tête d'Homme (man's head) offers a perilous perch for a superior 360° view.*

▶ *Go back to your car and continue along the D 127 for 500m/0.3mi. A path on the left climbs to a rocky outcrop (15min round trip on foot).*

The panorama embraces the Puy de Sancy and the mountains of Cantal, the River Dordogne and its tributaries, the Monédières range and the Plateau des Mille Vaches. From the D 979, as you travel towards Bort, keep an eye out for the pretty **Pierefitte Château** on the right, and more views of the lake and dam.

② **Along the Dordogne**

Round-trip of 95km/59mi – allow one day

Here the Dordogne used to flow through narrow gorges. The dams and reservoir lakes which now succeed one another down the valley, forming a gigantic water stairway 100km/60mi long, have altered the appearance of the countryside, however they often fit remarkably well into the beautiful settings. All the same try to avoid the seasons when the waters are low and the lower, erosion-worn slopes are visible.

▶ *Leave Bort-les-Orgues on the D 922 heading N then turn left onto the D 979.*

Belvédère des Aubazines

This viewpoint situated on the right side of the D 979 (picnic area) offers a view of the dam and its 1 400ha/3 460-acre lake.

▶ *Continue along the D 979 and turn left onto the D 127 2km/1.2mi further on.*

Saint-Nazaire Site★★

30min round trip on foot.

After parking the car, bear right along the ridge on the slope and later follow a path to the Calvaire, lined with the Stations of the Cross. Pass a statue of St Nazarius and make for the end of the promontory across the heather. A Calvary has been erected on the point from which there is a magnificent view of the Dordogne and Diège gorges.

▶ *Drive to St-Julien-près-Bort and continue along the D 127.*

The road crosses the Diège, climbs wooded slopes and, as far as Roche-les-Peyroux provides views of the river.

▶ *After Liginiac take the D 42E on your left.*

Along the Dordogne near St-Nazaire

Belvédère de Marèges

The road drops down to the **Marèges Dam** in a series of hairpin bends; 500m/550yd further, a belvedere affords a view of the dam and its lake hemmed in by steep banks forming a picturesque wild setting.

▶ *The D 42 leads to the D 20; 2km/1.2mi further on, turn right onto the D 183 towards Plage de Liginiac.*

Two beaches line the shores of Triouzoune Lake: Liginiac to the east and Neuvic to the west. The Neuvic d'Ussel Dam to the south contains this impressive reservoir covering 410ha/1 013 acres, ideal for water sports enthusiasts.

Puy de Manzagol

Alt 698m/2 290ft. From the summit (*viewing table*) there is a vast panorama of the Triouzoune Lake and the Massif Central.

▶ *The D 183 and then the D 982 on the left skirt the beautiful lake.*

Neuvic

This attractive resort, built on the hillside has a beach with a sailing school and a centre for water skiing. The village has retained its narrow streets lined with granite houses, its fortified gate and its church with a characteristic belfry-porch.

Musée de la Résistance Henri-Queuille – ⏲ *Open May-Oct, 10am-noon and 3-6pm; Nov-Apr, by prior arrangement.* ⊜*3€ (-12 years old: no charge).* ☎ *05 55 95 96 87.* This museum is dedicated to the Resistance movement in Corrèze where, in 1944, fierce fighting prepared the way for the liberation of the region.

Maison de l'Eau et de la Pêche - *Next to the church.* ⏲ *Open May to mid-Sep, daily except Sun, 10am-noon and 2-6pm; mid-Sep to Apr, daily except Sun and Mon, 10am-noon and 2-5pm.* ⏲ *Closed public hols (except 1 May).* ⊜ *2.30€.* ☎ *05 55 95 06 76. Near the church.* This information centre presents an exhibition devoted to fishing methods, water treatment and fish species that are commonly found in rivers. Excursions are organised on the themes of fishing and nature.

▶ *Drive S out of Neuvic along the D 982 towards Mauriac.*

Pont de St-Projet

This suspension bridge provides a good view of the reservoir.

▶ *Turn back and follow the D 168.*

Route des Ajustants★

The Ajustants Tourist Road follows the Dordogne Valley with its rock-strewn wooded slopes, providing beautiful views of the L'Aigle reservoir with its indented shoreline.

Belvédère de Gratte-Bruyère★

This is a magnificent viewpoint (*picnic area*) from which to see the Sumène flowing into the Dordogne.

▶ *Shortly before Sérandon, turn right onto the D 20E1.*

Ydes

This small village lies on the banks of the Sumène, in an area dotted with basalt peaks. The 12C church is typical of the Haute-Auvergne Romanesque style; the east end is decorated with carved modillions representing lively young faces. Note the interesting carvings adorning the west porch.

Insects of the World exhibition – *Entrance behind the town hall.* ♿ ◷ *Open Jul–Aug, 2–7pm.* ☞*3€.* ☎ *04 71 40 82 51.* ▥ This exhibition is mainly devoted to butterflies and moths. Note the size and colours of some of the remarkable specimens on display.

▶ *Return to the D 15 then bear left onto the D 130.*

Madic

This attractive village is the starting point of a pleasant walk round the lake of the same name.

▶ *The D 30 and the D 922 lead back to Bort-les-Orgues.*

Château de BOUGES★★

MICHELIN LOCAL MAP 323: G-4 – 10KM/6.2MI NE OF LEVROUX

Set in the heart of the Berry-Champagne region, this 18C château was built in the Italian style on the site of a former stronghold. Because of the arrangement of its pediments and façades, it closely resembles the Petit Trianon at Versailles.

Visit

◷ ☛ *Guided tour (45min) Jul–Aug at 11am, noon, 2.30pm, 3.30pm, 4.30pm and 5.30pm; Apr–Jun and Sep–Oct, daily except Tue at 11am, 2.30pm, 3.30pm and 4.30pm; Mar and Nov, Sat–Sun and public hols at 11am, 2.30pm and 3.30pm.* ◷ *Closed 1 May.* ☞*6.10€ (guided tours), 7.60€ (full visit, including kitchen and bathrooms).* ☎ *02 54 35 88 26.*

The château contains an interesting collection of 18C **furniture**★, particularly sofas and chairs (many of the pieces bear the marks of famous cabinetmakers), which was patiently assembled by the previous owners. Note in particular the small Louis XV salon, the games room with its fine furniture, the drawing room with its marble chimney-piece and astronomical clock, and the charming Louis XVI bedroom.

The outbuildings are vast edifices with tall mansard roofs and include fine stables with a **harness room** containing an important collection of saddles, harnesses and riding boots. In the wing set at right angles, there are several horse drawn carriages dating from the beginning of the 20C.

French style gardens and a 80ha/198-acre **park**★ planted with a variety of fine trees and with a pond bring the visit to an end.

BOURDEILLES★

POPULATION 777

MICHELIN LOCAL MAP 329: E-4

The impressive castle of Bourdeilles, with the village clustered at its foot, stands imperiously above the River Dronne. It was here that the famous chronicler, Brantôme, was born in 1540.

☻ **Don't Miss**: The village's medieval and Renaissance châteaux.

◷ **Organising Your Time**: Allow a couple of hours to explore the churches of the Boulou Valley.

A Bit of History

A coveted spot – In 1259 St Louis ceded Périgord and Bourdeilles, his most important barony, to the English. This incredible desertion made the country rise in revolt and divided the Bourdeille family: the elder branch supported the Plantagenets, and the Maumonts, the younger branch, the Capetians. A while later, after plots and lawsuits,

Géraud de Maumont, Counsellor to King Philip the Fair, who urged him on, seized the castle of his forebears. He turned it into a fortress. Then, to show his strength in Périgord, Philip the Fair set up a strong garrison within the fief of his enemies, the English.

The Renaissance touch – Credit for the plans for the 16C château must go to Jacquette de Montbron, wife of André de Bourdeille and sister-in-law to Pierre de Brantôme, with her active and informed interest in geometry and architecture.

Building was started in haste at the promise of a visit by Catherine de' Medici, but was abandoned when the visit was cancelled.

Visit

Château★

○*Open Jul-Aug,* ⟜ *guided tour (1hr) 10am-7pm; Apr-Jun, Sep to mid-Nov and Christmas hols, daily except Tue, 10am-12.30pm and 2-6pm; mid-nov to Mar, daily except Tue, Fri and Sat, 10am-12.30pm and 2-5.30pm.* ○ *Closed Jan and 25 Dec.* ⊜*5€.* ☎ *05 53 03 73 36.*

Cross the first fortified curtain wall, pass under the watch-path to get inside the second wall and enter the outer courtyard, in which there is a fine cedar.

Medieval castle – The 13C castle, built by Géraud de Maumont on older foundations, is an austere building surrounded by a quadrangular curtain wall. Inside the main building, exhibitions are held in a great hall. A 35m/115ft-high keep dating from the early 14C, with 2.4m/7ft-thick walls, towers above it. From the upper platform there is a good overall **view** of the castle and a sweeping, bird's-eye view of the River Dronne and the Renaissance castle.

Renaissance château – Sober and elegant in appearance, the 16C château houses remarkable **furnishings**★★ collected by two patrons who donated their collection to the Dordogne *département*. Displayed on three floors, they include more than 700 tables, credences, tapestries, armchairs, low-relief sculptures, paintings, weapons, chests, carpets.

Do not miss the **salon doré**★★, a sumptuously decorated room built to accommodate Catherine de' Medici, and above all the dining hall with its 16C carved **chimney-piece**★★★ decorated with palm leaves.

Emperor Charles V's bedroom

Éditions René, Marsac-sur-l'Isle

From the watch-path there is a lovely **view**⋆ of the castle and its setting, a Gothic bridge with cutwaters and a very attractive 17C seigneurial mill surrounded by the green waters of the River Dronne.

Excursions

Churches of the Boulou Valley

Round trip of 22km/14mi – allow 2hr

▶ *Leave Bourdeilles N on the D 106E2 towards Brantôme. Pass the rock formation known as the Forge du Diable (Devil's Forge), and take a small road on the left.*

St-Julien-de-Bourdeilles

In this modest hamlet is a small Gothic church with two lovely statues in polychrome wood and parts of a 17C altarpiece.

▶ *Continue N to Boulouneix.*

Boulouneix

A Romanesque chapel with a domed bell-tower stands in the middle of a cemetery. In the chancel, 17C mural paintings represent Mary Magdalene and St Jerome. The façade with two storeys of arcades is of Saintonge influence.

▶ *About 100m/109yd after the church, bear left towards Au Bernard.*

The road descends through the woods (hornbeam and filbert) to the marshy Boulou Valley. Numerous prehistoric sites have been discovered in the region.

Paussac-et-St-Vivien

Several 16C houses and a 13C-15C fortified church are of interest in this village. The church's defensive areas, built above the three domes covering the nave and chancel, can still be seen. The south wall is decorated with arcades. Inside, note the capitals decorated in low relief with naïve carvings, a large Christ in polychrome wood and a Louis XV-style pulpit.

▶ *Take the C 2 towards Brantôme; at Les Guichards turn right towards Les Chauses, leaving the road to Puy-Fromage on the left.*

From the road you will soon see Bourdeilles and its tall keep.

BOURGES ★★★

POPULATION 72 480

MICHELIN LOCAL MAP 323: K-4

From whichever direction you approach the city, the magnificent cathedral, classified by UNESCO as a World Heritage Monument, soars above the Berry-Champagne countryside, a striking symbol of Bourges' rich medieval past. Built on the slopes of a hill, the city is dissected by the waters of the Yèvre and Auron and a network of rivers and marshes. The commercial and industrial centre of the Berry, the city is the capital of the Cher *département*. ⧉ *21 r. Victor-Hugo (près de la cathédrale), 18000 Bourges, ☎ 02 48 23 02 60. www.ville-bourges.fr.*

▶ **Orient Yourself**: The city's tourist train provides a good introduction to the city. For a wonderful view of Bourges and its surrounding countryside, climb the 396 steps to the top of the cathedral's north tower.

🅿 **Parking**: There are several car parks dotted around the city (👍 *see city plan*).

☺ **Don't Miss**: Cathédrale St-Étienne; Palais Jacques-Cœur; Hôtel Estève; Les Marais.

▦ **Especially for Kids**: Muséum d'Histoire Naturelle and Musée de l'Homme.

A Bit of History

One of the loveliest towns in Gaul – Avaricum, town of abundant water, made its mark in history in 52 BC, during the tumultuous Gallic wars. The Bituriges, a powerful Celtic people (who gave their name to the town), took part in the resistance to Roman occupation. The celebrated warrior Vercingétorix had adopted a scorched-earth policy, destroying town and field before the invading army's advance. When he arrived in Bourges, the denizens begged him to leave their dwellings intact, and assured him that the town could never be taken, thanks to its strategic location atop a hill surrounded by rivers and marshland. Exception was made, Caesar's legions attacked, and the town, despite its bravest efforts, fell. Caesar estimated the population at 40 000: all were massacred. After a few days rest, the sated soldiers of the Roman empire moved on, leaving the shell of the looted, desolate city behind them.

Caesar reported that the town was "one of the loveliest in Gaul"; archaeological research has revealed that it was a busy iron craft and trade centre, but little is known of how it appeared before its defeat.

Bourges under Roman rule – Avaricum set about healing its wounds and once again rose to prominence as a capital city and trade centre. Prosperous and attractive, the town spread to the surrounding hillsides and monuments were erected. Digs have uncovered a 2C fountain and a monumental gateway which extended over 75m/80yd at the foot of the hill; they probably bordered a commercial avenue. The town boasted a vast amphitheatre, a river port with harbour and wharves, and necropolises on the outskirts.

Jean de Berry: a patron of the arts – The young duke, Jean de Berry, third son of King John the Good of France, made Bourges the capital of his duchy and a centre of the arts of utmost importance. From 1360 to 1416 the Duke, an inspired lover of the arts, spent a fortune as, with mad prodigality, he commissioned work from painters, illuminators such as Pol de Limbourg, the author of the Très Riches Heures (The Rich Hours), now to be seen in the Chantilly Museum, and Jacquemart de Hesdin, the author of the *Très Belles Heures* (The Beautiful Hours).

"A vaillans cœurs, riens impossible" – "To a valiant heart, nothing is impossible" was the motto of **Jacques Cœur**, Master of the Mint to King Charles VII of France at a time when that kingdom was largely occupied by the English.

This man of humble origin, son of a furrier, had an extraordinary life: amazingly gifted in commerce and trade, he soon made a colossal fortune. He armed merchantmen with the idea of seizing the markets of the eastern Mediterranean from the traders of Genoa and Venice; he set up counting-houses in Marseille and Montpellier, and bought houses and land; from being the man in charge of the finances of Bourges, he became, in 1442, counsellor to Charles VII and principal emissary for the kingdom's expansion of trade; finally he built a magnificent palace at Bourges, though he was to see little of it. Hated by many courtiers who were jealous of his political and diplomatic

BOURGES

Anatole-France Cours	YZ		Dr-Témoin R. du	Y	17	Mirebeau R.	Y	
Arènes R. des	YZ		Dolet Pl. Étienne	Z		Moyenne R.	YZ	
Armuriers R. des	Z	2	Dormoy Av. Marx	Y	19	Nation Pl. de la	Y	
Auron Bd d'	Z		Ducrot Av.	Z		Orléans Av. d'	Y	48
Avaricum Cours	Y		Équerre R. de l'	Z	20	Pelvoysin R.	Y	50
Baffier R. J.	Z		Fernault R.	Z		Poissonnerie R. de la	Y	52
Barbès R.	Z	4	Gambetta Bd	Y		Porte-Jaune R.	YZ	
Bardoux Pl. A.	Z		Gambon R.	Y		Poulies R. des	Y	
Beauvoir Cours	Y		George-Sand Escalier	Y	27	Prinal R. du	Y	55
Beaux-Arts R. des	Y	5	Gordaine Pl.			Rabelais Pl.	Y	
Berry Pl. du	Y		Hémerettes R. des	Z	29	République Bd de la	Y	
Bourbonnoux Prom.	YZ		J.-J. Rousseau R.	Z	33	Rimbault R. J.	Z	61
Branly R. É.	Y		Jacobins Cour des	Z	31	Sarrebourg R. de	Z	
Brisson Av. É.	Z		Jacques-Coeur R.	Y	32	Séraucourt Pl.	Z	
Calvin R.	Y	7	Jean-Jaurès Av.	Y		Séraucourt R. de	Z	
Cambournac R.	Y	8	Joyeuse R.	Y	35	Strasbourg Bd de	Y	71
Champ-de-Foire R. du	Z	12	Juranville Bd de	YZ		Thaumassière R. de la	Y	72
Chanzy Bd du Gén.	Y		Juranville Pl.	Z	36	Tory R. G.	Y	73
Chappe R. de la	Z		Lamarck Bd	Z		Vaillant R. Édouard	Y	
Clemenceau Bd	Y		Leblanc R. N.	YZ	40	Verdun Carref. de	Y	
Commerce R. du	Y	13	Linières R. de	Z	42	Victor-Hugo R.	Z	74
Cordeliers R. des	Z		Littré R.	Y		11-Novembre 1918 Av. du	Y	
Coursarlon R.	Y		Louis XI Av.	Z	43	3-Maillets R. des	Y	75
Cujas Pl.	Y	15	Mallet R. L.	Z	44	4-Piliers Pl. des	Z	76
Decouvoux Pl. Ph.	Y		Malraux Pl. André	Z		8-Mai-1945 Pl. du	Z	
			Marceau Rampe	Z	45	95e-de-Ligne av. du	Z	78

Cathédrale St-Étienne	Z		Jardin des Prés-Fichaux	Y
Digue de l'Yèvre	Y		Jardins de l'Archevêché	Z
Grange aux Dîmes	Z B		Les Marais	Y
Hôtel Cujas -			Maison de Pelvoysin	Y L
Musée du Berry	Y M¹		Maison dite	
Hôtel Lallemant -Musée des			"de Jacques-Coeur "	Z E
Arts décoratifs	Y M³		Musée des Meilleurs	
Hôtel des Échevins -			Ouvriers de France	Z M⁵
Musée Estève	Y M²			

Muséum d'Histoire naturelle — Z
Palais Jacques-Coeur — Y
Préfecture — Z P
Rempart gallo-romain — YZ Q
Église Notre-Dame — Y
Église St-Bonnet — Y
Église St-Pierre-le-Guillard — Z

offices, the honours he had bestowed upon him and the king's favour, he fell into disgrace, a victim of his own advancement. He was arrested in 1451 and condemned to perpetual banishment, confiscation of all his property and a heavy fine.

But this was not the end for Jacques Cœur: he escaped from prison, sought refuge in Rome and was given command by the Pope of a fleet of ships. It was while he was on the Ninth Crusade to liberate the Christian islands in the Greek archipelago, that he died in 1456 in Chios.

The university, a cradle of new ideas – The town of Bourges owes the foundation of its university in 1463 to Charles de Berry, Louis XI's brother. Its influence spread far beyond the duchy for over a century. The law school under such masters as Alciat (1529-33) and Cujas (1559-66) attracted many students some even from abroad. It was thus that German students coming from Heidelberg brought with them the new doctrines of Luther: Calvin, at that time a student at Bourges, learnt these new theories and began to form the outlines of the principles he was later to publish in his *Institutes of the Christian Religion*. His ideas on reforming the Church found many adherents and, in spite of persecution, soon gained support in Bourges and throughout Berry.

The duchy was thus divided and became a battlefield during the period of the Wars of Religion; the prosperity of the city, which had been much reduced by a terrible fire in 1487 which destroyed two-thirds of the town, came to an end.

Decline and expansion – By the mid-17C, Berry was in a sort of stupor which lasted two more centuries. Off the main routes, it was by-passed while towns like Tours and Orleans, on the River Loire, underwent economic expansion. The bourgeoisie were not drawn into industry and trade, as elsewhere, but lived lives circumscribed by regional politics and religion. As convents and churches proliferated, and the aristocracy grew poorer, Bourges gained a deplorable reputation as a lacklustre backwater.

The construction of the Berry canal (1819-42), the railway and the establishment of the armaments industry in Bourges under the Second Empire breathed new economic life into the region.

Since the end of the Second World War, Bourges has expanded rapidly. Many industries have arrived, creating thousands of jobs and the A 71 motorway has contributed to the lively dynamics of the town today.

A city of music – The cultural influence of Bourges is far greater than its small size might suggest. The capital of Berry is home to an unparalleled Maison de la Culture, a national music academy and a fine arts school reputed for mastery of earthenware techniques. The renowned musical festival, **le Printemps de Bourges**, is a yearly event drawing crowds of young fans of popular music.

Cathédrale St-Etienne★★★

The vigour of the architecture, the harmony of proportion and the richness of the decoration make one marvel before this cathedral.

Construction took place in two stages. From 1195 to 1215, the chevet and the chancel were built. The lower church had to be built outside the fortifications standing at that time, for lack of space within. The second stage, which lasted 35 years (1225-60), concerned the nave, the west front, the historiated stained-glass windows, the carvings decorating the doorways and the rood screen. The cathedral was consecrated on 13 May 1324.

Additions and restorations – The southern tower was consolidated during the 14C by a construction linked to the tower by a reinforced arcade known as the *pilier butant* – the buttress pile. Once the west front had been remodelled, it was possible to install the great window above the central door. The chapels between the buttresses were built in the 15C.

East end of Bourges Cathedral

S. Sauvignier/MICHELIN

Address Book

TOURIST INFORMATION

Guided tours – 🔍 Bourges, which has been officially designated as a *"ville d'art et d'histoire"*, offers guided tours (1hr 30min/2hr) with qualified local guides. *For information, contact the tourist office (☎ 02 48 23 02 60) or log onto www. bourges-tourisme.com*

P'tit train touristique – The city's tourist train provides a 45min overview of the city's history and architecture. Operates daily, Apr to early-Nov (departures every 15min from the tourist office). *For information, call ☎ 06 08 60 54 56.*

For coin ranges, see the Legend at the back of the guide.

EATING OUT

🍽 **Le Bourbonnoux** – *44 r. Bourbonnoux - ☎ 02 48 24 14 76 - restaurant. bourbonnoux@wanadoo.fr -* 🕐 *closed 11-21 Feb, 16-26 Apr, 16 Aug-3 Sep, Sun eve Nov-Jun, Sat lunchtime and Fri.* The restaurant is in a street lined with craft shops, just a few steps away from St-Étienne Cathedral. The welcome is warm and the dining room is pleasantly decorated with bright colours and exposed beams. Popular with locals.

🍽 **Le Bistro Gourmand** – *5 pl. de la Barre - ☎ 02 48 70 63 37 - reserv. recommended.* A delightful bistro specialising in regional and Lyonnais cuisine. The sober decor here is enhanced by gentle candlelight. The terrace looks onto the Église Notre-Dame.

🍽 **La Table Savoyarde** – *14 r. Florentin-Labbé - ☎ 02 48 24 57 94 -* 🕐 *closed the first 3 weeks in Aug, Sun lunchtime and Mon.* As the name suggests, the focus here is on the cuisine of Savoy, with a menu that includes cheese fondues, raclettes, tartiflettes etc. Wooden skis, clogs, cow bells and other typically Savoyard objects adorn the cool stone vaults of this former coal cellar.

🍽 **La Courcillière** – *R. de Babylone - ☎ 02 48 24 41 91 -* 🕐 *closed Wed, Sun eve and Tue eve.* Located in the Les Marais district just a stone's throw from the city centre, this pleasant, rustic restaurant has a terrace by the water facing the gardens. Down-to-earth and reasonably priced cuisine.

🍽 **D'Antan Sancerrois** – *50 r. Bourbounnoux - ☎ 02 48 65 96 26 -* 🕐 *closed 1-20 Aug, Christmas-1 Jan, Sun and Mon.* This pretty bistro used to be home to a 15C alderman who kept company with the Duchesse de Berry. The handsome rustic decor features an amusing collection of porcelain tureen lids. Traditional fare and good service.

WHERE TO STAY

🛏 **Chambre d'hôte Château de Bel Air** – *Lieu-dit le Grand-Chemin - 18340 Arcay - 16km/10mi S of Bourges on the D 73 - ☎ 02 48 25 36 72 -* 🕐 *open all year -* 🚭 *- 6 rooms.* Surrounded by spacious grounds, this 19C château is both calm and comfortable. The vast entrance hall leads to the dining room with its massive fireplace. Large rooms on the upper floor. Mountain bikes available for rent.

🛏 **Hôtel Christina** – *5 r. Halle - ☎ 02 48 70 56 50 - info@le-christina.com - 71 rooms.* This hotel is the perfect base for discovering the city centre. Two categories of well-maintained bedrooms are available: cosy and chic, or smaller and functional.

🛏 **Hôtel Les Tilleuls** – *7 pl. Pyrotechnie - ☎ 02 48 20 49 04 - lestilleuls.bourges@ wanadoo.fr -* 🅿 *- 39 rooms.* Situated in a quiet part of town, this hotel offers guests accommodation in the main building and an annex, where the rooms are less spacious, more basic, but with the benefit of air-conditioning. Children's play area in the garden. Solarium.

🛏 **Best Western Hôtel d'Angleterre** – *1 pl. des Quatre-Piliers - ☎ 02 48 24 68 51 -* 🕐 *closed 24 Dec-1 Jan -* 🅿 *- 30 rooms.* The city's former court of justice is located close to the Palais Jacques-Cœur. All necessary creature comforts in the bedrooms (most with air-conditioning), where the decor is sober yet modern. Buffet breakfast. Friendly staff.

BARS AND CAFÉS

Pub des Jacobins – *Enclos des Jacobins - ☎ 02 48 24 61 78 -* 🕐 *open Mon-Sat, 4pm-3am -* 🕐 *closed Sun.* This piano-bar is whole-heartedly devoted to jazz, as demonstrated by the photos of musicians covering the walls. Top-quality concerts are held here once a month. The pub specialises in cocktails.

Pub Jacques Cœur – *1 r. d'Auron - ☎ 02 48 70 72 88 -* 🕐 *open Mon-Sat, 10am-2am -* 🕐 *closed Sun.* This 16C half-timbered residence, now a pub, was built on the site where Jacques Cœur, a wealthy and influential 15C merchant and councillor to King Charles VII, was born. Sloping and lopsided, this antique building is the most photographed of Bourges. Concerts are frequently held here.

ENTERTAINMENT

Maison de la Culture de Bourges – *Pl. André-Malraux - ☎ 02 48 67 74 70 - www. mcbourges.com -* 🕐 *ticket office open Tue-Sat, 2-7pm -* 🕐 *closed 13 Jul-20 Aug and 1 May - ticket prices* 🎫. Opened by André Malraux, then Minister of Culture, this was the first Maison de la Culture in France. This lively and popular venue hosts plays, dance performances and classical music and jazz concerts. Cinema and café.

Les Nuits Lumières de Bourges – ☎ 02 48 23 02 60 - ⏰ *Every evening in Jul-Aug and during the Printemps de Bourges festival; May-Jun and Sep: Thu-Sat. No charge.* A walk through the historic city centre at night to view illuminated buildings (2hr 30min). Blue lanterns mark the way.

LEISURE ACTIVITIES

Base de Voile du Val-d'Auron – *23 chemin Grand Mazières* - ☎ 02 48 20 07 65. ⏰ *Open 9am-noon and 2-6pm.* ⏰ *Closed Oct-Apr and Mon.* This watersports centre at the Val d'Auron Lake covering 85 ha/210 acres offers a range of activities, including swimming, canoeing, fishing and rowing.

SHOPPING

The main shopping area is in the pedestrianised area that includes rue Coursarlor and rue Mirebeau (near the palais Jacques-Cœur), and rue Bourbonnoux and rue Moyenne (near the cathedral).

Markets – Every Saturday morning, the listed Halle au Blé comes to life with 200 stallholders selling all types of food. A permanent daily market is also held at the *Halle St-Bonnet* (⏰ open 7.30am-1pm and 3-7.30pm), selling fresh seasonal produce, local cheeses and other regional specialities. On Sunday mornings, stalls selling bric-a-brac, inexpensive clothes etc add to the charm of this popular market.

La Maison des Forestines – *3 pl. Cujas* - ☎ 02 48 24 00 24 - mdforestines@wanadoo.fr - ⏰ *open Mon, 3-7pm; Tue-Sat 9.30am-12.15pm and 2-7.15pm.* This chocolate/confectionery business founded in 1825 occupies an attractive Haussmann-style building. The shop, with its coffered ceiling and superb Gien china, produces irresistible house specialities such as the *Forestine*, a chocolate praline with a satiny sugar coating created in 1879, the *Amandine* and *Noisette* (created in 1885) and the *Richelieu*, a nougatine filled with an almond and pistachio creme, created in 1890.

Domaine de Coquin – ☎ 02 48 64 84 51 - ⏰ *open Mon-Fri, 8am-7pm, Sun and public hols, 9am-noon.* Francis Audiot is a wine-producer whose family has been producing excellent white wines for the past 150 years.

Épicerie du Berry – *41 r. Moyenne (îlot Victor-Hugo)* - ☎ 02 48 70 02 38. This small boutique at the foot of the cathedral only sells regional products such as *sablés de Nançais* (a type of shortcake biscuit), pasta from La Chapelle de St-Ursin, *tortillons* (goat's cheese pastries) and Monin syrups.

Misfortune came with the 16C; in 1506 the north tower collapsed and had to be entirely rebuilt; in 1562 a Protestant army pillaged the cathedral and destroyed the magnificent statues that adorned the west front; 200 years later the canons decided to remove the rood screen and the 18 stained-glass windows in the chancel. Restoration was undertaken during the 19C but much of it was unfortunate as balustrades, bell-towers and pinnacles were added to the building. During the 20C, pollution became the major threat and a preservation campaign was launched to fight this chemical enemy which destroys stone carvings.

Exterior

West front – Five **doorways** beneath individual gables stand in a line beneath the great stained-glass window, known as the *grand housteau* – the great western gable. The asymmetry of the doorways gives an impression of originality and great variety. A frieze of 62 low-relief sculptures runs between two lines of niches from left to right and depicts the life of Christ.

The theme of the **central doorway** is the Last Judgement. Great vitality and realism make the doorway one of the masterpieces of 13C Gothic sculpture.

The tympanum of **St Stephen's doorway** is devoted to episodes in the life and the martyrdom of St Stephen, patron of the cathedral.

The story of St Ursinus, the first bishop of Bourges, and of St Justus is depicted on the tympanum of **St Ursinus' doorway**.

The **Virgin's doorway** and **St Guillaume's doorway** (showing the archbishop of Bourges receiving offerings for the building of the cathedral) had to be partly rebuilt after the collapse of the north tower in the 16C.

Two **towers** of unequal height frame the five doorways. On the right, the so-called Deaf Tower (*Tour Sourde* – because no bell was hung), never completed, is architecturally more sober in style than the flamboyantly decorated Butter Tower on the left (*Tour de Beurre* – perhaps an allusion to the exemptions purchased by the faithful who preferred to continue to enjoy butter and cream during Lent, which helped to pay for the tower's construction).

▶ *Go round the cathedral by the north.*

North side – It is embellished by a 12C **doorway** which was incorporated in the present cathedral. The lintel is adorned with a frieze of flowers and foliage. On the tympanum are scenes from the life of the Virgin.

East end – The chevet is original in having little turrets above the radial chapels. The outline is harmonious and the double flying buttresses built above it add to its grace.

South side – This side is adorned with a 13C **doorway**. Christ appears in majesty on the tympanum, surrounded by the symbols of the Evangelists; angels and the prophets and kings of the Old Testament crowd the covings.

▶ *Enter the cathedral by the south doorway.*

Interior

Nave – St Stephen's Cathedral, which is 124m/407ft long, 41m/135ft wide and 37m/121ft high to the top of the inner vaulting, is one of the largest Gothic cathedrals in France (Gloucester Cathedral is 128m/420ft long and 44m/144ft wide). There are no transepts and this gives the nave with its four side aisles a feeling of greater majesty; the five aisles correspond to the five doorways.

The columns of the nave rise in a single thrust to a height of 17m/56ft and they are encircled by groups of smaller columns, some of which reach the vaulting. To extend the perspective the architect slightly increased the distance between the pillars in the chancel.

The building is original in having double side aisles of different height with windows on two levels; the five bands of light and shade thus created within the cathedral considerably enhance the architectural effect (*see cross section*).

A double ambulatory continues the line of the twin aisles. Five small radial chapels, each semicircular in shape, open on to the apse.

▶ *Turn right and enter the chancel via the second south aisle.*

Chapelle St-Jean-Baptiste – This chapel contains two beautiful frescoes dating from the late 1460s, depicting the Crucifixion and the Resurrection.

Chapelle des Tullier – The chapel is lit by fine Renaissance windows by Lescuyer.

Stained-glass windows★★★ – Although they have incurred some damage over the years, the collection of stained-glass windows in the cathedral is one of the most remarkable in France, dating from the 12C to the 17C. Apart from their striking colours, they illustrate the powerful narratives of Christianity in medieval France.

The five apsidal chapels and the windows between them are adorned with windows shaped to fit the architecture, and medallion windows, most of which were made between 1215 and 1225.

The works, donated by trade guilds (note the distinguishing medallions representing carpenters, barrel-makers and wheelwrights at the bottom of the window relating the story of St Joseph), are generally attributed to the three workshops under the hands of the masters whose names have not come down to us.

S. Sauvignier/MICHELIN

Joseph's dream

First the **master of the Last Judgement and the New Alliance**, employs a style both exuberant and majestic, apparent in the bodies and clothing draped over them.

The Good Samaritan master is also supposed to be the artist responsible for the execution of the intermediate windows representing the Passion and the Apocalypse, the windows of St Mary the Egyptian, St Nicholas and the martyrdom of St Stephen (radial chapels). The fanciful compositions include a variety of extravagant details.

The master of the St Stephen reliquaries illustrates some of the typical traits of Gothic representational art: over-long bodies

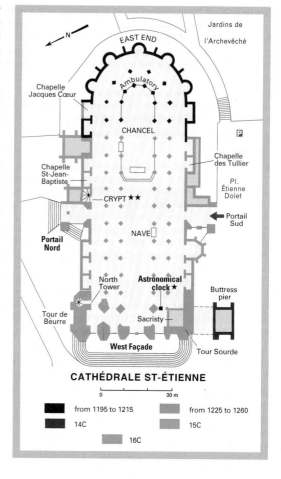

CATHÉDRALE ST-ÉTIENNE

from 1195 to 1215	from 1225 to 1260
14C	15C
16C	

on spindly legs, disproportionate heads, faces seeming to express displeasure, yet these windows are lively and evocative. The artist carried the message across through spontaneous gesture and unencumbered attitudes.

The **side chapels** (Chapelle Jacques-Cœur, Chapelle des Tullier, Chapelle St-Jean-Baptiste) illustrate three creative periods: the early 15C marked by the influence of the Duc de Berry's workshops (particularly that of André Beauneveu), the middle part of the 15C and the Renaissance.

Crypt★★ – ⏲ 🔍 *Guided tour (45min) Jul-Aug, 9.45am, 11am, 12.15pm, 2.15pm, 3.15pm, 3.45pm, 4.15pm, 5pm and 5.45pm; May-Jun, 10am, 11.15am, 2.30pm, 3.45pm and 5pm; Apr and Sep, 10.15am, 11.15am, 2.30pm, 3.45pm and 5pm; Oct-Mar, 10am, 11.15am, 2.30pm, 3.30pm and 4.30pm.* ⏲ *Closed 1 Jan, 1 May, 1 and 11 Nov, 25 Dec.* 🎫6.10€ *(-18 years old: no charge); combined ticket with the crypt, north tower and Palais Jacques-Cœur: 8.50€.* ☎ *02 48 65 49 44.* A long sloping gallery leads down to the vast late-12C crypt known as the Underground Church of the church of St-Guillaume. Twelve large windows light the sanctuary. Six massive pillars (2.10m/7ft in diameter) flanked by columns with crocheted capitals support the vaulted ceiling on diagonal ribs which, in turn, supports the cathedral above. The sturdy ribs set in five-sided formations shape counterbalanced curvatures (the same feature is seen in the ambulatory of the chancel). The marks on the floor were left there by the original building crew.

In the crypt, note the **recumbent white marble figure** of the Duke of Berry, the only vestige of a grandiose mausoleum (1422), sculpted by Jean de Cambrai. The tomb once stood in the Sainte-Chapelle at Bourges. The 14C windows of the prophets are from the same chapel. Fragments saved when the **rood screen** was destroyed in the 17C are on view. Set against the Gallo-Roman outer wall, a 16C Entombment consists of 10 statues under a canopy. Behind the sculpture, stairs lead to a little cradle-vaulted gallery, the only remains of the 11C sanctuary.

Ascent of the north tower – ⊙*Open Jul-Aug, 9.45am-6.15pm; Sep and Apr, 9.45-11.45am and 2-5.30pm; May-Jun, 9.30am-11.30am and 2-6pm; Oct-Mar, 9.30am-11.30am and 2-4.45pm.* ⊙ *Closed Sun morning, 1 Jan, 1 May, Whitmonday (morning), 15 Aug (morning), 1 and 11 Nov, 25 Dec.* ◉*4.60€ (under -18 years old: no charge).* ☏ *02 48 65 49 44.* The attempt to complete the northern tower at the end of the 15C met with catastrophe on 31 December 1506, which had an impact on the entire north-west corner.

Reconstruction lasted until 1540, carried out under the direction of architect Guillaume de Pelvoysin, who introduced new decorative elements in the Renaissance style. A spiral stair (396 steps) leads to the top (65m/213ft), where an excellent **view**★★ rewards those who venture up.

Organ – The organ case dates from 1663. The old pipes are still in place but the mechanism has been altered many times.

Astronomical clock★ – Designed by mathematician and astronomer Jean Fusoris in 1424, this magnificent clock (6.2m/20ft high) is set in a square frame, surmounted by a concave roof and a bell. The decorative elements were designed by Jean Grangier. The most remarkable aspect of this timepiece is the ingenious outfitting of the lower face, which relates astronomical data. An informed clock-watcher can get seven precise readings from the dial, six of them with one single hand. The outer dial (revolving once every 24 hours) gives the time in relation to the position of the sun. The inner ring (one revolution per month) represents the lunar cycle and indicates the number of days since the last full moon as well as the current phase of the moon. The central face (one full revolution per year) bears the 12 signs of the zodiac divided into days, thus giving the date. This disk also supports an opaque panel representing the night and a panel of golden rays symbolising the day. A sun figure moves up and down, marking its position in relation to the horizon, according to the solstices. The 12 daytime spaces indicate the current hour.

Palais Jacques-Cœur★★

⊙ ☛Guided tour (1hr). Open Jul-Aug, 9.30am-7pm; May-Jun, 9.30am-12.15pm and 2-6.15pm; Sep-Apr, 10am-12.15pm and 2-5.15pm. ⊙ Closed 1 Jan, 1 May, 1 and 11 Nov, and 25 Dec. ◉6.10€ (under17 years old: no charge). ☏ 02 48 24 79 41.

The architectural elegance, the richness and variety of decoration, make this one of the most beautiful and sumptuous secular buildings of the Gothic age. This splendid mansion was commissioned in 1443 for Charles VII's famous Master of the Mint, and was intended no doubt, as the place to which he would retire. It was completed in less than 10 years; the cost was 100 000 gold *écus*.

Jacques Cœur fell into disgrace in 1451 and so never enjoyed his completed palace. In 1457 it was restored to his heirs and from then on knew many changes of fortune. In 1679 it belonged to Colbert (statesman: 1619-83); soon afterwards it was acquired by the city of Bourges. Since 1925, when it was bought by the State, it has been completely restored.

Palais Jacques-Cœur

S. Sauvignier/MICHELIN

Exterior

Jacques Cœur's Palace consists of four main buildings round a central court. Whereas the west face, which may be seen from rue des Arènes, looks like the exterior of a fortress with massive towers and bare walls rising above the remains of the Gallo-Roman perimeter, the **east face** draws attention through the delicacy and richness of its decoration. This appears, in one instance, as a motif of hearts and shells – emblems from Jacques Cœur's coat of arms – adorning the mullioned windows of the top floor and the balustrade at the base of the eaves.

On either side of a balcony note the amusing figures of a man and a woman, the master and mistress of the house.

To the left of this wing, at the base of the octagonal staircase tower, Jacques Cœur's motto may be seen inscribed: *A vaillans cœurs, riens impossible* (To a valiant heart, nothing is impossible).

As you enter the **central court** there is a striking difference to be seen between the sober appearance of the galleries – no doubt kept for business by the Master of the Mint – and the rich decoration of the main living quarters containing the banqueting and ceremonial halls and the private apartments. Three staircase towers divide the façade. The central tower, which is hexagonal, is carved with exotic trees such as palms, oranges and dates, reminiscent of Jacques Cœur's distant travels, and bears another of the master's well known mottoes: *Dire, Faire, Taire* (Speak, Act, Be Silent).

Jacques, ever-valiant

S. Sauvignier/MICHELIN

Interior

A tour of the palace gives an idea of the luxury to which a wealthy burgher with a taste for beautiful things and practical sense could aspire.

On the ground floor, the taste for luxury produced the magnificence of the **dining hall** with its monumental chimney-piece (restored in the 19C) and a loggia to accommodate musicians; the practical sense comes out in the installation of running water, a **boiler room** and **bathroom** and the planning of staircases and corridors so that those wishing to take a bath could do so without going outside to adjoining buildings. Interesting architectural details may be seen in different parts of the buildings: armorial bearings, high and low-relief sculptures and bosses.

Of particular interest on the first floor are the **Salle des échevins** decorated with 17C murals depicting rural and hunting scenes, the **Treasury** which has a heavy iron door closed with a secret lock, the **Attic** with its wooden vaulting in the shape of an inverted boat keel, the **Reception hall** where Duke Jean's tomb has been reconstructed, the **Council chamber** which houses a model of the original palace, the **Galleries** where Jacques Cœur used to receive the town's merchants (note the two elaborately decorated fireplaces in the south gallery) and finally the **Chapel**; the two oratory chapels, contained within the thickness of the north and south walls on either side of the altar, could be heated and were probably used by Jacques Cœur and his wife.

Walking Tour of Old Town

The whole town centre comes under a preservation and renovation scheme which aims at restoring the **half-timbered houses**★ (many date from the 15C and 16C) to their former glory. The old district lying north of the cathedral offers a particularly pleasant stroll.

Jardins de l'Archevêché★

Designed in the 17C and extended in the 18C, these gardens feature splendid flower beds, fine shaded alleyways, ornamental ponds, bronze vases and a bandstand. From the garden's beautiful flower beds and shaded alleys, there is a good view of St Stephen's Cathedral, particularly of the great nave and chevet.

Place Étienne-Dolet

As you walk across the square, note on your left the façade of the former **archbishop's residence** which now houses the Musée des Meilleurs Ouvriers de France (🖰 *see below*). Walk the length of the **cathedral**★★★ and admire the successive doorways.

Grange aux Dîmes

Opposite the cathedral's north doorway at the corner of rue Molière, this massive tithe barn with its buttresses and stairway designed as a half-timbered balcony was used to store the dues paid to the church.

▷ *Take a short walk down rue des Trois-Maillets then turn left and go through a porch.*

Promenade des Remparts★

Visible in several places, the ramparts are clearly distinguished along the **Promenade des Remparts** behind and below the cathedral. Ingeniously integrated into the fabric of the contemporary town, the dressed stone wall dates back to the 3C, when it was erected for protection against barbarian invasions. Some of the façades lining this leafy walkway date from the Middle Ages (12C-15C).

▷ *Take the George Sand stairs on the left.*

This passageway, known as casse-cou (breakneck) – one understands why on rainy days – runs through the ramparts and leads to place George-Sand. Cross **rue Porte-Jaune** and admire the massive cathedral towers on your left. Next, rue St-Michel-de-Bourges leads into the town centre's high street; note **Louis XI's statue** near the neo-Gothic post office dating from 1926.

▷ *Follow rue Moyenne and turn right onto rue Mayet-Genetry.*

The lovely **Fontaine Bourdaloue** adorns place de la Préfecture.

▷ *Walk along rue des Armuriers.*

Jacques Cœur's "Birthplace"

A half-timbered, corbelled house, standing at the corner of rue d'Auron and rue des Armuriers, bears an inscription describing it as the house in which Jacques Cœur was born (c 1395-1456). In fact it was built early in the 16C on the site of a house which came to Jacques Cœur through his marriage.

▷ *Follow rue d'Auron and turn right onto rue des Arènes.*

Église St-Pierre-le-Guillard

According to legend, funds for building the church were provided by the Jew, Zacharie Guillard, whose mule knelt before the Holy Sacrament as it was being carried by St Antony of Padua through Bourges in about 1225.

A massive belfry-porch leads to the nave flanked by side aisles to which chapels were added in the 15C. The sexpartite vaulting of the nave rests on crocheted capitals above slim columns.

▷ *Continue along rue des Arènes then turn right.*

Rue des Linières

This steep street is paved with attractive cobblestones.

Place des Quatre-Piliers

Three splendid 17C and 18C mansions, Hôtel Témoin (the former library), Hôtel Bengy and Hôtel Méloizes, overshadow the fountain decorating the square.

▷ *Follow rue Jacques-Cœur.*

Palais Jacques-Cœur★★

Walk to place Jacques-Cœur to admire Jacques Cœur's statue and the remarkable façade of his mansion, restored in 1998, which reveals the elegance and wealth of decoration of this 15C residence (⚭ *see above*).

▷ *Retrace your steps and go down some stairs on your right, leading to the lower part of town.*

Place du Berry

Facing you is the west front of Palais Jacques-Cœur built on the remains of the Gallo-Roman ramparts: it looks like a fortress flanked with massive towers… a strange contrast with what you saw higher up!

▷ *Walk along rue des Arènes towards the Palais de Justice.*

Hôtel Cujas★

This elegant building was designed in about 1515 by Guillaume Pelvoysin for Durando Salvi, a rich Florentine merchant who had settled in Bourges. The famous jurist Cujas bought the mansion and finally died there in 1590. Since 1891 it has been owned by the city which uses it to house the Berry Museum (⚭ *see Sights*).

▷ *Walk across place Planchat to rue Pelvoysin.*

Maison de Pelvoysin

An interesting group of old, half-timbered houses stand at the corner of rue Pelvoysin and rue Cambournac. Next to these is the house of Pelvoysin, the cathedral architect. It is built of stone and now houses the savings bank. The street was so narrow when it was being built, that the architect designed the front to stand at an angle to the street thus giving the house an appearance of greater width and dignity. Inside there is a fine chimney-piece. The courtyard can best be seen from rue Cambournac.

Église Notre-Dame

The church was almost entirely gutted by the fire of 1487 which destroyed two-thirds of the town. When it was rebuilt many modifications were made to the original plan including the addition of side aisles and the square tower which rises at the north end of the west front. The church is therefore a mixture of styles: the nave has ogive vaulting with emblazoned keystones, the south door is Renaissance and adorned with a statue of the Virgin Mary. In the south aisle, opposite the door, a **white-marble baptismal font** adorned with fleurs-de-lis bears an inscription from the *Romance of the Rose*, the French medieval poem which inspired Chaucer (and which he translated in part).

▷ *Walk across place de la Barre.*

Rue Mirebeau

This pleasant pedestrianised street is lined with timber-framed houses whose ground floor is often occupied by shops. Opposite passage casse-cou (yet another one) you can see the doorway of the former Augustine convent. Enter the courtyard to admire the trapezium-shaped cloisters.

▷ *Walk up the steep dark passage casse-cou (Mirebeau stairs); once at the top, turn right onto rue Branly.*

Hôtel des Échevins★

Formerly the town hall, this building now houses the Musée Estève. There is a striking difference in architectural style between the two parts of the building:
– the living quarters at the far end of the courtyard date from 1489 and were built in the Flamboyant Gothic style. A fine **octagonal tower**★★ juts out from the façade and, rising to a height of three storeys, contains a circular staircase which gives access to each floor. Note the arches embellished with foliated crotchets in a variety of leaf motifs which include thistle, oak, cabbage and tapering maple;
– the gallery on the left was built in 1629 by the architect Jean le Juge in the Classical style: open arcades with hanging keystones separated by Corinthian pilasters; lattice windows alternating with recesses.
This former town hall now houses the Musée Estève.

▷ *Continue along rue Branly to place Cujas then turn onto rue des Beaux-Arts.*

Rue Coursalon

There is a fine view of place Gordaine along this lively pedestrianised street. Turn right onto a narrow street with a 15C house on the corner. It leads to the elegant Hôtel Lallemant.

▷ *Return to rue Coursalon.*

Place Gordaine

Situated at the intersection of the pedestrianised streets, this flower-decked square is popular with strollers. Note the stone on which Calvin used to stand to advocate the reformation.

▷ *Turn right onto rue Bourbonnoux.*

Hôtel Lallemant★

Altered in the 17C this mansion has been converted into a museum of decorative art. The site on which it was built straddled the Roman wall of the town and certain parts of the house are on different levels.

▷ *Turn onto the street facing the Hôtel Lallemant.*

Rue Joyeuse

Note the carved-wood pillar on the street corner; it supports the Maison des Trois-Flûtes (*now a bakery*). Walk up this peaceful street lined with private mansions.

▷ *Return to rue Bourbonnoux via place Louis-Lacombe.*

If you like cobblestones, walk along rue Moncenoux then turn right onto rue de la Thaumassière.

Rue Bourbonnoux

There are many craftsmen's workshops along this former high street lined with timber-framed houses. Further along it reaches the east end of the cathedral.

▷ *A small flight of stairs located between the cathedral and the adjoining gardens takes you back to the starting point of this walk.*

Les Marais

Before you take a stroll through the town's unusual wetlands, go into Église St-Bonnet, which somehow links the historic part of the city and the rural district known as Les Marais.

Église St-Bonnet

🕐*Open Jul-Aug, 10am-noon and 2-6pm; Sep-Jun, 2-5.30pm.* Construction began in 1510, using plans by the architect Pelvoysin. The 20C was marked by the addition of two bays to the western part and a neo-Flamboyant façade.

Inside, the most remarkable features are the **stained-glass windows** by Jean Lescuyer in three chapels (one shows the Holy Women in regional Berry headdress) and a work by the 17C local painter Jean Boucher.

▷ *From place St-Bonnet, walk along rue Voltaire towards the Marais, then cross boulevard du Général-Chanzy.*

Les Marais★

A pleasant walkway wanders through the wetlands and canals formed by the River Voiselle, a small tributary of the Yèvre, winding among the many garden plots held by the residents of Bourges. Between rows of poplars and willows, each garden reveals something of the personality of its tender: orderly tomato and bean plants, regal purple iris, rows and rows of strawberries, or perhaps a few bright marigolds set around an inviting hammock. A gate marks the border between the town and the Marais.

▷ *Go through the gate and walk along the narrow road on the left. At the end of the road, walk across the footbridge (on your left) then bear right.*

A path skirting the **Voiselle** and the Marais de Mariens leads to the River Yèvre.

Digue de l'Yèvre

Flat-bottomed boats are moored beneath a willow tree.

▷ *Retrace your steps and take the first path on the right.*

Place Gordaine

Rue de Babylone

There is a fine view of the cathedral to your left. On the right, beyond the Marais Hauts the horizon is barred by the town's northern suburb and the convent of the Sisters of Charity.

▶ *Follow avenue Marx Dormoy on the left then turn right beyond the bridge onto cours Beauvoir.*

Jardin des Prés-Fichaux★

A beautiful garden has been laid out on marshland between the river and the close of St-Ambroise Abbey where the Protestants used to gather in the 16C to sing.
The designer has kept the avenue of plane trees and added a rose garden, French-style flower beds and ponds, to make a setting of pleasing perspectives through arches of clipped yew trees.

▶ *Return to place St-Bonnet along boulevard de la République.*

Just before you reach the square, note the lively covered market on your left.

Sights

Musée des Meilleurs Ouvriers de France

&. ① *Open Jul–Aug, 10am–12.30pm and 1.30–6pm; Apr–Jun and Sep–Dec, 10am–noon and 2–6pm; Jan–Mar, depending on exhibits.* ① *Closed Sun morning, Mon, 1 May, 1 and 11 Nov, and 25 Dec.* ☜*No charge.* ☎ *02 48 57 82 45.*

Housed in the former archbishop's residence, this unusual museum contains exceptionally fine objects made by gifted craftsmen.

Musée du Berry

①*Open Jul–Aug, daily except Tue, 10am–12.30pm and 1.30–6pm, Sun 1.30–6pm; Apr–Jun and Sep–Dec, daily except Tue, 10am–noon and 2–6pm, Sun 2–6pm; Jan–Mar, daily except Tue, 10am–noon and 2–5pm, Sun 2–5pm.* ① *Closed 1 Jan, 1 May, 1 and 11 Nov, and 25 Dec.* ☜*No charge.* ☎ *02 48 57 81 15 or 02 48 70 41 92.*

This quiet, unpretentious museum, housed in the Hôtel Cujas, contains **archaeological collections**★ (dating from prehistory to the end of the Gallo-Roman period), sculpture, furniture and pottery as well as a fine collection of **statues**★ including *The Prophets* (1382) by Jean de Cambrai and André Beauneveu and *The Weepers* from the Duke of Berry's tomb by Jean de Cambrai.

Musée Estève★★

&.①*Open Jul–Aug, 10am–12.30pm and 1.30–6pm, Sun 1.30–6pm; Apr–Jun and Sep–Dec, 10am–noon and 2–6pm, Sun 2–6pm; Jan–Mar, 10am–noon and 2–5pm, Sun 2–5pm.* ☞*Guided tour available (1hr) by prior arrangement.* ① *Closed Tue, 1 Jan, 1 May, 1 and 11 Nov, and 25 Dec.* ☜*No charge.* ☎ *02 48 24 75 38.*

Since 1987, this museum, located in the Hôtel des Échevins, has been home to a unique collection of 130 works in oil and on paper.
Born in Culan in 1904, **Maurice Estève** had no formal training as an artist. His work reveals a stunning evolution in technique, while themes from his native Berry are repeated over time: the home (curtains, window, table, other household objects), his grandmother (*Paysanne endormie aux rideaux verts*, 1924), the natural environment (*Châtaigneraie*, 1927).
In Paris, Estève worked under difficult conditions, but was able to absorb the influence of Surrealism and later, Cézanne. Until 1947, his work shifted between the figurative (*La Toilette Verte*, 1934) and the abstract (*Embarquement pour Cythère*, 1929), before settling on the latter course. Most of his paintings (*Skibet*, 1979, is one of the best examples) are a subtle combination or a juxtaposition of masses of colour.

Hôtel Lallemant★

This magnificent Renaissance mansion has retained the name of Jean Lallemant, the rich cloth merchant who had it built. It now houses the Museum of Decorative Arts.

Musée des Arts Décoratifs

①*Open Jul–Aug, daily except Mon, 10am–12.30pm and 1.30–6pm, Sun 1.30–6pm; Apr–Jun and Sep–Dec, daily except Mon, 10am–noon and 2–6pm, Sun 2–6pm; Jan–Mar, daily except Mon, 10am–noon and 2–5pm, Sun 2–5pm.* ① *Closed 1 Jan, 1 May, 1 and 11 Nov, and 25 Dec.* ☜*No charge.* ☎ *02 48 57 81 17.*

Le Printemps de Bourges

Created in April 1977, this musical event initially aimed at bringing together musicians overlooked by the Hit Parade and underplayed on the radio. The first year, 15 000 people flocked to hear such non-conformist French artists as Béranger, Font and Val, and Lavilliers. Two years later, ever more popular, the festival was extended to one week and welcomed other musical genres (rock, folk, jazz). Most of the spectators are young (75% between ages 15 and 25), and now number more than 100 000. Shows take place in a dozen different halls, and the street life is certainly as big an attraction as what goes on inside. Over the decades, some of the groups and individual artists who have won acclaim at Bourges are Téléphone, Charles Trenet, Claude Nougaro, Murray Head, Touré Kunda, Patricia Kass, Johnny Hallyday, Véronique Sanson, Joe Cocker, Miles Davis, Nina Simone, The Cure, U2, Frank Zappa, Khaled, and Rita Mitsouko. Some of the latest trends have included world music, rap and techno, and in its 20th year, the spring festival remains fresh and exciting. Play on!

A sloping ramp, covered with barrel vaulting and used to lead horses in and out of the building, goes through to the **main courtyard** which is on two levels. The large main building shows the styles of different architectural periods: the mullioned windows and arcades are 15C, the doors to the corridors and the window-frames of the bays above the passageway are 16C and the entablature and round frontons bearing the arms of the Dorsannes who once owned the mansion are 17C. Right round the courtyard at first-floor level is a kind of frieze of terracotta medallions portraying the heads of prominent personages of Antiquity. An Italian-style loggia, formerly used for summer dining, has 17C frescoes representing hunting scenes and a polychrome bas-relief dedicated to St Christopher.

On the top floor, one room houses a notable **collection of miniatures**★; toys, master craft pieces, models and various small-scale fancies, all perfectly executed and together providing an unusual and thorough summary of the history of furniture from Louis XV to Art Nouveau.

▶ *Return to the main building and take the spiral staircase opposite the information desk.*

Displayed in elegant rooms are enamels, porcelains and ivories, as well as Renaissance and 17C French and Flemish tapestries.

The **chapel** has a curious coffered ceiling decorated with the symbols of alchemy, philosophy and heraldry, including the coat of arms of the Lallemant family.

Musée d'Histoire Naturelle★

Kids ⚙ ⏱*Open daily, 2-6pm; school hols, 10am-noon and 2-6pm.* ⏱ *Closed 1 Jan, 1 May, 11 Nov and 25 Dec.* ⏺3.60€ *(child: 1.90€).* ☎ *02 48 65 37 34. www.museum-bourges.net.*

The Natural History Museum was created in 1927 and renovated in 1989. It is interactive, entertaining and educational, with an emphasis on the regional environment as well as the work of local naturalists and scientists.

Musée de l'Homme★

Kids This section of the Natural History Museum deals with the evolution of man. Various themes (the senses, digestion and demography) are dealt with in an entertaining way.

Excursion

Plaimpied-Givaudins
12km/7mi S.

The church is all that remains of a large abbey founded by Richard II, archbishop of Bourges. Construction began in the late 11C and went on for 100 years. Additions and renovations were made up until the 18C. The sculpted capitals are of particular interest. The oldest can be seen in the chancel. The pillar separating the nave from the south transept is surmounted by one of the most beautiful capitals, carved with a scene depicting Christ's Temptation.

BRANTÔME★★

POPULATION 2 043

MICHELIN LOCAL MAP 329: E-3

Brantôme lies in the charming Vallée de la Dronne. Its old abbey and picturesque setting★ make it one of the most delightful places in the Périgord. *Abbaye de Brantôme, 24310 Brantôme, ☎ 05 53 05 80 52. www.ville-brantome.fr.*

The Chronicler Brantôme

The literary fame of **Pierre de Bourdeille**(1538-1614), better known as Brantôme, brought renown to the abbey of which he was commendatory abbot.

He began life as a soldier of fortune and courtier, went to Scotland with Mary Stuart, travelled to Spain, Portugal, Italy and the British Isles and even to Africa. Wild adventures brought him into contact with the great and famous in an era rich in scandal. After fighting at Jarnac in 1569, he withdrew to his abbey and began his famous chronicles. He left the abbey to return to court as chamberlain to Charles IX. In 1584 a fall from his horse crippled him, he then left the restless and impetuous Valois court to retreat to the peace of his monastery and finish his chronicles.

Brantôme, whose fame lies in his *Les vies des hommes illustres et grands capitaines* (Lives of Illustrious Men and Great Leaders), was a lively, witty and sometimes cynical historian.

▶ **Orient Yourself**: A boat trip on the river is the perfect way to discover this charming town.

 Don't Miss: The abbey bell tower; the banks of the River Dronne; Grotte de Villars; Château de Puyguilhem.

 Especially for Kids: Musée "Rêve et Miniatures".

Visit

Banks of the River Dronne★★

The former abbey buildings, located at the foot of the cliff, overlook the island upon which the village has been built.

Clocher (Belfry)★★

 Open early-Jul to Aug, guided tour (1hr 15min), 11am-7pm, Sun 2.30-6pm; mid-Jun to early-Jul and early to mid-Sep, daily except Tue and Sat, 10.30-noon and 2-6pm, Sun, 2.30-6pm. 6€. ☎ 05 53 05 80 63.

Brantôme on the banks of the Dronne

J. P. Clapham/MICHELIN

Address Book

RIVER TRIPS

Boat trips *(45min)* with on-board commentary operate May-Sep. Departures from quai du Pavillon Renaissance. ➸*6.50€ (child: 4.50€).*

For coin ranges, see the Legend at the back of the guide.

EATING OUT

➸➸**Les Ondines Salon de Thé** – *13 bd de Coligny* - ☎ 05 53 46 60 30 - ◔ *closed 1 Nov-Easter except weekends.* The summer terrace of this tea room overlooking the abbey enjoys a bird's-eye view of the Dronne. Home-made pastries and a choice of top-quality foies gras.

➸➸**Les Jardins de Brantôme** – *33/37 r. P.-de-Mareuil* - ☎ 05 53 05 88 16 - ◔ *closed Wed (except 15 Jul-Aug) and Thu - reserv. required.* In the summer months, enjoy the terrace or sit under the trees in the garden of the former 18C stagecoach inn. In cooler weather, the spacious dining room is welcoming. Traditional regional cooking with vegetables fresh from the garden.

➸➸**Au Fil du Temps** – *1, chemin du Vert-Galand* - ☎ 05 53 05 24 12 - *fildutemps@ fildutemps.com* - ◔ *closed 6 Jan-6 Feb, Sun eve and Mon.* This elegant bistro occupies an attractively restored 14C posthouse. One dining room with a rotisserie, where the decor is kitchen inspired, the second is more elegant in feel. Grilled dishes and typically Périgord cuisine.

➸➸**Au Fil de l'Eau** – *21, quai Bertin* - ☎ 05 53 05 73 65 - *fildeleau@fildeleau.com* - ◔ *closed Nov-Mar, Sun eve and Wed (except July-Sep).* A charming bistro with a fishing theme. Terrace overlooking the river. The culinary emphasis here is on fried fish *(fritures)* and regional cuisine.

➸➸**L'Auberge Périgourdine** – *24800 Vaunac - 8km/4.8mi S of Thiviers on the N 21* - ☎ 05 53 55 05 41 - *auberge-perigourdine@ wanadoo.fr* - ◔ *closed last week of May, 1st week of Jun, 1-15 Oct, 26-30 Dec, Fri eve and Sun eve.* On the edge of the village, this restored inn is full of rural charm, with its exposed beams, bright tablecloths and hearty regional cooking.

WHERE TO STAY

➸**Chambre d'hôte Ferme des Guézoux** – *24800 Vaunac - 9km/5.4mi S of Thiviers on the N 21* - ☎ 05 53 62 06 39 - *3 rooms.* The hay barns of this isolated farm have been transformed into guest rooms with kitchens; a small chalet is also available. Simple pine furnishings typical of the local area.

➸➸**Chambre d'hôte Les Habrans** – *In a lane across from the gendarmerie - 1km/0.6mi from the centre of town* - ☎ 05 53 05 58 84 - ◔ *closed 1 Nov-May -* ⚹ *- 5 rooms.* This 17C house on the banks of the River Dronne has simple, tasteful rooms with views over the water. Breakfast outdoors in fine weather.

➸➸**Chambre d'hôte Doumarias** – *Doumarias - 24800 St-Pierre-de-Côle - 12km/7.2mi E of Brantôme on the D 78* - ☎ 05 53 62 34 37 - *doumarias@aol.com* - ◔ *closed 15 Oct-1 Apr -* ⚹ *- 6 rooms.* The ruined towers of the Château de Bruzac are just across from this charming house covered with Virginia creeper. A majestic lime tree reigns supreme over the inner courtyard. Quiet, unpretentious rooms and a pretty garden with a pool. Friendly welcome.

➸➸**Chambre d'hôte La Maison Fleurie** – *54 r. Gambetta* - ☎05 53 35 17 04 - ◔ *closed Feb school hols -* ⚹ *- 5 rooms.* This 19C house, with its handful of attractive, comfortable rooms is right in the centre of town. Copious breakfasts, served in the courtyard in fine weather. Four holiday cottages are also available for rent. No-smoking policy. Small swimming pool.

SHOPPING

Markets – Traditional market on Friday mornings. Farmers' market on Tuesday morning in Jul-Aug. *Marché au gras* (selling duck and goose products) Friday mornings from Nov-Feb. Truffle market from Dec-Feb.

EVENTS

Sinfonia - This Baroque music festival takes place in Brantôme at the end of August and early September. ☎ 05 53 04 78 78.

The bell tower was built apart from the church upon a sharp rock towering 12m/39ft high, beneath which are vast caves. It was erected in the 11C and is the oldest gabled Romanesque bell tower in the Limousin style. It was made of four storeys, each stepped back and slightly smaller than the one below, and topped with a stone pyramid. The ground floor is roofed with an archaic dome where the evolution from the square to the ellipse is obtained from triangular ribs held up by marble columns, an architectural element most likely recovered from a Merovingian construction. The three other storeys are opened by round arched bays supported on columns with simply decorated capitals.

Old abbey

Brantôme Abbey, which was founded by Charlemagne in 769, under the Benedictine rule, to house the relics of St Sicaire, attracted a multitude of pilgrims. Sacked by the Normans, it was rebuilt in the 11C by Abbé Guillaume. In the 16C, it became a commandery headed by Pierre de Mareuil as abbot (he had constructed the most interesting of the buildings); later his nephew, Pierre de Bourdeille, became the administrator.

The present buildings were remodelled in the 18C by Bertin, administrator of Périgord and extensively restored in the 19C.

Abbey church – Angevin vaulting, a compromise between cross-ribbed vaulting and a dome, replaced the two original domes of this abbey church in the 15C. The nave is plain and elegant; a bay in the form of a cross and three depressed-arched windows below it illuminate the flat east end.

The baptistery is adorned with a 14C bas-relief in stone of the Baptism of Christ. Another bas-relief, this time dating from the 13C and showing the Massacre of the Innocents, may be seen underneath the porch above the font, which rests on a fine Romanesque capital.

Near the main doorway go into the 16C cloistral gallery from where it is possible to get a glimpse of the former chapter-house; its palm tree vaulting is supported by a central column.

Convent buildings – These now house the town hall and the **Fernand-Desmoulin Museum** which displays works by this local painter. A monumental staircase leads to the former monks' dormitory (note the remarkable timber work), where temporary exhibitions are regularly held.

Du Creusé au Construit (Troglodyte tour)

&. ⏰ *Open Jul-Aug, 10am-7pm; Apr-Jun and Sep, daily except Tue 10am-12.30pm and 2-6pm; Oct-Mar, daily except Tue, 10am-noon and 2-5pm.* ⏰ *Closed Jan (excluding school hols), 1 Jan and 25 Dec.* ⊜6€. ☎ 05 53 05 80 63.

The hermits who had converted the fountain of the rock, originally a place of pagan worship, to Christianity were succeeded by monks, who initially occupied the caves in the rock face. Later on they continued to use the caves as outbuildings, or as refuges when the abbey buildings came under attack (in the 11C, 12C, 14C and 17C). The tour shows the monks' calefactory and the lavacrum, the remains of the abbey mill and the troglodyte dovecote. The fountain of the rock, dedicated to St Sicaire, is still believed to have life-giving properties and the power to cure infant diseases in particular. The awesome atmosphere of the Cave of the Last Judgement, decorated with an epigrammatic Triumph of Death and an Italianate Crucifixion sculpted in the 15C, is an indication of the sort of spirituality that pervaded in the monastic community of Brantôme for a 1 000 years.

Pont coudé

Walk through the gardens adorned by the Fontaine Médicis towards the Renaissance house with mullioned windows. A 16C elbow bridge with asymmetrical arches gives access to the **Jardins des Moines** (Monks' Gardens).

"Venice of the Perigord"

On leaving the Jardins des Moines, cross the bridge to reach quai Bertin where the old houses with their flower-covered balconies and trellises are reflected in the tranquil mirror of water. Follow the numbered panels marking the tour of the town and providing information about the different architectural styles (*a map is available at the tourist office*).

Musée "Rêve et Miniatures"

8, rue Puyjoli (the high street leading to the abbey). &. ⏰ *Open Jul to Aug, noon-6pm.* ⊜5.80€ *(3-10 years old: 3€).* ☎ 05 53 35 29 00.

🧒 This museum displays a plentiful collection of miniature houses filled with furnishings in silver, china and glass, with all the relevant details. The scale of the models is 1:12. A series of reconstructions describes the evolution of style from the Middle Ages through Art Deco. Another series, a proven child-pleaser, arrays imaginary habitats where animals are the denizens.

Excursions

Château de Puyguilhem★

🕐 *Open Jul-Aug,* 👥*guided tour (45min), 10am-7pm; Apr-Jun, Sep to mid-Nov and Christmas school hols, 10am-12.30pm and 2-6pm; mid-Nov to Mar, daily except Mon, Fri and Sat, 10am-12.30pm and 2-5.30pm.* 🕐 *Closed Jan and 25 Dec.* 🎫*5.20€.* ☎ *05 53 54 82 18. 12km/7.5mi NE. Drive 3km/1.9mi along the D 78 then turn left towards Champagnac just before the bridge on the River Dronne.*

This 16C château is typical of those built in and around the Loire Valley in the days of François I. The towers, balustrades, sculpted chimneys and mullioned windows create a graceful exterior impression. Inside, the **chimney-pieces**★ are particularly impressive, as are the panels representing six of the Labours of Hercules and the massive beams made of chestnut.

Grottes de Villars★★

🕐*Open Jul-Aug,* 👥*guided tour (1hr, last entrance 30min before closing), 10am-7.30pm; Apr-Jun and Sep, 10am-noon and 2-7pm; Oct, 2-6.30pm.* 🎫*6.50€ (5-12 years old: 4,20€).* ☎ *05 53 54 82 36. 16km/10mi NE; 4km/2.5mi beyond Puyguilhem.*

The tour follows galleries linking several chambers dug out by an underground river. Among the most remarkable formations are yellow and ochre draperies (up to 6m/20ft long), two small rimstone pools, and very finely-wrought stalactites hanging from the ceiling. The first chambers are stunning for the brightness of the white concretions composed of almost pure calcite. Halfway through the tour, a *son et lumière* show provides a dramatic overview of the main stages which led to the formation of the cave. Prehistoric paintings done in manganese oxide probably date from the same period as the paintings at Lascaux (17 000 years old). The calcite flows which cover up sections of them help to authenticate their age. A video presentation, which can be viewed before or after the tour, provides a good insight into the local geological features.

Thiviers

26km/16mi E along the D 78.

This busy little town is known for its markets and fairs. The **Musée du Foie Gras** (♿🕐*Open mid-Jun to mid-Sep, 9am-7pm (last entrance 30min before closing); May to mid-Jun, 10am-noon and 2-6pm, Sat, 9am-1pm and 2-6pm, Sun, 10am-1pm and 2-6pm; mid-Sep to Apr, daily except Sun, 10am-noon and 2-6pm, Sat, 9am-1pm and 2-7pm.* 🎫*1.50€ (child: no charge).* ☎ *05 53 55 12 50),* to the right of the tourist office, has an exhibit devoted to **foie gras**. Thiviers is one of the main production areas.

La BRENNE★★

MICHELIN LOCAL MAP 323: C/E-6/7

The northern limit of La Brenne is marked by the River Claise, and the eastern limit by the Fôret de Lancosme. The Vallée de la Creuse borders La Brenne to the west and south. The region's main feature is its 7 500ha/18 533 acres of lakes.

At the end of 1989, the **Parc Naturel Régional de la Brenne** was created, covering 1 660km2/640sq mi and involving 47 different local governments and 32 000 inhabitants. For information on tourist and cultural activities here, head for the **Maison du Parc**.

The natural environment is a haven for wildlife, in particular some 100 species of birds. A good observation point is the **Réserve Naturelle de Chérine.** 🏛 *Maison du Parc, Le Bouchet, 36300 Rosnay,* ☎ *02 54 28 12 13. www.parc-naturel-brenne.fr.*

👁 **Don't Miss**: Étang de la Mer Rouge.

🕐 **Organising Your Time**: Allow at least half a day to explore this fascinating area.

A Bit of History

Land of a thousand lakes – La Brenne is a land of legends: it has inspired painters and poets; fairies, elves and sorcerers as well. The name recalls Geoffroy de Brenne, lord of Mézières in the 13C. Once neglected woodlands and moors, the area was cleared out by monks who engineered the ponds for the purposes of cultivating fish to enjoy on meatless fast days. Later, in the 19C, the region was further improved, removing the risk of malaria; roads were laid and swampy lands drained, opening the land to agriculture. Today the area is a patchwork of mixed uses.

The ponds and lakes mark the landscape and symbolise the close ties linking man and nature in this region, in addition to providing a rich ecosystem and a lovely setting. The waters are also a major factor in the local economy, for over 1 000t of fish (carp, roach, tench, pike, bass and eel) are drawn out annually. Every year, a sluice gate is opened to drain the waters.

Excursion

Round-trip Starting from Le Blanc

80km/50mi – allow half a day

Le Blanc

This busy burg is a commercial centre for the area, attracting fairs and markets, drawing regional inhabitants to its shops and cinemas. The upper town is a picturesque labyrinth of old houses, whereas the lower town gathers around **St-Génitour**, the church dedicated to the 4C martyr and **cephalophore** saint (which is to say he was decapitated, but nonetheless picked up his severed head and walked to the church, where he was buried) reputed for curing diseases of the eye.

Écomusée de la Brenne – ⏱*Open Jul-Aug, 9.30am-7pm; May-Jun and Sep, daily except Mon, 9.30am-12.30pm and 2-6pm; Oct-Apr, daily except Mon, 10am-noon and 2-5pm.* ⏱ *Closed 1 Jan, 11 Nov and 25 Dec.* 🎫*3.40€.* ☎ *02 54 37 25 20.*

This ethnographic museum, housed in Château Naillac, illustrates the history of the Brenne region and its population, bird life, the thousand lakes, the first settlers, smithies, local agriculture and architecture.

▸ *Leave Le Blanc to the N on the D 975, then turn right after crossing the railway.*

Étang de la Mer Rouge

The Red Sea pond is believed to have been given its name by a former owner, Aimery Sénébaud, on his return from the Holy Land, where he had been imprisoned beside the Red Sea. It is the biggest lake in La Brenne, and has a surface area of 180ha/445 acres. It provides a natural refuge for migrating waterfowl. The church of Notre-Dame-de-la-Mer-Rouge, rebuilt in 1854, stands on a headland to the south and is the site of a yearly pilgrimage. The statue of the Virgin, miraculously found in the hollow of an oak tree by Aimery in the 13C, was stolen and later replaced by a copy which is kept in the church in Rosnay, and is brought out for the pilgrimage.

Château du Bouchet

⏱ *Open Jul-Aug,* ⟿*guided tour (1hr, last entrance 30min before closing), Sun and Mon, 2.30-6.30pm; holidays in May, 2.30-6.30pm.* 🎫*5€ (guided tour); 2€ (exterior only).* ☎ *02 54 37 80 14.*

This impressive medieval fortress, occupied by the English during the Hundred Years War, was restored in both the 15C and 17C. For 300 years it belonged to the Rochechouart-Mortemart family and for a while served as the residence of the Marquise de Montespan who was born a Rochechouart-Mortemart and was the daughter and sister of the lords of Le Bouchet (her portrait hangs inside the castle). You may walk round the outside of the castle and visit the keep, terrace and part of the ground floor. From the keep and the terrace there is a view of the Brenne countryside and the Red Sea pond.

▸ *Drive past the Maison du Parc. Turn left at the intersection with the D 44 then right onto the D 17A at Le Maupas. There is a parking area a little farther on.*

Étang Massé

⟿*Guided tours.* ⏱*Open Feb-Oct, 9am or 6pm, by prior arrangement.* 🎫*5.30€ (child: 2.30€). Information and reservations,* ☎ *02 54 28 11 04.*

In the early morning or late evening, the observation post overlooking the lake is the perfect spot to watch one of the richest natural spectacles in La Brenne, with wading birds such as bitterns and small bitterns and European pond turtles visible here.

Address Book

For coin ranges, see the Legend at the back of the guide.

EATING OUT

Le Bellebouche – *Base de Loisirs de Bellebouche - 36290 Mézières-en-Brenne - 9km/5.5mi E of Mézières towards Châteauroux on the D 925 -* ☎ *02 54 38 30 77 - open weekends in May and every day in Jul-Aug.* This outdoor recreation centre has a restaurant on site. Located in a natural setting on the edge of the lake, its terrace is a pleasant place to relax, unwind and enjoy views of the neighbouring pine forest. Contemporary, reasonably priced cuisine.

Espace Dégustation de la Maison du Parc – *Hameau du Bouchet - 36300 Rosnay -* ☎ *02 54 28 53 02 - closed 1 Jan and 25 Dec -* . This renovated farmhouse, part of the old château, serves an interesting choice of copious, inexpensive local specialities (fried fish, cheeses, bread, rillettes etc). Terrace with views of the lake.

Auberge de la Gabrière – *2 La Gabrière - 36220 La Gabrière - 9km/5.5mi S of Mézières. Head towards Le Blanc, then La Gabrière along the D 15 and D 17 -* ☎ *02 54 37 80 97 - closed Mon in Jul-Aug, Tue eve and Wed - reserv. recommended at weekends.* This spacious, country restaurant is well-situated opposite the Étang de la Gabrière. The menu features a good choice of freshwater fish, as well as game in season. Very popular at weekends. Basic rooms.

Au Bœuf Couronné – *9 pl. du Gén.-de-Gaulle - 36290 Mézières-en-Brenne -* ☎ *02 54 38 04 39 - closed 20 Nov-31 Jan, Sun eve and Mon except public hols.* A variety of harnesses adorn the dining room of this restaurant, a former 17C posthouse, on the village square. A good choice of fixed-price menus, including one for children. A few modest guest rooms are also available.

WHERE TO STAY

Auberge Saint-Hubert – *8 pl. de l'Église - 36800 Migne -* ☎ *02 54 37 86 09 - closed Christmas to New Year and Fri - 13 rooms.* Given the discreet façade, the interior of this inn is unexpectedly charming. The bedrooms, identical in size and comfort, have been tastefully personalised. A hunting scene embellishes one of the dining rooms. In winter, dine to the sound of live background piano music.

Chambre d'hôte La Presle – *Rte de Châteauroux - 36290 Mézières-en-Brenne - turn left after leaving the village -* ☎ *02 54 38 12 36 - closed 15-30 Sep - - 3 rooms.* This attractive small farmhouse dating from the 17C offers guests a choice of three comfortable bedrooms with Louis XV furniture, delicate English wallpaper, and views over the garden or surrounding fields. Communal breakfast around a large table.

SPORT AND LEISURE

Base de Loisirs de Bellebouche – *10km/6mi E of Mézières-en-Brenne along the D 925 - 36290 Mézières-en-Brenne -* ☎ *02 54 38 32 36 - open May-Jun and Sep, weekends 2-6pm; mid-Jul to mid-Aug, 10.30am-7pm; first 2 weeks of Jul and last two weeks of Aug, 2-6pm - parking Jul-Aug: 4€ - no dogs allowed.* A natural sandy beach (no lifeguards). Three nature trails for hikers, mountain bikes and horses, including a fitness trail. Discovery trail (7.5km/4.5mi, 3hr) around the lake, with three observation areas (the best views are from the southwest). Pedalos and kayaks available for hire.

Centre Équestre Poney-Club de la Virevolte – *Le Fresne - 9km/5.4mi E of Rosnay and 11km/6.5mi N of Le Blanc on the D 17 - 36300 Douadic -* ☎ *02 54 37 10 28 - except for school holidays, daily except Tue; during school holidays, daily (Jul-Aug: daily except Sun) - closed first two weeks in Sep, Christmas and New Year's Day.* Isabelle and Jean-Charles Liva lead trips in the heart of the Land of a Thousand Lakes (Le Pays aux Mille Étangs), and offer riding lessons for children.

Domaine Ste-Marie – Éric Aphatie - *36290 Mézières-en-Brenne - open Mar-Nov, daily by prior arrangement -* ☎ *02 54 38 01 18.* Take a horse-drawn carriage ride with Mr. Aphatie (father or son), who will tell you about the history of La Brenne, its local customs and point out the many species of birds that can be seen here.

▶ *Slightly farther on, the Blizon discovery trail branches off on the left.*

Sentier découverte de l'Étang du Blizon
1.5km/0.9mi, allow 30min.

Informative panels on the theme of "dragonflies and frogs" line this discovery trail which skirts the edge of the Blizon lake.

▶ *Turn left at the end of the D 17A. Leave the car in the Étangs Foucault parking area on the right.*

WILDFOWL OF THE BRENNE

Short-toed eagle

Reed bunting

Heron

Black-taled Godwit

R. Corbel/MICHELIN

Étangs Foucault

A look-out post, located at the end of the marked path, offers good views of ducks, ospreys, herons, egrets etc.

▶ *Turn back and follow the D 15 to Mézières-en-Brenne.*

Mézières-en-Brenne

The most important town in Brenne is built on the banks of the Claise whose course is marked by a line of poplars. The **church** belfry, flanked by two stone turrets, has a porch ornamented with sculpture. The nave has wooden vaulting with painted uprights and crossbeams. Note the beautiful stained glass of the Renaissance chapel to the right of the chancel.

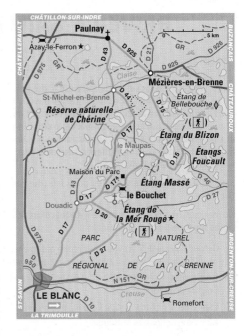

The remaining stained-glass windows date from the 14C and 16C. Some were restored in the 19C. The stalls were originally in the Abbaye de St-Cyran.

Maison de la Pisciculture de Brenne

Open mid-Mar to Oct, daily except Tue, 2-6pm (last entrance 30min before closing); Nov to mid-Mar, by prior arrangement with the tourist office. Closed 1 Jan, 1 May and 25 Dec. 2.20€. ☎ 02 54 38 12 24.

Established in one of the last vestiges of the 11C stronghold, this nature museum is one of the branches of the Écomusée de la Brenne. The exhibits displayed inside are related to fish and fishing in the region. In addition to aquariums, displays recount the history of the village and provide information on techniques for catching local fish.

Église de Paulnay

The **church** dating from the 12C and 13C has an interesting Romanesque **doorway**★. Three rows of finely sculptured covings are supported on elegant capitals. Inside the oven-vaulted chancel and the narrow bay are decorated with lovely ochre-coloured frescoes. The modern Stations of the Cross carved in wood and painted are the work of a monk from Fontgombault Abbey.

▶ *Drive S along the D 43 to St-Michel-en-Brenne then turn onto the D 44.*

Réserve Naturelle de Chérine

Open Jul-Aug, guided tour (2hr), Thu 6-8pm, by prior arrangement; Apr to Jun, Wed and Sat, 10am-noon, guided tour, Thu 4-6pm, by prior arrangement. 5.30€ (child: 2.30€). ☎ 02 54 28 11 02.

From the edge of a 26ha/64-acre lake, nature lovers can observe at leisure the amazing diversity of this unspoilt ecosystem, which shelters colourful bird life (including purple herons, wild ducks and tits).

▶ *Return to Le Blanc along the D 17.*

BRIVE-LA-GAILLARDE

POPULATION 49 141

MICHELIN LOCAL MAP 329: K-5

Brive, which owes its suffix La Gaillarde –"the bold"– to the courage displayed by its citizens during sieges in centuries past, is a busy town standing in the alluvial plain of the River Corrèze. As a result of its fertile soil, the surrounding area is an important centre for market gardening and fruit growing. Located at the crossroads of the Bas-Limousin (Lower Limousin), the Périgord and the limestone plateaux of the Quercy, the town is an important railway junction with a thriving economy.

Since 1982, an important annual book fair (the Foire du Livre) has been held in the town.

No mention of Brive can be made without reference to its rugby union team, one of the most respected in France.

▶ **Orient Yourself**: Start your tour of the old town at the tourist office in place du 14 Juillet, where you can also park your car (⏱ see town plan).

⊙ **Don't Miss**: Hôtel de Labenche; Basse Vallée de la Corrèze; Causse Corrézien; Gouffre de la Fage.

▨ **Especially for Kids**: Lac de Causse, in the Vallée de la Couze.

⏱ **Also See**: Collonges-la-Rouge.

A Bit of History

A brilliant career – Guillaume Dubois (1656-1723), the son of an apothecary from Brive, took the Orders and became tutor to Philip of Orléans. He became prime minister when Philip was appointed regent during the minority of Louis XV. Offices and honours were heaped upon him; he became Archbishop of Cambrai and then a cardinal. He made an alliance with England, which thus ensured a long period of peace in France.

A glorious soldier – Guillaume-Marie-Anne Brune (1763-1815) enlisted in the army in 1791 and rose to become a general commanding the army in Italy in 1798. Following victories in Holland and Italy he was appointed ambassador to Constantinople. Elected Maréchal de France in 1804, he was banished by Napoleon soon afterwards for his republican attitude. He became the symbol of the Revolution and died, a victim of a Royalist mob, in 1815 at Avignon.

Walking Tour of Old Town

The old town located in the heart of the city, bounded by a first ring of boulevards, has been successfully restored. The buildings, old and new, create a harmonious ensemble of warm beige sandstone and bluish tinted rooftops.

▶ *Start from the tourist office (place du 14-Juillet). Follow avenue de Paris then rue de Toulzac across boulevard Anatole-France and turn immediately right onto rue de Corrèze.*

Chapelle St-Libéral

This Gothic chapel is the venue of temporary exhibitions throughout the year.

▶ *Continue along rue de Corrèze then follow rue Majour.*

Collégiale St-Martin

In this church, only the transept, apse and a few of the capitals are Romanesque, the traces of a 12C monastic community. Inside, over the transept crossing, is an octagonal dome on flat pendentives, characteristic of the Limousin style. The nave and side aisles are 14C. The chancel was faithfully rebuilt by Cardinal Dubois in the 18C; note the 12C baptismal font, decorated with the symbols of the Evangelists. From the outside admire the historiated capitals and modillioned cornice of the apsidal chapels.

Archaeological Crypt – Vestiges of previous churches have been uncovered beneath the chancel, including the primitive construction dating from the 5C over the tomb of St Martin the Spaniard, who brought the Gospel to the town but was massacred by its inhabitants.

▶ *On coming out of the church, take rue des Échevins on the left.*

Address Book

For coin ranges, see the Legend at the back of the guide.

EATING OUT

Chez Francis – 61 av. de Paris - ☎ 05 55 74 41 72 - ⏱ closed Feb school hols, 2-17 Aug, Sun, Mon and public hols - reserv. required. An authentic Parisian bistro in the centre of town. Simple but tasty traditional cuisine.

La Toupine – 11 r. Jean-Labrunie - ☎ 05 55 23 71 58 - ⏱ closed Feb school holidays, 9-24 Aug, Wed evening and Sun - reserv. required. A popular local haunt in the old town serving good value-for-money cuisine.

La Potinière – 6 bd de Puyblanc - ☎ 05 55 24 06 22 - restaurantlapotiniere@ wanadoo .fr - ⏱ closed Sun eve (except Aug). This old house with painted shutters is decorated in warm tones, with tables set out around an attractive bar counter. Traditional cuisine, including a number of grilled dishes. Attractive shaded terrace.

Ferme-Auberge de Baudran – Rte d'Estivals - 19600 Nespouls - 15km/9mi S of Brive. Take the A 20 and D 19E, then turn onto the N 20 - ☎ 05 55 85 81 45 - 🍽 - open Fri eve to Sun lunchtime - reserv. recommended. This delightful farm-inn is the perfect place to enjoy delicious local cooking, including foie gras, confits, lamb etc.

Le Relais du Quercy – 19500 Meyssac - ☎ 05 55 25 40 31 - ⏱ closed 15-30 Nov. Choose between the comfortable dining room or attractive terrace to sample typical cuisine prepared using the best local ingredients A few guest rooms are also available. Piano-bar.

Les Arums – 15 av. Alsace-Lorraine - ☎ 05 55 24 26 55 - ⏱ closed 1-10 Mar, 1-15 Sep, Sat lunchtime, Sun eve and Mon (excluding public hols). A recently modernised restaurant in the heart of Brive serving contemporary dishes in an elegant dining room or private garden. Attractive choice of menus.

WHERE TO STAY

Collonges – 3 pl. Winston Churchill - ☎ 05 55 74 09 58 - 24 rooms. A family-run hotel set back slightly from the main boulevard encircling the centre of town. Cosy lounge-bar and modern, functional bedrooms.

Le Teinchurier – Av. du Teinchurier - 3km/1.8mi W of the centre on the Périgueux road - ☎ 05 55 86 45 00 - 40 rooms - ⏱ closed 24 Dec-1 Jan, Sat and Sun. On the outskirts of town with easy access from Clermont, Cahors and Bordeaux. Pastel shades in the contemporary dining room, where the focus is on unpretentious local cuisine. Spacious, functional bedrooms with good soundproofing.

Chambre d'hôte À la Table de la Bergère – Belveyre - 19600 Nespouls - 15km/9mi S of Brive. Take the A 20 (Nespouls exit), the D 19 and then turn right onto the D 920 - ☎ 05 55 85 82 58 - 🍽 - 5 rooms. This bed and breakfast on the Causse Corrèzien is nestled amid a landscape of oak trees, meadows and typical stone huts. Pleasant rooms, tasty local cuisine and a friendly welcome.

La Truffe Noire – 22 bd Anatole-France - ☎ 05 55 92 45 00 - contact@la-truffe-noire.com - 27 rooms. The Black Truffle occupies a 19C regional-style house on the edge of the old town. Welcoming lounge with an imposing fireplace, and attractive guestrooms furnished with a contemporary feel. The pleasant dining room and shaded terrace are the setting for Corrèze specialities (including the trademark truffle).

MARKETS

Marché Brassens - place du 14-juillet - ⏱ open Tue-Sat, 7.30am-12.30pm. This wonderful covered market sells a huge range of local products. A relaxed atmosphere and a fun place to start your day.

Duck and goose markets - These typical markets are held four times a year between Dec and Feb.

SHOPPING

Distillerie Denoix – 9 bd du Mar.-Lyautey - ☎ 05 55 74 34 27 - www.denoix.com - ⏱ Tue-Sat 9am-noon and 2.30-7pm; Jul-Aug: daily. Founded in 1839, this distillery produces and markets Le Suprême de Noix walnut liqueur and Le Quinquinoix, an aperitif also made of walnuts. Violette de Brive mustard is also sold here.

Domaine de Lintillac – 19270 Ussac - ☎ 05 55 87 65 24 - ⏱ open Mon-Fri, 8am-1pm and 2-6.30pm; Sat, 8am-noon - ⏱ closed public hols. This reputable company sells foie gras, pâtés, confit, cassoulet and other specialities from the southwest direct to the public. The owner also owns restaurants in Paris, Lille and Brussels.

Chocolaterie Vimbelle - 18 and 29 rue Gambetta - ☎ 05 55 24 13 44 - ⏱ open Tue-Sat, 8am-12.30pm and 2.30-7pm; Sun, 8.30am-1pm. One of the few traditional chocolate-makers still plying their trade in Brive. Forty sorts to choose from, plus nougat, tarte tatin and delicious cakes.

Tour des Échevins

In the narrow rue des Échevins stands a town house with a fine corbelled Renaissance tower pierced by mullioned windows.

▷ *Retrace your steps and turn right.*

Place Latreille

This square was once the spiritual and commercial heart of the city and is still surrounded by old houses. The house known as **Tours St-Martin** dates from the 15C and 16C.

▷ *Continue straight on along rue du Docteur-Massénat then turn right onto rue Raynal.*

Positioned at the corner of rue Raynal and rue du Salan is the 18C Hôtel Desbruslys.

▷ *Walk along rue Raynal and enter the Hôtel de Labenche through the small door on the left.*

Hôtel de Labenche★

From the inner courtyard, the view encompasses the two buildings standing at right angles, which support the arcaded gallery. The pinkish colour of the stone enhances the fine decoration of the edifice. Built in 1540 by Jean II de Calvimont, lord of Labenche and the king's keeper of the seals for the Bas-Limousin, this mansion is a magnificent example of Renaissance architecture in Toulouse style and is the most remarkable secular building in town. From the inside courtyard the two main buildings can be seen set at right angles, above which are large arches. The roseate hue of the stone enhances the beauty of the building's decorative elements: mullioned windows adorned with festoons and slender columns and surmounted by busts of men and women set in niches.

Inside, it has been converted into a museum.

▶ *Continue along boulevard Jules-Ferry and turn left onto rue du Dr-Massénat.*

Logis de l'Abbesse des Clarisses (Residence of the Mother Superior of the Order of St Clare)

This Louis XIII building is distinguished by its dormer windows with semicircular pediments decorated with keel-shaped spheres.

▶ *Turn right onto rue Teyssier.*

Ancien Collège des Doctrinaires

This college was maintained by the Brothers of Christian Doctrine, who were as much open-minded humanists as men of faith, and its prosperity increased up until the Revolution. Today these 17C buildings house the town hall. The façade on rue Teyssier is of fine Classical arrangement and the wall decorated with a colonnade overlooks an inner courtyard.

▶ *Turn right.*

Place Jean-Marie-Dauzier

On this large square, modern buildings (Crédit Agricole bank) and old turreted mansions form a harmonious architectural unit.

The 16C **Maison Treilhard** consists of two main buildings joined by a round tower, decorated by a turret.

▶ *Retrace your steps, walk back to the collegiate church across place de l'Hôtel-de-Ville, then turn right onto rue de Toulzac.*

Sights

Musée de Labenche★

♿ 🕑*Open Apr-Oct, 10am-6.30pm; Nov-Mar, 1.30-6pm. Temporary exhibitions, daily except Tue, 10am-noon and 1.30-6.30pm.* 🕑 *Closed Tue, 1 Jan, 1 May, 1 Nov and 25 Dec.* ✍*4.56€, no charge last Sun of the month.* ☎ *05 55 24 19 05.*

The Roman-style **main staircase** of the Hôtel de Labenche, with brackets carved as busts of warriors and ladies, exudes the same exuberance as the outside. Among the 17 rooms displaying the collections, pay particular attention to the Counts of Cosnac room decorated with a marvellous set of **tapestries**, known as the Mortlake tapestries, made in the 17C using the widely renowned techniques of English high-warp tapestry. In the Cardinal Dubois room, there is the tomb of the pilgrim to Santiago de Compostela and a wonderful 11C silver and bronze **eucharistic dove** hanging above the altar, in which the sacred Host used to be kept. One of the main attributes of this museum is the successful reconstruction of the various series of excavations.

Mortlake tapestry

Musée de Labenche, Brive

Musée de la Résistance et de la Déportation Edmond-Michelet

🕑 *Open daily except Sun, 10am-noon and 2-6pm.* 🕑 *Closed public hols.* ✍ *No charge.* ☎ *05 55 74 06 08.*

The museum traces the history of the Resistance movement and deportation with paintings, photographs, posters and original documents relating to the camps, especially Dachau, where Edmond Michelet, former minister under General De Gaulle, was interned.

Excursions

1 Basse Vallée dela Corrèze★

Round tour of 45km/28mi – allow 3hr

▷ *Take the N 89 NE towards Tulle.*

Aubazine★

👋 *See AUBAZINE.*

▷ *Drive E along the D 48.*

Puy de Pauliac★

30min round trip on foot. Altitude 520m/1 706ft.

The footpath makes its way through heather and chestnut trees, leading upwards to reveal a splendid **view**★. A **viewing table** helps to identify the Roche de Vic to the south-east and to the north, the Monédières range.

The **Parc du Coiroux** has been developed around a large lake with swimming beaches and sailing, golf and tennis facilities.

▷ *Return to Aubazine. Drive SE along the D 130 and the D 175 to Lanteuil, then drive back to Brive along the picturesque D 921.*

2 Les Terres de Monsieur de Turenne★

Round trip of 55km/34mi – allow 4hr

This trip crosses the central area of the old viscounty of Turenne, which was not united with the French crown until 1738 (👋 *see TURENNE*). Beyond Turenne, the wooded hills of the Limoges region give way to the first limestone plateaux of the Quercy region.

▷ *Leave Brive-La-Gaillarde travelling SE on the D 38 towards Meyssac.*

Château de Lacoste

This former stronghold, built of local sandstone, has a main building flanked by three 13C towers. It was completed in the 15C with an elegant turret and a polygonal staircase.

At **Noailhac** you enter the region of red sandstone, which is used to build the lovely warm-coloured villages of the area. Soon Collonges-la-Rouge, perhaps the best-known, can be seen against a backdrop of greenery.

Collonges-la-Rouge★★

👋 *See COLLONGES-LA-ROUGE.*

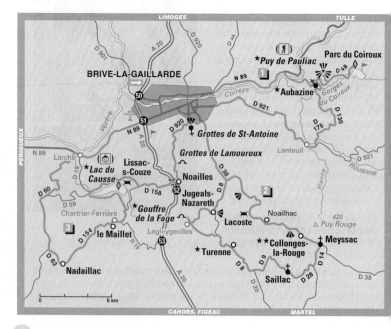

Meyssac

Meyssac is in the centre of hilly countryside where walnut and poplar trees, vineyards and orchards prosper. Like Collonges-la-Rouge, the town is built of red sandstone.

The **church** is an unusual mixture of architectural elements: a Gothic interior, a belfry-porch fortified by hoarding and a limestone doorway in the Romanesque Limousin style, adorned with small capitals decorated with animals and foliage.

Near the church, the **18C covered market**, which has a timberwork roof resting on alternating pillars and columns, is set in the middle of a square surrounded by elegant town houses, some of which have towers.

The picturesque nature of this village is confirmed by some of the houses, which are half-timbered with overhanging storeys and porch roofs.

The red earth, known as Collonges clay, is also used in pottery manufacture, which has developed in Meyssac.

▶ *Leave Meyssac S on D 14, towards Martel. After 2km/1.2mi, turn right on the D 28.*

Saillac

The village nestles among walnut trees and fields of maize. Inside the small Roman-esque church is a doorway, preceded by a narthex, with a remarkable **tympanum**★ in polychrome stone, relatively rare in the 12C. The tympanum is held up by a pier, composed of twisted columns adorned with foliage and hunting scenes, which probably came from a pagan monument.

In the chancel, topped by a dome on pendentives, are elegant historiated capitals. The village has retained its old mill (🕒 *Open daily,* 🐁 *no charge*); walnut oil is pressed here every other year during the Walnut Festival on the first Sunday in October.

▶ *Leave Saillac travelling NW to reach the D 19, then turn SW towards the D 8.*

Turenne★

🖐 *See TURENNE.*

▶ *Continue along the D 8. After 3km/1.8mi, turn left towards Lagleygeolles.*

Gouffre de la Fage★

🕒 *Open Jul-Sep,* 🚶 *guided tour (1hr, last entrance 30min before closing), 9.30am-1pm and 2-7pm; Apr-Jun, unaccompanied tour, 2-6.30pm; early-Sep to mid-Oct, unaccompanied tour, 2-6pm; Nov school hols, Tue and Thu, 3pm.* 🐁 *5.50€ (child: 3.50€).* ☎ *05 55 85 80 30.*

The underground galleries in this chasm form two separate groups, which can be visited one after the other. A staircase leads into the chasm, which was created by the collapse of the roof section. The first group of chambers, to the left, contains fine draperies in the form of jellyfish in beautiful rich colours. In the Organ Hall (Salle des Orgues), the concretions are played like a xylophone.

The second group, with many stalagmites and stalactites, also has a forest of needle-like forms hanging from the roof.

The cave is occupied by a very large colony of bats, including six different species. Return to Lagleygeolles, and take the left turn that will bring you to D 73.

Jugeals-Nazareth – The village of Nazareth was founded by Raymond I of Turenne on his return from the First Crusade. He built a leper-house which he entrusted to the care of the Knights Templars. Beneath the town hall there are several vaulted chambers, each equipped with a well and closed off with a railing, in which the lepers used to stay.

As you leave town to the N on D 8, a scenic overlook comes into view on the right. At the Monplaisir crossroads, D 38 goes back to Brive-la-Gaillarde.

③ Le Causse Corrèzien★

Round trip of 45km/29mi – allow 3hr

▶ *Leave Brive on the D 920 S, towards Cahors.*

The road rises above the Brive basin.

Grottes de St-Antoine

These caves, hollowed out of sandstone, were used as a retreat by St Antony of Padua while he was living at Brive. They form an open-air sanctuary. Franciscans still provide hospitality for today's pilgrims. Follow the Stations of the Cross to the top of a hill to get a good view of Brive.

▶ *Take the small signposted road to the left.*

Grottes de Lamouroux

This picturesque group of caves arranged in five tiers was used by man in times of danger.

Noailles

Noailles, lying in a pleasant setting of green hills, is overlooked by its castle and church perched on a hill.

The Renaissance **château**, seat of the De Noailles family, is decorated with pinnacle windows, which have pediments ornamented with angels bearing the De Noailles coat of arms.

The **church**, topped with a Limousin-style bell gable, has a Romanesque apse and chancel with realistic historiated capitals (cripples on crutches) on slender columns. In the pointed-vaulted nave are memorial plates of the De Noailles family. There is a painting by Watteau's teacher Claude Gillot (*Instruments of the Crucifixion*).

▶ *Leave Noailles on the D 158 heading W.*

The road climbs towards the lake and Corrèze Causse, an area of white limestone and with here and there a dip filled with red clay and covered with juniper bushes and stunted oak trees.

Lissac-sur-Couze

Set back from the lake, this elegant manor, flanked by battlemented turrets, was a military tower in the 13C and 14C. The church beside it has a bell gable.

Lac du Causse★

Kids Also known as the Lac de Chasteaux, this superb stretch of water (90ha/222 acres), set in lush green countryside in the lovely Couze Valley, is a recreation centre (swimming, sailing, water-skiing, windsurfing, sculling etc).

▶ *Leave Lissac on the D 59 SW.*

The itinerary runs along the lake shore, revealing its extent and beauty.

▶ *Turn right off the D 19 onto the D 154 towards Chartrier-Ferrière.*

Le Maillet

The limestone walls of the houses in this hamlet are constructed in a traditional way using house martin mortar, that is lumps of clay pressed into cracks. The vivid red of the clay gives a lot of character to the scene.

▶ *Continue along the D 154.*

Nadaillac

This charming country village is famous for its high-quality truffles. Some of the medieval houses have typical *lauzes*-covered roofs. The fortified church is entered through a deep-set doorway preceded by a vaulted passageway. The pre-chancel is covered by a dome on pendentives.

▶ *Leave Nadaillac on the D 63.*

Further on, scenic road D 60 weaves in and out of the départements of the Dordogne and Corrèze at their borders.

▶ *In Larche, take the N 89 back to Brive.*

Le BUGUE

POPULATION 2 778

MICHELIN LOCAL MAP 329: G-6

This busy agricultural centre is situated at the gateway of the Périgord Noir, on the north bank of the Vézère, near its confluence with the Dordogne. A wide variety of leisure and cultural activities are available in and around the town, including museums, caves, castles etc.

- **Don't Miss**: Gouffre de Proumeyssac; Cingle de Trémolat; Aquarium du Périgord Noir; Village du Bournat; Les Grottes de Maxange; Limeuil.
- **Organising Your Time**: Allow a full day to explore the Vézère and Dordogne valleys.
- **Especially for Kids**: Aquarium du Périgord Noir; Maison de la Vie Sauvage-Musée de Paléontologie; Village du Bournat.

Sights

Aquarium du Périgord Noir★

Open Jul-Aug, 9am-7pm; Jun, 10am-6pm; Apr-May and Sep, 10am-6pm; mid-Feb to Mar and Oct to mid-Nov, 10am-5pm. 8.20€ *(children aged 4-16: 5.80€).* 05 53 07 10 74. www.parc-aquarium.com

This has been designed to make visitors feel as if they were moving below the surface of the river. The open-topped aquariums have natural lighting and open onto large windows. They contain fresh water fish, crustaceans and invertebrates from various parts of Europe. Of particularly impressive dimensions are the gleaning catfish, originating from the centre and east of the continent (some of the larger specimens are over 1.5m/5ft long), white and silver grass carp and sturgeons. There is a separate display on the breeding cycle of the salmon.

Address Book

For coin ranges, see the Legend at the back of the guide.

EATING OUT

Cygne – 2 le Cingle - 05 53 07 17 77 - t-raux@wanadoo.fr - closed 1-15 Oct, 20 Dec-5 Jan, Sun eve and Mon out of season. This old family home on the edge of town has been converted into a hotel with a country feel. Plain but well-kept rooms, a warm dining room with a stone fireplace, plus a veranda and shady terrace.

Le Chai – Pl. du Port - 24510 Limeuil - 05 53 63 39 36 - closed Dec-Jan. This former wine storehouse at the confluence of the Vézère and Dordogne has been converted into a restaurant decorated in yellow and blue tones and adorned with an old fireplace and oven. Pleasant garden terrace. Salads, crêpes and pizza feature on the menu.

WHERE TO STAY

Camping St-Avit Loisirs – 24260 St-Avit-de-Vialard - 7km/4.3mi NW of Le Bugue on the D 710 and a minor road - 05 53 02 64 00 - contact@saint-avit-loisirs.com - open 15 Apr to 28 Sep - reserv. recommended - 350 pitches. Large pitches, comfortable facilities and a range of services are the main features of this campsite in a lovely location near a 100-year-old farm surrounded by oak and chestnut trees. Bungalows and hotel

accommodation packages are also available. Several swimming pools, one of which is covered.

Maison Oléa – La Combe de Leygue - 5km/3mi E of Le Bugue on the D 703 towards Sarlat and then a minor road to the left - 05 53 08 48 93 - - 5 rooms. A peaceful stay is assured in this modern building which takes its inspiration from local architecture. The ground floor is embellished with Moorish touches and a lovely veranda which is used as a winter garden. The spacious rooms face south and overlook the swimming pool and the Vézère Valley.

LEISURE ACTIVITIES

Canöes des Courrèges – 05 53 08 75 37. Canoes for hire on the Dordogne and the Vézère.

A Canoë Raid – Campeyral - 24170 Siorac-en-Périgord - 05 53 31 64 11 - www.a-canœ-raid.com - open daily, Easter-Oct, 9am-2pm. Full-day and overnight canoe and kayak trips on the Dordogne and the Vézère.

Canoë Rivière Loisirs – 24510 Limeuil - 05 53 63 38 73 - www.canœs-rivieres-loisirs.com - open 9am-6.30pm. Canoe, touring and mountain-bike hire. Boat trips from Limeuil (at the confluence of the Dordogne and the Vézère) exploring the superb landscapes of the Périgord Noir.

Maison de la Vie Sauvage-Musée de Paléontologie

Open Jul-Aug, 10am-1pm and 3-7pm; Apr-Jun and Sep, Tue and Sat, 9.30am-12.30pm and 3-6pm, other days (except Mon), 2-6pm; Oct-Mar, school hols and Sun, 3-6pm. Closed 1 Jan and 25 Dec. ☎ 05 53 08 28 10.

Vie Sauvage – The focus of this section is birds, including a collection of stuffed and mounted specimens, their habits and habitats in Europe.

The displays address aspects such as the how and why of feathers, beaks, and song; techniques for flying, hunting and fishing. Migratory routes and their many dangers are described.

One section is devoted to the evolution from fish to reptiles, and another to mammals.

Musée de Paléontologie – Four exhibit rooms house the collection of over 3 000 items, grouped together in families: ammonites, trilobites, gastropods, rudistae, and so forth.

Village du Bournat★

Open May-Sep, 10am-7pm; mid-Feb to Apr and Oct to mid-Nov, 10am-5pm. 12€ high season; 8.70€ low season (child: 6€). ☎ 05 53 08 41 99.

This is a reconstitution of a regional village-farm at the turn of the last century with its school, chapel, town hall, wash-house, wine cellar. In each of the buildings, figures stage the joys and chores of the past: harvest supper, a wedding celebration, washerwomen at work. Bakers, smithies and other craftsmen perpetuate their traditional tradecraft, also highlighted by the collection of farm tools and machinery. There is a fun fair in season.

Caves

Caverne de Bara-Bahau

Open Jul-Aug, guided tour (30min, last tour 30min before closing), 9.30am-7pm; Feb-Jun, 10am-noon and 2-5.30pm; Sep-Dec, 10am-noon and 2-5pm. Closed Jan. 5.50€ (child: 3.50€). ☎ 05 53 07 44 58.

Just west of Le Bugue, the cave, which is about 100m/300ft long, ends in a chamber blocked by a rock fall. On the roof of the chamber, amid the protrusions in the rock face, may be seen drawings made with sharpened flints and fingers (Early and Middle Magdalenian Culture) discovered in 1951 by the Casterets; they depict horses, aurochs, bison, bears and deer.

Grotte de St-Cirq

6km/3.6mi NE on the D 31. Open Jun-Sep, guided tour (30min), daily except Sat, 10am-6pm; Oct-May, daily except Sat, noon-4pm. 4€ (child: 1€). ☎ 05 53 07 14 37.
In a small cave underneath an overhanging rock engravings from the Middle Magdalenian Period, representing horses, bison and ibex, have been discovered. However, the cave is best-known for the painting of the Man of St-Cirq (at times inappropriately called the Sorcerer of St-Cirq), one of the most remarkable representations of a human figure found in a prehistoric cave.

A small museum exhibits fossils and prehistoric tools.

Gouffre de Proumeyssac★★

3km/2mi S via the D 31E. Open Jul-Aug, guided tour (45min), 9am-7pm; May-Jun, 9.30am-6.30pm; Mar-Apr and Sep-Oct, 9.30am-noon and 2-5.30pm; Feb and Nov-Dec, 2-5pm. Closed Jan and 25 Dec. 7.90€ (-15 years old: 5.30€). Descent via lift by reservation only: 15€ (-15 years old: 10€). ☎ 05 53 07 27 47. www.perigord.com/proumeyssac.

A tunnel drilled into a hill, overlooking the Vézère, leads to a platform built half way up the chasm. This platform offers a view of this underground dome which is decorated, particularly at the base of the walls, with fine yellow and white concretions. Water seeps through abundantly, adding to the stalactites which, in some places, are very numerous and form draperies, pure coloured stalagmites and fantastic shapes such as the eccentrics and triangular crystallisations that are building up from the floor of the caves. All these concretions are revealed in turn by a *son et lumière* presentation. A short film explains the formation of the cave and a second *son et lumière* presentation takes place after the descent into the depths of the chasm.

The minute basket suspended in mid-air was until 1952 the only way of getting into the chasm. The 52m/171ft descent in complete darkness at the mercy of the fluctuations in temperament of the mule which was working the winch must have been an unforgettable experience for the four tourists allowed down each time with their guide. This primitive lift is available once more (*apply in advance*).

Outside, a landscaped area dotted with explanatory panels offers visitors an insight into the geological features of the site.

In summer, concert and shows are organised inside the chasm.

A woodland trail (30min there and back) leads to a spot overlooking the Vézère which offers a fine panorama of the river. Panels dotted along the way offer information on the main tree species in the Périgord.

Excursion

From the Vézère to the Dordogne

80km/50mi round tour – allow one day

▶ *Drive SE out of Le Bugue along the D 703.*

Campagne

At the opening of a small valley stands a small Romanesque church preceded by a belfry.

The **castle** of the lords of Campagne, built in the 15C, was restored in the 19C. The towers with crenellations and machicolations which flank the living quarters and the neo-Gothic elements give the castle the appearance of an English manor house. The last Marquis de Campagne gave the castle to the State in 1970.

▶ *Continue E along the D 35.*

St-Cyprien

St-Cyprien clings to the side of a hill near the north bank of the Dordogne, in a setting of hills and woodlands characteristic of the Périgord Noir. It is dominated by the massive outline of its **church**, the old houses of the village clustered close around. The large church was built in the 12C and restored in the Gothic period; the belfry keep is Romanesque. Inside, the enormous main body of the church has pointed vaulting. A wealth of 17C furnishings include altarpieces, a pulpit, stalls, an organ loft and a wrought-iron balustrade.

Close to the village are the carefully restored ruins of the **Château de Fages**.

▶ *Leave St-Cyprien travelling SW along the D 703E. The road skirts the north bank of the Dordogne. Turn left onto the D 703.*

Siorac-en-Périgord

This small village, sought after for its beach, has a 17C castle and a small Romanesque church.

The castle now houses the **Musée des Arts Culinaires** which displays utensils, crockery, objets d'art and furniture connected with kitchens and tableware. &⊙*Open mid-Jun to mid-Sep, 10am-7pm; Easter to mid-Jun, 10am-noon and 2-6pm; mid-Sep to Oct, by prior arrangement.* ⊚*5€.* ☎ *05 53 31 63 69.*

▶ *Return to the D 703E and continue to follow the River Dordogne.*

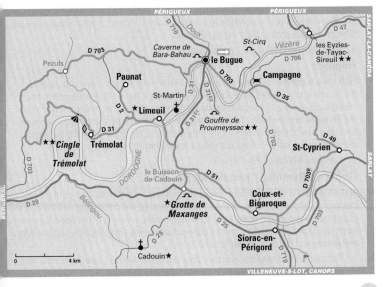

Coux-et-Bigaroque

This village consists of two formerly independent parishes. Note the carved doorway of the Romanesque church of Coux and the picturesque streets of Bigaroque.

▶ *Continue your journey along the Dordogne via the D 51 then turn left onto the D 51E to Le Buisson-de-Cadouin. Turn left beyond the railway line then left again and drive on for another 1.5km/0.9mi.*

Les Grottes de Maxange★

🕐 *Open Jul-Aug, 9am-7pm; Apr-Jun and Sep, 10am-noon and 2-6pm; Oct, 10am-noon and 2-5pm.* ⊙6.50€ *(6-12 years old: 4€).* ☎ *05 53 23 42 80.*

These caves, discovered in a quarry in 2000, consist of galleries dug out of the yellow limestone by the sea when it withdrew, and later obstructed by alluvial deposits which it was necessary to clear away. The different deposit strata can be seen in the lower gallery, whereas the upper gallery contains a great variety of concretions (including stalactites and stalagmites), some of them with strange shapes and colours.

▶ *Return to the D 51.*

Limeuil★

Walk up the main street. Built on a steep promontory, this old village, arranged in tiers overlooking the confluence of the River Dordogne and River Vézère, occupies a picturesque **site**★. Its two bridges, unusually set at right angles and spanning each of the rivers, mark the confluence. Traces of its past as a fortress town can be seen on climbing up the ancient narrow streets to the site of the old castle and church.

Limeuil's role as arsenal and watchtower established itself quite early on, thanks mainly to its strategic position, which aroused desire and envy in those who saw it. At one point the militant peasants known as *Croquants* gained control of the town during an uprising. Limeuil was also for many centuries a port and safe haven for heavy barges (*canoes for hire*).

The village has retained traces of the former walled town along the pedestrianised streets leading up to the church. The imposing house with mullioned windows situated next to the 16C fortified harbour gate was the seat of the boatmen's guild. Immediately to the left, the town hall is housed in a former convent. The Grand Rue leads to the Récluzou gate with a pointed arch on the outside and a rounded one on the inside. From the **Parc du Château** (a former mansion remodelled in the early 20C) there is a fine panoramic view of the confluence of the Dordogne and Vézère. 🕐 *Open Jul-Aug, guided tour daily except Sat, 10am-7pm; at other times between Easter and early Nov, call* ☎ *05 53 63 38 90.*

The cliff road (D 31) overlooks the Limeuil meander.

▶ *2km/1.2mi further on turn right onto the D 2.*

Paunat

This modest village has retained an imposing church, once part of a monastery under the control of the powerful abbey of St-Martial in Limoges.

The austere-looking **Église St-Martial** was built in the 12C and remodelled in the 15C. The fortified belfry-porch, featuring two domed storeys, is an unusual example of Romanesque architecture in the Périgord.

▶ *Turn back and take the D 31 on the right.*

Trémolat

Built on a meander in the Dordogne, this charming village was made famous by the shooting of Claude Chabrol's film *The Butcher*. It has a 12C Romanesque church which represents a condensed version of all the religious architectural features of the Périgord region: heavy fortifications are combined with a vaulting system supporting a row of three domes and a huge defensive chamber covering the whole of the interior; the latter served as a refuge for the entire village.

▶ *Continue NW and follow the river.*

Cingle de Trémolat (Trémolat Meander)★★

At the foot of a semicircle of high, bare, white cliffs highlighted by clumps of greenery, the river coils in a large loop, spanned by bridges of golden stone and reflecting lines of poplars. Beyond the wonderful stretch of water, which is often used for water sports and rowing regattas, on the convex bank lies a vast mosaic of arable fields and meadows (Trémolat Water Sports Centre).

▶ *The road offers fine glimpses of the valley. Just before Mauzac, turn right onto a minor road leading to the D 703 which takes you back to Le Bugue.*

CADOUIN★

POPULATION 335

MICHELIN LOCAL MAP 329: G-7

The Abbey of Cadouin, founded in a narrow valley near the Forêt de Bessède in 1115 by Géraut de Sales, was occupied soon after by the Cistercians and was extremely prosperous during the Middle Ages, particularly as a place of pilgrimage. A small village, with its old covered market, has grown around the church and cloisters, which were restored after the Revolution.

On 14 October 1890, the cinematographer and film critic Louis Delluc was born in a house on Cadouin's market square.

Don't Miss: Abbey church and cloisters.

Especially for Kids: Musée du Vélocipède.

A Bit of History

The Holy Shroud of Cadouin – The first written mention of the Holy Shroud appeared in 1214 in an act decreed by Simon de Montfort. This linen cloth adorned with bands of embroidery had been brought from Antioch by a priest from the Périgord and was believed to be the cloth that had been wrapped around Christ's head.

The shroud became an object of deep veneration and attracted large pilgrimages, bringing great renown to Cadouin. It is said that Richard the Lion Heart, St Louis and Charles V came to kneel before it in reverence. Charles VII had it brought to Paris and Louis XI to Poitiers.

Tradition versus Science – In 1934, two experts attributed the Holy Shroud of Cadouin to the 11C, as the embroidered bands bore Kufic inscriptions citing an emir and a caliph who had ruled in Egypt in 1094 and 1101. The bishop of Périgueux therefore had the pilgrimage to Cadouin discontinued.

Visit

Abbey

Church★ – The building, completed in 1154, presents a massive, powerful west front divided horizontally into three sections: the middle section,

---

WHERE TO STAY

Camping La Grande Veyière – 24480 Molières - 4km/2.5mi W of Cadouin along the D 25 and D 27- ☎ 05 53 63 25 84 - la-grande-veyiere@wanadoo.fr - ◐ open Apr-2 Nov - reserv. recommended - 64 pitches. This hilltop campsite is next to an attractive traditional farm, whose outbuildings have been converted into a shop and bar. Spacious, well-shaded pitches, plus a swimming pool and play area for children.

Abbey church and cloisters

J. Damase/MICHELIN

opened by three round-arched windows which light the church's interior, divides upper and lower arcaded sections.

This austere architectural plan, where decoration is limited virtually to the play of light on the stone, emphasises the ornamental effect brought about by the gold colour of the Molières stone.

The finely proportioned building broke away from Cistercian architecture with its interior plan: a chancel with an apse between two apsidal chapels, a dome at the transept crossing capped by a pyramidal bell tower roofed with chestnut shingles, and a more elaborate interior decoration (windows surrounded by mouldings, carved capitals). Nonetheless, the harmonious proportions and the grandeur of the construction emanate a spirituality entirely in keeping with Cistercian sanctuaries.

Cloisters★★ – ♿ ◷*Open Jul-Aug, ⌖guided tour (45min), 10am-7pm; Feb-Jun, Sep to mid-Nov and Christmas hols, daily except Tue, 10am-12.30pm and 2-6pm; mid-Nov to mid-Dec, daily except Tue, Fri and Sat, 10am-12.30pm and 2-5.30pm. ◷Closed Jan and 25 Dec. ☞5.20€. ☎ 05 53 63 36 28.* Thanks to the generosity of Louis XI, the cloisters were built at the end of the 15C in the Flamboyant Gothic style. The work, in fact, continued to the middle of the 16C, as the Renaissance capitals of some of the columns bear witness. Despite the damage suffered during the Wars of Religion and the Revolution, the cloisters were saved and restored in the 19C, owing to the enthusiastic attention they were given by historians and archaeologists alike.

Fine doors, adorned with coats of arms, pendants carved into people and lively little scenes and a large fresco of the Annunciation make it a fascinating visit. Four small columns cast in the form of towers are decorated with themes from the Old and New Testaments (Samson and Delilah, Job etc).

The chapter house and two other rooms have been set up as a **Musée du Suaire** (Shroud Museum), where the restored relic is on display, forming the centrepiece of an exhibition to mark the eight centuries of pilgrimage and religious fervour that it provoked.

Musée du Vélocipède

Kids ◷*Open 10am-7pm (last entry 1hr before closing). ☞6€(child: 3€). ☎ 05 53 63 46 60.*

France's biggest bicycle museum occupies an outbuilding of the convent with a display of about 100 models. Huge pennyfarthings, distinguished by the large front wheel and very small rear wheel, other old bicycles and tricycles represent the finest hours of technology and inventions in this field since the middle of the 19C. The beginnings of competitive cycling are represented by the model from the Paris-Brest return race of 1891 and a bicycle from the first ever Tour de France in 1903.

CAHORS★★

POPULATION 20 003

MICHELIN LOCAL MAP 337: E-5

The town of Cahors, impressively enclosed by a meander in the River Lot, still retains precious vestiges of its glorious past. **Boulevard Gambetta**, a typically southern French avenue lined with plane trees, cafés and shops, is the town's main thoroughfare. The busy, bustling atmosphere here reflects the fact that Cahors remains an important commercial and administrative centre.

The former capital of the Quercy is an excellent starting point for tours of the Célé and Lot valleys, where options include tours of the famous Cahors vineyards, boat trips along the River Lot, and visits to some of the region's famous underground caves. ▯ *Pl. F.-Mitterrand, 46004 Cahors, ☎ 05 65 53 20 65. www.quercy-tourisme. com/cahors.*

▸ **Orient Yourself**: Take a boat trip on the River Lot to discover this charming town and valley from a different perspective.

▯ **Parking**: A number of car parks are dotted around the centre (&see town plan).

⊕ **Organising Your Time**: Allow a full day to explore the Célé and Lot valleys.

⊝ **Don't Miss**: Pont Valentré; Cathédrale St-Étienne (north door and cloisters).

▦ **Especially for Kids**: Musée de Plein Air du Quercy, in Cuzals.

& **Also See**: Grottes du Pech-Merle; Château de Cénevières; St-Cirq-Lapopie.

A Bit of History

The Sacred Spring – A spring, discovered by Carthusian monks, led to the founding of Divona Cadurcorum, later known as Cadurca and later still as Cahors. First the Gauls and then the Romans worshipped the spring with a devotion which was confirmed by the discovery in 1991 of a great number of coins dating from the beginning of Christianity, which had been thrown into the fountain as offerings. The town grew rapidly in size: a forum, a theatre, temples, baths and ramparts were built. This spring still supplies the town with drinking water.

The Golden Age – In the 13C Cahors became one of the great towns of France and experienced onsiderable economic prosperity due in no small part to the arrival of Lombard merchants and bankers. The Lombards were brilliant businessmen and bankers, but also operated somewhat less reputedly as usurers.

The Templars, in turn, came to Cahors; gold fever spread to the townspeople and Cahors became one of the leading banking cities of Europe. The word cahorsin, which was what the people of Cahors were called, became synonymous with the word usurer.

War and Decline – At the beginning of the Hundred Years War, the English seized all the towns in the Quercy. Cahors alone remained impregnable, in spite of the Black Death which killed half the population.

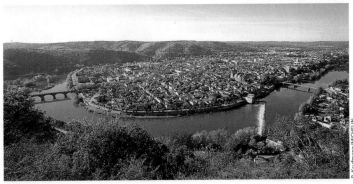

Cahors is tucked into a meander of the River Lot.

In 1360, under the Treaty of Brétigny, Cahors was ceded to the English. By 1450, when the English left the Quercy, Cahors was a ruined city.

Cahors and the Reformation – After several decades of peace, Cahors was able to regain some of its past prosperity; unfortunately in 1540 the Reformation reached the city and rapidly caused dissension among the population. In 1560 some Protestants were massacred.

Twenty years later the town was besieged by the Huguenots, led by Henri de Navarre. The assault lasted three days and ended in the ransacking of the city.

Native Sons – These include Pope John XXII (1316-34), founder of the successful university in Cahors in 1332 (which was combined with that of Toulouse in the 18C), the poet Clément Marot (1496-1544) and **Léon Gambetta** (1838-82), an outstanding lawyer and statesman. This ardent patriot played an active part in the downfall of Napoleon III and in the proclamation of the Third Republic on 4 September 1870.

During the Franco-Prussian War, Gambetta escaped from Paris, under enemy siege, in a balloon in October 1870, floating over the German lines and landing in Tours where he was able (in his capacity as War Minister) to organise the country's defence against the Prussian Army; an armistice was signed in 1871.

There is scarcely a town or city in France which has not paid homage to this republican statesman by naming a street or square after him.

Visit

Pont Valentré★★

The Valentré bridge is a remarkable example of French medieval military architecture. The three towers, with machicolations and crenellated parapets, and the pointed cutwaters breaking the line of the seven pointed arches, give it a bold and proud appearance.

The best view of the bridge and its towers, which rise 40m/130ft above the river, is from a little way upstream on the north bank of the Lot.

The original appearance of the Pont Valentré was considerably modified in 1879 when the bridge was restored; the barbican, which reinforced the defences from the town side, was replaced by the present-day gate.

The bridge was originally an isolated fortress commanding the river; the central tower served as an observation post, the outer towers were closed by gates and portcullises. A guard house and outwork on the south bank of the Lot provided additional protection. The fortress impressed the English during the Hundred Years War, and Henri de Navarre at the time of the siege of Cahors (1580); it was, consequently, never attacked.

Pont Valentré

S. Sauvignier/MICHELIN

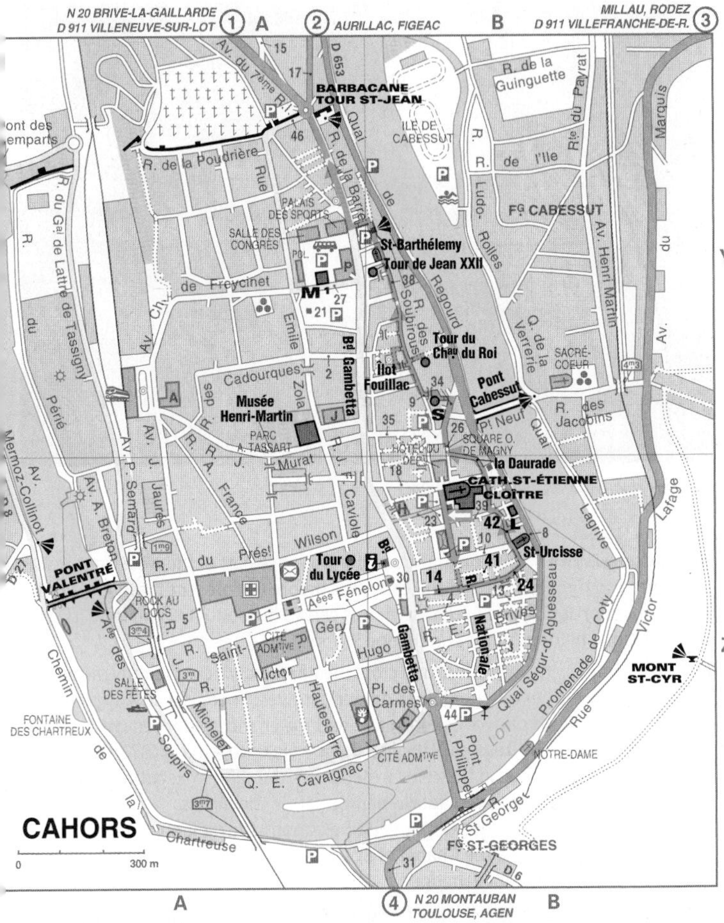

CAHORS

Augustins R. des	AY	2	Dr-Bergounioux R.	BZ	14	Mitterrand Pl. F.	BZ	30
Badernes R. des	BZ	3	Dr-J.-Ségala R. du	AY	15	Monzie Av. A.-de	BZ	31
Blanqui R.	BZ	4	Évêques Côtes des	AY	17	Pelegry R.	BY	34
Bourthoumieux R. P.	AZ	5	Foch R. du Mar.	BZ	18	Portail-Alban R. du	BY	35
Champollion Quai	BZ	8	Gambetta Bd	AY,BZ		St-Barthélemy R.	BY	38
Château-du-Roi R. du	BY	9	Gaulle Pl. Ch.-de	AY	21	St-James R.	BZ	39
Clemenceau R. G.	BZ	10	Joffre R. du Mar.	BZ	23	St-Priest R.	BZ	41
Delmas R. du Col.	BZ	13	Lastié R.	BZ	24	St-Urcisse R.	BZ	42
			Marot R. Clément	BY	26	Vaxis Cours	BZ	44
			Mendès-France R. P.	AY	27	Villars R. René	AY	46

Maison de Roaldès	BZ	L	Tour du Collège Pélegry	BY	S
Musée de la Résistance, de la Déportation et de la Libération	AY	M1			

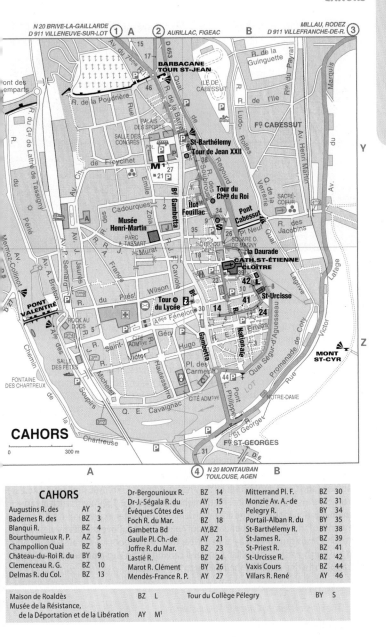

Cathédrale St-Étienne★

The clergy built this church as a fortress to provide a place of safety in troubled times, as well as to bolster prestige. At the end of the 11C, Bishop Géraud of Cardaillac began to build a church on the site of a former 6C church. Much of Bishop Géraud's church remains standing to this day. The trefoiled south door dates from 1119. The north door is 12C; the restoration work on the original east end dates from the 13C. The west front was built early in the 14C, and the paintings inside the domes and in the chancel were completed at the same time. The Flamboyant-style cloisters and some of the outbuildings were commissioned at the beginning of the 16C by Bishop Antoine de Luzech.

Exterior – The west front is made of three adjoining towers. The central one has a belfry above it and opens with double doors. On the first floor, the rose window is surrounded by blind arcades. In spite of windows with twin bays completing the decoration, the appearance of the façade remains austere and military.

Northern doorway of St-Étienne Cathedral

North doorway★★ – This Romanesque door was once part of the west front; it was transferred to the north side of the cathedral before the present façade was built. The tympanum depicts the Ascension. It was carved in about 1135 and from its style and technique belongs to the Languedoc School.

Interior – Enter by the west door and cross the **narthex** which is slightly raised; the nave is roofed with two huge domes on pendentives. There is a striking contrast between the nave, in pale-coloured stone, and the chancel, adorned with stained glass and paintings. The frescoes of the first dome were uncovered in 1872; these show the stoning of St Stephen in the central medallion, the saint's executioners around the frieze and eight giant-sized figures of prophets in the niches.

The chancel and the apse have Gothic vaulting. Among the radiating chapels, which were added in the 15C, is the Chapel of St Antony, which opens onto the chancel through a beautiful Flamboyant door.

Cloisters★ – Dating from 1509, these Renaissance cloisters were built after those of Carennac and Cadouin, with which they have a number of stylistic similarities. Access to the cloisters is through a door on the right of the chancel. They are still rich in carved ornamentation in spite of considerable damage. The galleries are roofed with stellar vaulting; of the decorated pendants, only one remains above the north-west door, showing Jesus surrounded by angels. Near the chancel door is a spiral staircase, and on the north-west corner pillar a graceful carving of the Virgin of the Annunciation, wrapped in a fine cloak, her hair falling to her shoulders.

Walking Tour

▸ *The cloisters lead to Chapelle St-Gausbert.*

Chapelle St-Gausbert

🕐 *Open Jun-Sep, 10am-12.30pm and 3-6pm.* ☎ *05 65 23 07 50.*

16C paintings in the style of the Italian Renaissance decorate the ceiling of this former chapter house, whereas 15C paintings representing the Last Judgement adorn the walls. The chapel also contains the Cathedral Treasury.

Enter the inner court of the former arch-deaconry of St John through the door in the north-east corner of the cloisters. Note the lovely Renaissance decoration.

▸ *On leaving the cathedral, follow rue Nationale past the covered market.*

Rue Nationale

This was the main thoroughfare of the active Badernes Quarter. At no 116, the panels of a lovely **17C door** are decorated with fruit and foliage.

Across the way, the narrow **rue St-Priest** has kept its medieval appearance. It leads to place St-Priest which boasts a beautiful outside wooden staircase in Louis XIII style (no 18).

▸ *Turn right.*

Rue du Docteur-Bergounioux

At no 40 a 16C town house has an interesting Renaissance façade opened by windows influenced by the Italian Renaissance style.

▶ *Retrace your steps and continue straight on.*

Rue Lastié

At no 35 note the Rayonnant-style windows.
At no 117, a 16C house has kept its small shop on the ground floor above which are twin bays.
At the far end of the street, the pretty brick houses have been recently restored.

▶ *Turn left.*

Rue St-Urcisse

The late-12C church of St-Urcisse is entered through a 14C doorway. Inside, the two chancel pillars are decorated with elegant historiated capitals.
Note the 13C half-timbered house (no 68) with its *soleilho* (open attic), in which laundry was hung out to dry.

▶ *Turn right.*

Maison de Roaldès

The mansion is also known as Henri IV's Mansion because it is said that the king of Navarre stayed there during the siege of Cahors in 1580.
The house dates from the end of the 15C and was restored in 1912. In the 17C it became the property of the Roaldès, a well-known Quercy family.
The north side, overlooking the square, has different ornamental motifs – Quercy roses, flaming suns, lopped off trees – used by the Quercy School of the early 16C.

▶ *Turn back then right onto rue de la Chantrerie.*

La Daurade

This varied set of old residences around the Olivier-de-Magny square includes the Dolive House (17C), the Heretié House (14C to 16C) and the so-called Hangman's House (Maison du Bourreau), with windows decorated with small columns (13C).

▶ *Turn right then walk down the street on the right.*

Pont Cabessut

From the bridge there is a good **view**★ of the upper part of the city, the Soubirous district. The towers bristling in the distance are: Tower of the Hanged Men or St John's Tower, the bell tower of St-Bartholomew, John XXII's Tower, Royal Castle Tower and the Pélegry College Tower.

Tour du Collège Pélegry

The College was founded in 1368 and at first took in 13 poor university students; until the 18C, it was one of the town's most important establishments. The fine hexagonal tower above the main building was constructed in the 15C.

▶ *Follow the narrow lane to the left; it runs onto rue du Château du Roi. Turn right then right again past the prison.*

Tour du Château du Roi

Near Pélegry College stands what is today the prison and was once the governor's residence. Of the two towers and two main buildings erected in the 14C, the remaining massive tower is known as Château du Roi.

▶ *Return to the prison, follow the street opposite and turn right.*

Ilôt Fouillac

This area, once insalubrious, has undergone an extensive programme of redevelopment. By getting rid of the most run-down buildings, a square has been cleared. Its sides are decorated with **murals**, and it is brightened by a particularly interesting **musical fountain**.

▶ *Turn right towards rue des Soubirous.*

Tour Jean-XXII

This tower is all that remains of the palace of Pierre Duèze, brother of John XXII. It is 34m/112ft high and was originally covered in tiles. Twin windows pierce the walls on five storeys.

Address Book

For coin ranges, see the Legend at the back of the guide.

EATING OUT

Le Dousil – *124 r. Nationale* - ☎ *05 65 53 19 67* - ◷ *closed 10 days in Feb, 10 days in Oct, Sun and Mon.* This wine bar near the town's covered market offers an extensive list of over 100 vintages. The decor includes a traditional zinc counter and stone walls. The menu includes a choice of sandwiches, *charcuterie* and daily specials.

Le Rendez-Vous – *49 r. Clément-Marot* - ☎ *05 65 22 65 10* - ◷ *closed 29 Apr-14 May, 28 Oct-12 Nov, Sun and Mon - reserv. recommended.* Located close to the cathedral, Le Rendez-Vous has developed a reputation for its modern cuisine. The mix of colourful contemporary decor and old stonework combine well in the dining room and mezzanine extension. Attractive à la carte and fixed menu options.

La Garenne – *In Saint-Henri, 7km/4.5mi N towards Brive* - ☎ *05 65 35 40 67* - ◷ *closed Feb, 1-15 Mar, Mon eve and Tue eve (except Jul-Aug) and Wed.* This typically Quercy-style building once served as a stable. Cosy interior decor featuring exposed beams, stone walls, attractive, locally made furniture and typical country objects. The main attraction here is the delicious regional cuisine.

Auberge du Vieux Douelle – *46140 Douelle - 8km/5mi W of Cahors on the D 8* - ☎ *05 65 20 02 03* - *aubergededouelle@aol. com* - ◷ *closed over Christmas week.* The dining room in the vaulted cellar of this popular inn, known locally as "Chez Malique", is decked out with bright red tablecloths. Meats are grilled over a wood fire; salads and a buffet are also available. Terrace and pool in the summer. A few rooms available.

WHERE TO STAY

Hôtel Les Chalets – *46090 Vers - 14km/8.7mi E of Cahors on the D 653* - ☎ *05 65 31 40 83* - *les.chalets.vers@wanadoo.fr* - ◷ *closed Jan Sun evenings and Mon Oct-Apr - 23 rooms.* This small modern hotel situated in an attractive leafy setting is particularly welcoming. The bedrooms, with balconies or small gardens, overlook the river. A quiet and peaceful retreat, with gentle background noise courtesy of a waterfall. Swimming pool in summer.

Chambre d'hôte Le Clos des Dryades – *46090 Vers - 19km/11.4mi NE of Cahors on the D 653, towards St-Cirq-Lapopie and the D 49 road to Cours* - ☎ *05 65 31 44 50* – ◷ *closed 15 Nov-15 Feb - 5 rooms.* Nestled deep in the woods, this house with its tiled roof is the perfect place to get away from it all. The rooms are comfortable and the large swimming pool is a great place to cool off on a hot summer's day. Two self-catering cottages are also available.

Chambre d'hôte Les Poujades – *Flaynac - 46090 Pradines - 5km/3.1mi N of Cahors on the D 8* - ☎ *05 65 35 33 36* - – 2 rooms. A flower garden and shady trees surround this typical Quercy house, from where you can enjoy a wonderful view of the Château de Mercuès, the Cahors vineyards and the outskirts of the town. The decor is a little on the sombre side, but is compensated by the warm welcome. One holiday cottage available.

Hôtel A l'Escargot – *5 bd Gambetta* - ☎ *05 65 35 07 66* - ◷ *closed Feb school hols, Dec and Sun out of season - 9 rooms.* Near the Tour Jean-XXI, this hotel occupies the old palace built by the pontiff's family. Functional bedrooms with colourful furnishings, plus a renovated breakfast room.

Chambre d'hôte Domaine de Labarthe – *46090 Espère - 8km/5mi NW of Cahors on the D 911* - ☎ *05 65 30 92 34; reserv. required - 3 rooms.* Guests at this manor house, complete with dovecote, are assured the warmest of welcomes. The rooms are pretty, and fresh flowers and biscuits await you on arrival. All the rooms open onto the garden and pool.

SHOPPING

Market – *Pl. de la Halle.* A traditional market is held on Wednesday and Saturday mornings, with numerous stalls run by farmers selling a range of local produce.

Les Délices du Valentré – *21 bd Léon-Gambetta* - ☎ *05 65 35 09 86* - ◷ *open Tue-Sun.* This pastry chef makes Coque de Cahors, a brioche with candied citron and flavoured with orange water, and Cabecou, a chocolate sweet.

Château de Haute-Serre – *Georges Vigouroux - 8km/5mi S of Cahors on the D 6 towards Lalbenque - 46230 Cieurac* - ☎ *05 65 20 80 20* - *g-vigouroux.fr* - ◷ *open 10am-noon and 2-6pm* - ◷ *closed holidays from 1 Nov to the day before Easter.* This estate, in a wonderful location on a hill with views of vineyards and the Causses du Lot, is one of Cahors' best-known wineries. Guided tours of the cellars and vineyards.

LEISURE ACTIVITIES

L'Archipel – *Quai Ludo-Rollès. Water sports and leisure centre* - ☎ *05 65 35 05 86 / 31 38* - ◷ *closed mid-Sep to mid-Jun.* This summer pool offers lots of fun activities for kids, including slides, hydro-massage, bubble baths, fountains and a games area.

Stade Nautique de Regourd – *Base Nautique de Regourd* - ☎ *05 65 30 08 02 or 05 65 22 15 23* - *fabian.gouthier@free.fr* - ◷ *open Oct-May, Sat, Sun and public hols, 3-6pm; Jun and Sep, Wed, Sat and Sun, 2-7pm; Jul-Aug, Mon-Fri , 3-7pm, Sat-Sun,*

2-8pm - ⏱ closed Nov-May. Water-skiing, wakeboarding and kneeboarding.
Alliance Nautique Cahors – Port Bullier - ☎ 06 80 14 96 77 - ⏱ open Easter-15 Sep - 30min: 18€; 1hr: 28€; 1hr 30min. Hire a small, quiet and easy-to-handle electrically powered boat to explore the River Lot from a different perspective. No permit required.

EVENTS

Festival de Blues - mid-Jul. ☎ 05 65 35 99 99.

Festival du Quercy Blanc - late-Jul to mid-Aug. ☎ 05 65 31 83 12.

Église St-Barthélémy

This church was built in the highest part of the old town, and was known until the 13C as St-Etienne de Soubiroux, *Sancti Stephani de superioribus* (St Stephen of the Upper Quarter), in contrast to the cathedral built in the lower part of the town. The church was rebuilt to its present design in several stages. It now contains a rectangular belfry-porch with three lines of bays of depressed arches one above the other. The belfry, the base of which dates from the 14C, has no spire, and it is built almost entirely of brick.

The nave, with its ogive vaulting, was designed in the Languedoc style. In the chapel nearest the entrance, on the left, a marble slab and bust call to mind that John XXII was baptised in this church.

The cloisonné enamels on the cover of the modern baptismal font depict the main events in the life of this famous Cahors citizen.

The terrace near the church affords a good view of the Cabessut suburb and the Lot Valley.

▷ *Walk to boulevard Gambetta and head N.*

Barbican and Tour St-Jean★

The ramparts, constructed in the 14C, completely cut the isthmus formed by the meander of the River Lot off from the surrounding countryside. Remains of these fortifications can still be seen and include a massive tower at the west end, which sheltered the powder magazine, and the old gateway of St-Michel, which now serves as entrance to the cemetery. It is on the east side, however, where the N 20 road enters the town, that the two most impressive fortified buildings remain: the barbican and St John's Tower. The barbican is an elegant guard house which defended the Barre Gateway; St John's Tower or the Tower of the Hanged Men (Tour des Pendus), was built on a rock overlooking the River Lot.

Sights

Musée de la Résistance, de la Déportation et de la Libération

⏱Open 2-6pm (mornings by prior arrangement). ⏱ Closed 1 Jan, 1 May and 25 Dec. ⊜No charge. ☎ 05 65 22 14 25.

Housed in six rooms, this museum illustrates the birth of the Resistance movement in the Lot region, deportations and persecutions which followed, fighting for the Liberation of France and the epic journey of the Free French from Brazzaville to Berlin. Eighteen models of war planes are also displayed and newspapers dating from that period are available to visitors.

Musée Henri-Martin

⏱ Open daily except Tue, 11am-6pm; Sun and public hols, 2-6pm. ⏱ Closed 1 Jan, 1 May and 25 Dec. ⊜3€ (child: 1.50€). ☎ 05 65 30 15 13.

This museum is housed in the former Episcopal palace. One room is devoted to the works of the painter Henri Martin (1860-1943), a member of the pointillist movement. The museum also presents high-quality temporary exhibitions (contemporary photographs, major 20C and contemporary painters).

In addition, the museum owns important archaeological and historical collections connected with the Quercy region which, it is hoped, will be shown when the premises have been fully renovated.

Excursions

La Croix de Magne Viewpoint★
5km/3mi.

▷ *From the western end of the Valentré Bridge, turn right and then immediately left; take the first left after the agricultural school, and left again at the top of the rise.*

Around the cross, a **view**★ extends in all directions over the plateau, to the River Lot, Cahors and the Valentré Bridge.

Viewpoint to the North of the Town

▷ *5km/3mi along rue du Docteur-J.-Ségala which turns right off the N 20 just beyond the Tour St-Jean.*

This road offers fine views of the Lot Valley and the surroundings of Cahors, including the old town built like an amphitheatre, with its pinnacles, crenellated towers and Valentré Bridge.

Mont St-Cyr Viewpoint★

▷ *7km/4mi via the Louis-Philippe Bridge and the D 6 which you leave after 1.5km/1mi to reach the mount, keeping to the left.*

From the top (viewing table) there is a good **view**★ of Cahors; the contrast between the old and the new quarters of the town, which are separated by boulevard Gambetta, Cahors' main artery, is striking. In the background the distinctive shape of Valentré Bridge can be seen.

Château de Mercuès

▷ *6km/3.7mi NW along the D 911.*

Once the property of the count-bishops of Cahors, the château is now a hotel. It occupies a remarkable site overlooking the north bank of the Lot. In 1212 the château was a fortified castle, it was then enlarged in the 14C, besieged several times during the Hundred Years War and the Wars of Religion, altered in the 15C and converted in the 16C into a château with terraces and gardens. It was not restored completely until the 19C. There is an outstanding **view**★ of the valley from the château.

West of Mercuès the road leaves the valley for a short distance to cross a flourishing countryside of vineyards and orchards; then the road returns to the river, following it closely.

◉ **Château de Roussilon** – *9km/5.4mi N on the N 20.* and **Château de Cieurac** – *12km/7.5mi S via the D 6.*

Confluence of the Célé and the Lot★★
125km/78mi round tour – allow one day

▷ *Leave Cahors travelling NE along the D 653 towards Figeac.*

Laroque-des-Arcs

This village's name is a reminder of the aqueduct which crossed the Francoulès Valley and supplied water to Cahors. A three-tiered bridge bore the aqueduct which transported water over 20km/12mi from Vers to Divona (ancient Cahors). The consuls of Cahors had it demolished in 1370. An old tower perched on a rock beside the Lot enabled guards to watch the river traffic and exact tolls.

▷ *Continue along the D 653.*

Notre-Dame-de-Vêles

This small pilgrimage chapel was built in the 12C and has a lovely square bell tower and a Romanesque apse.

▷ *From Vers, keep following the Dordogne along the D 662.*

Starting from Conduché, where the Célé flows into the Lot, D 41 goes up the valley. The road is squeezed between the river bed and the cliff face, which rises on one side like a wall and at times even overhangs the road below. Many crops grow in the valley with maize tending to replace tobacco.

Cabrerets

Cabrerets, set in a rocky amphitheatre, occupies a commanding position at the confluence of the River Sagne and River Célé.

There is a good overall **view**★ of Cabrerets and its setting from the left bank of the Célé, which is reached by crossing the bridge. Opposite stand the ruins of the **Château du Diable** (Devil's Castle), or Castle of the English, clinging to the formidable

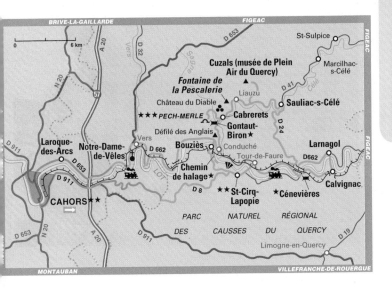

Rochecourbe cliff. This eagle's eyrie, a typical clifftop castle, served as a base from which the English could pillage the countryside during the Hundred Years War.

On the far left is the impressive mass of the 14C and 15C **Château des Gontaut-Biron**★ overlooking the valley. A big corner tower flanks the buildings that surround an inner courtyard.

▶ *Take the D 198 up the valley of the Sagne to Pech-Merle Cave.*

Grottes du Pech-Merle★★★

See Grottes du PECH-MERLE.

▶ *Shortly after Cabrerets the cliff road crosses the face of high stone cliffs.*

Fontaine de la Pescalerie

This is one of the most attractive sights of the Célé Valley; a beautiful waterfall pours out of the rock wall close to the road. It marks the surfacing of an underground river that has cut its way through the Causse de Gramat. Beside the waterfall stands an ivy-covered mill, half-hidden by trees.

▶ *Continue along the D 41, then 1.5km/0.9mi beyond Liauzu, turn left onto a minor road.*

Cuzals

Musée de Plein Air du Quercy (Quercy Open-Air Museum) – Kids All the aspects of life in the Quercy region, from before the Revolution until the Second World War, are illustrated in the park, covering 50ha/124 acres. Visitors are offered an authentic, scientific approach to the area's cultural heritage.

Furniture, machinery, a rather unsettling dentist's surgery dating from 1900, milliner's and baker's shops, and of course examples of Quercy architecture, regional crop specialities as well as a collection of pieces of improbable-looking agricultural equipment are on display. In summer, people from local communities gather together to operate the exhibits; including the thresher, the mill, the bread oven; teams of tireless oxen take children for rides.

A 3km/1.9mi-long discovery trail offers an insight into man's impact on the local environment.

▶ *Return to the D 41 and turn left.*

Sauliac-sur-Célé

This old village clings to an awe-inspiring cliff of coloured rock. In the cliff face can be seen the openings to the fortified caves used in time of war as refuges by the local inhabitants. The more agile climbed up by way of ladders; invalids and animals were hoisted up in great baskets.

▶ *As you leave Sauliac, turn right onto the D 24 which crosses the Célé.*

Beyond Sauliac the valley widens out. Crops and pasture land grow well on the alluvial soil of the valley bottom. The road climbs onto the causse, runs across it then down into the Lot Valley.

Bouziès – Towpath with a bas-relief by Monnier

▶ *From St-Martin-Labouval, follow the north bank of the Lot.*

Larnagol

This village has retained some fine 16C and 17C façades. The castle and its buttressed keep overlook the upper part.

▶ *Leave Arnagol S and cross the river.*

Calvignac

This old village, where a few traces of its fortress may still be seen, is perched on a spur on the river's south bank.

▶ *Staying on the same bank take the D 8 which leads to Cénevières.*

Château de Cénevières★

👁 *See Château de CÉNEVIÈRES.*

▶ *Cross the River Lot and pick up the D 662 towards St-Cirq-Lapopie.*

From Pont de Tour-de-Faure, admire St-Cirq-Lapopie in its remarkable setting on the river's south bank.

St-Cirq-Lapopie★★

👁 *See ST-CIRQ-LAPOPIE.*

Beyond St-Cirq-Lapopie, the D 40, which is built into the cliff, has been designed as a tourist route. There is a good **view**★ of the confluence of the Lot and the Célé from a small viewpoint, the **Belvédère du Bancourel**.

Bouziès

On the bank opposite the village, the **Défilé des Anglais** (Englishmen's Gorge) is the most famous of the fortified gullies constructed during the Hundred Years War in cave-like openings which could only be accessed by a rope-ladder. Towering over the deep valley, the Château de Conduché overlooks the confluence of the River Célé and River Lot.

Towpath along the Lot★ (Chemin de Halage)

▶ *Take the GR 36 trail off to the right of the car park by the moorings.*

After about 500m/547yd, the spectacular towpath comes into view, carved out of the rock because here, the cliff juts out over the river. In sections such as this, the barges coming up the Lot with their cargoes of salt, dried fish, spices or plaster could not be towed by the usual teams of horses or oxen, but had to be pulled along by strong fellows with a reputation for bad tempers and miserable lives. This pathway is now a marvellous walk. At the top of the first lock there is a 15m/9ft-long bas-relief, the work of contemporary artist D Monnier, decorating the limestone wall with fish and shellfish.

▶ *Rejoin the D 8 and turn right. The road runs onto the D 911 at Arcambal. This leads back to Cahors.*

CARENNAC★

POPULATION 373

MICHELIN LOCAL MAP 337: G-2

LOCAL MAP SEE VALLÉE DE LA DORDOGNE

Carennac is one of the most attractive sights along the Dordogne, its picturesque tiled houses and turreted mansions clustering around the old priory once occupied by the prelate and writer François de Salignac de la Mothe-Fénélon.

Visit

This charming village, where some of the houses date from the 16C, has barely changed since Fénelon's day. The Île Barrade, in the Dordogne, was renamed Calypso's Island, and visitors will still be shown a tower in the village which is called Telemachus' Tower in which, it is maintained, Fénelon wrote his masterpiece. The deanery was suppressed by order of the Royal Council in 1788, and put up for auction and sold in 1791. Of the old ramparts there remains only a fortified gateway, and of the buildings, only the castle and the priory tower are left.

▶ *Go through the fortified gateway.*

For coin ranges, see the Legend at the back of the guide.

WHERE TO STAY

◍◍◍ **Auberge du Vieux Quercy** – ☎05 65 10 96 59 - contact@vieuxquercy.com - 🕐 *closed 16 Nov-14 Mar, Sun eve and Mon from 15 Mar-30 Apr and 1 Oct-15 Nov -* 🅿 *- 22 rooms.* This quiet hotel with an attractive flower garden overlooks the village. Functional guest rooms with those in the single-floor annex looking onto the swimming pool. Summer terrace for outdoor dining.

Château

Next to the church of St-Pierre (👆*see below*), this 16C edifice consists of a main building flanked by corner turrets and a gallery built above the church's Gothic chapels. The severe façade looks over the Dordogne and Calypso Island.

Espace Patrimoine

🕐 *Open Jul-Sep, daily except Mon, 10am-noon and 2-6pm; mid-Apr to Jun and Oct, daily except Mon and Sat-Sun, 10am-noon and 2-6pm; public hols, enquire; rest of the year, daily except Sat-Sun, by prior arrangement.* ☎ *05 65 33 81 36. Stairs on the left of the doorway lead inside the castle.*

The three storeys of the château house a discovery area devoted to the River Dordogne where it passes through the Lot *département*. A **scale model** is enlivened by lights and sounds which create a picture of the Dordogne Valley from Biards to Souillac. The

Northern entrance to Carennac

S. Sauvignier/MICHELIN

François de Salignac de la Mothe-Fénélon

The priory-deanery at Carennac, which was founded in the 10C and attached to the famous abbey at Cluny in the following century, owes its fame to the length of time spent there by François de Salignac de la Mothe-Fénélon before he became archbishop of Cambrai. While he was still a student at Cahors, Fénélon used to enjoy spending his holidays at the house of his uncle, senior prior of Carennac. In 1681 Fénélon's uncle died and was succeeded by the young abbot, who remained at the priory for 15 years. Fénélon was greatly revered at Carennac; he enjoyed describing the ceremonies and general rejoicing that greeted his arrival by boat and his installation as commendatory prior. Tradition has it that Fénélon wrote *Télémaque* while living at Carennac. The description of the adventures of Ulysses' son was at first only a literary exercise, but was subsequently turned into a tract for the edification of the duke of Burgundy, Louis XIV's grandson, when Fénélon was appointed his tutor.

other rooms also use audio-visual programmes to explore various subjects: flora and fauna, regional arts, the history of navigation, prehistoric times (3-D projection).

Musée des Alambics et Aromathèque

🕐 *Open Mar-Dec, 10am-6pm; Sat-Sun, 10am-7pm.* 👓 *No charge.* ☎ *05 65 10 91 16.*

Adjacent to the park of the château, this museum is devoted to stills and aromatic plants; it offers guided tours with a demonstration of how lavender is distilled.

Église St-Pierre

In front of this Romanesque church dedicated to St Peter, stands a porch with a beautiful 12C carved **doorway**★. It is well preserved and from its style would appear to belong to the same school as the tympana of Beaulieu, Moissac, Collonges and Cahors. In a mandorla (almond-shaped glory) in the centre of the composition, is Christ in Majesty. His right hand is raised in blessing. He is surrounded by the symbols of the four Evangelists. On either side are the Apostles on two superimposed registers, and there are two prostrate angels on the upper register. The tympanum is framed with a foliated scroll in the Oriental style. Its base is decorated with a frieze of small animals. The continuation of the animals was pursued on a protruding band which doubled the doorway arch, of which a dog and bear can still be seen on the left.

Inside, the interesting archaic capitals in the nave are decorated with fantastic animals, foliage and historiated scenes.

▶ *On leaving the church, walk to the end of the priory courtyard.*

Cloisters – 🕐 *Open Jui, Aug, 10am-12.30pm and 2-7pm (last entry 15min before closure of tourist office); Apr-Jun and Sep-Oct, daily except Sun, 10am-noon and 2-6pm; Jan-Mar and Nov-Dec, daily except Sun, 10am-noon and 2-5pm.* 👓*2.50€.* ☎ *05 65 10 97 01. www.tourisme.carennac.com.* The restored cloisters consist of a Romanesque gallery adjoining the church and three Flamboyant galleries. Stairs lead to the terrace.

The chapter house, which opens onto the cloisters, shelters a remarkable **Entombment**★ (15C). Christ lies on a shroud carried by two disciples: Joseph of Arimathea and Nicodemus. Behind these figures, two holy women accompany the Virgin and the Apostle John; on the right, Mary Magdalene is wiping away a tear. The faces seem quite rustic in character.

▶ *Leave the priory and walk alongside the castle overlooking the Dordogne and Calypso Island. Take the first street on the left.*

A small public park gives access to a charming **Romanesque chapel**. Opposite stands a 16C house with a corner window.

▶ *Turn right to walk round the former priory and return to the castle.*

A bartizan still towers over the Pont de Carennac. On the other side of the bridge, another four-storey, 16C tower overlooks a small pier.

Château de
CASTELNAU-BRETENOUX★★

MICHELIN LOCAL MAP 337: G-2

LOCAL MAP SEE ST-CÉRÉ: EXCURSIONS

On the northern border of the Quercy stands Castelnau-Bretenoux Castle with the village of Prudhomat tucked beneath it. The great mass of the castle's red stone ramparts and the towers rise up from a spur overlooking the confluence of the Cère and the Dordogne. The scale on which the castle defence system was built makes it one of the finest examples of medieval military architecture.

Seen from the countryside more than 5km/3mi round, the castle, as Pierre Loti wrote, "is the beacon . . . the thing you cannot help looking at all the time from wherever you are. It's a cock's comb of blood-red stone rising from a tangle of trees, this ruin poised like a crown on a pedestal dressed with a beautiful greenery of chestnut and oak trees." 🛈 *Av. de la Libération, 46160 Bretenoux,* ☎ *05 65 38 59 53.*

> 🚫 **Don't Miss**: The view from the ramparts of the Château Fort.
> ♿ **Also See**: Rocamadour; Gouffre de Padirac; Beaulieu-sur-Dordogne.

A Bit of History

Turenne's egg – From the 11C onwards the barons of Castelnau were the strongest in the Quercy; they paid homage only to the counts of Toulouse and proudly styled themselves the Second Barons of Christendom. In 1184 Raymond de Toulouse gave the suzerainty of Castelnau to the viscount of Turenne. The baron of Castelnau refused to accept the insult and paid homage instead to Philip Augustus, king of France. Bitter warfare broke out between Turenne and Castelnau; King Louis VIII intervened and decided in favour of Turenne. Whether he liked it or not the baron had to accept the verdict. The fief, however, was only symbolic: Castelnau had to present his overlord with... an egg. Every year, with great pomp and ceremony a yoke of four oxen bore a freshly laid egg to Turenne.

Visit

Château Fort

🕐*Open Jul-Aug,* 👥*guided tour (30min, last entrance 1hr before closing), 9.30am-7pm; May-Jun, 9.30am-12.30pm and 2-6.30pm; Sep-Apr, 10am-12.30pm and 2-5.30pm.* 🕐 *Closed 1 Jan, 1 May, 1 and 11 Nov, 25 Dec and Tue from Oct-Mar.* ⊜*6.10€ (under 18 years old: no charge).* ☎ *05 65 10 98 00.*

Château de Castelnau-Bretenoux

Round the strong keep built in the 13C, there grew up during the Hundred Years War a huge fortress with a fortified curtain wall. The castle was abandoned in the 18C and suffered depredations at the time of the Revolution. It caught fire in 1851 but was skilfully restored between 1896 and 1932.

Exterior – The ground plan is that of an irregular triangle flanked by three round towers and three other towers partially projecting from each side. Three parallel curtain walls still defend the approaches, but the former ramparts have been replaced by an avenue of trees.

From along the ramparts there is a far-reaching **view**★of the Cère and Dordogne valleys to the north; of Turenne Castle set against the horizon to the north-west; of the Montvalent Amphitheatre to the west; and of Loubressac Castle and the Autoire Valley to the south-west and south.

A tall square tower and the seigneurial residence, a rectangular building still known as the *auditoire* (auditorium), suggest the vast scale of this fortress; the garrison numbered 1 500 men and 100 horses.

Interior – In addition to the lapidary depository, containing the Romanesque capitals of Ste-Croix-du-Mont in Gironde, many other rooms should be visited on account of their decoration and furnishings done by the former proprietor, a singer of comic opera, Jean Moulierat, who bought the castle in 1896.

The former chamber of the Quercy Estates General is lit by large windows; the pewter hall and the Grand Salon contain Aubusson and Beauvais tapestries; the oratory has stained-glass windows dating from the 15C and two 15C Spanish altarpieces.

▶ *Leave the castle and turn left, down to the collegiate church.*

Collégiale St-Louis

The church was built in 1460 by the lords of Castelnau in red-ferriferous stone, at the foot of the castle. A few canons' residences can be seen nearby.

▶ *Enter the church.*

The lords' chapel has lovely quadripartite vaulting, the pendant of which is emblazoned with the Castelnau coat of arms. The chancel houses two 15C works of art in polychrome stone; a Virgin in Majesty and a depiction of the Baptism of Christ.

Château de CASTELNAUD★★

MICHELIN LOCAL MAP 329: H-7

LOCAL MAP SEE VALLÉE DE LA DORDOGNE

The impressive ruins of the Château de Castelnaud stand on a wonderful **site**★★ commanding the valleys of the Céou and the Dordogne. Right opposite stands the Château de Beynac (*see BEYNAC-ET-CAZENAC*), Castelnaud's implacable rival throughout the conflicts of the Middle Ages.

▶ **Orient Yourself**: Take a boat trip on the Dordogne to get a wonderful photo of the castle.

Don't Miss: The view from the terrace.

Especially for Kids: Musée de la Guerre au Moyen Âge, inside the castle.

Also See: Beynac-et-Cazenac; la Roque-Gageac; Domme; Sarlat.

A Bit of History

In 1214 Simon de Montfort (c 1165-1218, father of the English statesman and soldier) took possession of the castle, whose occupants had taken the side of the Cathars. In 1259 St Louis ceded the castle to the king of England who held it for several years. During the Hundred Years War the castle constantly changed hands between the French and the English. When at last peace was declared the castle was in terrible condition. During the whole of the second half of the 15C the castle was under reconstruction. Only the keep and curtain wall have kept their 13C appearance. In the 16C the castle was once again transformed in various ways, and the artillery tower was added. After the Revolution it was abandoned and later used as a stone-pit.

In 1969 a major restoration program was undertaken which has enabled most of the buildings to be rebuilt.

Château de Castelnaud

Visit

Château – Musée de la Guerre au Moyen Âge

🕐*Open Jul-Aug, 9am-8pm; Apr-Jun and Sep, 10am-7pm; Feb-Mar and Oct to mid-Nov, 10am-6pm; mid-Nov to Jan, 2-5pm; Christmas school hols, 10am-5pm.* ⊗*7€; Jul-Aug, reduced rate before 1pm, 5.60€ (10-17 years old: 3.50€).* ☎ *05 53 31 30 00. www.castelnaud.com*

Castelnaud is a typical example of a medieval fortress with its powerful machicolated keep, curtain wall, living quarters and inner bailey. Nonetheless, certain parts of the castle – artillery tower, loopholes – which were added later reflect the evolution of weapons in siege warfare. Reconstructed hoarding, later replaced by machicolations, and audio-visual presentations offer an insight into siege warfare tactics in the Middle Ages; housed in a small room, a model illustrates the siege of Castelnaud in 1442, when Charles VII attempted to boot the English out of France once and for all.

The castle is entirely devoted to medieval warfare. A great variety of weapons and objects connected with warfare are on display: 15C and 16C guns in the artillery tower; bows, crossbows and defensive weapons used by bowmen in the lower part of the keep; catapult, battering ram and trebuchet in the siege-warfare room; 15C-17C swords in the sword room.

Another room houses the reconstruction of an armourer's workshop. One room on the ground floor contains a wide choice of comic strips and books about the Medieval period.

Reconstructions of siege apparatus, including a 12C mangonel, or ballista, and other stone-casting devices are displayed in various parts of the castle. At the beginning of the 13C, for instance, a trebuchet could throw a stone weighing as much as 100kg/220 pounds over the walls of a besieged castle. In the 15C, these weapons, which were difficult and dangerous to operate, were replaced by artillery.

From the ward the view extends southwards over the Céou Valley. From the east end of the terrace there is an exceptional **panorama**★★ of one of the most lovely views of the Dordogne Valley.

In July and August, visitors can also visit the castle at night (🕐 *open Mon-Fri, from 8.30pm*). A new play, based on historical figures, is performed every year in the torch-lit rooms.

> **WALNUTS**
>
> **Écomusée de la Noix du Périgord** – *Ferme de Vielcroze - 24250 Castelnaud -* ☎ *05 53 59 69 63 - ecomuseedelanoix@ wanadoo.fr -* 🕐 *open Easter-1 Nov, 10am-7pm -* 🕐 *closed 12 Nov-early Apr -* ⊗ *4€ (child: 3€).* A restored farm is home to this museum entirely devoted to walnuts, in which exhibits and educational displays explain the cultivation and uses of this precious local product. On-site shop, plus a scenic path through the huge walnut grove surrounding the museum.

Château de CÉNEVIÈRES ★

MICHELIN LOCAL MAP 337: G-5 – 7KM/4MI E OF ST-CIRQ-LAPOPIE

LOCAL MAP SEE CAHORS

This imposing castle perches on a sheer rock face overlooking the Lot Valley from a height of more than 70m/230ft.

Also See: St-Cirq-Lapopie; Grotte du Pech Merle.

A Bit of History

As early as the 8C the dukes of Aquitaine had a stronghold built here. In the 13C the lords of Gourdon had the keep built. During the Renaissance, Flottard de Gourdon, who had participated in the campaigns in Italy with François I, completely remodelled the castle. His son, Antoine de Gourdon, converted to Protestantism and participated alongside Henri IV in the siege of Cahors in 1580. He pillaged the cathedral in Cahors and loaded the high altar and altar of the Holy Shroud onto boats returning to Cénevières Castle. The boat carrying the high altar sank in a chasm along the way. Before his death Antoine built a small Protestant church, which is in the outer bailey. He died childless, his widow remarried and a new lineage took over Cénevières. The château was pillaged during the French Revolution, but escaped arson.

Visit

The outside of the castle boasts a 13C keep and 15C wings joined by a 16C Renaissance gallery. The gallery is held up by Tuscan columns and above it are dormer windows. The moat, once crossed by a drawbridge, is now filled in. Inside, the ground floor includes the vaulted salt room and kitchen. The keep has a trap door, which permits a glimpse of the three floors of underground cellars. The adjacent chapel, still consecrated, houses the altar of the Holy Shroud.

On the first floor the great drawing room, with a lovely Renaissance painted ceiling and recently discovered murals, contains 15C and 16C Flemish tapestries and the shrine of the Holy Shroud brought back from Cahors. Various objects are displayed in the following room: a Spanish helmet, a mould for cannon balls, letters from famous people found among the family archives and family trees. The owner is only too pleased to tell you about it.

The small alchemy room is decorated with fascinating 16C naïve frescoes illustrating Greek mythology. The alchemist's oven has a representation of the philosopher's stone.

Finally, from the terrace there are commanding views of the Lot Valley and the hanging village of Calvignac, perched on the hillside.

CHÂLUS

POPULATION 1 759

MICHELIN LOCAL MAP 325: C-7

The old city of Châlus dominated by its keep, recalls the memory of **Richard the Lion Heart's** tragic death. On every side are the solid granite masses, densely wooded, of the Châlus Hills, last buttresses of the Massif Central.

- **Don't Miss**: Château du Haut-Châlus.
- **Also See**: Parc Naturel Regional Périgord-Limousin; Montbrun; Château de Brie.

A Bit of History

A fatal siege – The tale is told of how in 1199 a serf belonging to Adhemar V, viscount of Limoges, discovered a fabulous treasure trove of "ninepins and large balls, all in solid gold" (these items now figure in the arms of Châlus together with a long bow). The viscount of Limoges hid the treasure in his castle at Châlus. Nevertheless rumours of the find reached Richard the Lion Heart, king of England and lord of Western France.

Richard demanded his share of the booty as overlord, and when his vassal refused to give it up, it provided him with a pretext for punishing his vassal for siding with the king of France while he was a prisoner in Germany and he laid siege to Châlus. While he was directing the attack on the castle, he was struck on the shoulder by a quarrel from a prototype of a new crossbow. Richard refused to dress the wound which turned black, the poison went to his heart and the end came. So died, at 42, one of the greatest men of the Middle Ages.

The castle defenders paid dearly for the death of the king: all were hanged except the sharp-eyed archer – he was flayed alive in spite of the fact that he was pardoned by the king on his death bed.

Visit

Château du Haut-Châlus★★

🕐 *For information on opening times, contact the tourist office.* ☎ *05 55 78 51 13. www.chateaudechalus.com.*

The remains of the castle, also known as Châlus-Chabrol, stand on rising ground in the upper part of the village.

Donjon – This cylindrical keep (25m/82ft high and 10m/33ft in diameter), an excellent illustration of feudal military architecture, dates from the 11C. Originally, it had four levels, but the highest one, crowned by machicolations, fell in 1870. A metal stairway leads up and in: the only entrance to the keep is 6m/20ft above ground.

A very narrow passage opens on to a vaulted room (8.5m/18ft high); an opening set in the floor provides a view of the lower room, used for storage. The knights and soldiers were quartered on the upper floors, reached by a stairway safely ensconced in the thick walls. The view from the top platform stretches far, to the Tadoire Valley, Puyconnieux and the fields of Limousin.

The castle ruins

E. Larribère/MICHELIN

The keep's thick, smooth walls of gneiss stone, rising vertically, were a good protection against attack by battering ram, axe and fire.

A short distance from the keep are vestiges of the **chapel** where King Richard's remains were brought. At the time, the chapel was Romanesque; in the 15C a side chapel was added (one arch still stands).

Main building – Perhaps the most spectacular part of the tour is the exhibit on the discovery of architectural remains from the 11C and 13C. The main building opens onto a 13C room which contains a Romanesque column squeezed into a wall erected at a later date. In the next room, you can see the other side of it, as well as two Romanesque windows. The walls are hung with the coats of arms of the castle's different owners.

A little corridor leads to the oldest section, dating from the 11C. Beyond an escape shaft tucked into a nook in the fortifications, a six-sided room forms the base of a corner tower; note the vaulted ceiling and the loopholes. Beside this tower room, a smaller room dissimulates another shaft, 16m/52ft high, and the entrance (walled off) to the watch-path. The lower level, once open to the air, was the ground floor.

The 17C wing features two drawing rooms furnished in 17C-18C style and an 18C oak staircase leading to a large exhibition hall where a collection of fancy dress for the Venice Carnival is displayed.

The barn houses a small museum devoted to the regional craft performed by feuil-lardiers, hoop-wood makers who used chestnut to make the circular strips used for holding together barrel staves.

Gardens – A medieval herb garden surrounding a central closed fountain has been laid out on the esplanade, in front of the castle, whereas the French-style garden with its rosemary maize, its rose trees and hornbeams, is laid out at the foot of the 17C building.

Maison du Châtaignier

Along the N 21, next to the tourist office. ⚐ ⊙Open Jun to mid-Sep, 10.30am-12.30pm and 2.30-6.30pm; the rest of the year, daily except Sat-Sun, 10am-noon and 2-6pm. ⊜2.30€ (child: 1.60€). ☎ 05 55 78 51 13.

This exhibition centre, devoted to chestnut trees and their various uses, offers visitors interactive terminals and video presentations as well as a reconstructed hoop-wood maker's hut.

Château de Châlus-Maulmont

⊙Open Jul-Aug, daily except Tue, ⌁guided tour (1hr), 2-6pm. ⊜No charge. Further information is available from the tourist office, ☎ 05 55 78 51 13.

Located in the town centre, this castle is undergoing restoration work following the collapse of part of its 13C keep. It houses a small museum on local history and gastronomy.

Excursions

Parc Naturel Regional Périgord-Limousin

24300 Abjat-sur-Bandiat. ☎ 05 53 60 34 65.

Created in 1998, this regional nature park covers 180 000ha/695sq mi within a triangle formed by the towns of Périgueux, Limoges and Angoulême. Its aims are to protect and enhance the natural and cultural heritage, to contribute to the economic and cultural development of the area and to attract new inhabitants and new activities to the Périgord-Limousin region. Various brochures are devoted to the local architectural heritage, traditional crafts, outdoor activities and accommodation available within the park.

Montbrun★

▶ *7km/4.3mi SW along the D 6BIS and the D 64A.*

This imposing castle stands deep in a valley, where it reflects in the waters of a pond surrounded by lawns and trees. Edified in the 12C, it once defended the borders of the ducal realm of Aquitaine, and still boasts a moat, high walls and an impregnable square keep surmounted by machicolations. Closed to visitors.

▶ **Château des Cars** - *8.5km/5.3mi NE. ⊙ Open Jul-Aug, daily except Tue 10am-noon, 2-6pm. ⊜2€ (-12 years old: no charge). ☎ 05 55 36 90 22. Mostly in ruins (13C-16C); lapidary museum.*

▶ **Château de Lastours** – *13.5km/8.5mi E.* ⏰🕐 *Open mid-Jul to mid-Aug, daily except Mon 1-7pm; mid-Aug to mid-Jul, Sat-Sun and hols, 1-7pm. Preferably by prior arrangement.* ◉*3€.* ☎ *05 55 58 38 47.* Ruins of a 12C keep, 13C-16C buildings restored.

▶ **Château de Brie**★ – *8km/5mi NW.* 🕐*Open Apr-Oct,* ⛏*guided tour (45min), Sun and public hols, 2-7pm.* ◉*4.50€ (child: 3€).* ☎ *05 55 78 17 52.* This fortified house was built around 1500; 16C-18C furnishings, Gothic granite stairway.

Abbaye de CHANCELADE★

MICHELIN LOCAL MAP 329: E-4 – 7KM/4MI NW OF PÉRIGUEUX

The abbey appears as a peaceful haven tucked into the foot of the green slopes overlooking the Beauronne. Today, it continues in its role as an active spiritual centre.

🕮 **Don't Miss**: The Baroque music festival which takes place in late August and early September.

🕭 **Also See**: Périgueux; Brantôme.

A Bit of History

Founded in the 12C by a monk who adopted the rule of St Augustine, the abbey was protected by the bishops of Périgueux and later answered directly to the Holy See. It therefore prospered and was accorded considerable privileges: asylum, safety and franchises. From the 14C the abbey's fortunes declined; the English captured it, sent the monks away and installed a garrison. During the Wars of Religion, the abbey buildings were partly destroyed by the Protestants from Périgueux.

In 1623 Alain de Solminihac, the new abbot, undertook the reformation and restoration of Chancelade. He was so successful that he was named bishop of Cahors by Louis XIII. The abbey was able to function calmly until the Revolution, when it became national property.

Visit

Church

The lower part of the church is all that remains of the original 12C church. The Romanesque doorway features an elegant arcade, showing Saintonge influence, underlined by a modillioned cornice. The other parts of the church date from the 17C: beneath the square bell tower, made up of three tiers of arcades, the nave was re-vaulted with pointed vaulting and the original east end was demolished.

Conventual buildings – These buildings, added in the 17C, include the abbot's lodgings and the outbuildings around the courtyard and garden, which comprise the 15C pointed barrel-vaulted laundry room (now an exhibition hall), stables, workshops and a fortified mill. Adjoining the courtyard is the garden.

A **museum** of religious art, housed in the basement of the abbot's lodgings, displays reliquaries, statues, altarpieces and paintings, including a Christ outraged believed to be the work of Georges de la Tour.

Chapelle St-Jean

This small, charming parish church was consecrated in 1147. A bas-relief of a lamb carrying a cross (the Benedictine Pax) adorns on the west front. There is a fine ovenvaulted apse, decorated with a modillioned cornice.

La CHÂTRE

POPULATION 4 547

MICHELIN LOCAL MAP 323: H-7

La Châtre is built on a hill overlooking the Indre Valley, in the centre of the area known locally as the Vallée Noire (Black Valley) beloved by George Sand (see NOHANT). It is a dark green countryside of wooded farmland that the "good woman of Nohant" described in so many of her novels. Only the old castle keep recalls the fact that the town had a military origin and was a Roman encampment (castrum, which became Châtre over time).

- **Organising Your Time**: Allow a full day to explore the rural backwaters of the Berry as described in the works of George Sand.
- **Don't Miss**: Musée George-Sand et de la Vallée Noire.
- **Also See**: Nohant.

Visit

Around the church, and towards the river, the **old town** invites strolling. Start from square George-Sand and walk by the town hall, the former Carmelite abbey church (14C carved doorway) and the fine Villaines mansion (now the municipal library). From there you have a choice of picturesque streets and several interesting old houses to admire: the **Maison Rouge**, a fine 16C timber-framed residence (place Laisnel-de-la-Salle) and private mansions in Classical style further on along rue de **Bellefond**. A fine Gothic **statue** of the Virgin Mary stands on place Notre-Dame; it once decorated a fortified gate located here. From place de l'Abbaye, overlooking the River Indre, walk down the stairs lined with flower beds, which lead to the **Pont aux laies**, an old humpback bridge offering a charming view of the picturesque surroundings: at the river's edge, former tanneries with their typical sheltered porches are quiet today, and the water runs clear beneath them.

Address Book

For coin ranges, see the Legend at the back of the guide.

EATING OUT

Le Duplex – *22 r. Ajasson-de-Gransagne - ☎ 02 54 48 00 28 - closed Mon out of season and Sun.* This recently restored 17C manor house has retained its original stones and beams. Two dining rooms decorated in attractive rustic style serving unpretentious traditional cooking. Bar-disco in the basement.

Ferme-Auberge de Poumoué – *Poumoué - 36400 Le Magny - 7km/4.2mi SW of La Châtre along the D 72 - ☎ 02 54 48 22 95 - closed Dec, Sat eve, Sun lunchtime, Tue-Thu from Sept-15 Jun - reserv. recommended.* An 18C farm-inn where the emphasis is on excellent local cheeses and *charcuterie*, both produced from the goats raised on the property. In winter, hearty soups are cooked over an open fire.

WHERE TO STAY

Camping Intercommunal le Val Vert – *3km/1.8mi SE of La Châtre along the D 943 and the D 83A towards Briantes - ☎02 54 48 32 42 - open Jun-Sep - 77 pitches.* This simple but pleasant campsite stands in a verdant setting close to the town and the River Indre.

Hôtel Notre Dame – *4 pl. Notre-Dame - ☎02 54 48 01 14 - closed Feb schoool hols - 19 rooms.* Located in a quiet neighbourhood in the heart of the old town, this small hotel offers guests simple yet well-maintained rooms, almost all of which overlook an inner courtyard.

Chambre d'hôte et Ferme-Auberge Montgarni – *36230 Sarzay - 1.5km/0.9mi S of Sarzay along the D 41 towards Chassignolles - ☎02 54 31 31 05 - reserv. recommended - 5 rooms.* Comfortable bedrooms, delicious cuisine based on home produce and friendly hosts are the hallmarks of this 19C property in the middle of the countryside. Farm products are also on sale here.

Sights

Donjon

"The prison at La Châtre, an old feudal fortress in the control of provincial lords, was then nothing more than a huge square tower, blackened by the centuries and standing straight upon the rock on the side of a narrow ravine where the River Indre flows amid luxuriant green" (George Sand, *Mauprat*). Built in the 15C by Guillaume III de Chauvigny, used as a prison from 1743 to 1934, it now houses a museum.

Musée George-Sand et de la Vallée Noire

Open Jul-Aug, 9am-7pm; Apr-Jun and Sep, 10am-noon and 2-6.30pm; Oct-Mar, 10am-noon and 2-5pm. ☉ *Closed Jan and 25 Dec.* ₪4.20€. ☎ *02 54 48 36 79.*

In a modern building, located next to the keep, 3 000 stuffed and mounted birds, collected from the late 18C and early 19C, are on display. This ornithological museum includes species now extinct or threatened, as well as birds of prey and sea birds. The upper floor is devoted to George Sand and her guests at Nohant, including portraits, letters, first editions, novels and mementoes of her personal friends. Exhibits on the other floors evoke the folklore and art of the Black Valley.

Église St-Germain

This is a modern church. The porch and tower fell down in 1896, carrying the 12C nave with them. Inside, the pillars and Romanesque capitals have been reconstructed. A 14C *Pietà*, from the Carmelite convent, is in the Lady chapel on the left of the chancel; the painting, *Pentecost*, is by Jean Boucher.

Excursions

Église de la Berthenoux

12km/7.5mi NE via the D 940 and the D 68.

The church is a vast 12C edifice surmounted by a powerful belfry crowning a fine dome resting on squinches. The capitals in the transept are adorned with carved figures, animals and foliage.

1 George Sand Tour

60km/37mi – allow one day

This tour wanders through the countryside that served as backdrop for Sand's novels set in rural Berry. Their settings have changed but little in the past century. Still "vivid and sombre in colour . . . the melancholy far distant views".

▶ *Leave La Châtre travelling NE on the D 940 towards Bourges. Drive along the car-racing track and turn left.*

Château d'Ars

Surrounded by a large park, this 16C castle was chosen by George Sand as the setting for her novel *Les Beaux Messieurs de Bois-Doré*. It now houses the George Sand and Romanticism International Centre (exhibitions).

▶ *Drive to the D 943 and turn towards Châteauroux.*

Château de Nohant★

👣 *See NOHANT.*

▶ *Turn back and continue along the D 943.*

Fresques de Vic★

The village built along the Roman road (its Latin name Vicus means village), contains a small Romanesque church, **Église St-Martin**, decorated with interesting frescoes brought to light in 1849.

The **frescoes** adorn both sides of a wall that divides the chancel from the nave, as well as the walls of the chancel itself and the wall

Northern wall

S. Sauvignier/MICHELIN

and vaulting of the apse. Redemption is shown as the main theme throughout the life of Christ from birth to death. Six colours are used in the paintings: carmine, red-ochre, yellow-ochre, ceruse white, black and grey-blue. Though the faces lack expression, the composition is so skilled, the movement of the figures so alive and the detail so accurate, these paintings form a group whose technique was later copied in the pictorial and sculptural art of Limousin and the South-west. Note on the wall facing the main door, Christ in Majesty with the Lamb of God in a medallion; on the right, a Descent from the Cross (representations of the sun and moon); on the vaulting of the apse, the four Evangelists and Christ in Majesty; on the north wall of the chancel, the Washing of the Feet, Judas' Kiss, Simon Carrying the Cross and episodes in the life of St Martin; on the south wall, Jesus entering Jerusalem; facing the altar, the Last Supper.

▶ *Cross the D 943 (minor road opposite rue de l'Église).*

St-Chartier

🕐*Unaccompanied tour of the park. Open Jun-Aug,* 🚶*guided tour of the château (1hr), by prior arrangement (except 1-20 Jul during "Les Rencontres du Festival").* 🎫*2€.* ☎ *02 54 31 10 17.*

The interesting small church and château (restored in the 19C) can be admired as you go through the **park**. In July, there is an international meeting of string-instrument makers.

▶ *Rejoin the D 943 via the D 69.*

Corlay

This inspired the landscapes described in *Fanchon the Cricket*; a rest area overlooks the green Indre Valley *(for a closer look, drive down the D 69).*

▶ *Turn left onto the D 38 5km/3mi further on.*

La Mare au Diable

🚶 A forest clearing off the D 38 was probably the site of the marsh known as the haunted pool *(La Mare au Diable)*, the title of one of Sand's most famous novels.

Château du Magnet

The 15C castle stands surrounded by greenery, in a pastoral landscape.

▶ *D 19 on the left runs through charming countryside crisscrossed by hedges.*

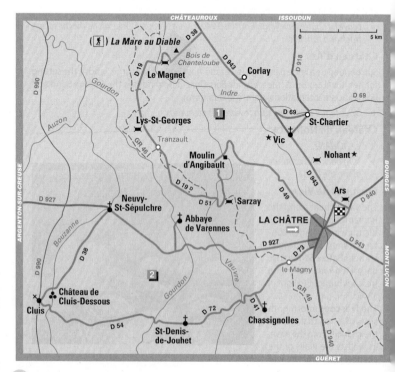

Château de Lys-St-George

The château, whose towers rise straight up out of the moat, combines the architectural severity of a medieval fortress with the charm of the Renaissance. From the terrace (*visitors are allowed up to the postern but not across the moat*), you will see the 15C façade and the Gourdon Valley.

▶ *Continue along the D 19 and turn left 3km/1.9mi beyond Tranzault.*

Château de Sarzay

🕐*Open 9am to dusk.* ⊛*6€ (child: 4€).* ☎ *02 54 31 32 25.*

A proud feudal domain whose tall round towers have tiled roofs. The ground-floor rooms have been restored and furnished. Blanchemont Castle in George Sand's novel *The Angibault Miller* is based on Sarzay.

▶ *Drive N along the D 41.*

Moulin d'Angibault

Stop by the mill which stands on the Vauvre, a tributary of the Indre (*festivities, dancing, evening gatherings in summer*).

▶ *Take the D 49 back to La Châtre.*

2 Southwest Boischaut

50km/31mi – allow 4hr

▶ *Leave La Châtre by D 73 SW towards le Magny.*

Église de Chassignolles

Tour by prior arrangement. Contact Mme Aussire, ☎ *02 54 48 31 77.*

The **church** is crowned by a large belfry-tower. A small Renaissance door with an emblazoned pediment opens into the north transept.

▶ *Turn back and continue along the D 72.*

St-Denis-de-Jouhet

The Gothic church has a shingle-covered steeple as well as 12C and 13C stained-glass windows.

▶ *Leave the village via the D 54.*

Cluis

The chancel of the 13C **church** ends with two apses bearing noteworthy capitals. The side chapel of the fourth bay houses a splendid 14C white-marble **Virgin and Child**★. Aubusson tapestries hang in the 16C town hall. The 17C covered market is surmounted by a pinnacle.

▶ *Drive NE along the D 38.*

Cluis-Dessous

Among the ruins of the medieval castle, one can still see part of a curtain wall, a gate flanked by two towers and a central building. A Gothic chapel stands nearby.

▶ *Continue along the D 38 towards Mouhers.*

Neuvy-St-Sépulchre

🕐 *Unaccompanied visit, daily 9-7pm.* 🔍*Guided tours possible by prior arrangement. Contact Monsieur Morin,* ☎ *02 54 30 86 28.*

This small town gets its name from the **basilica** modelled on the Holy Sepulchre in Jerusalem. It consists of a rectangular structure joined more or less happily to a circular one. The first was completed in 1049. The vast **rotunda**★ on the other round side is 22m/72ft across; the upper part was restored by Violet-le-Duc in the 19C.

▶ *Drive E out of Neuvy along the D 927.*

Abbaye de Varennes

🕐*Open Jun-Sep.* ⊛*No charge.* ☎ *02 54 31 30 59.*

The abbey, founded in 1148 is not far from the road, at the bottom of a dale. The 13C buildings are open to the public. The church dates from the 12C, and is remarkable for the purity of its Cistercian architecture. George Sand wrote of the abbey in her novel *Les Beaux Messieurs de Bois-Doré* (1857).

▶ *Rejoin the D 927 which leads back to La Châtre.*

COLLONGES-LA-ROUGE★★

POPULATION 413

MICHELIN LOCAL MAP 329: K-5 – LOCAL MAP SEE BRIVE-LA-GAILLARDE

Collonges the Red, built of red sandstone, is set with its small manor houses, old houses and Romanesque church in a countryside characteristic of the Quercy region, with juniper bushes, walnut plantations and vineyards all around. A historic atmosphere pervades the streets of this lovely old village. 🅘 *Pl. de l'Ancienne-Gare, 19500 Collonges-la-Rouge,* ☎ *05 55 25 47 57.*

- 🅿 **Parking**: Cars are not allowed in the village during the summer. Use the car park by the old station.
- 👁 **Don't Miss**: The Église St-Pierre, with its impressive tympanum and bell tower; Castel de Vassinhac; tympanum in the church at Saillac.
- 👶 **Also See**: Brive-la-Gaillarde.

A Bit of History

The village developed in the 8C around its church and priory, a dependency of the powerful Charroux Abbey in the Poitou region. In the 13C, Collonges was a part of the viscounty of Turenne and thus received franchises and liberties. Much later on, in the 16C, Collonges was the place chosen by prominent denizens of the viscounty for their holidays. For their pleasure, they erected charming manors and mansions flanked with towers and turrets, which give the town its unique image.

The old centre displays a harmonious use of traditional materials, and a fluent interplay of proportions, creating an architectural symphony.

Visit

▶ *Start near the old station (ancienne gare) and take rue de la Barrière on the left.*

Maison de la Sirène

This 16C corbelled house, with a porch and beautiful lauze roof, is adorned with a mermaid holding a comb in one hand and a mirror in the other. The interior has been reconstructed as the inside of a Collonges house of olden days.

Further along, the pointed gateway arch (Porte du Prieuré) marks the entrance of the former Benedictine priory, which was destroyed during the Revolution.

Hôtel des Ramades de Friac

The *hôtel*, crowned by two turrets, was once the town house of the powerful Ramades de Friac family.

Go past the Relais de St-Jacques-de-Compostelle – the name recalls that Collonges was a pilgrims' stopping place along the famous route to Santiago de Compostela – and through a covered passageway and soon afterwards in an alley, on the right, there is an old turreted house.

Château de Benge

Set against a backdrop of poplar and walnut trees is this proud towered and turreted manor house with its lovely Renaissance window. The lords of Benge were top of the league of the famous Collonges vineyards, until these were decimated by phylloxera.

Porte Plate

This flat gateway, so named because it has lost its towers, was part of the town walls protecting the church, cloisters and priory buildings.

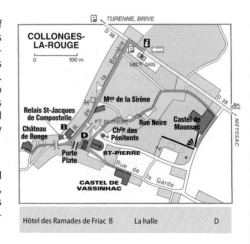

Hôtel des Ramades de Friac B   La halle   D

Halle

The covered market, with its massive framework supported by strong pillars, served as a central granary store and shelters the communal oven.

The **Église St-Pierre**★ stands opposite.

Castel de Vassinhac★

This elegant manor house was owned by Gédéon de Vassinhac, lord of Collonges, captain-governor of the viscounty of Turenne. Built in 1583, the manor house bristles with large towers and turrets with pepper-pot roofs. Despite a large number of mullioned windows, its defensive role is obvious from its many loopholes and castellated turrets.

Chapelle des Pénitents

The chapel was built in the 13C and modified by the Maussac family during the 17C, at the time of the Counter-Reformation.

Rue Noire

This street cuts through the oldest part of Collonges, where old houses can be seen set back one from the other, ornamented with turrets and towers and adorned with wisteria and climbing vines.

Castel de Maussac

This building is embellished with a turret and a porch roof above the main door. A barbican projects from the square tower, which is overlooked by a dormer window. Before the Revolution this manor house was the refuge for the last member of the Maussac family, who emigrated to Italy where he became the chaplain to Napoleon's sister, Princess Pauline Borghese.

Continue further south along the street to enjoy a pretty **view**★ of Collonges, Vassinhac Manor and the bell tower.

Sights

Musée des Arts et Traditions Populaires

Open Easter -1 Nov, 10am-noon and 3-6pm. 2€. Visits by prior arrangement; contact Madame Faucher, ☎ 05 55 84 08 03.

A traditional local interior has been reconstructed inside the Maison de la Sirène.

Église St-Pierre★

The church, which dates from the 11C and 12C, was fortified during the Wars of Religion in the 16C. It was at this time that the great, square keep was strengthened by a defence chamber communicating with the watch-path, and that the tympanum was placed in the new gable out of harm's way. It was restored to its original place in 1923.

Tympanum★ – Carved in the white limestone of Turenne, the 12C tympanum stands out among all the red sandstone. It depicts the Ascension (or perhaps the second coming of Christ) and was apparently carved by sculptors of the Toulouse School. The upper register shows the figure of Christ surrounded by angels, holding the Gospels in one hand, the other raised in benediction. The lower register shows the saddened Virgin surrounded by the eleven Apostles. The whole tympanum is outlined by a pointed arch ornamented with a fine border of carved animals.

Bell tower★ – The 12C bell tower is in the Limousin style: two lower square tiers pierced with round-arched bays are surmounted by two octagonal tiers flanked by gables.

Interior – In the 12C, the church had a cruciform plan around the transept crossing. The dome above the transept crossing rests on 11C pillars. Modifications were made in the 14C and 15C, when side chapels were added as well as a second nave in the Flamboyant style.

Château de COMMARQUE ★

MICHELIN LOCAL MAP 329: H-6

LOCAL MAP SEE LES EYZIES-DE-TAYAC

The impressive remains of Commarque castle stand on the south bank of the River Beune.

▶ **Orient Yourself**: From the castle keep, there is a fine view of the valley and of the elegant 15C-16C Château de Laussel perched on a cliff across the river.

👓 **Also See**: Jardins d'Eyrignac; Beynac-et-Cazenac; Sarlat; Les Eyzies-de-Tayac.

A Bit of History

Commarque was built as a stronghold in the 12C and 14C and for a long time it belonged to the Beynac family. In 1968, Hubert de Commarque, a descendant of the original owners decided to give the site a new lease on life. When he started, the keep and the chapel alone could be seen above the vegetation. The whole of the site is now visible, but the restoration work undertaken 35 years ago is far from completed!

Visit

🕐 *Open Jul-Aug, 10am-8pm (last entrance 1hr before closing); May-Jun and Sep, 10am-7pm; Apr, 10am-6pm. ☞5.60€ (under 10 years old: no charge). ☎ 05 53 59 00 25. www.commarque.com*

Cave dwellings nestle at the foot of the castle: note the drip-mouldings carved in the rock to deflect rain from the rock face. Inside the walls are fitted with rings and putlock holes to which hoarding was fixed.

The tour of the fortified village begins with the well-preserved chapel (note the transverse arches); next come four mansions (a fifth is still buried) once occupied by noblemen. The *Maison du four* features a bread oven. The *Maison à contreforts* (buttressed house) illustrates the successive building periods: a troglodytic base, a 10C-11C wall, a 15C fireplace and 16C murals. Along a narrow street, which has been cleared, visitors can see the beginning of a stone-slab roof. Separate entrances indicate that each household was independent. The Hôtel de Commarque where the Commarque family lived while the castle was occupied by the Beynacs, is preceded by a courtyard.

The double keep (the extension is visible on the front) comprises the 14C great hall covered with a five-rib vault: the carved pendant brackets are well preserved and the keystone represents a helmet bearing the arms of Pons de Beynac (these are reproduced on the ground). Note the 12C colonnaded window and the chessboard in front of it. It is possible to climb to the top of the 34m/112ft-high tower to admire the panoramic view.

COUSSAC-BONNEVAL ★

POPULATION 1379

MICHELIN LOCAL MAP 325: E-7

The castellated towers of the Château de Bonneval rise on a height overlooking the village of Coussac in a typically Limousin countryside where fields divided by small streams alternate with hedges and chestnut coppices. It is the native hearth of the Bonneval family.

😊 **Don't Miss**: The inside of the château; the Lanterne des Morts.

A Bit of History

Achmet-Pasha – Claude-Alexandre de Bonneval was born in Bonneval Castle in 1675 and at an early age showed his desire to be a fighting man. He fought in the Italian Campaigns (1701-06) then offered his services to the Austrian Emperor, becoming a general in the army. After a personal quarrel he again became a soldier of fortune, this time in the lands of the Ottoman Empire. He offered his talents to the Turkish ruler, reorganised the Turkish Army and led it in decisive victories against the Austrians. He was by this time a general in the artillery and took the title of Achmet-Pasha, Pasha of the three tails, an honour which gave him precedence over ordinary pashas. But in spite of all his efforts he was never able to return to France and died in Constantinople at the age of 72.

Visit

Château★

 Guided tour (45min, last entrance 30min before closing), Jul-Sep, 2.30-7pm; mid-Mar to Jun and Oct, daily except Mon, 2.30-6pm. 10€ (child: 5€). 05 55 75 24 15.

The castle was built in the middle of the 14C and the inside was altered in the 18C and 19C. The plan is square with an inner courtyard: the corner towers are crowned with machicolations and topped with pepper-pot roofs; the keep and the Devil's Tower (Tour du Diable) adjoin another tower.

Inside the castle there are furnishings dating from the period of the Renaissance to the Directory (16C to the end of the 18C). Remarkable tapestries and Louis XVI woodwork, portraits, engravings and contemporary documents recall the life of Bonneval-Pasha.

Church

A small 12C building, renovated in the 15C, in which there are remains of a fresco (south transept), a 16C polychrome, wooden bas-relief, a *Pietà* and a painting by Lebrun, *God the Father* (17C).

Lanterne des Morts★

This imposing Lantern of the Dead dates from the 12C and was restored in the 14C. It once marked the cemetery entrance. The small door was used to insert a lamp, which was then raised up to the top of the structure, where light could shine through the openings. The light served several purposes: symbolically, it paid homage to the dead and reminded the living of their fate; in the dark medieval night, it guided lost travellers.

For coin ranges, see the Legend at the back of the guide.

WHERE TO EAT

 Les Voyageurs – 21 av. du 11-Novembre-1918 - 05 55 75 20 24 - closed 2 weeks in Jan, 2 weeks in Nov, Sun eve (except Jul-Aug) and Wed. This old Limousin-style house is right by the château. The cuisine (including the famous local beef) served in the rustic dining room is unpretentious and reasonably priced. Seven rooms, some overlooking the garden.

WHERE TO STAY

 Chambre d'hôte Le Moulin de Marsaguet – 3.6km/2.2mi N of Coussac along the D 17 towards La Roche-l'Abeille, then the D 57 - 05 55 75 28 29 - closed end Sep to mid-Apr - 3 rooms. The hosts at this large 18C bed and breakfast property also run the farm. Farm-produced cuisine, including duck, foie gras, veal and pork. The 13ha/32.5-acre lake is popular for fishing, swimming and boat trips.

CROCQ

POPULATION 546

MICHELIN LOCAL MAP 325: L-5

This little medieval stronghold, its cobbled streets intact but its fortifications long since fallen, is located on a high point, surrounded by woodlands, meadows and lakes.

▶ **Orient Yourself**: Climb the towers of the castle for an impressive view of the surrounding area.

 Don't Miss: The triptych in the Chapelle Notre-Dame-de-la-Visitation.

 Also See: Pays de Franc-Alleu; Plateau de Millevaches; Lac de Vassivière; Le Puy de Dôme; Clermont-Ferrand.

S. Sauvignier/MICHELIN

View of the town of Crocq

A Bit of History

Formerly under the feudal wing of Auvergne, Crocq made up one side of a defensive triangle, with Auzanac to the north-east and Herment to the south-east, which controlled the Clermont-Limoges road. Facing the stronghold of St-Georges-Nigremont (👉 *see below*) on high ground, Crocq was the leading line of defence against attacks from the Limousin region.

The town gave its name to the peasant-rebels known as croquants.

Visit

Chapelle Notre-Dame-de-la-Visitation

Founded at the end of the 12C, this small Romanesque edifice was thoroughly remodelled in the 15C and 16C, and restored in the 19C. It is surmounted by a belfry-gable and a lantern of the dead, removed to the top of the building.

Inside, there is a remarkable **triptych**★ painted on wood, installed on the northern wall in 1995. This work, designed around 1530, relates the life of St Eligius in seven panels. An interesting feature on the representation of the Last Supper is the fork pictured on the back (whereas this utensil was not in common use before the 17C).

Castle towers

Connected by a curtain wall, these towers are the only vestiges of the defensive castle built in the second half of the 12C, which fell in 1356 under assault by the troops of Edward, the Black Prince. Recently restored, the towers have been fitted with stairs making it possible to reach the orientation table in the eastern tower. The table indicates the sites in the vast **panorama**★: the Combraille to the north; the Dôme range and the Puy de Dôme to the east; the Dore range and the Sancy peak to the south-east; the Millevaches plateau to the south-west.

For coin ranges, see the Legend at the back of the guide.

EATING OUT

🍽️🍷 **L'Assiette de Lille** – *23260 St-Maurice-près-Crocq - 5km/3mi W of Crocq along the D 10 -* ☎ *05 55 67 47 12 -* ⏰ *closed Christmas and New Year -* 🖼️. Don't be put off by the rather austere granite façade of this former school house – the inside is truly charming, with its decor of spring colours, baskets, old photos, copperware and dried flowers for decor. The cuisine is traditionally French, with some specialities from the north.

WHERE TO STAY

🛏️ **Auberge de St-Éloi** – *Route de Clermont -* ☎ *05 55 67 40 14 -* ⏰ *closed 23 Sep-21 Oct and Mon eve -* 🅿️ *- 6 rooms.* An old inn with half a dozen small rooms, all with en-suite facilities and creaking floors! A friendly welcome and cuisine based on fresh local ingredients.

Excursion

Le Pays de Franc-Alleu★

Round-trip of 45km/27mi – allow 3hr

The name of this region recalls the Hundred Years War, which devastated it; in 1426, as compensation, an exemption from duties (*alleu*) was granted.

▸ *Leave Crocq on the D 996. Drive past the stadium, then turn left towards Dimpoux and park the car at Laval.*

A pleasant lane bordered by beech and pine leads to a heath carpeted in fern. After 1km/0.5mi, in a little copse, stands the **Urbe dolmen**.

You can return to Laval by continuing down the lane, which shortly leads back to the road.

There is a good view of Crocq as you head back to the D 996.

▸ *At the crossroads, turn left on the D 996.*

After 2km/1.2mi through the heart of the Urbe Forest, look for a little road on the right which leads to the **church** (*Information at the town hall, ☎ 05 55 67 40 32*) of **Montel-Guillaume**, with its curious polychrome statues.

▸ *Return to the D 996 and turn right (1km/0.6mi) on the D 29.*

At St-Agnant-près-Crocq, follow the D 31 as it winds around ponds and lakes (Étang de la Motte is especially inviting). Nearby, the 15C **Château du Theil** (*not open to the public*) is well sheltered behind its wall.

▸ *At Magnat-l'Étrange, turn N on the D 90.*

St-Georges-Nigremont

Where the Limousin hills (the region known as the Montagne) meet the Millevaches plateau, St-Georges-Nigremont holds the summit of a mount (referred to as *Nigers Mons* in Latin texts) which faced a Gaulish *oppidum*. This hillside fort served as an important religious and administrative centre under the Merovingian and Carolingian dynasties. From the terrace near the church, a wide **panorama** (*orientation table*) extends north-east to Crocq and beyond to the Combraille hills; to the south-east, the hills of Auvergne are visible.

▸ *Continue along the D 90 then turn right on the D 10. At Pontcharraud, take the D 21 SE for 7km/4.2mi, then turn left on the D 28.*

The road leads back to Crocq by way of the hamlet of Naberon, once home to a Knights of Malta commandery.

Ruines de CROZANT★

MICHELIN LOCAL MAP 325: G-2

The massive Crozant fortress, known as the key to the Limousin, rises, still impressive though in ruins, from a rocky promontory commanding the confluence of the Creuse and the Sédelle.

▸ **Orient Yourself**: The most spectacular view of Crozant, the castle ruins and the Creuse Valley, with the river cutting its way through the ravines, appears as you approach from the east along the D 30.

☺ **Don't Miss**: A tour inside the ruined fortress; a boat trip on the lake.

☺ **Also See**: Confluence of the two Creuse rivers; Argenton-sur-Creuse.

A Bit of History

During the Middle Ages, the castle was merely a wooden construction. In the 13C, the Comte de la Marche, Hughes X de Lusignan, husband of Isabelle d'Angoulême, reinforced it and the building began to take on the appearance of a fortress. It measured 450m/490yd in length; the ramparts were more than 1km/0.6mi round with 10 towers to defend them – six facing the Creuse, four the Sédelle.

Strong in his position, Hughes X revolted against Blanche de Castille and then St Louis. Crozant eventually fell to the royal troops, whereas the Count and his father-in-law and ally Henry III of England were defeated at Saintes in 1242. The French king took

For coin ranges, see the Legend at the back of the guide.

EATING OUT

Le Lac – *At the Pont de Crozant - 23160 Crozant - 1km/0.6mi E of Crozant along the D 72 and D 30 -* ☎ *05 55 89 81 96 -* ◔ *closed Feb, 1-7 Mar, Sun eve, Wed eve and Mon.* Enjoy a meal in this pleasant restaurant before taking a boat trip on the lake. Traditional and contemporary cuisine. A few guest rooms are also available here.

BOAT TRIPS

L'hôtel du Lac - *23160 Crozant -* ☎ *05 55 89 81 96 -* ◔ *Apr to Oct,* ⌂ *guided tours (1hr 15min) at 2.45pm and 4pm (Jul-Aug, at 2.45pm, 4pm and 5.30pm). Minimum of 20 people required.* These cruises on Lac d'Éguzon provide a different perspective of the ruins and the river.

possession of the castle for eight years, ordering Hughes X to bear the expenses of upkeep and protection. Several thousand men could be garrisoned in the citadel which, a century later, was to resist the attacks of Edward the Black Prince.

In 1436, the castle changed hands, from the Bourbons to the Armagnacs. Charles VII had it repaired, but Louis XI confiscated it along with the rest of the county, in order to hand it back to the Bourbons. After the treason of Constable Charles de Bourbon (one of the most highly placed officials in the kingdom), the county was definitively confiscated. The Wars of Religion and an earthquake in 1606 brought calamity and destruction; by 1640, when Louis XIII sold the property to Henri de St-Germain, it was a ruin.

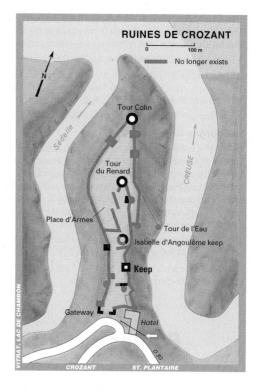

RUINES DE CROZANT

No longer exists

Tour Colin

Sédelle

CREUSE

Tour du Renard

Place d'Armes

Tour de l'Eau

Isabelle d'Angoulême keep

Keep

VITRAT, LAC DE CHAMBON

Gateway

Hotel

D 50

CROZANT ST. PLANTAIRE

Visit

◔ *Open Jul-Aug, 10am-noon, 2-7pm, Sat-Sun and holidays: 10am-7pm; Apr to Jun and Sep: 2-6pm, Sat-Sun and holidays: 10am-noon, 2-6pm; Oct-11 Nov: Sat-Sun and holidays 2-6pm.* ⌂ *2€.* ☎ *05 55 89 09 05.*

In its heyday, visitors to the castle passed through the Charles VII gate to enter the first courtyard. The **square keep**, in the second courtyard, was the 12C castle; 13m/42ft on each side, it had no abutments.

Modified in the 13C and 15C, it had three upper storeys and served as the seigniorial abode. It was surrounded by a curtain wall. A steep ramp leads to the third courtyard, the twin-walled section built by Hughes X.

The platform built on the rocky spur (18×120m/20×165yd) was used as a parade ground.

The base of the massive tower built by Isabelle d'Angoulême in the 13C stands on a rise 5m/16ft high. The line of towers continued to the end of the point, where the ground floor of the Tour Colin is intact.

Excursions

Vallée de la Creuse★

  See ARGENTON-SUR-CREUSE: Excursions.

Fresselines

8km/5mi SE along the minor road skirting the cemetery.

Maurice Rollinat, the poet who was George Sand's godson, worked and died in this town. Painters still live and work in this village.

A rocky path leads from the church to the **confluence of the two Creuse rivers**★ (*1hr round trip on foot*), in picturesque surroundings. Claude Monet loved to set up his easel here. Footbridges span the Petite Creuse, offering fine views. The path eventually leads to the D 44.

Villejoint, les Jardins Clos de la Forge

  From mid-Jun to mid-Sep: daily except Mon 2-5pm. ~Guided tour (2hr) 5pm, by prior arrangement 2 weeks in advance. ⌂4.50€ (-7 years old: no charge), 6.50€ guided tour. M. Allaert, ☎ 05 55 89 82 59 or M. Sautot, ☎ 05 55 89 83 64. 5km/3mi S along the D 913 towards Dun-le-Palestel; turn right in Maisons.

These gardens offer a pleasant combination of natural growth and careful planning: trimmed arbour, water garden, backwater through which runs a footbridge on piles, wasteland and a patch of blueberries.

Château de CULAN★

MICHELIN LOCAL MAP 323: K-7

The powerful medieval fortress of Culan stands four square with its massive round towers looking straight down into the gorges of the River Arnon. The the stark façade, relieved only by its many mullioned windows, rises out of a tangled undergrowth and clings to the rock commanding both the ravine and the road.

▸ **Orient Yourself**: The best view of the castle **site**★ is from the place where the bridge crosses the river along the D 943 from Montluçon.

 Especially for Kids: A visit inside the castle.

  Also See: Épineuil-le-Fleuriel, the childhood home of the writer Alain-Fournier, author of Le Grand Meaulnes.

Visit

  ~Guided tour of the château (45min) Jul-Aug 10am-7pm; Apr-Jun and Sep to 1 Nov: 10am-noon, 2-6pm. ⌂Gardens and château 7.50€ (4-14 years old: 4.50€); medieval gardens and Musée des Hourds only, 6€ (child: 4€). ☎ 02 48 56 66 66. www.chateau-de-culan.com.

Culan Château

E. Larribère/MICHELIN

Captured by Philip Augustus in 1188, it was reconstructed in the 13C and considerably altered during the 15C. At that time, 300m/984ft of wall surrounded the 3 000m²/323 000sq ft area. Admiral Culant, faithful partisan of Joan of Arc, welcomed her to his home in 1429; Louis XI was a guest in 1465. The castle was later bought by Sully who subsequently sold it to the Prince of Condé; in the 17C it passed into the hands of Michel Le Tellier, father of the Minister Louvois.

Interior

The rooms reflect different periods of the castle's history: Admiral Culant's room (Gothic chest sculpted in folds); the archives room (war chest with seven locks); four guard-rooms where you can admire the wooden galleries and the three-layered, star-shaped timber frame; a diorama explaining the revolt known as *la Fronde* and the siege of the castle; the red salon (18C Aubusson tapestry); the George Sand room; Sully's Intendants' room (massive chimney).

▷ *After the tour, go to the end of the terrace where there is a good view of the Arnon Valley.*

Church

One doorway and the crypt of the former chapel are Romanesque; the rest of the building dates from the 15C.

Excursion

Épineuil-le-Fleuriel
19.5km/12mi E.

Located on the edge of the region known as the Bourbonnais, Épineuil was the childhood home of author **Alain-Fournier** from 1891 to 1898. Readers of his most famous work *Le Grand Meaulnes* will recognise the fictional Sainte-Agathe, where the story was set. The novel (written in 1913, translated as *The Wanderer* in early editions and later as *The Lost Domain*), about the transition from the innocence of childhood to the excitement of adolescence, blends memory, dream, and reality.

L'École du Grand Meaulnes

🕐 *Open Jul-Aug, 10am-7pm; Apr-Jun and Sep-Oct: daily except Tue 10am-noon, 2-6pm; Nov to mid-Nov: daily except Tue 10am-noon, 2-5pm. ◎5.40€ (child: 3.10€). ☎ 02 48 63 04 82.*

The universe of the author, and of the young heroes of *Le Grand Meaulnes* is re-reated here in the schoolhouse ( *a guided tour, in French, makes use of headphones*), the town hall, and the schoolmaster's apartments. In one room, exhibits trace the author's life. Alain-Fournier is also remembered as a poet and a journalist. The author was killed in the First World War.

DOMME★★

POPULATION 987

MICHELIN LOCAL MAP 329: I-7 – LOCAL MAP SEE VALLÉE DE LA DORDOGNE

Domme, the Acropolis of the Dordogne, is remarkably situated on a rocky crag overlooking the Dordogne Valley. This exceptional site inspired many artists including the writer Henry Miller. 🅸 *Pl. de la Halle, 24250 Domme, ☎ 05 53 31 71 00.*

🅿 **Parking**: A number of car parks are available within the walls of the bastide (🕐 *see town plan*). You can also park outside of the walls and catch a tourist train to the centre.

👁 **Don't Miss**: The view from the Belvédère de la Barre.

👁 **Also See**: Sarlat-la-Canéda; la Roque-Gageac.

A Bit of History

A royal bastide – Domme was founded by Philip the Bold in 1283 in order to keep watch on the Dordogne Valley and check the desire for expansion of the English established in Gascony. The king granted the town important privileges including that of minting coins and Domme played an important role during the Hundred Years

The bastide high above the Dordogne

War. In the 17C, its wine-growing and river-trading activities were thriving and its markets were renowned throughout the region.

Captain Vivans' exploit – While the struggles of the Reformation were inflaming France, Domme kept up resistance against the Huguenots who were overrunning Périgord. Yet, in 1588, the famous Protestant Captain **Geoffroi de Vivans** captured the town by cunning.

One night he and 30 of his men climbed along the rocks of the cliff face known as the *Barre*, a place so precipitous that it had not been thought necessary to protect it, and entered the sleeping town. Vivans and his men created an infernal racket and during the ensuing confusion opened the tower doors to their waiting army. The inhabitants were too sleepy to resist, and Vivans thereupon became master of the town for the next four years. He installed a garrison, burned down both the church and the Augustine priory and established the Protestant faith. However, noting the increasing success of the Catholics in Périgord, he determined to sell the *bastide* to his rivals on 10 January 1592. The unwary purchasers found nothing but ruins.

Visit

The Bastide★

Domme is far from presenting the perfect rectangular plan of the bastide as such – it is more in the form of a trapezium. The surrounding fortifications have been adapted to the terrain; inside the fortified town, the streets follow a geometric plan, as far as possible.

▶ *Start from the tourist office and follow rue Mazet (running parallel to Grand'Rue) then rue Porte Delbos.*

Porte del Bos

This gateway, which has a pointed arch, was once closed with a portcullis. Walk inside the ramparts to the 13C **Porte de la Combe**.

▶ *Walk toward the town along rue de la Porte-de-la-Combe.*

The street is lined with many fine houses. The beauty of the gold stone and the flat brown tiles is often enhanced by the addition of elegant wrought-iron balconies and brightened by climbing vines and flower-decked terraces. Note the lovely fountain on the left.

▶ *Rue de la Porte-des-Tours on the right leads to the Porte des Tours.*

Porte des Tours

🕐 🚶 Open Jul-Aug, guided tour by prior arrangement at 10.30am, 2.30pm and 5pm. 🎫6€ (5-14 years old: 3.50€). ☎ 05 53 31 71 00.

This late-13C gateway is the most impressive and best preserved of the town's gateways. On the side of place des Armes, the wall is rectilinear but on the outside, the gateway is flanked by two massive semicircular rusticated towers, built by Philip the

Fair and originally used as guard-rooms. Between 1307 and 1318 Knights Templars were imprisoned there and left their mark with graffiti.

▷ *Turn left.*

Rue Eugène-le-Roy

During the period he spent in a house along this street (*plaque*), Eugène le Roy wrote two of his masters-works: *L'ennemi de la mort* (The Enemy of Death) and *Le moulin du Frau* (Frau Mill).

Place de la Rode

This is the place where the condemned were broken on the wheel. The *Maison du batteur de monnaie* (Money Minter's House) is decorated with fine Gothic apertures.

Grand'Rue

This shopping street is lined with shops displaying many of the culinary specialities of Périgord. Note the elegant mullioned windows of the house standing on the corner of rue Geoffroy-de-Vivans.

▷ *Walk to rue des Consuls via rue Geoffroy-de-Vivans.*

Rue des Consuls

The Hôtel de Ville (town hall) is located in a 13C building, which was once the Seneschal law courts.

▷ *Walk along Grand'Rue to the town centre.*

Place de la Halle

In this large square stands an elegant 17C covered market (*halle*). Facing it is the 15C **Maison du Gouverneur** (Governor's House) flanked by an elegant turret. It now houses the tourist office.

Église

Destroyed during the Wars of Religion, the church was rebuilt in the 17C and the belfry-porch was added in the 19C.

Sights

Belvédère de la Barre

From the promontory, the **view**★★★ embraces the Dordogne Valley from the Montfort meander in the east, to Beynac in the west.

Changing with the time of day – hazy in the early morning mist, bright blue between lines of green poplars in the noonday sun, a silver ribbon in the evening light – the Dordogne winds its way through the carefully cultivated fields (maize, tobacco, cereals) dotted with villages and farms. Of all the creative artists who have come here seeking inspiration, Henry Miller was perhaps the most affected, describing the area as the nearest thing to Paradise on earth.

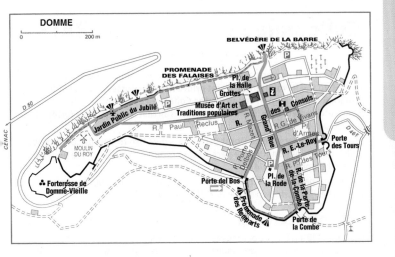

The esplanade at the end of the Grand'Rue offers the best panorama of the valley below.

▶ *Follow the Promenade des Falaises, a cliffside walk along the promontory.*

Jardin Public du Jubilé

These attractive gardens (*viewing table*), are situated between the town and the tip of the promontory, on the site of the entrenched camp installed here in 1214 by Simon de Montfort. He had just beaten the Cathars and razed their fortress **Domme-Vieille**, leaving but a few ruins standing (*these are not accessible; it is only possible to walk as far as the Moulin du Roy which overlooks the Dordogne Valley*).

Caves

🕐⌖⌖*Open Jul-Aug, guided tour (30min), 10am-7pm; Feb-Jun, Sep to mid-Nov and Christmas hols, 10am-noon and 2-6pm.* 🕐 *Closed the rest of the year and Sat in Feb, Mar, Oct and Nov.* ⌖6€ *(child: 3.50€).* ☎ *05 53 31 71 00.*

The entrance is in the covered market converted into an entrance hall. The panoramic lift which brings visitors up at the end of the visit offers a magnificent view of the Dordogne Valley but, unfortunately spoils the cliffside.

These caves served as refuge for the townspeople of Domme during the Hundred Years War and the Wars of Religion.

So far about 450m/490yd of galleries have been cleared for the public to visit; the chambers are generally small and are sometimes separated by low passages. The ceilings in certain chambers are embellished with slender white stalactites. There are also places where stalactites and stalagmites join to form columns or pillars. The Salle Rouge contains some eccentrics.

Bison and rhinoceros bones, discovered when the caves were being prepared for tourists, are displayed precisely as they were found.

Musée d'Art et Traditions Populaires

🕐*Open Jul-Aug, 10.30-7pm; Apr-Jun and Sep, 10.30am-12.30pm and 2.30-6pm.* ⌖3€. ☎ *05 53 31 71 00.*

In an old house on place de la Halle, this museum presents a retrospective of every day life in Domme: displays of typical furnishings, clothing, farm tools. Amid the archives and photographs documenting the town's past, note the royal missives according special privileges and exemptions to the inhabitants of Domme.

Collégiale St-Pierre du DORAT★★

MICHELIN LOCAL MAP 325: D-3

As the seat of the principal seneschalsy, or governorship of Basse-Marche from the 16C to the Revolution, Le Dorat prides itself on possessing one of the most remarkable buildings in Limousin, the Collegiate Church of St Peter. The Porte Bergère, complete with its machicolations, is all that remains of the fortifications built about 1420.

Every seven years the Le Dorat ostensions give rise to unique ceremonies in which guards of honour take part – sappers and drummers in the uniforms of the First Empire (1804-14).

The natural pastureland of the region is the ideal landscape for the breeding of sheep and cattle. 🏛 *17 pl. de la Collégiale, 87210 Le Dorat,* ☎ *05 55 60 76 81. www.ledorat.com*

Collegiate Church

In about 1100, on the site of a monastery built in the 10C and probably destroyed in the 11C, construction began simultaneously at the east and west ends of a church of impressive proportions (77m/253ft long, 39m/128ft wide at the transept) which, after 50 years of work, bore the appearance we see today. A collegiate church is a church other than a cathedral that has a chapter of canons, or a church under the pastorate of more than one minister.

Exterior

The collegiate church, which is built in fine grey granite, is striking in size and pleasing in proportion. The west front opens with a wide, **multifoil doorway** showing a Mozarabic influence which was perhaps inspired by the pilgrims who had journeyed to Santiago de Compostela. The doorway's festooned covings bring a joyful and original touch, lightening the stark façade.

An elegant **octagonal belfry** on three tiers of unequal height surmounted by a soaring spire topped with a 13C copper-gilt angel, rises above the transept.

From below place de l'Église at a former churchyard where the roads from Guéret and Bellac meet, there is a good overall view of the **chevet**, the arrangement in tiers of the apse, the apsidal chapels and the stone belfries. The central apsidal chapel supports a semicircular tower which formed part of the 15C town's defence system. Two rectangular abutments shore up each apsidiole; each of the bays has a single Limousin-style arch.

At the entrance, in the axis of the nave, the large granite baptismal font is pre-Romanesque, embellished on both sides with fancy tailed lions.

Interior

From the first bay which has a dome above, and is 12 steps above the level of the rest of the nave, one is struck immediately by the majesty of the building. The four bays following are broken barrel vaults on joists. Narrow aisles provide support for the central arching. The transept crossing, above which rises a tall dome on pendentives, is lit by Romanesque windows.

The arcades in the chancel rest on foliated capitals; two chapels hold shrines to St Israel and St Theobald.

Crypt

🕐 Open Jun-Sep, guided tour, daily except Sun and public hols, 10am-noon and 2.30-6pm; visits by prior arrangement at the tourist office. No charge. ☎ 05 55 60 76 81.

The crypt is reached from the south transept. It extends the length of the chancel and resembles it in plan and proportion. This fine 11C sanctuary, dedicated to St Anne, has columns whose primitive capitals are roughly hewn, one however is sculpted. The apsidal chapel contains fragments of 13C statues.

Sacristy

🕐 Open Jul-Sep, 2.30-6pm. For further information, contact the tourist office, ☎ 05 55 60 76 81.

It houses a small religious museum; this exhibits a multicoloured statue of St Anne and a *Pietà* dating from the 15C and a 13C reliquary cross with two crosspieces, which belonged to the treasure of the collegiate church.

Vallée de la DORDOGNE★★★

MICHELIN LOCAL MAP 329: I-7 TO L-7

The Dordogne is one of the longest rivers in France and is said to be the most beautiful. The variety and beauty of the countryside through which the river flows and the architectural glories that mark its banks make the valley a first-class tourist attraction.

- **Organising Your Time**: Allow a full day to explore the Quercy stretch of the Dordogne and a half a day to explore the Périgord Noir stretch of the river.

- **Don't Miss**: Souillac, Grotte de Lacave; Domme; la Roque-Gageac; Château de Castelnaud; Château des Milandes; Jardins de Marqueyssac; Beynac-et-Cazenac; Sarlat-la-Canéda.

Geographical Notes

A lovely journey – The Dordogne begins where the Dore and the Dogne meet at the foot of the Sancy, the highest peak in the Massif Central. Swift flowing and speckled with foam, the river calms down for a short while after Beaulieu as it crosses the rich plain, where it is joined by the River Cère, which rises in Cantal. From this point the Dordogne is a truly majestic river, though it remains nonetheless swift and temperamental. The *causses* (limestone plateaux) of Quercy bar its way and so in true Herculean style it cuts a path through the Montvalent Amphitheatre. Having reached the Périgord plateaux beyond Souillac, the river begins to flow past great castles, washing the base of the rocks on which they perch. Starting at Limeuil, where the river is joined by the Vézère, the valley widens out and, after crossing some rapids, reaches Bergerac and then the Guyenne plains with their vineyards. At the Ambès Spit, the Dordogne completes its 500km/310mi journey; joins the Garonne and the two flow on together as the Gironde.

The unpredictable Dordogne – The Dordogne flows swiftly through both the mountains and the plains, but its volume is far from constant. Winter and spring rain storms and the melting of the snows on the Millevaches Plateau and the mountains of Auvergne bring floods almost every year which are sudden, violent and at times devastating.

Excursions

1 Dordogne in the Quercy★★★

1 *Round tour from Souillac – 85km/53mi – allow one day*

Souillac★
See SOUILLAC.

▶ *Drive NE out of Souillac along the D 703.*

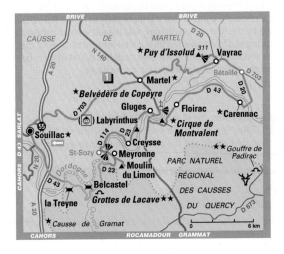

Address Book

For coin ranges, see the Legend at the back of the guide.

EATING OUT

La Ferme de Maraval – D 46 - 24250 Cénac-St-Julien - S of Cénac, on the route de Gourdon - ☎ 05 53 30 26 95 - maraval@ perigord.com - closed Mon except Jul-Aug - reserv. required. This former barn has been converted into a pleasant restaurant with exposed beams and stone walls. An interesting collection of old farming implements is on display. Regional cuisine.

Ferme-Auberge Montalieu-Haut – 24250 St-Cybranet - 8km/5mi SW of Domme on the D 50 and then the D 57 (towards Daglan) - ☎ 05 53 28 31 74 - closed Nov-May and Mon in Jul-Aug - reserv. required. A tranquil rural setting in which to enjoy regional specialities and fresh produce direct from the farm. Four holiday cottages available with splendid views across the valley. Swimming pool.

La Treille – At the dock - 46200 Meyronne - ☎ 05 53 28 33 19 - hotel@ latreille-perigord.com - closed 11 Nov-31 Mar, Sun eve and Mon. This family home was built in 1866 and is now covered with Virginia creeper. The dining room extends to a pleasant leafy veranda and terrace, where the focus is on reasonably priced local cuisine. A few recently decorated rooms are also available here.

WHERE TO STAY

Hostellerie Fénelon – 46110 Carennac - ☎ 05 65 10 96 46 - contact@ hotel-fenelon.com - closed 6 Jan-20 Mar, 17 Nov-20 Dec, Fri, Sat lunchtime and Mon lunchtime (except Jul-Aug) - 15 rooms. A large Quercy-style house with a friendly atmosphere, with some rooms overlooking the river. Exposed beams, attractive stonework, a welcoming fireplace and a scattering of objects recalling life on the farm add charm to the dining room, where you can enjoy traditional regional cuisine while admiring views of the countryside.

Relais du Touron – Route de Sarlat - 24200 Carsac-Aillac - ☎ 05 53 28 16 70 - contact@lerelaisdutouron.com - closed 13 Nov-28 Mar - 18 rooms. In a pretty wooded park, this attractive traditional house and its annex provide a choice between simple, rustic-style rooms and more modern ones embellished with Moorish-inspired furnishings. A pleasant veranda opens onto the pool. Regional cuisine.

Martel★

See MARTEL.

▶ Continue along the D 703 to Vayrac and turn N along the D 20 towards Brive-la-Gaillarde. Turn left onto the D 119 before leaving the town.

Puy d'Issolud★

The plateau near Vayrac, of which the highest point is Puy d'Issolud with an altitude of 311m/1020ft, is bordered by steep cliffs overlooking little tributaries flowing into the Dordogne.

From the plateau there is an extensive, albeit piecemeal **view**★ of the Dordogne. Puy d'Issolud was surrounded, at the time of the Gauls, by such solid earthworks and dry-stone defences that it was one of the most redoubtable *oppida* of Quercy, and is said to have been the former **Uxellodunum**, site of the last Gaulish resistance to Caesar after Alésia. Some historians place Uxellodunum at Capdenac or Luzech, but archaeological research suggests that it is more likely to be the Puy d'Issolud.

The battle, led by the Roman legionaries, was waged with unbelievable ferocity and, after a spring had been diverted through underground caverns, causing those defending Uxellodunum to believe that their gods had deserted them by cutting off their water supply, ended in another defeat for the Gauls.

▶ Return to Vayrac.

Vayrac

Located in place Luctérius, the **Musée Uxellodunum** (Open Jul-Aug, 9am-noon and 3-6pm. Closed Sun, public hols and the weekend after 15 Aug. 1€. ☎ 05 65 37 30 03) displays prehistoric and Gallo-Roman finds discovered in and around the Puy d'Issolud oppidum.

▶ Continue along the D 703 towards Puybrun. In Bétaille, turn right onto the D 20.

Carennac★

See CARENNAC.

▶ Leave Carennac to the NW via the D 43 which runs alongside the south bank of the river.

Beyond Carennac, the Dordogne cuts a channel between the Martel and Gramat *causses* before entering the beautiful area of the Montvalent Amphitheatre.

Floirac

A 14C keep is all that remains of the old fortifications. North of the village stands a lovely 15C chapel.

Cirque de Floirac★

The road is very picturesque, running for the most part beside the river, though sometimes running along a ledge above it. There are attractive views of the valley and the *causse* cliffs from every bend.

▷ *Take the D 140 towards Gluges then turn right on the D 32 after crossing the river.*

Belvédère de Copeyre★

There is a good **view**★ of the Dordogne, the Floirac Amphitheatre and Puy d'Issolud from a wayside cross standing on the edge of the cliff.

Gluges

This village (with old houses) lies in a beautiful **setting**★ beside the river at the foot of the cliffs.

▷ *Leave Gluges SW along the D 43 and continue along the D 23 carved out of the cliff.*

Creysse

The charming village of Creysse with pleasant, narrow streets, brown-tiled roofs, houses bedecked with climbing vines and flights of steps leading to their doors, lies at the foot of the rocky spur, on which stands a pre-Romanesque church, the former castle chapel, with its curious twin apses. The 12C church and the remains of the 15C castle are reached by a stony alleyway, which climbs sharply to a terrace. It is from a little square shaded by plane trees, near the war memorial, that you get the best overall view of the village.

▷ *Drive NW out of Creysse along the D 114 and, in Sozy, turn left onto the D 15.*

Meyronne

From the bridge over the Dordogne, there is a pretty **view** of the river and the village – former home of the bishops of Tulle – with its charming Quercy houses built attractively into the cliffs.

▷ *Continue SE along the D 15 then turn right 1km/0.6mi further on.*

Site du Moulin du Limon

The ruins of an old mill and a chasm overgrown with greenery form a charming setting.

▷ *Return to Meyronne and turn left onto the D 23.*

The road subsequently follows the course of the Dordogne through beautiful countryside of rocks and cliffs, then crosses the River Ouysse near Lacave.

Grottes de Lacave★

🕐 ⸙ *Open Jul-Aug, guided tour (1hr 30min), 9.30am-12.30pm and 1.30-6pm; Apr-Jun and Sep, 9.30am-noon and 2-6pm; last two weeks of Mar and Oct to Nov, 10am-noon and 2-5pm.* 🕐 *Closed Nov school hols to mid-Mar.* 7.20€ *(4-14 years old: 5€).* 05 65 37 87 03. www.grottes.lacave.com.

Near the valley of the Dordogne as it makes a deep cut through the Gramat Causse, a series of caves was discovered in 1902 by Armand Viré, a student of the geographer and speleologist EA Martel, at the foot of the cliffs beside the river.

The galleries open to visitors are 1.6km/1mi long (*complete tour, on foot*) and divide into two: concretions and stalactites prevail in the first; in the second, underground rivers run in between natural rimstone dams (*gours*) and flood out into placid lakes.

In the **Salle des Merveilles**, black light first shows up the "living" part of the stalactites; then normal lighting enhances the reflection of the concretions in the still water of the lake.

Château de Belcastel

A vertical cliff dropping down to the confluence of the Ouysse and the Dordogne is crowned by a castle standing proudly in a remarkable **setting**★. Only the eastern part of the main wing and the keep date from the Middle Ages; most of the other buildings were rebuilt later.

Château de Belcastel and the River Dordogne

▶ *D 43 cuts across the meander of the Dordogne and runs towards Pinsac. Turn left just before the bridge.*

Château de la Treyne

🕐 *Open Jul-Aug, 9am-noon and 2-6pm.* ✑*5€.* ☎ *05 65 27 60 60.*

The château stands perched on a cliff, which on one side overlooks the east bank of the Dordogne and on the other side a vast park. Burned by the Catholics during the Wars of Religion, the château was rebuilt in the 17C.

The park (French gardens) and chapel (where exhibitions are held) are open to the public.

▶ *The D 43 leads back to Souillac. If you wish to enjoy the Dordogne a while longer, turn left at Port de Souillac and return to Souillac via Cieurac.*

② Dordogne in the Périgord★★★

② *Round tour from Sarlat – 70km/44mi – allow half a day*

Sarlat★★★

👁 *see SARLAT-LA-CANÉDA.*

▶ *Drive S out of Sarlat along the D 46, cross the Dordogne then turn right onto the D 50.*

Soon after Vitrac, Domme comes into view on its rocky promontory.

Domme★★

👁 *See DOMME.*

▶ *Continue along the D 50.*

Cénac

The only remaining evidence of the large priory built in Cénac in the 11C is the small **Romanesque church** which stands outside the village. Even the church did not escape the Wars of Religion, and only the east end escaped the depredations of the Protestants serving under Captain Vivans in 1589.

Go into the churchyard to get an overall view of the east end with its fine stone roof and its column buttresses topped with foliated capitals. Inside, in the chancel and the apse, there is a series of interesting historiated capitals.

▶ *Continue along the D 50 to St-Cybranet then follow the D 57 towards Sarlat and turn left before the bridge.*

Château de Castelnaud★★

🖐 *See Château de CASTELNAUD.*

▶ *Rejoin the D 57 (on the left) then drive straight on along the D 53 which follows the south bank of the Dordogne.*

Château de Fayrac

The castle is tucked amid the greenery on the south bank of the Dordogne opposite Beynac-et-Cazenac. A double curtain wall surrounds the interior courtyard, which is reached by two drawbridges.

▶ *Continue along the D 53.*

Château des Milandes★

🕘*Open Jul-Aug, 9.30am-7.30pm (last entrance 30min before closing), night visits Tue; May-Jun and early Sep to mid-Oct, 10am-6.30pm; Apr and mid-Oct to early Nov, 10am-6.15pm, Sat 2-6pm.* ⊜*7.50€ (child: 5.50€).* ☎ *05 53 59 31 21. www.milandes.com*

Built in 1489 by François de Caumont, the estate remained the property of this family until the Revolution and was eventually purchased by the well-known American singer, Josephine Baker or *La Perle Noire* as she was known in her Paris cabaret heyday in the 1920s and 1930s. It was here that she sought to create a world village, gathering together and adopting children of different races, religions and nationalities and bringing them up to promote mutual understanding.

Joséphine Baker adapted the interior decoration to her own taste as visitors can gather from walking through various rooms devoted to the different periods of the singer's life. The exhibition includes unreleased photos, stage costumes, posters, as well as spoken commentaries with the artist singing in the background.

An unrelated addition to the tourist attraction are the falconry demonstrations staged in the gardens surrounding the château. Visitors may also stroll through the 7ha/17-acre park beyond.

▶ *Rejoin the D 53 then turn right onto the D 50 and right again 4.5km/2.8mi further to Allas-les-Mines. Cross the Dordogne and turn right onto the D 703 which follows the north bank of the river.*

J. Damase/MICHELIN

Château des Milandes

Josephine Baker

1906, St Louis, Missouri – 1975, Paris, France

An early symbol of the beauty and vitality of artistic expression in the American black community, Josephine Baker was also an honoured hero of the Second World War, winning the Croix de Guerre for her work as a member of the Free French forces and the Résistance. She began her theatrical career in her early teens, eventually earning a place as a chorus girl in the revue *Shuffle Along*, which brought her to New York City. Still a very young woman, she stirred sensation in Paris with her *danse sauvage*, playing on colonial fantasies and high-octane sexuality, while learning much about the world, her art, and herself. She got star billing for her performance at the Folies-Bergère, clad in the famous banana skirt. Baker became a French citizen in 1937. When war broke out, she used her special position as a European entertainer (albeit one who had caused much scandal in cities more conservative than libertine Paris) to carry secret messages and to help spirit friends out of France to safety. She retired at age 50, but, short of funds and determined to continue building her dream and her family at Les Milandes, she returned to the stage within a few years, and worked tirelessly up until the day of her death.

Beynac-et-Cazenac★★

See BEYNAC-ET-CAZENAC.

▶ *Continue along the D 703; turn left past the railway line onto the D 49 towards Sarlat then right onto the D 57.*

Jardins de Marqueyssac★★

Kids ⏱Open Jul-Aug, 9am-8pm (last entrance 1hr before closing); Apr-Jun and Sep, 10am-7pm; Feb-Mar and Oct to mid-Nov, 10am-6pm; mid-Nov to Jan, 2-5pm. ⭐6.60€ (under 7 years old: 3.30€) or 11.20€ (under 7 years old: 5.60€) for a combined ticket with Castelnaud. ☎ 05 53 31 36 36. www.marqueyssac.com

Situated at the tip of a rocky promontory, the splendid 22ha/54-acre park offers a pleasant mixture of natural vegetation, essentially holm oaks, and hand-trimmed box shrubs forming patterns, and includes a terrace, a waterfall as well as three walks (linked by footpaths) leading to a belvedere. If you are short of time, you could take a round-trip of the gardens by heading towards the belvedere along the cliff walk and taking a free barouche ride back along the main alleyway. The shaded paths wending their way through the gardens are lined with panels detailing the local flora, fauna and history and there is a playground for children. From the belvedere, there are striking **views**★★ of nearby villages and castles: La Roque-Gageac, Beynac, Castelnaud and the Dordogne meanders.

▶ *Rejoin the D 703 (on the left).*

Note, on your left, the **Château de la Malartrie**, a castle built in the 20C, greatly influenced by the 15C style.

La Roque-Gageac★★

See La ROQUE-GAGEAC.

▶ *Drive 2km/1.2mi along the D 703 and turn left onto the D 46 which leads back to Sarlat.*

EYMET

POPULATION 2 552

MICHELIN LOCAL MAP 329: D-8

On the border of the Bergerac and Agen regions, Eymet is a small Périgord town famous for its gourmet food factories which preserve goose and duck liver (foie gras), galantines and ballottines, and local specialities on view in the window of any shop selling cold-cuts worthy of the name *charcuterie*.

- **Don't Miss:** The weekly Thursday market.
- **Also See:** Bergerac.

A Bit of History

The bastide – Founded in 1256 by Alphonse de Poitiers, the *bastide* was ruled by several seigneurial families – even though it was granted a charter guaranteeing privileges and liberties in 1271 – who were alternately in allegiance with the king of France and the king of England. Consequently, it had an eventful history during the Hundred Years War and the Wars of Religion. The ramparts were razed under Louis XIII.

Visit

Place Centrale

The arcaded square is lined with old half-timbered or stone houses, some of which have mullioned windows. In its centre is a 17C fountain.

A walk through the streets reveals the chequer-board plan of the town.

> **Market** – According to locals, the weekly Thursday market has taken place here since 1270. If you miss it, you can also shop in Figeac on Tuesday evenings in July and August.

Église

It was built on the site of a former Bene-dictine church belonging to Moissac Abbey.

Donjon (Keep)

This 14C tower is all that remains of the castle.

Moulin

The lower parts of the mill date from the 13C. Up until 1902 when the river traffic stopped altogether, boats were moored along the quays situated downstream.

EYMOUTIERS

POPULATION 2 115

MICHELIN LOCAL MAP 325: H-6

The only part of the Monastère d'Eymoutiers still standing is the collegiate church built from the 11C to the 15C. The village developed on a height overlooking the River Vienne.

- **Don't Miss:** The view from Mont Gargan; Vallée de la Maulde.
- **Especially for Kids:** Cité des Insectes.
- **Also See:** Lac de Vassivière.

Visit

Église

The greatest part of the nave and the belfry-porch are Romanesque. The elegant chancel is lit by 15 remarkable stained-glass windows dating from the 15C. Note the tall carved-wood Christ facing the pulpit. The church also contains a fine 13C reliquary **cross**★.

Address Book

For coin ranges, see the Legend at the back of the guide.

WHERE TO STAY

◔ **Chambre d'hôte Le Verrou** – *Le Bourg - 87120 Nedde - 10km/6mi E of Eymoutiers along the D 992 -* ☏ *05 55 69 98 04 -* ◔ *closed Jan-Feb -* ⚘ *- reserv. required in winter - 4 rooms.* You'll find delightful bedrooms with wood furnishings and embroidered linens in this bed and breakfast near the Lac de Vassivière, where the inner courtyard and its flower-filled garden exude tranquillity. For meals, you can choose between the crêperie and the family dining room where the menu is on based on carefully selected local products.

EXCURSIONS

L'Escale – *7km/4.5mi E of Peyrat-le-Château along the D 13 and D 222 - Rte circumlacustre - Lieu-dit Auphelle - 87470 Peyrat-le-Château -* ☏ *05 55 69 41 35 -* ◔ *open daily Apr-Oct, 8am-9pm -* ◔ *closed Nov to Palm Sunday.* The owners of this bar-restaurant organise regular excursions on Lac de Vassivière, including lunch on board. If you prefer to stay on dry land, enjoy a leisurely drink on the terrace.

GUIDED TOURS

Eymoutiers – At Easter *(Wed at 10am; 3€)* and in July and August *(Mon at 10am; 3€),* the tourist office in Eymoutiers organises walking tours (1hr 30min) of the town's main sights, providing a fascinating insight into the town's history and architecture.

Pays Monts et Barrages – In July and August, you can enjoy a guided tour *(4€)* of this area of mountains *(monts)* and dams *(barrages)* covering 30 or so communes between Limoges and Vassivière in the company of a qualified local guide.

The summer programme for this area includes themed hikes, evenings with storytellers, and days in which you can help restore local buildings. *For further information, contact the Syndicat Intercommunal Monts et Barrrages in Bujaleuf,* ☏ *05 55 69 57 60, or log onto www.vpah.culture.fr.*

Espace Paul Rebeyrolle

 ♿ ◔*Open Jun-Sep, 10am-7pm (last entrance 30min before closing); Oct-May, 10am-6pm.* ◔ *Closed Christmas hols and 1 May.* ◉*4€.* ☏ *05 55 69 58 88.*

The building houses 43 works by the figurative artist born in 1926, obsessed by all the suffering in the world. Rebeyrolle is also a nature lover whose pastoral compositions are inspired by local landscapes.

Espace Minéralogique

Opposite the Espace Paul Rebeyrolle. ♿ ◔*Open Jun-Sep, 10am-noon and 2.30-7pm.* ◉*2.50€ (child under 10: 1.50€).* ☏ *05 55 69 27 74 or contact the tourist office,* ☏ *05 55 69 27 81.*

Guided tours by members of an association dedicated to the study of minerals inform visitors about their specificities, their different uses and the discovery of dinosaurs' eggs and enable visitors to see tiny minerals through special binoculars.

Excursions

Chaud

▷ *13km/8mi SE along the D 992. In Nedde, bear right onto the D 81 then, after crossing the river, turn right onto the D 81A.*

Located on the edge of the Millevaches plateau, this village houses a centre devoted to the natural environment of the Limousin region.

Cité des Insectes

Kids ◔ *Open Jul-Aug, 10am-1pm and 2.30-6.30pm; Easter to end of Jun and Sep-1 Nov, Sat-Sun and public hols, 10am-1pm and 2.30-6.30pm.* ◉*4.50€ (child: 3€).* ☏ *05 55 69 10 87.*

A typical Auvergne barn houses themed exhibitions, an ant hill, a room where exotic insects are being bred and a presentation of bees. The garden, which contains aromatic and melliferous plants, enables visitors to watch insects in their natural environment (pond, woods etc)

Mont Gargan

23km/14mi SW along the D 30. Alt 731m/2 398ft.

The road climbs steeply at first, leading to the summit which is crowned by the ruins of a chapel. As you go round the chapel, you see a vast **panorama**★★, south-east over the Monédières Massif, north over the hills of Marche and west to the Limousin Mountains.

In July 1944, it was the site of fierce fighting between German troops and members of the Resistance led by Georges Guingouin.

Vallée de la Maulde

70km/44mi round-trip – allow half a day

▶ *Drive NW out of Eymoutiers along the D 14.*

Bujaleuf

Bear left to reach the bridge spanning the reservoir from which you can enjoy a good **view**★ of the two shores of the lake forming the recreation centre.

Beyond Bujaleuf, the D 16 descends into the valley affording lovely views of the stretches of water and the mountains on the horizon.

Barrage de Fleix

Set in a fine wooded site, the slim form of the dam (50m/164ft long and 16m/53ft high) is supported by vertical buttresses.

Barrage du Martineix

A similar construction to the previous one, this dam stands in a wild but picturesque site.

▶ *Drive along the D 13 towards Peyrat.*

Shortly after Clédat, the D 5 runs past Mont Larron.

▶ *Turn right onto the D 5A1 towards St-Julien-le-Petit then left just beyond the cemetery.*

Usine et Barrage du Mont-Larron (Power Station and Dam)

This stark looking building is the control centre for the series of dams. To the right of it a path, tarred to begin with, leads to the foot of the massive dam which is of the vaulted type. A path to the right climbs to the crest of the dam which is 183m/600ft long.

▶ *Turn left onto the D 233 just before Artigeas.*

Peyrat-le-Château

In this rolling landscape where broom and heather alternate with pine and beech, the remains of a castle stand by a lake; the square keep of this fortress was once the home of the Lusignan family. The church was destroyed by fire in 1184, and rebuilt in the Gothic style (keystones carved with symbolic ornamentation).

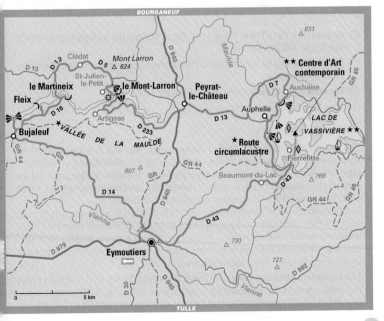

Musée de la Résistance – ⏱*Open Jun-Aug, 10am-noon and 4-6.30pm; May and Sep, 3-5.30pm.* 🕐 *Closed Tue.* ⚙*2.30€ (under 12 years old: no charge).* ☎ *05 55 69 75 11 or 05 55 69 48 75.*

This small museum is devoted to the local resistance movement, named Maquis Guingouin after its leader, and to the Limousin Resistance in general. There is a wealth of information about local leaders, the action taken, weapons…

Maison des Moulins – Kids ⏱ *Guided tour (1hr 15min, last entrance 1hr before closing), Jul-Aug, daily (except Sat), 2.30-6pm; May-Jun and Sep, Sun, 3.30-6pm.* ⚙*4.50€.* ☎ *05 55 69 26 05.*

There was a flour mill on the site until 1900; it was replaced by a paper mill which closed down in 1934. The mill museum contains 13 scale models (1:10) illustrating various mills: windmill, tide mill, noria…which can be seen working.

There is a picnic area on the banks of the River Maulde.

▶ *Leave Peyrat to the E along the D 13 then turn left onto the D 7 towards Royère; 5km/3mi further on, turn right to the Vassivière dam.*

A short distance beyond Auchaise, the **route circumlacustre**★, which skirts the west shore of Vassivière Lake via **Auphelle**, offers pleasant views of the lake and its islands.

Lac de Vassivière★★

👣 *See Lac de VASSIVIÈRE.*

▶ *Drive to Beaumont-du-Lac via the D 43 which leads back to Eymoutiers.*

Les EYZIES-DE-TAYAC★★

POPULATION 909

MICHELIN LOCAL MAP 329: H-6

The village of Les Eyzies occupies a grandiose setting of steep cliffs crowned with evergreen oaks and junipers, at the confluence of the River Vézère and River Beune. The poplar-lined River Vézère winds between meadows and farmland, sometimes narrowing to flow between sheer, vertical walls of rock 50-80m/ 164-262ft high. Shelters cut out of the limestone base served as dwelling places for prehistoric people; caves located higher up on the cliff face were used as sanctuaries. The discovery within the last 100 years of many such dwellings within a limited radius of Les Eyzies has earned the town the title **European Capital of Prehistory.** 🛈 *Pl. de la Mairie, 24620 Les Eyzies-de-Tayac, ☎ 05 53 06 97 05. www.leseyzies.com.*

🕐 **Organising Your Time**: Allow a full day to explore the archaeological sites in the Beune and Vézère valleys.

👁 **Don't Miss**: Musée National de la Préhistoire; Grotte du Grand Roc; Grotte de Font-de-Gaume.

Kids **Especially for Kids**: Roc de Cazelle; Préhisto Parc.

👣 **Also See**: Site de la Madeleine.

A Bit of History

The capital of prehistory – During the Second Ice Age and at the time when the volcanoes of Auvergne were active, prehistoric people abandoned the northern plains and headed for the warmer areas of the south. The lower Vézère attracted the migrants because of its easily accessible natural caves and overhanging rocks, which could be hollowed out into shelters without much difficulty.

People used these cave dwellings for tens of thousands of years and left in them traces of their daily tasks and passage such as bones, ashes from their fires, tools, weapons, utensils and ornaments. As their civilisation evolved, so did animal species: after elephants and cave bears came bison, aurochs, mammoths and, later still, musk-oxen, reindeer, ibex, stags and horses.

The archaeologists' paradise – Methodical study of the deposits in the Les Eyzies region has considerably increased our knowledge of prehistory. The Dordogne *département* has greatly contributed to the study of prehistory with more than 200 deposits discovered there, of which more than half are in the lower Vézère Valley. Following these discoveries, two great periods of the Paleolithic Age were defined and named after the cave deposits – Mousterian and Magdalenian. Discoveries followed thicker and faster as Les Eyzies proved to be one of the richest prehistoric sites in the world.

The Village

Musée National de la Préhistoire (National Museum of Prehistory)★

🕐 Open Jul-Aug, 9.30am-6.30pm; Jun and Sep, daily except Tue, 9.30am-6pm; Oct-May, daily except Tue, 9.30am-12.30pm and 2-5.30pm. 🕐 Closed 1 Jan and 25 Dec. ⊗4.50€, Sun 3€ (under 18 years old: no charge), no charge 1st Sun of the month. ☎ 05 53 06 45 45. ⟳ Guided tours by prior arrangement. ☎ 05 53 06 45 65.

The museum is in the old castle of the barons of Beynac. The 13C fortress, restored in the 16C, clings to the cliff half way up, beneath a rocky outcrop, overlooking the village. From the terrace, there is a good **view** of Les Eyzies and the valleys of Vézère and Beune.

Room 1 illustrates the evolution of flint-cutting from around 2.5 million years BC and the successive civilisations through displays of tools dating from the major Paleolithic periods.

Room 2 forms the most fascinating part of the museum: it contains an impressive collection of modern man's first works of art, including a low-relief carving known as the **Devil's Furnace** (around 20000 BC). Other carved stone blocks (36000-26000 BC) depict animals and various symbols.

There is a remarkable group of small statues of women with striking similarities.

Room 3 displays new acquisitions and illustrates the quaternary fauna discovered in palaeontological sites.

Room 4, devoted to anthropology and funerary rituals, contains the reconstruction of a woman's tomb from St-Germain-la-Rivière. Also presented are the animals hunted by prehistoric man.

Address Book

For coin ranges, see the Legend at the back of the guide.

EATING OUT

⊗⊗**Hostellerie du Passeur** – Place de la Mairie - 24620 Les Eyzies-de-Tayac - ☎ 05 53 06 97 13 - www.hostellerie-du-passeur.com - 19 rooms . This handsome house covered in Virginia creeper stands in the heart of Les Eyzies. Stylish, cheerful rooms all sporting bright colours, some overlooking the cliffs. At dinner, choose from the classical dining room with its stone fireplace, the bright conservatory or the shady terrace facing the Vézère. Traditional cuisine.

⊗⊗**Auberge de l'Étang Joli** – 4km/ 2.5mi S of Les Eyzies on the D 706 and a minor road - ☎ 05 53 35 29 87 - reserv. required in winter. Far from the tourist crowds, this peaceful Périgord inn has an attractive flower garden and terrace. Regional cooking, prepared with care by the exuberant patronne.

⊗⊗ **La Métairie** – On the D 47 - 7km/4.3mi E of Les Eyzies-de-Tayac - ☎ 05 53 29 65 32 - bourgeade@wanadoo.fr - 🕐 closed Sun eve out of season, Mon, and Wed lunchtime. This farm once belonged to the Château de Beyssac and is built around a courtyard-terrace. The old feeding troughs in the dining room are an appropriate reminder of the building's past history!

WHERE TO STAY

⊗ **Le Panoramique** – Beune - 3.9km/ 2.3mi SE of Les Eyzies-de-Tayac on the D 47 towards Sarlat then the D 48 towards St-Cyprien - ☎ 05 53 06 98 82 - 🍽 - 4 rooms. A pleasant park with trees forms an oasis of quiet around the three regional-style houses. The decor of the guestrooms is plain; two have panoramic terraces overlooking the site of Les Eyzies. Breakfast served on the veranda. Two self-catering cottages.

⊗⊗ **Hôtel Le Moulin de la Beune** - ☎ 05 53 06 94 33 - www.moulindelabeune.com - 🕐 closed 2 Nov-31 Mar - 🅿 - 20 rooms. The guest rooms at this former mill on the River Beune are traditional and comfortable. Wood and stone are the predominant themes in the dining room, where you can admire the mill's old waterwheel mechanism. Waterfront terrace.

SHOPPING

The farmers' market is open daily in the summer season, selling a range of local crafts and produce.

Outside the National Museum of Prehistory

The new buildings erected at the foot of the castle will provide space for the expansion of the present exhibitions and the introduction of audio-visual presentations and interactive terminals. The first gallery will deal with the main prehistoric civilisations from 400000 to 10000 BC; the second gallery will illustrate prehistoric life through objects presented in a reconstructed real-life situation.

Grotte de Font-de-Gaume★

🕐 👁👄 *Open mid-May to mid-Sep, guided tour (45min, last entrance 1hr 30min before closing), daily except Sat 9.30am-5.30pm; mid-Sep to mid-May, daily except Sat 9.30am-12.30pm and 2-5.30pm. By prior arrangement only.* 🕐 *Closed 1 Jan, 1 May, 1 and 11 Nov, and 25 Dec.* 👓 *6.10€.* ☎ *05 53 06 86 00.*

▶ *Leave the car by the road to St-Cyprien opposite a cliff-spur. A path takes you up 400m/440yd to the cave entrance.*

The cave runs back in the form of a passage 120m/130yd long with chambers and other ramifications leading off it. Detailed examination and study of the paintings date them as belonging to the Middle Magdalenian period (16000-13000 BC). Some were probably drawn at the same time as those at Lascaux (Upper Magdalenian period). Beyond a narrow passage, known as the Rubicon, are many multicoloured paintings, often superimposed on one another; all the drawings of horses, bison, mammoths, reindeer and other deer indicate great artistic skill and, after Lascaux, form the finest group of polychrome paintings in France. The frieze of bison, painted in brown on a white calcite background, is remarkable.

Abri Pataud (Pataud Shelter)

🕐 *Open Jul-Aug, daily 10am-7pm; Apr-Jun, Sep to mid-Nov and Christmas school hols, daily except Mon, Fri and Sat, 10am-12.30pm and 2-6pm; mid-Nov to Mar, daily except Mon, Fri and Sat-Sun, 10am-12.30pm and 2-5.30pm.* 🕐 *Closed 1 Jan and 25 Dec.* 👓*5.20€.* ☎ *05 53 06 92 46.*

A museum on site shows objects and bones discovered during excavation work; note in particular two large stratigraphic sections and 14 archaeological layers (Aurignacian, Gravettian and Solutrean, 35000-20000 BC) where bones, flints and the remains of fireplaces can be seen in place, as well as a carved Venus in the Gravettian layer and the vivid low-relief carving of an ibex dating from the Solutrean period.

Abri de Cro-Magnon (Cro-Magnon Shelter)

This cave was discovered in 1868 and it revealed, in addition to flints and carved bones of the Aurignacian and Gravettian Cultures, five adult skeletons which were studied by Paul Broca, the surgeon and anthropologist who founded the School of Anthropology in France. The discoveries made in this cave were of prime importance for prehistoric studies, since they were the first remains of *Homo Sapiens* to be found. A commemorative plaque is all that is left of the site today.

Église de Tayac

🕐 *Open Jul-Aug, Sun 3-6pm, by prior arrangement with the tourist office.* ☎ *05 53 06 97 05.*

The warm, gold-coloured stone enhances this 12C fortified church. Two towers roofed with *lauzes* frame the main body of the church. The tower above the doorway serves as the bell-tower.

The doorway is intriguing; the first scalloped arch gives it an Eastern air whereas the two outermost columns, with Corinthian capitals of white marble, show Gallo-Roman influence.

Inside, the arrangement of the three naves, divided by large arcades resting on piers, and the timberwork ceiling are features rarely found in Périgord.

Excursions

Along the D 47

Musée de la Spéléologie (Museum of Speleology)

🕐 *Open May-Jun, daily except Sat-Sun and public hols, 1-6pm.* ⌾*3€.* ☎ *05 53 24 24 20.*

The museum is installed in the rock fortress of Tayac, which overlooks the Vézère Valley. The four chambers, cut out of the living rock, contain a selection of items pertaining to speleology: caving equipment, exhibits describing the geological formations and plant and animal life in local caves as well as several models.

Abri du Poisson (The Fish Shelter)

🕐 *Same opening times and conditions as the Gisement de Laugerie-Haute (👍 see below).* ⌾ *2.50€.*

A 1.05m/3.3ft-long fish has been carved on the roof of a small hollow. It is a species of salmon which was very common in the Vézère until quite recently. It dates from the Gravettian Period (about 23000 years BC), and is one of the oldest cave sculptures yet discovered. A hand can be seen not far from the fish.

Grotte du Grand Roc (Grand Roc Cave)★★

🕐 ⌱*Open Jul-Aug, guided tour (30min) 9.30am-7pm; Apr-Jun and Sep-Oct, 10am-6pm; Feb-Mar, 1-11 Nov and Christmas hols, 10am-5pm.* 🕐 *Closed 1 Jan and 25 Dec.* ⌾*7€, 8€ combined ticket with shelter and caves (child: 3.50€).* ☎ *05 53 06 92 70. www.grandroc.com*

There is a good **view**★ of the Vézère Valley from the stairs leading up to the cave (discovered in 1924) and the platform at its mouth. The length (40m/45yd) of tunnel enables one to see, within chambers that are generally small in size, an extraordinary display of stalactites, stalagmites and eccentrics resembling coral formations, as well as a wonderful variety of pendants and crystals.

Abris Préhistoriques de Laugerie Basse (Lower Laugerie Deposit)

♿ 🕐 *Open Jul-Aug, 9.30am-7pm; Apr-Jun and Sep-Oct, 10am-6pm; Feb-Mar, 1-11 Nov and Christmas school hols, 10am-5pm.* 🕐 *Closed the rest of the year, 1 Jan and 25 Dec.* ⌾*6€ (child: 3€) combined ticket for cave and shelters.* ☎ *05 53 06 92 70. www.grandroc.com.*

Prehistoric bones, stone tools and other artefacts were discovered in this deposit, downstream from the Upper Laugerie Deposit. They are in various museums and private collections, but an exhibition centre here contains reproductions of the best of them.

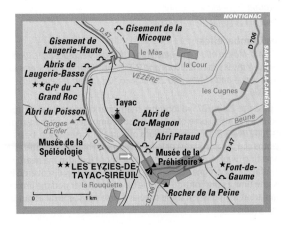

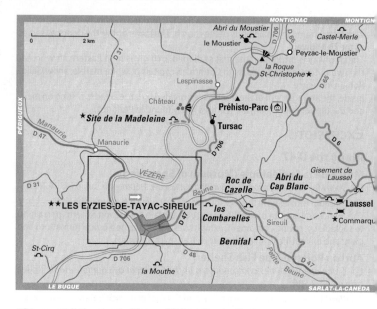

Gisement de Laugerie Haute (Upper Laugerie Deposit)

🕐 ⚒ Open daily except Sat, guided tour (1hr), by prior arrangement only. 🕐 Closed 1 Jan, 1 May, 1 and 11 Nov, and 25 Dec. Contact the Grotte de Font-de-Gaume. ☎ 05 53 06 86 00.

Scientific excavations going on for over a century in a picturesque spot at the foot of high cliffs have revealed examples of the work and art of prehistoric people at different stages of civilisation.

The work has demonstrated the importance of this area, inhabited continuously from the middle of the Perigordian to the middle of the Magdalenian period; that is to say, during the 25000 years of the Upper Paleolithic Age.

The establishment of a time line startles the imagination, clearly illustrating the painfully slow progress of the human race through these millennia. Note the drip stones or channels cut in the rock in the Middle Ages to prevent water from running along the walls and entering the dwellings.

Gisement de la Micoque (La Micoque Deposit)

🕐 Open daily except Sat, by prior arrangement only (2 weeks in advance). 🕐 Closed 1 Jan, 1 May, 1 and 11 Nov, and 25 Dec. ⚒ For further information and prices, call ☎ 05 53 06 86 00.

This deposit revealed many items belonging to periods known as the Tayacian, Micoquian and Mousterian Ages. Some of the finds are exhibited at Les Eyzies National Museum of Prehistory.

Along the River Beune and River Vézère

50km/31mi round-trip – allow one day

▶ Drive E out of Les Eyzies along the D 47.

Grotte des Combarelles

🕐 ⚒ Open mid-May to mid-Sep, guided tour (1hr), daily except Sat, 9.30am-5.30pm; mid-Sep to mid-May, 9.30am-12.30pm and 2-5.30pm. By prior arrangement only. 🕐 Closed 1 Jan, 1 May, 1 and 11 Nov, and 25 Dec. ⚒6.10€ (under 18 years old: no charge). ☎ 05 53 06 86 00.

A winding passage 250m/275yd long has many markings on its walls for the last 120m/131yd of its length, some of which are superimposed one upon another. The drawings include nearly 700 representations of animals (horses, bison, bears, reindeer and mammoths can be seen at rest or in full gallop) and human caricatures. Note the shapes suggesting dwellings which are similar to those found in the nearby Font-de-Gaume, Bernifal and Rouffignac caves. The Combarelles cave, discovered in 1901 at about the same time as the Font-de-Gaume Cave, demonstrated the importance of Magdalenian art at a time when some scholars were still sceptical about the worth of prehistoric studies.

A second passage with similar cave drawings shows traces of domestic settlement and the tools of Magdalenian inhabitants.

▶ *Continue along the D 47 towards Sarlat.*

Roc de Cazelle

Open Jul-Aug, 10am-8pm; May-Jun and Sep, 10am-7pm; Mar-Apr and Oct-Nov: 10am-6pm; Dec-Jan, 11am-5pm. 6€ (5-13 years old: 3€). 05 53 59 46 09. rocde-cazelle.com

Kids This cliff site offers an insight into our ancestors' life from the Paleolithic period to the mid-20C. A marked path leads visitors past scenes of prehistoric daily life to the monolithic dwelling occupied until 1966 by a farming couple. Children will appreciate the quality of the reconstructions, the sound effects and the animals hidden in the forest as well as the adventure trail.

Grotte de Bernifal

10min on foot. Open Jul-Aug, guided tour (1hr), 9am-6pm; Jun and Sep, 10am-noon and 2-6.30pm. 5€. 05 53 29 66 39.

Cave paintings and delicate carvings from the Middle Magdalenian period (16000-13000 BC) are spread over about 100m/330ft. They include mammoths, horses, human figures, a bear and shapes suggesting dwellings.

▶ *Continue along the D 47 which follows the River Petite Beune and turn left 2km/1.2mi further on. Beyond Sireuil, drive N to join the D 48 on the right.*

Abri du Cap-Blanc (Cap-Blanc Shelter)

Open Jul-Aug, guided tour (30min) 10am-7pm; Apr-Jun and Sep-Oct, 10am-noon, 2-6pm. 5.60€ (child: 3.30€). 05 53 59 21 74.

Excavation of a small Magdalenian deposit in 1909 led to the discovery of **carvings**★ in high relief on the walls of the rock shelter. Two bison and in particular a frieze of horses were carved in such a way as to use to full advantage the relief and contour of the rock itself. A human grave was discovered at the foot of the frieze.

▶ *Drive on along the D 48 for 1.5km/0.9mi and turn left onto the D 6 to Moustier; 9km/5.6mi further on, turn left again onto the D 706 towards Les Eyzies.*

Préhisto Parc

Kids *Open Jul-Aug, 10am-7pm; Apr-Jun and Sep, 10am-6.30pm; mid-Feb to end of Mar and Oct to mid-Nov, 10am-5.30pm. 6€ (child: 3€). 05 53 50 73 19.*

In a small cliff-lined valley, carpeted with undergrowth, a discovery trail reveals about 20 reconstituted scenes of Neanderthal and Cro-Magnon daily life: mammoth hunting, cutting-up of reindeer, cave painting, burial customs etc.

▶ *Continue along the D 706 for 500m/547yd then turn right onto a minor road which soon crosses the River Vézère. Turn left in Lespinasse.*

A day in the (Cro-Magnon) life

J. Damase/MICHELIN

Site de la Madeleine★

See Site de la MADELEINE.

▶ *Turn back then right onto the D 706.*

Tursac

The **church** is dominated by a huge, forbidding bell-tower. There is a series of domes, characteristic of the Romanesque Périgord style, covering the church.

The road once more scales the cliff, giving good views of Tursac village and the Vézère Valley.

▶ *The D 706 leads back to Les Eyzies.*

FELLETIN

POPULATION 1 892

MICHELIN LOCAL MAP 325: K-5

This small industrial town, lying in hilly surroundings 10km/6mi south of Aubusson, owes its prosperity to tapestry weaving and claims to have woven the largest tapestry ever made (22×12m/72×40ft) which hangs in Coventry Cathedral. The city's oldest district, perched on an outcrop, has retained many 18C houses.

▸ **Orient Yourself**: Felletin is an excellent base for exploring the mountainous landscapes of the Limousin.

🕐 **Organising Your Time**: Allow a full day to explore the Montagne Limousine region.

☺ **Don't Miss**: A tour of one of Felletin's tapestry workshops.

☝ **Also See**: Aubusson.

A Bit of History

The birthplace of tapestry – Felletin owes its long-standing tradition to a group of Flemish weavers who settled there in the 14C and brought fame to the place from the 15C onwards. In 1689 Felletin became a royal manufacture, entering into fierce competition with the nearby town of Aubusson. Today, the former rivals have joined forces and contribute to the renewal of tapestry weaving undertaken by Jean Lurçat.

Visit

Filature Terrade

🕐 ✎ *Open Jul-end of Aug, guided tour (1hr), Thu 10.30am; rest of the year by prior arrangement with the tourist office (minimum 5 people).* ✎4€. ☎ 05 55 66 54 60.

A guided tour of the tapestry workshops and of a wool mill gives an insight into the various stages of tapestry making.

Église du Moûtier

The three-tiered square bell-tower, dating from the 15C, dominates the whole town; the third tier, decorated with gargoyles and statues is surmounted by an openwork balustrade and topped with a lantern. Note the Flamboyant windows superposed above the Gothic doorway.

The 15C frescoes decorating the nave are particularly noteworthy: they depict St Martin giving half his coat and St Laurent being martyred. There are traces of medieval murals in the transept. Do not miss the ornate 17C altarpiece and the 19C stalls.

Église Notre-Dame-du-Château

🕐 *Themed exhibitions on tapestries; Jul-Aug 10am-noon and 2-6.30pm; May-Jun and Sep, 2-6pm.* ☎ *05 55 66 54 60.*

This Gothic church dates from the late 15C; its typical Languedoc style is unusual in the Limousin region.

Diamanterie

🕐 🐾 *Open Jul-Aug, guided tour (1hr), Wed and Fri, 3pm.* 👝*3€. For further information, contact the tourist office,* ☎ *05 55 66 54 60.*

These works located on the edge of the River Creuse, belonged to a cooperative of diamond cutters who worked for the jewellery trade up to the 1950s then for various industries until 1982. A guided tour of the site enables visitors to discover the workshop and its machinery, the turbine used to produce electricity.

Excursion

La Montagne Limousine★

75km/47mi round-trip – allow one day

▷ *Drive SW out of Felletin along the D 992.*

The road winds pleasantly along the Gourbillon Valley, amid prairies and woodlands.

St-Quentin-la-Chabane

Surrounded by hilltops, this hamlet takes its name from one of them, the Puy de Cabanne. The 13C **church** has a Limousin-style door and bell gable. The nave is vaulted with diagonal ribs. Beneath the chancel, an 11C crypt, Notre-Dame-de-Sousterre, harbours a Black Virgin.

▷ *Continue along the D 992 for 5km/3m, then take the D 59A to the right, towards La Nouaille.*

Domaine de Banizette★

🕐 🐾 *Open Jul-Aug, last 2 weekends in Jun and the first 3 weekends in Sep, guided tour (1hr 15min) at 3pm, 4.15pm and 5.30pm; May-Jun and Sep-Oct, Sun and public hols, 3pm.* 👝*6€ (-8 years old: no charge).* ☎ *05 55 83 28 55.*

This 17C lordly manor, which has been partially transformed into a museum of rural life, shows what a big farm must have been like at the beginning of the 20C, the dawn of the mechanical age. The vaulted sheep barn, the mill, the wash-house, the big oven with its special chambers for pastries and patés, the stables with the original cobblestones, the dovecot, the woodshed, sharecroppers' land and immense grain storage barn, characteristically gathered around a closed courtyard, form a remarkable, well-restored ensemble. The flower garden featuring a central fountain and the three, marked forest trails are also interesting.

▷ *Leave the manor and turn right on the D 59. At St-Marc-à-Loubaud, turn left and take the D 16 towards Gentioux.*

Site du Pont de Sénoueix★

This ancient Roman bridge over the Taurion has only one original arch left. The carefully mounted stones defy time, while the trickle of water at the river's source seems to mark it.

Pont de Sénoueix

S. Sauvignier/MICHELIN

Gentioux

As of the 11C, Gentioux attracted stonemasons from around the Creuse. The 13C **church**, rebuilt in the 15C by the Knights of Malta is adorned with curious 16C sculptures; in the chancel, note the low-relief sculptures and grimacing faces.

In the cemetery, the most remarkable tomb stands in homage to local sculptor Jean Cacaud.

The town's monument to the fallen of the First World War is unique and moving in its pacifist expression: a child in wooden shoes and a school smock, beret in hand, raises a clenched fist in front of the inscription *Maudite soit la guerre* (Cursed be war).

▸ *Leave Gentioux on the D 8 towards Pigerolles. After 3km/1.8m, turn left on the D 35.*

Maison des Chevaliers de Pallier

🕐 ━▣ *Open mid-Mar to mid-Nov, 10am–6pm; guided tours available in Jul–Aug.* ✍4€ *(unaccompanied visit),* 5€ *(guided visit) or* 5€ *(park).* ☎ *05 55 67 91 73.*

Built in the 12C by the Knights Templar, the chapel's façade is admirable, and the belfry gable stands out clearly against the sky. The doorway is flanked by two buttresses and crowned with a pointed arch and 14C sculpted tympanum. Inside, to the right of the stone altar, there is a small Templar's cross on the floor.

In the cemetery, there is a double-sided cross dating from the 16C, and an intriguing, loaf-shaped stone carved with three symbols: a square (for the Holy Scriptures), a circle (religion), and eight loops (eternity).

The chapel is atop a hill just above the 18C home of the Jabouille family of Royal Notaries, an example of the master craftsmanship of Gentioux stone-masons. Several displays relate the history of the Templars in the Creuse region.

The **medieval garden**★ is particularly interesting since it illustrates the symbolic meaning of gardens during the Middle Ages: thus the boxwood maze represents the mistakes man makes before he reaches truth. The garden consists of five parts: medicinal-herb patch, vegetable patch, orchard, flower garden and secluded spots.

▸ *1km/0.6mi before the town of Le Rat, take a small lane on the right, marked Chapelle. Park your car just beyond the turn-off and continue on foot.*

Site du Rat★

🚶 *1.2km/0.7mi on foot there and back (follow the path which climbs on the left).*

The short walk leads to one of the loveliest **sites** on the plateau. A magnificent row of ancient trees shades the path to the 17C granite **Chapelle St-Roch**. Some of the boulders may have been placed there in Celtic times, for purposes which remain enigmatic to us today. Beyond the moss-covered chapel, a path through the pine and heather leads to a group of massive boulders which invite the visitor to climb their broad backs and admire the wide open view over the hushed moorlands.

▸ *Continue along the same road and turn left in Malsagnes.*

Pigerolles

During winters when snow is plentiful, this village is an ideal cross-country ski resort. In summer, it offers pleasant hikes across the plateau.

▸ *Take the D 8 towards La Courtine.*

Féniers

Note yet another fine example of a belfry-porch. Follow the D 26 along the Gioune gorge and admire the lovely views of the Auvergne mountain range.

Gioux

Granite table in the village and Gallo-Roman site (IC and 3C AD) in Maisonnière, 1.5km/0.9mi to the north.

▸ *Take the D 35 and the D 982 back to Felletin.*

FIGEAC★★

POPULATION 9 606

MICHELIN LOCAL MAP 337: I-4

Sprawled along the north bank of the Célé, Figeac developed at the point where the Auvergne meets Upper Quercy. A commercial town, it had a prestigious past as is shown in the architecture of its tall sandstone town houses. 🛈 *Hôtel de la Monnaie, pl. Vival, 46102 Figeac, ☎ 05 65 34 06 25.*

🅿 **Parking**: A number of car parks are dotted around the centre (♿ *see town plan*).

⊙ **Don't Miss**: The old town; Hôtel de la Monnaie; Chapelle Notre-Dame-de-Pitié; Place des Écritures

♿ **Also See**: Célé and Lot valleys.

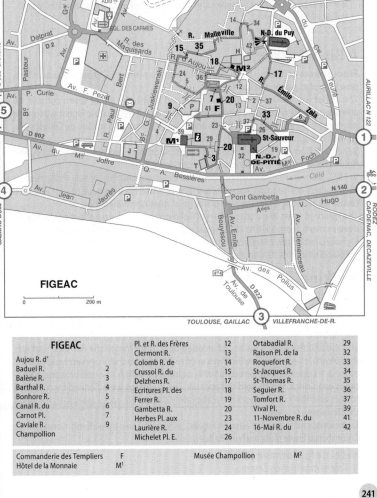

FIGEAC

0   200 m

FIGEAC		Pl. et R. des Frères	12	Ortabadial R.	29
		Clermont R.	13	Raison Pl. de la	32
Aujou R. d'		Colomb R. de	14	Roquefort R.	33
Baduel R.	2	Crussol R. du	15	St-Jacques R.	34
Balène R.	3	Delzhens R.	17	St-Thomas R.	35
Barthal R.	4	Écritures Pl. des	18	Seguier R.	36
Bonhore R.	5	Ferrer R.	19	Tomfort R.	37
Canal R. du	6	Gambetta R.	20	Vival Pl.	39
Carnot Pl.	7	Herbes Pl. aux	23	11-Novembre R. du	41
Caviale R.	9	Laurière R.	24	16-Mai R. du	42
Champollion		Michelet Pl. E.	26		

Commanderie des Templiers	F	Musée Champollion	M²
Hôtel de la Monnaie	M¹		

Jean-François Champollion

Champollion, the outstanding Orientalist, whose brilliance enabled Egyptology to make such great strides, was born at Figeac in December 1790. At the beginning of the 19C, Ancient Egyptian civilisation was still a mystery, since the meaning of hieroglyphics (the word means sacred carving) had not yet been deciphered.

By the time Champollion was 14, he had a command of Greek, Latin, Hebrew, Arabic, Chaldean and Syrian. After his studies in Paris, he lectured in history, at the youthful age of 19, at Grenoble University.

He set himself the task of deciphering a polished basalt tablet, showing three different inscriptions (Egyptian hieroglyphics, demotic – simplified Egyptian script which appeared around 650 BC – and Greek), which had been discovered in 1799 by members of Napoleon's expedition to Egypt near Rosetta in the north-west Nile delta, from which it derives its name – the **Rosetta Stone**.

However, he was not able to carry out his research on the stone itself, which had been seized by the English while at war with France (it is now in the British Museum, London), but had to make do with copies. Drawing on the work of a predecessor, the English physicist Thomas Young (1773-1829), who had succeeded in identifying genders and proper nouns, Champollion gradually unravelled the mystery of hieroglyphics.

In 1826, he founded the Egyptology Museum at the Louvre Palace, Paris, and became its first curator. He left for Egypt on a two-year mission and deciphered many texts while he was there. In 1831, he was appointed professor of Archaeology at the Collège de France, however he gave only four lectures before dying a year later, worn out by all his hard work.

A Bit of History

From abbots to king – Figeac began developing in the 9C around a monastery, which itself expanded in the 13C.

The abbot was the town's lord and governed it with the aid of seven consuls. All administrative services were located inside the monastery. Because Figeac was on the pilgrimage route running from Le Puy and Conques and on to Santiago de Compostela, crowds of pilgrims and travellers flocked through it.

Benefiting from the town's geographical situation between Auvergne, Quercy and Rouergue, local craftsmen and shopkeepers were prosperous.

In 1302, following a disagreement between the abbot and the consuls, Philip the Fair took control of the town, represented by a provost. He won back the inhabitants' favour by allowing them the rare privilege of minting royal money.

The Hundred Years War and the Wars of Religion had an adverse effect on the town's development. From 1576 to 1623 Figeac was a safe stronghold for the Calvinists, until Richelieu broke their fortifications up. Prosperity continued in the 18C and 19C as mills and tanneries settled along the canal.

Walking Tour of Old Figeac★★

The old quarter, surrounded by boulevards which trace the line of the former moats, has kept its medieval town plan with its narrow, twisting alleys.

The buildings, built in elegant beige sandstone, exemplify the architecture of the 12C, 13C and 14C. Generally the ground floor was opened by large pointed arches and the first floor had a gallery of arcaded bays. Underneath the flat tiled roof was the *soleilho*, an open attic, which was used to dry food, laundry or even hand-crafted objects. Its openings were separated by columns or pillars in wood or stone, sometimes even brick, which held the roof up. The buildings were flanked by corbelled towers and their doorways were elaborately decorated; spiral staircases heralded the Renaissance style.

Traditional crafts are still alive in Figeac, as you can see by walking down rue de Colomb, rue Émile-Zola and rue Baduel.

Hôtel de la Monnaie (Mint)★

🄸 *Tourist Information Centre*

This late-13C building, restored in the early 20C, exemplifies Figeac's secular architecture with its *soleilho*, pointed arches on the ground floor and the depressed arched windows placed either singly, paired or grouped in the façade. It is interesting to compare the façade, overlooking the square, which was rebuilt with the elements of the former consul's house of the same period, with the other plainer façades. The octagonal, stone chimney was characteristic of Figeac construction at one time, but very few examples remain.

The name *Oustal dé lo Mounédo* owes its name to the Royal Mint created in Figeac by Philip the Fair. It has since been established that the stamping workshop was located in another building and that this handsome edifice was the place where money was exchanged. It now houses the Musée du Vieux Figeac (see Sights).

▶ *Take rue Orthabadial and turn right onto rue Balène.*

Rue Balène

At no 7 stands the 14C Palais Balène, which houses the community hall. Its medieval fortress-like façade is lightened by an ogive doorway and chapel windows with decorated tracery.

At no 1, the 14C Hôtel de Viguier d'Auglanat, once the home of an influential family, is decorated with a lovely basket-arched doorway and castellated turret.

Rue Gambetta

This is the old town's main street. The houses at nos 25 and 28 are half-timbered, with decorative brickwork, and have been beautifully restored.

▶ *Continue via rue Gambetta and place aux Herbes to place de la Raison.*

Église St-Sauveur

This used to be an abbey church, the oldest parts of which date from the 11C. It has kept its original cross plan: a high nave with 14C chapels off the aisles. The nave is unusual for the lack of symmetry between its north and south sides. The south side includes: in the lowest section, rounded arcades; in the middle section, a tribune with twinned bays within a larger arch; and in the upper section, 13C clerestory windows.

The chancel, surrounded by the ambulatory, was rebuilt in the 17C. Four Romanesque capitals, remnants of the earlier doorway, support the baptismal font.

Chapelle Notre-Dame-de-Pitié★

This former chapter-house became a place of worship after the departure of the Protestants in 1622. A sumptuous carved and painted **wooden decor**★ was added to it, apparently the work of the Delclaux, a family of master painters from Figeac. To the right of the altar there is a striking panel depicting the infant Jesus asleep on the cross, dreaming of his future Passion.

▶ *Walk northwards along rue Tomfort then turn right.*

Rue Roquefort

The house with the bartizan on a carved corbel belonged to Galiot de Genouillac, Grand Master of the Artillery of François I.

▶ *Follow rue du Canal to rue Émile-Zola.*

Rue Émile-Zola

The oldest street in the town still has ogival arcades and an interesting sequence of Renaissance doorways from no 35 to 37.

▶ *Turn right.*

Rue Delzhens

No 3, the Provost's House (**Hôtel du Viguier du roy**) has a square keep and a 14C watch turret. It has been restored and converted into a hotel.

▶ *Walk up the street.*

Église Notre-Dame-du-Puy

The church is on a hill which gives a good view of the town and its surroundings. The Protestants used it as a fortress, strengthening the façade with a watch room.

This Gothic building underwent many alterations in the 17C; it has an enormous altarpiece carved in walnut dating from the end of the 17C, which frames two pictures representing the Assumption and the Coronation of the Virgin.

▶ *Go back down the hill along rue St-Jacques.*

Address Book

For coin ranges, see the Legend at the back of the guide.

EATING OUT

À l'Escargot – *2 bis av. Jean-Jaurès -* ☎ *05 65 34 23 84 -* ⏱ *closed 21 Dec-10 Mar and Thu - reserv. recommended.* The regular clientele of this unassuming restaurant flock here for the simple, family-style fare and friendly ambience. Three generations of women have run the kitchen here.

La Dînée du Viguier – *R. Boutaric -* ☎ *05 65 50 08 08 -* ⏱ *closed 23 Jan-15 Feb, 15-22 Nov, Sun eve out of season, Sat lunchtime and Mon.* The restaurant in the Château Viguier du Roy combines medieval decor (high ceilings, painted beams and stone fireplace) with contemporary cuisine.

Ferme-Auberge Domaine des Villedieu – *46100 Boussac - 8km/5mi SW of Figeac on the D 13 and then the D 41 -* ☎ *05 65 40 06 63 - reserv. required .* An enchanting 18C farmhouse deep in the country. In keeping with their farming background, the owners serve their own produce in the wood-floored dining room and on the outdoor terrace. The restored farm buildings have been converted into a number of attractive guestrooms.

WHERE TO STAY

Champollion – *3 pl. Champollion -* ☎ *05 65 34 04 37 - 10 rooms.* The memory of the famous Egyptologist is everywhere in the centre of town, including this hotel, the town's medieval meat market. Although on the small side, the bedrooms are modern and well-maintained.

Le Pont d'Or – *2, av Jean-Jaurès -* ☎ *05 65 50 95 00 - www.hotelpontdor.com - 10 rooms.* A welcoming stone house on the banks of the Célé, with some rooms offering balconies overlooking the river. A yellow and orange colour scheme, contemporary furniture and immaculate bathrooms. Fitness room and rooftop swimming pool. In summer, breakfast is served on the riverside terrace.

LEISURE ACTIVITIES

Domaine de Loisirs du Surgié – *Chemin Moulin Surgie -* ☎ *05 65 34 59 00 - www. domainedesurgie.com -* ⏱ *open May-Sep, 11am-8pm.* This large (14ha/34.5-acre) outdoor watersports and leisure area is on the banks of the River Célé to the northeast of Figeac.

SHOPPING

Market – The town's weekly market is held on Saturdays (the largest one is the last Saturday of the month). Evening markets are held on Thursdays in July and August.

Rue Malleville and Rue St-Thomas

Both these streets pass under a covered passageway painted with the coat of arms of the Hôtel de Laporte (17C).

Rue du Crussol

The courtyard of the 16C Hôtel de Crussol (no 5), now a terrace-bar, features a gallery over the courtyard stairway.

▶ *Take rue Laurière then rue Bonhore.*

At the far end of **rue Caviale**, opposite no 35 (**l'Hôtel d'Ay-de-Lostanges**), starts the street leading to the **Maison du Roi**, so-called because Louis XI is supposed to have stayed there in 1463.

▶ *Walk along rue Caviale.*

Place Carnot

Formerly place Basse, this was headquarters to the wheat exchange, which was destroyed in 1888. In the north-west corner, with a small side turret, is the **house of Pierre de Cisteron**, Louis XIV's armourer.

▶ *From place Carnot, after crossing the narrow, medieval-looking rue Séguier, go through a porch to get to place des Écritures.*

Place des Écritures, Figeac

J. Damase/MICHELIN

Place des Écritures★

Surrounded by medieval buildings, this square has an enormous (14×7m/46×23ft) **replica of the Rosetta Stone** underfoot. This was sculpted in black granite from Zimbabwe by the American conceptual artist Joseph Kossuth. Unveiled in 1991, this significant contemporary work of art is more clearly understood from the hanging gardens overlooking the square. The French translation of the inscriptions is carved on a glass plaque kept in a small neighbouring courtyard.

Place Champollion

Two contrasting buildings overlook the square: a 14C private mansion and the town's oldest house dating from the mid-12C, known locally as the Maison du Griffon.

▷ *Return to place Vival via rue Gambetta and rue du 11-Novembre.*

Sights

Musée Champollion★

⊶ *Closed for renovation.*

The museum is being extended: the collections will, in future, be displayed in Champollion's birthplace and in the adjacent building. This new exhibition area, devoted to "signs and writing", will illustrate the history of writing from its invention to the present around five main themes: Champollion's life and work, the invention of writing, the Chinese specificity, the alphabet: a revolution, writing in the West over the past 3 000 years.

Musée du Vieux Figeac - Hôtel de la Monnaie

🕐 *Open Jul-Aug, 10am-7.30pm; May-Jun and Sep, 10am-noon and 2-6.30pm, Sun 10am-1pm; Oct-Apr, daily except Sun and public hols, 10am-noon and 2.30-6pm.* ⊗2€. ☎ *05 65 34 06 25.*

The museum displays sculpture from religious and secular buildings (the door of the Hôtel de Sully), sarcophagi, grain measurements, old coins, the town seal originating from the period when the town had its seven consuls and furniture.

Commanderie des Templiers

🕐*Open mid-Jul to Sep, 11.30am-1pm and 3-7pm; Jun to mid-Jul and Oct-Nov, by prior arrangement.* 🕐 *Closed Mon.* ⊗5€. ☎ *05 65 50 27 08.*

This group of buildings dating from the mid-14C boasts a beautiful Gothic façade. The first building consists of two roofed towers, the second building features a half-timbered structure. Inside, it was remodelled to present the interior of a commandery of the Knights Templars.

A remarkable 15C wooden staircase leads to the first floor where the guard-room, the chapter-house and the chapel are to be found. The latter are connected by oratory hatches. On the second floor a wooden balcony links the monks' dormitory with the commander's residence in which there is also a private chapel.

Excursions

Aiguilles de Figeac

These two octagonal-shaped, false obelisks to the south and west of the town measure (base included) respectively 14.50m/47ft and 11.50m/38ft. It is believed that they marked the boundaries of the land over which the Benedictine abbey had jurisdiction.

The **Aiguille du Cingle**, also known as Aiguille du Pressoir, can be seen from the D 922, south of Figeac. The more remote **Aiguille de Lissac** is located in a wooded area near the Nayrac district (*footpath*).

Cardaillac

11km/7mi N of town along the N 140 and then the D 15.

This village is the home territory of the Cardaillacs, one of the most powerful Quercy families.

The district, where the fort stands, is located on a rocky spur above the town. Of this triangular shaped fortification, dating from the 12C, there remain two square towers: the Clock or Baron's Tower and Sagnes Tower (*only the latter is open to visitors*). The two tall rooms with their vaulted ceilings are reached by a spiral staircase. From the platform there is a lovely view of the Drauzou Valley and the surrounding countryside.

Musée Éclaté

🕐 📷 Open first two weeks of Jul and end of Aug to mid-Sep, guided tour (1hr 30min), daily except Sat, at 3pm; mid-Jul to end of Aug, daily except Sat, at 3pm and 4.30pm; Oct-Jun, by prior arrangement one day in advance. ☎ 05 65 40 10 63 or 05 65 40 15 65.

This museum consists of several different sites scattered (*éclaté*) around the village in a determined effort to integrate evidence of the past firmly into the modern life of the village. Exhibits represent the village school, local crafts and the rural way of life. A study of the manufacture of wine-growers' baskets, once a speciality of Cardaillac, is given pride of place.

Capdenac

7km/4.3mi SE.

Capdenac-le-Haut, perched on a promontory and enclosed by a meander in the River Lot, occupies a remarkable **site**★. This small town, which still looks much the way it did centuries ago, overlooks Capdenac-Gare, a busy railway junction which has developed in the valley.

The **ramparts** are vestiges of the 13C and 14C outer walls and the citadel as well as the Northern Gate (Comtale), the village entrance, and the Southern Gate (Vijane). The **keep**, a powerful square tower flanked by turrets (13C-14C), houses the Tourist Information Centre and a small **museum** which recounts Capdenac's history.

Célé and Lot Valleys★

95km/59mi round-trip – allow one day

▶ Drive W out of Figeac along the D 41 towards Cahors.

Espagnac-Ste-Eulalie

In this delightful village built in the picturesque setting of a series of cliffs, the houses with their turrets and pointed roofs are grouped round the former priory known as the **Ancien Prieuré Notre-Dame-du-Val-Paradis**, founded in the 12C; during the Hundred Years War the convent suffered considerably; the cloisters were destroyed and the church was partly demolished. It was rebuilt in the 15C, however, and the community carried on until the Revolution. The buildings are now occupied by a rural centre and holiday rentals (*gîtes communaux*), managed by the local authorities.

The church in Espagnac

The present Flamboyant-style **church** has replaced the 13C building (only the walls of the nave, a doorway and ruined bays remain). Note the unusual pentagonal east end and belfry-tower.

▶ Return to the north bank and continue along the D 41.

Brengues

This small village is in a pleasant setting, perched on a ledge overlooked by a vertiginous bluff.

St-Sulpice

The houses and gardens of this old village lie within the shadow of an overhanging cliff. The approach is guarded by a 12C castle which was rebuilt in the 14C and 15C. It is still the property of the Hébrard family of St-Sulpice.

Marcilhac-sur-Célé

🕐 See MARCILHAC-SUR-CÉLÉ.

The D 17 runs round the Bout du Rocher cliff. The landscape is dotted with dolmens, ruins, caves and a few farms. The shaded road runs down the slopes offering fine views of the Lot Valley.

Cajarc

The town was brought into the public eye when President Pompidou had a house here. Near the church, the Hébrardie Mansion with Gothic windows is all that remains standing of a 13C castle. Inaugurated in 1989, the **Centre d'Art Contemporain Georges-Pompidou** (& *Open Jun-Aug, 1-7pm; Sep-May, daily except Mon, 2-6pm. No charge. For annual closing and holiday periods, call 05 65 40 78 19) organises retrospective exhibits of the works of contemporary European artists: Hartung, Bissière and Soulages have been featured, ranking Cajarc among the foremost centres of contemporary art in the region.

▸ *Drive S out of Cajarc along the D 24 towards Villefranche-de-Rouergue; cross the river and turn left onto the D 127.*

The road, which follows the south bank of the Lot, overhangs the river to start with, then immediately after Saujac rises and winds round to overlook a wooded gorge, before reaching the top of the *causse*.

Saut de la Mounine★

There is a good **view**★ of the valley from the top of this cliff rising 155m/509ft above the river. The end of the spur overlooks a wide bend in the river as it encircles a mosaic of fields. Over on the left, on the far bank, stands Montbrun Castle.

The curious name, Saut de la Mounine – the little monkey's leap – comes from a rather strange legend. The lord of Montbrun decided to punish his daughter for her love of another lord's son and ordered her to be hurled from the top of the cliff; a hermit, appalled at this cruel idea, disguised a small blind monkey (*mounine* in the language) in women's clothes and hurled it into the air. When he saw the object falling the father immediately regretted his brutal action; on seeing his daughter alive and well he was so overjoyed that he forgave her.

▸ *Return to Cajarc and drive E along the D 662 towards Figeac.*

Montbrun

The village of Montbrun rises in tiers on a rocky promontory encircled by steep cliffs. It looks down on the Lot and faces the Saut de La Mounine (*see below*). Towering over the village are the ruins of a fortress that belonged to one of Pope John XXII' s brothers, and then to the powerful Cardaillac family.

▸ *Continue along the D 662.*

Château de Larroque-Toirac

 Open Jul to early Sep, guided tour (45min), 10am-noon and 2-6pm. 4.50€ (child: 2€). 06 12 37 48 39 or 06 60 08 80 10.

This 12C fortress belonged to the Cardaillac family who, during the Hundred Years War, took an active part in the region's resistance to English domination. From the church square (*parking area*), a surfaced path leads to the castle. The visit starts

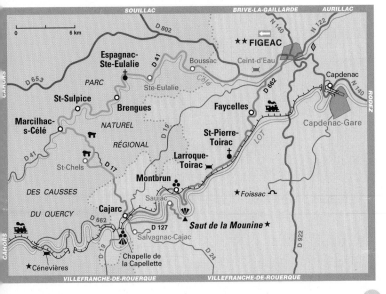

with a round tower built at the beginning of the Hundred Years War to withstand artillery fire, newly introduced in siege warfare. Note the charming heart-shaped opening. The 15C seigneurial residence is reached through two successive courtyards. A spiral staircase, located in an adjacent tower, leads to the different levels; there is a Romanesque fireplace in the guard-room and a Gothic one in the great hall; the original kitchen can also be seen. To the east stands the enormous late-12C keep which was greatly reduced in height during the Revolution.

Several caves, once used as dwellings, can be seen in the cliff at the back of the castle.

▶ *Continue along the D 662.*

St-Pierre-Toirac

Tour by prior arrangement; contact Monsieur Durand. ☎ 05 65 34 23 18.

This small village, on the north bank of the Lot, contains an interesting **church**, its architecture dating from the 11C and 14C. The Romanesque apse alone belies the fortified appearance of this building which served as a defence point with its massive crenellated keep and upper floor. The short nave has cradle vaulting and primitive style capitals. Recently discovered Merovingian sarcophagi have been placed behind the church.

▶ *Continue along the D 662.*

Faycelles

This village overlooking the Lot Valley once belonged to Figeac Abbey. A peaceful atmosphere pervades the old streets, the fountain near the Maison du Fort, a former property of the lord of Larroque-Toirac, place de la Barrière (the old city toll) and the suburb of Les Carbes on the south-eastern edge of the village.

▶ *The D 662 leads back to Figeac.*

Grottes de FOISSAC ★

MICHELIN LOCAL MAP 338: E-3

Discovered in 1959, Foissac Caves have a total of 8km/5mi of galleries. The underground stream, which flows through the caves, is a tributary of the Lot, joining it near Balaguier.

▶ **Orient Yourself**: The Grottes de Foissac are situated 15km/9mi south of Figeac.

⚸ **Also See**: Figeac.

Visit

🕐 ⌀ *Open Jul-Aug, guided tour (1hr, last entrance 1hr before closing), 10am-7pm; Jun and Sep, 10am-12.30m and 2-7pm; Apr-May and Oct, daily except Sat, 2-7pm; Nov-Mar, by appointment.* 🕐 *Closed 1 Jan, 1 and 11 Nov, and 25 Dec.* ⌀ *7€ (child: 5.30€).* ☎ *05 65 64 77 04.*

During the visit note the gleaming white stalactites and the lovely rock formations in the Obelisk Chamber (*Salle de l'Obélisque*); and the reflections, the stalagmites and ivory tower-like formations in the Michel Roques Gallery. In one gallery, known as the Cave-in Gallery (*Salle de l'Éboulement*), there is a roof covered with round mushroom-like formations, thus proving that the stalactites were in the gallery well before earthquakes changed the aspect of the cave. Bulbous stalactites known as onions (*Oignons*) are also worth noting.

Grottes de Foissac

These caves were inhabited during the Copper Age (2700-1900 BC), when they were used as quarries, caves and a cemetery, as evidenced throughout: the hearth, copper utensils and large rounded pieces of pottery. Also visible are human skeletons, some of which are accompanied by offerings suggesting some sort of ritual burial, and the imprint of a child's foot, fixed here in the clay 4 000 years ago.

A prehistoric park illustrates the daily life of Copper-Age man.

GIMEL-LES-CASCADES ★★

POPULATION 630

MICHELIN LOCAL MAP 329: M-4

Gimel stands in a remarkable **setting** ★, one of the most picturesque of the Bas-Limousin, near Tulle and the Corrèze Valley. The Montane flows over the tumbling rocks of a wild ravine and hurls itself down waterfalls 143m/469ft high. 🛈 *Le Bourg, 19800 Gimel-les-Cascades,* ☎ *05 55 21 44 32.*

▶ **Orient Yourself**: The walk to the falls provides excellent views.

👁 **Don't Miss**: The waterfalls; the shrine of St-Stephen in the Église St-Pardoux.

⚸ **Also See**: Tulle; Vallée de la Corrèze.

Sights

Cascades★★

🚶 *1hr round trip on foot (quite strenuous).*
🕐*Open Mar–Oct, 10am–6pm (7pm, Jul–Aug);
Wed, 11am–6pm.* 🎫*4€.* ☎ *05 55 21 26 49.*

▸ *Follow one of the marked pathways
through the Parc Vuillier or Parc Blavi-
gnac.*

The *Grande Cascade* (also known as the
Grand Saut) tumbles down 45m/145ft; the
next falls, *la Redole*, is 27m/90ft high. The
two cascades one above the other are an
impressive sight. The third one, with its
amusing name of *Queue de Cheval* (Pony
Tail), appears suddenly, spouting from a little rocky promontory; it plunges 60m/200ft
into the deep ravine of Hell's Swallow Hole
(le Gouffre de l'Inferno).

Grande Casade

J. Malburet/ICHELIN

Trésor de l'église St-Pardoux★

The **Shrine of St Stephen**★★, a decorative chest from the late 12C, is embellished
with Limoges enamels, the figures are in relief, with eyes of precious stones. The
silver-gilt **reliquary bust** is a 14C homage to St Dumine, a soldier from Clovis' army
who retreated to the Montane ravines as a hermit; note the 14C champlevé enamel
pyx (receptacle for the Eucharist) and a 13C gilded copper **monstrance** (vessel in
which the consecrated host is exposed for veneration).

GOURDON★

POPULATION 4 882

MICHELIN LOCAL MAP 337: E-3

**Gourdon is the capital of the green undulating countryside called Bouriane. The
town, situated on the borders of Quercy and Périgord, is arranged in tiers up the
flank of a rocky hillock, upon which the local lord's castle once stood. Follow the
circular route of avenues which have replaced the old ramparts for pleasant views
of the hills and valleys of Bouriane.**

▸ **Orient Yourself**: Gourdon is situated 26km/16mi south of Sarlat and 44km/27.5mi
north of Cahors.

🕐 **Organising Your Time**: Allow half a day to explore the Bouriane region.

😊 **Don't Miss**: Rue de Majou; the baptismal font in the Église des Cordeliers; the
view from the Esplanade.

🌿 **Also See**: Grottes de Cougnac; Les Arques; Cahors; Sarlat.

Visit

Rue du Majou★

The 13C fortified gateway, Porte du Majou, leads to the street of the same name.
This picturesque and narrow street was once the high street; all along it there are
old houses with overhanging storeys and ground floors with large pointed arches.
No 17, Anglars Mansion, has pretty mullioned windows.

▸ *The street leads to the esplanade where the town hall (right) and St Peter's Church
both stand.*

Hôtel de Ville (Town Hall)

This former 13C consulate, enlarged in the 17C, has covered arcades which are used
as a covered market.

Address Book

For coin ranges, see the Legend at the back of the guide.

EATING OUT

🍴🍴 **Domaine du Berthiol** – *route de Cahors* - ☎ 05 65 41 33 33 - domaineduberthiol@wanadoo.fr - 🕐 *closed 1 Jan-31 Mar.* Located on the outskirts of town in the middle of a beautifully maintained park. Two contemporary dining rooms where the menu shows a marked preference for local produce. 29 rooms also available here.

WHERE TO STAY

🏠🏠 **Chambre d'hôte du Syndic** – *Le Syndic - 46300 Payrignac - 6km/3.6mi NW of Gourdon on the D 704 towards Sarlat, then a minor road the left* - ☎ 05 65 41 15 70 - 🍴 *- 6 rooms.* This family home is typical of the region and stands in an elevated position with views of the countryside and the Germaine Valley. The rooms are comfortable, spacious and calm, with some under the eaves. The fireplace in the dining room provides a welcome winter glow. Friendly atmosphere.

🏠🏠🏨 **Hostellerie de la Bouriane** – *Pl. du Foirail* - ☎ 05 65 41 16 37 - hostelleriela-bouriane@wanadoo.fr - 🕐 *closed 15 Jan-10 Mar, Sun eve and Mon from 15 Oct-30 Apr -* 🅿 *- 20 rooms.* Outside of the town centre, this hotel is a quiet retreat with a pleasant sheltered terrace. The rooms are traditional and bright, with those on the upper floor crowned by sloping ceilings. The dining room is adorned with reproductions of paintings and Aubusson tapestries. Good traditional French food at reasonable prices.

SHOPPING

Farmers' market - Thursdays in July and August, 8.30am-1pm.

ENTERTAINMENT

Les Médievales - This festival is held in the streets of old Gourdon on the first weekend and Monday of August. ☎ 05 65 27 52 50.

Les Enchantements de la Flûte - This chamber music festival takes place in mid-July. ☎ 05 65 41 20 06.

Église St-Pierre

The church (dedicated to St Peter), built in the 14C, used to be a dependency of Le Vigan Abbey. The doorway is decorated with elegant archivolts and is framed by two tall asymmetrical towers. The large rose window is protected by a line of machicolations, a reminder of former fortifications. The vast nave has pointed vaulting; 17C wood panels, carved, painted and gilded, decorate the chancel and the south transept.

▶ *Go round the left of the church outside and go up the staircase leading to the esplanade where the castle once stood.*

Esplanade

A **panorama**★ unfolds from the terrace (*viewing table*): beyond the town and its roofs, which can be seen in tiers below the massive roof of the church (St-Pierre) in the foreground, one can see the churchyard, a forest of cypress trees, and then the plateaux stretching out around the valleys of the Dordogne and the Céou.

▶ *Return to place de l'Hôtel-de-Ville and go round the outside of the church starting from the right.*

There are some old houses opposite the east end, including one with a lovely early-17C doorway. Opposite the south door of the church take rue Cardinal-Farinié which goes downhill and contains old houses with mullioned windows and side turrets.

GOURDON

Briand Bd A.	2
Cardinal-Farinié R. du	4
Cavaignac Av.	5
Dr-Cabanès Bd	7
Gaulle Pl. Ch.-de	8
Gourdon R. B.-de	9
Hôtel-de-Ville Pl. de l'	10
Libération Pl. de la	12
Mainiol Bd	14
République Allées de la	17
Zig-Zag R.	18

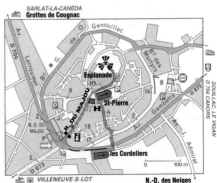

Below stands the Église des Cordeliers.

Église des Cordeliers

🕐 ━*The former church is now used for concerts and exhibits in Jul-Aug. Tours available by advance appointment at the tourist office.* ☎ 05 65 27 52 50.

The church which used to be part of the Franciscan monastery is worth a visit, despite being slightly marred by a massive belfry porch which was added in the 19C. At the entrance, in the middle of the nave, stands a remarkable 14C **baptismal font**★. The outside is decorated with trefoiled blind arcades. The fine seven-sided apse is lit by 19C stained-glass windows.

Excursions

Grottes de Cougnac★

3km/2mi N on the D 704. 🕐 ━*Open Jul-Aug, guided tour 10am-6pm; mid-Apr to Jun and Sep, 10-11.30am and 2.30-5pm; Oct, daily except Sun, 2-4pm.* ▦6€ (child: 4€). ☎ 05 65 41 47 54.

These caves are fascinating for two reasons: their natural rock formations and their Paleolithic paintings similar to those of Pech-Merle (25000 to 18000 BC).

The caves, consisting of two chasms about 200m/220yd apart, spread their network of galleries beneath a limestone plateau.

The first cave consists of three small chambers; closely packed and sometimes extremely delicate stalactites hang in profusion.

The second cave is bigger and has two remarkable chambers: the **Pillar Chamber**★ (Salle des Colonnes) is made particularly striking by the perspectives offered by columns reaching from floor to ceiling, and the **Hall of Prehistoric Paintings** (Salle des Peintures Préhistoriques) contains designs in ochre and black featuring ibex, mammoths and human figures.

Les Prades

7km/4.3mi NE.

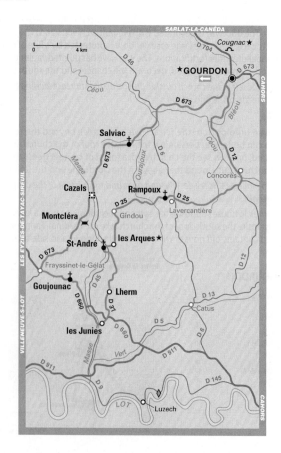

Musée Henri-Giron

&⌚Open Jun-Sep, daily except Mon, 10am-6pm; Oct-May by advance appointment; contact Monsieur Hoving. ✆2.30€. ☎ 05 65 41 33 78.

The museum's collection includes about 40 of this Belgian painter's works. His style reflects a classic heritage and Flemish influence, all the while integrating remarkably modern subjects, including some unsettling interpretations of feminine forms.

Le Vigan

5km/3mi E on the D 673.

The Gothic **church**, all that remains of an abbey founded in the 11C, became a regular chapter for canons in the 14C. The spectacular east end, overlooked by a tower rising from the transept crossing, has defensive turrets tucked in between the apsidal chapels. There is fine pointed vaulting over the nave. ⌚*Open weekday afternoons. For further information, contact the presbytery,* ☎ *05 65 41 12 90.*

Chapelle de Notre-Dame-des-Neiges

1.5km/1mi SE. ⌚ Tour by advance appointment at Gourdon town hall. ☎ 05 65 27 01 10.

Set in the small valley of the Bléou, this 14C chapel, a pilgrimage centre which was restored in the 17C, has a 17C altarpiece. A miraculous spring flows through the chancel.

La Bouriane

85km/53mi round-trip – allow half a day

The region known as La Bouriane extends from Gourdon to the Lot Valley and west of N 20. It is a region where the limestone formation disappears under a bed of sideritic sand (iron carbonate bearing), which is a lovely red and ochre colour. The rather infertile soil nevertheless allows the cultivation of chestnut, pine and walnut trees. There are vineyards on the south-facing slopes.

A great number of rivers carve through the plateau creating a hilly, wooded countryside scattered with farms.

▸ *Leave Gourdon W on the D 673.*

Salviac

The Gothic church has some lovely 16C stained-glass windows depicting scenes from the life of St Eutrope.

Cazals

This old *bastide*, built in 1319 on behalf of the King of England, is designed around a large central square. An old castle overlooks a stretch of the River Masse offering recreation facilities.

▸ *Continue along the D 673.*

Château de Montcléra

The fortified entrance gate dates from the 15C. Behind it are a square keep and residential quarters flanked by round, machicolated towers.

▸ *Continue along the D 673 to Frayssinet-le-Gélat then turn left onto the D 660.*

Goujounac

There used to be a Romanesque priory around the church, but there are now only a few vestiges of this. On the south wall of the church, the Romanesque **tympanum**, depicting Christ in Glory giving the sign of God's blessing surrounded by the symbols of the four Evangelists, is the work of a Quercy artist who was probably influenced by the tympanum at Beaulieu-sur-Dordogne.

▸ *Continue along the D 660 and turn right onto the D 45.*

Les Junies

The 15C castle flanked by round towers is decorated with elegant Renaissance windows.

Set apart from the village, the 14C church, an austere building, is of massive proportions. It was part of a priory, which was attached to the Dominican order in 1345, and had been founded by one of the local lords, Gaucelin des Junies, Cardinal of Albano.

▸ *Leave Les Junies travelling N along the D 37.*

Lherm

This little village of white-limestone houses with steeply pitched roofs covered with small brown tiles is dominated by a bell-tower, a turret and several dovecotes. In a small isolated, wooded valley, the **church** (Notre-Dame-de-l'Assomption), once a priory, has a Romanesque apse and a plain barrel-vaulted nave of ashlar-stone. The chancel contains a profusely decorated altarpiece of gold and carvings against a blue background, a rather grandiose, local interpretation of the Baroque style. The building was altered in the 16C; there is a fine Renaissance-style door.

▶ *Continue N on the D 37.*

Église St-André-des-Arques

See Les ARQUES.

Les Arques★

See Les ARQUES.

▶ *Leave Les Arques travelling SE along the D 150 and continue beyond Maussac. Turn left onto the D 47 2km/1.2mi further on; the road leads to the D 25.*

Rampoux

There is an interesting 12C Romanesque church here, made of red and white stone, which used to be a Benedictine priory. Inside, the 15C frescoes illustrate the life of Christ in naïve style.

▶ *Continue E on the D 25. Turn left towards Concorès 2km/1.2mi beyond Lavercantière, then follow the D 12 back to Gourdon along the River Céou and River Bléou.*

GUÉRET

POPULATION 14 123

MICHELIN LOCAL MAP 325: I 3-4

Guéret stands on a plateau stretching as far as the Forêt de Chabrières in close proximity to the Vallée de la Creuse.

▶ **Orient Yourself**: The town is located 66km/41mi west of Montluçon and 93km/58mi northeast of Limoges.

⊙ **Organising Your Time**: Allow half a day to tour the Pays des Trois Lacs, and half a day to explore the Haute Vallée du Taurion.

⊛ **Don't Miss**: The enamel work in the Musée d'Art et d'Archéologie de la Sénatorerie.

▦ **Especially for Kids**: Parc Animalier des Monts de Guéret; Observatoire-Planétarium des Monts-de-Guéret.

A Bit of History

The town developed around a monastery founded there in the 8C by a count from Limoges, in a place known as Garactus, at the foot of a hill called Grandcher. In 1514, Guéret became the capital of the county of La Marche, and has been an administrative centre ever since.

Sights

Musée d'Art et d'Archéologie de la Sénatorerie

⊙*Open May-Oct, daily except Tue, 10am-noon and 2-6pm; rest of the year, daily except 2nd and 4th weekends of each month, 2-6pm.* ⊙ *Closed on public hols.* ⊚2.50€, *no charge 1st Sun of the month.* ☎ *05 55 52 07 20.*

The museum is in a fine 18C Classical building surrounded by a large flower garden.

Archaeology – There is a collection of local archaeological finds from prehistoric times to the Middle Ages. One room displays Chinese works of various periods as well as Japanese prints and objets d'art.

Sculpture – Monumental sculptures depicting **Gaulish deities** and Gallo-Roman funerary stelae are exhibited in the basement.

Other works from the Middle Ages to the 20C, including *Eve* by Rodin and a *Bust of Rodin* by Camille Claudel, are displayed in various parts of the museum.

Precious items and decorative arts – The museum houses a magnificent collection of Limousin **champlevé enamel work**★ from the 12C to the 15C. Note in particular a processional cross, pyxes (to hold the host) and the collection of shrines (chests and boxes). The vivid colours of the enamels harmonise with the gilding and polished stones. Scenes depicted

Malval shrine

Musée de la Sénatorerie, Guéret

include the Crucifixion (early 13C), the Adoration of the Magi (late 13C), the Stoning of St Stephen (late 12C), also known as the Malval Shrine, and the Martyrdom of St Thomas Becket (late 12C).

Several of the painted enamel pieces (15C-18C) can be attributed to great masters of the art, namely Limosin, Laudin and Nouailher.

There are also displays of glazed earthenware from Nevers, Moustiers, Rouen, Strasbourg and Delft as well as Italian majolica earthenware and glassware.

Paintings – This section displays works by 17C French, Flemish and Dutch artists as well as more recent works by Guillaumin, Suzanne Valadon and Marinto, among others.

Hôtel des Moneyroux

This Late Gothic-style building, contemporary with the Palais Jacques Cœur in Bourges (👉 *see BOURGES*), consists of two buildings joined by a corner turret.

The right wing was built after 1447 by Antoine Alard, lord of Moneyroux; his successor, Pierre Billon, had the other wing built at the beginning of the 16C. The façade is pierced by many mullioned windows and is topped by dormer windows ornamented with finials and pinnacles.

Excursions

Forêt de Chabrières

🏃 The forest is dense with pine, oak, beech and birch trees; bracken forms a thick carpet underfoot. There are many marked footpaths and mountain-bike tracks offering various possibilities: one of them starting from the animal park runs past stones which have given rise to legends (10km/6.2mi, itinerary no 24, explanatory panels and brochure available at the tourist office). Stonemasonry works established along the road leading to Le Maupuy, testify to the importance of this activity in the past.

Les Loups de Chabrières, Parc Animalier des Monts de Guéret

Along the road to Bourganeuf. 🕑*Open Jun-Aug, 10am-7pm (9pm, Wed and Sat in Aug); Sep-May, Wed, Sat-Sun, public hols and school hols, 1-5pm. Wolves are fed at 4pm. Night visits (Les bruits de la nuit), Wed and Sat (by appointment).* 🕑 *Closed Jan and 25 Dec.* 📷*7€ (4-12 years old: 5.50€).* ☎ *05 55 81 23 23.*

Kids Located in the heart of the forest, this animal park offers (from the wooden watch-path) a fine panoramic view of the Puy de Dôme and Massif du Sancy, as well as a glimpse of the wolves in the pen below… A trail later offers visitors the possibility of observing them more closely. A tour of the museum provides information on popular beliefs, on myths connected with wolves and on their future. If you are keen to get to know them better, don't miss their feeding time at 4pm.

Observatoire-Planétarium des Monts-de-Guéret

In the Parc Animalier des Loups de Chabrières. 🕑*Planetarium and slide show (La planète aux mille regards) by appointment. Open Jul-Aug, 4.30pm; Sep-Jun, Wed and Sat, 2.30pm.*

5€ (-15 years old: 3€). Solar observatory and slide show (Notre étoile le soleil), Jul-Aug, Thu, 10.30am; Sep-Jun, Sat, 10.30am. Night observation, Jul-Aug, Thu-Fri, 9pm; Sep-Jun, Fri-Sat, 9pm. ⊘ Closed Jan and 25 Dec. 9.50€ (-15 years old: 5€). ☎ 05 55 81 23 23. Located in the Parc animalier des Loups de Chabrières.

This centre offers various activities including: observation of the sun, planetarium shows and a diorama.

Le Maupuy

A rocky plateau 685m/2 247ft high, its summit, together with its neighbour the Puy de Gaudy (621m/2 037ft), forms a natural barrier protecting Guéret. The view from the top provides surprising contrasts in landscape all around.

Haute Vallée du Taurion

88km/55mi round trip – allow 3hr

▶ *Leave Guéret travelling S on the D 940 to Sardent.*

Sardent

The Chapel of St-Pardoux, 2km/1mi outside of the village, rises up on the right. The site is lovely, and popular with pilgrims who come for the virtues attributed to the water.

▶ *Drive E along the D 50 to Maisonnisses.*

Maisonnisses

Near the source of the River Gartemps, the village was once a headquarters for the Knights Templars. Only the church has survived; it contains a **recumbent figure**★ discovered in 1830 and replaced in its wall-niche tomb in 1955. It probably represents a 13C Knight.

▶ *Leave the village on the D 34, travelling S to St-Hilaire-le-Château.*

Pont Peri

A footpath leads to this Roman bridge spanning the Gosne. In the picturesque setting, admire the vaulting arch formed by massive hewn stones.

▶ *Return to St-Hilaire-le-Château, then take N 141 towards Bourganeuf.*

Pontarion

Settled along the banks of the Taurion, the salient feature of the hamlet is the 15C **château**, its corner towers and battlements. The south façade faces the river and can be admired from the water's edge. Nature lovers will enjoy the arboretum, belvedere, garden and nature trail at the foot of the castle.
The **church** (13C) has a characteristic Limousin doorway, decorated with a frieze. Inside, the tombstones honour stonemasons.

▶ *After crossing the River Taurion, turn left on the D 13.*

Nécropole des Sagnes

A path leads through the woods (800m/875yd) to this Gallo-Roman site used for funeral ceremonies. The burial grounds contained incinerated remains in 300 tombs, some in the form of funerary urns.

▶ *Continue along the D 13.*

Pierre aux Neuf Gradins

Walk under oak trees along a steep path to this mysterious and lovely site (there is an easier access from the north along a signposted path).

▶ *Continue along the D 13 as far as Soubrebost.*

Soubrebost

Inside the church, note the interesting 13C **Virgin with Child**, a copper-clad wooden statuette.

▶ *Continue on the D 13, turn right on the D 37 then right again on the D 8 to Bourganeuf. Return to Guéret along the scenic D 940A which runs onto the D 940.*

Pays des Trois Lacs★

75km/47mi round-trip – allow half a day

▶ *Drive W out of Guéret along N 145 towards La Souterraine.*

Église de St-Vaury

The church contains, at the back of the altar, a bas-relief cut in limestone, depicting scenes from the Passion. There are also two small 13C enamelled reliquaries.

▷ *Continue NE along the D 48. The road veers to the left 3km/1.9mi beyond Longe-chaud.*

Le Vignaud

🚶 *1hr30min on foot there and back from a place known as Courtille.*

A marked path leads to the Jupille meander where it is possible to see peregrines wheeling over the rocks, in search of some prey.

▷ *Continue along the D 48.*

Le Bourg-d'Hem

This village is picturesquely situated on a height overlooking the Creuse Valley; there is a fine **view** from the square behind the church.
Two nearby lakes, Lac de l'Age and Lac de Chézelles, offer swimming, fishing and hiking facilities.

▷ *Drive E along the D 33.*

Anzême

This pleasant little village boasts a fine bell-tower clad with chestnut-wood shingles. From the square in front of the church, there is a fine view over the gorge of the River Creuse and the **Pont du Diable**.

▷ *Turn back then right after the bridge.*

Lac de Champsanglard

This is the largest (55ha/136 acres) of the three reservoirs along the River Creuse. Water sports are available at Chambon, near the dam.

▷ *Drive on to Champsanglard then follow the D 14 which runs onto the D 6 and turn left 1km/0.6mi further on.*

Jouillat

The local **church** (12C-13C) has a single nave which ends in an apse with five arcades (sculpted capitals). A 13C **fresco** representing Christ decorates the chancel vaulting. Outside, on the southern side, a Carolingian tomb is embellished by a pattern of squares and rosettes, and a crouching lion in granite.
The **château** is an attractive 15C square building, flanked by corner towers.

▷ *Take the D 940 towards Guéret.*

Église de Glénic

⛔ *Closed for restoration.*

Perched on a promontory above the Creuse, the Romanesque **church** was fortified during the Hundred Years War. The east end is protected by towers; the other corners have corbelled turrets; the fourth bay and the chancel are elevated. In the 15C, the nave was lengthened and diagonal ribbed vaulting added. Beyond the 12C doorway, surmounted by a niche with a Romanesque statue of the Virgin, a 14C fresco faces the entrance, illustrating the fall of Adam and Eve.

▷ *Drive E along the D 63A.*

Église d'Ajain

The **church** (13C) was fortified with a watch-path atop the battlements, and buttressed watchtowers. In the nave with its diagonal rib vaulting, a cornice runs the length of the walls above expressive grimacing faces (mascarons).

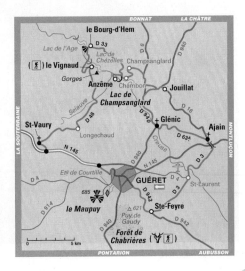

▷ *Leave Ajain travelling S along the D 3.*

Ste-Feyre

🕐 ⚫ *Guided tour of the château (1hr), mid-Jul to Aug, 2-7pm.* ⊗*5€.* ☎*05 55 81 15 52.*

The town is dominated by the **château**, erected in the 18C. The **church**, built in the 13C and fortified in the 14C, has an elegant Limousin-style doorway on the west front. The single nave has four bays; the last of these forms the chancel. It is flanked with an aisle on the south side (16C) and has three chapels on the north side (15C). In one of these chapels, note the polychrome stone statuary also dating from the 15C: St Anne, the Virgin and Child.

▷ *The D 942 takes you back to Guéret.*

Château de HAUTEFORT★★

MICHELIN LOCAL MAP 329: H-4

The proud outline of Hautefort Château dominates the skyline, reminiscent more of the royal palaces of the Loire Valley than of the fortresses of Périgord. 🔲 *Pl. René-Lavaud, 24390 Hautefort,* ☎ *05 53 50 40 27.*

▷ **Orient Yourself**: The castle is situated 41km/25.5mi east of Périgueux.

🕹 **Don't Miss**: The superb timberwork in the northwest tower.

🕐 **Also See**: Périgueux.

A Bit of History

The strategic position of the Hautefort site on a hill in the middle of an immense amphitheatre was certainly exploited very early on: in the 9C the viscounts of Limoges are known to have built a stronghold here. During the Middle Ages several castles succeeded one another, leaving some traces (the courtyard's west corner tower). The defensive position of the castle was strengthened in the 16C (barbican flanked by two crenellated bartizans and equipped with a drawbridge) during the tumultuous years of the Wars of Religion. Complete reconstruction of the castle in the 17C led to a harmonious combination of architectural styles – Renaissance and Classical – which contributes to the building's original and elegant appearance.

In 1929, Baron Henri de Bastard and his wife bought the castle and decided to restore it; they also had the French-style gardens laid out. In 1968, fire swept through the main building but the two wings were spared. Since then, the fine interior has been restored to its original state.

Château de Hautefort

J. P. Clapham/MICHELIN

Bertrand the Troubadour

The first castle of Hautefort was built by the Limousin family of Las Tours. In the 12C it passed by marriage to the house of De Born, of whom Bertrand, the very same mentioned by Dante in the Divine Comedy, is the most well-known member. **Bertrand de Born**, the famous troubadour who was much admired in the courts of love, became a warrior-knight when the need arose to defend the family castle against his brother Constantine. He succeeded in having Henry II acknowledge his rights in 1185. However, in 1186 Constantine returned to Hautefort and razed the castle to the ground. Renouncing everything, Bertrand withdrew to take monastic orders.

Visit

Castle

🕐 ⌀ *Open Jun-Sep, guided tour (1hr, last entrance 1hr before closing), 9.30am-7pm; Apr-May and Sep, 10am-12.30pm and 2-6.30pm; Feb-Mar and Oct-Nov, 2-6pm.* ⌀8€. *Garden:* ♿ *unaccompanied tour.* ☎ 05 53 50 51 23.

The terraces of the castle are laid out as French-style gardens, planted with flowers and box trees forming geometric patterns and offering views of the 30ha/74-acre English-style park where visitors can take a pleasant stroll.

Interior – The northwest tower has beautiful chestnut **timberwork**★★, the work of the Compagnons du Tour de France guild. It gives access to the watch-path dismantled in the 17C. Facing it is the chapel tower which contains 16C-18C religious gold plate.

The flower-decked gallery of the main building leads to a grand staircase giving access to various rooms, including Marie de Hautefort's bedroom furnished in Louis XV style.

The great hall boasts two **monumental walnut fireplaces** (replicas of the original 17C fireplaces) facing each other. The tapestry room contains four Flemish tapestries saved from the fire by a member of staff who threw them out of the window.

Ancien hospice

The former chapel of an almshouse, founded by the Hautefort family in 1669, stands on the village square, south of the castle. The edifice, shaped like a Greek cross, features a fine dome covered with slates and surmounted by a lantern.

It houses the **Musée de la Médecine** which displays a reconstructed ward and presents an exhibition devoted to the progress of medicine in the 19C; another room illustrates dental care from 1870 to the present. 🕐 ⌀ *Open Jul-Sep, 10am-7pm (guided tours possible - 1hr 15min); Apr-Jun and Oct-Nov, Mon-Fri, 10am-noon and 2-6pm. ⌀4.50€ (under 12 years old: no charge).* ☎ 05 53 50 40 27 or 05 53 51 62 98.

ISSOUDUN

POPULATION 13 685

MICHELIN LOCAL MAP 323: H-5

Issoudun goes back to Gaulish times (Uxellodunum comes from a Celtic term meaning a high, thus fortified, site) and later, during the Middle Ages, was the stake in many a battle, the most famous being that between Philip Augustus and Richard the Lion Heart. The town was besieged several times, as well as set on fire.

The town keeps alive the memory of the journey to the castle abbey made by Louis XI, who had a special devotion to Our Lady. Every year on 8 September in the basilica of Notre-Dame-du-Sacré-Cœur the traditional pilgrimage is celebrated.

▶ **Orient Yourself**: Issoudun is situated 35km/22mi south of Vierzon and 37km/23mi west of Bourges.

Ⓟ **Parking**: A number of car parks are dotted around the centre (&see town plan).

Ⓞ **Organising Your Time**: Allow a half day to explore the Chœurs and Bommiers forests.

🏛 **Don't Miss**: The Musée de l'Hospice St-Roch, including its Tree of Jesse carving and apothecary.

Kids Especially for Kids: Moulin de Nouan.

👁 **Also See**: Bourges; Vierzon.

A Bit of History

Balzac and Issoudun – Honoré de Balzac (1799-1850) stayed at Frapesle Castle, near Issoudun, where he wrote most of *César Birotteau* and also collected the information he needed to write *La Rabouilleuse (The Black Sheep)*. Issoudun has retained the peculiar street names which appear in Balzac's works: rue du Boucher-Gris (Drunken Butcher Street), rue à Chercher (Hard to Find Street).

Walking Tour

▶ *Start from place St-Cyr.*

Église St-Cyr

There is a very fine 14C-15C **stained-glass window** in the nave. It is divided into five vertical sections and in addition to depicting the Crucifixion contains medallions illustrating scenes from the lives of St Cyran and St Juliet. The marble high altar is surmounted by an unusual cross with Jesus Christ on both sides and by six gilt-wood candelabras offered by Louis XIV. The choir and the Rosary Chapel contain fine sculptured stalls. Above the west door is a Deposition painted by Boucher of Bourges in 1625.

▶ *From the church, walk up to place du 10 juin.*

Beffroi

The belfry, flanked by two round towers of unequal size, once served as a gateway (12C) through the castle wall to the town. Dismantled during the Wars of Religion, it was restored in the Renaissance style and used as a prison until 1914. The clock still strikes the hours and keeps good time.

Place des Miroirs

The façade of the **Hôtel de Ville** (town hall) dates from 1731; it is attached to a modern building and fronted by a courtyard designed by Marin Kasimir. This work, known as La Place des Miroirs, is made of eight glassed-in spaces surrounded by steps and waterworks. The artist created anthropomorphic symbols to compose the eight letters of the town's name. If you can't find the "I", it's because you are "I" – in the artist's scheme, the viewer represents this letter.

Tour Blanche

Ⓞ*Open Jul-Aug, 2-6pm, Sat-Sun and public hols, 2-7pm); Apr-Jun and Sep, daily except Mon, 2-6pm, Sun and public hols, 2-7pm. Evening shows, Jul-Aug, Wed-Sat; May-Jun and Sep, by advance appointment. ⊙3€ for tour and show (12-18 years old: 2€). ☎ 02 54 03 22 15.*

La place des Miroirs

The tower, standing in the middle of the town hall gardens, was built at the end of the 12C by Richard the Lion Heart. The inside is octagonal, the outside nearly circular; it is 28m/92ft high and the walls are 3.5m/12ft thick.

The four floors in the tower may be visited: the 8m/26ft-high former cellars (audio-visual presentation about Richard the Lionheart and Philip-Augustus), a lofty vaulted hall where the original entrance was located (presentation of King Arthur's legends), a room devoted to the Hundred Years War and an exhibition area displaying a model of the 17C town. From the top platform there is a view over the town and the country that lies between the valleys of the Indre and the Cher.

Parc François-Mitterrand

Access via the panoramic lift built within the fortifications. This pleasant park is easily reached from all parts of town; the greenery stretches across both sides of the river.

Musée de l'Hospice St-Roch★

&⚹ ⊙ *Open Apr-Oct, Wed-Sun 10am-noon and 2-7pm, Mon-Tue, 2-7pm; Nov-Mar, daily except Mon-Tue, 2-6pm, Sat-Sun and public hols, 10am-noon and 2-6pm.* ⊙ *Closed Jan, 1 May, 1 and 11 Nov, 24-27 and 31 Dec.* ✆No charge. ☎ *02 54 21 01 76. www.issoudun.fr.*

The museum is housed in the former hospital (Hôtel-Dieu) which is built on piles over the River Théols in a picturesque setting. St Roch (St Rock) is legendary for healing victims of the plague in the 14C. Stricken himself, he was succoured by a dog, and is often pictured with one in paintings and statuary.

Sculpture – After an overview of the history of Issoudun and a presentation of the Celtic archaeological collection, the sculpture collection gives an insight into local monuments which have disappeared: capitals, statues of the Virgin Mary, columns dating from the 8C to the 15C. The men's ward (**salle des hommes**) gives access to

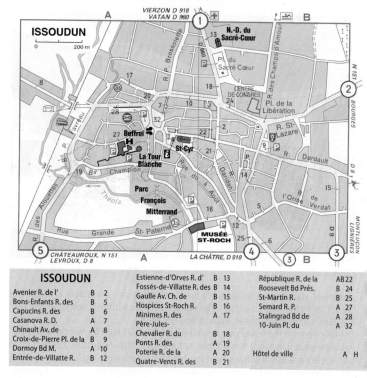

ISSOUDUN		
Avenier R. de l'	B	2
Bons-Enfants R. des	B	5
Capucins R. des	B	6
Casanova R. D.	A	7
Chinault Av. de	A	8
Croix-de-Pierre Pl. de la	B	9
Dormoy Bd M.	A	10
Entrée-de-Villatte R.	B	12

Estienne-d'Orves R. d'	B	13
Fossés-de-Villatte R. des	B	14
Gaulle Av. Ch. de	B	15
Hospices St-Roch R.	B	16
Minimes R. des	A	17
Père-Jules-Chevalier R. du	B	18
Ponts R. des	A	19
Poterie R. de la	A	20
Quatre-Vents R. des	B	21

République R. de la	AB	22
Roosevelt Bd Prés.	B	24
St-Martin R.	B	25
Semard R. P.	A	27
Stalingrad Bd de	A	28
10-Juin Pl. du	A	32
Hôtel de ville	A	H

the **chapel** built around 1500. The door connecting the chapel to the men's ward has a wooden shutter which could be opened during Mass, so that the patients could attend the service. The most outstanding items are two large carvings of the **Tree of Jesse**★★; they were made at the end of the 15C and represent the genealogical tree of Christ, showing the ancestors of the Virgin and figures of the prophets, kings and knights. The details in the robes and the expressive faces are remarkable; carved in local stone which hardens as it is exposed to the air, the statues were originally painted, as was the rest of the chapel. There are also two Flamboyant stained-glass windows depicting Louis XI and Charlemagne and a group of emblems carried by members of the guilds during official processions.

Ancient medecine – The last wing, the women's ward (**salle des femmes**), displays a collection of instruments used by surgeons, dentists and gynaecologists. The **Apothicairerie**★ (pharmacy), facing a garden where medicinal herbs are cultivated, houses a valuable pharmaceutical collection including 350 Nevers porcelain jars, rare painted boxes and other unusual items.

Modern wings – Inaugurated in 1995 and 2002, they house exhibitions of contemporary art, collections of Oceanian art and graphic arts. Note the bronze sculpture by Étienne Martin (*Le Puits-Fontaine*) opposite the information desk.

Basilique Notre-Dame-du-Sacré-Cœur

This late-19C neo-Gothic basilica is a popular place of pilgrimage as the numerous ex-votos testify (every year on 8 September). The stained-glass windows are particularly interesting: abstract designs in various hues of blue along the aisle, more classical designs in the nave and chancel.

Excursion

Forêt de Chœurs and Forêt de Bommiers
Round trip of 60km/37mi – allow 3hr

Located in the *départements* of Indre and Cher, these lovely forests cover more than 7 500ha/18 525 acres; 75% of the trees are oaks.

▶ *Leave Issoudun travelling E on the D 8 towards St-Ambroix. In St-Hilaire, take the D 84E.*

Bordered by woods, the route goes along the picturesque Arnon Valley. Above the river bank rise the vestiges of the **Abbaye de la Prée** (*concerts in season*), founded in the 12C.

Moulin de Nouan

⏰ 🚶 *Guided tour (15min mill + 45min tour) when the sails are unfurled or by appointment.* 💶 *2.50€.* ☎ *02 54 03 18 72. www.moulindenouan.fr.st*

Kids An unusual site in the region, this windmill mainly served to back up the many watermills, which are often stilled in summer when rivers and streams are low. Built in 1810, the mill was recently restored and its sails turn again on festive occasions. A lonely sentinel stands on the edge of the wood: the **Tour de la Croisette**. Built on the mound of a vanished feudal castle (vestiges of the moat remain), the tower now houses an exhibit on local fauna.

▷ *Return to the road, turning right on the D 9.*

Mareuil-sur-Arnon

Snug among the copses, this village was one of the metallurgical centres of the upper Arnon Valley. All that remains of the old forge is a tall brick chimney alongside the lake which supplied water to the works. South-west of the town of Mareuil, this 3ha/7.5-acre lake now serves as a **recreation centre**.

▷ *Outside of Mareuil, take the D 18 to the right.*

Abbaye de Chezal-Benoît

Founded in 1093 by the monk André de Vallombreuse, this former Benedictine monastery, now a psychiatric hospital, has kept the 12C nave of the church and the community buildings.

The façade is embellished by the foliage designs on the Romanesque capitals, and fluted pilasters (a rarity in Berry). The interior is pure Romanesque style: the blind nave is indirectly lit by the side windows. The foliated, spiral scrolls on the capitals are the precursor of the Gothic-style crocket (leafy projections). The modification of the supporting structure and the evolution of the sculpted decor show that construction was still taking place in the second half of the 12C.

▷ *Leave Chezal travelling SW on the D 65E.*

Travel along the southern edge of the **Forêt de Chœurs**, where many forest roads and trails lead to the central point known as the Croix Blanche.

▷ *At Pruniers, turn right on the D 925.*

Bommiers

This 12C **Église St-Pierre** is representative of the lower Berry by the clearly Benedictine plan (note the unusual *secretaria*, vaulted niches used as a sacristy, linking the chancel to the apsidal chapels in the transept). The capitals, also 12C, create an admirable ensemble: Christ handing over the Keys to St Peter and the Law to St Paul; the lively silhouettes seem to stretch out, the facial expressions underlined by lead set deep in the eyes. Other capitals bear a mixed arrangement of flowers, people and imaginary animals. The 48 magnificent **stalls**★ (1511-15) are from the chapel and the Minimes convent in Bommiers. Above the entranceway, the wooden Madonna dates from the 15C.

▷ *Take the D 925 towards Lignières. 1km/0.5mi before Pruniers, turn left on the D 68.*

The road back to Issoudun crosses the **Bommiers Forest** as far as **St-Aubin**, where the church shelters a 15C sculptural ensemble: St Anne, the Virgin and the Infant Jesus. After crossing the Cousseron, the road crosses the ancient Roman road known as the **Levée de César**, which linked Argentonmagus (♿ *see St-MARCEL*) to Bourges.

LABASTIDE-MURAT

POPULATION 690

MICHELIN LOCAL MAP 337: F-4

Labastide-Murat, which stands at one of the highest points on the Gramat Causse, was originally called Labastide-Fortunière, but changed its name to Murat in honour of the most famous of its sons.

The modest house in which Joachim Murat was born, in the south-west part of town, as well as the château that he had built for his brother André, preserve the memory of one of the French Empire's (1804-14) most valiant soldiers.

▶ **Orient Yourself**: The village is situated 25km/15mi south of Rocamadour and 32km/20mi north of Cahors.

◔ **Organising Your Time**: Allow a full day to explore the Parc Régional des Causses du Quercy and the Causse de Gramat.

⊛ **Don't Miss**: The Sunday morning market in July and August and the regional fair on the second and fourth Monday of every month.

⌚ **Also See**: Cahors; Rocamadour, Sarlat.

A Bit of History

The miraculous destiny of Joachim Murat – Murat was born in 1767, the son of an innkeeper. He was destined for the Church, but at 21 decided instead to be a soldier. The campaigns in Italy and Egypt enabled him to gain rapid promotion under Napoleon, whose brother-in-law he became by marrying the First Consul's sister, Caroline; he was promoted to Marshal of the Empire, Grand Duke of Berg and of Cleves and King of Naples. The phenomenal bravery he displayed on all the battlefields of Europe and his influence over his troops, at whose head he unhesitatingly charged into battle, made him a legendary hero.

His glory faded with that of his master, whom he abandoned in the dark days of the Empire. His miserable end in 1815 was in keeping with the diversity in his life: after the Bourbons had returned to Naples, he tried to reclaim his kingdom, but was taken prisoner and shot.

Visit

Musée Murat

◔ ⌖ *Open Jul-Sep, guided tour (1hr), daily, 10am-noon and 3-6pm.* ⊛ *3€.*

The museum is in the house where Murat was born. The 18C kitchen, the inn's saloon and a large genealogical tree on which 10 European countries and several royal families are represented are on display to visitors. On the first floor there are mementoes of the King of Naples and of his mother.

> **SHOPPING**
>
> **Fairs** – The 2nd and 4th Monday of every month.
> **Market** – A farmers' market is held from 9am-noon every Sunday in July and August.

Excursions

Parc Régional des Causses du Quercy

BP 10, 46240 Labastide-Murat, ☎ 05 65 24 20 50.

Created in 1999, the nature park covers 1 760km2/680sq mi situated between Figeac and Cahors on the south bank of the River Dordogne. It includes 97 municipalities and over 25 000 inhabitants. The aim of the park is to safeguard this rural environment by stopping the population drain and installing long-term development which implies the conservation of existing ecosystems and of the cultural heritage, the preservation of agricultural traditions and high-quality crafts and the promotion of environment-friendly tourism.

Southern Section of the Causse De Gramat

60km/37mi round-trip – allow half a day

▶ *Drive S out of Labastide-Murat along the D 32.*

St-Martin-de-Vers

In this small village the houses with brown-tiled roofs cluster round the old priory church and its asymmetrical bell-tower.

▶ *Drive E along the D 13 and turn left onto the D 10 3km/1.9mi further on, then left again onto the D 17.*

Soulomès

The Knights Templars built a commandery here in the 12C. The chancel of the church contains interesting 15C and 16C frescoes depicting episodes of Christ's life.

▶ *Leave Soulomès to the S along the D 17 and turn left onto the D 71 1km/0.6mi further on.*

Désert de la Braunhie

Here, drystone walls seem to stretch forever into the distance, and the scrubby vegetation includes oaks, maples and stunted walnut trees, or stony heath with junipers and thorn bushes.

Caniac-du-Causse

Beneath the church, the **crypt** (*light switch at the bottom of the stairs to the right*) was built by the monks of Marcilhac-sur-Célé in the 12C to shelter the relic of St Namphaise, an officer in the army of Charlemagne who became a hermit and whom the inhabitants of Braunhie held in great esteem. He was supposed to have hewn the so-called St Namphaise's lakes out of the rocks himself; the sight of these underlines the aridity of the area. This diminutive crypt has an unusual vault and an attractive central colonnade.

Planagrèze discovery trail – *An interesting brochure is available at the Maison de la Braunhie, beneath the town hall in Caniac-du-Causse and at the tourist office in Labastide-Murat.* ☎ *05 65 31 16 03.*

🚶 *7.5km/4.6mi round-trip on foot.*

▶ *Follow the D 42 towards Fontanes-du-Causse.*

This is the highest part of the Causse de Gramat, with numerous nooks and crannies caused by water infiltrating the limestone. The trail reveals the local fauna and flora, and offers an insight into the geology and history of the area.

▶ *Return to Caniac-du-Causse and continue along the D 71 to Quissac.*

The road runs across the most arid part of the Braunhie.

Quissac

Besides attractive farmhouses, the village of Quissac has retained its *travail à bœufs*, a farrier's sling used for shoeing oxen, at one time common throughout the communities of the plateau.

▶ *Drive W along the D 146. In Fontanes-du-Causse, turn left onto the D 2 and, 4.5km/2.8mi beyond Montfaucon, turn left onto the D 17.*

Château de Vaillac

The massive outline of the castle towers above the village. Built in the 15C and 16C, the stronghold comprises a large building flanked by four towers and a keep. The stables were later extended to accommodate some 200 horses and a new building was erected to lodge the owner's large family. The castle is one of the finest examples of military architecture of the Quercy region dating from the end of the Hundred Years War.

▶ *Return to Labastide-Murat along the D 10.*

Grotte de LASCAUX★★

MICHELIN LOCAL MAP 329: I-5

Lascaux Cave ranks among the finest prehistoric sites of Europe by dint of the number and quality of its paintings. *Pl. Bertran-de-Born, 24290 Montignac,* ☎ *05 53 51 82 60. www.bienvenue-montignac.com et www.culture.fr/culture/arcnat/lascaux/fr/index.html.*

▶ **Orient Yourself**: The cave is situated 2km/1.2mi south of the village of Montignac, and 26km/16mi north of Sarlat.

Especially for Kids: The prehistoric site of Régourdou.

Also See: Montignac; Les Eyzies-de-Tayac; Sarlat.

A Bit of History

Discovery of the cave – The cave was discovered on 12 September 1940 by four young boys looking for their dog, which had fallen down a hole. With a makeshift lamp, they found an extraordinary fresco of polychrome paintings on the walls of the gallery they were in. The teacher at Montignac was immediately told of the discovery, and he just as quickly notified Abbé Breuil. The abbot arrived and examined the paintings with meticulous care, baptising the cave the Sistine Chapel of Périgord.

In 1949 the cave was officially opened to the public. Over 15 years, more than a million people came to admire the famous Lascaux paintings. But, unfortunately, in spite of all the precautions taken (weak lighting, air conditioning, airlock), the carbon dioxide and the humidity resulted in two damaging effects: the green effect (the growth of moss and algae) and the white effect (less visible but much more serious as it leads to a build-up of deposits of white calcite).

In 1963, in order to preserve such a treasure, it was decided to close the cave to the public (a limited number of researchers are allowed in every year). Ten years later, to relieve public disappointment, a project was put forward to build a replica; Lascaux II was opened in 1983, under the care of the Dordogne Tourist Administration.

As early as 1966, The National Geographic Institute (*Institut Géographique National – IGN*) had accomplished a precise photographic survey of Lascaux using three-dimensional scenes of the cave and stereo images. This survey enabled a shell to be constructed in reinforced concrete – similar to the process used in shipbuilding.

Once the cave walls were reproduced, the painter Monique Peytral copied the cave paintings using slides and the results from numerous surveys she had made. She used the same methods and materials (pigments, tools etc) as the cave artists.

The Cave

The cave, carved out of Périgord Noir limestone, is a relatively small cavity, 250m/820ft long. It is made up of four galleries, the walls of which are covered with more than 1 500 representations, either engraved or painted. These works were created from around 17000 BC, during the Magdalenian Culture, a period when the climate was relatively mild as the presence of deer testifies.

At that time the cave was open to the outside air. Some time after the cave artists had decorated the cave, the entrance collapsed and a flow of clay tightly closed off the cave.

The airtight entrance and the impermeable ceiling are the reasons for the lack of concretions and the perfect preservation of the paintings fixed and authenticated by a thin layer of natural calcite.

The simplified scene of a wounded bison and a falling man offers one of the rare representations of a human figure. This collection of paintings is truly unique in the history of prehistoric art, in regard to the state of preservation, the number of works created over a long time span, and the precision of execution.

A wide range of fauna is depicted on the cave walls, mainly animals hunted during the early Magdalenian period: aurochs, horses, reindeer, bison, ibexes, bears and woolly rhinoceroses appear side by side or superimposed, forming part of extraordinary compositions. The hunter in difficulty theme is also to be found in the **Grotte du Villars**, probably decorated at the same time as Lascaux. Part of the drawings in the **Font-de-Gaume** cave may also belong to the same period.

The Lascaux style – There is a definite Lascaux style: lively animals with small, elongated heads, swollen stomachs and short legs, and fur illustrated by dabs of coloured pigment. The horns, antlers and hoofs are often drawn in three-quarter view at times even full face – whereas the animal itself is drawn in profile; this procedure is known as the turned profile. In addition, the artists used the wall contours to give relief to the subject matter. But the most important feature is the movement conveyed by the paintings to the point that the animals seem to be leaping all around the visitors.

Visit

Lascaux II★★

Open Jul-Aug, guided tour (45min), 9am-8pm; May-Jun and Sep, 9.30am-6.30pm; Oct to mid-Nov: 10am-12.30pm and 2-6pm; mid-Nov to Apr: daily except Mon, 10am-noon and 2-5.30pm. Closed 25 Dec. NB: from Apr-Sep, tickets are sold in Montignac, under the arcades next to the tourist office. Tickets go on sale at 9am and are sold until 2,000 have been issued for the day (in high season, this allocation sells out very quickly). 8€ (child: 4.50€). 05 53 05 65 65.

Located some 200m/219yd from the original cave, the facsimile reconstitutes two galleries from the upper part of the cave; the Bulls' Hall and the Axial Gallery, which contain the majority of the cave paintings at Lascaux. Airlock antechambers retrace the cave's history in explanatory exhibits and present items discovered in the cave's archaeological strata (tallow lamps, coloured powders, flints used by the engravers); a model of the scaffolding used; an explanation of the dating methods used; and displays on flint and bone knapping. The re-creation of the unique atmosphere of the original cave has been made possible purely by real technological prowess and rigid scientific discipline.

In the **Bulls' Hall** (La Rotonde), the paintings are on the calcite-covered upper part of the wall and the vaulting, so that the animals seem to be running along the natural rim as if along the horizon line. The graphic composition here is wonderful. The second animal, the only imaginary animal figure painted at Lascaux, has been nicknamed the unicorn because of the odd-looking horns above a bear-like muzzle, on a body not unlike that of a rhinoceros. Among the other animals represented there are some magnificent black bulls, one of which is 5.5m/17ft long, red bison, small horses and deer.

The **Axial Gallery** (Le Diverticule axial) contains a vault and walls covered with horses, cows, ibexes, bison and a large deer. A charming frieze of long-haired ponies (dubbed Chinese horses by the first chroniclers because of their resemblance to figures from ancient Chinese vases), a great black bull and a large red pony, seeming to sniff at a branch, bear witness to a very developed style of art.

Excursions

Régourdou

500m/550yd from Lascaux. You are advised to leave your car in the Lascaux car park. Open Jul-Aug, guided tour (45min), 10am-7pm; Sep-Nov and Feb-Jun, 11am-6pm. 4.80€. 05 53 51 81 23.

This prehistoric site, which goes back to the time of Neanderthal man and is therefore much older than Lascaux, was discovered in 1954; numerous objects and bones were brought to light, including a skeleton, Régourdou Man (70000 BC) and now displayed in the Périgord Museum in Périgueux. All these discoveries are representative of the Mousterian industry. In the cave, now open to the air, near the burial ground of the Régourdou Man, a pile of bear bones was found, which some specialists have interpreted as evidence of a bear burial ground.

A **museum** presents various elements found on the site and elsewhere, which help to illustrate the evolution of man from the Stone Age to the Iron Age.

Montignac

2km/1.2mi NW along the D 704E. See MONTIGNAC.

LEVROUX

POPULATION 2 914

MICHELIN LOCAL MAP 323: F-5

Set between the wooded landscape of the Boischaut and the rich farmlands of the area known as Champagne Berrichonne, Levroux is in the heartland of tradition. In addition to producing especially savoury goat cheeses, it is also home to tawing (a form of leather processing using alum and salt) and parchment enterprises.

▶ **Orient Yourself**: Levroux is situated 20km/12mi north of Châteauroux and 55km/34mi southwest of Vierzon.

⊘ **Don't Miss**: The stalls and organ case in the Collégiale St-Sylvain.

⏱ **Also See**: Château d'Argy; Château de Bouges; Château de Valençay; Palluau-sur-Indre.

A Bit of History

A land steeped in history – The area has been inhabited since prehistoric times; the settlement of Levroux appeared at the end of the Celtic period. It was certainly one of the *oppida* burned to the ground by Vercingétorix as Caesar's armies approached in 52 BC. Once the *Pax Romana* was established, Levroux grew quickly, spreading from the towers on the hill to the area where the city now stands. The historical interest of this sector is such that the district of Levroux has become one vast archaeological site. Besides the Gallo-Roman theatre, several villas have been discovered and are now being carefully unearthed.

In the Middle Ages, the town grew around the feudal château of the princes of Châteauroux and the church of St-Sylvain, the site of pilgrimages. During the Hundred Years War, local residents took refuge behind a fortified wall (one of the gates remains). There are several well-preserved 15C and 16C buildings in Levroux.

Visit

Collégiale St-Sylvain★

In the early 11C, Eudes de Déols founded a collegiate church (home to a chapter of clergymen sharing authority) in Levroux and made a special land grant to the canons. Thus, part of the town took on a separate status and became a place of refuge and asylum for fugitives and serfs.

The church was built in two stages beginning in the late 12C. The crypt, the apse and the large bell-tower came before the vaulting in the nave and the construction of the porch, undertaken around 1263.

EATING OUT

⊜⊜**Relais St-Jean** – *34 r. Nationale* - ☎ *02 54 35 81 56 - relais.saint.jean@free. fr -* ⏱ *closed 7-11 Feb, 23 Aug-12 Sep, Tue eve Oct-May, Sun eve and Wed.* Modern cuisine is the order of the day in the wood-floored dining room of this 19C house. A porch leads to a pleasant flower-decked courtyard terrace which comes into its own in the summer months.

The east end of the church is a heptagonal apse flanked by a square bell-tower. The southern doorway is embellished with 21 different figures, including a devilish face with a beard and horns. The main doorway bears a much-damaged tympanum; the sculpted imagery represents the Resurrection of the Dead and the Last Judgement. Inside, the nave and side aisles are impressive for their soaring height. The chancel was built in transitional Romanesque-Gothic style; note the keystone in the sanctuary, showing Christ bestowing blessings. The vaulted apse is supported by ribs and statuary columns.

Note the late-15C **stalls**★ with their humorous carvings depicting virtues and vices and, in the baptismal chapel, a 15C polychrome wood carving representing the Holy Trinity. The restored late-15C **organ case**★ is one of the three Gothic organ cases left in France.

Maison de Bois (Maison St-Jacques)

This wooden house was built between 1536 and 1547. Located in a street which leads to the façade of St-Sylvain, it is decorated with angelic carvings and the blazons of François I and Henri de Valois (later to become Henri II), as well as curious figures in the angles (note the **"wild man"** covered with leaves). The house was once used as a hospice for pilgrims on their way to Santiago de Compostela.

Porte de Champagne

Close to the church, this former town gate (1435-1506) was turned into a prison at the beginning of the 19C. It is framed by round towers and roofed with dark brown tiles.

Musée du Cuir et du Parchemin

Open mid-Jun to Aug, 10am-12.30pm and 2.30-6pm. 2.50€ (-12 years old: no charge). 02 54 35 63 39.

In the tourist office, this small temporary museum is devoted to the techniques of dressing hides by the dry process known as tawing, and to the manufacture of parchment.

S. Sauvignier/MICHELIN

A "wild man" on the Maison de Bois

Colline des Tours

1km/0.6mi N. Access from the intersection of the D 956 and the D 2 by a steeply rising path.

Atop this hill, an ancient fortified burg has left vestiges which include ramparts in a characteristic Gaulish style: the drystone construction was reinforced with cross-beams. The ruins of the 14C château built by Bertrand de La Tour d'Auvergne paint a lonely picture. Two round towers guard the old entranceway and the main building (Gothic doorway); there is a good **view** of Levroux from this site.

Excursions

Châteaux of the Boischaut and Champagne Berrichonne

Around Levroux, several interesting châteaux are found in the areas known as the Boischaut and Champagne Berrichonne.

Château de Bouges★★

9.5km/6mi NE. *See Château de BOUGES.*

Château de Valençay★★

22km/13.7mi N. *See Château de VALENÇAY.*

Palluau-sur-Indre★

25km/15.5mi W along the D 28 and the D 15.

Perched on a rocky crest above the Indre Valley, the **château** is set in a lovely park; the living quarters are in the Gothic style (13C), protected by two defensive towers. The 12C keep is known as the Tour de Philippe Auguste, in memory of the sovereign's visit in 1188. From the terrace, the view extends over the valley.

The former **St Laurence Priory** (turned into dwellings) contains remarkable Romanesque frescoes; note, in particular, a magnificent **Virgin in glory**★ decorating the oven vaulted apse and a Christ in glory in the chancel.

Ancienne Abbaye de St-Genou

3km/2mi SE of Palluau.

The church was once part of a Benedictine abbey, founded in 828. The place was then known as Strata (currently Estrées). The relics of St Genou held within gave the church its name. Genou was sent to evangelise Gaul by Pope Sixtus II, was made bishop of Cahors, and died near Estrées.

Begun in 994, the church was consecrated in 1066. The abbey went into decline in the early 16C, gradually falling into ruin. The archives were destroyed in 1580, the nave knocked down in 1676. One hundred years later, only a few monks were left and the monastery was closed. It was completely restored soon after being registered as a historic building (1882).

Only the transept and the choir, in the Berry Romanesque style, give a clue to the church's past.

Beyond the triumphal arc, the vast choir has an oven-shaped vault. The monumental columns have remarkable **capitals** with fantastic animal figures, biblical scenes (Adam and Eve, Daniel in the lion's den) and episodes from the life of St Genou.

Château d'Argy★

16km/10mi SW along the D 926 and the D 63. ⏱ ⚑Open Jul-Aug, guided tour (45min), daily, 10am-noon and 2-6pm; Apr-Jun and Sep-Oct, Sat-Sun and public hols, 2-6pm. 4€ (no charge on Indre heritage day in Jun). ☎ 02 54 84 21 55. www.clubduvieuxmanoir. asso.fr

Restored by the Club du Vieux Manoir association, the château and the 17C fortified farm buildings now serve as a training centre for the club, focusing on the theme architecture and environment.

Fortified in the 12C, this impressive château, renovated in the 16C by Charles de Brillac, companion-at-arms to Louis XII, is set in a 40ha/99-acre park. The square, 15C keep is an excellent example of military architecture, with its trefoil machicolations and guard towers. A curtain wall connects the keep and the Brillac Tower, where the upper levels have retained chimney-pieces embellished with seigniorial monograms. The moat was filled in during the French Revolution. Under the Second Empire, the south-western section was rebuilt and the towers fitted with windows.

In the courtyard, the **Louis XII-style gallery**★, carefully restored, contrasts with the severity of the outer walls: the flowery ornamentation of the brackets, the slender columns rising to pinnacles and the superposition of the galleries belie Italian influence. Nearby, a mill and a building housing a museum devoted to rural traditions (*traditions paysannes*) date from the 19C. In the barn, an exhibit of furnishings from the National Archives displays monumental items from the time of Napoléon III designed to store maps. The cast-iron stairway is also worthy of note.

LIMOGES★

POPULATION 133 968

MICHELIN LOCAL MAP 325: E-6

A ford across the Vienne and two stepped plateaux that could be put to defensive use are the reason for Limoges' existence. In the Gallo-Roman period when the town was known as Augustoritum, it spread out in an amphitheatre along the right bank of the river. In the Middle Ages two separate and rival townships developed: the **Cité épiscopale** grouped round its cathedral built on a low shelf overlooking the Vienne, and the **Château**, the busy commercial town on the opposite slope in the shadow of the powerful abbey of St-Martial.

The city's industrial rise is largely due to its porcelain and enamel works and shoe factories. Limoges also boasts a university (and hence plays an important cultural role in the region) and is the administrative capital of Limousin. The building of the A 20 motorway has put Limoges in closer contact with Paris in the north and Toulouse in the south.

▸ **Orient Yourself**: The centre of Limoges extends across the north bank of the River Vienne.

🅿 **Parking**: A number of car parks are dotted around the centre (*see city plan*).

The White Gold of the Limousin

In Europe, porcelain was imported from China until the late 17C, when the Sèvres manufacture bought the secret of hard-paste porcelain, which required 50% of kaolin, a rare white form of clay. In 1766, kaolin of remarkable purity was discovered in various parts of Limousin and, after encouraging experiments had been carried out at the Royal Factory at Sèvres, Turgot, who was then general intendant of Limousin, set up a porcelain works in 1771. This was under the patronage of the count of Artois and marked the beginning, for Limousin ceramics, of an era of prosperity which was hardly interrupted even by the troubled years of the Revolution. After 1815 the industry concentrated round Limoges which, because of its position on the Vienne, could land the wood for the kilns from lumber rafts floated down river.

Nowadays, more than 50% of all the porcelain made in France comes from Limoges, a world famous manufacturing centre.

Address Book

For price ranges, see the Legend at the back of the guide.

EATING OUT

🍽 **Chez François** – *Pl. de La Motte, Halles Centrales - ☎ 05 55 32 32 79 - closed 5-25 Aug, Sun and public hols.* Housed in the Halles de Limoges, a listed historical monument, this friendly bistro bases its menu on produce from the market. From the dining room, decorated with a fresco of sculpted wood, you can see the chef at work. Good value for money. Opens at 5.30am.

🍽 **Chez Alphonse** – *5 pl. de la Motte - ☎ 05 55 34 34 14 - closed Mon eve, Sun and public hols.* Tucked away behind the *halles*, this bistro is a popular local haunt. Tables decorated with chequered tablecloths and a menu which is written up on the blackboard.

🍽🍽 **Le Pont St-Étienne** – *8 pl. de Compostelle - ☎ 05 55 30 52 54 - closed Christmas-1 Jan - reserv. required at weekends.* Attractive bay windows with views of the old stone bridge and the river. The à la carte menu features a number of imaginatively named dishes. Summer terrace.

🍽🍽 **Les Petits Ventres** – *20 r. de la Boucherie - ☎ 05 55 34 22 90 - closed 8-15 Jan, 2-17 May, 5-22 Sep, Sun and Mon.* Classic French cuisine is to the fore in these two typical 15C houses, run by two young and enthusiastic owners. The cuisine is high on quality with traditional dishes based on liver, tongue, pig's trotters, tripe etc.

🍽🍽 **Le Bœuf à la Mode** – *60 r. François-Chenieux - ☎ 05 55 77 73 95 - closed 1 to late-Aug, Sat lunchtime and Sun.* If you love eating meat, then this is definitely the place for you! Excellent cuisine served in a friendly and traditional ambience.

🍽🍽 **L'Escapade du Gourmet** – *5 r. des 71ème-Mobiles - ☎ 05 55 32 40 26 - closed 10-26 August, Sat lunchtime, Sun eve and Mon.* A Belle-Époque decor of wood, frescoes, moulded ceilings and coloured glass is the backdrop to this popular traditional restaurant located between the château and the Cité Episcopale. Classical French cuisine. Good value for money.

WHERE TO STAY

🛏 **Hôtel de la Paix** – *25 pl. Jourdan - ☎ 05 55 34 36 00 - 31 rooms.* This Napoléon III-style hotel in the heart of the city features an entertaining phonographic collection. Bright and airy bedrooms, some with wicker furnishings. Friendly atmosphere.

🛏🛏 **Hôtel Jeanne-d'Arc** – *17 av. du Gén.-de-Gaulle - ☎ 05 55 77 67 77 - hoteljeanned'arc.limoges@wanadoo.fr - closed 20 Dec-7 Jan - ⓟ - 50 rooms.* This pleasant, well-located hotel is close to the city's famous train station. The well-mantained bedrooms and pleasant breakfast room have managed to retain their old French charm.

🛏🛏 **Chambre d'hôte M. et Mme Brulat** – *Imp. du Vieux Crezin - 87220 Feytiat - 5km/3mi E of Limoges. Take the A 20, exit 35, and head towards Feytiat; in Crézin follow signs to Le Vieux Crézin - ☎ 05 55 06 34 41 - 3 rooms.* Peace and quiet reign supreme in this large stone house in the middle of the country, yet just 10min from the centre of Limoges. Comfortable bedrooms, relaxing lounge, and a games room with billiards and darts. Friendly family atmosphere.

BARS AND CAFÉS

La Parenthèse – *Cours du Temple - 22 r. du Consulat - ☎ 05 55 33 18 25 - closed Sun and evenings.* This tea room sells home-made pastries and serves family-style meals at lunchtime. Either sit outdoors in the 16C courtyard or in the dining room painted with a mural of Montmartre. A restful and relaxing retreat.

Brasserie Artisanale St Martial – *8 pl. Denis-Dussoubs - ☎ 05 55 79 37 98 - open Mon-Thu, 3.30pm-1am; Fri-Sat, 3.30pm-2am - closed Sun and 15 Aug.* This brewery (in the true sense of the term), established over 10 years ago, perpetuates an old local tradition. Beer has been brewed in the region since the 18C; in the 19C there were no fewer than 50 brewers in the Limoges area.

Café des Anciennes Majorettes de la Baule – *27 r. Haute-Vienne - ☎ 05 55 34 34 16 - open Tue-Wed, 10.30am-1am; Thu-Sat, 10.30am-2am - closed mid-Jul to mid-Aug.* This renowned local bar is the venue for regular concerts and plays.

L'Irlandais – *2 r. Haute-Cité - ☎ 05 55 32 46 47 - open Apr-Oct, daily, 10am-2am; Nov-Mar, Mon-Sat, 4pm-2am, Sun, 2pm-midnight; concerts Wed-Sun; Thu, Irish evening with live music.* This Irish pub is run by a fisherman from Brittany who has travelled the world and has already established a bakery and a pub in Ireland, and a concert violinist who has played in royal circles. Over the past three years they've hosted jazz, Celtic music and other concerts here. Juggling shows on the terrace during the summer months.

ENTERTAINMENT

Cinemas - The main cinemas are around place Jourdan (Colisée et Lido) and Denis-Dussoubs (Grands Écrans). The Théâtre Municipal (rue Jean-Jaurès) hosts performances of ballet, opera, musicals and pop concerts. For theatre, head for La Limousine (rue des Coopérateurs) and Expression 7 (rue de la Réforme).

SHOPPING

Most of the city's shops are located in the area around the castle. The main boutiques selling porcelain are along boulevard Louis-Blanc and along the streets heading west from the city centre. Discount shops selling seconds and end-of-line products include Michel Morel (boulevard Louis-Blanc) and Cygne Bleu (place des Jacobins). Art et Feu (rue de la Boucherie) sells original enamel works.

Le Pavillon de la Porcelaine – *Av. du Prés.-John-Kennedy -* ☎ *05 55 30 21 86 - pavillon-porcelaine@haviland-limoges.com -* 🕐 *open daily, 9am-7pm -* 🕐 *closed Sun in Jan, 1 Jan, 1 May and 25 Dec.* This factory outlet belongs to Haviland, the American family which settled in Limoges in 1842 and began crafting prestigious porcelain sets for kings, queens and other famous names. The visit includes the museum and a demonstration of porcelain production, which includes a film on a large screen. A wide choice of table and decorative ware is on sale in the boutique.

Paul Buforn – *4 pl. de la Cité -* ☎ *06 70 54 30 40 -* 🕐 *open Tue-Sat, 10am-12.30pm and 2-7pm -* 🕐 *closed Oct and public hols.* This impassioned enameller will delight in telling you all about his profession, its tradition and its techniques. He can also provide information about enamel-making workshops, as well as offer advice and appraisals on individual antique pieces. In the past, Limoges was home to a hundred or so enamel artisans, a number that has dwindled to just thirty today.

Buissières – *27, r. Jean-Jaurès -* ☎ *05 55 34 10 44 -* 🕐 *open Mon-Sat, 9am-7pm.* This chic confectioner, established in 1848, is one of Limoges' must-see places where the Art-Deco decor is almost worth a visit on its own. Evocatively named chocolates, pastries and desserts, including the house speciality black chocolate with chestnut cream.

GUIDED TOURS

The tourist office is able to provide information on guided, theme-based visits (2hr) of the old town, which take place during school holidays. *5€.* ☎ *05 55 34 46 87.*

😊 **Don't Miss**: Musée Adrien-Dubouché; Cathédrale St-Étienne; Église St-Michel-des-Lions; Musée de l'Émail; Jardins de l'Évêché; Cour du Temple; Rue de la Boucherie; Chapelle St-Aurélien; Gare des Bénédictins.

📷 **Especially for Kids**: Planète Aquarium Limousin.

👁 **Also See**: Oradour-sur-Glane; Brienne and Briance valleys.

A Bit of History

Limoges in Gallo-Roman days – Limoges appears to have entered history in the last decade of the 1C BC.

The presence of the Roman military road, Agrippa's Way, the existence of a natural crossing point of the River Vienne, and the south-eastern exposure of the hillside most appropriate for settlement certainly contributed to the birth of the Augustoritum. This new town followed a well-ordered grid plan based on two central, perpendicular roads. The town quickly acquired a number of significant structures such as the stone bridge (later to become the Pont St-Martial), a forum, a theatre, baths, aqueducts, an amphitheatre, a temple, a triumphal arch, and so on. The forum was located on the site of the current town hall, between rue des Récollets and the rue Timbaud. Below, the baths welcomed visitors (place des Jacobins, archaeological excavation from 1967 to 1978) in three immense heated rooms, an exercise room, and assorted outbuildings. The amphitheatre (now the site of the Orsay garden), built on a rise on the outskirts, was 137x116m/449x380ft, making it one of the largest in Gaul. Despite the many facilities offered, Augustoritum was thinly populated: never more than 6 000 inhabitants. Archaeological research has shown gaps in the ancient urban fabric, which indicate that the town was not fully built up.

At the end of the 4C, the barbarian invasions squeezed the town in upon itself, as people gathered around the St-Étienne hilltop and settled behind ramparts, thus forming the core of the *Cité*.

An enthusiastic reformer – In 1761, a young magistrate by the name of **Turgot** became general intendant of Limousin, one of the poorest regions in France. He was an admirer of the enlightened philosophers of his time and seized this opportunity to put his theories into practice and to modernise the region. He built a network of modern roads, developed new industries (including the porcelain industry following the discovery of kaolin deposits), encouraged farmers to grow potatoes and even tried his hand at town planning, replacing the fortifications of Limoges with wide boulevards, building a college and a hospital.

Famous citizens of Limoges – Many of the sons of Limoges have gained fame. Among the artists are **Leonard Limosin** (1505-76) enameller and painter in ordinary to the king's royal chamber, who won favour with four monarchs. By his skill in engraving, painting and decoration he became one of the leaders of the great school of enamel artists of the 16C whose fame, through the Laudin dynasty, lasted until the 18C. The painter Auguste Renoir (1841-1919), one of the masters of the Impressionist School, worked for some time at the beginning of his career as a painter of porcelain.

Among statesmen, Pierre Vergniaud (1753-93) was the most famous orator of the Girondin Group in the Convention; there was also Sadi Carnot (1737-1894) who became president of the Republic.

Limousin Porcelain and Enamels

Musée Municipal de l'Évêché - Musée de l'Émail★

Open Jul-Sep, 10am-noon and 2-6pm; Oct-Jun, daily except Tue, 10am-noon and 2-5pm (6pm in Jun). Closed 1 Jan, 1 May, 1 and 11 Nov, and 25 Dec. No charge. ☎ 05 55 45 98 10.

The museum is housed in the former archbishop's palace. This elegant 18C building in grey granite near the cathedral was designed by Joseph Brousse.

Enamels – The museum has some 500 **Limousin enamels**★ dating from the 12C to the 21C. The Middle Ages was an especially rich period for this type of art, well represented in the museum's display cases.

Cloisonné enamels use an early technique where thin strips of metal are soldered to a metal base to outline the design. Although this process works well for gold, it is less effective for copper and soon came to be replaced by **champlevé**, where the lines of the design were cut away from the surface, and the enamel applied to the recesses.

In the museum, notable examples include the Thomas Becket shrine dating from around 1200 and a plaque illustrating the Visitation from 1770 to 1775.

The third technique is that of **painted enamels**; the design is painted on the enamel covering the copper plate.

In the series of painted enamels are two plaques by Monvaerni (late 15C), a **Nativity triptych** (1515-20), the **altarpiece from Mesnil-sous-Jumièges** (1525-30), a rare example of this type of item to have survived, a monumental statue representing the death struggle of the legendary Trojan priest **Laocoön** by Pierre Courteys (c 1560), works by Léonard Limosin, and pieces from the 17C and 18C by the Laudins, including the **twelve Caesars medallions**. Two rooms display contemporary enamel work. Limoges is still an international centre of enamel art, as witnessed in the Bie*nnale International de l'Art de l'Émail*, a major exhibition.

Egyptology – The two rooms in the Egyptology section present a particularly rich collection of terracotta figurines and bronze statuettes.

F. Magnoux/Musée de l'Évêché, Limoges

Musée de l'Évêché – Toy box

A Mini-Guide to Limoges Porcelain

True porcelain (hard-paste): resonant when struck, is translucent and made from ground feldspathic rock and the special white clay known as kaolin. Also called china, because that is where it was first made.

Artificial porcelain (soft-paste): made using clay and ground glass, it has a softer body and can be cut with a file, whereas true porcelain cannot. Dirt accumulated on an unglazed base can only be removed with difficulty; on true porcelain it comes off easily.

Bone china: developed by Josiah Spode the Second, it contains calcined bones in a hard-paste formula, which makes it chip-resistant. Especially popular in England and the United States.

Earthenware: opaque and porous, this, the most common type of pottery, is made from clay baked at low temperatures.

Stoneware: fired at high temperatures until it is vitrified (glasslike and nonporous), it does not require a glaze; lead, salt and feldspathic glazes are used for decorative effects. Stoneware also originated in China, and came to Europe in the 17C, but by the early 19C its popularity had been superseded by porcelain.

Faience: tin-glazed earthenware made in France, Germany, Spain or Scandinavia. In Italy, it is called Faenza majolica (the town of Faenza, the origin of the name, was a major production centre in the Renaissance). Manufactured in the Netherlands or England, it is referred to as delft, after the Dutch city famous for its production.

Creamware: this fine white English lead-glazed earthenware (also produced briefly in France) is more durable and less expensive to produce than faience. Wedgwood and Leeds are the best-known manufacturers.

Lapidary museum – The fine vaulted cellars which were formerly the bishop's palace kitchens complete with chimneys, ovens and well, make a good setting for the ancient and medieval exhibits of the lapidary museum. These include Iron Age funerary items from Glandon, stone lions, funerary chests, gravestones and statues, characteristic of local Gallo-Roman works in granite. The Middle Ages are represented by a collection of sarcophagi, a 9C mosaic from the tomb of St Martial, Romanesque and Gothic capitals, low-relief sculptures and various fragments from the 13C through the 16C.

Ancient Limoges – Scale models illustrate the evolution of the city from its founding up to medieval times. A rare **fresco** (early 2C), discovered on the site of a villa gives a hint of the beautiful decor found inside a luxurious residence: yellow and ochre traces on a red and black background, animal motifs (deer, cats, eagles).

French painting – This collection includes 17C-18C works (*Bataille de Constantin* by Charles Le Brun), landscapes of Limoges and the area by Courtot, and canvasses by Renoir (*Portrait de Mademoiselle Laporte*), Guillaumin, Pascin and Suzanne, Valadon.

Musée Adrien-Dubouché★★

🕐 *Open Jul-Aug, daily except Tue, 10am-5.40pm; Sep-Jun, daily except Tue, 10am-12.25pm and 2-5.40pm.* 🕐 *Closed 1 Jan, 1 May and 25 Dec.*≈4€ *(child: no charge), no charge 1st Sun of the month.* ☎ *05 55 33 08 50. www.musee-adriendubouche.fr*

The museum, founded in 1845, became a national museum in 1881 and is named after the director Adrien Dubouché, who provided it with the foundation of its collections. Today the collection, which includes items dating from the pottery of ancient times to porcelain from factories in production at Limoges today, shows the evolution of ceramics and glassware in France and throughout the world.

Ground floor – To the left of the vestibule and its bronze statue (1898 of Adrien Dubouché), eight display cases are given over to fine earthenware, popular in the 19C, and to clay pieces formed from slip (*Vase aux musiciennes* by Aube). A collection of pieces by **Théodore Deck** (1823-91) recalls his important role in ceramic arts in the 19C. Stoneware comes next, from 15C Germany to 19C France, with famous names including Delaherche, Decoeur, Chaplet and Moreau-Nélaton. Pottery pieces in the collection date from Ancient Greece and Rome and carry through to the 19C. One room provides explanations of the manufacturing techniques of the four major families of ceramics (pottery, earthenware, stoneware and porcelain) using illustrations, machines (for applying colour lithography), kiln models and an audio-visual presentation.

The right-hand wing displays 19C porcelain. One thousand two hundred pieces of Limoges porcelain amply demonstrate the reason for the worldwide renown of porcelain manufactured here since 1771. Notice the enormous service in a rice grain pattern from the Pouyat company, the unusual series of dishes from the First World

War and the Art Deco collection. Visitors can compare Limoges porcelain with items produced at the same time elsewhere in France or in other countries.

Salon d'honneur – This room houses Chinese porcelain. Tang earthenware, Song porcelain, Yuan blue and white ware, 17C and 18C white China, and coloured ware known as *famille verte* and *famille rose* complete this collection of precious items from the Far East.

First floor – The history of ceramic manufacture, from its origins in the Middle East to Medieval times, is traced in the **right wing**. Ceramics arrived in Europe through Spain, reaching Italy by the end of the Middle Ages, where new techniques and artistic effects developed rapidly. During the second half of the 16C, the craft spread throughout Europe: in France in Nevers (blues), Lyon, and Rouen; in Spain in Talavera and Alcora; in the Netherlands in **Delft**, where the production sought to rival chinaware imported by the East Indian Trading Company; and in Germany. In France, the 17C and 18C were high points for ceramic design and manufacturing. Each sizeable city had a production centre, distinguished by unique patterns and colours as well as the quality of the ceramics: **Moustiers** (Provence) invented the first polychrome motifs, while chinoiserie became fashionable in many different places, including Limoges.

The **left wing** contains the collection of 18C porcelain. The **soft-paste porcelain** technique (which does not use kaolin) was perfected in the 17C. First produced in Rouen, major manufacturing took off in Saint-Cloud as of 1677. Several centres in the Paris region became well known for their wares: Chantilly, Mennecy, Vincennes and **Sèvres**.

The first **hard-paste** porcelains manufactured in Europe were made in the **Meissen** factory in Saxony in 1710, when Bötttger and Tschirnhaus discovered a source of kaolin in Aue. The factory produced chinoiserie motifs on tableware and later branched out into figurines and statuary. Kaolin was found near Limoges in 1768, enabling the development of hard-paste production in Sèvres, Paris, Lille, Bordeaux, Orléans and Valenciennes.

Manufacture Bernardaud

27 avenue Albert-Thomas. ○ ✿⌖ *Guided tour (45min), Jun-Sep, 9-11.15am and 1-4.15pm; the rest of the year by prior arrangement.* ⊙4€. ☎ 05 55 10 55 91.

This porcelain manufacture founded in 1834 has become one of the leaders in the production of tableware. The bulk of the output today comes from a factory in Oradour-sur-Glane; however, the former works have been preserved and are open to visitors. Guided tours reveal the mysteries of porcelain manufacturing: designers and decorators can be seen at work, the different manufacturing stages are explained and the kiln with its 33m/108ft-long tunnel is on show.

Four des Casseaux

Access via quai Louis-Goujaud or rue Donzelot. ○*Open Jun-Aug, daily except Mon, 2-6pm; Mar-May and Sep-Oct, daily except Sun, 2-6pm; Nov-Feb, daily except Sun, 2-5pm.* ○ *Closed holidays.* ✿⌖*Guided tour (1hr) by prior arrangement.* ⊙4€, *unaccompanied tour* 2€. ☎ 05 55 33 28 74.

Built in 1844, this round kiln was intended for firing porcelain. There were originally six kilns on this site, set up in pairs inside factory buildings. The kiln is 19.5m/64ft high. The lower part, heated to a temperature of 1 400°C/2 552°F, has 1m/3.28ft-thick brick walls reinforced with iron. The upper part, used for the first baking at 950°C/1 742°F, was surmounted by a high chimney closed by a valve.

Today, gas-fired kilns allow continuous baking to take place.

La Cité

Situated on a height overlooking the River Vienne, the Cité is the historic district of Limoges.

Built in 1210 to provide access to the Cité, the humpback **Pont St-Étienne** is made up of eight pointed arches. There is a nice view of the Cité from the bridge.

Cathédrale St-Étienne★

St Stephen's was successor to a Romanesque church of which only a part of the crypt and the lower storeys of the belfry remain. The Gothic cathedral was begun in 1273; the chancel was completed at the beginning of the next century; the 14C saw the building of the south and north transepts and the first two bays of the nave had been constructed by the end of the 15C. Jean de Langeac undertook the completion of the cathedral in 1537, but he died in 1541 and work was stopped once more; Monsignor Dusquesnay completed the church between 1876 and 1888.

Exterior – The **St John Doorway**★ is really the cathedral's main entrance. It is of very fine-grained granite and was constructed between 1516 and 1530 when the Flamboyant style was at its peak. Two pierced galleries divide the façade into three tiers. A statue of Christ stands at the pier; the entire tympanum is adorned with a background of blind arcades filled in with richly coloured mosaics. An elongated gable frames the archivolt and rises to the base of the large rose window. The two Renaissance wooden doors are carved to show scenes from the lives of St Martial and St Stephen.

The **belfry** is square and 62m/204ft high. The lower three storeys are Romanesque, but the lowest has been submerged in stonework added to support the tower. The next four storeys are Gothic, of which the three uppermost are octagonal, a design often found in Limousin architecture. The belfry stood apart from the nave until last century when a modern narthex and three bays were added.

Interior – The nave gives an impression of unity of style even though it took 600 years to build. The boldness and elegance of line of the roof vaulting are wonderful; the triforium is constructed to act as a base for the clerestory windows.

The rood screen★ (at the end of the nave under the organ-loft), built for Jean de Langeac by artists from Touraine in 1533, once separated the chancel from the nave. This limestone screen is topped by a gallery with pendants decorated with statues of the Six Virtues. The niches on either side of the door are framed by columns and pilasters. The ensemble is decorated in a rich Italian style. The low-relief sculptures at the base depict mythological scenes – note Hercules' labours.

The three **tombs**★ that stand round the chancel are of considerable decorative interest:

♦ the tomb of Raynaud de la Porte (14C), bishop of Limoges;

♦ the tomb of Bernard Brun in the pure 14C French style, adorned with four low-relief panels and;

♦ the **tomb of Jean de Langeac**, built in 1544, an example of the Renaissance style at its most delicate. Fourteen carved panels depict scenes of the life of St John as described in the Book of Revelation. It is in effect an adaptation of the little Passion by Dürer, translated to stone with exceptional spirit and feeling for movement.

Jardins de l'Évêché (Bishop's Palace Gardens)★

These pleasant gardens rise in terraces above the Vienne and provide a good view of the cathedral and the palace. They include a themed garden and a "wild" garden featuring five natural environments typical of the region.

Medieval bridge across the Vienne and the Cathedral

S. Sauvignier/MICHELIN

Jardins de l'Évêché

Château District

The neighbourhood known as Le Château rose up long ago around the abbey of St-Martial and the château. Today it serves as Limoges' downtown, busy with shops and activity.

▶ *From place St-Pierre, walk north towards rue St-Martial.*

Remains of the abbey of St-Martial

Once located outside the city walls, place de la République stands over the site of a Gallo-Roman necropolis where St Martial was buried. His tomb was highly venerated and a chapel was built above it in the 6C. The chapel's keepers adopted the Benedictine rule in 848, and the abbey grew, becoming affiliated with Cluny in 1063. During the Middle Ages, it was the site of intensive religious, cultural and artistic activity. Between the 9C and the 12C, the scriptorium produced such masterpieces as the so-called *manuscrit de la Seconde Bible*, now in the French National Library. Yet thereafter the abbey declined and its buildings were destroyed during the Revolution. On place de la République, markings on the ground illustrate the size of the former abbey church.

Three churches rose around St Martial's tomb: the Basilique du Sauveur, St Pierre and St Benoît.

▶ *Cross rue Jean-Jaurès and follow rue du Clocher then turn right onto rue Gaignolle.*

Place du Présidial

Note, at the corner of rue Haute-de-la-Comédie, the former **hôtel Maledent** which dates back to 1639. Admire the pretty **place Fontaine-des-Barres** (16C) below. The north doorway of the church of **St-Michel-des-Lions** opens on to this square where the 17C-18C royal administrative buildings remain standing.

▶ *Walk down rue Ferrerie then along rue du Temple.*

The Butchers' Guild

Since 930, *Messieurs les Bouchers de Limoges* have administered a trade guild in the former rue Torte (now rue de la Boucherie). When the relics of St Aurélien (the bishop who succeeded St Martial) were discovered in 1315, the butchers of the city obtained the right to adopt the saint as their patron. They created a brotherhood which, in 1475, built the Chapelle St-Aurélien to receive the relics in a shrine. In the 16C, six families in the guild took control of the brotherhood (today, members are still elected by a secret ballot for a seven-year term). Since the time of Henri IV, the brotherhood has had the privilege of offering the keys to the city to visiting dignitaries. At the dawn of the 21C, the millenary tradition persists.

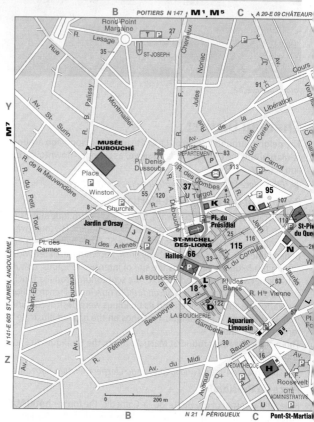

Cour du Temple★

Rue du Consulat, lined with 18C buildings, is linked to rue du Temple by a narrow passage (at no 22), which opens on to 16C half-timbered houses and arcaded galleries, known as the temple courtyard.

▶ *Continue along rue du Consulat then rue des Halles.*

Les Halles

Built at the end of the 19C, the covered market stands on **place de la Motte**, probably named for the *motte*, or hillock, where the viscounts' castle once stood. A decorative porcelain frieze depicts market produce.

Rue de la Boucherie★

This picturesque street is lined with half-timbered houses, some of which still have the accoutrements of the 80 butchers' shops which once operated there. On the last Sunday in October, a regional festival known as the *Frairie des petits ventres* brings back the memory of bygone activities.

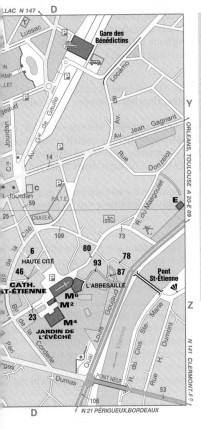

Place de la Barreyrrette

The name of this square comes from the fence (*barrière*) around the holding pen for animals awaiting slaughter. The pens disappeared when the municipal slaughterhouse was opened in 1832.

Chapelle St-Aurélien★

A 14C monolithic cross marks the entrance to this unusual little building dating from 1475. Founded to hold the relics of St Aurélien, the chapel was sold at an auction in 1795 and secretly purchased by the butchers' guild which still maintains it today. The ex-votos and gilded wooden statues inside sparkle in the light from votive candles.

▶ *Walk across place des Bancs to rue Haute-Vienne.*

Boulevard Louis-Blanc

Take a stroll along the porcelain avenue. The square in front of the town hall is adorned with a porcelain fountain!

▶ *When you reach place Wilson, turn left onto rue du Collège.*

Pavillon du Verdurier

🐾 *During exhibits, or included in the guided tours organised by the Office de tourisme.*

Built after the First World War to store meat which was in short supply at the time, this edifice looks rather unusual with its mosaics and floral friezes on a ceramic background. It has been turned into an exhibition hall.

▶ *Return to your starting point via place St-Pierre on the right.*

Additional Sights

Cité des Métiers et des Arts

🕐 *Open late-Jun to mid-Sep, 10.30am-1pm and 2.30-7pm (last entrance 20 min before closing); mid-Sep to Nov and Easter-Jun, Wed and Sat-Sun, 2-6pm.* 🕐 *Closed 1 Nov-Easter, and 1 May.* 🎟️ *4€ (children 12 and over: 2€).* ☎ *05 55 32 57 84 or 05 55 34 19 12 (tourist office).*

This centre, located in the Bishop's Plalace gardens, presents the work of the **Compagnons du Tour de France** (journeymen touring France after their apprenticeship) and of France's finest workers in the building trade. On the mezzanine are illustrated the different stages a young *compagnon* has to go through to master his trade.

Église St-Pierre-du-Queyroix

The flamboyant façade dates from 1534. The 13C bell-tower is well proportioned; it served as a model for the towers of two other churches in Limoges, St-Michel and St-Étienne.

Inside, the church forms an irregular rectangle of surprising width; from the 12C, it has preserved its enormous cylindrical pillars with flattened capitals embellished with palmettos. To the right of the choir, the brightly coloured window was created in 1510 by Jean Pénicaud and has since been restored; it shows Death and the Crowning of the Virgin.

Notice the wooden Christ (14C), very expressive, on the wall behind the main altar and, at the end of the second aisle, a 17C gilded wooden altar screen decorated with paintings. The church possesses a collection of reliquaries.

Crypte St-Martial

🕐 🐾 *Open Jul-Sep, unaccompanied visit, 9am-12.30pm and 2-7pm; for information on guided tours (1hr), contact the tourist office.* 🎟️ *No charge (guided tours 5€).* ☎ *05 55 34 46 87.*

The current stairway was added in the 13C, with the Chapelle de l'Ange, to improve the flow of pilgrims. Martial and his two companions (Alpinien and Austriclinien) were laid to rest in the two big tombs measuring more than 2.80m/9ft long, still on view. In the 9C, Martial's remains were exhumed and placed in a gold reliquary on the main altar in the new basilica. The bird mosaic was also created at this time. In the opposite corner stood the tomb of St Valérie; according to legend, she was beheaded by her fiancé, Governor Étienne.

The second room or sanctuary contains the enormous granite tomb known by the name of Tève-le-Duc, dating from the 4C.

Beyond, there is a large room which lies underneath and shores up the churches of St-Pierre and St-Benoît, installed on the Gallo-Roman ruins and on the site of an early Christian cemetery, as the numerous tombs testify.

Église St-Michel-des-Lions★

Construction began in 1364 and continued during the 15C when the north doorway was built, and the 16C when a west bay was added. The plan is rectangular, characteristic of churches used for public gatherings more generally.

Outside near the belfry door on the south side can be seen the two lions carved in granite which have given the church its name. It is believed that in the Middle Ages these lions served to mark limits of jurisdiction of the abbots of St-Martial and the viscounts of Limoges. The upper octagonal tiers of the tower are braced by four walled turrets; a tall spire, topped with a pierced copper ball, rising to a height of 68m/223ft. The north doorway is delicately ornamented.

Three parts of equal height resting on slender columns (some are offset on the outside) make up the interior. On either side of the chancel, at the end of the aisles, lovely 15C windows show the life of the Virgin Mary and that of John the Baptist. Behind the high altar, a monumental altar of carved stone supports a 19C gilded wooden reliquary shrine which contains relics of St Martial including the saint's head.

To the right of the first bay, a wall-niche contains a 13C reliquary in gilded silver and cut crystal.

Maison Traditionelle de la Boucherie

🕐*Same opening times as the Abbaye St-Martial.*

The butcher's stall at no 36 is now devoted to preserving the heritage of the meat trade in Limoges. In the kitchen (also a shop), visitors can admire the butcher's block and its accessories, a 19C icebox and a hearth where tripe was simmered to perfection. The back room was used for slaughtering and as a stable. Upstairs are the furnished rooms where about 25 lived at a time (family, apprentices and employees) and an attic space used for salting meat and drying skins. Exhibits relate the activities of the trade guild and a few culinary clues.

Planète Aquarium Limousin

♿🕐*Open 10.30am-6.30pm (last entrance 30min before closing).* ⊚*6€ (4-15 years old: 4.50€).* ☎ *05 55 33 42 11.*

🄺🄸🄳🅂 Set up beneath place Haute-Vienne on the site of an old reservoir, the aquarium has made use of the vaulted architecture to welcome European freshwater fish, tropical species, piranhas and more.

Espace FRAC

▷ *From place Denis-Dussoubs, follow rue François-Chenieux then turn left onto avenue G.-et-V.-Lemoine and left again onto impasse des Charentes.*

♿🕐*Open daily except Sun and Mon, 10am-6pm; Sat, 2-6pm.* 🕐 *Closed public hols.* ⊚*1.50€.* ☎ *05 55 77 08 98.*

The Fonds Régional d'Art Contemporain (regional collection of contemporary art), created in 1982 is located in a former grocery warehouse. The 45m/148ft-long basement hall makes an unusual exhibition area for the permanent collections as well as for temporary exhibitions.

Gare des Bénédictins★

This is one of the landmarks of Limoges. Built from 1923 to 1929, it stands as a symbol of the town's prosperity and expansion between the two World Wars. Its architectural features are enhanced by the green open space of the Esplanade du Champ-de-Juillet, laid out at the same time.

Musée des Distilleries Limougeaudes

52 rue de Belfort (not on the map). Same directions as the Espace FRAC, but continue to place Sadi-Carnot. ♿🕐*Open daily except Sun and Mon, 8.30-noon and 2-6pm.* 🕐 *Closed public hols.* ⊚*No charge.* ☎ *05 55 77 23 57.*

The distillery museum is steeped in local traditions as well as the fragrance of the sweet liqueurs produced here. Tools and alembics, bottles and posters are among the items on display. Chestnut liqueur (*Feuillardier*) and other house specialities are on sale.

S. Sauvignier/MICHELIN

Gare des Bénédictins

Musée de la Résistance

♿🕐*Open Jul to mid-Sep, 10am-11.45am and 2-6pm; Jun, daily except Tue, 10am-11.45am and 2-6pm; mid-Sep to May, daily except Tue, 2-5pm.* 🕐 *Closed 1 Jan, 1 May, 11 Nov and 25 Dec.* ⊚*No charge.* ☎ *05 55 45 63 40.*

During the Second World War, Limoges was hard hit by the numerous deportations and massacres in the region (👣 *see ORADOUR-sur-GLANE and TULLE*). In the series of rooms which make up the museum, posters, maps, documents and photos are among the items on exhibit, evoking the dark days of the war. Courageous women and men of Haute Vienne, led by Georges Guingouin, were some of the first in France to band together in the Resistance movement to combat the barbarism of Nazism.

Excursions

1 **From Vienne to Briance★**

Round trip of 90km/54mi – allow 2hr 30min

▶ *Leave Limoges on the N 21 towards Périgeux.*

This road is picturesque and goes up the valley of the Briance, winding its way through meadows. At **Pont-Rompu** hamlet, there is a view on the right of a picturesque old bridge with pointed cutwaters on which passed the ancient Roman way from Limoges to Bordeaux.

Église Abbatiale de Solignac★

◔ *See Église Abbatiale de SOLIGNAC.*

▶ *Follow the D 32 to Le Vigen then turn left onto the D 704. A short distance beyond the railway bridge, turn right onto the D 65 towards Boisseuil.*

Parc Zoologique et Paysager du Reynou

◔*Open Apr-Sep, 10am-8pm (last entrance 2hr before closing); Oct-Mar, Wed, Sat-Sun and public hols, 10am-5.30pm; school hols, 10am-5.30pm. ◌9€ (child: 6.50€). ☎ 05 55 00 40 00. www.parczooreynou.com*

Laid out in 1870 for Haviland, the porcelain manufacturer, the landscaped park is planted with 150 different species of trees (including cedars and sequoias) surrounding a castle. Kids In a nearby **zoo**, 120 species of animals from the five continents roam around relatively freely.

▶ *Turn back and continue along the D 32.*

Château de Chalusset

⊶*Access to the ruins is strictly forbidden for safety reasons; however, a footpath enables visitors to walk right round. It is also possible to visit the medieval village of Le Bas-Cha-lusset and the Tour Jeannette. ◔⊶Unaccompanied visits all year; possibility of guided tours mid-Mar to mid-Nov. For information, call ☎ 05 55 00 96 55.*

The impressive ruins of Chalusset Castle are a perfect example of medieval military architecture in their plan and position on a rock promontory, which juts forward to the point where the River Briance and River Ligoure meet. The castle was built in the 12C and in 1577 it fell into the hands of the Huguenots who used it as a base for their battles against Limoges. The troops of Limoges took the notorious castle by force and dismantled it (1593).

Only traces remain of the three outer walls, the square towers, the keep and the ramparts, but these traces, in spite of the overgrowth and the accumulation of earth and stones are still impressive in scale.

In Le Chatenet, the picturesque D 39, on the left (towards St-Léonard-de-Noblat), crosses the River Vienne. Turn left on reaching the confluence of the Vienne and the Maulde, overlooked by the **Château de Muraud** perched on a promontory.

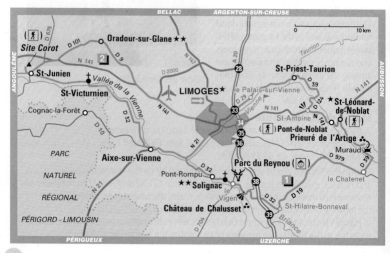

Vallée de la Maulde

The road runs up the Maulde Valley through a rocky, wooded gorge. The river has been transformed by the French electric company into a giant, watery staircase, with remote-controlled dams. The **Barrage de l'Artige**, the last dam of the series, serves to regulate the flow of water coming from the others upstream. The road overlooks the dam and affords a fine view of the valley and the ruins of the former priory of Artige.

Ancien Prieuré de l'Artige

A narrow road opposite the dam to the left leads to the entrance of the Priory.
Founded in the 12C and secularised shortly before the Revolution, part of it was subsequently left to fall into ruin. From the road you can see the vast buildings with their round tiled roofs, the arcades between the chapter-house and the cloisters, and the remains of emblazoned doors which create a romantic scene.
The road (D 39) follows the Vienne, framed by overhanging rocks, then rises above the river.

St-Léonard-de-Noblat★

See ST-LÉONARD-DE-NOBLAT.

Pont-de-Noblat

In the Vienne Valley, on the outskirts of town, this area has developed on both sides of the river. A 13C bridge spans the water; old houses line the time-worn path known as the *Pavé*.

Promenade du Chêne de Clovis – Between the bridge and the church, a steep path leads to a plateau where a castle once stood. The archaeological site encompasses a feudal hillock and a view on the river below.

▶ *The the N 141 crosses the Vienne and follows the river valley before it rises up to a plateau. At St-Antoine, take the D 124 for a panoramic view of the Ambazac hills, then turn left on the D 39, a lovely country road.*

St-Priest-Taurion

This town rests peacefully at the fork of the River Taurion and River Vienne, in a green valley cut across with dams.

▶ *After Le Palais, take the D 29 along the valley back to Limoges.*

2 La Vallée Ténébreuse

Round trip of 90km/56mi – allow 3hr

▶ *Leave Limoges travelling W on the N 141 towards Angoulême.*

Oradour-sur-Glane★★

See ORADOUR-SUR-GLANE.

St-Junien

See ST-JUNIEN.

Site Corot

See ST-JUNIEN: Excursions.

Église de St-Victurnien

The altar screen in the **church** has a 14C decorative painting illustrating the Passion and the Resurrection. Also worthy of note are the 13C enamel shrine, the 14C polychrome Virgin and Child, and, in the cemetery (*road to Oradour*), a lantern of the dead.
The winding road follows the river and rises up above the valley, revealing beautiful views.

Aixe-sur-Vienne

This town is one of the gateways of the Parc naturel régional Périgord-Limousin. Every seven years, during the *Ostensions* (*see Introduction*), 20 reliquaries are carried in a procession to Notre-Dame-d'Arliquet by representatives of the different trades, lit by torches as they return at night.

Maison de la Porcelaine – Open Jul-Aug, guided tour (30min) at 10am, 11am, 3pm, 4pm and 5pm; Sep, Dec and Apr-Jun, at 10am and 3pm; Oct-Nov, daily except Sat-Sun at 10am and 3pm. Closed 1 Jan, 1 May, 1 Nov and 25 Dec. No charge. ☎ 05 55 70 14 68. A visit to this workshop provides an insight into the art of porcelain making.

▶ *Return to Limoges via the D 32 and the N 21.*

LUZECH

POPULATION 1 647

MICHELIN LOCAL MAP 337: D-5

Luzech has grown up on the narrowest part of a tongue of land almost completely encircled by a loop in the River Lot. The isthmus at this point is some 100m/110yd wide. The town is crowned by the old castle keep. To the north lies the Roman city of Impernal and to the south the Pistoule Promontory, washed by the waters of the river as it sweeps round the bend. A reservoir has been formed by the construction of a dam upstream from the peninsula, and a water sports centre has been set up there (*boat tours*).

▶ **Orient Yourself**: Luzech is situated 27km/17mi west of Cahors.

🕐 **Organising Your Time**: Allow a full day to explore the lower reaches of the Lot valley.

🖐 **Don't Miss**: The commanding view of the town, the Pistoule promontory and the Lot valley from the Pech de l'Impernal (🕐 *see below*).

🕐 **Also See**: Château de Bonaguil; Cahors.

A Bit of History

Pech de l'Impernal – A natural defensive position, this rise has been inhabited since prehistoric times; Gauls, recognising its potential, transformed the plateau into a powerful stronghold. A citadel (the square keep can still be seen) was built below it in the Middle Ages. In 1118, Richard the Lion Heart was master of the citadel. Luzech became the seat of one of the four baronies of Quercy and was much sought as a prize by the English in the Hundred Years War. Nevertheless, the town resisted all attacks and became an important central stronghold. During the Wars of Religion, it remained a faithful bastion of Catholicism under the bishops of Cahors.

Excavations of the Impernal site have revealed walls and traces of buildings dating from the Roman and Gaulish periods.

Walking Tour

▶ *Start from the top of the Impernal.*

Viewpoint★

From the top of the Pech de l'mpernal, the view encompasses Luzech clustered at its foot, as well as the Promontoire de la Pistoule, slicing through the wide alluvial plain like a ship's prow, and the Lot winding between rich and fertile crops.

▶ *Follow the marked path (GR) down to the town.*

Keep

▶ *Entrance via place des Consuls.*

The entrance used to be through the small, pointed-arched doorway opening onto the first floor. From the terrace of the 12C keep there is a bird's-eye view of the brown-tiled roofs of the town, tucked amid meadows and crops with a row of hills along the horizon.

Old Town

In the old district known as the *faubourg du Barry*, picturesque alleyways link rue du Barry-del-Valat with the quays.

Around place des Consuls, on the other side of place du Canal, several examples of medieval architecture are still to be seen: Penitents' Chapel (12C), Capsol Gateway with its brick pointed arch and Consuls' House with its elegant twinned windows.

Additional Sight

Musée Archéologique Armand-Viré

🕐 *Open Jul-Aug, 9am-12.30, 2-5.30pm, Sat 9.30am-12.30, 2-4pm, Sun 10am-noon; Sep-Jun: daily except Sun and Mon 9.30am-12.30, 2-5.30pm, Sat 9.30am-12.30.* 🕐 *Closed Christmas to Jan and holidays.* 🐌 *2€.* ☎ *05 65 20 17 27.*

Established in the fine vaulted cellar of the old Consuls' House (13C), now the tourist office, the museum retraces the history (from the Paleolithic Age to the Gallo-Roman times) of the site of Luzech. The items displayed (excavated from the Impernal site and the cave found on the hillside) include the exceptional **scale model of the Column of Trajan**★, and an unusual Gallo-Roman hinged spoon, of bronze and iron.

Address Book

For coin ranges, see the Legend at the back of the guide.

EATING OUT

Auberge Imhotep – *La Rivière Haute - 46140 Albas - 4km/2.5mi W of Luzech on the D 8 - ☎ 05 65 30 70 91 - ⏰ closed Sun eve and Mon - reserv. recommended*. Imhotep is best-known as the great architect of ancient Egypt. But he also invented the method of gavage - force-feeding of geese to yield delicious foie gras. This and other regional dishes are available, as well as a vegetarian menu, all at reasonable prices.

Le Gindreau – *46150 St-Médard - 8.5km/5mi NE of Castelfranc via the D 911 and D 5 - ☎ 05 65 36 22 27 - le.gindreau@wanadoo.fr - ⏰ closed 1-17 Mar, 18 Oct-18 Nov, Mon and Tue - reserv. required Sun and public holidays*. Nestled among the chestnut trees on top of a hill, this restaurant was once the village school. The dining room is cosy, with its attractive woodwork and paintings on the walls. Elegant cuisine with a contemporary twist.

WHERE TO STAY

Chambre d'hôte Marliac – *46140 Bélaye - 15km/9mi W of Luzech via the D 8 and the D 50 towards Montcuq - ☎ 05 65 36 95 50 - ⏰ closed early Nov to the end of Mar - 5 rooms*. It is well worth the climb up the twisting road that leads to the lovely B&B. Unpretentious and comfortable rooms, and a quiet atmosphere in which to relax and enjoy good food. Swimming pool.

Chambre d'hôte Château de la Coste – *46700 Grezels - 16km/10mi W of Luzech on the D 8 - ☎ 05 65 21 38 28 - gervaiscoppe@wanadoo.fr - ⏰ closed Sep-Jun - reserv. required - 4 rooms*. This B&B occupies an authentic medieval château in a delightful spot above the Lot Valley. The guestrooms, varying in size, each have their own individual feel. The view from the foot of the fortress is quite splendid.

Hôtel Source Bleue – *46700 Touzac - 8km/5mi W of Puy-l'Évêque along the D 8 - ☎ 05 65 36 52 01 - sourcebleue@wanadoo.fr - ⏰ closed 16 Nov-9 Apr - 17 rooms*. This hotel-restaurant occupies

three former paper mills. Elegant, personalised bedrooms. The dining room, housed in a 17C outbuilding, serves traditional cuisine.

Château Onésime – *Les Cambous - 46220 Prayssac - 15km/9mi NW of Luzech along the D 8 as far as Anglars and then the D 67 towards Prayssac - ☎ 05 65 36 54 57 - jeanphilippe-christine.becht@wanadoo.fr - 4 rooms*. This charming 18C manor house is located in the heart of the Cahors vineyards. Spacious rooms decorated with individual touches. Swimming pool, sauna, jacuzzi, an elegant lounge and grounds that blend into the surrounding countryside. Appetising cuisine. Cooking classes and wine tastings also available.

SHOPPING

Markets – *In Duravel*: evening market on 13 July; wine and regional products fair on 14-15 Aug. *In Prayssac*: Pays du Lot farmers' market, Sun mornings in July and August.

Château de Chambert – *Marc and Joël Delgoulet, Les Hauts-Coteaux - 46700 Floressas - ☎ 05 65 31 95 75 - chateaudechambert.com - ⏰ open Mon-Sat, 8.30am-12.30pm and 2-6.30pm*. The wines produced here have won a number of prestigious awards. Tours of the cellars and tastings available.

Clos Triguedina – *Jean-Luc Baldès - 46700 Puy-l'Évêque - ☎ 05 65 21 30 81 - ⏰ open Mon-Sat, 9am-noon and 2-6pm*. The Baldès family is proud of its eight centuries of wine-growing on this 60ha/150-acre property. Their Clos Triguedina wine is considered one of the best wines produced in the Quercy. Visits of the cellars, winery and family museum.

LEISURE ACTIVITIES

Boat trips on the Lot – *Departures from the Base Nautique de Caix - Jul and Aug, 4.15-6.30pm - ☎ 05 65 20 18 19*. Cruises last 1hr 30min.

Safaraid Canoës Kayaks – *Pl. du Canal - ☎ 05 65 30 74 47 - www.canœ-dordogne.com - ⏰ open daily, 9am-6pm - ⏰ closed Nov-Mar*. Safaraid offers several locations for hiring canoes and kayaks on the Lot, Célé (Bouziès, Marcillac) and Allier (Lavoûte-Chilhac) rivers.

Excursions

Notre-Dame-de-l'Île

1.2km/0.8mi S along the D 23.

The chapel, set in a calm landscape of vineyards and orchards against a backdrop of hills along the course of the Lot, stands at the furthest point of the isthmus. This Flamboyant Gothic sanctuary is a pilgrimage centre, which dates back to the 13C.

Albas

Église de Cambayrac

8km/5mi S along the D 23 and D 67.

The hamlet possesses an odd-looking church identifiable from afar by a belfry-wall with a shape reminiscent of a French policeman's hat. Inside, the Romanesque apse and the side chapels were recovered in the 17C with an unusual marble and stucco decor in the Classical style.

Lower Reaches of the Lot

85km/52mi round-trip – allow one day

As the Lot flows between the tall limestone cliffs of the Quercy causse, its thousand curves provide a never-ending variety of magnificent views.
Follow the south bank for the best views of the valley.

▷ *Drive W out of Luzech along the D 8.*

Albas

From its past as the seat of the bishops of Cahors, this small town has retained ruins of the Episcopal castle and a network of narrow streets lined with old houses.

▷ *Continue along the D 8.*

Anglars-Juillac

A Crucifixion adorns the church's Renaissance doorway.

▷ *Continue along the D 8 and turn left onto the D 50, 2.5km/1.5mi further on.*

Bélaye

Once the fief of the bishops of Cahors, Bélaye stands on top of a hill. An extensive **view**★ of the Lot Valley unfolds from the top of the spur and from the upper square of this little village.

▷ *Rejoin the D 8 and turn left.*

Grézels

🕐 *Open Jul-Aug, lecture tour (1hr 30min) 4.30pm; wine museum: 3-6pm.* ◉4€. ☎ 05 65 21 34 18 or 05 53 21 38 28.

Overlooking the village is the feudal **Château de La Coste**, which was razed and rebuilt on several occasions. The bishops of Cahors possessed a fief which extended over the Lot Valley from Cahors to Puy-l'Évêque, and Grézels marked the limits of their territory; therefore, a stronghold was built to defend the entrance to their fief. During the Hundred Years War, it was transformed into a fortress. It was severely damaged during the different wars, then restored in the 14C and 16C. After the Revolution it was abandoned.
The curtain wall and crenellated corner towers are the oldest parts of the castle.

▷ *Continue along the D 8.*

The Pont de Cour-
benac offers the
best overall **view** of
Puy-l'Évêque (*see
below*).

▶ *Continue along
the D 8 to Tou-
zac, cross the
river and turn
left onto the
D 911 then right
to Cavagnac.
Drive N to the
D 673, turn
left then right
2.5km/1.5mi fur-
ther on (D 158).*

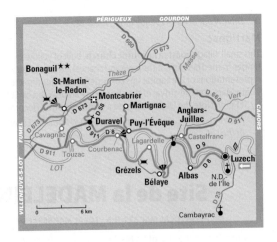

Château de Bonaguil★★

See Château de BONAGUIL.

▶ *Return to Couvert (D 158) then turn left to St-Martin-le-Redon 500m/547yd further on.*
Admire the splendid **view**★ of Bonaguil Castle in its lovely green setting (*parking*).

St-Martin-le-Redon

This charming village is known for the St-Martial mineral spring, reputed to cure skin ailments.

▶ *Leave St-Martin on the D 673 towards Gourdon.*

Montcabrier

The *bastide* was founded in 1297 by Guy de Cabrier, who gave it his name. It was granted a charter of franchises by Philip the Fair. Overlooking the square, several old houses (including the 16C house of the king's court) are laid out in the regular pattern of the original plan. The church, partly rebuilt in the 14C, has a Flamboyant doorway (restored) surrounded by a fine open-bayed bell-tower. Inside, a plain 14C statue of St Louis, the parish's patron saint, is surrounded by ex-votos. This statue was the object of a local pilgrimage.

▶ *Drive SE along the D 68 and turn right onto the D 58 1km/0.6mi further on.*

Duravel

The 11C **church** (*keys available from the tourist office*) has historiated capitals decorating the chancel. There is an archaic crypt supported by columns with rough-hewn capitals. The bodies of St Hilarion, St Poémon and St Agathon lie buried at the back of the apse.
The ostension, or solemn exhibition of relics to the faithful, is held every five years.

▶ *Drive S along the D 911.*

Puy-l'Évêque

Guided tours of the church by advance appointment at the church office, pl. du Rampeau, L'Abbé Charpentier, 46700 Puy-l'Évêque.

This small town, which took its present name (*évêque* – bishop) when it came under the lordship of the bishops of Cahors, occupies one of the most picturesque sites in the valley downstream from Cahors; from the far side of the bridge into town, admire the old houses in golden stone.
The **church** was built on the north-east side of the town, at the furthest point in the defence system of which it was itself a part. In front of the church stands a massive belfry-porch flanked by a turret and buttresses. The magnificent doorway is surmounted by a pediment adorned with statues. The nave was built in the 14C and 15C and ends in a polygonal apse. In the churchyard there are many old tombs, and on the left of the church stands a wayside cross ornamented with archaic-style sculpture.

▶ *Walk back towards place du Rampeau and place du Mercadiel. Beyond Grande-Rue is a maze of twisting lanes clinging to the promontory.*

The **keep**, all that remains of the Episcopal castle, dates back to the 13C.
From the **Esplanade de la Truffière**, next to the keep, admire the terraces and hillsides covered with vines, and the wide alluvial valley carpeted with fields.

▶ *Drive N out of Puy-l'Évêque along the D 28.*

Martignac

This small village boasts a fine rustic **church**, built of yellow stone and surmounted by a timber-framed bell-tower. The nave and chancel are decorated with 15C frescoes: realistic representations of the capital sins contrast with scenes depicting the Coronation of the Virgin Mary and the arrival of the chosen in Paradise, led by St Michael and welcomed by St Peter. Note the Deposition and a group of angels decorating the chancel.

▶ *Return to Puy-l'Évêque then follow the D 911 back to Luzech along the north bank of the Lot.*

Site de la MADELEINE★

MICHELIN LOCAL MAP 329: H-6 – LOCAL MAP SEE LES-EYZIES-DE-TAYAC

The location of the site of La Madeleine (*access from Les Eyzies via Tursac and the bridge to L'Espinasse*) **stands out very clearly, from the point where the wooded plateau meets the Vézère's alluvial plain below. The terrain is formed by the river's narrowest and most distinctly shaped meander. On the rock above stand the remains of a medieval castle, built in the 13C and abandoned in the 17C.**

Visit

Troglodyte Village

🕐☎⌂*Open Jul-Aug, guided tour (1hr), 9.30am-7pm; Sep-Jun, 10am-6pm.* ∞*5€ (child: 3€).* ☎ *05 53 46 36 88.*

Located midway up the cliff, this village was probably occupied from the end of the 10C (Viking invasions) to the 20C. The village consists of some 20 dwellings carved out of the rock near a spring and protected by a narrow fortified entrance; about 100 people could live there, both during troubled times and times of peace. A chapel consecrated to St Mary Magdalene, which was enlarged and had ogive vaulting added to it in the 15C, gave the site its name.

At the foot of the cliff lies the **prehistoric deposit** which established the characteristics of the Magdalenian culture; this culture predominated during the last 60 centuries of the Upper Paleolithic Age (15000-9000 BC). The richness and quality of the items discovered by Lartet and Peyrony in 1863 (for example the ivory plaque of an engraved mammoth) is remarkable. The majority of the objects are exhibited in the museums at Les Eyzies and St-Germain-en-Laye, west of Paris.

Cliff dwellings at the site de la Madeleine

J. Damase/ MICHELIN

MARCILHAC-SUR-CÉLÉ

POPULATION 194

MICHELIN LOCAL MAP 337: G-4 – LOCAL MAP SEE FIGEAC

Marcilhac is built in the centre of an amphitheatre of cliffs in the enchanting Célé Valley. Interesting old houses surround the ruins of a Benedictine abbey.

▶ **Orient Yourself**: The village is located halfway between Cahors to the west and Figeac to the east.

⊚ **Don't Miss**: The ruins of the Benedictine abbey.

⟳ **Also See**: Cahors; Figeac; St-Cirq-Lapopie.

A Bit of History

An eventful past – In the 11C the modest sanctuary of Rocamadour was under the care of Marcilhac Abbey, which let it fall into ruins. Noticing this negligence some monks from Tulle installed themselves in the sanctuary. However, in 1166 the discovery of the body of St Amadour turned the sanctuary into a rich and famous pilgrimage centre. Marcilhac recalled its rights and

expelled the Tulle monks. Soon afterwards the abbot of Tulle threw out the Marcilhac monks and again occupied Rocamadour. Lawsuits were filed fast and furiously. The case was acrimonious, and the bishop of Cahors, the papal legate, the archbishop of Bourges, even the Pope himself, were all called on to give judgement, but avoided reaching a decision; finally, after 100 years of squabbling, Marcilhac accepted an indemnity of 3 000 sols and relinquished its claim to Rocamadour.

Marcilhac Abbey flourished until the 14C, but during the Hundred Years War it was virtually destroyed by marauding bands of Englishmen and French mercenary troops. After the Reformation, the abbey, a ghost of its former self, fell into the hands of the Hébrards of St-Sulpice; the monks had to give up the monastic way of life and be put up in local people's homes. The abbey church was secularised in 1764.

Visit

Old Abbey

The abbey church is made up of two very distinct parts:

Romanesque section – The west porch and the first three bays of the nave are open to the sky. They are flanked by a tall square tower, which was probably fortified in the 14C. A round-arched door on the south side is topped with sculpture forming a **tympanum** and depicting the Last Judgement: Christ in Majesty, with figures on either side, thought to be representing the sun and moon, appears above St Peter, St Paul and two thick-set angels with open wings. These carvings are archaic in style, obviously reflecting the decor of gold and silverwork, and would appear to date from the 10C.

▶ *Go through this doorway and enter the church to the right.*

Gothic section – This part of the church, closed to the west from the fourth bay on, dates from the 15C and is built in the Flamboyant style. The chancel has stellar vaulting and is encircled by an ambulatory. A Baroque stall decorated with the Hébrard family crest has a fabulous **misericord** (a hinged shelf which supports someone standing) carved with the head of an angel. A chapel on the left of the chancel has 15C frescoes: Christ giving Blessing with the Twelve Apostles; under each Apostle is his name and a phrase which characterises him. The coat of arms in the centre of each triad is that of the Hébrards of St-Sulpice.

▶ *On leaving the church, turn right (from the second Romanesque bay) onto the path to the chapter-house.*

Chapter house – The 12C building has very delicate Romanesque capitals alternately made of grey-blue limestone and rose-coloured stalagmite stone.

▶ *Go towards an esplanade shaded by plane trees; a round tower marks the site of the abbot's house. By the banks of the Célé (right), the line of the rampart wall is interrupted by a postern. Return to the Romanesque ruins.*

MARCILLAC-LA-CROISILLE

POPULATION 778

MICHELIN LOCAL MAP 329: N-4

This small village, built on a granite plateau, grew at the point where Roman roads once converged. This peaceful holiday resort is situated near the Barrage de La Vallette and the Barrage de Meyrignac, both of which offer a range of leisure activities, including swimming and sailing.

▶ **Orient Yourself**: The village is situated 27km/17mi to the east of Tulle.

🕐 **Organising Your Time**: Allow half a day to explore the nearby Dordogne valley.

🚲 **Don't Miss**: A boat trip on the Dordogne; Barrage de l'Aigle.

👣 **Also See**: Gimel-les-Cascades; Tulle.

Visit

Barrage de La Valette
5km/3mi SW along the D 131E2.
The River Doustre goes through a gorge on its way to join the Dordogne near Argentat. Walk along the top of the dam for a fine view of the reservoir framed by hills over a distance of 8km/5mi.

Château de Sédières
7km/4.5mi W along the D 978 and D 135 E. 🕐 *Open Jun-Sep, unaccompanied visit (last entrance 45min before closing), 10am-noon and 2-7pm (*👣*guided tours possible); rest of the year, please enquire.* ⊚*3€ (child: 1.50€).* ☎ *05 55 27 76 40.*

This elegant Renaissance château stands in a pleasant setting near a waterfall. It comprises the fortified gatehouse, the main building and the high square keep. The main façade is crowned with machicolations in striking contrast with the large windows and their pediments decorated with scallops. Inside, note the carved fire-places of the reception rooms and the vaulting with pendentives of the guard-room.

Excursions

The Dordogne Valley★
75km/47mi round-trip – allow half a day

▶ *Leave Marcillac travelling NE along the D 978.*

Spontour
🕐 *Excursions operate Apr-Oct (please enquire for times). Three departure points: Pont de Chambon, Pont du Sablier and Beaulieu sur Dordogne.* ⊚*6€ (Pont de Chambon, Pont du Sablier), 5€ (Beaulieu).* ☎ *05 55 28 86 45.*

From the bridge, admire the village where you can still enjoy a taste of the past by boarding a traditional *gabarre* for a trip on the river.

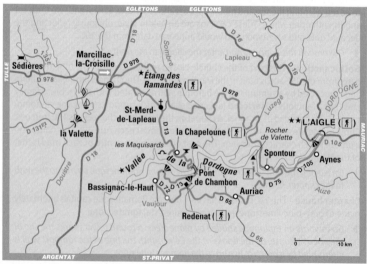

▶ *Cross the Dordogne and turn left onto the D 105.*

Aynes

The granite houses with their slate roofs are grouped round the chapel. The road, which is now laid out as a corniche road, provides views from different angles of the L'Aigle Dam.

Barrage de L'Aigle★★

The dam impresses by its size and the boldness of concept. Two ski-jump flood control gates can let through 4 000m³/880 000gal per second.

Belvédère

▶ *Leave the car opposite the L'Aigle Dam and go on foot up the D 16 to the belvedere built below the dam (the path lies between two road tunnels).*

From the belvedere there is a good **view**★ of the dam as a whole and the valley below it.

▶ *Turn back then left onto the D 75 just before the Spontour Bridge.*

The road climbs and offers fine glimpses of the River Dordogne and the village of Spontour.

🚶 As you come out of a bend, note the parking area and viewpoint, which is the starting point of a pleasant walk (*1hr 30min there and back*) to the **Rocher de la Valette**.

Auriac

The church of this charming village contains a 17C carved-wood crozier.

▶ *Drive W along the D 65 towards St-Merd-de-Lapleau then turn onto the road on the left of the calvary (opposite the cemetery).*

Redenat

🚶 This is the starting point of two pleasant walks (*marked paths*) through woodland. The first leads to a prehistoric **standing stone**; the second (*to the east*) leads down to a **waterfall** near the Chambon Bridge.

▶ *Continue along the road to the D 72 via Vaujour.*

Bassignac-le-Haut

Near the church stands a 16C limestone wayside cross; the four sides of the shaft are carved with scenes from the life of Jesus.

From the **belvedere**★ situated to the north of the village (D 13), you can appreciate a meander of the Dordogne; the road to Chapeloune offers other fine views.

Pont de Chambon

This is the ideal place for a break, particularly for anglers; boat trips aboard a traditional gabarre are available.

▶ *Continue along the D 13 on the opposite bank.*

La Chapeloune

Two walks offering fine views start nearby.

Viewing table – 🚶 *To the S, 30min there and back from the D 13*. A forest road leads down to a clearing affording a splendid view of the Chastang reservoir and the Cantal mountain range.

Grotte des Maquisards

🚶 *To the N, 1hr 30min there and back starting from the parking area (D 13)*.

Enjoy this typical scrubland and the fine view but beware, the last 200m/220yd to the cave are only suitable for experienced hikers.

St-Merd-de-Lapleau

Note the shape of the belfry-porch of the church with its row of four bays, each fitted with a bell.

▶ *Continue along the road running alongside the church.*

Étang des Ramandes★

🚶 This is the ideal place for relaxing or taking a walk (*2hr*) through the 260ha/642-acre forest planted with pines and spruce.

▶ *Rejoin the road which leads back to Marcillac-la-Croisille.*

MARTEL ★

POPULATION 1 467

MICHELIN LOCAL MAP 337: F-2 – LOCAL MAP SEE VALLÉE DE LA DORDOGNE

Martel built on the Upper Quercy causse to which it has given its name (Causse de Martel) is known as the town of the seven towers. It still contains many medieval buildings. Today fine foods are part of its reputation: it is a central market for walnuts, and small industries process and preserve local gourmet products.

▶ **Orient Yourself**: Martel is located 15km/9.5mi east of Souillac and 20km/12mi north of Rocamadour.

◉ **Don't Miss**: Places des Consuls; Hôtel de la Raymondie.

🅺 **Especially for Kids**: Reptiland.

◔ **Also See**: Collonges-la-Rouge; Gouffre de Padirac; Souillac; Rocamadour; Turenne.

A Bit of History

The three hammers – After stopping the Saracens at Poitiers in 732, **Charles Martel** chased them into Aquitaine. Several years later he struck again and wiped them out. To commemorate this victory over the infidels and to give thanks to God, Charles Martel had a church built on the spot; soon a town grew up around the church. It was given the name of Martel in memory of its founder and took as its crest three hammers, which were the favourite weapons of the saviour of Christianity.

Martel and the Viscounty of Turenne – The founding of Martel by the conqueror of the infidels is probably based more on fiction than on fact. However, it is known that the viscounts of Turenne made Martel an important urban community as early as the

---

Address Book

For coin ranges, see the Legend at the back of the guide.

EATING OUT

🍴 **Ferme-Auberge Le Moulin à Huile de Noix** – *Rte de Bretenoux - 3km/1.9mi E of Martel on the D 803 - ☎ 05 65 37 40 69 - closed 11 Nov-25 Mar and Mon - 🍴 - reserv. required.* Enjoy a delicious meal in the unique setting of this 17C walnut-oil mill. On Tuesday and Thursday afternoons visitors can learn how oil was once pressed according to traditional methods. Small shop selling products made on the property.

🍴 **Au Vieux Four** – *Av. Augustin-Garcia - 46110 Les Quatre-Routes - 8km/5mi NE of Martel on the D 96 - ☎ 05 65 32 01 98 - closed Mon - reserv. required Sat and Sun.* A warm welcome awaits in this small, simply decorated restaurant. A refined menu with dishes based on high-quality fresh ingredients. In winter, enjoy home-made bread baked in the impressive oven. Five recently renovated rooms are also available.

WHERE TO STAY

🛏 **Chambre d'hôte Cabrejou** – *46600 St-Denis-lès-Martel - 3km/1.9mi E of Martel on the D 703 - ☎ 05 65 37 31 89 - 🍴 - 7 rooms.* This attractive farm, which grows tobacco and walnuts, also offers a handful of plain but comfortable rooms, some of which are located in the annex. Pleasant garden. Meals available during the tourist season.

🛏 **Chambre d'hôte La Cour au Tilleul** – *Av. du Capitani - ☎ 05 65 37 34 08 - 🍴 - 3 rooms.* An attractive B&B whose façade dates from the 12C. Cosy rooms all have character. In fine weather, enjoy a hearty breakfast in the lovely inner courtyard, beneath the shade of the lime tree *(tilleul)*.

SHOPPING

Markets and fairs – Traditional market under the *halle* on Wednesdays and Saturday mornings. Walnut market in July. Truffle market in December and January. Wool fair on 23 July.

Chemin de Fer Touristique du Haut-Quercy "Le Truffadou" – *Steam train: Sun and public hols, Apr to end of Sep and Wed in Jul and Aug, departures at 11am, 2.30pm and 4pm; diesel train: Jul and Aug, Mon, Tue, Thu and Fri, departures at 11am, 2.30pm and 4pm; Apr-Jun and Sep, Tue and Thu, 2.30pm - ☎ 05 65 37 35 81.* This rail line runs from Martel to St-Denis-près-Martel, along cliffs 80m/250ft above the valley. A great way of discovering the Dordogne, its châteaux, and the history and culture of the area. Guided commentary (approx. 1hr).

12C. In 1219, Viscount Raymond IV granted a charter establishing Martel as a free town – exempt from the king's taxes, and with permission to mint money. However the town stayed faithful to the king. Very quickly Martel established a town council and consulate and thus became the seat of the royal bailiwick and of the seneschalship. It established a court of appeal which handled all the region's judicial matters; more than 50 magistrates, judges and lawyers were employed. It reached its peak at the end of the 13C and beginning of the 14C. Like the rest of the region, the town suffered during the Hundred Years War – batted backwards and forwards between English and French rule – and during the Wars of Religion – pillaged by the Huguenots. In 1738, when the rights of Turenne were sold to the king (👉 see TURENNE), Martel lost its privileges and became a mere castellany.

The rebellious son – At the end of the 12C, Martel was the scene of a tragic series of events which brought into conflict **Henry II Plantagenet**, king of England and lord of all western France, his wife **Eleanor of Aquitaine** and their four sons. The royal household was a royal hell. Henry could no longer stand the sight of Eleanor, and shut her up in a tower. The sons thereupon took up arms against their father, and the eldest, **Henry Short Coat**, pillaged the viscounty of Turenne and Quercy. To punish him, Henry Plantagenet gave his lands to his third son, Richard the Lion Heart, and stopped the allowance paid to his eldest son. Henry Short Coat found himself penniless, surrounded and in an altogether desperate situation: to pay his foot-soldiers he plundered the treasure houses of the provincial abbeys. He took from Rocamadour the shrine and the precious stones of St Amadour, whose body was profaned, and he sold Roland's famous sword Durandal. But as he was leaving Rocamadour after this sacrilegious act, the bell miraculously began to toll: it was a sign from God.

Henry fled to Martel and arrived there with a fever; he felt death to be upon him and was stricken with remorse. He confessed his crimes while Henry II was sent for, to come and forgive his son on his death bed; the King was at the siege of Limoges and sent a messenger with his pardon. The messenger found Henry Short Coat lying in agony on a bed of cinders, a heavy wooden cross upon his chest. Shortly afterwards he died, a last farewell to his mother Eleanor on his lips.

Walking Tour

Former perimeter walls

Wide avenues, fossé des Cordeliers and boulevard du Capitani, have been built on the site of the old ramparts (12C-13C). The machicolated **Tournemire Tower**, which used to be the prison tower, and the Souillac and Brive Gateways (found at the end of Route de Souillac and rue de Brive; *not on the town plan*) hark back to the time when

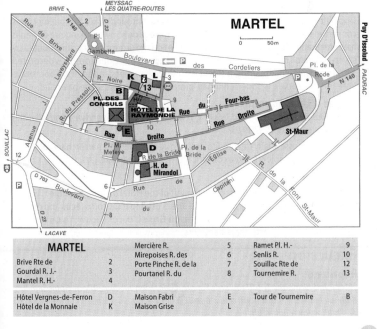

MARTEL		Mercière R.	5	Ramet Pl. H.-	9
		Mirepoises R. des		Senlis R.	10
Brive Rte de	2	Porte Pinche R. de la	7	Souillac Rte de	12
Gourdal R. J.-	3	Pourtanel R. du	8	Tournemire R.	13
Mantel R. H.-	4				

| Hôtel Vergnes-de-Ferron | D | Maison Fabri | E | Tour de Tournemire | B |
| Hôtel de la Monnaie | K | Maison Grise | L | | |

Martel was a fortified town, well protected by double perimeter walls. The second perimeter wall, built in the 18C, enclosed the suburbs.

▶ *Leave the car in the car park along the north wall. Pass between the post office and the Tournemire Tower to enter the old town.*

Rue du Four-Bas

There are still some Renaissance houses along this street, which is spanned by an archway.

▶ *Follow the street towards place de la Rode.*

Église St-Maur

This Gothic church (13C-16C) has some interesting defensive features; huge buttresses converted into defence towers, machicolations protecting the flat east end and a 40m/131ft-high bell-tower which looks more like a keep.

Beneath the porch is a fine historiated Romanesque **tympanum** depicting the Last Judgement. It shows Christ seated, His head adorned with a cruciform halo, His arms stretched wide to show His wounds; two angels hold the instruments of the Passion while two others sound the trumpets of the Resurrection. The width of the nave is striking. The chancel with its stellar vaulting is lit by a large 16C **stained-glass window** showing God the Father, the four Evangelists and scenes from the Passion.

▶ *Return to the town centre via rue Droite.*

Rue Droite

There are old town houses all along this road, one of which, Hôtel Vergnes-de-Ferron, is adorned with a lovely Renaissance door.

▶ *From place de la Bride, take rue de la Bride.*

Hôtel de Mirandol

This 15C town house features a great square tower with a spiral staircase.

▶ *Rue de la Bride leads to place M.-Meteye; turn right then left.*

Maison Fabri

The tower, called Court-Mantel after Henry Short Coat since he died here in 1183, has windows with frontons decorated with balls at the intersections of their cornices on all five floors.

Place des Consuls★

In the centre of the square is the 18C **covered market**. The timbering is supported on great stone pillars. On one side the old town measures can be seen.

Hôtel de la Raymondie★

Once the fortress of the viscounts of Turenne, built around 1280, this building was converted into a Gothic mansion in the 14C. The **façade**★ overlooking rue de Senlis has remarkable apertures; a row of ogive arches on the ground floor is surmounted by seven quatrefoil rose windows. The main entrance on place des Consuls is decorated with the town's coat of arms, a shield with three hammers. In the first-floor rooms note the two carved wooden chimney-pieces and the Renaissance bas-relief.

Musée d'Uxellodunum

⏱*Open Jul-Aug, 9am-noon and 3-6pm.* ⏱ *Closed Sun, public hols and weekend following 15 Aug.* ⌔1€. ☎ 05 65 37 30 03.

This museum, essentially devoted to prehistoric and Gallo-Roman archaeology, also houses medieval objects and a collection of 17C-18C chemist's jars.

Rue Tournemire

This attractive little street leads off to the left of the Hôtel de la Raymondie. The 13C **Hôtel de la Monnaie** with intersecting turrets used to mint coins (écus and denier) for the viscounty of Turenne. The 16C **Maison Grise** is decorated with a carved bust and a heraldic shield with three hammers.

Excursion

Reptiland

2km/1.2mi along the N 140 towards Figeac. ⏱ ♿*Open Jul-Aug, 10am-6pm; Sep-Jun, daily except Mon, 10am-noon and 2-6pm.* ⏱ *Closed Jan.* ⌔ *6.50€ (child: 4€).* ☎05 65 37 41 00. www.reptiland.fr.

Kids 92 species of snakes, lizards, crocodiles, tortoises etc. Explanatory panels provide information about their natural environment and their feeding and breeding habit. The owner, Pancho Gouygou, tries to show the peaceful disposition of his guests rather than their dangerous or spectacular side. He even claims to be able to cure anyone suffering from a morbid fear of snakes!

MEHUN-SUR-YÈVRE ★

POPULATION 7 212

MICHELIN LOCAL MAP 323: J-4

This charming old town on the banks of the River Yèvre and the Berry Canal is a centre of porcelain manufacture. Jean de Berry's castle, where Joan of Arc met the King of France, towers above the river.

▶ **Orient Yourself**: Mehun is situated 13km/8mi northwest of Bourges and 17km/10.5mi southeast of Vierzon.

🕐 **Organising Your Time**: Allow an hour or two to explore the Fôret d'Allogny and half a day to tour the Reuilly-Quincy vineyards.

😊 **Don't Miss**: Mehun's old town.

🕯 **Also See**: Bourges; Vierzon.

A Bit of History

Mehun's Golden Age – The third son of King John the Good, **Duke Jean de Berry** (1340-1416) was a lavish patron of the arts and admirer of the art of manuscript illumination. He rebuilt Mehun Castle in 1386 and it was here amid a brilliant court that he welcomed writers such as Froissart, miniaturists like the Limbourg brothers and André Beauneveu. The latter, who was also a sculptor and architect, worked for a lengthy period at the castle. The Duke was on friendly terms with them all and often invited them to visit his menagerie or his luxurious bath pavilion. Duke Jean de Berry left the castle to his grand-nephew Charles VII, who received Joan of Arc here in the winter of 1429 and 1430.

Visit

Porte de l'Horloge

A 14C gateway (restored) at the top of rue Jeanne-d'Arc.

Rue Jeanne-d'Arc

This street leads down towards the Yèvre between old houses which sometimes have wells in front of them. No 87, the house where Joan of Arc stayed, has elegant bays with trilobed arches; to the left is the esplanade leading to the castle.

Jardin du Duc-Jean-de-Berry

Fine views can be had of the public washing boards and a 12C watermill. A shaded promenade running alongside the Berry Canal affords views of the castle and church.

Pôle de la Porcelaine

🕐♿ *Open Jul-Aug, 10am-noon and 2-6pm; May-Jun and Sep, daily except Mon, 2-6pm; Mar-Apr and Oct, Sat-Sun and public hols, 2-6pm.* 🕐 *Closed Nov-Mar.* 🚌 *4.55€ (under 10 years old: no charge).* ☎ *02 48 57 06 19.*

Near the castle, a glass building displays fine porcelain items, both rare and unusual (china, a 1900 fountain, a pedestal table, a funerary plaque etc). A 10min *son et lumière* show illustrates the transformation of kaolin into porcelain.

Musée Charles VII

🕐⚔ *Guided tours. Same opening times and charges as the Pôle de la Porcelaine.*

Of this marvellous fairy tale castle, visited and admired by Claus Sluter and Holbein, sculptor and painter respectively, there remain two round towers, one of which is named after Charles VII (extensively restored). Vaulting springers and some of the chimney-pieces can still be seen. The original plan of the castle is still visible – note the position of the bastion jutting out like a spur towards the river. A miniature of the

Address Book

For coin ranges, see the Legend at the back fo the guide.

EATING OUT

Les Abiès – *86 av. Jean-Chatelet - ☎ 02 48 57 39 31 - les.abies@wanadoo.fr - ⏰ closed 23 Feb-17 Mar, 29 Jul-6 Aug, 20-29 Oct, evenings (except Fri and Sat) and Mon.* This elegant residence nestled at the heart of a garden planted with trees is embellished with a terrace and a spacious contemporary dining room with a maritime feel (fresco and live lobster tank). A good choice of reasonably priced traditional dishes.

WHERE TO STAY

Chambre d'hôte Villemenard – *18500 Vignoux-sur-Barangeon - 6km/4mi N of Méhun. Take the D 79 towards Vouzeron - ☎ 02 48 51 53 40 / 06 72 79 79 37 - villmenard@wanadoo.fr - ⊠ - 6 rooms.* The surrounding lakes, river and park planted with old trees add to the charm of this imposing 19C property. Entrance decorated with elegant painted tiles, spacious and comfortable rooms, and a lounge with billiard table. Two self-catering gîtes separate from the main building are also available for rent.

SHOPPING

Magasin d'usine Pillivuyt – *Allée de la Manufacture - ☎ 02 48 67 31 63.* ⏰ Open Tue-Fri, 10am-noon and 2.30-6.30pm; Sat, 10am-12.30pm and 2.30-7pm - ⏰ closed public hols. This factory outlet sells white and coloured porcelain sets and kitchen items.

Porcelaines Deshoulières – *5 r. Louis-Grandjean - 6km/4mi NW of Mehun on the D 60 - 18500 Foëcy - ☎ 02 48 53 04 55.*

Domaine des Bruniers – *Rte de Lury - 18120 Quincy - ☎ 02 48 51 34 10 -* ⏰ open by prior arrangement. The expressive and intense white wines produced on a plateau alongside the River Cher are made from Sauvignon grapes and sold under the Quincy appellation.

Domaine Bernard Aujard – *2 r. du Bas-Bourg - 4km/2.4mi outside of Reuilly - 18120 Lazenay - ☎ 02 48 51 73 69 -* ⏰ open daily, 8am-noon and 2-7pm - ⏰ closed Sun afternoons and afternoons of public hols. The wines sold here are part of the Reuilly appellation. The estate's most renowned product is a fruity rosé produced from pinot gris grapes.

duke of Berry's *Très Riches Heures* (Rich Hours) now in the Condé museum of Chantilly (north of Paris), executed by the Limbourg brothers, shows the castle as it existed in the 15C. Dismantled in the 17C the castle slowly fell into ruins. Excavations have revealed that more than 10 castles were built on the site between the 10C and the 15C.

Collégiale Notre-Dame

The construction of this church, Romanesque in style with the exception of the chapel added in the 15C, started with the chancel (11C) which has a horseshoe shape. The façade is preceded by a belfry-porch ornamented on the north side by a cross interlacing, in the centre of which is the Holy Lamb.

At the entrance to the nave, on the left beside the baptismal font, is a 15C relics cupboard, which was fitted in the 17C with a carved wooden door representing the Education of the Virgin. In the northern mart of the nave, there is a Crucifixion painted by Jean Boucher from Bourges, the master of Mignard. There are also modern ceramic stations of the cross.

Excursions

Forêt d'Allogny

Round trip of 40km/25mi – allow 1hr

▶ *Leave Mehun along the D 79 N.*

Note *La Pierre de Lu*, a great conglomerate made up of flint nodules, to the right of the road.

▶ *Turn right to Allouis and left onto the D 20 to Allogny.*

This wooded massif, a dark mass on the plateau which acts as a watershed, dominates the Cher and Barageon valleys. This densely forested area is mainly composed of oaks with isolated clumps of Norwegian pines, hornbeams, birch and beech.

The D 56 between Allogny and St-Martin-d'Auxigny traverses the forest. From the slope reaching down to St-Martin there is a fine view of the smiling and fertile Moulon Valley, a striking contrast to the dark and mysterious forest.

▶ *Return to Mehun via the D 68.*

Reuilly-Quincy Vineyards
Round trip of 62km/39mi – allow half a day

▷ *Drive S out of Mehun along the D 35 to Ste-Thorette and turn right onto the D 23 then left onto the D 114 towards Plou.*

Jardin Conservatoire de Plantes Aromatiques et Tinctoriales du Prieuré de Manzay

🕐 ✆ *Open Jul-Aug, daily except Tue, 3-7pm; May-Jun and Sep-Oct, Sat-Sun, 3-7pm.* 5€ *(-12 years old: no charge).* ☎ *02 48 57 34 53.*

Situated on the edge of the Font-Moreau woods, this garden occupies more than 1ha/2.5 acres of the grounds of St-Laurent-de-Manzay priory founded in the 13C. It contains all the main plants used for seasoning and dyeing since prehistoric times.

▷ *Continue along the D 114.*

Chârost

The origins of this hamlet go back to the Bronze Age. In Antiquity and the Middle Ages, Chârost enjoyed prosperity, as witnessed in the remains of its feudal castle, the defensive wall (northern gateway to the city) and especially its church.

Église St-Michel – *Apply in advance to the town hall.* This abbey church is a vast Romanesque edifice (12C), built of ferrous limestone. A wide nave, the timber framework dating from the 19C, leads to a hemispherical sanctuary: the transept and apsidal chapels have vanished. Note the high, narrow arch joining the chancel to the nave (northern side), typical of churches in the Berry. The capitals in the chancel are enlivened with human and animal figures.

Outside, above the entrances, a large cross with an intertwining motif supports the Pascal Lamb.

Go round the building and into the **cemetery**. From there, observe the apse and the wealth of carved ornamentation, as well as the marks left by the former arms of the transept and the apse (among the admirable capitals, look for the harpy – half woman, half bird – bearing a wheel).

▷ *Leave Chârost W on the D 2.*

Diou

This well-groomed village on the banks of the Théols is a pleasant stopover. Near the pretty church of St-Clément (13C), a lawn rolls down to the water's edge, where a mill straddles the river, with a dovecot alongside.

▷ *Leave Diou travelling N on the D 918 towards Mehun.*

Château de la Ferté

⚷ *Not open to visitors.*
This is a lovely classical manor with four corner towers, dating from 1659.

Reuilly

This village is known for its wines (*Appellation d'Origine Contrôlée*), grown in vineyards spreading over the *départements* of Indre and Cher. Along the banks of the Théols and the Auron, 132ha/326 acres from Lury to Diou (Preuilly alone is isolated to the east) produce mostly white wine from Sauvignon grapes.

▷ *Drive E along the D 20 towards Mehun.*

Quincy

The vineyards of Quincy and Brinay spread over 180ha/445 acres on the west bank of the River Cher. They produce one of the most distinctive white wines of the Loire region: very dry, crisp without being sharp, with a fairly high alcohol content, it is at its best during the first two years.

Château de MEILLANT★★

MICHELIN LOCAL MAP 323: L-6 – LOCAL MAP SEE ST-AMAND-MONTROND

The Château de Meillant, half-hidden by trees in its park, reveals the beauties of its architecture only a little at a time; the plain front seems, by contrast, to enhance the elegance and rich decoration of the east façade which is adorned with all the beauty of line of the Late Gothic period graced by Italian influence.

▸ **Orient Yourself**: The castle is located 7.5km/4.5mi north of St-Amand-Montrond and 39km/24mi south of Bourges.

🕐 **Organising Your Time**: Allow a full day to explore the Célé and Lot valleys.

😋 **Don't Miss**: A guided visit inside the castle.

👣 **Also See**: St-Amand-Montrond; Bourges.

A Bit of History

The Amboise family – Pierre of Amboise obtained the Meillant lands by his marriage in 1453. His son, Charles I, wished to modernise the castle which was a massive structure flanked by high towers. But death came and to his grand-son, Charles II, fell the honour of completing the work on the château. Charles II was to become grand-master, marshal and admiral of France. As governor of Milan, Charles II made such gains in Italy that he was able to complete the work planned for Meillant and also that for Chaumont in the Loire Valley.

Louis XII wrote to Charles II: "I came to see you in your château of Meillant, but you were not home. I got bogged down in the mud, and the devil take me if I ever return." Fortunately, the roads in these wetlands have been upgraded since then!

In the 18C, the property passed onto the Béthune-Charost family, and in the 19C to the Mortemarts. Among the famous Mortemart ancestors in the 17C were Marie-Madeleine, abbess of Fontevrault and Françoise Athénaïs, Marquise de Montespan and the mother of eight children by Louis XIV. The château was entirely restored in 1842.

Visit

🕐 Open Jul-Aug, guided tours (45min), 9.30am-6pm; May-Jun and Sep, 9.30am-noon and 2-6pm; rest of the year, 9.30am-noon and 2-5.30pm. ⏺7€ (child: 5€). ☎ 02 48 63 32 05.

Exterior

The feudal character of the château can now only be seen in the southern front. The towers, though stripped of their watch-paths, still stand guard with narrow loopholes.

The east façade is very different and approaches the château of the Loire in the richness of its decoration: two staircase turrets jut out from the main building and seem to have concentrated in them all the exuberance of the last blaze of the flowery Gothic style. The pierced balustrade running at the base of the eaves, the carved dormer windows, the chimneys ornamented with flamboyantly decorated balustrades are all overshadowed by the incredibly intricate decoration of the Lion's Tower by Giocondo, one of Michelangelo's assistants.

This tower, which owes its name to the lion, cast in lead, on its topmost lantern turret, strikes the onlooker by the close juxtaposition of contrasting carvings: twisted small columns, hearts entwined, mono-

The Lion's Tower

E. Larribère/MICHELIN

grams and crests with interlaced C's – the initials of Charles of Amboise – mountains on fire, the emblem of the château of Chaumont (*chaud mont* means hot mountain), and figures looking out of false windows as at Jacques Cœur's Palace in Bourges. A pretty 16C well and an elegant chapel of the same period, with buttresses topped by pinnacles, complete this harmonious group of buildings.

Interior

Among the rooms containing remarkable furniture and furnishings are: the main dining hall (*Grand Salle à manger*), where the walls are covered in Cordoba leather; the great salon (*Grand Salon*), where a beautiful chimney-piece is surmounted by a balcony once used as a musician's gallery. Note the 17C tapestries brought from Bruges and a portrait of Charles VII, long attributed to Clouet, hanging next to one of *La Montespan*, Louis XIV's favourite, and the Smyrna carpet. Beyond the library, replete with rare books and overlooking the chapel, is the so-called **Cardinal d'Amboise Bed Chamber**, perhaps the loveliest room in the château. Note the splendid 17C Flemish furnishings, tortoise shell encrusted with ivory; a wooden **statue** from Germany dated 1568, representing God the Father welcoming His Son. The Protestant origins of the statue recall the visit of Calvin in 1529. The final rooms on the tour are the Louis XII room with its chimney-piece and Aubusson tapestry and the guard-room, also hung with tapestries (17C Flemish) and arms. The recumbent figure represents François de Rochechouart-Mortemart.

In the courtyard, visit the **chapel**: interesting 16C stained glass; above the altar is an altarpiece of the Rhenish School on painted and gilded wood, depicting scenes from the Passion.

Tours de MERLE★★

MICHELIN LOCAL MAP 329: N-5 – LOCAL MAP SEE ARGENTAT

The remains of this feudal fortress stand on a spur surrounded by a meander of the River Maronne.

▶ **Orient Yourself**: For a wonderful view of the **ruins**★★, approach the Tours de Merle from the north, park by the side of a bend in the road and walk along a path to the viewpoint, nestled amid lush vegetation.

A Bit of History

An Impregnable lair – At the juncture of Auvergne and Limousin, the site was an obvious choice for defensive purposes. The promontory (200×40m/656×131ft) rises 30m/98ft above the river, and sits 150m/492ft below the high plateau. This type of border fortress takes best advantage of the lay of the land; it is, in theory, inaccessible, and commands a vast area around itself.

The lords of Merle were the most feared in the region in the Middle Ages and the family jealously guarded this the surest of strongholds.

Alongside the 11C castle rose the castles of the younger sons until by the 14C the Merle domain was divided into seven. During the Hundred Years War the English managed to force the stronghold to surrender in 1371 but gave it back at the request of Pope Gregory XI. The advent of artillery changed the fortune of this fortress which could be bombarded from neighbouring heights; made vulnerable, the old fortresses were one by one abandoned.

Tower Tour

🕐 *Open Jul-Aug, 10am-6pm; May-Jun and Sep, 2-6pm; Feb-Apr and Oct-Nov, Sun, public and schools hols, 2-6pm.* ✆*Prices not reported (under 8 years old: no charge). ☎ 05 55 28 22 31 or 05 55 28 27 67. www.st-geniez-o-merle.com.*

Merle is made up of a series of seven castles, like pearls on a rope, strung from north to south. On two terraces, three distinct units in various states of disrepair can be distinguished, made up of keeps, towers, and main buildings dating from the 12C through the 15C.

EATING OUT

🍽 **La Vieille Auberge** – *19220 St-Geniez-Ô-Merle - 5km/3mi NW of Les Tours de Merle via D 111 - ☎ 05 55 28 20 60 -* 🕐 *closed Jan, Mon eve and Tue.* Located a few miles from the medieval site, this charming country inn built in the early 20C is a pleasant rural stopover. Simple decor and regional cuisine including cabécou (the local goat's cheese), magret and confit de canard. Swimming pool.

B. Kaufmann/MICHELIN

The fortress

The entrance is on the northern side. After passing through the vestiges of the chapel of St-Léger, visitors enter the old castle of Hugues and Fulcon de Merle, which occupies the highest point of the site: Romanesque keep (*terrace access*) and main buildings. The second section is made up of two square towers with castellated crowns, on the far end of the platform: the Noailles and Pesteils towers. From the top of the second tower, there is a good view over the whole site. A mysterious and magical air floats around the impressive façades broken into bits, fireplaces suspended in mid-air, stairways to nowhere.

MEYMAC

POPULATION 2 627

MICHELIN LOCAL MAP 329: N-2

Perched on the edge of the Millevaches Plateau, Meymac is one of the prettiest villages in Corrèze, its streets and old houses clustered around the old abbey of St-André. In bygone days, the mountain folk came to town to trade their wool, cheese and chestnuts for products manufactured on the plains. Today, forestry is at the forefront of the local economy; a technical school trains future foresters. Rural and rustic, Meymac is an attractive tourist site, in lovely surroundings.

▶ **Orient Yourself**: Meymac is located 49km/30.5mi northeast of Tulle.

🕐 **Organising Your Time**: Allow a full day to explore the Plateau de Millevaches.

😊 **Don't Miss**: The Black Virgin in the abbey church.

👣 **Also See**: Tourbière de Longéroux; Etang des Oussines.

Visit

Old Town

The *vielle ville* is a charming place for a stroll. To the left of the church, an early-19C **covered market**, its framework resting on granite pillars, is set in a square formed by the buildings of the Hôtel-Dieu, erected in 1681.

Follow the street up towards the **clock tower**, which once guarded the castle gate, and discover the sculpted doorways (15C-16C), stair towers with pepper-pot caps, granite houses with steeply sloping slate roofs. Past the clock tower, a fountain embellishes a pretty little square.

Abbey Church

In 1085, Archambaud III founded a Benedictine abbey on the site of a church his forefathers had built.

The church was under construction in the 12C, and was finished in the 13C after modifications to the initial plans were made. There are some unusual aspects to the plans: a deviation of the transept arms, an irregular alignment of the apse and its chapels. The belfry-porch has a multifoil doorway in the Limousin style, an arch on either side. The porch is adorned with Romanesque capitals carved in the archaic style. The nave has ogive vaulting and continues into a chancel which is equally wide. Note a 12C **Black Virgin**★ on the pillar to the left of the chancel. Except for the turban on her head, the statue is typical of Auvergne in the posture and position of the long, protective hands.

Fondation Marius-Vazeilles

🕐 *Open Jul-Sep, 10am-noon and 2-6.30pm; mid-May to Jun and first half of Oct, 2.30-6.30pm, Sat-Sun and public hols, 10am-noon and 2.30-6.30pm.* 🕐 *Closed Tue.* ⊚ *2.30€.* ☎ *05 55 95 19 15 or 05 55 46 19 97.*

Established in a building beside the abbey, the foundation owns interesting archaeological collections illustrating human settlements and life on the Millevaches Plateau from prehistoric times (stone tools) and the Gallo-Roman period (funerary items, vestiges from habitations) to the Middle Ages.

Centre d'Art Contemporain

🕐 *Open Jul-Aug, 10am-1pm and 2-7pm; Sep-Jun, 2-6pm.* 🕐 *Closed Mon and mid-Dec to mid-Feb.* ⊚*4€.* ☎ *05 55 95 23 30.*

In the southern wing of the old cloisters of the abbey of St-André, the art museum presents one-person shows devoted to young artists as well as retrospectives (François Bouillon, 1990, Jesus Rafaël Soto, 1992, Gérard Garouste, 1996) and thematic exhibitions on trends in contemporary art. The monumental sculpture in front of the centre is by Robert Jakobsen.

Excursions

Lac de Sechemailles
2km/1.2mi SW via the D 76.

The road to Tulle goes to Sechemailles Lake (42ha/104 acres), where a large wooded shoreline and various amenities attract holidaymakers.

Douglaseraie des Farges
3km/1.9mi NW via the D 109.

A path starting near the Viaduc des Farges runs through a forest (20ha/49 acres) of conifers rising to a height of 40m/131ft!

Plateau de Millevaches★
98km/61mi round-trip – allow one day

▶ *Leave Meymac travelling N along the D 36.*

Mont Bessou
With the Puy Pendu just across the way, this is the highest point on the plateau (977m/3 205ft). Above the forest, a television transmitter rises; the 67ha/165 acres are now a municipal park. An artificial lake offers a shady resting area. A road goes all the way round the mount.

▶ *Continue to the D 979 and turn towards Bugeat; 3km/1.9mi further on, turn right onto the D 109 to Celle.*

Tourbière du Longéroux★
The source of the Vézère is located in this 255ha/630-acre conservation area. At Le Longéroux, the average thickness of the peat is 2m/6.56ft and the study of fossilised pollen shows that the bog is 8 000 years old. The heath is home to a well-adapted fauna (lizards, vipers, meadow pipits) and the favourite hunting ground of the short-toed eagle. The discreet presence of otters is a sure sign of the quality of the area's fresh-water supply. Three marked paths offer nature lovers the opportunity of exploring this wild area: 200m/220yd there and back, 5km/3mi there and back (yellow markings), 20km/12mi round trip (blue markings).

▶ *Continue to St-Merd-les-Oussines and turn right onto the D 164 towards Millevaches.*

Étang des Oussines★
This site is also the favourite haunt of otters. A path runs round the 15ha/37-acre lake filled with water from the River Vézère.

The Longéroux peat bog

S. Sauvignier/MICHELIN

▶ *Go back to the D 164 and turn right 1.5km/0.9mi further on.*

Église de Chavanac

The small 13C-14C church houses a stone polychrome statue, known as **la Dansarelle**, said to represent Salomé, the bewitching biblical figure who charmed Herod into bringing her the head of John the Baptist on a platter.

▶ *Continue along the D 36 towards Felletin.*

Millevaches

This little village (alt 912m/2 992ft) sits in the middle of the plateau of the same name, and is indeed characteristic of the region.

▶ *Continue along the D 36 for 3km/1.9mi.*

Plateau d'Audouze

The streams that run down from the western and northern slopes of the Audouze Plateau provide the waters for the River Vienne; the streams from the eastern and southern slopes those for the Diège, a tributary of the Dordogne. The Ardouze Beacon (Signal d'Ardouze) which is out of bounds (*military area*) towers over the plateau.

▶ *Continue along the D 36 then turn right onto the D 174.*

Arboretum de Saint-Setiers

🚻⏱*Open mid-May to Sep, 10am-noon and 2.30-6pm; Oct to mid-May, by prior arrangement.* ⊛*5€ (6-12 years old: 2.50€).* ☎ *05 55 95 61 75.*

The owner of a tree nursery has opened his park to the public. A stroll along alleyways lined with a variety of trees, enables visitors to discover more than 100 species, including a Douglas pine planted in 1895 and now more than 50m/164ft high. A former greenhouse contains an exhibition on the economical use of wood and offers a detailed study of 24 tree species.

Before leaving, make a detour via the D 174E3: the road starts climbing behind the town hall to a spot above the village which affords a magnificent **panorama**★★ of the Massif Central (*picnic area*).

▶ *Turn back then follow the D 174E1.*

Peyrelevade

This attractive town with its slate-roofed houses welcomes tourists. The church and the Templar's Cross date from the 13C.

If you like peat bogs, make a detour (3km/1.9mi N along the D 78) to Négarioux.

▶ *Continue along the D 21 for 2km/1.2mi then bear left onto the D 160.*

Tarnac

The **church** (*when the church is closed, contact Mme Banette, 2 r. du Four*) in this village is party Romanesque and partly Gothic. The northern doorway is adorned with sculpted covings and medallions; St George appears on the right, St Gilles on the left. In the village, note the two ancient oaks and the lovely Fontaine St Georges.

▶ *Continue along the D 160.*

Bugeat

Near the source of the river, this sizeable town sits

between the Millevaches Plateau and the Monédières hills. The Gallo-Roman vestiges reveal that people have lived here for a long time, despite the rugged climate. The proximity of the forest and rivers make Bugeat a centre for sports and recreation.

▷ *Leave Bugeat towards Meymac then turn left onto the D 164. In Fournol, turn right onto a minor road which joins the D 78 via Les Fargettes.*

Vestiges gallo-romains des Cars★

In the middle of nowhere, **Gallo-Roman vestiges** emerge from the greenery. The ashlar stone blocks now in a pile were once part of a temple and mausoleum.

The **temple** was rectangular, with a semicircular apse; visitors can still see the foundations, the podium and the monumental staircase.

The **mausoleum** was certainly very large, with a funeral urn in its centre.

The impressive **tank** above (it weighs about 8t) was a reservoir which supplied water to the building.

The so-called **thermes** were probably not public baths, but more likely a luxurious private residence built in the mid-2C and abandoned at the end of the 3C. Elements found on the site demonstrate the penetration of Roman civilisation in this hidden corner of the world: a hypocaust (a heating system: hot air circulated through brick pipes), a mosaic, marble panelling and fragments of painted walls.

▷ *Continue along the D 78. Shortly before Pérols-sur-Vézère, turn left onto the D 979 towards Meymac, drive for 8km/5mi then turn right onto the D 979E.*

Belvédère de la Route des Hêtres

The panoramic **view**★ extends over the Vallée des Farges, with Mont Bessou to the east and Meymac and Sechemailles Lake to the south.

Château de MONBAZILLAC★

MICHELIN LOCAL MAP 329: B-7 – LOCAL MAP SEE BERGERAC.

Emerging from the undulating vineyards, this château rises proudly on the edge of a limestone plateau overlooking the Dordogne Valley. It is owned by the Monbazillac Wine Cooperative, which restored and refurbished it. Monbazillac, like Bergerac, actively supported the Reformation and supplied wine to Protestants who had sought refuge in the Netherlands.

🙂 **Don't Miss**: The tour inside the castle and a visit to the wine museum.

👣 **Also See**: Bergerac.

Visit

Château

🕐 *Open Jul–Aug, 10am-7.30pm; Jun and Sep, 10am-12.30pm and 1.30-7pm; May and Oct, 10am-12.30pm and 2-6pm; Apr, 10am-noon and 2-6pm; Nov-Mar, daily except Mon, by prior arrangement.* 🕐 *Closed Jan.* ✆5.49€ *(child: 2.59€).* ☎ *05 53 61 52 52.*

This relatively small château was built in 1550 and is surrounded by a dry moat. Its elegant silhouette is eye-catching, the architectural style half-way between a defensive castle and a Renaissance château. There are machicolations and a crenellated watch-path around the main building, which is flanked at each corner by a massive round tower.

The façade is pierced by a double row of mullioned windows and a doorway with Renaissance-style ornamentation. Two tiers of dormer windows can be seen above the machicolations. The grey patina of the stone blends well with the brown tiled roofs of the turrets and pavilions.

Château and vineyards at Monbazillac

From the north terrace there is a good view of the vineyard and of Bergerac in the distance.

The **Great Hall**, its painted ceiling decorated with gilt foliated scrolls, has a monumental Renaissance chimney-piece, 17C furnishings and two beautiful Flemish tapestries of the same period.

Several rooms are open on the first floor; note in particular the viscountess of Monbazillac's **bedchamber** furnished in Louis XIII style.

Cave de Monbazillac – Musée du Vin

🕐*Same opening times and charges as the château.*

Partly hollowed out of the rock, these cellars house a small **wine museum** displaying harvesting and winemaking equipment used in the past, as well as a **Musée du Protestantisme et du Meuble périgourdin** (Museum of Protestantism and of Furniture from Périgord). There is also a restaurant giving onto the main courtyard.

Excursion

Vignoble de Monbazillac

Round trip of 15km/9.3mi – allow 1hr.

▷ *Leave Monbazillac N on the D 13. Turn left onto the D 14 then left again onto the D 933 1.5km/0.9mi further on. Drive just over 2km/1.2mi along this road then turn left.*

Moulin de Malfourat

The mill, now without its sails, stands on top of a hillock. From the viewing table there is a **panorama**★ of the Monbazillac vineyard and Bergerac and the Dordogne Plain to the north.

MONPAZIER★

POPULATION 516

MICHELIN LOCAL MAP 329: G-7

Monpazier was one of the **bastides** built to command the roads going from the Agenais region to the banks of the Dordogne. The square, surrounded by arcades, the **carreyrous** (alleyways), the old houses, the church and the ruined fortifications make it the best preserved of all the Périgord *bastides*.

▷ **Orient Yourself**: Monpazier is situated 46km/29mi northeast of Villeneuve-sur-Lot and 50km/31mi southwest of Sarlat-la-Canéda.

⊚ **Don't Miss**: Place des Cornières.

A Bit of History

A difficult start – The *bastide* of Monpazier was founded in 1284 by Edward I, king of England and duke of Aquitaine. This *bastide* was designed to complete the process of defence and colonisation of Périgord begun in 1267 with the founding of Lalinde, Beaumont, Molières and Roquépine. To this end Edward I allied himself with Pierre de Gontaut, lord of Biron. Many difficulties soon arose: delays in the building, disagreements between the lord of Biron and the people of Monpazier and renewed hostilities between the king of England and Philip the Fair.

Monpazier receives royalty – The Reformation, in which the marshal of Biron played a prominent part, marked the beginning of a violent era. In 1574, the town was betrayed and fell into the hands of the well-known Huguenot leader, Geoffroi de Vivans, who later won fame with the capture of Domme.

Buffarot the Croquant – After the Wars of Religion were over, the peasants rose again in revolt. The rebels, known as *croquants*, held a great gathering at Monpazier in 1594. The revolt flared up again in 1637. Led by a man named Buffarot, a local weaver from Capdrot, 8 000 peasants rampaged through the countryside plundering the castles.

Address Book

For coin ranges, see the Legend at the back of the guide.

WHERE TO EAT

🍴 **Privilège du Périgord** – *58 r. Notre-Dame -* ☎ *05 53 22 43 98 -* 🕐 *closed Dec-Feb and Mar - reserv. recommended.* This former 18C coaching inn covered in Virginia creeper has an attractive rustic-style dining room. In warm weather dine amid the greenery in the pleasant courtyard. Traditional dishes from the southwest.

WHERE TO STAY

🛏 **Camping Le Moulin de David** – *3km/1.8mi SW of Monpazier on the D 2 -* ☎ *05 53 22 65 25 - courrier@moulin-de-david.com -* 🕐 *open 17 May-6 Sep - reserv. recommended - 160 pitches - restaurant.* This popular campsite is set around an old mill in a pretty valley with a brook running through it. Friendly, quiet, comfortable and well maintained. Good sports facilities and an excellent range of services. Mobile homes and tents available.

🛏 **Edward 1er** – *5 r. St-Pierre -* ☎ *05 53 22 44 00 - info@hoteledward1er.com -* 🕐 *closed 13 Dec-26 Feb -* 🅿 *- 13 rooms.* The building's towers give this manor house the appearance of a small castle. Cosy, English-style interior, quiet rooms, plus a swimming pool and small garden.

SHOPPING

Markets and fairs – Traditional market on Thursday morning in place des Cornières. Large fair on third Thursday of the month as well as 8 July and 6 August. Wild mushroom market in October (depending on harvest) under the *halle* from 3pm onwards.

Atelier-Galerie Mariannick-Desaive – *30 r. St-Jacques -* ☎ *05 53 74 30 07 -* 🕐 *open mid-Jun to mid-Sep, 10am-1pm and 2.30-7.30pm - closed Sun afternoon.* Art gallery.

Verrerie d'Art de Monpazier (M. Pascal Guernic) – *13 r. St-André - 50km/30mi from Bergerac, Sarlat, Cahors and Villeneuve-sur-Lot -* ☎ *05 53 74 30 82 - www.artisans-d-art. com/guernic -* 🕐 *open mid-Sep to mid-Jun, 10am-12.30pm and 2.30-6.30pm (Sun and public hols, 3-7pm); mid-Jun to mid-Sep, 10am-12.30pm and 2.30-7pm -* 🕐 *closed Mon (mid-Sep to mid-Jun), Jan and Mar, 1 Jan and 25 Dec.* This glass-blower displays an interesting collection of original works in his workshop.

The soldiers of the duke of Épernon pursued them and, after some difficulty, captured Buffarot. He was brought back to Monpazier, tortured and broken on the wheel in the main square.

Visit

Bastide

🕐 🚶 *Guided tours, Jul-Aug, Tue and Fri, 2.30pm; Sep-Jun by prior arrangement.* 🎫 *4.60€. Contact the tourist office.*

The general layout of the *bastide* is still in evidence, as are three of its original six fortified gateways. Several houses still have their original appearance.

The town is in the shape of a quadrilateral (400×220m/1 312x722ft), the main axis running north-south. Streets are laid out from one end to the other, parallel with the longer sides, and four transverse roads run east to west, dividing the town into rectangular blocks. Originally all the houses had the unique characteristic of being of equal size and separated from each other by narrow spaces or *androscus*, to prevent the spread of fire. There is a panoramic view of the Dropt Valley from the Jardin des Franciscains to the south-east of the *bastide*.

Place des Cornières★

The main square's rectangular shape echoes the *bastide* itself. On the south side stands a covered market housing the antique weights and measures. Round the edge, the arcades or covered galleries are supported on arches, some of which are pointed, and have angle irons (*cornières*). The houses overlooking the square were built between the Middle Ages and the 17C.

▷ *Leave the square via a cut-off corner in a wall to the left.*

Église St-Dominique

This interesting church was built in the 13C and remodelled several times: the doorway dates from the 14C, the rose window and the gable were all rebuilt in the 16C. The wide nave has pointed vaulting and extends into a polygonal east end.

▷ *Turn right as you come out of the church.*

The distinctive geometry of a bastide is clear in this aerial view

Chapter house

This 13C house stands near the church. It was used as a tithe barn. Paired windows light the upper floor.

Atelier des bastides

🕐 *Jun-Sep: 10am-12.30, 3-6.30pm.* 👓 *No charge.* ☎ *05 53 27 09 25. Behind the church.*

This centre, devoted to *bastides*, offers extensive information: photos, models, archaeological evidence. Temporary exhibitions are organised in summer.

Château de **MONTAIGNE**

MICHELIN LOCAL MAP 329: B-6

Lovers of literary history will find the spirit of the great essayist Montaigne in the tower library of this château, where he was able to meditate and write in peace.

▶ **Orient Yourself**: The castle is located 9km/5.5mi northeast of Castillon-la-Bataille.

👓 **Also See**: St-Emilion.

A Bit of History

A Renaissance man – The essayist **Michel Eyquem de Montaigne** (1533-92) was born and died in this château; in his lifetime he served as a member of the Parliament of Bordeaux, was twice elected mayor of that city, and participated in high-level diplomatic negotiations during the Wars of Religion.

In 1571, at the age of 38, Michel de Montaigne took refuge in his family home in Périgord to reflect and write, as well as to care for his property. He continued to perform civic duties when called upon, and travelled throughout Europe (his travel journal was published posthumously in 1774). His personal life was saddened by the loss of his one great friend (Étienne de la Boétie, to whom the essay *On Friendship* is dedicated), an uninspiring marriage, and the death in infancy of five of the six daughters he fathered.

Visit

Tour Historique de Montaigne

🕐 *Open Jul-Aug, guided tour of the tower (45min), 10am-6.30pm; May-Jun and Sep-Oct, daily except Mon and Tue, 10am-noon and 2-6.30pm; Jan-Apr and Nov-Dec, daily except Mon and Tue, 10am-noon and 2-5.30pm; school hols, 10am-noon and 2-5.30pm.* 🕐 *Closed 25 Dec, 1 Jan and 5 Jan.* 👓 *5€.* ☎ *05 53 58 63 93.*

"…I myself am the matter of my book."

Montaigne's *Essays* have been widely read and highly influential in the world of letters. Among his Anglophone readers were John Webster, William Shakespeare, Lord Byron, Ralph Waldo Emerson, Virginia Woolf, TS Eliot and Aldous Huxley. He is recognised as the inventor of the essay form. The original title of the works, *Essais*, signifies attempts, which reveals his penchant for exploration of the mind: "*to follow a movement so wandering … to penetrate the opaque depths of its innermost folds, to pick out and immobilise the innumerable flutterings that agitate it.*"

Many readers have been charmed by Montaigne's unassuming self-portrait of a doddering country gentleman ("*I want death to find me planting my cabbages*"), full of contradiction. In fact, he was active in public life, following a tradition begun by his grandfather, and viewed public service as a noble duty. Today's readers will find him remarkably timely in his defence of cultural relativism and tolerance, personal dignity and fidelity to nature.

The main building was rebuilt after fire ravaged it in 1885; the **library tower**, Montaigne's domain, was saved. From his room above the chapel, the philosopher attended services by means of an opening in the wall (he died while hearing Mass thus). On the top floor, his famous **library**, is lined with books and decorated with Greek and Latin inscriptions.

Outside, visitors can admire a landscape little changed since the author's day: wooded hillsides, vineyards which produce a popular white wine, the outline of the feudal keep of Gurson on the horizon.

Château de MONTAL★★

MICHELIN LOCAL MAP 337: H-2 – LOCAL MAP SEE ST-CÉRÉ: EXCURSIONS

The Château de Montal is a harmonious group of buildings with pepper-pot roofs camped on a wooded hillside near the charming Bave Valley. A nine-hole golf course has been laid at the foot of the castle.

▸ **Orient Yourself**: The castle is located 3km/2mi west of St-Céré.

⊘ **Don't Miss**: A guided tour inside the castle to admire the Renaissance staircase.

⌚ **Also See**: Gouffre de Padirac; Rocamadour; Figeac.

A Bit of History

The wonder of a mother's love – In 1523 Jeanne de Balsac d'Entraygues, widow of Amaury de Montal, governor of Haute-Auvergne, had a country mansion built on the site of a feudal stronghold for her eldest son, Robert, who was away fighting in Italy for François I. The chatelaine had the best artists and workmen brought from the banks of the Loire to Quercy, and by 1534 the masterpiece begotten of a mother's loving pride was there for all to see.

Hope is no more – Everything was ready to welcome home the proud knight. But days, then years passed; Marignano, Pavia, Madrid are far away; the mother waited day after day for her eldest son's arrival. Alas, Robert's body was all that returned to the castle. The beautiful dream crumbled. Jeanne had the high window from which she had watched for her son blocked up and she had carved beneath it the despairing lament Hope is No More (*plus d'espoir*).

Jeanne's second son, Dordé de Montal, a church dignitary, was absolved from his ecclesiastical duties by the Pope in order that he might continue the family line; he subsequently married and had nine children.

Death and resurrection – Montal was declared a national asset but became uninhabitable as a result of the spoliation it suffered during the Revolution; finally in 1879 it fell into the hands of a certain Macaire. This adventurer, permanently short of cash, made a bargain with a demolition group and divided the palace into lots; 120t of carved stone were parcelled up and sent to Paris. The masterpieces of Montal were then auctioned and dispersed throughout the museums and private collections of Europe and the United States. In 1908 Montal rose from its ruins; a new and devoted owner set about finding and buying back at ransom prices all the Montal treasures, until he had refurbished the castle. He donated it to the State in 1913.

Visit

🕐 ☞ *Open week before Easter to early-Nov, guided tour (45min), daily except Sat, 9.30am-noon and 2.30-6pm (last entrance 1hr before closing).* 🕐 *Closed 1 May.* ☜5€ *(child: 2.50€).* ☎ *05 65 38 13 72.*

Exterior

Steeply pitched *lauzes* roofs and massive round towers with loopholes give the castle its fortress-like appearance. But this forbidding exterior accentuates the contrast with the inner courtyard, designed with all the graceful charm of the Renaissance.

Montal consists of two main wings set at right angles and linked at the corner by a square tower containing the staircase. The façade of the main building with all its rich decoration is one of the castle's most glorious features.

The frieze – Above the ground floor windows and doors, runs a 32m/105ft-long frieze. It is a marvel of ornamental diversity: cupids, birds and dream-like figures appear beside shields and a huge human head. There are also the initials of the founder and her sons: I (Jeanne), R (Robert) and D (Dordé).

The busts – On the first floor mullioned windows alternate with false bays with intricately carved pediments, which contain seven busts in high-relief, all masterpieces of realism and taste. Each statue is a likeness of a member of the Montal family; from left to right they are: Amaury with a haughty air, wearing a hat; Jeanne, his wife and the founder of the castle, with the air of a holy woman transfixed in eternal sorrow; Robert, the eldest son killed in Italy, wearing a plumed hat in the style of François I; Dordé, the second son, shown as a young page.

The dormers – There are four, and their decoration brings to mind those of Chambord; the dormer gables have small supporting figures on either side and the niches contain statues.

Interior

The entrance is at the corner, where the wings meet, through a door flanked by pilasters and topped with a lintel supporting several niches.

Renaissance staircase★★ – The staircase is built in the fine gold-coloured stone from Carennac, beautifully proportioned and magnificently decorated. Admire the fine carving beneath the stairs: ornamented foliage, shells, imaginary birds, initials and little figures form a ceiling, with decoration which completes that of the lierne and tierceron vaulting of the vestibules. This masterpiece of sculpture combines elegance with fantasy.

The **guardroom**, vaulted with basket-handled arches, contains a lovely chimney-piece. The Stag Room (**Salle du Cerf**) and the other rooms house fine pieces of furniture (mainly in the Renaissance and Louis XIII styles), altarpieces, paintings and plates attributed to Bernard Palissy, as well as tapestries from Flanders and Tours, which constitute a marvellous collection.

Detail of the façade

MONTIGNAC

POPULATION 3 023

MICHELIN LOCAL MAP 329: H-5

Lying along the banks of the River Vézère, Montignac consists of a group of houses around a tower, a last reminder of the fortress which once belonged to the counts of Périgord. In only a few years, this pleasant hamlet has become a busy tourist centre, thanks to the nearby Lascaux Cave. The small town spreads on both banks of the River Vézère: on the west bank lies the "feudal village" with its network of narrow medieval lanes, and on the east bank lies the "suburb", once a trade centre and river port.

▶ **Orient Yourself**: Montignac is located just 2km/1.2mi from the Lascaux caves and 25km/15km northwest of Sarlat.

🕙 **Organising Your Time**: Allow a full day to explore the Vézère valley.

😊 **Don't Miss**: Grotte de Lascaux.

Especially for Kids: La Roque St-Christophe.

⌚ **Also See**: Sarlat-la-Canéda; Périgueux.

A Bit of History

The presence of man in the area has been traced back to the Paleolithic era. The site was later occupied by the Romans and the fortress, built in the early part of the Middle Ages, turned Montignac into a stronghold. Taken and dismantled several times during successive wars, the castle was finally destroyed in 1825.

Walking Tour of Old Town

▶ *Start from the tourist office (east bank).*

The tourist office is housed in the former St John's hospital dating from the 14C (note the gallery). Église St-Georges, an extension of the hospital chapel, now houses temporary exhibitions. Follow **rue de la Pègerie** ★ opposite: it is lined with medieval houses, including a fine 13C timber-framed house at the end of the street. Continue towards the river and admire, on the opposite bank, the houses built on piles and their wooden galleries. Walk to the old stone bridge and cross the river to Pautauberge square, where there is a bust of Eugène Le Roy, the "novelist of Périgord" who spent the last years of his life in Montignac. Exit the square opposite the 17C Hôtel de Bouillac, turn left then right onto rue des Jardins offering a fine **view** ★ of Montignac. Continue along rue de la Tour which skirts the 11C castle (all that remains are the keep and part of the ramparts) and walk down towards the church. Note the fine house with its wooden gallery on the left. Return to the old bridge along the quays.

Address Book

For coin ranges, see the Legend at the back of the guide.

EATING OUT

😋 **Auberge de Castel Merle** – 24290 Sergeac - 10km/6.2mi S of Montignac on the D 65 - ☎ 05 53 50 70 08 - 🕙 closed late Sep-Mar, Tue lunchtime and Mon - reserv. required in summer. This charming and peaceful inn perched on the cliffs above the River Vézère enjoys superb views of the valley. In summer, dine on the red and white tablecloths on the shaded terrace. The auberge also has a number of cosy, rustic-style bedrooms.

WHERE TO STAY

😋 **Relais du Soleil d'Or** – R. du 4-Septembre - ☎ 05 53 51 80 22 - 🕙 closed 12

Jan-17 Feb - 🅿 - 32 rooms. This former coaching inn is an ideal base from which to visit nearby Lascaux. Rooms overlooking the garden are preferable. The dining room-veranda faces the swimming pool and outdoor terrace. Traditional cuisine. Bistro menus at lunchtime.

😋😋 **Hôtel de la Roseraie** – Pl. d'Armes - ☎ 05 53 50 53 92 - laroseraie@fr.st - 🕙 closed 8 Nov-1 Apr - 14 rooms. A large old house on a quiet square, with attractive rooms decorated with floral fabrics and painted wooden furniture. The dining rooms and terrace overlook a charming rose garden. Swimming pool.

SHOPPING

Markets - Walnut and chestnut market on Wednesdays in October and November.

Excursions

Grotte de Lascaux★★
2km/1.2mi SE along the D 704E. *See Grotte de LASCAUX.*

La Grande Filolie
5km/3mi E along the D 704; not open to the public.

Set in the hollow of a small valley, this charming castle dating from the 14C and 15C consists of a group of overlapping buildings and towers linked together. This building, part-castle, part-farm, is built in golden-coloured limestone and covered with a superb roof of *lauzes*. The castle includes the nobles' residence, a 15C quadrangular building flanked at each end by a square machicolated tower, a Renaissance wing, a gatehouse with a bartizan, and a chapel, which has at one end a round tower with a very pointed roof.

Fanlac
7km/4.3mi W.

This charming village was chosen by Eugène Le Roy as the setting of his most famous novel, *Jacquou le Croquant.*

Vallée De La Vézère★
55km/34mi round-trip – allow one day

From Montignac to Les Eyzies the road closely follows the course of the river, which is lined with magnificent poplars. This is the most attractive part of the valley.
Drive SW out of Montignac along the D 706 towards Les Eyzies.

Le Thot, Espace Cro-Magnon★
🕐*Open Jul-Aug, 10am-7pm; Apr-Jun and Sep, 10am-6pm; Oct to mid-Nov, 10am-12.30pm and 2-6pm; mid-Nov to Mar, daily except Mon, 10am-12.30pm and 2-5.30pm.* 🕐*Closed Jan, 25 Dec.* �®*5€.* ☎ *05 53 50 70 44.*

🄺🄸🄳🅂 The museum displays a large overview of the expression of prehistoric people through painting, sculpture, graffiti etc; prehistoric cultures are placed in the historical context of civilisation, its evolution and driving forces. These topics are developed with the aid of modern technology; re-creations, enormous slide shows, film and so on. Dramatic re-creations of camp sites from the upper Paleolithic period make the visit both exciting and instructive.

The **park** is especially well-designed, and is home to a number of species which inhabited the area in prehistoric times, such as the aurochs, European bison and Prjewalski's horses. Species which no longer roam the planet, the mammoth and the woolly rhinoceros, are represented by animatronics.

Workshops are regularly organised by the Espace Cro-Magnon (reservations essential).

▸ *Continue along the D 706.*

Château de Losse★
🕐➛*Open Jun-Aug, guided tour (45min) of the grand logis, 10am-7pm; mid-Apr to end of May, Easter weekend and Sep, 11am-6pm. Unaccompanied tour of the park and ramparts.* ⌐*6.50€ (child: 4€).* ☎ *05 53 50 80 08.*

This elegant 16C building set amid greenery is perched high on a rock above the right bank of the River Vézère. A terrace adorned with a balustrade, supported by a fine basket-handled arch, projects in front of the main building, which is flanked by a round tower at one corner. A fixed bridge, which has replaced the original drawbridge, gives access to the main courtyard past a fortified gatehouse.

Exterior – A walk along the ramparts offers a good overall view of the fortifications; from the **Tour Sainte-Marguerite**, now a dovecote (*video presentation of period costumes*), an alleyway lined with boxwood hedging leads to the **Tour de l'éperon** housing a steam room and resting room. Look down on the **Jardin bas**: two symmetrical beds planted with lavender and rosemary bushes, separated by a small canal. Nearby is an **outbuilding** presenting video films about castles in Périgord and stone-slab roofing methods. Further on are the **Jardins en terrasse** inspired by 17C bowers.

Interior – Splendid furnishings (16C Italian cupboards and coffers, Louis XIII furniture) and in particular **tapestries** make for fine decoration. Note the fresh colours of the Flemish tapestry, illustrating the traditional preparation for a tournament, and the Florentine tapestry depicting the Return of the Courtesan; both are 17C. A fine wax portrait of Henri IV can be seen in the wood-panelled green drawing room, restored to its original colour.

▷ *Drive onto Thonac then turn right onto the D 45.*

Plazac

The Romanesque church, in the centre of a churchyard planted with cypress trees, stands on a hillock overlooking the village. The 12C belfry-keep is roofed with *lauzes* and embellished with blind arcades resting on Lombard bands.

▷ *Drive S along the D 6.*

Le Moustier

This village, at the foot of a hill, contains a famous prehistoric shelter **(Abri du Moustier** – ⏰*open daily except Sat by reservation only (minimum 2 weeks in advance). ⏰ Closed 1 Jan, 1 May, 1 and 11 Nov, and 25 Dec. ⊜2.50€. For information, call ☎ 05 53 06 86 00).* The prehistoric finds made here include the skeleton of a Neanderthal man and many flint implements. A culture in the Middle Paleolithic Age was named Mousterian after the finds.

An interesting 17C carved confessional can be seen in the village church.

▷ *From the village, drive towards Chabans passing the Côte de Jor, which affords a remarkable panoramic view of the Vézère and St-Léon-sur-Vézère.*

Château de Chabans

⏰*Open Jul-Aug, 2-8pm; May-Jun and Sep, daily except Sat, 2-7pm. ⊜7€. ☎ 05 53 51 70 60.*

An avenue lined with ancient trees leads to this imposing castle still protected by defensive walls. The round tower dates from the 15C whereas the remainder of the edifice was rebuilt in the 16C and 17C. The castle was tastefully restored at the end of the 20C.

French and Italian-style gardens have been laid out in front of the entrance, in the inner courtyard and along the west front where they are embellished by fountains. The extensive park offers visitors a pleasant stroll along shaded alleyways.

The rooms contain period furniture and have magnificent **stained-glass windows**★ dating from the 15C to the 19C. Ancient **tapestries and embroideries**★ hang on the walls. One room illustrates the role of the castle in the Resistance movement and another is devoted to temporary exhibitions.

▷ *Return to Le Moustier. Cross the Vézère then turn left onto the D 66.*

La Roque St-Christophe★

⏰━━*Open Jul-Aug, guided tour (1hr, last entrance 45min before closing), 10am-7pm; May-Jun and Sep, 10am-6.30pm; Mar-Apr and Oct, 10am-6pm; Nov-Feb, 11am-5pm. ⏰ Closed 1 Jan and 25 Dec. ⊜6.50€ (child: 4€). ☎ 05 53 50 70 45.*

Kids This long and majestic cliff rises vertically (80m/262ft) above the Vézère Valley over a distance of more than 900m/0.5mi. It is like a huge hive with about 100 caves hollowed out of the rock on five tiers. Excavations along its foot have shown that the cliff dwellings were inhabited from the Upper Paleolithic Age onwards.

In the 10C the cliff terraces served as the foundation for a fortress which was used against the Vikings and during the Hundred Years War (accommodating up to 1 500 people), and then subsequently destroyed during the Wars of Religion, at the end of 16C. The drainage channels and water tanks, the fireplaces, the stairways and passages hollowed out of the rock all show that St Christopher's Rock was the site of continued, lively human activity. A house leaning against the cliff was reconstructed according to methods used in the 10C and 13C; in the **Cuisine de l'an mil** (the AD 1000 kitchen) are displayed replicas of archaeological finds. On the **Grande terrasse**, visitors can see a reconstruction of a medieval building site and a model of the whole site.

From this terrace, admire the **view**★ of the green Vézère Valley.

▷ *Continue along the D 66.*

Peyzac-le-Moustier

The **Musée du Moustier** illustrates the evolution of living beings as well as technical progress from the first creatures going back to some 600 million years to the Gallo-Romans. The park contains the sculpture of a dinosaur (11m/36ft long and 5m/16.5ft high) and several megaliths. ♿⏰*Open mid-Jun to mid-Sep, 9am-7.30pm; mid-Sep to mid-Jun, by prior arrangement (2 weeks in advance); contact Mr Quinsac-Mandeix. ⊜2.50€. ☎ 05 53 50 81 02 or 05 53 04 86 21 (out of season).*

▶ *Leave Peyzac to the S and join the D 65.*

St-Léon-sur-Vézère★

See ST-LÉON-SUR-VÉZÈRE.

▶ *Return to Peyzac, turn left and follow the D 65.*

Sergeac

This village is pleasantly situated beside the Vézère at a spot where tall cliffs follow the line of the valley.

The village of Sergeac, which has an interesting and delicately carved 15C cross standing at its entrance, also contains old houses roofed with *lauzes* and a turreted manor house, the remains of a commandery, which once belonged to the Knights Templars. The restored Romanesque **church**, despite its porch of fine ochre-coloured stone and recessed arches, still retains a fortified appearance with its loopholes, machicolations and bell-tower. A rounded triumphal arch supported by twinned columns opens onto the chancel, which has a flat east end, and is adorned with carved capitals.

Castel-Merle

This site, which is well-known to the specialists, was for a long time closed to the public. Some of the finds – bones, flints, headdresses – are exhibited in the museums of Les Eyzies, Périgueux and St-Germain-en-Laye (west of Paris).

Near the site, a small local **museum** exhibits a number of interesting artefacts from the Mousterian Age to the Gallo-Roman era. Note the handsome necklaces, found during the excavations, made of stone and bone beads, teeth and shells. *Guided tours (1hr), by prior arrangement, one day in advance; contact Mr Castanet, le Bourg, 24290 Sergeac. ☎ 05 53 50 77 45.*

Several shelters *(abris)* can be visited, one of which contains wall sculptures (bison, horses) from the Magdalenian Age (*open Apr-Oct, guided tour (1hr), 1.30-7pm. 5€. ☎ 05 53 50 79 70).* In the Souquette shelter a section of strata is shown with the different levels from the Aurignacian Age to the modern era.

▶ *Drive back to Montignac along the D 65 which follows the east bank of the Vézère offering a fine view of Losse Castle.*

MONTPEZAT-DE-QUERCY★

POPULATION 1 378

MICHELIN LOCAL MAP 337: E-6

On the edge of Limogne Causse, this picturesque small Lower Quercy town with its covered arcades and old half-timbered or stone houses owes its fame to the 14C collegiate church of St Martin and to its artistic treasures.

▶ **Orient Yourself**: Montpezat-de-Quercy is located 29km/18mi south of Cahors and 32km/20mi north of Montauban.

🐾 **Don't Miss**: The 16C tapestries in the Collégiale St-Martin.

⏱ **Also See**: Cahors; Montauban.

A Bit of History

The Des Prés family – Five members of this family from Montpezat became eminent prelates.

Pierre Des Prés, cardinal of Préneste (now Palestrina in Italy), founded the collegiate church of St Martin, which he consecrated in 1344; his nephew, Jean Des Prés, who died in 1351, was bishop of Coïmbra in Portugal and then of Castres in France. Three other members of the family were consecrated bishops of Montauban: Jean Des Prés (1517-39), who gave his famous Flemish tapestries to the collegiate church at Montpezat, Jean de Lettes (1539-56) and Jacques Des Prés (1556-89). Jacques was a warrior-bishop, and committed persecutor of the Huguenots. He fought on for 25 years, his diocese being one of the most ardent Protestant strongholds, and was killed in an ambush at Lalbenque, some 15km/10mi from Montpezat.

Visit

The *bastide* is laid out in tiers above the ramparts. The central place de la Résistance is surrounded by arcades and half-timbered houses. The 19C town hall replaces an older building. To the north, the 12C cloisters of the former Couvent des Ursulines were remodelled in the 20C and now house a school. Behind the collegiate church stand the 15C canons' living quarters: these timbered houses used to be linked by a gallery running along the first floor.

Collégiale St-Martin

This church, dedicated to St Martin of Tours, was built in 1337 by an architect from the papal court at Avignon. It is comparatively small in size and has many of the characteristics of a Languedoc building: a single nave with no side aisles and chapels separated by the nave's interior buttresses.

Address Book

For coin ranges, see the Legend at the back of the guide.

EATING OUT

🍽️ **Le Salmière** – *46500 Miers - 6km/4mi west of Padirac via the D 673 and D 20 -* ☎ *05 65 33 49 30.* During their heyday, the 16C thermal baths here received visits from Madame la Pompadour and politicians from the Fourth Republic. Nowadays you can visit the former spa and then enjoy a meal on the shores of the lake. Traditional cuisine based around local products.

🍽️ **Auberge de Mathieu** – *300m from the entrance to the cave - 46500 Padirac -* ☎ *05 65 33 64 68 - cathy.pinquie@ wanadoo.fr -* ⏱ *closed 16 Nov-14 Mar and*

Sat in Mar and Nov. A choice of local and more traditional fare is served in this inn just a few minutes' walk from the cave. The handful of simple but well-maintained rooms provide a good base for exploring the local area.

WHERE TO STAY

🛏️ **Chambre d'hôte Pech Lafon** – *Domaine de Lafon, Pech de Lafon - 2km/1.2mi along the D 20 towards Molières, then turn left and continue for 2km/1.2mi towards Mirabel -* ☎ *05 63 02 05 09 -* ⏱ *closed first 2 weeks of March, last 2 weeks of Nov -* 🛏️ *- 3 rooms.* This 19C manor house enjoys a superb view of the surrounding countryside. The spacious rooms have been superbly decorated by the owner - a painter and former theatre set designer.

Nave – Unity, simplicity and harmony make a striking impression as visitors enter the nave. Its pointed vaulting has hanging keystones painted with the founder's coat of arms. The side chapels contain several notable religious objects: a 15C Virgin of Mercy in polychrome sandstone (first chapel on the south side), three 15C-16C Nottingham alabaster altarpiece panels depicting the Nativity, the Resurrection and the Ascension (second chapel on the south side), a 14C alabaster Virgin and Doves (second chapel on the north side), and 15C wooden caskets with gold inlay work (fourth chapel on the north side).

Tapestry representing St Martin dividing his cloak

Tapestries★★ – These 16C tapestries, which were specially made to fit the sanctuary, are nearly 25m/82ft long and 2m/6ft high. They were woven in workshops in the north of France and consist of five panels, each divided into three pictures. Sixteen scenes altogether depict the best-known historic and legendary events in the life of St Martin, including the dividing of his cloak, many of the various cures performed by the saint and his victorious struggle with the devil. Each scene is accompanied by a quatrain in old French woven at the top of the panel.

The excellent condition of these tapestries, the vividness and richness of their colouring and the fact that they are still hanging in the exact spot for which they were designed all contribute to their outstanding interest.

Recumbent figures★ – Although the body of Cardinal Pierre Des Prés lies beneath the paving before the chancel, his statue and tomb carved in Carrara marble were placed on the right of the chancel entrance in 1778. Opposite, making a pair, lies the recumbent figure of his nephew Jean Des Prés, which is a masterpiece of funerary statuary.

As you come out of the church, take the rampart walk on the left to admire the fine view of the village and of the hills facing it.

Excursions

Église de Saux

▶ *5km/3mi N. Leave Montpezat-de-Quercy along the D 20 towards Cahors, then turn left 2km/1.2mi further on.*

Once the centre of a large parish, this church now stands isolated in the middle of the woods. The plain interior consists of three domed bays decorated with beautiful 14C and 15C **frescoes**. The best preserved are in the chancel and show Christ in Majesty with the symbols of the four Evangelists, the Crucifixion and scenes from the Childhood of Jesus. In the south chapel the legend of St Catherine is depicted; in the north chapel, the legend of St George.

Molières

▶ *13km/8mi W along the D 20.*

The village grew during the 13C when Alphonse de Poitiers made it into a *bastide*. The covered market has gone, but Molières has retained its characteristic town plan and part of its ramparts, the bulk of which was destroyed during the Revolution. The promenade offers a view of the Étang de Malivert. Two 19C wrought-iron footbridges linking the ramparts to some houses testify to the town's past prosperity. In addition to the two half-timbered houses located beyond the town hall, note the brick-built arch with a bell hanging from it: it stands to the north, where the clock tower used to be. The 13C bell-tower to the south was remodelled in the 17C.

MOUTIER-D'AHUN ★

POPULATION 195

MICHELIN LOCAL MAP 325: J-4

The village of Moutier-d'Ahun lies between Guéret and Aubusson, near the upper valley of the Creuse which is spanned by an old bridge bristling with cutwaters. The village clusters round the church which contains remarkable 17C woodwork.

▶ **Orient Yourself**: The village is located 20km/12mi southeast of Guéret and 24km/15mi northeast of Aubusson.

⊙ **Don't Miss**: The woodwork and stalls in the village church.

⚑ **Also See**: Aubusson.

A Bit of History

An abbey's fortunes and misfortunes – Shortly before the year 1000 Boson, count of Marche, gave a church consecrated to Our Lady, which he owned on the banks of the Creuse, to Uzerche Abbey as a first step towards founding a Benedictine monastery. The monastery became independent of its mother house and took the name Moutier d'Ahun; in the 12C the monks replaced Boson's church by a larger building.

But the Hundred Years War put an end to this long period of prosperity; the abbey church was first destroyed by the English, it had scarcely been resurrected from the ruins, when the nave was pillaged and set on fire during the Wars of Religion.

It was in 1610 that the woodwork to ornament the chancel was made. When the monks fled at the time of the Revolution, the woodwork was whitewashed but later regained its glory through patient restoration by the Abbé Malapert, priest of Moutier-d'Ahun.

Visit

Church

🕐 *Open mid-Jun to mid-Sep, 10.30am-12.30pm and 2.30-6.30pm; mid-Mar to mid-Jun and mid-Sep to mid-Nov, daily except Mon and Tue (except public hols), 2-5pm; mid-Nov to mid-Mar, daily except Mon and Tue, 2-4pm.* ⊙2.30€. ☎ 05 55 62 45 63.

The church is now partly Romanesque (transept crossing, belfry and chancel), and partly Gothic (15C west door). The western doorway, built in granite, is adorned with six covings embellished with little figures – prophets and angels jostle jugglers, musicians and dancers. The nave and the arms of the transept have been destroyed.

The crossing is surmounted by a square Romanesque belfry, pierced by three double bays on each side, supported by slender columns with smooth capitals.

A Gallo-Roman funerary plaque is set into the façade, a figure and inscription carved upon it.

Pass below the grand cupola supported by squinches to reach the chancel under the arch made of three arcades in juxtaposition. The chancel's eastern end is flattened, and the two chapels were embellished with ribbed vaulting in the 15C.

Outside, traces of the 14C fortifications can still be seen on the chevet.

Woodwork ★★ –

The woodwork and the stalls entirely occupy the walls of the apse and chancel. All the carving was commissioned by the monks of Moutier-d'Ahun and was done between 1673 and 1681 by the master-crafts-man of Auvergne, Simon Baüer.

Stall in the chancel

B. Kaufmann/MICHELIN

On either side of the high altar, whose base was covered with 17C Cordoba leather, are the two parts of a huge altar screen. These consist of ornately carved, twisted columns bearing a broken pediment. The part of the chancel next to the altar screen is panelled with decorated woodwork which forms a monumental door which in turn gives access to a 15C chapel. The 26 stalls are magnificently sculptured portraying animals, flowers and fantastic scenes. The screen enclosing the chancel is surmounted by a double figure of Christ carved from the trunk of an oak tree. The lectern is made up of two lions back to back with the pulpit resting on their paws.

Items from the old monastery may be seen in the sacristy. They include 12C statues in multicoloured granite of St Benedict and St Antony the hermit, 15C and 17C reliquaries and, above all, a wonderful Christ skilfully carved in boxwood (17C).

Musée des Outils et Techniques

Open mid-Jun to mid-Sep, 2-7pm. 2.50€. ☎ 05 55 62 45 63.

The watermill, which was once surrounded by craftsmen's workshops, today houses a collection of tools illustrating various ancient crafts. A temporary exhibition is devoted to arts and crafts.

NANÇAY

POPULATION 784

MICHELIN LOCAL MAP 323: J-2

This village in the Sologne region is home to many artists' studios, as well as one of Europe's most modern astronomical observatories.

▶ **Orient Yourself**: Nançay is situated 15km/9.5mi northeast of Vierzon.

Especially for Kids: Planetarium; Ciel Ouvert en Sologne.

Also See: Vierzon.

Sights

Grenier de Villâtre

Open mid-Mar to mid-Dec, Sat-Sun and public hols, 9.30am-12.30pm and 2.30-7.30pm, Mon-Fri by prior arrangement (2 weeks in advance). 5€ (child: 2.50€). ☎ 02 48 51 80 22. www.capazza-galerie.com

Established in the nicely restored stables of the château, the Galerie Capazza exhibits sculptures, pottery, drawing etc created by 65 different artists. One of the rooms, the **Musée Imaginaire du Grand Meaulnes**, is full of memories of Alain-Fournier, evoked by the family memorabilia on display: photographs, model of a scene from the novel, small furnishings.

Station de Radioastronomie

2km/1.2mi north along the D 29 towards Souesmes. Open Jul-Aug, guided tour (1hr 15min), 9am-noon and 1.30-5.30pm, Sat-Sun, public hols and zone B school holidays, 10.30am-12.30pm and 2-7pm; Sep-Jun, daily except one day per week (unspecified), 9.30am-noon and 1.30-5.30pm, Sat-Sun, public hols and zone B school holidays, 10.30am-12.30pm and 2-7pm. For information on dates of closure, please enquire. 6.50€ (child: 5€). ☎ 02 48 51 18 16. www.cielouvert.obs-nancay.fr

Created in 1953 by the École Normale Supérieure, the station came under the authority of the Paris Observatory in 1956. The main field of study involves radio waves from around the universe, which provide useful information on the solar system, distant galaxies and interstellar matter. Three of the instruments used in the research are the radio telescope (one of the largest in the world in terms of its sensitive surface), the radioheliograph (for studies of the solar corona and other measurements of the sun), and the network of 144 antennae for capting decametric radio waves (mainly emitted by the planet Jupiter).

Ciel Ouvert en Sologne

Open Jul-Aug, 9am-noon and 1.30-5.30pm, Sat-Sun, public hols and zone B school holidays, 10.30am-12.30pm and 2-7pm; Sep-Jun, daily except one day per week (unspecified), 9am-noon and 1.30-5pm, Sat-Sun, public and school holidays, 10.30am-12.30pm and 2-7pm. Permanent and temporary exhibitions (length of visit: 1hr). ◷ For dates of annual closure, please enquire. ⌾3€ (child: 2€). ☎ 02 48 51 18 16. www.cielouvert. obs-nancay.fr

Kids Protected from interference by a Faraday cage, this building, dedicated to the stars, houses all the equipment necessary for the would-be astronomer to make numerous experiments.

Planetarium

&.◷Film (50min), Jul-Aug, 9am-noon and 1.30-5.30pm, Sat-Sun, public hols and zone B school holidays, 10.30am-12.30pm and 2-7pm; Sep-Jun, daily except one day per week (unspecified), 9.30am-noon and 1.30-5.30pm, Sat-Sun, public hols and zone B school holidays, 10.30am-12.30pm and 2-7pm. ◷For dates of annual closure, please enquire. ⌾6.50€ for planetarium and exhibitions (child: 5€). ☎ 02 48 51 18 16. www.cielouvert.obs-nancay.fr

Kids The planetarium is the ideal place to learn all about the stars and their location in our universe.

Radio telescope

NEUVIC

POPULATION 3 315

MICHELIN LOCAL MAP 329: D-5

This peaceful village lies on the south bank of the River Isle which flows along the edge of the Forêt de la Double sprinkled with lakes and dotted with half-timbered clay houses.

▸ **Orient Yourself**: Neuvic is located 24km/15mi southwest of Périgueux and 32km/20mi north of Bergerac.

◷ **Organising Your Time**: Allow a full day to explore the Forêt de la Double.

Kids **Especially for Kids**: Parc Botanique; the wild boar enclosure near the Grand Étang de la Jemaye.

◔ **Also See**: Périgueux; Bergerac.

Visit

Château de Neuvic

◷⌁Open Jul-Aug, guided tours (1hr, last entrance 30min before closing) at 2.30pm, 4pm and 5.30pm; rest of the year, please enquire. ⌾5.50€ château and botanical gardens (child: 3€). ☎ 05 53 80 86 65.

A walkway lined with trees leads to this handsome building on the left bank of the River Isle; it is currently in use as a medical training centre. Built in 1530, the castle has retained its machicolated watch-path which is more of a decorative than a defensive feature; two main buildings surround a square keep erected at the beginning of the 16C. Inside, there are 16C and 18C frescoes to be seen.

Parc Botanique

◷Open Jul-Aug, 10am-7pm; mid-Apr to Jun and Sep to mid-Oct, 10am-noon and 1.30-6.30pm. ⌾3.80 €. Guided tour by prior arrangement. ☎ 05 53 80 86 65. www.chateau-parc-neuvic.com

Kids The castle grounds have been laid out as botanical gardens (6ha/15 acres) housing some 1 500 plant species (oak, dogwood, spindle tree, lilac, roses etc).

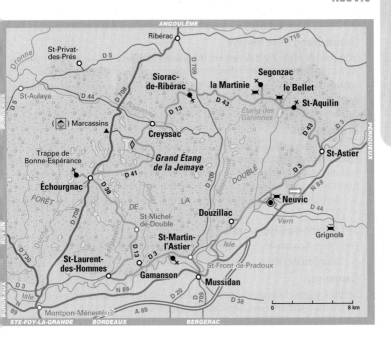

Excursions

Forêt de la Double

95km/59mi round-trip – allow one day

▷ *Drive N out of Neuvic, cross the River Isle then follow the D 3 to the right.*

St-Astier

Lying on the banks of the River Isle, the old town centre contains a few remaining Renaissance houses. It is overlooked by the church, supported by massive buttresses, and a magnificent 16C **bell tower** adorned with two tiers of blind arcades. The cement works near the River Isle give the appearance of an industrial town.

▷ *The D 43 climbs out of St-Astier on a series of steep hairpin bends to reveal beautiful views of the town before descending into the forest.*

St-Aquilin

The church, built in a transitional Romanesque Gothic style, contains a remarkable gilt-wood altarpiece.

▷ *Drive 700m/766yd along the D 43 and turn right.*

Château du Bellet

The fine tiled roofs, massive round towers and separate dovecot of this castle, built on the side of a hill, come into view on the right.

▷ *Continue along the D 43 and turn right onto the D 104 3km/1.9mi further on.*

Segonzac

As you enter the village, note the **Château de la Martinie**, a 15C building remodelled several times and finally converted into a farm.
The Romanesque **church** (11C-12C) was altered and enlarged in the 16C. The **apse** is remarkable for its oven-vaulting and richly sculpted capitals.

▷ *Return to the D 43 (right).*

Siorac-de-Ribérac

Overlooking a small valley, the fortified Romanesque church has a single nave partly surmounted by a dome.

▷ *Drive W out of Siroac and turn left onto the D 13, then right onto the D 44 towards St-Aulaye.*

Creyssac

Surrounded by the waters of a small lake, the elegant square dovecot makes a pleasant sight.

▷ *200m/220yd further on take the left fork towards Grand étang de la Jemaye.*

Grand Étang de la Jemaye

In the middle of the Forêt de Jemaye, the lake has been set up as a water sports centre with a beach and facilities for fishing, windsurfing and a splashing good time.

Nearby, at the intersection of the D 108 and the D 708, a **wild-boar and heron pen** can be seen close to the road.

▷ *Return to the road and turn right.*

Échourgnac

Not far from this village (along the D 38) stands a **Trappist monastery** (Trappe de Bonne-Espérance). The monastery was founded in 1868 by Trappist monks from Port-du-Salut in Normandy. They set up a model cheese-making farm, collecting milk from the neighbouring farms. Their Trappe cheese is very similar to Port Salut.

▷ *Drive SE out of Échourgnac along the D 38 to St-Michel-de-Double and turn onto the D 13.*

St-Laurent-des-Hommes

This village boasts a few splendid traditional houses of the Double region.

▷ *Drive E on the D 3.*

Gamanson

Set back slightly from the road, this hamlet constitutes the richest collection of traditional half-timbered and clay-walled houses of the Double region.

▷ *Turn back and continue along the D 3 (left).*

St-Martin-l'Astier

The unusual outline of the Romanesque **church** in the middle of the cemetery is right at the extremes of most Double architecture. The **bell-tower** and **chancel** are octagonal; the latter is covered by a dome supported on eight engaged columns.

▷ *Continue along the D 3 and cross the River Isle.*

Mussidan

This old Huguenot city on the banks of the River Isle was laid to siege on several occasions during the Wars of Religion. The siege in 1569, which was particularly bloody, inspired one of Montaigne's famous Essays (*L'Heure des Parlements Dangereuse*).

Musée des Arts et Traditions Populaires du Périgord André-Voulgre – Open Jun to mid-Sep, guided tour (1hr), 9.30am-noon and 2-6pm; Mar-May and mid-Sep to Nov, Sat-Sun and public hols, 2-6pm. 3€. 05 53 81 23 55. Displayed in the lovely Périgord mansion where Doctor Voulgre lived, this collection is rich and varied; it includes furniture, objects and tools, as well as a still, a steam engine and stuffed animals collected by the doctor during his lifetime.

▷ *Drive NE out of Mussidan along N 89 and turn left onto the D 3E5 3km/1.9mi further on.*

Douzillac

Have a look at the town hall with its pepper pot and wooden balcony. The outline of the 16C **Château de Mauriac** situated near the D 3, on the way to Mauriac, is reflected in the calm waters of the River Isle.

▷ *Continue along the D 3 to return to Neuvic.*

NOHANT★

POPULATION 481

MICHELIN LOCAL MAP 323: H-7 – LOCAL MAP SEE LA CHÂTRE

Near the Indre Valley, in this quaint Berry village clustered round a little square where century-old elms shade the church and its rustic porch, stands the manor where George Sand grew up.

▶ **Orient Yourself**: Nohant is situated 6km/4mi north of La Châtre.

☺ **Don't Miss**: The Maison de George Sand.

A Bit of History

The passionate life of George Sand (1804-76) – Amandine-Aurore-Lucile Dupin was born to scandal. Her father was an army officer, grandson of the celebrated Marshal General of France, Maurice de Saxe (albeit through an illegitimate branch of the family tree). Her mother, Sophie, was a camp follower, wed to the Lieutenant just before their daughter's appearance. The accidental death of her father did nothing to calm the stormy family atmosphere created by the circumstances of Aurore's birth. Her wealthy grandmother agreed to raise her, on the condition that Sophie stay out of sight. Thus, in her early childhood, Aurore developed a sense of rebellion, a sensitivity to injustice and social charade (indeed, the famous Marshal himself was an illegitimate son of the monarch), but also a deep attachment to nature and the Berry countryside which would later mark her work. She was married at 18 to Baron Casimir Dudevant and had two children, Solange and Maurice. Profoundly unhappy, she left her husband, established herself in Paris with Jules Sandeau in 1831, and out of financial necessity began writing for the satirical review *Figaro*. Her first independently written novel, *Indiana* (1832, English translation 1978), was an immediate popular success. She thereafter kept up a prolific pace of literary production to support herself and her children.

Her encounter with the poetic author Alfred de Musset and their trip to Venice fuelled her romantic works, most notably, *Lélia* (1833, English translation 1978), which amazed readers with its frank discussion of women's sensual feelings and a passionate call for the right to emotional satisfaction.

Sand's reputation for iconoclasm sprang from such themes and also from exaggerated reports of her unconventional behaviour: she smoked regularly and in public, occasionally dressed like a man and carried on love affairs with Musset, Prosper Mérimée and Frédéric Chopin. Yet she remained an idealist, convinced of the virtues of marriage between equals, and enraged at the prevalent social system which made such marriages impossible.

An uncommon woman – And yet, Sand was truly inhabited by the great ideas of moral progress that animated her times. France's leading woman author produced what are sometimes called socialist novels, including the *Consuelo* cycle (1842-44, English translation 1870). Dedicated to the advance of democracy, she put her pen to political pamphlets, created a local newspaper, and rejoiced when the French monarchy fell and the Second Republic was established. The return of Napoleon III so disappointed Sand that she withdrew to the estate at Nohant.

She continued to write successful plays and the ever-popular pastoral or rustic novels with their tender descriptions of the Berry countryside: *The Haunted Pool* (1846, English translation 1976), *The Country Waif* (1847, English translation 1976), and *Fanchon the Cricket* (1848, English translation 1977). Many readers enjoy her letters and journals, as well as her masterful autobiography, *Histoire de ma vie* (*My Life*, English translation 1979) and the travel essays collected under the title *Lettres d'un voyageur* (Letters of a Traveler, 1834-36). In her final years, she undertook charitable works which earned her the affectionate title *la bonne dame de Nohant* (the good lady of Nohant).

With 70 novels, 50 volumes of other writing and 25 plays to her credit, George Sand has been an inspiration to many women writers, including Elizabeth Barrett Browning and George Eliot; her work has been praised by the likes of Turgenev and Flaubert.

Visit

Maison de George Sand★

🕒➤ *Guided tour (1hr, last entrance 1hr before closing), Jul-Aug, 9.30am-6.30pm; May-Jun, 9.30am-noon and 2-6.30pm; Apr and Sep, 10am-12.30pm and 2-6pm; Oct-Mar, 10am-12.30pm and 1.30-5pm.* 🕒*Closed 1 Jan, 1 May, 1 and 11 Nov, and 25 Dec.* ⊚6.10€

(-17 years old: no charge). ☎ 02 54 31 06 04.

This country estate was built around 1760 on the site of an old château, and became the property of Mme Dupin de Francueil in 1793. Now a museum, it is devoted to the memory of George Sand and her many guests: composers Chopin and Liszt,

The blue room

novelists Balzac and Flaubert, painters Delacroix and Fromentin among them. The old-fashioned charm of Sand's home has remained unchanged since the 19C, and the visitor almost expects to find the author herself sitting at her desk.

The ground floor has eight rooms including the boudoir with its painted woodwork, where Sand's career began and *Indiana* took shape. "I was living in my grandmother's old boudoir … It was so small that with my books, my herbarium, and my rock collection, there was no room for a bed. I had a hammock installed instead. My table was made of a wardrobe which could fold out like a writing desk."

The theatre was built in 1849, for family entertainment. The puppet theatre, set up in 1854 still has many marionettes carved by young Maurice; Sand's son left other traces of his artistic temperament in the paintings hanging in the vestibule, the salon, and Aurore Lauth-Sand's room.

The salon, an inner sanctum, is the expression of family harmony, as suggested by the portraits on the walls.

The upper floor consists of a vestibule, antechamber, George Sand's room, where she passed away on 8 June 1876, her writing room, which was Chopin's room until 1846, the library, and Aurore Lauth-Sand's room (the château's last resident, she died in 1961), which was once occupied by George Sand and her mother.

The grounds of the house are lovely as well, and a visit to the family cemetery reveals George Sand's tomb in the centre of the plot, carved in Volvic stone.

Abbaye de NOIRLAC★★

MICHELIN LOCAL MAP 323: K-6 – LOCAL MAP SEE ST-AMAND-MONTROND

Between the River Cher and the Meillant Forest, this 12C-14C abbey, one of the best-preserved monasteries in France, is well worth a visit. In this exceptional setting, Gregorian chants, concerts and other cultural events take place.

A Bit of History

The foundation – This abbey was founded around 1130 by Robert of Clairvaux, St Bernard's cousin, on the right bank of the Cher, on the site known as Maison-Dieu on the edge of the wood, and later came to be known as Noirlac.

The first years were trying, and the monks knew hardship and hunger. In 1149, Bernard himself went begging for a royal grant of wheat. But the situation finally improved: Ebbes V of Charenton made a significant gift which ensured the continuity of the community. The hard-working monks went to work on the land, clearing and building, and prosperity was just around the corner. By its fiftieth year, the abbey had a vast domain.

From destruction to restoration – After the surge of recruits in the 12C and 13C, fewer monks inhabited Noirlac in the 14C, and commercial activities there slowly came to a halt. After the Hundred Years War, a stroke of bad luck befell the community in 1510: the abbot would be appointed by the king, and was to manage the place in absentia. Shortly thereafter, the Wars of Religion brought about further destruction.

As the French Revolution drew near, only six monks were left at Noirlac. Declared national property, the abbey was sold. Sold again in 1820, it became a porcelain manufactory. Prosper Mérimée discovered it in 1838, but not until 1909 did the Cher *département* acquire it for 46 000 francs. Restoration began slowly; the buildings were still in use for humanitarian purposes until 1949. In 1950, a vast restoration programme got underway, and the extraordinary results captivate visitors today.

Visit

Abbey

🕐*Open Jul-Aug, 9.45am-6.30pm; Apr-Jun and Sep, 9.45am-12.30pm and 2-6.30pm; Oct-Nov and Feb-Mar, 9.45am-12.30pm and 2-5pm.* 🕐*Closed Dec and Jan.* 🎫*For entrance fees, please enquire.* ☎ *02 48 62 01 01.*

The buildings are set up in a typical Cistercian pattern.

Church – Work started in 1150 and lasted for 100 years, thus illustrating the passage from Romanesque to Gothic style. The sanctuary was built first, followed by the nave and the side aisles. The simplicity of line and the lovely pale stone add to the beauty of the architecture and to the sense of peace. In accordance with the rule of the order, sculpted ornamentation was barred: the capitals are plain and the windows uniformly grey in tone.

The nave, with its ribbed vaulting, is linked to the side aisles, which have ogive vaulting with great pointed arches, and rests on square pillars; the transverse ribs are supported by engaged columns with a simple tapered pedestal just above floor level.

The chancel, lower than the transept, is the oldest part of the building.

Abbey buildings – The other buildings were erected at various times: late 12C (east wing and lay brothers' building); first part of the 13C (refectory); second part of the 13C and early 14C (cloister galleries). Other works were carried out in the 18C (staircase with wrought-iron banister (1), dormitory rooms).

The cloisters and adjacent buildings – The rectangular buildings (38×33m/125×108ft) probably replaced an earlier construction. At the heart of the abbey, it provides access to all the other areas. The east and south galleries have the most ornate carvings and all have fine ogive vaulting and rich ornamentation which contrasts with the simplicity of the church: corbels decorate the springing of the arches and capitals with different plant motifs crown the small pillars.

The chapter-house has a rounded doorway flanked by twin windows; the six square bays are divided by polygonal columns. There is a great chimney-piece (2) in a corner of the heated common room which is roofed with flattened pointed vaulting. The refectory, a tall room crowned with eight ogive domes and palm leaf mouldings adorning the capitals of the three columns, is lit by four large windows surmounted by two multilobed rose windows.

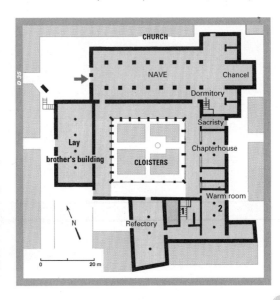

Only a portion of the **lay brothers' building** still stands. It was the economic centre of the monastery. The vast cellar is divided in two by a row of four pillars which support the vaults of the bays. On the upper floor, the lay brothers had their dormitory; it was used as attic storage space in the 18C and today serves as an exhibit area.

ORADOUR-SUR-GLANE★★

POPULATION 2 025

MICHELIN LOCAL MAP 325: D-5 – LOCAL MAP SEE LIMOGES

Ruined, fire-scarred walls and a cemetery stand in memory of 642 victims of a brutal attack by a detachment of SS troops, one of the cruellest events of the Second World War. An oddly peaceful impression seizes the visitor to this commemorative site, despite the fact that part of the horror of the massacre was that Oradour had been chosen for its very innocence and insignificance, the better to terrorise the French. The atrocity took place just four days after the announcement of the allied landing in Normandy. *Pl. du Champ-de-Foire, 87520 Oradour-sur-Glane, ☎ 05 55 03 13 73.*

▸ **Orient Yourself**: The town is situated 24km/15mi northwest of Limoges.

🔊 **Don't Miss**: The ruins of the old town and the Centre de la Mémoire.

🕯 **Also See**: Limoges; Parc Naturel Régional Périgord-Limousin.

A Bit of History

10 June 1944 – The people of Oradour, a large Limousin village, were going about their daily affairs on a busy Saturday morning. There were visitors from the city out for a day in the country, and visitors from the outlying farms had come to town for the day; a party of teenage cyclists was passing through. At 2 pm, as a cordon of German soldiers closed all the exits, a column of lorries and armoured cars entered the village.

Curiosity soon gave way to fear. On Nazi orders everyone gathered on the fairground: men, women and 247 schoolchildren brought there by their teachers. The women and children were locked in the church, the men in the barns and garages. Grenade explosions and machine-gun bursts killed a great many; fire and dynamite completed the massacre. One woman managed to get out of the burning church through a window in the east end; a young boy and a few men were the only others to escape death.

The ruins stand to commemorate the victims

Visit

Centre de la Mémoire

Access to the ruins of the martyred village. ⏰*Open Jul-Aug, 9am-7pm (last entrance 1hr before closing); Mar-Jun and Sep-Oct, 9am-6pm; Feb, Nov and early Dec to mid-Dec, 9am-5pm.* 🎟6€. ☎ *05 55 43 04 30.*

This centre, located close to the ruins, houses a permanent exhibition about the rise of Nazism and 10 June 1944.

The ruins

▸ *Entrance via the Centre la Mémoire.*

Access via the Centre de la Mémoire. Go through the outer walls and along the streets of the ruined village. For a guide apply to the old church, where 500 women and children died. A visit to the Maison du Souvenir which contains objects which did not perish in the flames, and to the cemetery where the remains of the victims lie, is a moving experience.

The New Oradour

Nearby, a new Oradour has been built. The modern church with its luminous stained-glass windows and square belfry may surprise at first, but it has been designed to blend harmoniously with the neighbouring buildings and surrounding countryside.

Jardins du Prieuré Notre-Dame d'ORSAN★★

MICHELIN LOCAL MAP 323: J-6 – 10KM/6MI SE OF LIGNIÈRES

LOCAL MAP SEE ST-AMAND-MONTROND

On the border of the Cher and Indre *départements*, between St-Amand-Montrond and La Châtre, a former priory is home to a medieval garden; its design is loosely based on illuminations and miniatures created by monks of the time.

▸ **Orient Yourself**: The priory is situated 10km/6mi southeast of Lignières.

Don't Miss: The magnificent gardens, including the vegetable labyrinth and the rose garden.

A Bit of History

Founded in the 12C by Robert d'Abrissel, the priory is said to possess a relic (the heart) of the founder, who died here in 1116. Pillaged and destroyed in 1569, the priory was rebuilt in the 16C and 17C, before the French Revolution brought about the end of its religious vocation for all time.

Visit

♿⏰*Open early Apr to early Nov, 10am-7pm.* 🎟8€ *(child: 4.50€).* ☎ *02 48 56 27 50. www.prieuredorsan.com*

In medieval times, religious communities tended gardens planted to correspond to biblical themes. Generally, the plots were encompassed by buildings and a row of oaks. Gardeners provided for both earthly and spiritual nourishment in the choice of vegetables and the planning of green spaces appropriate for meditation.

The garden in the middle of the monastery, was a natural cloister, a place of prayer and spiritual renewal. Marked out by four squares of grapevine, two grassy paths intersect; at the central point, a fountain symbolises the source of the waters of earthly paradise.

Eight gazebos provide access to the many adjacent gardens: herbs, small fruits, orchards, the **vegetable labyrinth**, the aromatic garden (near the kitchens), the **rose garden** (a

EATING OUT

🍽🍽🍽 **La Table d'Orsan** – *In the priory - 18170 Maisonnais -* ☎ *02 48 56 27 50 -* ⏰ *closed 2 Nov-2 Apr, lunchtime in Apr, Sep and Oct (except Sat-Sun) and public hols.* Fresh produce from the medieval garden and local markets are to the fore in this restaurant in a wing of the former priory.

Medieval splendour revived at Notre-Dame d'Orsan

harbour of peace dedicated to the Virgin), the pergola and the olive garden (symbol of mercy), the flower beds and the secret gardens.

To the north of the gardens, a path (1.2km/0.7mi) passes through the gate and invites walkers to discover the typical landscape of the Boischaut-Sud region.

Gouffre de PADIRAC★★

MICHELIN LOCAL MAP 337: G-2

The Padirac Chasm provides access to wonderful galleries hollowed out of the limestone mass of Gramat Causse by a subterranean river. A visit into the vertiginous well and a tour of the mysterious river and the vast caves adorned with limestone concretions leave visitors with a striking impression of this fascinating underground world.

▶ **Orient Yourself**: Padirac is located 13km/8mi east of Rocamadour.

◉ **Don't Miss**: The guided tour inside the chasm.

◔ **Also See**: Rocamadour; Parc Naturel Régional des Causses du Quercy.

A Bit of History

From legend to scientific exploration – The Padirac Chasm was a source of superstitious terror to the local inhabitants right up to the 19C, as people believed that the origin of this great hole was connected with the devil.

St Martin, so the tale went, was returning from an expedition on the causse where he had been looking unsuccessfully for souls to save. All at once his mule refused to go on; Satan, bearing a great sack full of souls which he was taking to hell, stood in the saint's path. Jeering at the poor saint Satan made the following proposition: he would give St Martin the souls he had in his sack on condition that St Martin make his mule cross an obstacle that he, Satan, would create on the spot. Whereupon he hit the ground hard with his foot, and a gaping chasm opened up. The saint coaxed his mule forward and the beast jumped clear with such force that its hoof prints are still visible. Satan, defeated, retreated to hell by way of the hole he had created.

The chasm served as a refuge for the people living on the causse during the Hundred Years War and the Wars of Religion, but it would appear that it was towards the end of the 19C, following a violent flooding of the river, that a practicable line of communication opened between the bottom of the well and the underground galleries. The speleologist, **Édouard A Martel**, was the first to discover the passage in 1892. He then undertook nine expeditions and finally reached the Hall of the Great Dome.

Padirac was opened for the first time to tourists in 1898. Since then, numerous speleological expeditions have uncovered 22km/13.5mi of underground galleries.

The 1947 expedition proved by fluorescein colouring of the water that the Padirac river reappears above ground 11km/7mi away where the Lombard rises and at St George's spring in the **Montvalent Amphitheatre** near the Dordogne. During the expeditions of 1984 and 1985, a team of speleologists, paleontologists, prehistorians and geologists discovered a prehistoric site, 9km/5.5mi from the mouth of the hole, on an affluent of the Joly, with bones of mammoths, rhinoceroses, bison, bears, cave-dwelling lions and deer, all of which were found to date from between 150 000 and 200 000 years ago. Amid the bones found were chipped flints dating from between 30 000 and 50 000 years ago. Copies of some of the bones are exhibited in the entrance hall.

> 🛏 **Padirac Hôtel** – *At the entrance to the cave -* ☎ *05 65 33 64 23 - padirac-hotel@wanadoo.fr -* ⏱ *closed early Nov-31 Mar -* 🅿 *- 22 rooms. A small quiet hotel with simple but clean rooms. Restaurant and snack bar, plus an ice cream counter in summer. Good value for money.*

Visit *1hr 30min*

⏱ Guided tours (1hr), Jul, 9am-6pm; Aug, 8.30am-6.30pm; Apr-Jun and Sep, 9am-noon and 2-6pm; Oct, 10am-noon and 2-5pm. ⊚8€ (children aged 6-12: 5€). ☎ 05 65 33 64 56. www.gouffre-de-padirac.com

Two lifts and some staircases lead into the chasm, which is 32m/105ft in diameter, and to the pyramid of rubble, debris of the original caving-in of the roof. From the bottom of the lift (75m/247ft), there is a striking view of walls covered by the overflow from stalagmites and by vegetation and of a little corner of the sky at the mouth of the hole. Stairs lead down to the underground river, 103m/338ft below ground level. At the bottom, the 2km/1.25mi underground journey begins, 500m/547yd of which are by boat and 400m/438yd on foot.

Galerie de la Source – This chamber is at the end of an underground canyon, the roof of which gets gradually higher and higher; it is 300m/984ft long and follows the upper course of the river that hollowed it out. At the far end is the landing-stage.

Rivière Plane – A flotilla of flat-bottomed boats offers an enchanting journey over the astonishingly translucent waters of this smooth river. The depth of the river varies from 50cm/20in to 4m/13ft, but the water temperature remains constant at 11°C/51.8°F. The height of the roof increases progressively to reach a maximum of 78m/256ft; the different levels of erosion corresponding to the successive courses of the river can be seen from the boat. At the end of the boat trip admire the **Grande Pendeloque** (Great Pendant) of **Lac de la Pluie** (Rainfall Lake). This giant stalactite, the point of which nearly touches the water, is simply the final pendant in a string of concretions 78m/256ft in height.

Pas du Crocodile – A narrow passage between high walls links the underground lake and the chambers to be visited next. Look to the left at the magnificent column known as the Grand Pilier, 40m/131ft high.

Salle des Grands Gours – A series of pools separated by gours, natural limestone dams, divides the river and the lake into basins; beyond them cascades a 6m/20ft waterfall. This is the end of the area open to tourists.

Lac Supérieur – This lake is fed only by water infiltrating the soil and falling from the roof; its level is 20m/66ft above that of the River Plane. Gours ring the lake's emerald waters.

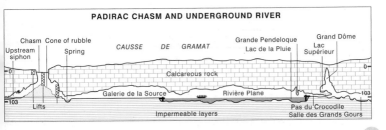

PADIRAC CHASM AND UNDERGROUND RIVER

Salle du Grand Dôme – The great height of the roof (91m/295ft) is most impressive in this, the largest and most beautiful of the Padirac caverns. The viewpoint, built halfway up, enables visitors to appreciate the rock formations and the flows of calcite decorating certain parts of the walls. The return trip (to the landing-stage) offers interesting views of the great pillar and the great pendant. From the end of the Galerie de la Source, four lifts (to avoid the walk up 455 steps) lead back to the entrance.

Grotte du PECH MERLE★★★

MICHELIN LOCAL MAP 337: F-4 – LOCAL MAP SEE CAHORS

Prehistoric people performed religious rites in this cave, which was only rediscovered thousands of years later in 1922. Not only is its natural decoration interesting, there are also wall paintings and carvings which are of great documentary value to prehistorians.

▶ **Orient Yourself**: The cave is located 7km/4.5mi north of St-Cirq-Lapopie and 32km/20mi east of Cahors.

☺ **Don't Miss**: A guided tour inside the cave.

♨ **Also See**: St-Cirq-Lapopie; Cahors.

A Bit of History

The underground explorers – Two boys of 15 and 16 were the heroes of the Pech Merle Cave rediscovery. Inspired by the expeditions and discoveries made throughout the region by Abbé Lemozi, the priest from Cabrerets who was a prehistorian and speleologist, the boys explored a small fault known only to have served as a refuge during the Revolution. The two friends ventured forward, creeping along a narrow, slimy trench pitted with wells and blocked by limestone concretions. After several hours their efforts were rewarded by the sight of wonderful paintings.

Abbé Lemozi, who soon afterwards explored the cave scientifically, recognised the importance of the underground sanctuary. It was decided to open it to tourists. In 1949 the discovery of a new chamber led to the finding of the original opening through which men had entered the cave about 16 000 to 20 000 years ago.

Visit 1hr 45min

Cave

🕐☛*Open mid-Apr to Oct, guided tour (1hr); tickets on sale from 9.30am-noon and 1.30-5pm. Access limited to 700 visitors per day (in July and August it is advisable to book 3 days in advance). ☞7€ (child: 4.50€), combined ticket with the Musée de Préhistoire.* ☎ *05 65 31 27 05. www.pechmerle.com.*

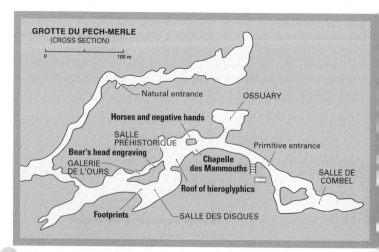

GROTTE DU PECH-MERLE
(CROSS SECTION)

0   100 m

Natural entrance · OSSUARY · Horses and negative hands · SALLE PRÉHISTORIQUE · Primitive entrance · Bear's head engraving · GALERIE DE L'OURS · Chapelle des Mammouths · SALLE DE COMBEL · Roof of hieroglyphics · Footprints · SALLE DES DISQUES

R. Delon/Castelet

Prehistoric painting

In addition to the interest it offers lovers of speleology who can marvel at the caverns of vast size communicating with each other through wide openings and decorated with beautiful concretions, the Pech Merle Cave offers prehistorians the sight of highly advanced paintings and engravings and material traces of prehistoric man's sojourn there.

The upper level of the **Chapelle des Mammouths** (Chapel of Mammoths or Black frieze) is decorated with drawings of bison and mammoths outlined in black and forming a frieze 7m/23ft long by 3m/10ft high.

The **Salle des Disques** is patterned with many strange concretions that look like discs; their formation might be due to the superposition of two slabs joined by a very thin layer. The footprints made by a prehistoric individual can be seen, petrified forever in the once wet clay of a *gour* (natural dam).

Further on the **Galerie des Ours** contains huge, impressive columns, eccentrics with delicate protuberances that defy the laws of gravity and cave pearls, with colours ranging from the shining white of pure calcite to red-ochre caused by the presence of clay and iron oxide in the limestone.

Beyond the Salle Rouge, visitors go down a narrow passageway, which contains an engraving of a bear's head, to the lower level of the **prehistoric gallery**, where one wall is decorated with the **silhouettes of two horses**, with dots patterning them and the surface around them, mysterious symbols and outlined hand prints, known as negative hands. These prints were made by stencilling in different pigments around the hands placed flat against the rock. The horses are depicted with distorted silhouettes (similar to those at Lascaux): a huge body and a tiny head. These prints and the roof of hieroglyphics once decorated a sanctuary older than that of the Chapel of Mammoths.

In the last cave to be visited, **Salle de Combel**, are the **bones of cave bears** and the roots of an oak tree that bored down into the cave in search of moisture.

Musée Amédée-Lémozi

 ♿⏰*Same opening times and charges as the Grotte du Pech-Merle (combined ticket).* ☎ *05 65 31 23 33.*

This is a research and information centre on prehistory in Quercy. There is an attractive and informative display of bones, tools, weapons, utensils and works of art from 160 different prehistoric sites, dating from the Lower Paleolithic Era to the Iron Age. Photographs of the decorated caves in the region (in particular Pech Merle and Cognac) are also exhibited. The museum visit ends with a film on Paleolithic art in Quercy.

PÉRIGORD NOIR★★

MICHELIN LOCAL MAP 329: G/I-6/7

This beautiful region, lying between the River Vézère and River Dordogne, is called Périgord Noir (Black Périgord), the word black referring to the dark colour of the forest cover consisting mainly of oaks, chestnut and sea pines. ⓘ *R. de Tourny, BP 144,, 24200 Sarlat-la-Canéda,* ☎ *05 53 31 45 45. www.sarlat-tourisme.com.*

🕐 **Organising Your Time**: Allow a full day to explore this delightful region.

🔎 **Don't Miss**: Sarlat-la-Canéda; Jardins d'Eyrignac; Cingle de Montfort; Château de Montfort.

Excursions

Round-trip from Sarlat★★

75km/47mi – allow one day

The houses, castles, châteaux, manor houses and churches along this route have walls of golden-coloured local limestone and steeply pitched roofs covered with lauzes or small flat tiles in a warm brown hue. These architectural elements, combined with the rolling, wooded countryside, make a harmonious picture.

Sarlat★★★ – 🕐 *See SARLAT-LA-CANÉDA.*

▷ *Leave Sarlat travelling SE along the D 704 towards Gourdon. As you leave town, turn right to La Canéda.*

Site de Montfort★

Occupying an advantageous site on the River Dordogne, Montfort has given its name to one of Périgord's most famous meanders.

Cingle de Montfort★ – From the cliff road (D 703 – car park), there is a splendid **view**★ of this meander in the river, known in French as the *Cingle de Montfort*, encircling the Tursac peninsula and its walnut tree plantations; the château clings to its promontory.

Château de Montfort★ –The castle stands in a grandiose **setting**★, which aroused the envy of those who wished to rule Périgord; its history consisted of a long series of sieges and battles. Seized by the formidable Simon de Montfort in 1214 and razed to the ground, it was rebuilt and then later destroyed three times – during the Hundred Years War (1337-1453), under Louis XI (1461-83), and again by order of Henri IV (1562-1610). The renovation work carried out in the 19C gives it the whimsical look of a stage setting for light opera.

▷ *Drive NW along the D 703.*

The village of Monfort below the château

Carsac-Aillac

The modest but delightful church of Carsac, built in lovely golden stone, stands in a country setting not far from the Dordogne.

The porch in the façade has five recessed arches resting on small columns. The massive Romanesque bell tower and the apse are roofed with *lauzes*.

The nave and the lower aisles had stellar vaulting decorated with elegant discs or bosses added to them in the 16C. A small dome on pendentives rises above the transept crossing. The chancel ends in a Romanesque apse with oven vaulting and is adorned with interesting archaic oriental-style capitals.

The **Stations of the Cross** are the work of the artist Zack. Unpretentious and austere in design, the work includes texts from the writings of Paul Claudel (diplomat and author: 1868-1955).

▷ *Leave Carsac travelling S along the D 704 to St-Rome and follow the signposts to the Jardins d'eau.*

Jardins d'Eau★

🕐 *Open May-Oct, 9am-8pm.* 🎫 *5€ (children aged 11-16: 2.50€).* ☎ *05 53 28 91 96 or 06 08 92 37 82.*

This 3ha/7.50-acre water garden was laid out along the riverside. The reception area is surrounded by a pond covered with exotic water lilies; it is home to a colony of frogs and five different kinds of dragonflies. Note that *gambusia*, commonly known as mosquito fish, are very efficient at keeping mosquitoes under control. The great white-water-lily pond, spanned by a Japanese bridge, evokes one of Monet's paintings, whereas the five varieties of iris bring Van Gogh to mind. On your way down, you will see part of a 4km/2.5mi long Roman aqueduct. The largest lotus flowers (2m/6.5ft high with leaves 70cm/28in in diameter) grow near the fountain, next to six varieties

---

Address Book

🪙 *For coin ranges, see the Legend at the back of the guide.*

EATING OUT

🍽🍽 **Auberge du Sol** – *24590 St-Crépin-et-Carlucet - 2km/1.2mi W of Salignac on the D 60 -* ☎ *05 53 28 80 51 -* 🕐 *closed 1 week in Jun, 14-28 Oct and Mon except public hols - reserv. required.* Don't look for the menu, as there isn't one! A charming inn with exposed beams and a large stone fireplace, where the emphasis is on delicious regional fare.

🍽🍽 **La Meynardie** – *24590 Salignac-Eyvigues - 2.5km/1.5mi NW of Salignac on the D 62 and then a minor road -* ☎ *05 53 28 85 98 - lameynardie24@wanadoo.fr -* 🕐 *closed late Nov to mid-Feb, Tue (except Jul-Aug) and Wed.* This restaurant deep in the countryside occupies an old farm. Dining room with exposed beams, a stone floor and walls, and an open fire. In fine weather, you can enjoy the reasonably priced and well-presented cuisine on the terrace.

WHERE TO STAY

🏕 **Camping La Bouquerie** – *24590 St-Geniès - 12km/7.5mi NW of Salignac via the D 60 and D 61 -* ☎ *05 53 28 98 22 - labouquerie@wanadoo.fr -* 🕐 *open 5 Apr-27 Sep - reserv. recommended - 183 pitches - restaurant (open evenings only).* A pleasant, well-maintained campsite with good facilities including swimming pools and shaded pitches. Mobile homes available for rent.

🏠🏠 **Chambre d'hôte Le Moulin de la Garrigue** – *24590 Borrèze - 9km/5.5mi SE of Salignac on the D 62 -* ☎ *05 53 28 84 88 -* ✍ - *5 rooms.* This pretty 19C mill is surrounded by woodland. The rooms are simple and functional, with mezzanines. Helpful owners who will point you in the right direction for good local restaurants, walks and other activities in the area. Swimming pool in the garden.

🏠🏠 **Chambre d'hôte Les Granges Hautes** – *Le Poujol - 24590 St-Crépin-et-Carlucet - 12km/8mi NE of Sarlat towards Brive and then Salignac -* ☎ *05 53 29 35 60 -* 🕐 *closed 13 Nov-15 Mar - 5 rooms.* A stylish property with non-smoking rooms decorated with charm and elegance. A lovely garden where you can relax in the shade or take a dip in the saltwater pool. Friendly hosts who will make you feel at home.

SHOPPING

Domaine de Béquinol – *Béquignolles - 24370 Carlux -* ☎ *05 53 29 73 41 - open Mon-Fri, 9am-noon and 1.30-5pm -* 🕐 *closed end Aug-early Sep and public hols.* This shop sells sweets and liqueurs made from walnuts, including Arlequines de Carlux, Nogaillous du Périgord, Bouchées aux noix, Noir et Noix and Béquinoix (an aperitif). Products on sale throughout the Perigord and Quercy, as well as at the Écomusée de la Noix in Castelnaud.

of white lilies. Take the footbridge wending its way above the lotus pond then touch and smell the water lilies floating on the tiered ponds among smaller water plants. All the varieties growing in the garden can be bought from the nursery.

▷ *Rejoin the D 704, cross the River Dordogne and turn left onto the D 50.*

Château de Fénelon★

🕙*Open Jul-Aug, 9.30am-7pm; Mar-Jun and Sep-Oct, 10am-noon and 2-6pm; Nov-Feb, 2-5pm.* 🚷 *For information on entrance fees, please enquire.* ☎ *05 53 29 81 45.*

François de Salignac de Lamothe-Fénelon, later to become the duke of Burgundy's mentor and author of *Télémaque*, was born here on 6 August 1651 and spent his early childhood within these walls. His family had been feudal lords since the 14C and remained so until 1780.

Built near Ste-Mondane village, on a hill overlooking the Dordogne and the Bouriane Forest, The 14C castle underwent substantial alterations in the 17C. Its triply fortified walls give it the appearance of being a very powerful fortress. The residential buildings and towers are still covered with *lauze* slate roofs. A beautiful **staircase** with two bends gives access to the main courtyard. On the right, beneath the gallery is a 96m/315ft-deep well dug out of the rock. From the terrace, there is a fine view of undulating countryside.

Inside, the bedroom where Fénelon was born, the Louis XVI and Empire rooms, the kitchen hollowed out of the rock and a collection of medieval military miscellany are all open to visitors.

▷ *Follow the D 50 to St-Julien-de-Lampon then drive over to the north bank of the river via the D 61.*

The crossing of the Dordogne is guarded by the **Château de Rouffillac**; its attractive outline can be seen rising out of the green oak trees.

Carlux

Overlooking the valley from its commanding position, the village still has some old houses and a small covered market. A rare Gothic chimney, jutting out from a gabled wall, adds a touch of the unexpected to the scene. Two towers and an imposing curtain wall are all that remains of the large castle, which once belonged to the viscounty of Turenne. From the castle terrace, there is a lovely **view** of the valley and the cliffs, which were used as the castle foundations.

▷ *Take the road behind the castle and follow the signposts for "Jardins de Cadiot."*

Jardins de Cadiot★ – 🕙 *Open May-Oct, 10am-7pm.* 🚷*5€ (child: 2.50€). ☎ 05 53 29 81 05.* This private 2ha/5-acre garden is surrounded by an oak wood. The tour starts with the vegetable garden and continues through 10 areas of different colours: the peony garden, the

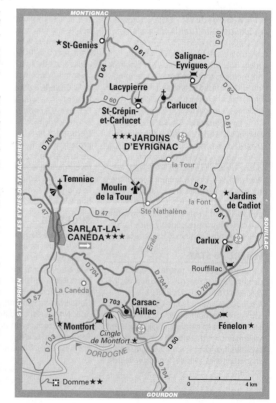

hornbeam maze, the rose garden containing 500 species of roses, the poetry garden, the English garden and the French garden, each having its own attraction.

▶ *Continue along the D 61 towards Salignac and turn left onto the D 47 3km/1.9mi further on. Turn right in Ste-Nathalène and drive towards Proissans.*

Moulin de la Tour

   ♿ ○ ⚲ *Open Jul-Aug, guided tour (30min) Mon, Wed, Fri, 9am-noon and 2-7pm, Sat 2-7pm; Jun and Sep, Wed and Fri, 9am-noon and 2-7pm, Sat 2-7pm; Apr-May, Wed and Fri, 9am-noon and 2-7pm; Oct-Mar, Fri, 9am-noon and 2-7pm.* ○ *Closed 1 Jan, 1 Nov and 25 Dec.* ⚲4€ *(under 6 years old: no charge).* ☎ 05 53 59 22 08.

The 16C watermill, driven by the flow of the River Enea, continues the traditional manufacture of walnut and hazelnut oils. There used to be many grain mills in Périgord which were also adaptable for the production of walnut oil during the winter. The mechanism of this mill is 150 years old. The tour of the mill explains the different stages.

▶ *Return to Ste-Nathalène. Shortly before reaching the village, turn left towards the hamlet of La Tour.*

Jardins d'Eyrignac★★★

♿ ○ ⚲ *Open Jun-Sep, guided tour (1hr), 9.30am-7pm; Apr-May, 10am-12.30pm and 2-7pm; Oct-Mar, 10.30am-12.30pm and 2.30pm to dusk.* ⚲8€ *(child: 4€).* ☎ 05 53 28 99 71. www.eyrignac. com.

Laid out in the 18C by the Marquis de la Calprenède, these gardens were remodelled many times during the 19C and finally given their present aspect in the 1960s by Gilles Sermadiras de Pouzols de Lile. Five gardeners work full time to look

The Eyrignac gardens

after the 4ha/10-acre gardens. The result is a happy compromise between the French-style garden and Tuscan topiary art, rich in evergreens which make for year-round delight. The grassy paths are bordered with well-trimmed yew, creating little green chambers; there are pine hedges, shapely boxwood bowers, apple trees in quincuncial arrangements (four trees in the corners and a fifth in the middle); cypress groves, urns, pools and dainty pavilions ornament the grounds of the 17C mansion, built in pale Sarlat stone. The latest addition to this enchanting place is the **Jardin blanc** (white garden); alleyways lined with white roses lead to five ornamental pools representing the five senses against a background of white rambling roses.

▶ *Rejoin the D 61 and turn left.*

Salignac-Eyvigues

The market square, the façade of the 13C convent (Couvent des Croisiers), and the neighbouring streets, in particular rue Sainte-Croix, are a charming sight, just a few yards away from the entrance to the castle.

Château – ⚬ *Closed for restoration.* There is a good overall view from the D 60, east of the village, of this medieval fortress which still belongs to the family of the archbishop of Cambrai, François de Salignac de la Mothe-Fénelon.

The castle, which was built between the 12C and 17C, is encircled by ramparts. Mullioned windows lighten the façade of the main building, which is flanked by round and square towers. The whole building is enhanced by the warm colour of the stone and the lovely stone slab (*lauzes*) roofs.

▶ *Drive W along the D 60 (Sarlat) and turn left as you leave the village.*

Carlucet

The church of Carlucet has an unusual 17C cemetery. Some of the tombs have been set in carved recesses in the curtain wall.

▶ *Drive SW out of Carlucet along a small winding road.*

St-Crépin-et-Carlucet

The charming **Château de Lacypierre** was built at the end of the 16C on the spot where a fortified building had once stood. The square main building is entirely roofed in lauzes and framed by turrets. 👍🕐🏷️ *Open Easter to 1 Nov, guided tour of the château by prior arrangement (book 2 days in advance), unaccompanied tour of the park and the exhibition on the restoration of the castle.* ⌔*5€.* ☎ *05 53 29 39 28.*

▶ *Continue N along the D 60 to Salignac and turn left onto the D 61 2km/1.2mi further on.*

St-Geniès★

This is one good example of the Périgord Noir's many beautiful villages with its golden limestone houses covered in *lauzes*, the ruins of a Romanesque keep and the 15C castle next to the church. Access to the church is through a fortified belfry-porch, which was added in the 16C.

Located at the top of a mound behind the post office, the **Chapelle du Cheylard**, a small Gothic chapel, is decorated with lovely 14C **frescoes**★ depicting the life of Christ and lives of popular saints.

▶ *Leave St-Geniès travelling S along the D 64 towards the D 704 and follow signs for Sarlat. Turn left at Les Presses.*

Temniac

The chapel of Notre-Dame, set on a hill overlooking Sarlat, offers a good **view**★ of that town. Once a pilgrimage centre, this 12C structure has certain Romanesque Périgord School characteristics: a nave vaulted with two domes and a pentagonal chancel. A black Virgin, the object of pilgrimages, is to be found in the crypt, which has archaic-style ogive vaulting.

Near the chapel stands the curtain wall of a castle (*restoration work in progress*), which was once a commandery of the Knights Templar before it became the residence of the bishops of Sarlat.

▶ *The D 57 leads back to Sarlat.*

PÉRIGUEUX★★

POPULATION 63 539

MICHELIN LOCAL MAP 329: F-4

Built in the fertile valley of the River Isle, Périgueux is an ancient town. Its long history can be traced in its urban architecture and its two distinctive districts, each of which is marked by the domes of its sanctuary: the Cité district, overlooked by St Stephen's tiled roof, and the Puy St-Front district, with the Byzantine silhouette of the present cathedral bristling with pinnacles. There is a good overall view of the town from the bridge beyond Cours Fénelon to the south-east. Périgueux's gastronomic specialities, with truffle and foie gras occupying prize position, have become famous around the world and attract many visitors.

▶ **Orient Yourself**: Périgueux is located on the banks of the River Isle, 48.5km/30mi north of Bergerac and 22km/14mi south of Brantôme.

🅿 **Parking**: The town has three large underground car parks in place Montaigne, place Francheville and along the esplanade du Théâtre (first 35min free of charge). Free outdoor car parks can also be found along the river, along part of the allées Tourny and on place Mauvard.

🕐 **Organising Your Time**: Once you have spent time exploring the town, allow a half day to explore the Périgord Blanc.

😊 **Don't Miss**: St-Front district; the cathedral; Musée du Périgord.

👍 **Also See**: Abbaye de Chancelade; Brantôme; Bergerac.

Address Book

For coin ranges, see the Legend at the back of the guide.

EATING OUT

☐ **Au Temps de Vivre** – *10 r. St-Silain -* ☎ *05 53 09 87 18 - ⏰ closed evenings, Sun and Mon - reserv. recommended.* Tucked away in a pleasant street in the old town, this restaurant serves daily specials, plus a selection of savoury and sweet pies. In the afternoon, tea and pastries are served here. The decor is enlivened by the attractive wooden tables and painted chairs.

☐ **Au Bien Bon** – *15 r. des Places -* ☎ *05 53 09 69 91 - ⏰ closed during Feb school hols and in early Nov, Sat lunchtime, Sun, Mon and public hols - ⬜.* The menu here is firmly influenced by seasonal local products. Dine in the rustic interior or outdoors on the summer terrace.

☐☐ **Le 8** – *8 r. Clarté -* ☎ *05 53 35 15 15 - yannick.guichaoua@wanadoo.fr - ⏰ closed 13-20 Apr, 2-10 Aug, 26 Oct-3 Nov, 25 Dec - 3 Jan, Sun and Mon - reserv. required.* This small, cosy restaurant near the cathedral has established an excellent local reputation for its authentic regional cuisine and an excellent pâté de Périgueux.

☐☐ **Le Clos Saint-Front** – *5 r. de la Vertu -* ☎ *05 53 46 78 58 - ⏰ closed for several days in early Nov.* This old house, with its exposed beams, fireplace and Louis XVI furniture, is now home to an elegant restaurant which is resolutely devoted to Périgourdine cuisine with an inventive twist. Attractive summer terrace with shade provided by linden, banana and liquidambars trees.

☐☐☐ **Hercule Poireau** – *2 r. de la Nation -* ☎ *05 53 08 90 76 - ⏰ closed 24-27 Dec, 31 Dec-3 Jan and Sat-Sun.* The name of this restaurant expresses the good humour of its owners: Hercule Poirot was, of course the Agatha Christie detective of Murder on the Orient Express, among other mysteries. The restaurant, in a vaulted 16C cellar, is popular with locals, who come here for the varied menu which includes several healthy options.

WHERE TO STAY

☐☐ **Comfort Hôtel Régina** – *14 r. Denis-Papin (opposite the train station) -* ☎ *05 53 08 40 44 - comfort.perigueux@wanadoo.fr - ⬜ - 45 rooms.* It is easy to spot this hotel as you exit the station, thanks to its newly repainted yellow façade. The rooms are small, functional and colourful. Buffet breakfast. Friendly service and a good location.

☐ **Chambre d'hôte La Calade** – *Le Bourg - 24420 St-Vincent-sur-l'Isle - 15km/9mi N of Périgueux on the N 21 towards Limoges, then turn right onto the D 705 -* ☎ *05 53 07 87 83 - j.hottiaux@libertysurf.fr - ⏰ closed 1 week at the end of Dec - ⬜ - 5 rooms.* This farm was built around 1750. The guestrooms, either in the main building or a restored barn, are furnished with a mixture of family items, old and new. A large chestnut tree provides welcome shade in the garden.

☐☐ **Hôtel L'Écluse** – *24420 Antonne-et-Trigonant - 10km/6mi NE of Périgueux on the N 21 -* ☎ *05 53 06 00 04 - contact@ ecluse-perigord.com - ⬜ - 43 rooms.* The River Isle flows gently past the small beach on the hotel property. The rooms on the main façade have balconies which overlook the river. Dine on the terrace in summer.

SHOPPING

Le Relais des Caves – *44 r. du Prés.-Wilson -* ☎ *05 53 09 75 00 - relais.aupert@ wanadoo.fr - ⏰ open Tue-Sat, 9am-12.30pm and 2-7.30pm; holidays: mornings only.* The friendly proprietor sells a wide selection of wines from across France, including a few very special vintages. Other local specialities such as fruit preserved in Bergerac wine, wine jam and foie gras are also sold here.

Stéphane Malard – *8 r. de la Sagesse -* ☎ *05 53 08 75 10 - ⏰ open mid-Jun to mid-Sep, Tue-Sun, 6.30am-12.45pm and 3.30-7.30pm; mid-Jul to the end of Aug, 6.30am-7.30pm; rest of the year, open Tue-Sat.* Behind the window arcades of his shop, Stéphane Malard sells some of the region's finest delicacies, including confits, foies gras, duck magret and wines. What he doesn't prepare himself, he sources with the greatest care.

La Ferme Périgourdine – *9 r. Limogeanne -* ☎ *05 53 08 41 22 - laferme.perigourdine@ wanadoo.fr - ⏰ open in summer, daily 7am-12.30pm and 2.30-7.30pm; rest of the year, daily except Sun, Mon and public hols.* The Thieullent family claims that local cheeses are too fatty, and prefer to ripen and sell cheeses from other parts of France. You will find their careful selection of quality products at the daily morning market (except Monday) on place du Coderc.

Markets – *Pl. de Clautre: Wed and Sat morning; pl. de la Clautre (food), pl. Bugeaud and pl. Franche-Ville (clothing): every morning; pl. du Coderc (food); duck and goose product market (marché au gras) from Dec-Feb.*

BARS AND CAFÉS

Tea for Tous – *Pl. St-Louis -* ☎ *05 53 53 92 86 - open Tue-Sat, 10am-7pm - ⏰ closed Sun and Mon.* In a building dating from the 16C, this charming tearoom draped in red and yellow fabric offers a selection of teas from the prestigious company Mariage, perhaps accompanied by a delicious home-made pastry. In fine weather, you can sit outside on place Saint-Louis.

Bar St-Silain – *7 pl. St-Silain* - ☎ *05 53 05 02 23* - ⏱ *open in summer, daily, 10am-2am; rest of the year, Tue-Sat, 9.30am-7pm.* More than a café, this is an outdoor experience! The setting is idyllic, with cane chairs set out on cobblestones under the trees.

Café de la Place – *7 pl. du Marché-au-Bois* - ☎ *05 53 08 21 11* - ⏱ *open daily, 9am-2am* - ⏱ *closed Christmas and 1 Jan.* Once known as the café for intellectuals, this café is perhaps the most popular in the town. Choose between the lovely outdoor terrace or the early-19C interior.

The Star Inn – *17 r. des Drapeaux* - ☎ *05 53 08 56 83 www.thestarinnfrance.com* - ⏱ *open in summer, 8pm-2am; rest of the year, Mon-Sat, 8pm-1am.* The Anglo-Irish owners have created a home-away-from-home for their compatriots, with regular events found in a typical British or Irish pub. Three rooms, with lots of old stone, dark wood, tall bookcases and photographs of sailors adorning the walls. Pleasant terrace for the summer months. The inscription next to the bar, "Chevaliers de la Royale Champagne", was carved in the stone in 1778.

LEISURE ACTIVITIES

Gabarre Vésunna – *Quai de l'Isle* - ☎ *05 53 24 58 80* - *departures every hour in summer from 11am-6pm* - *services do not operate from mid-Sep to mid-June* - ☎ *6.50€ (child: 4€).* This 50min cruise on the river provides an excellent introduction to the town and its 2 000 years of history. On-board commentary.

A Bit of History

The wonderful Vésone – The town of Périgueux owes its foundation to a sacred spring known as the Vésone. It was near the stream, on the Isle's south bank, that the Gaulish Petrocorii (Petrocorii, which meant the four tribes in Celtic, gave its name both to Périgueux and Périgord) built their main *oppidum* (defensive town). After siding with Vercingetorix against Caesar, the Petrocorii finally had to accept Roman domination but in fact benefited greatly from the Pax Romana, which enabled the city to become one of the finest in all Aquitaine. Vesunna, as the town was then called, spread beyond the bend in the Isle; temples, a forum, basilicas and an arena were built and an aqueduct over 7km/4mi long was constructed to carry water to the baths. But in the 3C AD the city's prosperity was destroyed by the Alemanni, who sacked this town as well as 70 other towns throughout Gaul.

The unfortunate town – To avoid further disaster the Vesunnians shut themselves up in a narrow fortified enclosure; stones from the temples were used to build powerful ramparts and the arena was transformed into a keep.

In spite of all these precautions, the town suffered the alternate depredations of fire and pillaging by barbaric invaders such as the Visigoths, Franks and Norsemen. Such misfortune reduced Vesunna to the status of a humble village and finally even its name died; it was simply known as the city of the Petrocorii and *la Cité* eventually became the town's new name. St Front later established the town as an Episcopal seat and, in the 10C, it became the unassuming capital of the county of Périgord.

The ambition of Puy-St-Front – A little sanctuary containing the tomb of St Front, Apostle of Périgord, was built not far from the Cité. Initially the object of a pilgrimage, the sanctuary became a monastic centre. A busy market town, Puy St-Front, grew up round the monastery, soon eclipsing the Cité in size.

The townspeople of Puy St-Front joined the feudal alliances against the English kings, established an emancipated consular regime and then sided with Philip Augustus against King John of England.

Little by little, the expanding Puy St-Front annexed the Cité's prerogatives; there were more and more squabbles between the rivals. The Cité, unable to win against its neighbour who was under the protection of the king of France, was forced to accept union. On 16 September 1240, an act of union established that the Cité and Puy St-Front would now form one community governed by a mayor and 12 consuls, under the name of Périgueux. Nevertheless, each town kept its distinctive characteristics; the Cité belonged to the clerics and aristocrats whereas Puy St-Front belonged to the merchants and artisans.

Périgueux becomes Préfecture – In 1790, when the Dordogne *département* was created, Périgueux was chosen over Bergerac as Préfecture. The town, which had slowly become dormant, suddenly found itself the object of a building boom. The old districts were enhanced by the addition of avenues and new squares.

The transfer of stamp printing from Paris to Périgueux in 1970 (almost two centuries later) turned Périgueux into the main production centre of postal stamps (more than 3.5 billion per year!) for France and a dozen or so other countries.

St-Front District★★★

The old artisans' and merchants' district has been given a face-lift. A conservation program for safeguarding this historic area was set up, and the area has been undergoing major restoration. Its Renaissance façades, medieval houses, courtyards, staircases and shops are being gradually brought back to life; the pedestrian streets have rediscovered their role as commercial thoroughfares.

Place du Coderc and place de l'Hôtel-de-Ville are colourful and animated every morning with their fruit and vegetable market, whereas place de la Clautre is where the larger Wednesday and Saturday market is held. During the winter, the prestigious truffle and foie gras markets held in place St-Louis attract hordes of connoisseurs. In summer, the restaurants, overflowing onto the pavements, serve high quality Périgord cuisine in an atmosphere of days past.

Walking Tour

▶ *Start at Tour Mataguerre (tower) opposite the tourist office.*

Tour Mataguerre
Only as part of a guided tour of the town.

This round tower (late 15C) is crowned by a machicolated parapet and pierced by arrow-slits. It is the last of the 28 towers forming the defensive system of Puy St-Front in the Middle Ages. On the side of rue de la Bride part of the ramparts can be seen. The name Mataguerre is believed to have come from an Englishman who was imprisoned in the tower.

From the top (viewing table), there is a **view**★ of the old district with its tiled roofs, the towers of the noblemen's town houses, the domes of St-Front and the neighbouring hills, one of which is the well-known Écornebœuf Hill (*écorner* means to break the horns of an animal; *bœuf* means ox) so named because the hill was so steep that the oxen broke their necks...and lost their horns.

▶ *Follow rue de la Bride.*

Rue des Farges

At nos 4 and 6 stands the **Maison des Dames de la Foi** (House of the Women of Faith). The medieval (12C) layout of its façade is still visible: pointed arches on the ground floor, rounded arches on the upper storey and a loggia beneath the eaves. A small bell turret set in one corner brings to mind the fact that in the 17C the building was a convent, whose congregation gave the house its name.

▶ *Look down passage Taillefer before turning right onto the narrow ruelle des Farges which leads to place de Navarre. Walk up the stairs.*

Rue Aubergerie

At no 16, the **Hôtel d'Abzac de Ladouze** consists of great round arch, an octagonal tower and a corbelled turret, all characteristics of 15C architecture.

At nos 4 and 8 the **Hôtel de Sallegourde**, also 15C, has a polygonal tower surmounted by a machicolated watch-path.

▶ *Turn left.*

Rue St-Roch

At no 4 a small arcaded loggia is decorated with diamond-work. Further on, on the corner of rue de Sully, note the tastefully restored half-timbered house.

▶ *Bear left.*

Rue du Calvaire

The condemned, on their way to be executed on place de la Clautre, came up this street, their road to Calvary. At no 3 there is a lovely door ornamented with nailheads beneath a Renaissance porch.

The street leads to place de la Clautre which offers an interesting view of the imposing St Front Cathedral.

Cathédrale St-Front★★

This cathedral, now on UNESCO's World Heritage List, is one of the largest in Southwest France and one of the most curious.

A chapel was first built on the site of the saint's tomb in the 6C. The origin of the abbey established around the sanctuary is either Augustinian or Benedictine. In 1047 a larger church was consecrated. This second building was almost completely destroyed by fire in 1120, whereupon it was decided to construct an even bigger church.

PÉRIGUEUX

Abreuvoir R. de l'	CY 2
Amphithéâtre R. de l'	AZ 3
Aquitaine Av. d'	BYZ 4
Arènes Bd des	AZ 6
Arsault R. de l'	CY
Aubarède R.	CYZ
Aubergerie R.	BZ 9
Barbecane R.	CY 12
Barbusse Av. Henri	AY 13
Barris Pont des	CZ
Bert R. Paul	AZ
Bloy R. L.	CZ
Boétie R. de la	BZ
Bonnelie R. Sergent	CZ
Born Bd Bertran-de	BZ
Bride R. de la	BZ 15
Bugeaud Pl.	BZ
Calvaire R. du	BZ 16
Cavaignac Av.	AZ 18
Chanzy Carrefour	AY
Chanzy R.	AYZ
Cité R. de la	ABZ 23
Clarté R. de la	BZ 24
Claude-Bernard R.	AZ
Clautre Pl. de la	BZ 26
Clos-Chassaing	BY 27
Coderc Pl. du	BYZ 28
Combe-des-Dames R.	BY
Condé R.	BZ 29
Constitution R. de la	CY 30
Courier R. Paul-Louis	CY
Cronstadt R. de	AY
Daumesnil Av. et Pl.	BCZ 32
Daumesnil Galerie	BYZ 31
Deux Ponts R. des	AYZ
Durand Rd-Pt Charles	AZ 34
Eguillerie R.	BY 35
Faidherbe Pl.	CZ
Farges R. des	BZ
Fénelon Cours	BZ
Francheville Pl.	BZ
Gadaud R. A.	ABY
Gambetta R.	ABY
Goudeau Pl. Émile	CY 36
Guillier R.	ABZ
Guynemer R.	BY
Hôtel de Ville Pl. de l'	BZ 37
Jacobins R. des	AY
Juin Av. du Mar.	AY
Kléber R.	AY
Lacombe R.	CZ
Lakanal Bd	BZ
Lammary R.	BY 38
Lanxade Rd-Pt P.-	AY
Limogeanne R.	BY
Louis-Blanc R.	AY
Magne R. P.	CZ
Mangold R. Charles	BZ
Marché au bois Pl. du	BCY 63
Maurois Pl. André	BY 39
Metz R. de	AY
Mie R. L	BY
Miséricorde R. de la	BY 40
Mobiles-de-Coulmiers R.	AY 41
Montaigne Bd M.	BYZ

Montaigne Cours et Pl. M.	BYZ		Romaine R.	AZ
Musset R. A.-de	CY		Sagesse R. de la	BY 46
Notre-Dame R.	CY 42		St-Front R.	CY
Papin R. Denis	AY		St-Georges Cours et Pont	CZ
Plantier R. du	CYZ		St-Georges Pl.	CZ
Plumancy Pl.	AY		St-Louis Pl.	BY
Pompidou Av. G.	BV		St-Martin Pl.	AY
Port Allée du	AY 43		St-Pierre-ès-Liens R.	ABZ 47
Port-de-Graule R. du	CYZ 44		St-Roch R.	BZ 48
Prés R. des	CZ		St-Silain Pl.	BY 49
Président-Wilson R. du	AY		Ste-Marthe R.	CZ 50
Puebla R.	AY		Saumande Bd Georges	CYZ
République R. de la	BYZ 45		Solferino R.	AY
Rivière R. de la	CYZ		Stalingrad Bd de	CZ

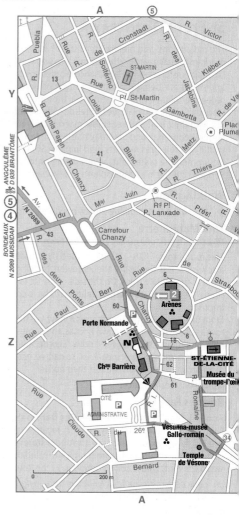

This third basilica, completed about 1173, was Byzantine in style, with a dome and with a ground plan in the form of a Greek cross. This architecture, which is uncommon in France, brings to mind St Mark's in Venice and the church of the Apostles in Constantinople. This was the first domed church to be built on the Roman road, which was still used in the Middle Ages by those travelling from Rodez to Cahors and on to Saintes.

In 1575, during the Wars of Religion, St Front was pillaged by the Huguenots, the treasure was scattered and the saint's tomb destroyed. Restoration was carried out with little regard for the original design.

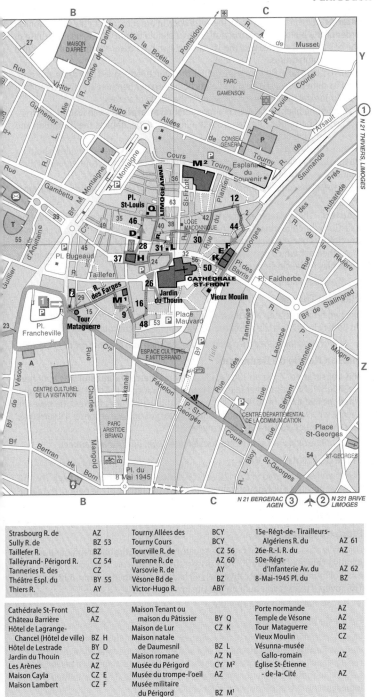

Strasbourg R. de	AZ	Tourny Allées des	BCY	15e-Régt-de- Tirailleurs-	
Sully R. de	BZ 53	Tourny Cours	BCY	Algériens R. du	AZ 61
Taillefer R.	BZ	Tourville R. de	CZ 56	26e-R.-I. R. du	AZ
Talleyrand- Périgord R.	CZ 54	Turenne R. de	AZ 60	50e-Régt-	
Tanneries R. des	CZ	Varsovie R. de	AY	d'Infanterie Av. du	AZ 62
Théâtre Espl. du	BY 55	Vésone Bd de	BZ	8-Mai-1945 Pl. du	BZ
Thiers R.	AY	Victor-Hugo R.	ABY		

Cathédrale St-Front	BCZ	Maison Tenant ou		Porte normande	AZ
Château Barrière	AZ	maison du Pâtissier	BY Q	Temple de Vésone	AZ
Hôtel de Lagrange-		Maison de Lur	CZ K	Tour Mataguerre	BZ
Chancel (Hôtel de ville)	BZ H	Maison natale		Vieux Moulin	CZ
Hôtel de Lestrade	BY D	de Daumesnil	BZ L	Vésunna-musée	
Jardin du Thouin	CZ	Maison romane	AZ N	Gallo-romain	AZ
Les Arènes	AZ	Musée du Périgord	CY M²	Église St-Étienne	
Maison Cayla	CZ E	Musée du trompe-l'oeil	AZ	- de-la-Cité	AZ
Maison Lambert	CZ F	Musée militaire			
		du Périgord	BZ M¹		

It was largely reconstructed by Abadie from 1852 onwards in the style of Second Empire pastiche. He was to use this restoration later as the inspiration for the design of the Sacré Cœur Basilica in Paris.

Exterior – Stand in place de la Clautre to have an overall view. Before the restoration, the domes, covered in stones and tiles, had small end ornaments. The façade overlooking place de la Clautre and the open bays were part of the 11C church. The beautiful tiered bell tower is all that remains of the 12C church, and is preserved more or less as it was originally. Abadie drew on its lantern as inspiration for the tall pinnacles which adorn the new domes.

Interior – *Enter the cathedral by the north door.* In order to respect the chronological order of the building's construction, visitors should first of all see, near the base of the bell tower, the remains of the 11C church; two bays covered with domes perched on tall column drums.

From its prestigious Romanesque model, the church redesigned by Abadie appropriated its dimensions, the boldness of its domes on pendentives and the strength of its odd-looking pillars carved in places in the shape of a cross.

Adorning the back of the apse is a monumental **altarpiece**★★ in walnut; this masterpiece of baroque sculpture, from the Jesuit College, depicts the Dormition and the Assumption of the Virgin.

Admire the **pulpit**★, a fine example of 17C craftsmanship, where Hercules is holding up the stand while two atlantes carry the sounding board. The five monumental brass chandeliers, hanging at each of the bays, were designed by Abadie.

☺ *A visit to the cathedral is included in the guided tour of the "Medieval and Renaissance town".*

Cloisters – The cloisters date from the 12C, 13C and 16C and are of a half-Romanesque, half-Gothic architectural style. The enormous pine-cone-like mass in the centre of the cloisters once crowned the bell tower; during the Revolution it was replaced by a weathercock which was later replaced by Abadie's angel. Several sarcophagi are on display in the cloisters' galleries.

▶ *Walk to the right of the building.*

Place du Thouin

The two bronze cannon with the inscription Périgueux 1588 were excavated at place du Coderc in 1979 on the site of the armoury in the old consulate.

▶ *Walk round the cathedral to place Daumesnil then turn left onto rue de la Clarté.*

Maison Natale de Daumesnil

This house, at no. 7, has an 18C façade. **General Pierre Daumesnil** was born here on 27 July 1776. This soldier followed Napoleon to Arcola, to Egypt and to Wagram, where he lost a leg. In 1814, while governor of the Vincennes fortress, he gave the enemy, who were laying siege and urging him to give up, the response: "I'll surrender Vincennes when you give me back my leg."

▶ *Continue along rue de la Clarté, turn left then right onto rue du Serment.*

Place de l'Hôtel-de-Ville

The town hall is located in the 17C and 18C **Hôtel de Lagrange-Chancel**. The 15C house at no 7 has a polygonal staircase tower characteristic of the period. Its machicolations are neo-Gothic.

▶ *Walk to the left of the town hall.*

Place du Coderc

Originally a field for keeping pigs, this square has become the geographic and administrative centre of the Puy St-Front district. In the early 19C the old consulate, the heart of municipal and legislative life, still had its square belfry, some 600 years old. The covered market was built on this site in c 1830.

▶ *Follow rue de la Sagesse opposite.*

Hôtel de la Joubertie

Visits as part of a guided tour of the town. Located at no 1, this mansion contains an elegant **Renaissance staircase**★, of a square design, decorated with a coffered ceiling depicting mythological scenes including Venus putting down her weapons, which symbolises the young wife entering the household. The intertwined H and S represent the initials of the Hauteforts and Solminihacs.

Place St-Louis

This square is known locally as Foie Gras Square, as it is here that the foies gras are sold in late autumn.

It features a modern fountain, decorated with a bronze sculpture by Ramon.

Maison Tenant or the **Maison du Pâtissier**, opposite, used to be the Talleyrands' town house; it consists of a residential part set at right angles, with an adjoining corbelled turret. The corner door, oddly enough, has a double squinch above it. A machicolated parapet runs around the small inner courtyard. The façade on rue Eguillerie has a marvellous Gothic window.

No 5 rue Lammary has an unusual superposition of mullioned corner windows.

▶ *Turn right.*

Rue Limogeanne★

In the past, this street led to Limogeanne Gate (Porte Limogeanne), which opened onto the Limoges road. The large pedestrian street is lined with numerous stores and several elegant Renaissance town houses.

In the courtyard of the **Hôtel de Méredieu** (no 12) there is a 15C carved doorway decorated with a coat of arms, which was added in the 17C.

At no 7, note the initials A C in the centre of the wrought-iron impost; these denote Antoine Courtois, the famous 18C caterer, whose partridge pâtés were the talk even of the Court of Prussia. His headquarters were in the cellars of this town house.

Maison Estignard (no 5) has an elegant Renaissance façade.

The Regional Department of Architecture is to be found at no 3. Behind the heavy balustrade above the doorway, the inner courtyard has a lovely door decorated with grotesques on the lintel and François I salamanders on the tympanum. The huge staircase is remarkable.

Lapeyre House (no 1), which is at the corner of place du Coderc, has a corbelled corner turret.

▶ *Retrace your steps and turn right onto impasse Limogeanne.*

Galerie Daumesnil★

It consists of a network of courtyards and small squares linked by alleyways. The buildings, which were grafted on over the centuries, have been demolished, creating open spaces and revealing the fine 15C, 16C and 17C façades.

▶ *Come out onto rue de la Miséricorde and cross rue St-Front.*

Walking along rue St-Front, developed in the 19C, notice on the left the unusual Masonic Lodge (Loge Maçonnique) perforated by openings like arrow slits. The sculptures on the façade represent masonic emblems.

Rue de la Constitution

At no 3 is the **doorway of the Hôtel de Crémoux** with a crocketed arch between tall pinnacles.

At no 7, the **Hôtel de Gamanson**, also called Logis St-Front, consists of two 15C wings set at right angles, linked by a staircase tower, flanked by a corbelled turret and perforated by mullioned windows. A 17C well is sheltered by a Moorish dome.

▶ *Turn left onto rue du Plantier then turn right.*

Rue Barbecane

The street owes its name to an old tower, now destroyed; all that remains is part of a wall. Before taking the stairs in rue de l'Abreuvoir, note the 19C façade of the Hôtel de Fayolle. Walk along the street then turn round to admire the 17C front of this mansion overlooking the river.

▶ *Turn right.*

Rue du Port-de-Graule

Just like rue Ste-Marthe which prolongs it, this street still has a medieval air about it with its large uneven paving stones, its low doors and the little staircase-alleyways that lead off it. In 1967, several scenes from the film of Jacquou le Croquant (based on local author Eugene le Roy's novel) were shot here.

▶ *Walk to boulevard Georges-Saumande on the left.*

Maisons de Lur, Cayla, Lambert

S. Sauvignier/ MICHELIN

The quays

Along the river there are several fine houses standing side by side. **Maison Lambert**, on the left of Pont des Barris, is called the House with Columns because of its gallery; it is a fine Renaissance town house with two wings set at a right angle and lit by mullioned windows. Next to it, **Maison Cayla**, also called the Consul's House, was built on the ramparts in the 15C. The roof is decorated with Flamboyant-style dormers. At the corner of avenue Daumesnil, the **Maison de Lur** dates from the 16C.

Continue along the quays; on the other side of avenue Daumesnil the half-timbered building, corbelled over the fortress wall, is a remainder of the **barn** attached to the cathedral, called the **Old Mill**, which once jutted out over the river.

▶ *Turn right onto rue de Tourville leading back to the cathedral.*

If you have enjoyed this walk through the medieval town, there are still plenty of narrow winding streets for you to explore.

Cité District★

This district, occupying the site of ancient Vesunna, has retained numerous Gallo-Roman ruins which testify to the town's importance under Roman occupation.

Walking Tour

▶ *Leave from the tourist office, follow rue de la Cité then turn right onto rue de l'Évêché.*

Arènes

A public garden occupies the space where the arena once stood. Built in the 1C, this amphitheatre, one of the largest in Gaul, had a capacity for 20 000 people. Great blocks of stone still mark the stairwells, the passages between banks of seating and the vaulting, but all of the lower part of the building is still buried below ground. Demolition of the arena began in 3C, when the amphitheatre was turned into a bastion and became part of the city ramparts. The arena was next transformed into a quarry, its stone being used to build houses in the town.

▶ *On leaving the amphitheatre, take rue de Turenne on the left.*

Porte Normande

This gateway formed part of the ramparts built in the 3C to protect the city from the hordes of barbarians sweeping across Europe. The story behind the name is that the gate is supposed to have played a part in the defence of the city against the Vikings who came up the River Isle in the 9C.

Maison Romane

This 12C (Romanesque) rectangular building is neighbour to the vestiges of a tower from the Gallo-Roman defence wall, jumbled up with bits of capitals, column drums and other architectural elements. An altar on which bulls were sacrificed was discovered here; it is now on display in the Gallo-Roman Museum (◖ *see below*).

Château Barrière

This castle has a 12C keep rising above one of the towers of the ramparts. It was altered during the Renaissance period but kept the lovely, main entrance door in the staircase tower. Destroyed by fire during the Wars of Religion, it was not rebuilt.

▶ *Cross the bridge on the right.*

Vesunna – Musée Gallo-Romain de Périgueux

◖*Open Jul-Aug, 10am-7pm; Apr-Jun, Sep to mid-Nov and Christmas hols, daily except Mon, 10am-noon and 2-6pm; Feb-Mar and mid-Nov to end of Dec, daily except Mon, 10am-12.30pm and 2-5.30pm.* ◖*Closed 1 Jan and 25 Dec.* ◖*5.50€ (children aged 6-12: 3.50€).* ☎ *05 53 05 65 65.*

Designed by Jean Nouvel, this museum houses the remains of an opulent Gallo-Roman residence covering 4 000m²/4 784sq yd. Built in the centre of a garden, it is like a large glassed-in inner courtyard reflecting the surroundings and blending perfectly with them. On one side, a mezzanine on two storeys overlooks the ancient *domus*. This section of the museum is devoted to the ancient town of Vesunna: a scale model of the town in the 2C shows how extensive it was in Roman times – the residence can easily be located near the sanctuary and the forum. The lapidary collection includes fine examples of architectural ornamentation and an altar used for bull sacrifice, originally in the temple.

Wooden footbridges enable visitors to wander through the house. Digs have revealed the presence of a 1C building, considerably extended in the 2C. Elaborate murals can be seen on the base of the walls of the primitive house. The frieze surrounding the central pond, on the other hand, was painted when the house was extended. Along the way, the daily life of the inhabitants is illustrated: hypocaust heating system, decoration, water distribution (oak water pump) and various handicrafts.

Tour de Vésone

Temple de Vésone

This tower, 20m/65.5ft high and 17m/56ft in diameter, is all that remains of the temple dedicated to the titular goddess of the city. The temple, which was built in the heart of the old Cité in the 2C AD, originally had a peristyle, and was surrounded by porticoes and framed by two basilicas. The tower is still impressive despite being damaged.

▸ *Cross the bridge and turn left along rue Romaine where the remains of a Roman wall (Late Empire) can be seen.*

St-Étienne-de-la-Cité★

🕐*Open daily except Sun and holidays, 8am-7pm.*

Built in the 11C on the site of the ancient temple of Mars, this church, the town's first Christian sanctuary, was dedicated by St Front to the martyr Stephen and was the cathedral church until 1669.

It included a row of four domed bays, one after the other, preceded by an imposing belfry porch. When the town was occupied in 1577, the Huguenots demolished all but the two east bays. The Episcopal palace, nearby, was also destroyed. Restored in the 17C, ravaged again during the Fronde, secularised during the Revolution, St Stephen's was consecrated anew at the time of the First Empire.

The church as it now stands is a good example of the pure Périgord-Romanesque style.

Inside, it is interesting to compare the architecture of the two bays built within a 50-year interval. The first (11C) is archaic, primitive, short and dark. The arches serve as wall ribs and the dome, the largest in Périgord, being 15m/49ft in diameter, is illuminated by small windows. The second bay is more slender. Its dome rests on pointed arches held up by square pillars, made less heavy in appearance by twinned columns.

Against the south wall of the first bay is an impressive 17C **altarpiece** in oak and walnut built for the seminary. Facing it is a carved arcade, part of the tomb of Jean d'Asside, bishop of Périgueux (1160-69), which now frames the 12C baptismal font.

A modern Stations of the Cross is the work of the painter J-J Giraud.

Sights

Musée du Périgord★

🕐*Open Apr-Sep, 10.30am-5.30pm, Sat-Sun, 1-6pm; Oct-Mar, 10am-5pm, Sat-Sun, 1-6pm.*
🕐*Closed Tue and public hols. ◉4€. No charge, noon-2pm, on Mon, Wed, Thu and Fri from Oct-May. ☎ 05 53 06 40 70.*

The Perigord Museum, located on allées de Tourny, on the site of what was an Augustinian convent, houses one of the most important **collections of prehistory** in France. It contains, in particular, a remarkable collection of engraved objects of the Magdalenian period (15000-12000 BC), found in various sites across the Dordogne region, as well as the fossilized skeleton of the Regour-dou man (Neanderthal man 70000 BC, ⓘ *see LASCAUX*) and of the Raymonden man (*Homo sapiens*, 15000 years old), The section of **non-European ethnography** displays daily-life objects and sculpture from Africa, Oceania and America.

The collection of **medieval exhibits** includes Limoges enamels, 11C capitals from the cathedral, the 13C Virgin altar-piece, the 13C Rabastens diptych, and a 15C liturgical cupboard which used to belong to Chancelade Abbey.

The **fine arts and decorative arts Department** (16C-20C), displays works by local artists next to works by French, European and Asian artists; note the portrait of Fénelon by F Bailleul (18C) and Sem by François Flameng (20C).

Musée du Périgord

Terracotta figures (16C) used as finials on roof cresting from the Château de la Borde at Festalemps

Musée Militaire du Périgord

🕐*Open Apr-Sep, daily except Sun and public hols, 1pm-6pm (last entrance 30min before closing); Oct-Dec, daily except Sun and public hols, 2-6pm; Jan-Mar, Wed and Sat, 2-5pm.* ☞*3.50€ (under 10 years old: no charge).* ☎ *05 53 53 47 36.*

Arms and weapons of all sorts, standards and uniforms evoke the military history of Périgord from the Middle Ages to today. The great military men of the region are also remembered. Particularly honoured is the 50th Infantry Regiment; note one of the regiment's flags, which Colonel Ardouin wrapped around his body to prevent it from falling into enemy hands after the surrender of Sedan.

Musée du Trompe-l'œil

🕐⁓*Guided tours, Apr-Sep, 10.30am-12.30pm and 2.30-6.30pm, Sun, 3-6pm; Oct-Mar, daily except Mon and public hols, 2-5.30pm, Sun, 3-5.30pm (by prior arrangement).* 🕐*Closed Mon and public hols.* ☎ *05 53 09 84 40.*

Located in the Gallo-Roman district, this museum relates the history of *trompe-l'œil* techniques from prehistoric times to the present, by means of panels illustrating each major period, with additional comments by the enthusiastic owner. An exhibition/sales area displays today's production and courses are organised by professionals.

Excursion

Périgord Blanc

Round-trip 56km/35mi – allow half a day

▶ *Leave Périgueux along the D 939 towards Brantôme.*

The region owes its name of Périgord Blanc to the colour of the local stone.

Abbaye de Chancelade★

ⓘ *See Abbaye de CHANCELADE.*

▶ *Leave Chancelade on the D 2 travelling N. The road between Chancelade and Merlande rises through a wood of chestnut and oak trees.*

Prieuré de Merlande

In a deserted clearing in Feytaud Forest stand a small fortified chapel and a prior's house, as solitary reminders of the Merlande Priory founded here in the 12C by the monks of Chancelade. Both have been restored. The chapel appears to be a fortress-like structure with its 4-sided plan and the little fort protecting its east end. The chancel, the oldest part, is slightly above the level of the nave and preceded by a rounded triumphal arch. It has barrel vaulting and a flat east end and is bordered by a series of blind arcades adorned with finely carved archaic **capitals**★; tangled-up monsters and lions devouring palm-leaf scrolls make up a bizarre but striking fauna.

▶ *Return to the D 2, turning left then right 2.5km/1.5mi farther on.*

Château-l'Évêque

The village took its name from the Episcopal castle. This has been altered several times since the 14C. It consists of an asymmetrical main building. The façades facing the Beauronne Valley have mullioned windows, and a machicolated watch-path runs around the line of the roof.

The parish church is where St Vincent de Paul, founder of missionary organisations to help the poor, was ordained by Monsignor François de Bourdeille in September 1600 at the early age of 20.

▶ *Leave the village travelling NE along the D 3E.*

Agonac

In a pleasant setting in the wooded hills of the area known as Perigord Blanc, the **Église St-Martin** gives this town its character. The square belfry and the buttresses (16C) were added to repair damage incurred during the Wars of Religion. The interior (late 11C and 12C) is typical of Romanesque churches in Périgord. The system of two-storey high defensive chambers encircling the 12C dome recalls the troubled times when churches were turned into fortresses. *Open mid-Jul to mid-Aug, guided tours by prior arrangement, daily except Sat-Sun and public hols, 4-6pm. ☎ 05 53 06 36 71.*

▶ *Continue E along the D 106.*

Sorges

This pleasant village has a century-old reputation for producing truffles, and a museum to honour them. The **Musée de la Truffe** in the tourist office tells you everything you ever wanted to know about this rare, delectable fungus, and directs you to a walking tour (*3km/1.9mi*) outside of town, where, if you are very lucky, you just might find one yourself. *Open mid-Jun to mid-Sep, 9.30am-12.30pm and 2.30-6.30pm (last entrance 30min before closing); Feb to mid-Jun and mid-Sep to mid-Nov, daily except Mon, 10am-noon and 2-5pm; mid-Nov to Jan, daily except Mon, 2-5pm. Guided tours, Jul-Aug, Tue and Thu, 2.30pm. Closed 1 Jan, 1 May, 1 Nov and 25 Dec. 4€ (10-15 years old: 2€). ☎ 05 53 05 90 11.*

Château des Bories

On the way back to Périgueux along the N 21. Open Jul-Aug, guided tour (45min, château and park), daily except Sun, 3-6pm. 4.50€ (children: 1.50€). ☎ 05 53 06 00 01.

A 15C-16C gem that boasts a splendid monumental staircase in the square tower, unusual vaulting over the guard-room and a fine Flemish tapestry in the long gallery.

Le QUERCY BLANC★

MICHELIN LOCAL MAP 337: C/E-5/7

Between the Lot and Tarn valleys, the region known as Quercy Blanc, so-called because of the white colour of the chalky soil, is characterised by low, long plateaux, arranged in rows (*serres*) with narrow, fertile valleys between them. The landscape and architecture are similar to that of the neighbouring Garonne region; red brick constructions, nearly flat roofs covered in pale-pink Roman tile. Vineyards (the highly appreciated Chasselas variety is grown in Moissac), plum trees, peach trees and melons thrive on the sunny hillsides; tobacco, sunflower and corn are grown on the valley floors. This mixed-farming land is dotted with windmills, dovecots, Romanesque churches and castles.

🕐 **Organising Your Time**: Allow two full days to explore this scenic region.

Excursions

1 Churches and Mills

60km/37mi round-trip from Castelnau-Montratier – allow one day

Castelnau-Montratier
A map of the town with useful information is available at the tourist office.

This hilltop *bastide* was founded in the 13C by Ratier, lord of Castelnau, who gave it his name. It replaced a small village, Castelnau-de-Vaux, which was destroyed by Simon de Montfort in 1214 at the time of the Albigensian Crusade. The town "**square**" is in the form of a triangle, surrounded by covered arcades and old houses. Note the **Église St-Martin** standing right at the end of the promontory.

North of the promontory are three **windmills**, one of which still works. Such mills with rotating caps were once common in Quercy.

▶ *Leave Castelnau S along the D 659 and turn left 3km/1.9mi farther on.*

One of three mills at Castelnau-Montratier

S. Sauvignier/MICHELIN

Église de Russac

The church has an oven-vaulted Romanesque east end decorated with carved modillions; the original north doorway was walled up. Inside, note the 16C fresco in the apse, particularly the central panel depicting St George slaying the dragon.

▸ *Rejoin the D 659, drive 1km/0.6mi towards Castelnau and turn right onto the D 26, then left onto the D 214 6km/3.7mi farther on.*

Flaugnac

This once fortified village occupies a picturesque site overlooking the Lupte Valley. In the 13C, a castle stood at the end of the promontory and the "suburbs", known as barris, stretched across the slopes.

▸ *Leave Flaugnac along the ridge, turn left onto the D 19 then right onto the D 64 6km/3.7mi farther on.*

Moulin de Boisse

🕒*For information about visits, contact the tourist office.* ☎ *05 65 21 84 39.*

There are demonstrations five times a year in this well-preserved mill built in 1669.

▸ *Continue along the D 64 then the D 55.*

Montcuq

Main town of a castellany to which Raymond VI, count of Toulouse, granted a charter of customary law in the 12C. Montcuq was the centre of many a bloody battle during the Albigensian Crusade, the Hundred Years War and the Wars of Religion. All that remains of this once fortified village is a tall castle keep (12C), on a hillock overlooking the Barguelonnette river and a few old houses between place des Consuls (near the town hall) and place de la Halle-aux-Grains.

▸ *Leave Montcuq travelling NW along the D 4 then the D 55.*

Château de Lastours

♿🕒*Open mid-Jul to mid-Aug, daily except Mon, 1-7pm; rest of the year, Sat-Sun and public hols, 1-7pm. Preferably by appointment.* 👛*3€.* ☎ *05 55 58 38 47.*

The two towers of the castle's defensive wall overlook the Séoune Valley. The main building dates from the 16C. Tour of the exterior: tower and ramparts.

▸ *Turn back then right onto the D 228 1km/0.6mi farther on.*

Ste-Croix

This village has retained many old houses nestling round the imposing church. Note the fine Romanesque doorway which once gave access to the cemetery.

▸ *Continue along the D 228 then turn left onto the D 953 to Montcuq. Drive S out of Montcuq along the D 28 and turn right onto the D 45 2km/1.2mi farther on.*

Église de Rouillac

The 12C church was remodelled in the 15C; several chapels and a bell-tower were added in the 19C. In the flat east end, there are traces of Romanesque frescoes depicting the Passion.

▸ *Continue along the D 45 then turn left towards St-Laurent-de-Lolmie; drive on for 2km/1.2mi, turn left onto the D 28, left again onto the D 57 then follow the D 104.*

Moulin de Brousse

🕒*Visits by prior arrangement.* ☎ *05 65 21 95 81.*

This watermill dating from the 13C has been worked by a family of millers since 1917: locally grown wheat is ground in the mill and bread is baked on the premises.

▸ *Turn right to return to Castelnau-Montratier.*

② Pays de Serres

70km/31mi round-trip from Lauzerte – allow one day

Lauzerte

This *bastide* was built in 1241 by the count of Toulouse and was occupied at one time by the English.

Upper Town – The pale-grey stone houses with their almost flat roofs are clustered round the church of St Bartholomew and a square, place des Cornières. This square, named after its covered arcades (*cornières*), still has one half-timbered house. Promenade de l'Éveillé, in the once wealthy middle-class district, has retained elegant residences, some half-timbered, some Gothic in style with twin windows and some

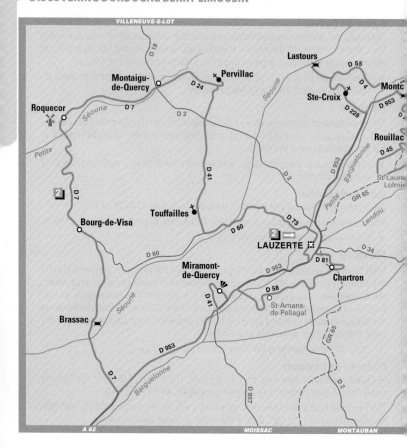

Renaissance with mullioned windows. The ground floors of several 13C and 14C houses in rue de la Garrigue and rue de la Gendarmerie were occupied by busy shops. Beyond the ramparts to the east stands the Église des Carmes, remodelled in the 17C and 19C.

The Via podiensis, which starts from Le Puy-en-Velay, runs through Lauzerte on its way to Santiago de Compostela. The landscaped **Jardin du Pèlerin** (Pilgrim's garden) laid out beneath the barbican is a kind of outdoor snakes and ladders (*ask for the dice at the tourist office*).

▷ *Leave Lauzerte travelling S along the D 2; turn left onto the D 953 then right onto the D 81 and right again towards Sainte-Amans-de-Pellagal 2km/1.2mi farther on.*

Chartron

This place boasts a fine square dovecot built on pillars. These are topped with a kind of cap (*une capel*) designed to prevent various rodents from getting in. The half-timbered dovecot is covered with flat tiles and surmounted by a lantern.

▷ *Turn left then immediately right 1km/0.6mi farther on and continue to Ste-Amans then head for Miramont.*

Miramont-de-Quercy

From the watch-path of this small village, there is a fine view of the valley.

▷ *On leaving Miramont, turn left onto the D 41 then right onto the D 953; drive on for 8km/5mi then turn right onto the D 7.*

Château de Brassac

◷☞Open Jul-Sep, guided tour of the château (1hr), 10am-8pm (last admission 1hr before closing); Apr-Jun, 10am-noon and 2-8pm; Oct-Mar, by prior arrangement. ⚫5€ (guided tour), 4€(unaccompanied visit). ☎ 05 63 94 59 67.

The 12C fortress, remodelled several times until the 16C, towers above the Séoune Valley. The quadrangular structure is flanked by four round towers. The towers and curtain walls have been brought down level with the bailey. During the Hundred

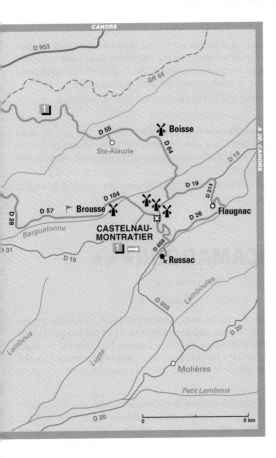

Years War, the stronghold fell successively into English and French hands. Besieged by Protestant troops during the Wars of Religion, burned down during the Revolution, Brassac was abandoned in the 19C.

A fixed stone bridge, which replaced the original drawbridge, leads into the bailey. The upper part consists of the 14C living quarters, flanked in the 15C by a polygonal tower containing a spiral staircase (*not open to the public*). The 16C fortress, built on the site of the former fortifications, is in the lower part; the guard-room can be visited.

▶ *Continue along the D 7 to Bourg-de-Visa.*

Bourg-de-Visa

The wrought-iron structure of a covered market surrounded by arcaded houses stands in the centre of the town hall square. A few ruins are all that remains of the former castle. Note the dovecot tower next to the church.

▶ *Continue along the D 7 and turn left after 10km/6.2mi.*

Roquecor

This village, perched on a rocky spur, towers above the Petite Séoune. Walk along rue des Coutelets, which starts opposite the town hall; the street is lined with old houses. Continue along rue du Barry and bear left towards the **wash-house**, past the ruined ramparts of the old town, to reach a troglodytic site known as the **Roc de la Nobis**.

▶ *Drive N out of Roquecor and turn right onto the D 7.*

Montaigu-de-Quercy

The village nestles round a promontory on which a castle once stood (*now occupied by a private property*). Follow rue des Frères-Quémeré to place de la Mairie: note the former wash-house and the 19C neo-Gothic church. Rue des Colombiers skirts the ramparts and rue des Anciens-Fours leads back to the town hall. Follow rue de la Fontaine to the right to take a look at the village fountain.

▶ *Drive NE out of Montaigu along the D 24 and turn left 2km/1.2mi farther on.*

Pervillac

This hamlet boasts a Romanesque **church** (*ask for keys at the Maison Fournier foie gras and wine shop, ☎ 05 63 94 39 20*) remodelled in the 19C, which houses well-preserved 15C murals depicting hell, purgatory and the virtues. The purpose of these sometimes rough drawings strikes one as being rather more didactic than artistic.

▶ *Turn back, then right towards Montaigu and first left (D 41) to Touffailles.*

Touffailles

The late-15C **Église St-Georges** overlooks the village (*on the right past the town hall*). The nave vaulting is decorated with 12 scenes depicting Christ's childhood and Passion. ⏱ ☞*Guided tour by prior arrangement at the town hall, Mon, Tue and Thu, 2-6pm, Fri, 2-4pm.*

▶ *Continue along the D 41 and turn left onto the D 60 then right onto the D 73 leading back to Lauzerte.*

ROCAMADOUR★★★

POPULATION 614

MICHELIN LOCAL MAP 337: F-3

Rocamadour, with its slender castle keep towering above it, comprises a mass of old dwellings, oratories, towers and precipitous rocks on the rugged face of a causse cliff rising 150m/492ft above the Alzou Canyon. This is one of the most extraordinary places in France; a historic site, and a place of pilgrimage steeped in beliefs and legends. ▯ *Maison du tourisme, 46500 Rocamadour, ☎ 05 65 33 22 00. www.rocamadour.com.*

▶ **Orient Yourself**: The best way to arrive in Rocamadour is along the L'Hospitalet road. From a terrace there is a marvellous **view**★★ of Rocamadour, with the Alzou winding its way through the bottom of a gorge, and the village clinging to the cliff face. The Cité Religieuse rises above the village, with the castle ramparts above it. There is another striking view of Rocamadour from the Couzou road (D 32).

🅿 **Parking**: There are several car parks in the valley as well as at L'Hospitalet.

🕐 **Organising Your Time**: Allow a full day to visit the village and Cité Religieuse and another half a day to explore the Causse de Gramat.

👁 **Don't Miss**: The Cité Religieuse; the ramparts; the view of the village from L'Hospitalet.

Address Book

TRANSPORT

Getting around by car – The streets of Rocamadour are pedestrianised. Access for vehicles is only permitted for hotel and restaurant customers.

Lift (Elevator) – *Open Jul-Aug, 8am-8pm; May-Jun, 8am-7pm; Feb-Apr and Sep to mid-Nov, 10am-5pm. 3€ return, 2€single (chidren under 8: no charge). ☎ 05 65 33 62 44.* Provides access to the village and the ecclesiastical city.

TOURS

Petit train de nuit – *Apr-Sep, departures from porte du Figuier at 9.30pm and 10pm. 5€ (child: 2.50€). ☎ 05 65 33 67 84 or 05 65 33 65 99.* Guided tours by little train in seven languages (30min).

For coin ranges, see the Legend at the back of the guide.

EATING OUT

⊜⊜ **Le Château** – *Rte du Château - ☎ 05 65 33 62 22 - hotelchateau@wanadoo.fr - 🕐 closed 8 Nov-21 Mar.* The traditional house is near the château, in a quiet setting. Oaks shade the large terrace and the dining area inside is embellished by a wooden sculpture of a shepherd. The rooms in the hotel are very comfortable whereas the annex offers simpler accommodation. The pool is nice and you can use it summer and winter alike.

⊜⊜ **Jehan de Valon** – *☎ 05 65 33 63 08 - hotel@bw-beausite.com - 🕐 closed 16 Nov-7 Feb.* Dining room with a view of the valley and a pleasant terrace shaded by lime trees. The menu features traditional regional dishes.

⊜⊜ **Le Bistrot Beau Site** – *Cité Médiévale - ☎ 05 65 33 63 08 - www.bw-beausite.com - 🕐 daily 7am-9pm - 🕐 closed*

Nov-Feb. With a shaded terrace above the valley, this chic bistrot lives up to its name. Tables are reserved for diners during meal times, but they also serve breakfast – what better way to start the day?

🍽 **Le Mas de Douze** – *Les Gîtes de Rocamadour - 4km/2.5mi E of Rocamadour on the D 673 -* ☎ *05 65 33 72 80 -* 🕐 *closed 15 Nov-15 Mar*. This restaurant provides some quiet relief from the tourist crowds, yet it is not too far away. The setting is country-style and the dishes hearty regional specialities. You can take a break on the terrace and a dip in the pool. There are eight cottage-bungalows in the park.

WHERE TO STAY

🏠 **Hôtel du Centre** – *Pl. de la République - 46500 Gramat -* ☎ *05 65 38 73 37 - le.centre@wanadoo.fr - 14 rooms*. The warm welcome in this family-style hotel in the town centre will charm you. The rooms with roughcast walls are serviceable. Traditional fare; children's menu.

🏠 **Hôtel Les Vieilles Tours** – *Rte de Payrac - 4km/2.5mi W of Rocamadour on the D 673 -* ☎ *05 65 33 68 01 - les. vieillestours@wanadoo.fr -* 🕐 *closed 16 Nov-26 Mar -* 🅿 *- 16 rooms*. The country house dates from the 16C and the hawk house from the 13C. The tower room is the nicest, if it's available, but the others are attractive too. Nice view of the valley from the garden. Pool. Meals served in the evening only.

🏠 **Le Troubadour** – *Belveyre - 2.5km/1.5mi NE of Rocamadour on the D 673 towards Brive -* ☎ *05 65 33 70 27 - troubadour@rocamadour.com -* 🕐 *closed 16 Nov-14 Feb -* 🅿 *- 10 rooms*. Seeking peace and quiet? Do not hesitate to book in this restored farmhouse. The garden, pool and surrounding countryside are part of the charm. Simple meals prepared for hotel residents only.

🏠 **Chambre d'hôte Moulin de Fresquet** – *46500 Gramat -* ☎ *05 65 38 70 60 - moulindefresquet@ifrance.com -* 🕐 *closed Nov-Mar -* 🚭 *- 5 rooms*. This very agreeable guesthouse, a renovated mill in a pretty park, is just a short walk from the centre of town. The rooms are stylish and comfortable (non-smoking) and look out over the garden. The welcome is warm and the food delicious.

🏠 **Domaine de la Rhue** – *6km/3.7mi NE of Rocamadour on the D 673 and then the N 140 -* ☎ *05 65 33 71 50 - domainedela-rhue@wanadoo.fr -* 🕐 *closed 18 Oct-1 Apr -* 🅿 *- 14 rooms*. Quiet nights guaranteed! The rooms are in the renovated stables of a prosperous 19C farm. The rustic furniture, original wooden beams and posts are in harmony with the view of the countryside. The swimming pool is a modern touch.

BARS AND CAFÉS

L'Esplanade – *L'Hospitaland -* ☎ *05 65 33 18 45 - bouz06@infonie.fr -* 🕐 *summer: daily 10am-12.30am; Feb-Mar, Oct-Nov except school holidays: closed evenings -* 🕐 *closed from mid-Nov to mid-Feb*. This new café has an exceptionally good view of the old city and surrounding mountains. The shaded terrace is an ideal spot to relax and admire the site.

Les Jardins de la Louve – *Pl. Hugon -* ☎ *05 65 33 62 93 -* 🕐 *in season: 10am-11pm-* 🕐 *closed mid-Nov to Jan except school holidays*. This elegant establishment is a 13C residence that was remodelled in the 15C. The interior is charming, with exposed beams and stone walls. A pleasant terrace under the trees is welcoming in fine weather. Choose from a selection of regional dishes, pizzas, ice cream and teas in the afternoon.

Pâtisserie Quercynoise – *Pl. St-Louis -* ☎ *05 65 33 63 09 -* 🕐 *Apr-Nov: daily 8am-midnight*. Take a break on the shaded terrace of the pastry-shop and brassiere, and pity the pilgrims of yore who doubtless did not enjoy such delights as they came to the end of their long and weary trail.

SHOPPING

Boutique du Terroir – *R. de la Couronnerie -* ☎ *05 65 33 71 25 - hours vary in different seasons –* 🕐 *closed 11 Nov-1 Apr and Sat except Jul-Aug*. This culinary artist has won many awards including the Gold Medal at the 1999 Salon Agricole. Foie gras, prepared dishes, black Périgord truffles… this attractive shop has a thousand and one delights, including prize-winning plum brandy.

Ferme Lacoste – *Les Alix -* ☎ *05 65 33 62 66 -* 🕐 *Mon-Fri 10am-noon, 2.30-6pm, Sat 10am-noon, 2.30-5pm, occasionally open Sun*. This handsome farm is home to 100 goats who live to maintain the reputation of the delicious cheese Cabécou de Rocamadour, also known simply as Rocamadour.

La Maison de la Noix – *R. de la Couronnerie -* ☎ *05 65 33 67 90*. This shop sells aperitifs, liqueurs, jams, oils, biscuits, sweets, mustards and vinegars made with walnuts.

Farmers' market - *In Miers (10km/6mi from Rocamadour)*. Fridays in July and August, 5-8pm.

LEISURE ACTIVITIES

Association Rocamadour Aérostat – *Domaine de la Rhue -* ☎ *05 65 33 71 50 - domainedelarhue@rocamadour.com -* 🕐 *daily by reservation only*. Rocamadour is the perfect place to try the most poetic of all forms of transportation – the hot-air balloon. Once the balloon is ready, you will rise up from the valley floor for a flight of about 45min around the site. Naturally, the company may cancel flights when the weather is inclement.

Especially for Kids: Rocher des Aigles; Féerie du Rail; Forêt des Singes; Parc Animalier de Gramat.

Also See: Gouffre de Padirac; Sarlat-la-Canéda.

A Bit of History

The enigmatic St Amadour – The identity of St Amadour, who gave his name to the sanctuary village, has never been firmly established. A 12C chronicler reported that in 1166 "as a local inhabitant had expressed the wish to be buried beneath the threshold of the Chapel of the Virgin, men began to dig a grave only to find the body of a man already buried there. This body was placed near the altar so that it might be venerated by the faithful and from that time onwards miracles occurred".

Who was this mysterious person whose tomb appeared to be so old? Conflicting theories have been put forward: some contend that he was an Egyptian hermit, others that it was St Silvanus.

The most widely accepted theory, since the 15C, is that the body was that of the publican Zaccheus, a disciple of Jesus and husband of St Veronica, who, when she saw Christ on His way to Calvary, wiped the blood and sweat from His face with her veil. Both Zaccheus and Veronica were obliged to flee Palestine and set up home in Limousin. On the death of Veronica, Zaccheus retired to the deserted and wild Alzou Valley to preach. All this is hearsay, but one thing is certain; there was a hermit, and he knew the rock well as it often sheltered him.

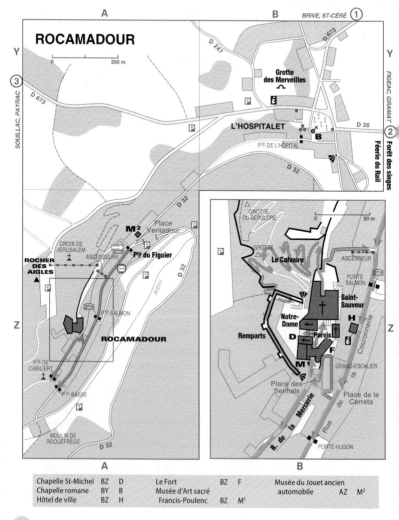

Chapelle St-Michel	BZ	D	Le Fort	BZ	F	Musée du Jouet ancien	
Chapelle romane	BY	B	Musée d'Art sacré			automobile	AZ	M²
Hôtel de ville	BZ	H	Francis-Poulenc	BZ	M¹		

The buildings cling to the cliff face

The Langue d'Oc expression – *roc amator* (he who likes the rock) – was adopted as the name of this village sanctuary, later becoming Roc Amadour and finally Rocamadour.

The fame of Rocamadour – From the time that the miracles began until the Reformation, the pilgrimage to Rocamadour was one of the most famous in Christendom. Great crowds would gather there. Thirty thousand people would come on days of major pardon and plenary indulgence. Since the village was too small to house all the pilgrims, the Alzou Valley was transformed into a vast camp. Henry Plantagenet, king of England, was miraculously cured and among the first to kneel before the Virgin; his example was followed during the Middle Ages by the most illustrious people including St Dominic, St Bernard, St Louis and Blanche of Castille, Philip IV the Fair, Philip VI and Louis XI. Veneration of Our Lady of Rocamadour was established at Lisbon, Oporto, Seville and even in Sicily; the Rocamadour standard, flown at the Battle of Las Navas at Tolosa, put the Muhammadans to flight and gave victory to the Catholic kings of Spain.

Pilgrimage and penitents – Ecclesiastical, and in some cases, lay tribunals used to impose the pilgrimage on sinners. It was a considerable penance. On the day of their departure, penitents attended Mass and then set forth dressed in clothes covered with large crosses, a big hat upon their head, a staff in their hand and a knapsack on their back. On reaching the end of their journey, pilgrims stripped off their clothes, climbing the famous steps on their knees in only a shirt, with chains bound round their arms and neck. Before the altar to the Black Virgin in this humiliating condition they pronounced their *amende honorable*. A priest recited prayers of purification and removed the chains from the penitents, who, now forgiven, received from the priest a certificate and a kind of medal in lead bearing the image of the miraculous Virgin, called a *sportelle*.

But the pilgrimages were not always motivated by piety; lords and town consuls sought the protection of Our Lady when making a treaty or signing a charter. Others came to Rocamadour to see the crowds or even to do a little business.

Decline and renaissance – Rocamadour reached its zenith in the 13C. Favours not even granted to Jerusalem were granted to it; money poured in, but wealth brought covetousness with it.

For 100 years the abbeys of Marcilhac and Tulle disputed who should own the church at Rocamadour; Tulle was finally awarded the honour after arbitration. During the Middle Ages, the town was sacked several times: Henry Short Coat, in revolt against his father Henry Plantagenet, pillaged the oratory in 1183; during the Hundred Years War, bands of English and the local soldiery plundered the treasure in turn; during the Wars of Religion the Protestant, Captain Bessonies, seized Rocamadour to desecrate it and lay it to waste; only the Virgin and the miraculous bell escaped. Rocamadour did not rise from its ruins; the abbey remained idle until it was dealt its final blow by the Revolution. In the 19C, the bishops of Cahors tried to revive the pilgrimage, and the churches were rebuilt. Though much of its splendour has vanished, Rocamadour has found again the fervour of its former pilgrims and is today a very respected pilgrimage centre.

The Ecclesiastical City

Access – *The ecclesiastical city is a pedestrian zone. It can be accessed from the plateau (car park) on foot or by lift (there is a charge; see Address Book), or from the Alzou Valley (car parks) on foot or by a small train (there is a charge) which runs to the village, and then from here to the ecclesiastical city either by the flights of stairs up the Via Sancta or by the lift.*

For guided tours of the Cité Religieuse, contact Le Relais des Remparts, Le Château, 46500 Rocamadour. ☎ 05 65 33 23 23.

Go through the **Porte du Figuier**, which was a gateway to the town as early as the 13C, and enter the main street which is now cluttered with souvenir shops.

Climb the 223 steps of the Great Stairway (Via Sancta). Pilgrims often make this ascent, kneeling at every step.

Porte du Fort

Five flights of stairs lead to a terrace on which stand the former canons' quarters, now converted into shops and hotels.

The terrace is called place des Senhals because of the pilgrims' insignia called *senhals* or *sportelles* that were made there.

The **Porte du Fort**, which opens under the palace perimeter wall, is an old entrance way leading to the sacred perimeter wall.

Parvis des Églises

The parvis (open space in front of the churches), which is also known as place St-Amadour, is fairly small and has seven churches: St Saviour's Basilica opposite the stairway; St Amadour's Church below the basilica; the Chapel of Our Lady or Miraculous Chapel on the left; the three chapels of St John the Baptist, St Blaise and St Anne (*visit possible only as part of a guided tour of the Cité Religieuse*) on the right; and the Chapel of St Michael standing on a terrace to the left.

Basilique St-Sauveur

This 11C-13C Romanesque-Gothic sanctuary has three naves of equal size, divided into two bays each by two massive columns. One of the basilica walls is made out of the cliff's living rock, upon which the arches of the end bay are supported. The mezzanine was added in the 19C to enlarge the basilica during the great pilgrimages.

Above the altar stands a fine **16C Christ**, in polychrome wood, with a cross which resembles a tree.

Eglise St-Amadour

Included in the guided tour of the Cité Religieuse. Open Jun to mid-Sep, 9am-5.30pm; rest of the year, daily except Sat-Sun. ∞5.40€. ☎ 05 65 33 23 23.

This 12C sanctuary lying below the basilica consists of a flat chevet and two bays with quadripartite vaulting. It used to be a place of worship: the body of St Amadour was venerated here.

Chapelle Notre-Dame

From the parvis, 25 steps lead to the Miraculous Chapel or Chapel of Our Lady, considered the Holy of Holies of Rocamadour. It is here that the hermit is believed to have hollowed out an oratory in the rock.

In 1476 the chapel was crushed by falling rocks; it was rebuilt in the Flamboyant Gothic style. This new chapel, sacked during the Wars of Religion and the Revolution, was restored in the 19C.

On the exterior façade, to the right of the Flamboyant doorway, part of the 13C fresco remains, illustrating the dance of death of the three living and three dead men: three menacing skeletons are ready to bury or kill their victims.

On the altar, in the semi-darkness of the chapel blackened by candle smoke, is the miraculous Virgin, also called **Black Madonna**★. This rustic-style reliquary statue, carved in walnut, dates from the 12C. It is small in size (69cm/27in). The rigidly seated Virgin holds the Infant Jesus, who has the face of an adult, on her left knee, without touching Him. It was covered with silver plating of which several fragments, blackened by candle smoke and oxidation, remain.

The interior is adorned with many votive offerings: ex-votos and chains worn by the penitents during certain ceremonies of repentance.

The miraculous **bell**, made of jointed iron plates and most likely dating from the 9C, hangs from the roof. It rang out of its own accord to foretell miracles, for example when sailors lost at sea invoked Our Lady of Rocamadour.

On leaving the chapel, stuck in the cliff face above the doorway, one can see a great iron sword, which legend identifies as **Durandal**, Roland's famous sword. The story goes that Roland, surrounded by the Saracens and unable to break his sword to prevent it falling into enemy hands, prayed to the Archangel Michael and threw him his sword, which in a single stroke implanted itself in the rock of Rocamadour, far from the Infidels.

To the right is St Amadour's grave, believed to have been dug out of the rock on the very spot where the saint's body was found.

Chapelle St-Michel

Included in the guided tour of the Cité Religieuse. ☎ 05 65 33 23 23.

This Romanesque chapel is sheltered by a rock overhang. The apse, which houses a small oratory, juts out towards the square. It was used for services by the monks of the priory, who had also installed a library there.

On the wall **outside** are two frescoes representing the Annunciation and the Visitation; the skill of the composition, the richness of colour – ochre, yellow, reddish-brown, and the royal blue background, protected from condensation and, therefore, well preserved – and the grace of movement all seem to point to the works having been painted in the 12C.

Below them, a 14C fresco depicts an immense St Christopher, patron saint of travellers and thus of pilgrims.

Inside, the chancel is adorned with paintings (not as well preserved as those outside): Christ in Majesty is surrounded by the Evangelists; farther down a seraph and the Archangel Michael are weighing souls.

Musée d'Art Sacré Francis-Poulenc★

Open Jul-Aug, 9am-6pm; Sep to mid-Nov and Mar-Jun, 10am-noon and 2-5pm. 4.80€. ☎ 05 65 33 23 30.

The museum of sacred art is housed in the former palace of the bishops of Tulle, a vast military-style building once used to accommodate illustrious pilgrims. Erected in the 14C, it was restored in the 19C by one of Viollet-le-Duc's students.

The museum is dedicated to the famous composer Francis Poulenc (1899-1963), who, having received a revelation during a visit to Rocamadour in 1936, composed *Litanies à la Vierge Noire de Rocamadour*. In the hallway various documents recount the history of Rocamadour and its pilgrimage, with the help of maps and a statue of St James as a pilgrim (Rocamadour was a pilgrims' stop on the way to Santiago de Compostela).

The vestibule displays objects from the sanctuary: 13C stained glass (the only remaining stained glass from the basilica), showing the death of St Martin, and the 17C reliquary casket of St Amadour, which once contained the relics of the saint's body (destroyed during the Wars of Religion).

The first gallery contains objects (ex-votos, paintings and items in carved wood) dating for the most part from the 17C. A naïve panel (1648) shows St Amadour hailing the Virgin with the Ave Maria; next to it, a baroque statue of Flemish origin represents the prophet Jonas as an old man writing.

The treasury contains fine items which came from the once fabulous treasure collection of the sanctuary. **Reliquary caskets** from Lunegarde and Laverhne (both 12C) and Soulomès (13C), ornamented with enamelwork, demonstrate the craftsmanship of the Limousin artist. Among the other works displayed note the 14C reliquary of St Agapit, in the form of a head. The next gallery contains 17C, 18C and 19C religious paintings.

On leaving the museum take the gallery, known as the tunnel, which passes beneath St Saviour's Basilica and go down onto the watch-path to the right.

The Village

Access – *The village is a pedestrian zone. It can be accessed from the plateau (car park) on foot or by lift (there is a charge; see Address Book), or from the Alzou Valley (car parks) on foot or by a small train (there is a charge) which runs to the village, and then from here to the ecclesiastical city either by the flights of stairs up the Via Sancta or by lift. A tourist train offers visitors a view of the village by night, with commentary.*

▶ *When you reach the end of the watch-path, walk to place des Senhals and turn left.*

Rue de la Mercerie

This former trading street is lined with tiered gardens. Note, on the right, the **Maison de la Pommette**, an old arcaded shop dating from the 15C and, slightly farther on to the left, a Romanesque house. The street leads to the 13C **Porte de Cabiliert**.

▶ *Return to place des Senhals, walk down the Grand Escalier and turn right.*

Le Coustalou

Once through the 13C Porte Hugon, one enters a picturesque medieval quarter. The half-timbered Maison de la Louve is the best preserved of the old houses built on the slope leading down to the Alzou. Beyond the Porte Basse, on the banks of the river, stands the old fortified mill, known as the Moulin de Roquefrège.

▶ *Retrace your steps to reach the Porte du Figuier.*

Hôtel de Ville

🕐 *Open mid-Jul to Aug, 10am-7.30pm; May to mid-Jul and end of Aug to mid-Sep, 10am-12.30pm and 1.30-6.30pm; Apr, 10am-12.30pm and 1.30-6pm; mid-Sep to mid-Nov, 10am-noon and 2-5.30pm; mid-Nov to Mar, 2-5pm.* 🕐*Closed 1 Jan and 25 Dec.* ⊜*2€.* ☎ *05 65 33 22 00.*

The town hall is located in a 15C house (restored), known as the Couronnerie or the House of the Brothers. In the council chamber there are two fine **tapestries**★ by Jean Lurçat which portray the flora and fauna of the causse.

The Plateau

Stations of the Cross

A 19C shaded Stations of the Cross winds up towards the ramparts. After passing the caves (*grottes*) of the Nativity and the Holy Sepulchre, visitors will see the great Cross of Jerusalem, brought from the Holy Land by the Penitential Pilgrims.

Ramparts

🕐*Open 9am-6pm.* ⊜*2.50€.* ☎ *05 65 33 23 23.*

These are the remains of a 14C fort which was built to block off the rocky spur and protect the sanctuary. Leaning against the fortress, the residence of the chaplains of Roc-Amadour was built in the 19C.

Rocher des Aigles

♿🕐*Open Jul-Aug, 1.30-5.45pm; Apr-Jun and Sep, 1.30-4pm, Sat-Sun, public and school hols, 1.30-5pm; Oct, 3-4pm, Sat-Sun, public and school hols, 2-5pm.* ⊜*6.50€ (child: 4€).* ☎ *05 65 33 65 45.*

🔳 The Eagles' Rock is a breeding centre for birds of prey. Regular demonstrations showing how they fly and how they hunt are popular with visitors. A running commentary helps them to understand the behaviour of these birds, some of which are endangered species.

▶ *To return to the village, go back to an esplanade which is on the same level as the Ecclesiastical City and take the lift to the main street near the Porte Salmon.*

Excursions

Moulin de Cougnaguet

10km/6.2mi W along the D 673. 🕐*Open Apr to mid-Oct, guided tour, 10am-noon and 2-6pm.* ⊜*3.50€.* ☎ *05 65 32 63 09.*

The rounded arches of this fortified mill span a derivation of the Ouysse in a cool, lush and charming **setting**. The mill was built in the 15C at the foot of a sheer cliff, on the site of a mill to which the water rights were granted in 1279. In the Middle Ages grain and flour, both highly sought-after commodities, needed to be particularly well-defended, as is illustrated by the impressive defence system here. The opening of the sluice gates hurled assailants to a watery fate. The mill has four millstones; one of which is still in working order.

Northern Part of the Causse de Gramat

70km/43.5mi round-trip – allow half a day

▷ *Drive N out of Rocamadour along the D 32.*

The Gramat Causse, which stretches from the Dordogne Valley in the north to the Lot and Célé valleys in the south, is the largest – and wildest – *causse* in Quercy. It is a vast limestone plateau which lies at an average altitude of 350m/1148ft and contains a variety of natural phenomena and unusual landscapes.

Autumn is the time to cross the *causse*, when the trees are donning their seasonal colours and shedding a golden light on the grey stones and rocks, with the maples adding a splash of deep red.

L'Hospitalet

The name of this village, clinging to Rocamadour's cliff face, comes from the small hospital founded in the 11C by Hélène de Castelnau to nurse the pilgrims on the road from Le Puy (Auvergne) to Santiago de Compostela. Only a few ruins of this hospital remain; the **Romanesque chapel**, which is set in the middle of the churchyard, was remodelled in the 15C.

L'Hospitalet is very popular with visitors for its **viewpoint**★★ which overlooks the site of Rocamadour. There is a large Tourist Information Centre (*syndicat d'initiative*).

Grotte des Merveilles

⏱🔦Open Jul-Aug, guided tour (30min), 9.30am-7pm; Apr-Jun and Sep to early-Nov, 10am-noon and 2-6pm (5.30pm, Oct). ⊙5.50€ (child: 3.50€). ☎ 05 65 33 67 92.

Discovered in 1920, the Cave of Wonders is small, only 8m/24ft deep, but has some lovely formations: stalactites, stalagmites and natural limestone dams reflecting the cave roof and its concretions.

On the walls are cave paintings dating back, most likely, to the Solutrean Period (c 20 000 BC), depicting outlined hands, black spots, a few horses, a cat and the outline of a deer.

▷ *Leave L'Hospitalet travelling E along the D 36.*

Féerie du Rail

On the road to Figeac. ♿⏱Open mid-Jul to Aug, performances (45min) at 9.45am, 10.45am, 11.30am, 1pm, 2pm, 3pm, 4pm, 5pm and 6pm (last week of Aug at 11am, 1.30pm, 2.30pm, 3.30pm, 4.30pm and 5.30pm); mid-Jun to mid-Jul, 11am, 2pm, 3pm, 4pm and 5pm; Apr to mid-Jun and Sep, 11am, 2.45pm, 3.45pm and 4.45pm; Oct, 3pm and 4.15pm; Nov school hols, 11am, 2.45pm, 3.45pm and 4.45pm. ⊙7.50€ (child: 5€). ☎ 05 65 33 71 06.

🧒 Visitors sit on bleacher seats which move, back and forth, alongside a giant scale model (85m²/915sq ft) including **animated miniatures**.

A fantastic **decor** represents city, country and mountainous landscapes, criss-crossed by a train network. Light and sound effects accent groups of automata playing out realistic scenes (marriage ceremony, ski run). Some of the animation is extremely detailed (circus, fun fair) and unusual (hot-air balloons taking off); these are also visible on a video monitor, for fuller appreciation.

Forêt des Singes

On the road to Figeac. ♿⏱Open Jul-Aug, 9.30am-6.30pm; Apr and first two weeks of Sep, 10am-noon and 1-5.30pm; last two weeks of Sep, 1-5.30pm, Sat-Sun, 10am-noon and 1-5.30pm; May-Jun, 10am-noon and 1-6pm; Oct, 1-5pm, Sat-Sun and public and school hols, 10am-noon and 1-5pm; first two weeks of Nov, 1-5pm. ⊙7€ (child: 4€). ☎ 05 65 33 62 72.

🧒 Living at liberty on 10ha/25 acres of woodland, the Monkey Forest, are 150 animals in an environment similar to the upper plateaux of North Africa, where they originated. The monkeys are Barbary apes and macaques, a species which is becoming extinct.

▷ *Continue along the D 36 to Rignac and turn left onto the D 20.*

Source Salmière

The beneficial properties of the Miers mineral water were discovered in 1624; rich in magnesium, it is used in the treatment of liver and urinary diseases and for its laxative properties.

Gouffre de Padirac★★

👣*See Gouffre de PADIRAC.*

▶ *Drive S to Padirac and turn right onto the D 673, then left onto the D 11 2km/1.2mi farther on.*

Gramat

Capital of the causse that bears its name, Gramat is also a busy commercial centre attracting agricultural fairs.

It is the ideal starting point for visits to Padirac, Rocamadour and the area that lies between the Lot and the Dordogne.

It was here that the French Centre de formation des maîtres-chiens de la Gendarmerie (Police Dog Handler Training Centre) was established in 1945.

▶ *Take the D 677 travelling SW and turn left onto the D 14 beyond the railway line.*

Parc Animalier de Gramat

◷*Open Easter to Sep, 9.30am-7pm; Oct to Easter, 2-6pm. ☜7.50€ (5-14 years old: 4.50€).* ☎ *05 65 38 81 22.*

Kids This nature park extends over 40ha/99 acres. It was acquired by the local authorities so that animals and plants could be observed in their natural environment.

A botanical park is home to trees and shrubs from the *causse* (durmast oak, dogwood, ash etc).

The animal park contains mainly European species living in semi-captivity in their natural habitat. Some of these animals – wild oxen, Przewalski's horses, ibexes, bison – are species which existed during prehistoric times.

A collection of farmyard animals includes a variety of domestic fowl, pigs etc.

Follow the signposted itinerary over 3km/2mi for an enjoyable and informative outing.

▶ *Turn back and pick up the D 677 on the left. In Le Bastit, turn right onto the D 50 then right again in Carlucet onto the D 32, which takes you back to Rocamadour.*

ROCHECHOUART

POPULATION 3 667

MICHELIN LOCAL MAP 325: B-6

Rochechouart Castle rises above a rocky promontory. On the last day of the ostensions (*see Introduction*), held once every seven years (*next in 2009*), a unique procession takes place; the participants wear special costumes and carry precious shrines.

▸ **Orient Yourself**: The best view of the town is from the D 3bis where it passes the foot of the cliff.

⊙ **Don't Miss**: The frescoes in the castle.

A Bit of History

A distinguished family tree – The Rochechouart family can be traced back beyond the year 1000: their first castle rose up near the monastic settlement governed by the Charroux Abbey. A son of the viscount of Limoges became the lord upon his marriage to Ève d'Angoulême, whose dowry was the Rochechouart title and property. The dynasty took an active part in the crusades. The château was completely rebuilt when Aquitaine shifted to the English crown.

Around 1205, Viscount Aymeric de Rochechouart married the heartbreakingly beautiful Alix de Mortemart. The castle steward, mad with love for the viscountess, tried to seduce her, but she repulsed his advances. In revenge the steward told his master that the viscountess had solicited him. The jealous and impulsive Aymeric had his wife thrown to a lion in the east tower. Two days later, when he went to contemplate his act of justice, he found the lion crouched docilely at his wife's feet. The guiltless woman was brought back into favour, truth and virtue won out and the steward was dispatched to the lion, which, this time, proved to be hungry.

In the struggle facing off Capetians and Plantagenets, the Rochechouart family sided with the king of France. One family member was killed at the Battle of Poitiers (1356), protecting the life of his sovereign liege, another was imprisoned by the prince of Wales. In the centuries following, the Rochechouart family continued to serve France, while the family tree branched out. The Mortemart line (*see Château de MEILLANT*) is also replete with history-making figures. The château was buffeted by wars and often threatened with ruin, but always saved – often with the help of Rochechouart wives who brought hefty dowries into their alliances. The French Revolution called for its destruction, but given the size of the buildings, the project was abandoned. In 1836, the State acquired the buildings and set up some offices within.

Visit

Church

This is the former priory church, consecrated in 1067; only the western doorway, the northern wall, and part of the transept and chancel have survived. The unusual belfry with its twisted spire was rebuilt in the 18C.

The Château

B. Kaufmann/MICHELIN

Rue Jean-Parvy

Note the 15C **Maison des Consuls**, and, further on, a corner tower which stood within the medieval city wall.

Château★

The castle stands in a remarkable **setting**★ above the confluence of the Graine and the Vayres and is mostly late 15C. The 12C keep which flanks the entrance fort, was razed level with the rooftops in the 16C.

The second tower at the left end of the façade bears a lion carved in granite in a niche, perhaps in homage to the beautiful Alix, or more likely the crusading viscounts of Limoges. A drawbridge leads to the entrance fort.

Cour d'honneur – The buildings which line the court on three sides were restored in the 18C and now house the offices of the sub-prefecture and a museum of contemporary art (see Sights). They are adorned with a gallery supported on elegant twisted columns. The fourth side is closed by a curtain wall. The Gothic doorway in the left-hand corner of the courtyard is a fine example of 15C architectural ornamentation.

Promenade des Allées

Leaving the château, the promenade is on the left, a shady terrace fragrant with age-old lime trees. From the site of the cross standing at the end of the walk, there is a good **view**★ of the valleys of the Graine and the Vayres and the front of the castle, framed by round towers and set with elegant windows with their stone cross-pieces intact. The view also enfolds the terraced gardens, accessible by a double flight of stairs, hidden by the greenery in season.

Sights

Musée Départemental d'Art Contemporain

 Open Mar-Sep, 10am-12.30pm and 1.30-6pm; Oct to mid-Dec, 10am-12.30pm and 2-5pm. Closed Tue. 4.60€. 05 55 03 77 77. www.musee-rochechouart.com

The Haute-Vienne General Council began building up the collection in 1985; today it is a significant centre for contemporary art. It focuses on three main themes: landscape, history and the realms of the imagination, illustrated by artists such as Christian Boltanski, Annette Messager and Richard Long. Raoul Hausmann (Berlin 1886-Limoges 1971), a major exponent of Dadaism, is particularly well represented.

Frescoes★ – Besides the main focus on contemporary art, the museum gives over two rooms to a remarkable group of 16C frescoes. The **salle d'Hercule** is decorated with rare murals painted in *grisaille*. Created by several artists, they may have been inspired by the low-relief sculptures in the Limoges Cathedral; almost like a comic strip, they illustrate the labours of Hercules. Nearby, the **salle des chasses** contains slightly older frescos, which depict scenes from a royal hunt: the cortege setting out, the sounding of the horn, the baying dogs and the banquet table. The attire, the setting – Rochechouart, the château and small town surrounded by ramparts, is easily recognizable – make these paintings an interesting study of the times of Louis XII.

Espace Météorite

 Open Apr-Jun, daily except Sat, 2-6pm; Jul to mid-Sep, 10am-12.30pm and 1.30-6pm, Sat-Sun and public hols, 2-6pm; mid-Sep to 23 Dec and end-Jan to end-Mar, daily except Sat-Sun and public hols, 2-6pm; school hols, daily except Sat, 10am-12.30pm and 1.30-6pm, Sun and public hols, 2-6pm. Closed 24 Dec-20 Jan and 1 May. 3.60€ (-15 years old: no charge). 05 55 03 02 70.

Rochechouart was built over a 20km/12mi-wide crater caused by a large meteorite which crashed in the area some 200 million years ago, releasing an energy 14 million times greater than the Hiroshima bomb.

Excursions

Cimetière de Rochechouart

To the northwest, on the road to Chabanais.

The cemetery houses a novel funerary monument shaped like a large cask. Closer inspection reveals that it honours the memory of Léonce Chabernaud, whose profession--you guessed it--was that of a wine merchant.

Biennac
2km/1mi E via the D 10.

The church dating from the 12C and 13C is topped with a hexagonal belfry and supported at each corner by buttresses. To reach the church pass a covered well and then go up the semicircular flight of steps.

La ROQUE-GAGEAC★★

POPULATION 449

MICHELIN LOCAL MAP 329: I-7 – LOCAL MAP SEE VALLÉE DE LA DORDOGNE

The village of La Roque-Gageac, huddled against a cliff which drops vertically to the River Dordogne, occupies a wonderful **site**★★ – one of the finest in this part of the valley, in which Domme, Castelnaud and Beynac-et-Cazenac are all within a few miles of each other. At the top of the cliff there are clear traces to remind visitors of the tragic day in 1957 when a huge block of rock came away from the cliff face, killing three inhabitants.

▶ **Orient Yourself**: The best view of La Roque-Gageac is from the west: the late afternoon sun highlights the tall grey cliff face covered with holm oaks, while the houses, with their stone slab (*lauzes*) or tile roofs, are reflected in the calm waters of the river below.

🐾 **Don't Miss**: A boat trip on the Dordogne.

👶 **Also See**: Sarlat; Domme.

The Village

Attractive little streets, in which the humble homes of peasants and craftsmen nestle side by side with the grander residences of the gentry, run tightly along the rocky bluff. One of them, leading off to the right of the Carrier hotel, climbs through luxuriant plant life to reach a kind of oasis backing onto the cliff face. It has taken Gérard Dorin 30 years to develop his exotic garden: the micro climate favours the growth of Mediterranean vegetation (olive, lemon and banana trees thrive here together with 20 varieties of palm trees).

WHERE TO STAY

🍽🍽🍽**Auberge La Plume d'Oie** – ☎ 05 53 29 57 05 - *walker.marc@wanadoo.fr* - 🕐 *closed 10 Jan-Feb, late-Nov to 20 Dec, Tue lunchtime and Mon out of season, and lunchtime in Aug-Sep – reserv. required.* A little village inn in an old renovated house, typical of the region. The dining room is bright and cheerful with blonde wooden beams, stonework and large bay windows. A few rooms with views of the Dordogne.

La Roque-Gageac

Nearby, the small late-Romanesque church has an interesting 17C west front.

Walk back down the street towards the troglodytic fort opposite. On your way, take a look at the **Manoir de Tarde**. Two pointed gabled buildings, with mullioned windows, stand next to a round tower. This charming manor house is associated with the Tarde family, the most famous member of which is the canon Jean Tarde, a 16C local humanist, historian, cartographer, astronomer and mathematician.

The impregnable **troglodytic fort** was built in the 12C and reinforced in the 17C before being dismantled in the 18C. A 140-step climb will take you within sight of what remains of the defensive system and the beautiful view will reward your efforts. ⏱Open Jun-Aug, 10am-7pm; Apr-May and Sep to mid-Nov, 10.30am-6pm. ✺4€ (6-10 years old: 1€). ☎ 05 53 31 61 94.

👀 Note the outline of the Château de la Malartrie on the right.

ROUFFIGNAC-ST-CERNIN-DE-REILHAC★

POPULATION 1 484

MICHELIN LOCAL MAP 329: G-5

Rouffignac lies at the heart of a region rich in archaeological and historic sites, including the splendid prehistoric cave of the same name. The church is all that escaped when the Germans set about burning the village in March 1944 as a reprisal; it has since been rebuilt and is now a peaceful holiday resort and the ideal starting point of excursions in the area.

- 🕐 **Orient Yourself**: The village is located 18km/11mi north of Les Eyzies de Tayac.
- 👀 **Don't Miss**: Grotte de Rouffignac.

Visit

Church

The church entrance is through an interesting belfry-porch containing a doorway built in the style of the Early Renaissance. It was constructed in about 1530 and is decorated with Corinthian capitals and surmounted by a finely carved lintel; the somewhat irreverent decoration – mermaids, busts of women – seems surprising in a place of worship.

The nave and aisles built in the Flamboyant style have pointed vaulting supported by round pillars reinforced by remarkable engaged twisted columns.

Excursions

Grotte de Rouffignac★

5km/3mi S along the D 32. �︎🕐⏱✺Open Jul-Aug, guided tour (1hr), 9-11.30am and 2-6pm; week before Easter to Jun and Sep-Oct, 10-11.30am and 2-5pm. ✺5.90€ (children 6-12 years old: 3.60€). Limited number of daily visitors. ☎ 05 53 05 41 71. www.grotteroufignac.fr/.

This dry **cave**, also known as Cro de Granville, was already well-known in the 15C. The galleries are more than 8km/5mi long. An electric train carries visitors to the main galleries. It is worth noting that this is one of the few prehistoric sites in the area which is fully accessible to persons of limited mobility. In 1956 Professor LR Nougier called attention to the remarkable group of paintings marked with black lines and **engravings**★ produced during the middle or upper Magdalenian period (around 13000 BC). These engravings are of horses, ibexes, rhinoceroses, bison and a great number of mammoths, among which may be seen the Patriarch and an amazing frieze depicting two herds locked in combat. There is an outstanding group of drawings on the ceiling of the last chamber.

ST-AMAND-DE-COLY★

POPULATION 356

MICHELIN LOCAL MAP 329: I-5

Tucked away in the fold of a small valley off the Vézère Valley is St-Amand-de-Coly its old *lauze*-roofed houses clustering round the impressive abbey church, where concerts take place during the Festival du Périgord.

🕸 **Don't Miss**: The village church.

🐚 **Also See**: Grotte de Lascaux; Sarlat.

Visit

Church★★

This church of fine yellow limestone is perhaps the most amazing of all Périgord's fortified churches. The Augustinian abbey of which it was once part saw its spiritual activity reduced during the Hundred Years War. Consequently, it transformed itself into a fortress. The highly elaborate defence system was designed to keep enemies at a distance, but also to drive them away should any forays be made into the church.

St-Amand-de-Coly village and church

J.P. Clapham/MICHELIN

The Huguenots occupying the church in 1575 were able to hold out for six days against 20 000 soldiers of the Périgord seneschal, who had powerful artillery backup.

An impression of tremendous strength is created by the **tower keep**, indented by the enormous pointed arch of the doorway which supports a defence room intended to prevent anyone approaching. The harmony of the apsidal chapels is a contrast to the severity of the high walls of the nave and transept. A watch-path runs around the building beneath the *lauze*-covered roof.

Purity of line and simplicity of **decoration**, both of which are usually to be found in Augustinian architecture, contribute to the beauty of the lofty space inside. The concern for protection also affected the interior design; remains of the defence system include a narrow passage enclosing the chancel, small look-out posts in the pillars of the crossing and the loopholes in the base of the dome.

The **Point Accueil-Information** opposite the church presents an audio-visual show on the abbey and its history. It is also the starting point of guided tours and a "Topoguide" detailing eight local rambles is on sale. ◐✦*Guided tours leave from here. For information, call* ☎ *05 53 51 04 56 or 05 53 51 67 50 (town hall).*

Excursion

Terrasson-Lavilledieu
15km/9.3mi E along the N 89.

Terrasson, built beside the Vézère, has old districts stretching in tiers up the side of a hill overlooking the south bank of the river. It is a busy little town with a prosperous trade in truffles and walnuts. A walk through the narrow streets will enable you to discover many half-timbered houses, the 15C church overlooking the town and the valley, the 12C cutwater bridge etc. There is an interesting **historical tour** *(free map available at the tourist office, ☎ 05 53 50 37 56)* of the town lined with explanatory panels.

Jardins de l'Imaginaire★

&◐✦*Open Jul-Aug, guided tour (1hr 15min), 9.50-11.50am, 12.50pm and 1.50-6.10pm; Apr-Jun and Sep, daily except Tue, 9.50-11.50am and 1.50-5.20pm; Apr and first two weeks of Oct, daily except Tue, 9.50-11.20am and 1.50-5.20pm. ∞6€. ☎ 05 53 50 86 82. www.ot-terrasson.fr*

This 6ha/15-acre terraced garden overlooking Terrasson and the valley, a contemporary creation, guides visitors to the realm of fantasy through its holy wood, its forest alive with elves and imps, its water garden, its rose garden (2 000 rose bushes), its arbour, its iris garden and its greenhouse lined with vegetation. A night show takes place in the garden every year, in summer.

Terrasson-la-Villedieu – Market on the old bridge

Roulland/Images Toulouse

ST-AMAND-MONTROND

POPULATION 11 447

MICHELIN LOCAL MAP 323: L-6

Capital of the region known as Val de Germigny, where the fields are dotted with white Charollais cattle, the village developed around a monastery, founded in the 7C by St Amand, a disciple of St Colomban. Later, a castle rose above it, on the hill known as Mont-Rond, and served to protect the growing town; it was destroyed in the 17C. A park, laid out on the hill top, offers a fine view of the town and its surroundings.

▶ **Orient Yourself**: The village is located 44km/27.5mi south of Bourges.

Don't Miss: Château de Meillant; Abbaye de Noiriac.

Also See: Bourges.

Address Book

WHERE TO STAY

Chambre d'hôte La Trolière – 18200 Orval - 4km/2.4mi W of St-Amand-Montrond towards Châteauroux then 500m after the last roundabout on the right - ☎ 02 48 96 47 45 - 3 rooms. This large bourgeois family home offers comfortable rooms in pastel tones decorated with etchings and porcelain pieces. You'll appreciate the pervasive quietude and charm of the site.

Chambre d'hôte Domaine de la Vilotte – Lieu-dit la Vilotte - 18170 Le Châtelet - 6km/3.6mi SE of Châtelet on the D 951 and a secondary road - ☎ 02 48 96 04 96 - closed Feb - 5 rooms. Hidden away in the Berry countryside, this 19C manor house is elegant and tasteful. The rooms are warm and welcoming, furnished with attractive antiques. The grounds boast a lovely rose garden and a lake where a boat is ready to amuse guests so inclined.

Visit

Église St-Amand

For information on opening times, call ☎02 48 96 16 19.

This interesting 12C Romanesque church with a Benedictine floor plan opens with a beautiful round arched doorway framed by two multifoiled bays. The nave with its barrel-vaulting, is rather dark. The transept crossing has pointed arches which certainly replaced an earlier cupola. In the 15C, side chapels were added. The capitals in the nave are interesting for their traditional Romanesque design: birds with long, twining necks, monstrous faces and acanthus leaves. In the south aisle note the fine late-16C carving of Christ Reviled and opposite, the early-16C stone figure of St Roch.

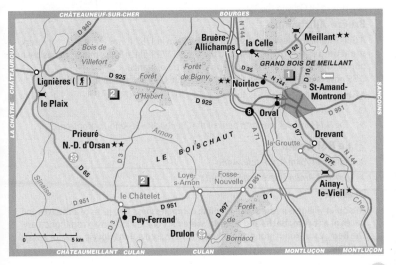

Musée St-Vic

◔*Daily except Tue, 10am–noon and 2–6pm; Sat–Sun and public hols, 2–6pm.* ◔*Closed 1 Jan, 1 May and 25 Dec.* ◉*2.20€.* ☎ *02 48 96 55 20.*

The 16C St-Vic Mansion, set amid a pleasant garden, was the town residence of the commendatory abbots of Noirlac (◔*see NOIRLAC*). The exhibit area presents a wide panorama of this region, rich in history and vestiges. There are rooms devoted to excavations and materials related to the old castle; to local ethnography (furnishings, pottery, headdresses); to the ceramic work of the potters of La Borne; to the work of the clog-maker Louis Touzet, as well as to regional landscapes painted by Brielman, Cals, Delavaux, Detroy, and Osterlind (the Crozant School).

Cité de l'Or

♿◔*Open Apr–Sep, 9.45am–6.30pm (last entrance 1hr before closing); Oct–Mar, 9.45am–5.30pm.* ◔*Closed Tue (except Jul–Aug), 1 Jan and 25 Dec.* ◉ *6€.* ☎ *02 48 82 11 33.*

This vast complex testifies to the importance of gold and jewellery in the town's economic development. There is a visual presentation of the history of gold at local level, but major gold rushes throughout the world, gold processing and jewellery techniques are also illustrated.

Excursions

1 Grand Bois de Meillant

25km/15mi – allow 3hr

▶ *Leave St-Amand along the D 10 towards Dun-sur-Auron.*

The road goes through the forest, Grand Bois de Meillant.

Château de Meillant★★

◔*See Château de MEILLANT.*

▶ *Leave Meillant heading SW along the D 92.*

La Celle

The 12C **church of St-Blaise**, originally a dependency of Déols Abbey has an impressive square belfry and an east end adorned with modillions and Romanesque capitals. The west front is adorned with unusual carvings, including roughly sculpted characters and bulls' heads, which denote a primitive style. The nave is supported by stout flying buttresses added in the 15C and 17C. Inside, the apsidal chapels are separated from the chancel by massive columns with interesting capitals depicting monsters, bearded faces, birds, lions, masks etc. The church contains the tomb of St Silvanus, the legendary apostle of Berry, whose relics were moved from Levroux to La Celle in the 15C.

Church of St-Blaise

B. Kaufmann/ MICHELIN

Bruère-Allichamps

A Gallo-Roman milestone was found in the town in 1757. It was erected in its present site at the junction of the N 144 and the D 92 in 1799. Since 1865, this point has been popularly held to mark the geographical centre of France.

D 35 now follows the course of the picturesque Cher Valley rich in meadowland.

Abbaye de Noirlac★★

◔ *See Abbaye de NOIRLAC.*

▶ *The N 144 follows the north bank of the Cher back to St-Amand-Montrond.*

2 Le Boischaut

Round-trip of 75km/47mi – allow 4hr

▶ *Leave St-Amand travelling S on the D 97.*

Drevant

This quiet village is infused with a feeling of timelessness. The ruins of a **theatre** and traces of a **forum, baths** and **temple**, were part of a Gallo-Roman rural sanctuary. The Berry canal runs through a park by the ruins, providing a lovely spot for a walk or picnic.

▶ *Continue S, cross the River Cher and turn left in La Groutte.*

Ainay-le-Vieil★

The **castle**★ is the town's proudest feature, its severe **medieval walls** (12C-14C) hiding a gracious Renaissance building within. The **hexagonal tower** (early 16C) is reminiscent of Meillant, and from the watch-path visitors can admire the moat and crenellated ramparts. The interior is beautifully decorated and furnished, and the **rose garden** in bloom is fragrant with its many varieties (the oldest is a variety first named in 1420). ◐ *Guided tour (45min, last entrance 45min before closing), Jul-Aug, 10am-7pm; Apr-Jun, daily, 10am-noon and 2-7pm; Feb-Mar, daily except Tue, 10am-noon and 2-7pm; Oct-Nov, daily except Tue, 2-6pm.* ◌7€ *(7-12 years old: 3.50€).* ☎ *02 48 63 50 03 or 02 48 63 36 14.*

▶ *Drive W along the D 1 then turn left onto the D 997 at the Fosse Nouvelle crossroads.*

Jardins Artistiques de Drulon

◐ *Open late-Apr to Sep, 10am-6pm; Oct, Sat-Sun, 10am-6pm.* ◌7€ *(4-12 years old: 2.50€).* ☎ *02 48 56 65 96.*

This extraordinary place, a 15ha/37-acre landscaped park surrounding a former 15C-17C hunting lodge, offers a variety of settings to about 100 sculptures by contemporary European artists: there is the flower garden, the greenery, the marsh skirted by footpaths and natural labyrinths and the secret garden with its fishponds. Inside the manor, four ground-floor rooms house the most fragile sculptures.

▶ *Rejoin the D 997 on the left and drive to Loye-sur-Arnon to pick up the D 951 on the left.*

Le Châtelet, Abbatiale de Puy-Ferrand

◐ *Open mid-Jun to Sep, Sat-Sun and public hols, 3-6pm. Guided tours available.* ☎ *02 48 56 21 73.* ☎ *02 48 56 29 35.*

The former abbey church of Puy-Ferrand, south of Le Châtelet, is a fine Romanesque building. The façade is ornamented with bays, finely carved capitals and geometrical designs.

▶ *Leave Le Châtelet travelling NW along the D 951 then turn right onto the D 65.*

Jardins du Prieuré Notre-Dame d'Orsan★

◌ *See Notre-Dame d'ORSAN.*

▶ *Follow the D 65 towards Lignières.*

Château du Plaix

◐ *Open mid-Jun to mid-Sep, daily except Tue, 2-6pm; Easter to mid-Jun and mid-Sep to early-Nov, Sat-Sun and public hols, 2-6pm.* *Guided tours available by prior arrangement.* ◌5€ *(under 12s: no charge).* ☎ *02 48 60 22 14.*

This small castle, surrounded by a moat, houses the **Musée des Arts et Traditions Populaires**: temporary exhibitions on various themes (such as cooking and toys) are organised every three years. Nearby, stands a typical Berry house with its 1850 interior: box bed in the living room, bakery, scullery.

Lignières★

In the heart of a landscape of well-kept family farms and meadows neatly bordered by hedgerows, this small town was a centre of Calvinism when the famous protestant reformer was a student in Bourges. The classical **château** (⊶ *closed to the public)* was designed by François Le Vau (exhibit in the orangerie), brother of the more famous Louis, who designed the Louvre, Vaux-le-Vicomte and Versailles. Near the bank of the River Arnon, there is a pretty 12C church containing fine 17C furnishings (pulpit, altarpiece and breast-feeding Virgin).

▶ *Continue E along the D 925.*

Église d'Orval

◐ *For information on opening times, contact the town hall,* ☎ *02 48 96 57 40.*

The church in town has a 13C reliquary cross in gold-plated silver, its crosspieces embellished with enamel.

ST-CÉRÉ★

POPULATION 3 515

MICHELIN LOCAL MAP 337: H-2

The lovely old houses of St-Céré cluster in the cheerful Bave Valley, at the foot of St Laurence's Towers. St-Céré stands at the junction of roads from Limousin, Auvergne and Quercy, but has become a good place to stay in its own right because of its pleasant site. It is also an excellent starting point for walks and excursions in Upper Quercy and its renowned festival is the rendezvous of music lovers.

🕐 **Organising Your Time**: Allow half a day to explore the Bave valley.

👁 **Don't Miss**: The Atelier-Musée Jean-Lurçat; Château de Montal; Château de Castelnau-Bretonoux.

A Bit of History

A prosperous town – In the 13C the viscounts of Turenne, overlords of St-Céré, granted a charter with franchises and many advantages to the town. Other charters added to the wealth of the town by giving it the right to hold fairs and establish trading houses. Consuls and officials administered the town, which was protected by St Laurence's Castle and a formidable line of ramparts. Even the Hundred Years War left the town practically unscathed. With the 16C dawned a new period of prosperity.

Jean Lurçat and St-Céré – Born in 1892 in the Vosges *département*, Jean Lurçat, whose parents had planned that he would become a doctor, directed his talents instead to painting, decoration of theatrical scenery, mosaics and ceramics. He soon became interested in tapestry as a medium; it is for his work on tapestry design and technique that he achieved world renown (👁 *see AUBUSSON*).

After a period spent in Aubusson, he participated in the Resistance movement and through this discovered the region of the Lot. He settled in St-Céré in 1945. It was in St Laurence's Towers that he set up his studio, and this is also where he lived until his death in 1966.

Lurçat had the Aubusson tapestry factory weave most of the tapestries for which he had painted the designs (cartoons).

Walking Tour of Old Town

The 15C, 16C and 17C houses give St-Céré a picturesque character all of its own. Some houses still have their half-timbered corbelled façades and fine roofs of brown tiles.

Address Book

👁 *For coin ranges, see the Legend at the back of the guide.*

EATING OUT

🍽🍽 **Le Victor Hugo** – *7 av. du Maquis* - ☎ 05 65 38 16 15 - tsmyth9816@aol.com - 🕐 *closed Sun eve and Mon - reserv. recommended.* This half-timbered 17C house sits on the banks of the River Bave. There is a nice restaurant with an outdoor terrace where you can enjoy a tasty meal without ostentation. Cute little rooms, some with a river view.

🍽🍽 **Les Prés de Montal** – *Rte de Gramat* - *2km/1.2mi W of St-Céré on the D 673* - ☎ 05 65 10 16 16 - lestroissoleils@wanadoo. fr - 🕐 *closed 10 Nov-31 Jan.* On the grounds of the Hôtel Les Trois Soleils de Montal, this restaurant offers poolside dining. Befitting the setting, grilled foods are the speciality. It is pleasant and relaxing

outdoors, but you may prefer a more elaborate meal in the hotel dining room.

WHERE TO STAY

🍽 **Chambre d'hôte Château de Gamot** – *46130 Loubressac - 5km/3.1mi W of St-Céré on the D 673 and D 30* - ☎ 05 65 10 92 03 - 🕐 *closed Oct-Apr -* 🖛 *- 7 rooms.* This guesthouse is in a charming 17C family manor house, in a pastoral setting. Some of the rooms do not have private baths, but all are spacious and comfortable. Two holiday cottages are also available.

🍽🍽 **Hôtel du Coq Arlequin** – *Av. du Dr-Roux* - ☎ 05 65 38 02 13 - 🕐 *closed 8-25 Mar and 1-28 Oct -* 🅿 *- 16 rooms.* In the breakfast room of this hotel in the centre of town, you can admire tapestries by Jean Lurçat and an amusing collection of ceramic roosters. The rooms are standard, a bit old-fashioned but well kept.

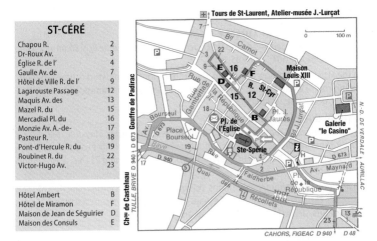

Place de l'Église

The church of Ste-Spérie was rebuilt in the 17C and 18C in the Gothic style. **The Hôtel de Puymule** (15C), in the square near the east end, is a turreted town house, with doors and windows decorated with ribbed arches.

▷ *From place de l'Église, walk along rue Notre-Dame and across rue de la République.*

Rue du Mazel

This street and the surrounding area form one of the most charming districts in the old town, with old houses and fine doorways. At the corner of rue St-Cyr, note the 15C **Hôtel Ambert** with its two corbelled turrets and Renaissance doorway.

Further along on the right, the narrow cobblestoned **passage Lagarouste**, with a stream down the middle, is overshadowed by tall corbelled houses.

▷ *Continue along rue du Mazel.*

Place du Mercadial

This was the market square where fishermen brought their catch to be displayed on the *taoulié*, a stone bench beside the 15C **Maison de Jean de Séguirier** at the corner of rue Pasteur. From this spot, there is a lovely view of the square surrounded by half-timbered houses against St Laurence's Towers. The **Maison des Consuls** has an interesting Renaissance façade overlooking rue de l'Hôtel-de-Ville.

▷ *Follow rue des Tourelles.*

Rue St-Cyr

On the corner of rue de l'Olie stands a lovely medieval house with three corbelled façades. Further on, in rue de l'Olie on the left, is the 15C Hôtel de Miramon flanked with a corner turret.

▷ *At the end of rue de l'Olie, turn right onto boulevard Carnot.*

Maison Jean de Séguirier

Maison Louis XIII

This fine mansion has an elegant façade adorned with a loggia.

▷ *Return to place de l'Église along the boulevards.*

Sights

Atelier-Musée Jean-Lurçat★

Open mid-Jul to Sep and during the Easter school holidays (zone B), 9.30am-noon and 2.30-6.30pm. 2.50€. 05 65 38 28 21.

In the artist's studio, now a museum, the ground-floor rooms (studio, drawing room, dining room) exhibit Lurçat's works (tapestries, designs, paintings, ceramics, lithographs, gouaches, wallpaper).

Galerie d'Art le Casino

Open Jul-Sep, 9.30am-noon and 2-6.30pm, Sun, 11am-7pm; May-Jun, daily except Tue, 9.30am-noon and 2-6.30pm, Sun 11am-7pm; Oct-Apr, daily except Tue and Sun, 9.30am-noon and 2-6.30pm. Closed 1 Jan, 1 and 11 Nov, and 25 Dec. No charge. 05 65 38 19 60.

In addition to temporary exhibitions, this gallery displays a large collection of **Jean Lurçat's tapestries**★. Hung on the walls, the tapestries combine a variety of forms and colours, depicting fantastic animals and cosmic visions.

Excursions

Site de Notre-Dame-de-Verdale★

9km/5.6mi E. Leave St-Céré travelling E on the D 673. After 2km/1mi, turn right on the D 30. 1km/0.5mi beyond Latouille-Lentillac a narrow road branches off to the left and runs along the river. Park the car in the area provided and continue on foot. 1hr round trip on foot.

Walk up a path, which runs beside the Tolerme, as it falls in cascades over the rocks. After crossing the stream twice on primitive wooden bridges the path climbs steeply, in a hilly setting.

Shortly, the pilgrimage chapel of Our Lady of Verdale appears perched on a rocky crag. From the site, there is an extensive **view**★ of the Tolerme gorges and the chestnut-covered hills.

▶ *23km/14.5mi E. Leave St-Céré travelling E on the D 673 and continue along the D 30.*

Lac du Tolerme

The lake, at 530m/1 739ft, is surrounded by greenery and covers 38ha/94 acres. At the lake there is a **recreation centre** open to visitors (*Parking fee in Jul-Aug. 5€. 05 65 40 31 26*). A lakeside footpath (4km/2.4mi) is a pleasant place to stretch your legs.

Lac du Tolerme

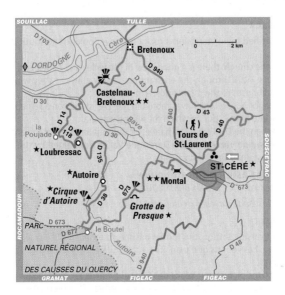

Vallée de la Bave

45km/28mi round-trip – allow 3hr

▶ *Leave St-Céré travelling W along the D 30.*

The towers of Montal Castle soon come into view on the left, rising above fertile fields and meadows interspersed with lines of poplars.

Château de Montal★★

See Château de MONTAL.

The road towards Gramat climbs above the Bave Valley, offering views of St Laurence's Towers.

▶ *Join up with the D 673 via St-Jean-Lespinasse.*

Grotte de Presque★

Open Jul-Aug, guided tour (45min), 9.30am-6.30pm; Mar-Jun, 9.30am-noon and 2-6pm; second half of Feb and Oct to mid-Nov, daily except Sat-Sun, 10am-noon and 2-5pm. 6€ (children 7-11 years old: 3€). ☎ 05 65 38 07 44 or 06 88 04 47 04. www.grottesdepresque.com

The cave consists of a series of chambers and galleries that extend 350m/380yd into the rocks. Concretions, especially strange-shaped stalagmite piles and thousand-faceted frozen falls along the walls, have built up in the different *salles* or chambers of the caves, named for the imagery evoked: Draperies, Salle Haute, Grande Cuve (basin), Marbre Rouge (red marble). Slender columns of astonishing whiteness stand at the entrance to the **Salle des Merveilles**★ (Hall of Wonders).

▶ *Continue along the D 673 towards Padirac then turn right onto the D 38.*

Cirque d'Autoire★

▶ *Leave the car in a parking area. Take, on the left of the road, the path that overlooks the River Autoire, which here forms a series of waterfalls (viewpoint).*

Cross the little bridge and go up the steep stony path cut in the rocks. Very soon a wonderful **view**★★ of the natural amphitheatre, the valley and the village of Autoire unfolds.

Autoire★

Autoire in its picturesque **setting**★ is typical of the character of the Quercy region. Enchanting scenes are revealed at every street corner: a fountain at the centre of a group of half-timbered houses; old corbelled houses with brown-tiled roofs; elegant turreted manors and mansions.

From the terrace near the church, which has a fine Romanesque east end, there is a good view of the Limargue Mill and the rocky amphitheatre that lies to the south-west.

▶ *Drive N along the D 135.*

Loubressac★

This old fortified town stands on a rocky spur overlooking the south bank of the River Bave.

From near the church, there is a good view of the valley and of St-Céré, marked out by its towers. Walk through the enchanting narrow alleys as they wind between brown-tiled houses to the castle's postern.

This 15C manor house, which was rebuilt in the 17C, stands on a remarkable **site**★ at the very end of the spur on which the village was built.

D 118 and then the D 14 from the hamlet of La Poujade descend towards the Bave Valley, giving fine **views**★ of the Dordogne Valley dominated by the impressive outline of Castelnau-Bretenoux Castle.

Château de Castelnau-Bretenoux★★

See Château de CASTELNAU-BRETENOUX.

▶ *Leave Castelnau travelling N along the D 14.*

Bretenoux

In its leafy riverside setting, this former bastide, founded in 1277 by a powerful lord of Castelnau, has kept its grid plan, its central square, covered arcades and parts of the ramparts.

After visiting the picturesque **place des Consuls** with its 15C turreted town house, go through a covered alley to the old manor at the corner of the pretty rue du Manoir de Cère. Turn right and right again returning via the charming quay along the Cère.

▶ *Drive 4km/2.5mi along the D 940 towards St-Céré and turn left onto the D 43 then right onto the D 40 5km/3mi beyond Belmont-Bretenoux.*

Tours de St-Laurent

Traffic on the private road branching off to the right is allowed. 🚶 *1hr on foot there and back.*

Perched on a steep hill which overlooks the town, the two, tall medieval towers and curtain wall are a familiar local landmark. They were acquired by Jean Lurçat in 1945. Although the road to the right is private, the restriction is not strictly enforced. From a track (*1hr on foot round trip*) skirting the ramparts, admire the **view**★ of the town, the Bave and Dordogne valleys and the surrounding plateaux.

▶ *The D 48 (left) leads back to St-Céré.*

ST-CIRQ-LAPOPIE★★

POPULATION 187

MICHELIN LOCAL MAP 337: G-5 – LOCAL MAP SEE CAHORS

St-Cirq-Lapopie (*Cirq* pronounced *Sear*), faces a semicircle of white cliffs and is itself perched (80m/262ft) on a rocky escarpment that drops vertically to the left bank of the Lot; it is a remarkable **setting**★. The present name of the site commemorates the martyrdom of the young St Cyr, killed with his mother in Asia Minor during the reign of Diocletian; his relics were brought back, it is said, by St Amadour. The La Popies, local lords in the Middle Ages, gave their name to the castle built on the cliff's highest point and, by extension, to the village that grew up at its foot.

▶ **Orient Yourself**: For a wonderful view of the River Lot, head to the top of La Popie Rock.

🕐 **Organising Your Time**: Allow a full day to explore the Célé and Lot valleys.

🌜 **Also See**: Grottes du Pech-Merle; Cahors.

A Bit of History

A contested stronghold – This rock commanding the valley has probably tempted would-be occupiers since Gallo-Roman times.

The history of the fortress is a long series of sieges and obscure battles until 1580 when Henri de Navarre, the future Henri IV, ordered that the walls of the valiant fortress which were still standing be knocked down.

Address Book

For coin ranges, see the Legend at the back of the guide.

EATING OUT

Le Gourmet Quercynois – *R. de la Peyrolerie* - ☎ *05 65 31 21 20* - 🕐 *closed mid-Nov to Jan.* A nice restaurant and an interesting wine museum have been set up in this village house owned by an oenologist. Naturally, the wine list is excellent and the choices go well with the regional cuisine on the menu. The decor of the dining room is a happy mixture of modern and old-fashioned styles.

L'Oustal – ☎ *05 65 31 20 17 - loustal. restaurant@wanadoo.fr* - 🕐 *closed 15 Nov-15 Dec - reserv. required.* This restaurant is small in size and big on quality. The menu features unpretentious regional dishes at reasonable prices. Afternoons, before dinner service starts, you can enjoy a drink on the terrace.

WHERE TO STAY

Auberge du Sombral Aux Bonnes Choses – ☎ *05 65 31 26 08* - 🕐 *closed 12 Nov-31 Mar and Wed from Sep to Jun - 8 rooms.* A country inn in the heart of a charming medieval hill village. Take a seat in one of the two dining rooms and admire the array of decorative objects. Country cooking. A few rooms available, under the eaves.

Hôtel La Pelissaria – ☎ *05 65 31 25 14* - 🕐 *closed 15 Oct-15 Apr* - 🅿 - *10 rooms.* If you love the old stone houses of this region, check in to this hotel. The medieval building has a garden with an exceptional view, and once the tourists leave the village, the evenings are calm. Nice rooms, small pool.

LEISURE ACTIVITIES

Kalapca – ☎ *05 65 30 29 51 or 05 65 24 21 01 - kalapca@wanadoo.fr.* On the River Lot and River Célé: recreational activities and canoe hire, with or without a guide.

The end of a craft – St-Cirq-Lapopie had a strong guild of woodturners dating back to the Middle Ages. Until the late 19C, there were a considerable number of craftsmen still to be seen working their primitive lathes; their industry added a colourful note to the old-fashioned village alleyways. The tap makers made taps for the casks, and the bushel makers candlesticks, rosary beads and crossbars for chairs. Their shopfronts set small and large arched openings side by side. Nowadays, other businesses take advantage of the distinctive architecture; there is only one woodworker left in St-Cirq.

The Village

It is a perennial pleasure to wander along narrow, steeply sloping streets lined with houses with lovely brown-tiled roofs. The corbelled façades and exposed beams of some of the houses are further ornamented with Gothic windows, or bays with mullioned windows in the Renaissance style. Most of the houses have been carefully restored by artists, particularly painters and craftsmen who have been attracted by the beauty of St-Cirq-Lapopie and the Lot Valley. Among the most famous are the writer André Breton, who lived on place du Carol in the old sailors' inn, and the painters Foujita, Man Ray, Henri Martin and Pierre Daura; the latter lived in the house with carved beams (his own work) in ruelle de la Fourdonne.

La Popie

▶ *Take the path that starts on the right of the town hall (mairie), to reach the castle ruins and the highest part of the cliff.*

From the cliff top (telescope), on which once stood the keep of La Popie Fortress, there is a remarkable **view**★★ right over the village of St-Cirq, with the church clinging to the cliff face, to a bend in the River Lot, encircling a patchwork of arable fields and meadows delineated by poplars, and to the north, the wooded foothills that border the Gramat Causse.

Fortified church

This 15C sanctuary stands on a rock terrace overlooking the Lot. A squat belfry-tower, flanked by a round turret, stands at the front end.
Inside, the main body of the church has pointed vaulting and contains several baroque statues. There is a good view from the terrace to the right of the church.

▶ *Walk down towards place du Carol and turn left (signpost).*

St-Cirq-Lapopie rises above the Lot

Château de la Gardette

🕐*Open mid-Jun to Sep, daily except Tue, 10am-12.30pm and 2.30-7pm; Apr to mid-Jun, daily except Tue, 10.30am-12.30pm and 2.30-6pm.* 🎫*1.50€.* ☎ *05 65 31 23 22.*

The two main buildings, each flanked by a bartizan, house the **Musée Rignault**, so named as the painter and collector left his works in legacy to the *département* of the Lot.

Exhibited are old furniture (Renaissance cabinet and sideboard, 14C dowry chest), 14C and 15C statues, lacquered items from China and frescoes dating from the Ming Dynasty. Temporary exhibitions are regularly held in the castle.

Belvédère du Bancourel

▶ *Follow the D 40 towards Bouziès for 300m/330yd to reach this rock promontory overlooking the Lot. A lay-by esplanade (car park) has been built where the D 8 branches off to the left from the cliff road.*

There is a **view**★ from Le Bancourel of the Lot Valley and St-Cirq, with the rock of La Popie rising up out of the village.

ST-JUNIEN

POPULATION 10 666

MICHELIN LOCAL MAP 325: C-5 – LOCAL MAP SEE LIMOGES

St-Junien is a busy town, known for its paper mills, taweries (leather dressing works) and particularly its glove factories. The collegiate church is Romanesque-Limousin in style.

▶ **Orient Yourself**: The town is located 12km/8mi northeast of Rochechouart and 27km/17mi west of Limoges.

🕼 **Don't Miss**: The Collégiale St-Junien and St-Julien's tomb.

🕼 **Also See**: Oradour-sur-Glane; Rochechouart; Limoges.

A Bit of History

St Junien, the miracle worker – In the early 6C, in a forest along the banks of the River Vienne, at Comodoliac, lived a saintly hermit named Amand. Drawn to the hermit and his reputation for holiness, a young man from Cambrai, Junien, joined him in his solitude. For some 40 years, Junien lived in this place, using waters from a sacred spring to cure those who came to see him, often from afar. His own reputation was so great that when he died, in 540, the bishop of Limoges personally presided over his funeral ceremonies and ordered the construction of a sanctuary above his tomb. A monastery grew up and a settlement around it: the town of St-Junien was born.

The development of glove-making – St-Junien lies in the centre of a livestock rearing region and therefore had on hand the necessary raw materials – kid and lambskin. In addition the waters of the Vienne possess exceptional properties for tanning. Glove-making began here in the Middle Ages and by the 15C had made the town famous. It is even said that Louis XI, on his return from Bayonne, was received in great style at St-Junien and permitted the master glover makers to present him with pairs of gloves.

Expansion of the industry has brought about many changes, but mechanisation is excluded as handwork alone can ensure a good finish. Today, 300 workers in seven workshops produce over 480 000 pairs of gloves each year, 45% of all French production.

The Ostensions of St-Junien

Every seven years, *Ostensions (next in 2009)* commemorate the memory of St Junien. When the ceremony is held the relics are shown and a picturesque spectacle unfolds: rich costumes are brought out, the main street is decorated with foliage and caged birds as a reminder of the forest in which the saint lived. The main events of the saint's life are evoked; music and ringing bells add an air of celebration.

Visit

Collégiale St-Junien★

🕒 *Open daily except Sun, 8am-noon.*

The nave and transept of this remarkable Romanesque-Limousin building are late 11C; the main part of the building was completed when the façade was added at the end of the 12C; the plain, square chevet is 13C. The central bell tower was rebuilt after it had fallen down in 1922.

The west doorway is divided into two bays and is framed by small columns. It is surmounted by a massive belfry-porch two storeys high, flanked by two stone bell-turrets.

Inside, the **nave** and the **chancel** are of equal length. The transept is punctuated by bays, one of which is quite narrow and extends the side aisle, and the chapels have primitive pointed arches. The crossing is surmounted by an octagonal cupola with flat pendants, pierced by four Limousin-style bays and a multifoil occulus. The capitals in the chancel are ornamented with common motifs: palmettos, animals, figures. The last two bays and the rose window in the east end were added in the 13C. There are traces of 12C and 13C **frescoes** in several places, in particular on the vaulting of the second bay of the nave. The third bay on the north side houses an enamelled 13C reliquary.

Behind the main altar is **St Junien's tomb**★, a masterpiece of 12C Limousin sculpture. Two-thirds of the tomb is of limestone adorned with sculpture; the remainder is only a plaster covering added last century

St Junien's tomb

when the high altar was moved and no longer formed part of the sarcophagus. On the east side, Christ is shown in glory surrounded by the symbols of the Evangelists; medallions depict the theological and moral virtues. On the north face the Virgin, within a glory, holds the Infant Jesus; seated on one side are the figures of twelve Old Men of the Apocalypse. On the opposite side the other twelve Old Men are portrayed together with a medallion of the Holy Lamb.

In the second bay on the northern side of the chancel is the **Chapelle St-Martial**. Of Gothic design, it once harboured the relics of the saint, whose life is depicted in the 13C frescoes which are only partly visible. A polychrome wall niche holds an early-16C Entombment; Christ is shown surrounded by seven figures (only St John has kept his head).

Chapelle Notre-Dame du Pont
🕐*Open Apr-Sep, 2-6pm.*

Standing on the right bank of the River Vienne beside a 13C bridge equipped with cutwaters is the elegant Chapel of Our Lady of the Bridge. There is a legend that the statue of the Virgin which now stands in the apse was originally found alongside the bridge on the river bank; the statue was immediately taken in solemn procession to the collegiate church, but the next day was found, once more, on the river bank. The people of St-Junien erected a chapel to the Virgin on the spot where the statue was found. The present church was built in the 15C on the site of the earlier sanctuary; it was enlarged and completed thanks to Louis XI, who came there twice on pilgrimage.

The overall architectural effect is of graceful flamboyance; a sculptured balustrade lines the base of the roof. The nave and two aisles of equal height are supported by elegant octagonal pillars; the vaulting is ornamented with finely carved keystones.

Excursions

Site Corot
2km/1.2mi NW along N 141. 15min round-trip on foot.

▶ *As you leave town, take a sharp right turn at the bend in the road, then turn left immediately on a small road. Follow this road as far as the porcelain factory and park at the entrance of the lane.*

Walk for a few minutes beside the river to reach the setting of the stream, flowing past rocks and trees, which inspired Corot and many other painters.

ST-LÉON-SUR-VÉZÈRE ★

POPULATION 419

MICHELIN LOCAL MAP 329: H-5

Built in a picturesque loop of the River Vézère, this charming village, overrun by greenery, possesses two castles and one of the finest Romanesque churches of Périgord. The village comes to life in August during the Festival Musical du Périgord Noir.

▶ **Orient Yourself**: The village is situated midway between the Grotte de Lascaux and Les-Eyzies de-Tayac.

◔ **Also See**: Sarlat.

Visit

Church ★

The church was part of a Benedictine priory which was founded in the 12C and depended upon the abbey at Sarlat. It was built on the ruins of a Gallo-Roman villa. The remains of one of the villa's walls can be seen on the river-side.

From the square, the apse, the perfectly smooth radiating chapels and the fine square two-storey arcaded bell tower form a harmonious unit. The church is roofed with the heavy limestone slabs (*lauzes*) of Périgord Noir.

Inside, the transept crossing is vaulted with a dome, whereas apsidal chapels are connected to the apse by narrow openings, known as passages *berrichons* as they are a feature of churches in the Berry region in particular. The apse and south radiating chapel are decorated with parts of Romanesque frescoes, in which red is predominant.

The 12C church

▶ *Walk along the river on the left.*

Château de Clérans

This elegant 15C and 16C palace, flanked with machicolated towers and turrets, stands on the banks of the river.

▶ *Go into the village.*

Château de la Salle

Standing on the square, this small castle built of dry-stone has a fine 14C square keep crowned with machicolations.

Chapelle du Cimetière

This small 14C chapel in the cemetery is roofed, like the church, with *lauzes*. An inscription in the *Oc* language above the door harks back to an extraordinary event; in 1233, a servant who had let fly an arrow onto the crucifix guarding the entrance to the cemetery dropped dead on the spot, with his head turned back-to-front. In 1890, the blasphemer's grave was excavated, and a skeleton with its skull back-to-front was unearthed. The cemetery still has a tall crucifix, and there are six tombs in the defence wall.

EATING OUT

◔◔ **Le Petit Léon** – ☎ 05 53 51 18 04 - ◔ *closed Sep-Jun*. This garden restaurant is a real find! White parasols shade the wooden tables under the apple trees. The dishes are inventive and tasty.

WHERE TO STAY

◔ **Camping Le Paradis** – 4km/2.5mi SW of St-Léon-on-Vézère along the D 706 - ☎ 05 53 50 72 64 - le-paradis@perigord. com - ◔ *open Apr-25 Oct - reserv. recommended - 200 pitches – restaurant.* "Paradise" is a good name for this campsite. Former farm buildings serve as facilities and the sites are attractively landscaped. Modern and comfortable. Pool, tennis court and play areas.

ST-LÉONARD-DE-NOBLAT★

POPULATION 4 764

MICHELIN LOCAL MAP 325: F-5 – LOCAL MAP SEE LIMOGES

Perched on a hilltop above a wide valley defined by the Vienne, Maulde and Taurion rivers, the bell tower of the old church in St-Léonard-de-Noblat is a remarkable example of Limousin-style Romanesque architecture.

The main industry in town is the manufacture of porcelain (four companies), and the valley is famed for its cattle. The distinctive, ruddy brown animals known as vaches limousines originate from the area around St-Léonard, which is an active export and breeding centre.

For visitors with a sweet tooth, St-Léonard is memorable for its *massepain*, a speciality found in local pastry shops, made with sugary crushed almonds.

▶ **Orient Yourself**: The town is located 21km/13mi east of Limoges.

🐾 **Don't Miss**: The collegiate church and belfry.

Kids **Especially for Kids**: Historail.

👣 **Also See**: Limoges.

A Bit of History

A hermit – Long before the Roman conquest, the road between Bourges and Bordeaux, crossing the Vienne near the village of Noblat, was well travelled. The road, watched over by a castle belonging to the bishops of Limoges, was used by pilgrims on their way to Compostela in the 12C.

The town was named after the hermit **Léonard**, godson of Clovis, who early in the 6C chose Pauvain Forest, which has since disappeared, as his place of retreat. He built a rustic sanctuary. His piety and the many miracles he performed made him one of the most popular saints in Limousin. A village was built alongside the retreat and took the name Noblat (derived from *nobiliacum*, meaning noble site). Léonard's help was invoked in protecting horses and seeking the release of prisoners. Because he was the patron saint of prisoners, it is the tradition in St-Léonard, in the month of November to celebrate the *Quintaine*. A small wooden fortress (representing a prison) or *Quintaine* is trampled down by riders on horseback armed with clubs.

A great scholar – Joseph-Louis **Gay-Lussac** was born in St-Léonard in 1778 (d 1850). He distinguished himself in physics and chemistry: he discovered the law of expansion of gases and made ascents in a balloon to examine whether the earth's magnetic attraction decreased as the altitude increased. Later he devised the law of gaseous combination. In 1809 he demonstrated that chlorine was an element and discovered boron and fluoboric acid. In addition to his scientific achievements and awards, Gay-Lussac represented the Haute-Vienne in the French *Chambre des Députés*.

Address Book

👣 *For coin ranges, see the Legend at the back of the guide.*

EATING OUT AND WHERE TO STAY

🍽️🍽️ **Le Gay Lussac** – 18 r. de l'Égalité - ☎ 05 55 56 98 45 - 🕐 *closed Christmas-1 Jan, Sun eve, Tue eve and Mon except 14 Jul-15 Aug*. This bistro-style restaurant is housed in a former bakery. The upstairs dining room tends to be used by locals who appreciate the simplicity of the setting and the cuisine.

🍽️🍽️ **Hôtel Grand St-Léonard** – 23 av. du Champs-de-Mars - ☎ 05 55 56 18 18 - *grandsaintleonard@wanadoo.fr* - 🕐 *closed 22-26 Jan, 12-19 May, Mon (🕐 open Mon eve from 15 Jun-15 Sep) and Tue noon - 13 rooms*. This old post house with an imposing façade is located in the centre of town. The pleasant rooms have been decorated with care, with the restaurant's dining room adorned with gleaming copper. Simple cuisine prepared from high-quality ingredients.

Visit

It is easy to imagine the layout of the medieval town: the ring of boulevards follows the path of the old defensive wall, whose vestiges can be seen on boulevard Carnot (south) and rue Jean-Jaurès (north-west). Some of the many old houses in this neighbourhood date back to the 13C.

In the days of the pilgrims, rue Georges-Perrin (then rue Aumônière) led from the Noblat Bridge to the centre of town; a 13C hospital gate still stands in this main street.

Medieval Town

Two names are mentioned for every street: the present name in blue and the medieval name in red.

The restored Romanesque church

B. Kaufmann/MICHELIN

Start from place Gay-Lussac (commemorative monument and birthplace of the scientist). This was the centre of activities during the Middle Ages: the town's butchers had their stand here; note the corner house dating from the 13C and featuring a large bay surmounted by two storeys with twinned windows. Follow rue Gay-Lussac to place de la République: no 18, known as the Maison de la Tour Ronde (16C), has a picturesque corbelled turret. On the corner of rue de la Halle, another 16C building, known as the Maison de la Tour Carrée, features a square bartizan. As you walk towards place Noblat, note the 13C house with its shop entrance surmounted by twinned windows.

Sights

Ancienne Collégiale★

Guided tours available by prior request via the tourist office.

This 12C former collegiate church (restored) remains a fine specimen of Romanesque architecture. The side walls and the chapel for the Holy Sepulchre go back to the 11C. It is said that Richard the Lion Heart contributed to the construction of the church on his release from prison in Austria.

Exterior – The **belfry★★**, built above a porch which is open on two sides and embellished with remarkable capitals, adjoins the third bay of the nave. The bell tower consists of four storeys built square, surmounted by two recessed storeys which are octagonal in shape. The transition from the square plan to the octagonal is managed by devising a sharply pointed gable for each of the four walls of the top quadrilateral. Each tier is adorned with beautiful blind arcades. The final touch of elegance is given by the stone spire which was constructed in the 12C.

Situated between the belfry and the transept, the **Rotonde du Sépulcre**, now restored to its original appearance, was probably built by a knight returning from the Holy Land.

The church's **west front**, built in the 13C, has a wide doorway flanked by small columns decorated with finely carved, crocketed capitals supporting the covings. The **east end** rises harmoniously in tiers and the chapels are roofed with rounded tiles.

Interior – The church went through several building stages (*see the scale model at the entrance*), which are apparent in the disunity of style within.

The powerful **nave** has groined, barrel and broken-barrel vaulting, the **crossing** is roofed with a high dome on pendentives placed atop a drum pierced by eight windows and smaller and less ornate domes rise above the end of each transept arm. The **chancel** (late 12C) is wider than the nave, and rather awkwardly linked to the transept; its complex design involves arches, each divided down its centre by a pillar or column supporting a suspension arch. The ambulatory has asymmetrical groined vaulting resting on elegant small columns which stand between the seven apsidal chapels.

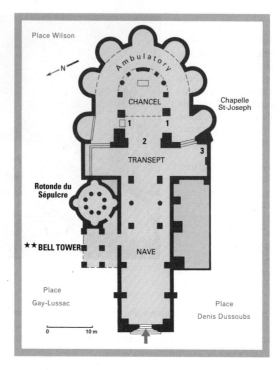

In the 17C, a new vault, higher than the cupola in the transept, was added on and the church had to be shored up. Two thin columns in the sanctuary were set into a chunky block and another such supporting block was added beneath the central arcade.

The 15C oak wood stalls (1) are sculpted with satirical motifs. On the gilded main altar (2), dating from the 18C, the relics of St Léonard are in a case below his statue. In the south transept, a wall niche holds the saint's tomb (3) and a revered lock bolt; the bolt is symbolic of St Léonard's power to intervene on prisoners' behalf (tradition also holds that it is effective in curing cases of sterility).

Musée Gay-Lussac

&⊙*Open Jul-Aug, 10am-noon and 2-6pm (last entrance 15min before closing); mid-Apr to Jun and Sep-Oct, Sun, 2-6pm. Closed Easter Sun and Whitsunday.* ☞*No charge.* ☎ *05 55 56 25 06.*

The museum devoted to this man of science is located in a former convent. His memory and accomplishments are recalled in documents, objects (a hot air balloon basket; the re-creation of a 19C chemistry laboratory) and instruments (barometer, oven etc).

Historail

On the D 39 S of town. ⊙*Open mid-Jun to Aug, daily except Sat-Sun, 2-6pm; rest of the year by prior arrangement.* ⊙*Closed on public hols.* ☞*4.50€ (children 8-16 years old: 3€).* ☎ *05 55 56 11 12.*

Kids The history of the iron horse is the subject of this museum's displays, which include genuine train parts as well as working models (six different scales; one of the models operates outdoors). Re-creations and simulations bring the heyday of rail back to life; in the yard, there are tracks, signals, a water tower, and engine motors.

ST-MARCEL ★

POPULATION 1 641

MICHELIN LOCAL MAP 323: F-7

The medieval hamlet of St-Marcel stands on a hill overlooking the right bank of the Creuse, on the site of the Gallo-Roman town of **Argentomagus**, high above the River Creuse.

An archaeological dig carried out on the site and in the surrounding area revealed traces of ancient monuments and a large number of items were excavated. Some of these are now part of the collections of the local museum.

▶ **Orient Yourself**: St-Marcel is situated on the northern outskirts of the town of Argenton-sur-Creuse.

◉ **Don't Miss**: Théatre du Virou; Musée Archéologique d'Argentomagus.

A Bit of History

Archaeological excavations – The site is remarkable for the preservation of its vestiges, which long slumbered beneath a vineyard. Several roads passed through the town, a pivotal point between the upper valley of the Creuse and the low wet lands of the Brenne; the river runs a regular course here and is navigable. The development of trade, the abundant game, the presence of water and wood (which made metal work possible), explain why this land was occupied so long ago, and the diversity of the archaeological discoveries. Magdalenian reindeer hunters dwelled in caves here (14000-8000 BC), whereas their Gallo-Roman successors built an *oppidum*, or fortified city, to live in. Following the Roman conquest (50 BC), **Argentomagus** (perhaps from the Latin argenteum, silver, or from the Gaulish man's name *Argentos* and *magus*, meaning market) underwent spectacular demographic and economic growth, as trade, crafts and especially metal working – the Bituriges (◉ see BOURGES) were specialists – developed. The site figures on a 15C reproduction of the road network of the lower Roman Empire known as the **Peutinger Table**, and is mentioned in a 4C text as the leading Gaulish arms manufactory. For two centuries, the town expanded well beyond the bounds of the original *oppidum*, although it never rated as a major city, covering no more than 70ha/173 acres with a population of 5 000.

Archaeological Site

◉ *No charge.* ☎ *02 54 24 47 31.*

In addition to the sections known as Mersans and Virou, other areas have been explored, including a necropolis, called Champ de l'Image (200m/220yd north-west of the museum).

Les Mersans

This plateau (27ha/67 acres), protected by cliffs and a moat, was the first urban core. Excavations have been ongoing since 1962. The so-called Sergius Macrinus house is on the site, as well as a religious enclave made up of two **temples** and a square edifice. In the Celtic tradition, very different from Greek and Roman styles, the fanum-style architecture of the temples consists of two square forms, one within the other, open to the east. The inner square (*cella*) held statues of gods; around, a gallery served as an ambulatory where, according to ancient documents, processions took place, following the path of the sun.

Along with most of the rest of the town, these temples were destroyed during a Barbarian invasion in 276.

During excavations, archaeologists discovered some lovely bronze statuettes: a goat lying down, an eagle, and the famous Mercury. Some 40 sacrificial pits have been found in the sanctuary. In one of them, the split skull of a sow and many pig bones were discovered along with a large cutlass. Near the big temple, a ring set in a slab was used for tying up animals.

EATING OUT & WHERE TO STAY

◉ **Le Boisseau** – *Rte de Châteauroux - 3.5km/2.1mi N of St-Marcel. Take the D 927, then head towards Châteauroux -* ☎ *02 54 24 12 33 -* ◉ *closed Sun eve and Mon.* An unpretentious restaurant surrounded by nature where the emphasis in the restaurant is on traditional fare. Renovated bedrooms.

To the east of the temple area, the forum and other ancient monuments are still buried. In 1967, a **monumental fountain** was discovered by chance. As the earth was removed, two large stairways appeared, leading down to a square pool 6m/20ft on each side. The water drained from here into a sewer, still in perfect condition, which has been uncovered along a 90m/295ft course. The exact purpose of this fountain (the largest of its kind from the period) is uncertain. It certainly played some cultural role, before it was filled in by metal workers, some time after 276.

Théâtre du Virou★

▶ *Return down the hill towards Argenton; turn right just before the railway bridge, go along for about 200m/220yd, then take a steep path on the right which goes up to the theatre.*

Until 1966, only a part of the outside wall was visible (the rest was underground), and this gave the parcel of land its name: *Virou*, something which rotates or revolves. Now the building has been entirely uncovered, revealing the two successive stages of construction: the first, rustic period, from the early 1C, and a second 2C part. The way the works of two centuries have been superimposed creates an interesting study for archaeologists. The first theatre, with poor acoustics, was typical of Gallo-Roman times in its horseshoe shape, small stage area, and wide orchestra section. Mime and dance were commonly performed in such theatres, where the Greek influence is strongly felt.

Simple in design, the theatre provided open-air seating, hewn out of the rock; spectators sat with their legs crossed in front of them.

The 2C improvements brought the theatre into line with Roman design: the circular seating (84m/275ft in diameter) could accommodate an audience of 6 000.

Musée Archéologique d'Argentomagus★

🕐♿*Open Jul-Aug, 9.30am-noon and 2-6pm; Sep-Jun, daily except Tue, 9.30am-noon and 2-6pm.* 🚫*Closed 24 Dec-19 Jan.* ✍*3€ (child: 1.50€), no charge 1st Sun of the month. Tactile exhibits for the blind and some explanations in braille.* ☎ *02 54 24 47 31. www. argentomagus.com*

Inside the modern building, a wide ramp spirals down to the archaeological crypt, where the collection includes items from the immediate area. Only the prehistoric section extends to cover the whole Creuse Valley.

The **prehistoric collections** take visitors back in time to a million years BC, to the period known as the lower Paleolithic. A hut from the **Lavaud** site, in Éguzon-Chantôme has been recreated. The prehistoric displays continue in chronological order and include: tools from a Solutrean find (18000-16000 BC) from Fressignes and the Roches shelter, in Pouligny-St-Pierre; and many items found in the **Garenne cave** (hills around St Marcel), dating from 14000 BC. Among these exceptional pieces, note the pendant with dancers, where six stylised female dancers hold hands in a prehistoric roundel; the Baptist, a human face on a pierced rod; the collection of 20 lamps.

The **Gallo-Roman section** is organised around themes: the city and its monuments (scale models); work, daily life, and trade (an interesting display of pottery and household utensils); funerary rites (re-creation of part of the Roman cemetery at Champ de l'Image).

The final room, devoted to **religious practices**, illustrates, with statuary, the coexistence of gods of many origins in Gaulish civilisation. Native, Greek and Eastern divinities are depicted; the small bronzes are most remarkable. Notice the masterly **Mercury**, made in the 1C, god of tradesmen and thieves, venerated in Argentomagus and throughout Gaul. Also on view: a Gaulish god sitting cross-legged, many mother goddesses, the Vergobret urn (named for a magistrate in independent Gaul), and a plaque commemorating the dedication of a temple.

Musée d'Argentomagus – Domestic altar

Gezell/MUSÉE D'ARGENTOMAGUS, St-Marcel

Finish the visit with a walk through the **crypte archéologique**, 150m/492ft along the vestiges of the north moat (the wall measures 20m/66ft long by 5m/16ft high), and past an area devoted to crafts (leather and dye workers' tanks) and shelters, where a rare domestic altar has been left in place (& *see photograph*).

Medieval Village

At the town hall and in the museum, a map is available for an interesting self-guided tour.

Church★

To the left of the nave, the **massive 14C bell tower** was used as a keep. The severe, shingled tower differs from others in the region in its defensive allure. The chevet dates from the 12C.

The **doorway** on the western façade has two rounded arches, topped by a band of mouldings with a diamond pattern. The narrow, almost rectangular stones are sculpted with Carolingian-style interlacing, geometric designs, and animal figures (lions, griffins, horses) standing alone or facing each other, inspired by Eastern tradition.

Some parts of the wall in the nave have been pierced with small, ceramic-lined holes, which serve to improve the acoustics, amplifying the resonance of religious chants.

At the end of the nave, to the left above the door, a 15C **Fresco of Our Lady** (Notre-Dame-de-Pitié) shows St Louis in a fur coat presenting a priest to the Virgin, who holds the Infant Jesus in her arms.

The chancel is ornamented with 16C **stalls** (restored), the work of Antoine Barbaud, prior of St-Marcel from 1484-1522, which are a good illustration of the transition from Gothic to Renaissance styles.

The **treasure** contains several processional crosses (13C), a 15C sculpted shrine representing the martyrdom of St Marcel and St Anastase (a scene which took place close by in the 3C, under the reign of Emperor Declus), a gilded copper shrine from the 13C adorned with Limoges enamel, the arm of St Marcel and a 14C reliquary.

Outside the church, the visitor can walk around the **medieval streets**: vestiges of the 15C fortifications, many entranceways surmounted by lintels, some with a tympanum bearing the arms of the household.

St-Marcel has retained a few characteristic wine-growers' houses with 18C galleries. There is one to be seen in rue de la Treille, next to the town hall and another one in rue du Parlement.

ST-YRIEIX-LA-PERCHE

POPULATION 7 251

MICHELIN LOCAL MAP 325: E-7

Bordering the Périgord Vert region, St-Yrieix (pronounced St-Irieh) stands at the centre of a rich stock rearing region and has a thriving cattle market. Nearby kaolin deposits are at the origin of Limoges porcelain.

- ⊙ **Don't Miss**: Collégiale du Moustier; Musée de la Porcelaine.
- & **Also See**: Coussac-Bonneval.

A Bit of History

The origins – A Gallo-Roman settlement named Attanum was probably the first on the site. Around 530, Aredius, a noble from the court of King Théodebert, friend of Grégoire de Tours and Fortunat de Poitiers, inherited his father's house and came to stay there. A pious man, he founded a sanctuary which welcomed monks and, in 572, wrote his last will and testament (a document which tells us much about Merovingian society), leaving most of his property to the abbey of St-Martin de Tours.

Near the monastery, a hamlet grew up, and took the name St-Yrieix, a transformation of Aredius, to which La Perche was added in the 15C.

From 1307, the town was partly subject to royal authority, but was dominated by the powerful canons of the church at Moûtier. After the Hundred Years War, which brought Du Guesclin to town, and the terrible plague of 1563, St-Yrieix became a full-fledged municipality in 1565. Henri IV stayed here just before the Battle of La Roche-l'Abeille, and visitors are still shown the room he slept in.

Darnet and kaolin – Limoges owes its position as china capital of France to St-Yrieix, where kaolin deposits were discovered in the 18C. Kaolin, already employed in China in the 7C, was named after a hill called Kao-ling. It was first used in Europe in 1710, in great secrecy, by the Meissen factory near Dresden. Experiments on this pure white clay had been conducted by manufacturers of the translucent soft-paste porcelain (see LIMOGES). Searches were being made all over South-west France, when, quite by chance, a surgeon by the name of Darnet who lived in St-Yrieix, came in touch with a chemist who was taking samples of clay and analysing them for the manufacturers. Darnet showed the chemist his wife's mixture for making her laundry snow white. Analysis revealed the pure kaolin content. In 1771 Darnet was charged by the king to supervise the mining of the kaolin. Thanks to Turgot, the general intendant of Limousin, development was encouraged and St-Yrieix became the source of kaolin for Limoges and the whole region. Since 1774, a porcelain manufacte has been operating in Seynie, 1km/0.5mi from St-Yrieix.

The last gold mine – Gold mining in France and in particular in the St-Yrieix area goes back to Roman times. However, this lucrative activity disappeared for centuries and was only rediscovered in 1866 when an engineer revealed that ancient fortifications were in fact disused gold mines going back to the Gallo-Roman period. Le Bourneix near St-Yrieix-la-Perche was the last working gold mine in the European Union. Eighty-five persons were employed on the site and the mine yielded around 2t of gold every year until il closed down in 2001.

WHERE TO STAY

Moulin de la Gorce – *87800 La Roche-l'Abeille - 12km/8mi northeast of St-Yrieix-la-Perche via the D 704 and the D 17 - 05 55 00 70 66 - moulingorce@ relaischateaux.fr - closed 30 Nov-2 Apr, lunchtime except Sat-Sun and public hols.* This charming hotel occupies a former 16C mill and its outbuildings near a lake popular with fishing enthusiasts. The restaurant is known to serve some of the best cuisine in the area.

Visit

Collégiale du Moustier★

The church stands on the site of the abbey founded by Aredius.

This vast edifice is a curious hodgepodge of Romanesque and Gothic styles: the Romanesque church, built in the 11C, was replaced by the larger building at the end of the 12C.

All that remains of the Romanesque church is the belfry-porch with its two narrow aisles. Massive, with stout buttresses capped with crenellations, it looks fortified. The south door, however, is ornamented with fine covings and is surmounted by a Christ in Majesty dating from the 12C set in delicate blind arcades.

The nave has ogive vaulting and is very wide but the length is limited to two bays. A huge transept is followed by a long chancel. The walls are decorated with elegant blind arcades. A gallery which circles the nave, transepts and chancel is supported by modillions ornamented with carved heads, animals and floral motifs some of which are very beautiful. In the chancel the gallery is bordered by a fine wooden rail.

Treasury – In a niche in the chancel, rests the reliquary head of St-Yrieix made of wood plated with chased silver; the beard and eyebrows are picked out in gold. The bust dates from the 15C whereas the necklace is probably 13C.

A niche in the nave contains a small 13C reliquary of enamelled gilt copper, adorned with 20 medallions showing angels with outstretched wings; a Eucharistic dove in gilded copper, with wings which open to reveal the Host; and a fabric banner adorned with pearls which was used to cover the dove.

Collegiale du Moustier, exterior

E. Larbere/MICHELIN

Tour du Plô

Near the collegiate church stands this 13C keep with twinned windows; it once formed part of the monastery's fortified precincts.

Musée de la Porcelaine

▶ *Head towards Limoges. After 2km/1mi, turn left towards the lake.*

Open Jul-Aug, 9am-noon and 2-6pm, Sun, 10am-noon, 2-6pm; Sep-Jun, daily except Sun, 9am-noon and 2-6pm. No charge. ☎ 05 55 75 10 38.

There is a rich collection dating from the 18C to the present day. Next to the soft paste porcelain from Vincennes, Arras and Strasbourg, are fine specimens in soft and hard paste from the count of Artois' factory. Presented in a glass case are items from Germany and England and two other cases display French ceramics of the 19C, mainly from Limoges. The absence of local production may seem surprising, but, although St-Yrieix did and still does manufacture porcelain, it is decorated at other factories.

SANCERRE★

POPULATION 1 799

MICHELIN LOCAL MAP 323: M, N-3 – LOCAL MAP SEE P 386

High above the banks of the River Loire, Sancerre roosts above St-Satur and St-Thibault. From this vantage point★, a wide panorama embraces the river and the Nivernais to the east, and Berry to the west. This little city, reigning over a land of trim vineyards and frisky goats, is renowned for its delicious white wine, flinty in flavour, and its little round cheeses, especially those from Chavignol. This creamy and savoury goat's cheese is so well-loved in France, that no one is put off in the slightest by its amusing name, *Crottin* (roughly translated as something you'd rather not step on in the barnyard). The steep streets of the town are enticing for their tempting food shops, restaurants and wine merchants.

▶ **Orient Yourself**: For a wonderful view of the surrounding area, head for the Esplanade de la Porte César.

Organising Your Time: Allow a full day to explore the Sancerrois region.

Don't Miss: The village's renowned vineyards.

A Bit of History

A strategic location – Sancerre, already well-known in Roman times as the site of an *oppidum*, has long stood watch over the Loire. It may have been the 9C residence of Robert le Fort, an early member of the Capetian dynasty. Later, the city played an important role in the Hundred Years War, as the gateway to Berry, placed between the Burgundians and the English. Charles VII, the so-called king of Bourges, assembled 20 000 warriors there, personally commanding them for a time.

Le Sancerrois – Vineyards and hillside of Sancerre

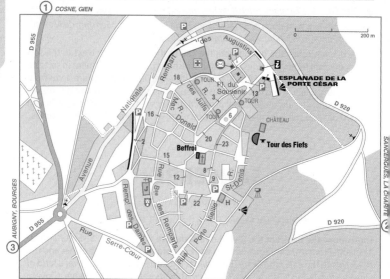

SANCERRE		Panneterie R. de la	9	St-André R.	18
Marché-aux-Porcs R. du	5	Pavé-Noir R. du	12	St-Jean R.	20
Nouvelle Place	6	Porte-César R.	13	St-Père R.	22
Paix R. de la	8	Porte-Serrure R.	15	Trois-Piliers R. des	23
		Puits-des-Fins R. du	16		

Having embraced the Reformists as of 1534, Sancerre became a stronghold of Protestantism, withstanding the assault of royal forces. The Treaty of St-Germain (1570) and the St Bartholomew's Day Massacre (1572) had no effect on those who held to their reformed views of religion, and refused to give in. Thus, on 3 January 1573, the Maréchal de La Châtre, accompanied by 7 000 men, laid siege to Sancerre. After an intense artillery preparation, an assault took place on three fronts, but the local resistance was strong. La Châtre decided to starve the people out by setting up a blockade. Inside the city walls, hungry people were eating ground slate, animal skins and leather. Capitulation came after seven long months of struggle. The population's surrender was accepted with honour, and they were allowed the freedom of their religion.

Sancerre wine – "Wine," wrote Balzac in 1844 in *La Muse du Département*, "is the main industry and the most important trading item of this land, which produces many generous vintages of rich bouquet, so similar to those of Burgundy that an untrained Parisian palate cannot taste the difference. Sancerre wines are therefore popular in Parisian cabarets where they flow steadily, which is a good thing, as they cannot be kept more than seven or eight years."

Vineyards are planted on every hill where the sun shines. The Sancerre label is only applied to white Sauvignon wines, and to red and rosé wines made from the Pinot grape.

Old Town

Visitors will enjoy strolling in the old neighbourhoods, where many of the interesting houses and vestiges are marked with informative signs. There are many architectural details to attract the eye; around the renovated Nouvelle Place, many shops sell local crafts and pottery.

Esplanade de la Porte César★★

From this terrace, there is a great **view**★★ over the vineyards, St-Satur and the viaduct, St-Thibault and the Val de Loire, and even farther afield to the Puisaye region of woods and lakes, between the Loire and the Loing, north-east of Sancerre; the first hills of the Morvan region also can be seen on the horizon.

Tours des Fiefs

⊙*Scheduled to re-open in 2006. For further details, call* ☎ *02 48 78 51 52.*
This 14C cylindrical keep is the only vestige of the château of the counts of Sancerre, a Huguenot citadel bitterly defended during the 1573 siege.

Address Book

For coin ranges, see the Legend at the back of the guide.

EATING OUT

Auberge Joseph Mellot – *16 Nouvelle Place* - ☎ *02 48 54 20 53* - *josephmellot@ jospehmellot.com* - *closed Feb and Tue and Wed out of season.* This restaurant run by a venerable family of wine-growers is a great place to stop for a meal. An authentic country inn, it serves generous portions of local specialities. Le goûter du vigneron and the sancerrois are special menus guaranteed to satisfy hearty appetites.

La Pomme d'Or – *Pl. de la Mairie* - ☎ *02 48 54 13 30* - *closed 25 Feb-5 Mar, public hol in early-Nov, Tue eve and Wed - reserv. required.* Its vineyard fresco gives this little neighbourhood restaurant near the town hall a bistro bent. Tasty cuisine at reasonable prices. The ideal occasion for sampling a glass of red, white or rosé Sancerre.

La Tour – *31 Nouvelle-Place* - ☎ *02 48 54 00 81* - *info@la-tour-sancerre.fr* - *closed 19 Dec-13 Jan.* The 14C tower of this traditional house still presides over the village square. Take your choice of two dining rooms: one, with a fireplace, is situated in the old section, whereas the other, upstairs, presents a panoramic view of the region.

Le Moulin du Grand Senais – *18300 Crézancy-en-Sancerre - 7km/4.2mi SW of Sancerre via the D 955 and D 22* - ☎ *02 48 79 06 64* - *closed Mon from Nov to Apr - reserv. recommended.* Lying in a small park

in the heart of the grapevines, this delightful inn is set in an enchanting environment. Have a seat by the pond or near the fireplace of the intimate dining room to enjoy the toothsome traditional cuisine and casual, friendly atmosphere. Three bedrooms available.

Le Laurier – *29 r. du Commerce - 18300 St-Satur - 3km/1.8mi NE of Sancerre on the D 955* - ☎ *02 48 54 17 20* - *closed 3 weeks in Mar, 3 weeks in Nov, Sun eve and Mon, and Thu eve in winter.* This former coaching inn is splendid in its cloak of Virginia creeper set off by blue shutters. The interior is charming too: exposed beams, woodwork, antique furniture and copperware. Traditional cuisine and simple rooms.

Côte des Monts Damnés – *18300 Chavignol - 4km/2.4mi W of Sancerre on the D 183* - ☎ *02 48 54 01 72* - *restaurantcmd@ wanadoo.fr* - *closed Feb, 22-30 Jun, Tue eve, Sun eve and Wed - reserv. required.* This little restaurant is on the main street of the wine-growing village. On the terrace or in the dining room, you can enjoy an appetizing selection of dishes.

WHERE TO STAY

Hôtel Panoramic – *Rempart des Augustins* - ☎ *02 48 54 22 44* - *panoramicotel@wanadoo.fr* - 57 rooms. The rooms of this hotel have an admirable view of the countryside and its vineyards. After exploring the nearby ramparts or having a dip in the pool, gourmand guests can satisfy their appetites in La Tasse d'Argent restaurant.

From the top, there is a wide **scenic view**★ of the Loire Valley and the hills of Sancerre.

Belfry

This old belfry, dating from 1509, serves the church of Notre-Dame de Sancerre.

Excursions

1 Le Sancerrois★

77km/48mi round-trip – allow 6hr

▶ *Leave Sancerre travelling SW on the D 955 towards Bourges. Shortly thereafter, turn right on the D 923.*

The road seems to part the waters of a sea of vineyards, then rises up into the so-called white hills, where hearty wines are produced in the clay and limestone soil.
At the intersection with the D 7, there is a splendid **view**★★ over Sancerre high atop its bluff, the vineyards, St-Satur and, beyond, the Loire Valley.

Chavignol

This lovely little wine-growers' village is nestled in a hollow with vineyards all around. The name is synonymous with one of France's tastiest and most popular cheeses, the little round goat's cheese known as Crottin de Chavignol.

▶ *Just outside the village, take a little road on the right which leads to the hamlet of Amigny.*

On the Sens-Beaujeu road, near the intersection with the D 85, there is a nice **view**★ of the village of Bué and the rolling countryside.

Château de Boucard

🕐 🚶 Open Apr-Sep, guided tour (40min, last tour 30min before closing), daily except Thu, 10am-noon and 2-6pm. ∞6.50€ (child: 3.80€). ☎ 02 48 58 72 81.

The castle, surrounded by a moat and well-kept outbuildings, was built between the 14C and the 16C. The furnished interior has several impressive chimneys (the one in the kitchen has a mechanical roasting spit) and a chapel which was specially redesigned to allow the Princesse de la Trémoille to attend Mass without leaving her bedroom.

▶ *Continue along the D 74.*

Jars

Visitors to this charming town will notice the manor house with its round towers and the 15C-16C church in pink and white stone. Walk round to the back of this building for a view over the countryside. 🕐*Open by prior arrangement with the town hall.* 🕐*Closed Wed and Sat afternoon and Sun.* ☎ 02 48 58 70 15.

▶ *Return to Le Noyer and drive SW along the D 55.*

Henrichemont

In the early 17C, Sully, minister to Henri IV, decided to carve out a little territory in Berry, which would serve as a refuge for his fellow Protestants. As he already owned a château in Chapelle-d'Angillon, he decided to build a town nearby, in a sandy, deserted place, which he called Henrichemont in honour of the king.
Never completed, the design for the town includes eight streets like spokes of a wheel, converging on a central square. A few 17C houses with arched doorways and the old well with its decorative moulding are intact. The region's soil lends itself well to earthenware manufacture, and several potter's workshops operate in and around Henrichemont (👁*see La Borne, below*).

▶ *Leave Henrichemont travelling E on the D 22.*

La Borne

Berry is a good place for potters because of the rich clay soil; the abundant timber was an important factor in the past, when wood-burning kilns were the rule. Gallo-Roman earthenware household objects are on display in the Berry Museum (👁*see BOURGES*). Here in La Borne, visitors can see more recent items in the **Musée de la Poterie** (🕐*open Easter to early-Nov, Sat-Sun and school hols, 3-7pm.* ∞3€. ☎ 02 48 26 98 31), established in an old chapel; or purchase local ceramics in the **exhibition-sales room** (🕐*open mid-Mar to Oct, Sat-Sun, public and school hols (zones B and C), 3-7pm; Nov to early-Jan, Sat-Sun, public and school hols (zones B and C), 2-6pm.* ∞*No charge.* ☎ 02 48 26 96 21).

Musée Vassil Ivanoff

🕐 ♿ Open May-Sep, daily except Tue, 2.30-7pm. ∞2.30€. ☎ 02 48 26 96 24.

This Bulgarian ceramic artist came to Paris in 1922 where he worked in interior decoration, fabric painting and photography. When he was 48 years old, strolling by the booksellers' stalls along the River Seine, he discovered a book on the *Art of Pottery*. He became interested in learning new techniques and was soon installed in La Borne, in a small house which doubled as his workshop. He built his own kiln and set to work, producing some 3 000 pieces before his death in 1973.
The museum houses a generous collection of the artist's work: vases, pots, cups, engraved plaques, pieces with tubular structures, some of them resembling figurative or abstract sculptures. The red enamels known as bull's blood are especially eye-catching. *His workshop can be seen on request.*

▶ *Leave La Borne travelling SE on the D 46.*

Église de Morogues

This 13C Romanesque church, fronted by an octagonal belfry-porch in reddish stone has a wonderful wooden dais inside, which was originally in the Sainte-Chapelle in Bourges. Three finely worked pinnacles rise above the chairs where the priests sat. On each side of the chancel stand two artfully crafted 14C polychrome statues: John the Baptist and St Symphorien; in the chapel to the left, a Virgin and Child.

▶ *Leave Morogues travelling W on the D 59.*

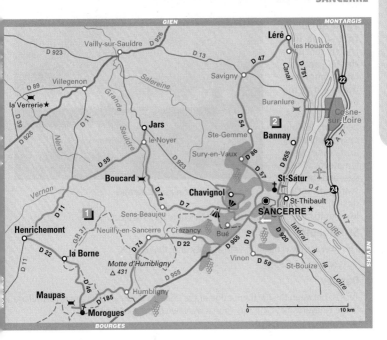

Château de Maupas

♿🕐⤴ *Guided tour (45min) Easter to Sep: 2-7pm, Sun and holidays: 10am-noon and 2-7pm.* ✆ *6.50€ (child: 4€).* ☎ *02 48 64 41 71.*

Set in the greenery of a forest, on the edge of a lake, the castle partly dates from the 13C (main building, two towers). It was rebuilt in the 15C, then transformed in the 17C and 18C, when it fell into the hands of the Maupas family. The furnishings are attractive, and pride of place is given to the **collection of plates**★ (880 pieces) dating from the 17C-19C. There are some fine old tapestries; the modern era is represented in the collection of toys; in the kitchen, copper pots gleam on their pegs.

▸ *Return to Morogues and take D 185 travelling NE.*

The ridge road which goes to La Borne runs by the **Motte d'Humbligny** (alt 431m/1414ft), the highest point in the Sancerrois region.

▸ *Leave Humbligny travelling NE on D 74.*

This is a lovely route along the Grande Sauldre Valley, as far as Neuilly-en-Sancerre, where D 22 goes back to Sancerre by way of the vineyards beyond Crézancy.

> 🕐 *For coin ranges, see the Legend at the back of the guide.*
>
> **EATING OUT**
>
> 🍽 **Auberge des Pellets** – *Les Pellets - 18220 Moroyues - 5km/3mi N of the Château de Maupas towards La Borne on the D 46 -* ☎ *02 48 26 90 68 -* 🕐 *closed Wed from 16 Sep-14 Jun, and Tue -* 🍴*.* This is the perfect place to try Crottin de Chavignol, a famous goat's cheese which is produced on the property. The dining room is adorned with old farming implements as well as tables once used as stands for sewing machines.

② Along Lateral Canal, East of Pays Fort

60km/36mi round-trip – allow half a day

▸ *Leave Sancerre travelling SW on the D 955, then turn left on D 10 towards Baugy.*

Cross the vintners' village of Vinon, and go on to St-Bouize to reach the road which runs alongside the **Loire lateral canal**. The canal, which is parallel to the river, has many locks; since 1836 it has enabled navigation from Roanne to Briare.

St-Satur

This village was once called Château-Gordon, until the relics of the African martyr Satyrus were brought here and it was renamed St-Satur.

Église St-Guine-fort – The first church went up in the 12C, and was later completely destroyed by the English. A new abbey church was begun in 1362, but only the chancel and apse were finished. Their size, and the pure soaring lines of the design can only

M. Guillot/MICHELIN

St-Satur – St-Thibault quais and the Loire

leave us to imagine the splendour of this unrealised project.

St-Thibault

This river port was bustling with activity until the mid-19C.

▶ *Continue on D 955.*

Bannay

Tucked between the northern edge of the Charnes wood and the canal, this village in the vineyards has a curious church with two pepper-pot roofs.

▶ *Continue along D 955.*

Facing the road which leads to Cosne-sur-Loire, the 15C Château de Buranlure has a lovely natural setting; the road then follows the canal for about 5km/3mi as far as the lock in the Houards.

Léré

On the border of the region known as the Pays Fort and the Val de Loire, this hamlet was once fortified, as the remaining round towers and curving rue des Remparts show.

Collégiale St-Martin – Heavily restored after the 16C, this edifice has kept its Romanesque apse, adjoining a 15C chancel; above the Gothic doorway, note the tympanum where a few sculpted figures remain intact. Despite the damage, one can still recognise St Martin sharing his cloak. Beneath the sanctuary, there is a **crypt**; the central part, a half circle, is divided into three naves with ribbed vaulting. ◷*Open Wed-Fri, 10am-noon and 2-5pm; Sat, 9am-noon.*

▶ *Leave Léré travelling SW on the D 47.*

Following the Judelle Valley as far as Savigny, the road goes through the eastern part of the **Pays Fort**, a verdant landscape of meadows and hedgerows. The villages, tucked in wooded groves, are often gatherings of houses occupied by members of an extended family (Henriots, Naudeaux, Thibauts) and built of local materials (wood, stone, cob).

The D 54 takes you back to the vineyard south of the typical village of Ste-Gemme.

▶ *Return to Sancerre on the D 86 (to Sury-en-Vaux) and the D 57.*

SARLAT-LA-CANÉDA★★★

POPULATION 9 707

MICHELIN LOCAL MAP 329: I-6

LOCAL MAPS SEE VALLÉE DE LA DORDOGNE AND PÉRIGORD NOIR

At the heart of Périgord Noir, Sarlat-la-Canéda (Sarlat for short) was built in a hollow surrounded by wooded hills. Its charm lies in its preservation of the past; it still gives the impression of a small market town – the home of merchants and clerks during the Ancien Régime (period before the Revolution) – with narrow medieval streets, restored Gothic and Renaissance town houses (*hôtels*) and its famous Saturday market. ▯ *R. de Tourny, BP 144,, 24200 Sarlat-la-Canéda, ☎ 05 53 31 45 45. www.sarlat-tourisme.com.*

▸ **Orient Yourself**: Sarlat is located 52km/32.5mi south of Brive-la-Gaillarde, 60km/37.5mi north of Cahors and 74km/46mi east of Bergerac.

🅿 **Parking**: There are a dozen car parks in Sarlat, four of which are free of charge (👃*see town plan*). In summer, traffic is banned from the town's historical quarter.

👀 **Don't Miss**: Old Sarlat; Place du Marché aux Trois Oies; Hôtel Plamon; Hôtel de Maleville; Maison de la Boétie; Saturday and Wednesday markets.

👃 **Also See**: Château de Puymartin; Beynac-et-Cazenac; Château de Castelnaud; La Roque-Gageac; Les Jardins de Marqueyssac; Domme.

A Bit of History

From abbey to bishopric – Sarlat grew up around a Benedictine abbey founded in the 8C and to which the relics of St Sacerdos, bishop of Limoges, and of his mother, St Mondane, had been entrusted under Charlemagne.

The abbots were all powerful until the 13C when internal strife and corruption caused their downfall. In 1299 the Book of Peace, an act of emancipation signed by the community, the abbey and the king, stated that the abbot might continue in his role of lord but that the consuls should be given all administrative power concerning the town itself. In 1317, however, Pope John XXII divided the Périgueux diocese and proclaimed Sarlat the Episcopal see of an area which extended far beyond the Sarladais region. The abbey church therefore became a cathedral, and the monks formed a chapter.

Sarlat's golden age – The 13C and early 14C had been a prosperous time for this active market town, but the Hundred Years War left it weakened and depopulated. Therefore, when Charles VII bestowed numerous privileges (new revenues and certain tax exemptions) upon Sarlat and its population to thank them for their loyalty and strong resistance against the English (despite Sarlat having been ceded to the English with the Treaty of Brétigny in 1360), the people of Sarlat began reconstruction. Most of the town houses to be seen were built between 1450 and 1500. This has created an architectural unity which is appreciated by the townspeople and tourists alike.

The magistrates, clerks, bishops, canons and merchants formed a comfortable bourgeois class which included such men of letters as Étienne de La Boétie.

The true and faithful friend – **Étienne de La Boétie**, who was born in Sarlat in 1530 in a house that can still be seen (👃*see below*), became famous on many counts. He proved himself to be a brilliant magistrate in the Bordeaux Parliament as well as an impassioned writer – he was only 18 when he wrote the compelling appeal for liberty, *Discourse on Voluntary Subjection or Contr'un* (Against One), which inspired Jean-Jacques Rousseau when he came to write the Social Contract. He formed a friendship with **Michel de Montaigne** that was to last until he died and which has been immortalised by posterity. Montaigne was at La Boétie's bedside when the young man died all too early in 1563; with his friend in mind, Montaigne wrote his famous *Essay on Friendship* in which he formulated the excellent sentiment: "If I am urged to explain why I loved him, I feel I can only reply: because he was himself and I am myself."

Old Sarlat★★★

Sarlat's old district was cut into two in the 19C by the Traverse (rue de la République), separating it into a more populated western section and a more sophisticated eastern section.

The town houses are quite unique: built with quality ashlar-work in a fine golden-hued limestone, with interior courtyards; the roofing, made of heavy limestone slabs (*lauzes*), necessitated a steeply pitched framework so that the enormous weight (500kg per m^2 – about 102lb per sq ft) could be supported on thick walls. Over the years new floors were added: a medieval ground floor, a High Gothic or Renaissance upper floor and Classical roof cresting and lantern turrets.

This architectural unit escaped modern building developments in the 19C and 20C because of its distance from the main communication routes. It was chosen in 1962 as one of the new experimental national restoration projects, the goal of which was to preserve the old quarters of France's towns and cities. The project, begun in 1964, has allowed the charm of this small medieval town to be recreated.

▶ *Start from place du Peyrou.*

Cathédrale St-Sacerdos

St Sacerdos' Church was built here in the 12C. In 1504 Bishop Armand de Gontaut-Biron had the church razed, in order to build a cathedral.

However, when the bishop left Sarlat in 1519, the construction work ceased for more than a century. Although the present church was built during the 16C and 17C, the base of the tower on the western front is Romanesque. Of its three storeys, the lowest is formed of blind arcades, the second has open bays, whereas the third is a 17C addition.

Inside, the most striking features are the elevation and harmonious proportions of the nave, which has ogive vaulting, and of the chancel surrounded by an ambulatory. Among the furnishings are an 18C organ loft and an organ by Lépine (a well-known 18C organ maker).

Ancien Évêché

To the right of St Sacerdos' Cathedral, is the former bishopric. Its façade has windows in the Gothic style on the first floor, Renaissance on the second floor and an Italian Renaissance loggia above, added by the Italian bishop Nicolo Goddi, friend of Catherine de' Medici. The interior has been converted into a theatre. *The tourist office is on the ground floor.*

Maison de la Boétie★

This house was built in 1525 by Antoine de La Boétie, a criminal magistrate in the seneschal's court at Sarlat, and is the birthplace of Étienne de La Boétie.

A large arch on the ground floor used to shelter a small shop; the two upper floors of Italian Renaissance style have large mullioned windows, framed by pilasters carved with medallions and lozenges. The steeply pitched, gabled roof is decorated with crockets, and on the slightly recessed left side there is a heavily ornamented dormer window.

Sarlat from above

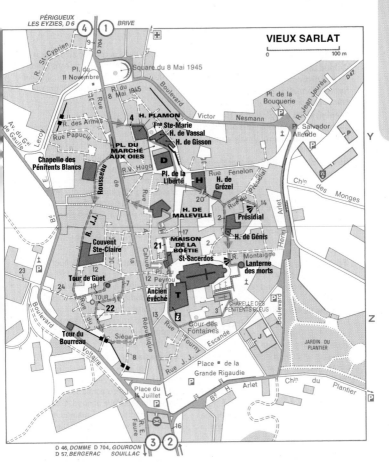

VIEUX SARLAT

Address Book

VISITS

Guided tours – Tours (1hr 30min) led by qualified local guides. Apr-Oct. 5€. For further information, contact the tourist office or log onto www.ot-sarlat-perigord.fr.

Evening visits – Organised by the tourist office, these fascinating visits provided a different perspective of this delightful town. Jun-Sep. 6€.

For coin ranges, see the Legend at the back of the guide.

EATING OUT

Auberge des Lys d'Or – Pl. André-Malraux - ☎ 05 53 31 24 77 - ⏰ closed Wed eve and Thu – reserv. recommended. This typical regional house is in a picturesque part of town where many old buildings still stand. The dining room is rustic and the dishes served there traditional: foie gras, confit, magret and pommes sarladaises.

Les Délices de Lauralice – Pl Beauvau - ☎ 05 53 30 29 00 - ⏰ closed 6 Jan-6 Feb. The local flavour is in the decor and on your plate in this restaurant. There are several dining rooms and a nice terrace in the courtyard. The prices are very reasonable.

Rossignol – 15 r. Fénelon - ☎ 05 53 31 02 30 - ⏰ closed Thu. A simple, family-run restaurant near the centre, with one rustic-style dining room. Copious and unpretentious local cuisine, including fish.

WHERE TO STAY

Hôtel Altica – Av. de la Dordogne - ☎ 05 53 28 18 00 - altica-sarlat@altica.fr - ⓟ - 50 rooms. This hotel (part of a chain) near the centre of Sarlat is conveniently located for those who wish to visit one of the prettiest towns in Périgord. The rooms are satisfactory for the price.

Hôtel des Récollets – 4 r. Jean-Jacques-Rousseau - ☎ 05 53 31 36 00 - contact@hotel-recollets-sarlat.com - ⓟ - 18 rooms. This unique hotel is in a former convent (17C). The rooms are not large, but they are quiet and all have been renovated with contemporary furniture, original beams and walls. Enjoy breakfast in a vaulted room or on the patio. Staff will help you carry your bags from the public parking lot.

Mas de Castel – 3km/1.8mi south of Sarlat via the D 704 and C 1 - ☎ 05 53 59 02 59 - castalian@wanadoo.fr - ⏰ closed 12 Nov-29 Mar - ⓟ - 13 rooms. An

attractive hotel occupying an old farm in a peaceful rural setting. Pastel tones and rustic furniture in the bedrooms, some of which are on garden level. Swimming pool.

SHOPPING

Markets – Traditional market in the streets of the old town on Saturdays, plus a smaller market in place de la Liberté on Wednesday morning. Covered market in the former Eglise Sainte-Marie, daily (except Monday and Thursday from early-Nov to Feb). Truffle and duck and goose product market on Saturday mornings from December to March. Walnut and chestnut market on Saturday mornings in October and November.

Francis Annet – R. Albéric-Cahuet - ☎ 05 53 28 88 17 - www.perigord.com/francis. annet - ⏰ open Apr-Sep, daily 10am-12.30pm and 2-7pm. Francis Annet is a professional photographer who has taken some wonderful images of the Périgord. A good address for postcards and photographs.

Chez le Gaulois – 1 r. Tourny - ☎ 05 53 59 30 64 -open daliy, Apr-Oct, 9am-midnight; rest of the year: Tue-Sat, 10am-10pm. The Gauls in the Asterix comic books were known for their love of good food, and here the tradition is maintained. You can savour some fine products of the region, and from other regions of France, including a great variety of jambons crus (the hams are hanging from the ceiling) , chestnut preserves and ice creams.

LEISURE ACTIVITIES

L'Étrier de Vitrac (École Française d'Equitation) – Pech de Pech - ☎ 05 53 59 34 31 / 06 87 76 90 34 - ⏰ open 9am-6pm; horse-riding lessons and treks. This equestrian centre is located in a pleasant wooded area. Lessons for all ages and abilities, including shorter rides and 4-day treks as far as Rocamadour.

Indian Forest – La Feuillade-Basse - 7km/4.2mi S of Sarlat-la-Canéda on the D 704 and D 704 A, towards Souillac - 24200 Carsac-Aillac - ☎ 05 53 31 22 22 - marcel. mondamert@wanadoo.fr - ⏰ open May-Oct. Enjoy tree-top adventure in this forest adventure centre. Several levels of difficulty. Sturdy shoes and suitable clothing required. Climbing equipment and tuition provided.

On the left of the house is **passage Henri-de-Ségogne**, between Hôtel de Maleville and La Boétie's House. The alleyway leads visitors through an arch, a passageway and a covered passageway.

Picturesque half-timbered buildings have been restored and, in summer, craft shops do a swift business.

Hôtel de Maleville★

This edifice is also known as the Hôtel de Vienne after the man who built it, Jean de Vienne. Born of humble parents in Sarlat in 1557, he successfully climbed the social ladder to become financial secretary under Henri IV.

Later, the town house was bought by the Maleville family; a member of this same family, Jacques de Maleville (&see DOMME), helped write the French *Code Civil*, the general rules of law.

The distinctive roof line of the Maison de la Boétie

Three existing houses were combined in the mid-16C to form an imposing mansion. In front of the tall, narrow central pavilion, like a majestic tower, is a terrace under which opens the arched main doorway surmounted by medallions depicting Henri IV and Marie de Medici. It is flanked by a corbelled turret which joins it to the left wing. The right wing, overlooking place de la Liberté, has a late Renaissance gable.

Insérer carnet pratique en habillage

▶ *Take the covered passage to the left of the entrance, then take rue du Minage opposite, follow rue de la République and turn right onto rue des Consuls.*

Rue des Consuls

The town houses in this street are beautiful examples of Sarlat architecture from the 14C-17C.

▶ *On the right after the bend.*

Hôtel Plamon★

As identified by the shield on the pediment above the doorway, this town house belonged to the Selves de Plamon family, members of the cloth merchants' guild. Because it is made up of a group of buildings built in different periods, it is a particularly interesting illustration of the evolution of the different architectural styles used in Sarlat construction.

The 14C ground floor opens through two large pointed arches. The first floor has three Gothic windows ornamented with High Gothic tracery, and the second floor has 15C mullioned windows.

Left of the town house is the very narrow Plamon Tower with windows which get smaller the higher up they are; this architectural ruse makes the tower seem much taller than it is.

On the corner of the street is a rounded overhanging balcony supported by a squinch. Go into the courtyard to admire the elegant 17C wooden **staircase**★.

Fontaine Ste-Marie

Opposite the Hôtel de Plamon, the fountain splashes in a cool grotto.

Place du Marché aux Trois Oies★

Appropriately called Goose Square, this is the place where on Saturdays from December to March people come from far and wide to haggle over the price of geese and, of course, of delicious goose liver (*foie gras*).

The square is an elegant architectural collection of turrets, pinnacles and corner staircases.

Hôtel de Vassal

Located on a corner of place des Oies, this 15C town house consists of two buildings at right angles flanked by twin corbelled turrets.

Beside it, the **Hôtel de Gisson** (16C) is made of two buildings joined by a hexagonal staircase tower with a remarkable pointed roof.

Place de la Liberté

Many pavement cafés liven up Sarlat's main square. The 17C **town hall** stands on the east side and the disused **Église Ste-Marie** (the chancel was demolished in the 19C) on the north side. The church is being converted by the architect Jean Nouvel in order to house a covered market, an exhibition area and a panoramic lift.

Typical house in old Sarlat

▷ *Leave place de la Liberté and walk along rue de la Salamandre.*

Hôtel de Grézel

Built at the end of the 15C, the town house straight ahead has a half-timbered façade with a tower and a lovely Flamboyant Gothic ogee-arched doorway.

The skill and artistry of the carpenter and roof-layer can be admired by looking further down onto several of the roofs: the fine layout of the *lauzes*, following the line of the roof perfectly down to where the roof widens and levels out (this is achieved by furring: nailing thin strips of board under the line of the roof; a technique used to compensate for the thickness of the walls).

Continue onto rue Présidial, then rue Landry (as far as no 7), until you can see the 17C tower of the **Présidial**, former seat of royal magistrates (now a restaurant).

▷ *Retrace your steps and turn left onto rue d'Albusse.*

At the corner of the dead end (where the old post house can be seen) stands the **Hôtel de Génis**, a massive, plain 15C building with an overhanging upper storey supported by seven stone corbels.

▷ *Follow rue Sylvain Cavaillez and enter the garden.*

Lanterne des Morts

Built at the end of the 12C, this mysterious cylindrical tower topped with a cone and split into tiers by four bands contains two rooms. The room on the ground floor has domed vaulting held up by six pointed arches; the other room is in the cone part of the tower, which was inaccessible.

A number of hypotheses have been put forward concerning the lantern's function: was it a tower built in honour of the visit of St Bernard in 1147 (he had blessed bread which miraculously cured the sick); or a lantern of the dead (but it is difficult to imagine how the lantern was lit because the top room was inaccessible); or a funerary chapel?

▷ *Go down the stairs and walk around the Chapelle des Pénitents Bleus (12C). Go into cour des Chanoines then cour des Fontaines. Rue Munz and rue Tourny lead back to place du Peyrou.*

West Side★

This part of town, on the opposite side of rue de la République (the so-called Traverse), is currently under renewal. Its steep and winding lanes are quieter, off the main tourist track, and offer another image of Sarlat.

▷ *Walk along rue de la République and turn left onto rue J.-J.-Rousseau.*

Chapelle des Pénitents Blancs

Used by the Order of Pénitents Blancs, the chapel was part of the religious establishment of the Pères Récollets. Construction began in 1622 and it was completed four years later. The intriguing doorway is composed of four fluted columns; the capitals and entablature are curiously designed.

Rue Jean-Jacques Rousseau

This is the main street in this part of town, and many attractive old houses grace it. At no 9, on the corner of Côte de Toulouse, there is an admirable 18C façade (Hôtel Monméja); at the intersection with rue de la Boétie, you can see the bartizan which marks the site of **St Clare's Convent**, a vast 17C building once occupied by the Poor Clares, and today provides low-rent housing. The garden is used during the theatre festival in the summer, and also hosts concerts and other cultural events.

▷ *Continue along rue du Siège then turn left onto rue Rousset.*

Tour de Guet

Overlapping the buildings, the watchtower is crowned by 15C machicolations and flanked by a corbelled turret.

▷ *Turn right onto rue du Cordil.*

Rue des Trois-Conils (des Trois Lapins)

This street bends sharply left around the foot of a house flanked by a tower, which once belonged to consuls related to the La Boétie family.

Tour du Bourreau

The Executioner's Tower, which was part of the ramparts, was built in 1580.

▷ *Walk along rue du Siège leading back to rue de la République.*

Excursions

Marquay

11.5km/7mi NW along the D 47 and the D 6.

This sought-after holiday resort surrounded by important Paleolithic sites has an unusual 12C church: the end of the transept arms form apsidal chapels.

Tamniès

15km/9.3mi NW along the D 47 and the D 6.

The 12C village church and former priory overlook the Beune Valley. There is a lake with leisure facilities nearby.

Southern Section of Perigord Noir★★★

70km/44mi round-trip – allow half a day

&See Vallée de la DORDOGNE.

Round-trip from Sarlat★★

75km/47mi – allow half a day

&See PÉRIGORD NOIR.

From Dordogne to the Beaune★

60km/37.3mi round-trip – allow half a day

▷ *Drive SW out of Sarlat along the D 57; turn right onto the D 703 shortly after Vézac.*

Beynac-et-Cazenac★★

&See BEYNAC-ET-CAZENAC.

▷ *Continue on the D 703 to St-Cyprien then turn right as you leave the village.*

Cazenac

This hamlet possesses a 15C Gothic church from which there is a lovely view of the valley.

▷ *Turn back and rejoin the D 703.*

St-Cyprien

&See Le BUGUE: Excursion.

▷ *Drive NE along the D 25.*

Chapelle de Redon-l'Espi

This remote Romanesque chapel is flanked by the ruins of a small monastery, destroyed during the Wars of Religion. The Virgin Mary is said to have appeared to a young shepherdess in the 19C, giving rise to a pilgrimage which still takes place in September.

▷ *Rejoin the D 25 (right), turn left onto the D 47 just beyond Allas then right 1.5km/0.9mi further on.*

Cabanes du Breuil

🕐♿*Open Jun-Sep, 10am-7pm; Mar-Apr and Oct to mid-Nov, 10am-noon and 2-6pm; mid-Nov to Feb, Sat-Sun, 2-5pm.* ✆4€. ☎ *06 80 72 38 59. www.cabanes-du-breuil.com*

The hamlet of Breuil has the richest collection of drystone buildings known as *caselles* (or *gariottes*) in Périgord. There are five huts, forming an architectural grouping unique in the region. A cultural centre is devoted to these huts.

▶ *Turn back and turn left onto the D 47 towards Sarlat; turn left again 3km/1.9mi further on.*

Château de Puymartin★

🕐🔍*Open Aug, guided tour (45min), 10am-6.30pm; Jul, 10am-noon and 2-6.30pm; Apr-Jun, 10am-noon and 2-6pm; Sep, 10am-noon and 2-6pm, Sat 2-6pm; Oct to mid-Nov, 2-5.30pm.* ✆6€ *(child: 3€).* ☎ *05 53 59 29 97.*

Constructed in the 15C and 16C, considerably remodelled in the 19C, the castle standing atop a steep hill consists of several buildings linked to towers, and protected by a curtain wall. The **interior decoration**★ is impressive: period furnishings, Aubusson tapestries, painted beams and paintings. Note, in particular, the charming **cabinet de meditation**★ adorned with mythological scenes.

▶ *The D 47 takes you back to Sarlat.*

Église abbatiale de SOLIGNAC★★

MICHELIN LOCAL MAP 325: E-6 – 13KM/8MI S OF LIMOGES

LOCAL MAP SEE LIMOGES

An interesting Romanesque church is all that remains of the once famous abbey founded in 632 by St Eligius near the green valley of the River Briance.

▶ **Orient Yourself**: The abbey is located 8km/5mi south of Limoges.
♿ **Also See**: Limoges; Oradour-sur-Glane.

A Bit of History

The great St Eligius – The legendary figure of St Eligius (St Éloi in France) dominated the Merovingian Age. This wise and saintly man was not only Dagobert's chief minister, but is also remembered as a goldsmith and loved as a man of inexhaustible charity.

He was born at Chaptelat in 588 and learned his skill as a goldsmith in the workshops at Limoges. He went to work in Paris; but it was due to the confidence in him of good King Dagobert – who is famous to all French school children thanks to a nursery rhyme on the theme of his knickers – that St Eligius was able to use his talents as a minister. St Eligius, though titular bishop of Noyon, felt the call of his native countryside and asked the king for land at Solignac on which to found a monastery where he could die in peace. "My king and master", the holy man said, "may you grant me this out of your bounty so that I may build a ladder, for by this ladder we shall climb to heaven, you and I." The king replied favourably to Eligius' request.

The abbey was built on a grand scale from the start, but in spite of its fortifications it did not escape the depredations of the Normans, the Saracens, the English and the Huguenots, each of whom plundered it in turn during its long history.

Stalls in the abbey church

E. Larribère/MICHELIN

Visit

Abbey Church

🕐➴⌕*Guided tours available. For information, contact the tourist office, ☎ 05 55 00 42 31.*

The present church dates from the first half on the 12C and is the Limousin church which is most influenced by the Périgord style of architecture.

Exterior – The big bell tower built at the same time as the abbey was replaced in the 19C by a belfry-wall. As you walk around the northern side of the church, admire the harmony of the construction: large buttresses and recessed columns reaching up to the ledge around the roof; on the lower part, groups of four arches falling alternately on plain pilasters and bases embellished with scrolling designs, crouching figures and monsters. Just above, the succession of windows and blind trefoils illustrates the influence of Mozarabic tradition (which qualifies styles originating with Christians who lived in the Iberian Peninsula after the Arab invasion of 711, and who

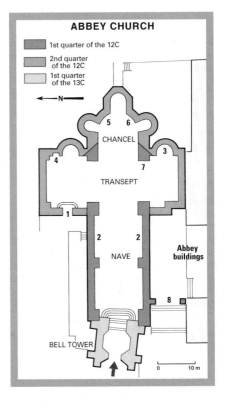

ABBEY CHURCH

■ 1st quarter of the 12C
■ 2nd quarter of the 12C
□ 1st quarter of the 13C

← N →

CHANCEL
5 6
4
3
7
TRANSEPT

1
2 2
NAVE   Abbey buildings

8

BELL TOWER

0   10 m

were thus exposed to Islamic culture and art forms). A bas-relief of Christ in Majesty (1) rises above the north-transept doorway.

Interior – *Go in through the door in the porch.* The main body of the church is covered over with vast semicircular domes. An elevated passageway runs down both sides of the nave and is supported by blind arcading which in turn is carried by engaged columns and pilasters. Note also the carved archaic capitals and modillions which become more intricate towards the chancel.

The stalls (2), on each side of the nave, mostly date from the 15C, the carved misericords – a small ledge which a worshiper could use to rest on while standing up – and arm rests depict foliage, animals and grimacing faces.

The transept is asymmetrical. The south arm is roofed with barrel vaulting; note the 18C polychrome Virgin carved in wood (3). In the north transept, which is covered with an ovoid cupola pierced by a round window, a glass case (4) contains works of art including the 12C reliquary-bust of St Théau in gilded copper and silver.

The chancel, covered with an imperfectly shaped cupola, is punctuated by seven arcades and three chapels. The capitals bear a variety of embellishments: palmettos, figures struggling with griffins, twining serpents etc. Two 17C frescoes represent the Temptation of Christ (5) and the Olive Garden (6). Some of the windows date from the 15C. On the right pillar, note the restored distemper painting (powdered colours and size mixed with water) of St Christopher (7), which probably dates from the 15C.

Monastery buildings – The buildings which were reconstructed in the 18C and ravaged during the Revolution, have been occupied since 1945 by student missionaries of the Oblate of Mary Immaculate.

The courtyard faces the south side of the church, which was connected to the cloisters by an archway leading from the second bay. The pointed arch (8), under which you pass as you go around towards the front of the buildings may have been another entrance to the cloisters, or else the entrance to a chapel.

SOUILLAC★

POPULATION 3 459

MICHELIN LOCAL MAP 337: E-2 – LOCAL MAP SEE VALLÉE DE LA DORDOGNE

At the confluence of the Corrèze and the Dordogne, in the centre of a fertile region, Souillac is a small town bustling with trade and tourists, bisected by the national route 20.

▶ **Orient Yourself**: Souillac is situated along the N 20, 29km/18mi east of Sarlat-la-Canéda and 39km/24mi south of Brive-la-Gaillarde.

◉ **Don't Miss**: The abbey church.

Kids Especially for Kids: Musée National de l'Automate.

◔ **Also See**: Grottes de Lacave; Rocamadour; Gouffre de Padirac; Sarlat-la-Canéda.

A Bit of History

When the Benedictines settled in the plain of Souillès – so-called after the local word *souilh*, meaning bog or marshland where wild boar wallow – story has it that they replaced the community established there previously by St Eligius. The monks drained the land continuously, transforming the marsh into a rich estate. Souillac Abbey was plundered and sacked several times by the English during the Hundred Years War, but rose from its ruins each time thanks to the tenacity of its abbots. Greater disasters, however, befell it during the Wars of Religion. The abbey was rebuilt in the 17C and attached to the Maurist Congregation, but it then ceased to exist during the Revolution, its buildings being used for storing tobacco.

Address Book

◔ *For coin ranges see the Legend at the back of the guide.*

EATING OUT

◒◒ **Les Ambassadeurs** – *12 av. du Gén.-de-Gaulle -* ☎ *05 65 32 78 36.* The façade of this restaurant features local stone, a red awning and a golden stew pot. The atmosphere is old-fashioned and the cuisine traditional French, with local highlights.

WHERE TO STAY

◒ **Belle Vue** – *68 av. J.-Jaurès -* ☎ *05 65 32 78 23 - hotelbellevue.souillac@wanadoo.fr -* 🕔 *closed 8-31 Jan, Feb and Sat-Sun in Mar -* 🅿 *- 25 rooms.* Conveniently located near the train station, this hotel offers rooms, which are plain and clean. In the garden, you can enjoy the use of tennis courts and a pool. A shop on the premises sells regional products.

◒◒ **Grand Hôtel** – *1 allée Verninac -* ☎ *05 65 32 78 30 - grandhotel-souillac@wanadoo.fr -* 🕔 *closed Nov-Feb -* 🅿 *- 44 rooms.* Go up to the rooftop terrace and enjoy a drink in the view of the city spread out at your feet. In the main building, the rooms are quite modern; in the 18C section, the rooms are more old-fashioned. The dining room has a veranda and there is a nice terrace under the plane trees.

◒◒ **Chambre d'hôte et Gîte Le Manoir** – *La Forge - 5km/3.1mi NW of Souillac on* the D 15 - ☎ *05 65 32 77 66 -* 🕔 *closed 30 Oct-15 Apr -* 🍽 *- 5 rooms.* In need of a little R&R? You will be able to relax in this attractive guesthouse or in one of the five comfortable holiday cottages (up to six people). Non-smokers only. Pool.

◒◒ **La Vieille Auberge** – *1 r. Recège -* ☎ *05 65 32 79 43 - r.veril@la-vieille-auberge.com -* 🕔 *closed 8 Nov-20 Dec, Sun eve, Mon and Tue lunchtime from Jan-Mar -* 🅿 *- 19 rooms.* This inn is just around the corner from the church, in a quiet neighbourhood. The rooms are practical; the 3rd floor rooms have sloping ceilings under the eaves. For a pick-me-up, dive into the pool – open air in the summer months – or use the exercise facilities.

SHOPPING

Distillerie Louis Roque – *41 av. Jean-Jaurès -* ☎ *05 65 32 78 16 - www.lavieilleprune.com -* 🕔 *open Mon-Sat, 8.30am-noon and 2-5pm -* 🕔 *closed public hols.* The heirs of Louis Roque make regional liqueurs and apéritifs using traditional recipes that have proved their worth over the century. The most famous elixir is *la vieille prune*. Visit the distillery and the museum and sample the wares, all free of charge.

LEISURE ACTIVITIES

Quercy Land – ☎ *05 65 32 72 61.* Canoe-kayak hire on the River Dordogne and water park.

East end of the old abbey church

J. Damase/MICHELIN

Visit

Former abbey church

Dedicated to Mary, Mother of Christ, this church became a parish church to replace the church of St Martin, which was destroyed during the Wars of Religion.

Built in the 12C, the church is related to the Romanesque cathedrals of Angoulême, Périgueux and Cahors with their Byzantine inspiration, but it is more advanced in the lightness of its columns and the height of its great arcades than the others. From place de l'Abbaye one can admire the attractive east end with its five pentagonal, apsidal chapels and an unusual tower on the other side of the building.

The back of the doorway★

This composition consists of the remains of the old doorway, which was badly damaged by the Protestants and had been placed inside the nave of the new church, when it was erected in the 17C.

Above the door, framed by the statues of St Peter on the right and St Benedict on the left, is a bas-relief relating episodes in the life of the monk Theophilus, deacon of Adana in Cilicia: a new abbot, misled by false reports, removes Theophilus from his office of treasurer of the monastery of Adana; Theophilus, out of resentment, signs a pact with the devil to regain his office (left). Repenting of his sins, Theophilus implores forgiveness and prays to the Virgin Mary (right) who appears before him in his sleep, accompanied by St Michael and two angels who guard her; they bring him the pact he made with the devil, and she shows how she has had his signature annulled and has obtained his pardon.

On the right side of the door is a fine bas-relief of the prophet **Isaiah**★★, striking in its expression.

The disfigured bell tower, which is all that remains of the church St Martin, is now the town hall belfry.

Musée National de l'Automate★

◷*Open Jul-Aug, 10am-7pm; Jun and Sep, 10am-noon and 3-6pm; Apr-May and Oct, daily except Mon, 10am-noon and 3-6pm; Nov-Mar, daily except Mon and Tue, 2.30-5.30pm.* ⊛*5€ (child: 2.50€).* ☎ *05 65 37 07 07.*

▶ *Enter by the parvis of the abbey church (Abbatiale St-Pierre).*

Kids The museum contains some 3 000 objects, including 1 000 automata donated by the **Roullet-Decamps** family, who for four generations were leaders in the field. In 1865 Jean Roullet created his first mechanical toy: a small gardener pushing a wheel barrow. In 1909 he created the first Christmas window display for the Bon Marché department store.

Note especially the **Jazz band** (1920), a group of electric automata with black musicians performing a concert.

Excursion

Quercy Stretch of the Dordogne★★★

1 *Round-trip of 85km/53mi - allow one day.*

↻*See Vallée de la DORDOGNE.*

TREIGNAC

POPULATION 1 415

MICHELIN LOCAL MAP 329: L-2 OR 522 FOLD 15

Treignac lies in the upper valley of the Vézère, at the foot of the Monédières mountains and downstream from a dam across the river. From the D 16 to the north, there is a fine view of the village and its picturesque setting.

▸ **Orient Yourself**: The village is situated 37km/23mi northeast of Uzerche.

▸ **Don't Miss**: Massif des Monédières; Suc-au-May.

▸ **Especially for Kids**: Maison de l'Arbre.

▸ **Also See**: Uzerche.

Heather and Bilberries

In late summer the slopes are covered with a carpet of pink heather. Slowly but gradually bilberries (known as blueberries in North America) are replacing the heather above 700m/2300ft, creating a new source of income and activity especially at harvest time. Picked with an adroit movement of the hand, the fragile berries are dispatched to markets, canning factories and pharmaceutical laboratories.

Lower Town

Vieux Pont Gothique

▸ *Access via a steep street.*

The old Gothic bridge spanning the fast-flowing Vézère affords a view of the castle ruins towering above the river, of the old slate-roofed houses and of the church.

Church

The square church covered with slates has a hexagonal bell tower; inside, note the pointed vaulting resting on massive pillars and the granite altar shaped like a dolmen. The modern stained-glass windows by Camille Fleury date from 1954 and 1960.

Upper town

This district, stretching between place de la République and place du Collège, comprises a number of turreted old houses with carved doorways (note the numerous shells reminding visitors that Treignac was once a stopover for pilgrims on the way to Compostela) and a 15C granite covered market.

Musée des Arts et Traditions Populaires de la Haute et Moyenne-Vézère

For information on opening times, contact the tourist office. ☎ *05 55 98 15 04.*

Located in the house of Marc Sangnier, the founder of the Auberges de Jeunesse (youth hostels), this museum contains ethnographic collections.

Excursions

Rocher des Folles

▸ *45min round trip on foot; the path starts at the SW end of the village.*

A pleasant marked stroll up to the Rocher des Folles – Crazy Women's Rock – affording fine views of Treignac, the gorge and wooded hills of the Vézère.

Lac des Bariousses

▸ *4km/2.5mi N along the D 940.*

The road goes along the shoreline of this lake and provides a lovely drive. The wooded site (chestnuts, oaks and evergreens) is the setting for a recreation centre.

Chamberet

▸ *10km/6.2mi NW along the D 16.*

Arboretum – *On the outskirts of the village, along the road to Eymoutiers; free access.* Located in the municipal park, this arboretum dating from 1994 consists of some 100 species of trees surrounding a pond (playground and picnic area).

Maison de l'Arbre – *Next to the arboretum.* 🕐 ♿ *Open Jul-Aug, 9am-noon and 2-6pm, Sat-Sun, 2-6pm; Apr-Jun and Sep-Oct, daily except Mon, 9am-noon and 2-6pm, Sat-Sun, 2-6pm.* 👓*3.50€ (6-18 years old: 2€).* ☎ *05 55 97 92 14.* **Kids** This "tree centre" provides comprehensive information about trees, but also about other living species and ecosystems connected with them including: lichens, mushrooms and peat bogs. There are attractive interactive panels for children as well as guided discovery trails and workshops (*from three years upwards*).

Barrage de Monceaux-la-Virole

▸ *17km/11mi NE along the D 940 and the D 160.*

The first of the dams on the Vézère straddles Lake Viam, where waterfalls once tumbled down. The view reveals the contrasts of the surrounding landscape.

Les Monédières★

50km/31mi round-trip – allow 3hr

Adjoining the Millevaches Plateau, the Monédières Massif, stretching between the upper valley of the Vézère and the River Corrèze, forms the southern bastion of the area known as the *montagne limousine*.

> **SHOPPING**
>
> **Ferme de la Monédière** – *La Monédière - 19390 Chaumeil -* ☎ *05 55 98 20 48 -* 🕐 *open late Jul-Aug.* This farm sells a selection of cheeses, jams, fresh fruit and fromage frais.

This relatively low massif (the tallest peak is the Puy de la Monédière with an altitude of 919m/3015ft) is a highly eroded mass of crystalline rocks.

Although the region is open to considerable oceanic influences, brought by the Westerlies, the climate is essentially a mountainous one with arduous snowy winters and short hot summers.

▸ *Leave Treignac travelling SE along the D 16 towards Égletons.*

Église de Lestards

Note the unusual thatched roof of the Romanesque church.

▸ *On leaving the village, turn right onto the D 32 then right again at Col des Géants onto the D 128 to Madranges.*

Col du Bos

▸ *Turn left onto the D 128E.*

The road, lined with conifers, soon runs into the open, affording a wide view across the heath.

Suc-au-May★★

▸ *Leave the car in the parking area; then 15min round-trip on foot.* Altitude 908m/2 979ft.

From the viewing table there is a **panorama** of the Limousin countryside and the Millevaches Plateau to the north-east. The Monédières Massif in the foreground has an undulating, severely eroded surface. In fine weather conditions, it is possible to see the three mountain ranges of the Auvergne region: the Monts Dore and Monts Dômes to the east and the Cantal Mountains to the south-east.

▸ *Return to Col de Bos and take the D 128 to the left.*

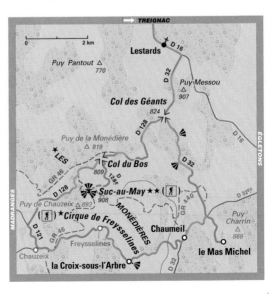

The road runs down amid meadows and conifers. Note to the right the long ridge of the **Puy Pantout** (770m/2 526ft).

▶ *At the end of the road, turn left onto the D 121.*

The road winds along the south facing slope where arable crops alternate with rough grazing and chestnut groves.

Cirque de Freysselines

This natural amphitheatre surrounds a small hamlet of the same name. Drive east through the village (D 121) for a better view of the cirque. The vegetation is remarkable: gorse, heather, fern, broom, birch trees, service trees and conifers.

🚶 A path (12km/7.5mi round-trip) runs round the cirque towards Suc-au-May.

La Croix-sous-l'Arbre

In a bend, to the right of the road, there is a fine view of Chaumeil (the main village in the area) and Puy de Sarran.

▶ *Continue along the D 121.*

Chaumeil

This attractive village, capital of the Monédières, with its sturdy granite houses roofed with slates or stones, is clustered round the 15C **church** adorned with a fine 16C porch. Inside the church, on the left of the chancel, there are a polychrome naïve *Pietà* (16C) in wood, a Madonna and child, and a reliquary.

All the local products can be found in the **Maison des Monédières** (gourmet food, handicraft) which holds regular painting exhibitions.

An artificial lake has been created just north of the village. Hikers can continue along the narrow road which climbs to the top of Suc-au-May (*6km/3.7mi*).

▶ *Continue N along the D 32.*

Le Mas Michel

At the crossroads take the narrow road leading to this hamlet, which lies at the foot of the Puy Charrin. Old cottages built of drystone make it worth a visit.

▶ *Turn back and continue along the D 32.*

Col des Géants

Beyond the pass, the road goes uphill amid conifers. There are fine glimpses of the **Puy Messou** (907m/2 976ft) to the right and the Suc-au-May to the left.

▶ *The D 32 and the D 16 lead back to Treignac.*

TULLE

POPULATION 15 553

MICHELIN LOCAL MAP 329: L-4

Tulle extends over a couple of miles, its main street following the course of the narrow and winding valley of the Corrèze and its old houses rising in terraces on the hillsides overlooking the river. From the centre of the city rises the elegant stone steeple of the cathedral of Notre-Dame. The administrative seat of the département of Corrèze, although it is not the largest city, Tulle is well-known in France as a centre for the manufacture of armaments and lace. ⓘ *2 pl. Émile-Zola, 19000 Tulle, ☏ 05 55 26 59 61.*

▸ **Orient Yourself**: The town is located 27km/17mi northeast of Brive-la-Gaillarde.

🕐 **Organising Your Time**: Allow half a day to explore the Upper Corrèze valley.

🚗 **Don't Miss**: Maison de Loyac; bell tower of the Cathédrale Notre-Dame.

🖐 **Also See**: Argentat; Brive; Beaulieu-sur-Dordogne; Collonges-la-Rouge; Gimel-les-Cascades; Uzerche.

A Bit of History

A Heavy Toll – During the Hundred Years War the town fell twice, in 1346 and 1369, to the English. Each time the invaders were driven away by the local militia.

During the Wars of Religion, Tulle sided with the papists. The Protestant army under the viscount of Turenne failed to take the city in 1577 but in 1585 Turenne came back and with bloody vengeance sacked the city after first assaulting it.

On 8 June 1944 Tulle was liberated by the men of the *maquis*, but the next day the Germans retook the town. Several hundred townspeople were arrested: 99 were hanged in the streets, the others were deported; 101 never came back. South of town (*N 89, the road to Brive*), a monument has been erected to the memory of the victims of Nazism.

Walking Tour of Old Town

This area, lying north of the cathedral and known as the Enclos (the Enclosure), retains a medieval atmosphere with alleys, stairways and old houses.

A short walk starting from the cathedral (*15min round-trip*) offers an overall view of the edifice.

Cathédrale Notre-Dame

In 1103, Abbot Guillaume wished his abbey, which was then very prosperous, to have a worthy setting, so he undertook the reconstruction of the church and the cloistral buildings. The 12C saw the building of the nave, the porch and the first storey of the belfry.

The **belfry**★ is 73m/240ft high; the three storeys are surmounted by an elegant octagonal spire surrounded by bell turrets. This spire, which dated from the 14C, was struck by lightning in 1645, but has been restored to its original form. The ogive-vaulted **porch** contains a tiers-point doorway, adorned with moulding and small columns in the Limousin style.

The interior decoration is plain, although the colours of the modern **stained-glass windows** by Jacques Gruber (1979) in the chancel are vivid: in the centre, Our Lady of Tulle; below, John the Baptist bearing the Lamb of God. The border shows: on the right, Bishop Dumoulin-Borie (a local missionary who suffered martyrdom in Tonkin) with St Sebastien below; on the left, St Jacques with, below, a hanged man commemorating the terrible events of 1944.

A much venerated **16C wooden statue of St John the Baptist** stands in the north aisle. Since the 14C, the inhabitants of Tulle have celebrated his birth with a procession known as *la lunade* (23 June).

Cloisters – Built in the early 13C, the building has been greatly damaged over time. Still standing are the west gallery and two bays in the north and east galleries. The south gallery was destroyed in the 19C for the purposes of a municipal theatre project. The two restored galleries have fine ribbed vaulting; admire the elegant sculptures on the capitals and keystones.

Address Book

For coin ranges, see the Legend at the back of the guide.

EATING OUT

La Ferme du Léondou – *19700 St-Salvadour - 12km/7.2mi N of Naves. Take the N 120, the D 53 towards Corrèze, then the D 173 -* ☎ *05 55 21 60 04 - jlfauvert@aol.com -* ⏰ *closed 1 Feb-8 Mar and Wed except for lunch in Jul-Aug.* Leave the beaten path to discover this old barn with its handsome wood troughs and grand fireplace. Local traditions are taken seriously in this kitchen, which serves specialities such as *flognarde* (baked apple pudding), guinea fowl with veal sweetbreads, *la poux* (buckwheat cakes or gruel), blood pudding with chestnuts, stuffed cabbage and goose conserves with cepes.

La Toque Blanche – *Pl. M.-Brigouleix -* ☎ *05 55 26 75 41 -* ⏰ *closed 20 Jan-3 Feb, 30 Jun-4 Jul, Sun eve and Mon.* This downtown restaurant gives diners a choice between the rustic dining room and the veranda. The white chef's cap - la toque blanche - rides atop the head of the son of the family, who concocts tasty cuisine that's good value for the price. A few rooms upstairs.

Le Central – *2 r. de la Barrière -* ☎ *05 55 26 24 46 - r-poumier@internet19.fr -* ⏰ *closed 28 Jul-10 Aug, Sun eve and Sat.* This impressive house near the Corrèze is home to this first-floor restaurant with an attractive dining room with exposed beams, stonework, lace tablecloths etc. Le Central enjoys an excellent local reputation for the quality of its traditional local cuisine. Brasserie on the ground floor.

WHERE TO STAY

Hôtel Bon Accueil – *10 r. Canton -* ☎ *05 55 26 70 57 -* ⏰ *closed 23 Dec-7 Jan - 12 rooms.* There's a medieval feel to this small, modest hotel thanks in part to the window and door frames dating from the 16C. Family ambience and cuisine at very inexpensive rates.

Chambre d'hôte Chez M. et Mme Perrot – *Gourdinot - 19460 Naves - 5km/3mi N of Naves via the N 120 and a side road -* ☎ *05 55 27 08 93 - brunhild.perrot@wanadoo.fr -* ⏰ *- 3 rooms.* Located in a pretty wooded valley, this old stone farm is run by convivial young owners. Pleasingly calm and cosy bedrooms. Regional dishes at the table d'hôte and home-made gingerbread served with a panoply of jams for breakfast.

BARS AND CAFÉS

La Taverne du Sommelier – *8 quai de la République -* ☎ *05 55 26 57 63 -* ⏰ *open daily 8.45am-1am.* This traditional brewery proposes a wide range of wines by the glass. The owner, Didier Bordas, was chosen as best young sommelier of France in 1983. A handsome terrace overlooking the Corrèze.

SHOPPING

Maugein Accordéon – *Route de Brive - Zone Industrielle de Mulatet -* ☎ *05 55 20 08 89 - accordeon.maugein@wanadoo.fr -* ⏰ *open Mon-Fri 9am-noon and 2-5pm; tours at 10am and 2.30pm -* ⏰ *closed last week of Jul, 3 weeks in Aug and public hols.* This brand of accordions was established in 1919. The manufacturer, who has been in business longer than any other French accordion maker still in activity, was the first to introduce the MIDI system accordion nationally, in September 1984.

Le Jardin du Centaure – *Les Chaussades - 19300 St-Yrieix-le-Déjalat -* ☎ *05 55 93 93 79 -* ⏰ *open daily except Sun; Jul-Aug,* *guided tour (2hr) Mon, Wed and Fri at 10am -* ⏰ *closed public hols in early-Nov. No charge.* Dominique Lepage, an organic farmer specialised in raising plants used for health and beauty aids or seasoning food, welcomes you to share his knowledge and passion for his aromatics: use in medicine and in cooking, origin of the names, mythology etc. You may visit the drying room; plants and herbal tea preparations for sale.

Le Poinct de Tulle *(Lace shop) - 2 r. des Portes-Chanac -* ☎ *05 55 26 77 29 -* ⏰ *open daily except Mon, 9am-noon and 2-6pm. No charge.* Cathy Vedrenne is an experienced lacemaker who can demonstrate and teach a rare technique using needles.

The east gallery (the farthest back) is the most elaborately decorated (note the angels on the keystones, capitals with human heads); the entrance to the chapter-house is guarded by two recumbent figures. The vaulted ceiling rests on two central pillars. On the north wall, two early-14C paintings depict Christ entering Jerusalem and the Last Supper.

Many vestiges are displayed along the galleries: a collection of 16C-18C firebacks, statues, copies of recumbent figures representing popes from Limousin, various stone fragments (capitals, ribs).

Maison de Loyac★

This is the most outstanding secular building in Tulle. Built in the early 16C it has an attractive façade: the windows and door are framed by small columns and are topped by acco-lades adorned with sculptured foliage, roses and animals.

> ▶ Take rue de la Tour-de-Maïsse, to the left of the building.

Maison de Loyac

JACASS/MICHELIN

Rue de la Tour-de-Maïsse

This street is a nar-row stairway, where the roofs of corbelled houses almost meet above the alley.

> ▶ Bear left again onto rue de la Baylie and yet again onto the sloping rue des Portes-Chanac.

Rue des Portes-Chanac

Along this steep street, you will notice among a group of old houses on the left, at no 9, a fine sculptured doorway belonging to a late Renaissance mansion.

Rue Riche

Note the carved façade at no 13.

> ▶ Rue Riche leads back to the cathedral.

Sights

Musée de Tulle

🕐 Open May-Sep, 9am-noon and 2-6pm, Wed and Sat, 2-6pm; Oct-Mar, 9am-noon and 2-5pm, Wed and Sat-Sun, 2-5pm. 🕐 Closed 1 Jan, 1 May, 1 Nov and 25 Dec. ⮾2.50€, no charge 1st Sun of the month. ☎ 05 55 26 91 05.

The museum adjoins the west gallery of the cloisters. The groundfloor is used for **temporary exhibitions**. The spiral staircase dates from the Middle Ages (note the engravings); it leads to the **first-floor** rooms, which display a collection illustrating the history, the **popular arts and traditions** of Tulle and its region. The collection includes watercolours by Gaston Vuillier, which depict the landscapes of Corrèze, and drawings showing the practice of witchcraft as well as the religious practices in the countryside in the late 19C. Local lacemakers are credited with having created the distinctive pattern which bears the name of the town. One of the rooms devotes pride of place to the **accordion**, for Corrèze was once well-known for the manufacture of these instruments. Those on display date from 1832 to 1950, and include the work of a local craftsman still in business. The second floor houses a collection of **swords and firearms** (partly made in the local manufacture founded in 1696, which became a royal manufacture in 1777), a display of regional **ceramics** and of **religious art**.

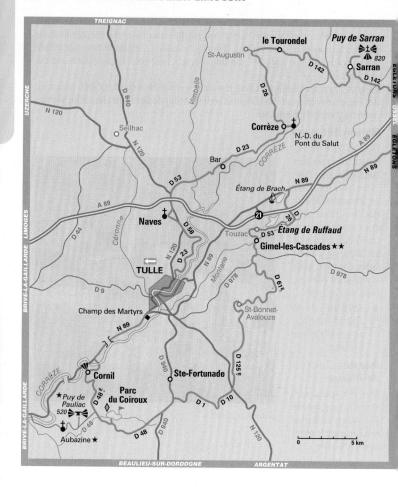

Excursions

Upper Corrèze Valley★

Round-trip of 140km/87mi – allow half a day

Surging forth to the west of Meymac, at an altitude of nearly 900m/2952ft, the River Corrèze crosses the Monédières range and digs a deep valley in the granite. It is the main artery of the *département* which bears its name, and passes through Tulle and Brive before joining forces with the Vézère.

▶ *Drive out of Tulle along N 89 towards Brive-la-Gaillarde.*

The road follows the west bank of the Corrèze and almost immediately runs by the **Champ des Martyrs**, a monument commemorating the massacre of 99 young men in Tulle on 8 and 9 June 1944.

The valley soon becomes narrower, flanked by steep wooded slopes dotted with boulders. There are many gneiss quarries along the river.

▶ *Continue along the N 89 towards Brive.*

Cornil

A four-storey square tower above the village, all that remains of the castle, rises next to the Romanesque church. There is a scenic overlook of the bend in the river.

▶ *In the village, take the D 48E.*

Parc du Coiroux

This park has been developed around a large lake with swimming beaches and sailing, golf and tennis facilities.

▶ *Outside Coiroux, turn left on the D 48.*

Ste-Fortunade

Near a much-restored 15C **castle** stands a small Romanesque church containing, on the left at the entrance to the south chapel, the **reliquary-head**★ of St Fortunade. This is a delightful 15C work in bronze.

▶ *Follow the D 940 for 1km/0.5mi, turn left onto the D 1 and follow the D 10 to Marc-la-Tour. Take the D 125E to St-Bonnet-Avalouze, continue along the D 61E to St-Martial-de-Gimel then drive along the D 53.*

Gimel-les-Cascades★★

See GIMEL-LES-CASCADES.

▶ *Take the D 53 towards Touzac.*

The road runs alongside the southern shore of the Étang de Ruffaud. This lovely stretch of water with bathing beaches lies in a romantic setting.
The **Étang de Brach**, 3.5km/2mi farther on, has boating facilities.

▶ *Continue on the D 26 to La Gare-de-Corrèze, then take N 89 right towards Égletons.*

Égletons

The tour of the **Centre de Découverte du Moyen Âge** (Middles Ages Discovery Centre) begins with a short video presentation devoted to Bernard Ventadour, the 12C troubadour. This is followed by an exhibition illustrating life in the Middle Ages: farming, building, the art of illumination, monasteries etc. Several workshops (illumination, stained glass, blacksmith's) are open in summer. ◐*Open Jun-Sep, 10am-noon and 2-5pm; Oct-May, 10am-noon and 2-5pm, 2nd and 3rd weekends of the month, 2-6pm.* ◑*Closed Mon.* ⊚*3€ (-10 years old: no charge).* ☎ *05 55 93 29 66.*

Sarran

President Jacques Chirac, a former MP for the Corrèze constituency, inaugurated his **Musée du Septennat** in the Village of Sarran in December 2000. The museum houses gifts and souvenirs collected by the president during his seven-year term of office. ◐&*Open Jul-Aug, 10am-12.30pm and 1.30-6pm; Mar-Jun and Sep-Dec, daily except Mon, 10am-12.30pm and 1.30-6pm; Jan-Feb, Sat-Sun and public hols, 10am-12.30pm and 1.30-6pm.* ◑*Closed 1 Jan and 24-25 Dec.* ⊚*4€.* ☎ *05 55 21 77 77.*

Puy de Sarran

A narrow, bumpy road, lined with conifers, climbs steeply over 1.5km/1mi to reach the summit at 820m/2690ft. The wayside crosses form an impressive calvary, dominating the surrounding mounts, bare of vegetation.

▶ *From the village of Sarran, take the D 135 for 1km/0.5mi, then turn left on the D 142 towards St-Augustin.*

Le Tourondel

This charming little village has an attractive château (⊶*not open to the public*) and a communal **bread oven**. The oven is in a thatched-roof shelter, where other items once used by local farmers are on display.

▶ *At the end of the D 142, turn left on the D 26.*

Corrèze

In this old hamlet the granite houses are topped with slate roofs; they cluster around the massive 15C church, next to the **Margot gateway**, last vestige of the fortifications which once surrounded the village. The 15C **Église St-Martial**, surmounted by an English-style tower, contains a fine 18C altarpiece.
A short distance away (600m/660yd via rue Talin), the **site**★ of the **chapelle Notre-Dame-du-Pont-du-Salut** offers a pleasant detour. The little chapel nestles between the rocks and the river, which is spanned here by an old bridge.

▶ *Take the D 23 towards Bar.*

The winding road tumbles over woods and fields. The village of **Bar** sits on a promontory overlooking the valleys of the River Vimbelle and the River Corrèze.

Naves

The 15C church, flanked by a fortified turret, contains a huge **reredos**★ in sculpted wood. The vertical imagery is centred around Christ; horizontally, the carvings detail the founding of the church (St Peter in chains).

▶ *Follow the D 58, then turn right onto N 120 for a short distance before turning left to pick up the D 58 again.*

The road winds down to the river, and follows its course as far as Tulle.

TURENNE ★

POPULATION 742

MICHELIN LOCAL MAP 329: K-5

LOCAL MAP SEE BRIVE-LA-GAILLARDE: EXCURSIONS

Pompadour pompe. Ventadour vente. Turenne règne. This old French pun defies translation, but can be loosely construed as crediting Turenne with noble dignity, whereas the other cities mentioned are just full of hot air. Today the ruins of the proud castle, once the stronghold of the viscounts of La Tour d'Auvergne, rise above the picturesque town.

▶ **Orient Yourself**: Turenne is situated 15km/9.5mi south of Brive-la-Gaillarde.

◉ **Don't Miss**: The castle; the view from the Tour de César.

◔ **Also See**: Brive; Collonges-la-Rouge.

A Bit of History

The small town with a great past – The incapability of the last Carolingians to govern the whole of their territories and the aptitude of the lords of Turenne for resisting Viking invasion seems to have been the root of the fief's emancipation from royal power. As early as the 11C, a fortress was set on the outlines of the Martel Causse. In the 15C, Turenne held sway over a third of Lower Limousin, Upper Quercy and the Sarladais region or 1 200 villages and a number of abbeys. The viscounty, in its heyday, enjoyed enviable privileges; like the king of France, the viscounts ruled absolutely, ennobling subjects, creating offices and consulates, minting money and levying taxes.

◔ *For coin ranges, see the Legend at the back of the guide.*

"THE CANONS' HOUSE"

🍽🛏🛏 **La Maison des Chanoines** – ☎ 05 55 85 93 43 - 🕐 *closed 11 Oct-9 Apr, Wed eve in Jun and at lunchtime (except Sun and public hols) - reserv. required.* Having entered this 16C house via a spiral staircase, choose between the vaulted dining room with its stone walls, or the terrace with its tiny garden and vegetable patch. Six quiet rooms.

Lower Town

At the foot of the hill is the Barri-bas Quarter, the old part of town.

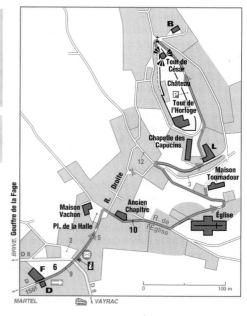

TURENNE	
Anciens-Combattants Pl. des	2
Beudin Av.	3
Charollais R. du Cdt	5
Foirail Pl. du	6
Leymarie R. F.-	9
Rouveyrol R. J.-	10
19-Mars-1962 R. du	12

Ancienne fonderie d'or	B
Hôtel Sclafer	F
Maison du Sénéchal	L
Échoppe du 15ème siècle	D

Turenne règne

Place du Foirail

The Hôtel Sclafer, with a loggia, was a residence for notaries in the 17C. Opposite, there is a small shop (15C) with a large arcade.

▶ *Walk along rue du Commandant-Charolais.*

Place de la Halle

The town houses around this square reflect the wealth of its inhabitants, especially **Maison Vachon**, the residence of the consuls of Turenne in the 16C and 17C.

Rue Droite

This narrow street, lined with old corbelled houses and small shops, climbs towards the castle.

▶ *Turn right onto rue Joseph-Rouveyrol.*

Rue Joseph-Rouveyrol

Note the **Maison de l'Ancien Chapitre** (Old Chapter-house), the tower of which is decorated with a lovely Flamboyant-Gothic-style doorway.

▶ *Continue straight on along rue de l'Église.*

Église

The construction of the church was decided upon by Charlotte de La Marck in 1593, the year Henri IV converted to Catholicism.

After Charlotte's death, Elizabeth of Nassau took over the project; and yet it was not consecrated until 1668. The church is in the form of a Greek cross, and has an unusual ornamentation – a yellow and white mosaic forming a network of prismatic ribbing.

La Tour d'Auvergne-Turenne Family

The name Turenne became famous through the family of La Tour d'Auvergne. In the 16C, Henri de la Tour d'Auvergne was leader of the Limousin Huguenots and the most valiant supporter of the Reformation. As a reward for his zeal, Henri IV allowed him to marry the heiress to the duchy of Bouillon, Charlotte de la Marck; the Turennes then went to live in Sedan and administered their viscounty, which remained sovereign, at a distance. Charlotte died three years after her marriage, leaving the titles of duke de Bouillon and prince of Sedan to her husband Henri, who remarried Elizabeth of Nassau. His youngest son, also a Henri, was to become the great **Turenne** (1611-75). His eldest son, who inherited the viscounty and title of duke de Bouillon, participated in the Fronde (an aristocratic rebellion against Mazarin with which Turenne had associated himself in its early days – 1648). In 1650 he welcomed two supporters of the Fronde, the princess of Condé and her son the duke of Enghien. The meeting was celebrated with such pomp and magnificence that it was baptised 'Turenne's Wild Week', and in consequence the people of Turenne were taxed for two years to refill the impoverished coffers.

The 17C and 18C furnishings include stalls and a high altar surmounted by a carved and gilded wooden altarpiece depicting the Passion of Christ. The trompe l'œil decoration between the twisted columns was added later on.

Just above the church, a vast building, the **Maison Tournadour** was once the town's salt storehouse.

Upper Town

Access is through the **fortified gateway** of the second of the three curtain walls which protected the castle. On the right the **Seneschal's House** has an elegant tower. On the left the **Chapelle des Capucins** (1644) houses exhibitions.

Château

Open Jul-Aug, 10am-7pm; Apr-Jun and Sep-Oct, 10am-noon and 2-6pm; Nov-Mar, Sun and public hols, 2-5pm. 3.20€. 05 55 85 90 68.

The castle was demolished by Louis XV after the viscounty became crown property. Only the Clock and Caesar's towers, at each end of the promontory, were spared. The **site**★ is remarkable. Once the fortified buildings and chapel (behind the Clock Tower) occupied the entire promontory.

Tour de l'Horloge

The Clock Tower was the castle keep, dating from the 13C. Only the guard-room with broken-barrel vaulting is open to visitors. Above it is the *salle du trésor* – the counting room or treasury.

Tour de César

This round tower with irregular stone bonding seems to date from the 11C. A staircase goes up to the top, from where there is a vast **panorama**★★ of the region. In the foreground below are the village's slate roofs, in the distance, beyond a green valley landscape, appear the Monts du Cantal to the east and the Dordogne Valley directly southwards (*viewing table*).

Go round the castle from the right. A series of manor houses, roofed with slate and flanked by squat towers have names which evoke their past purpose – the Gold Foundry, for example.

▷ *Return to the lower town along the lane separating the second and third curtain walls then via rue Droite.*

USSEL

POPULATION 11 006

MICHELIN LOCAL MAP 329: O-2

Built 631m/2 067ft above sea level on the edge of the Millevaches plateau, between the Diège and Sarsonne valleys, Ussel has kept a raiment of 15C-17C monuments, souvenirs of a prosperous past.

▷ **Orient Yourself**: The town is located 17km/10.5mi east of Meymac and 31km/19mi northwest of Bort-les-Orgues.

Old Town

Follow rue de la Liberté, behind the church, to place Joffre, where a fountain flows, and wander around the narrow surrounding streets. Many of the old houses have been restored; admire the turrets and decorative doorways.

Behind place de la République, the **Maison ducale de Ventadour** is an elegant Renaissance residence built by the dukes of Ventadour at the end of the 16C, to replace the austere feudal castle (now in ruins).

Rue Michelet

The 17C building at no 18 houses printing works and an exhibition hall.

Aigle Romain

The Roman Eagle monument, carved in granite, was discovered in the Peuch mill on the banks of the River Sarsonne.

Église St-Martin

Only the chancel and flat east end of this church date from the late 12C; the nave and side aisles were rebuilt in Gothic style; the west front and bell-tower (19C) are modern. Inside, the woodwork and stalls are 18C; there is a 16C polychrome *Pietà* carved in wood.

Musée du Pays d'Ussel

🕐*Open Jul-Aug, 10am-noon and 2-7pm.* 🎫*No charge.* ☎ *05 55 72 41 36.*

This museum, devoted to local crafts and traditional trades which are slowly dying out, is housed in the Hôtel Bonnot de Bay (early 18C). Old-fashioned workshops have been faithfully recreated, illustrating traditional crafts practised by the village smithy, the weaver (rare 18C loom), the clog-maker, the *galochier* (who made leather shoes with wooden soles), the milliner, the caner and basket-weaver, and the woodworker. Several rooms are devoted to *la bugeade* (washing linens and clothes), music, cooking and local furniture. One small room is set up like an old countryside café. On the floor above, a display case is given over to a presentation of selected local writers.

Chapelle des Pénitents

The religious life of the region is addressed by themes, including the historical context, parish services, processions and brotherhoods, popular devotions and religion as practised cradle to tomb.

There are some remarkable pieces of local art, a gilded and wood altar screen made in 1711; a painting (1664) by the Cibille brothers, *Pentecost*; and several painted wooden statues (the 17C praying angel is especially lovely).

In the ethnology section, there is a surprising 19C hearse, complete with a stuffed and mounted horse to draw it.

Chapelle N.-D.-de-la-Chabanne

▸ *1km/0.6mi S, access by rue Pasteur.*

From the esplanade near this pilgrims' chapel, there is an extensive **view**, reaching the Plateau des Millevaches (north-west), the Monts Dore (east), and the hills of Cantal (south-east).

UZERCHE★★

POPULATION 2 800

MICHELIN LOCAL MAP 329: K-3

Uzerche, a charming small Limousin town, stands on a promontory encircled by a bend in the River Vézère. On this picturesque site a surprising number of buildings are crowned with bell-turrets, watchtowers and pepper-pot roofs. "He who has a house in Uzerche, has a castle in Limousin"; the number of attractive mansions and old houses to be seen in the town confirms this popular old saying.
🛈 *Pl. de la Libération, 19140 Uzerche,* ☎ *05 55 73 15 71.*

▸ **Orient Yourself**: This small town is situated 30km/18.5mi northwest of Tulle and 38km/24mi north of Brive-la-Gaillarde.

🕐 **Organising Your Time**: Allow a full day to explore the Upper Vézère valley and the Gorges de la Vézère.

👁 **Don't Miss**: Eglise St-Pierre; the view of the town from the Ste-Eulalie district.

👜 **Also See**: Arnac-Pompadour; Coussac-Bonneval.

A Bit of History

The trick which always succeeded – In 732, the Saracens, after being beaten back by Charles Martel at Poitiers, attacked Uzerche. The town was protected by solid walls and 18 fortified towers and held out for seven years, but the population became decimated by famine and surrender seemed near until the besieged hit on a trick: they presented the emir of the Saracens with their last fatted calf, and with their last ration of corn. Amazed at such prodigality, the infidels raised the siege.

The Uzerche arms – tow bulls – recall this trick. The old town was never taken by force during any of the many sieges of the Middle Ages. Charles V, when he authorised the town to add three gold lilies to its arms, also gave it the appellation Uzerche the maid, and its crest *non polluta* (never sullied) confirms the glorious epithet.

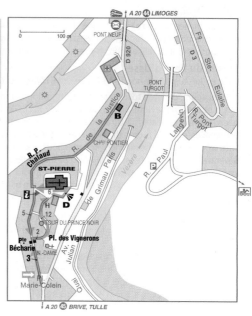

Upper Town

▷ *Leave from place Marie-Colein.*

Rue Gaby-Furnestin

On the left, you will see the 16C timbered house in which Alexis Boyer, surgeon to Napoleon I, was born. In this street which extends onto rue Jean-Gentet, note a group of renovated old houses with fine carved doorways.

Porte Bécharie

This fortified gateway is the only one of the old city gates still intact: a modern statue of the Virgin stands in a niche above the arched passageway. Adjoining the gateway is a building known as the Château Bécharie, which is flanked by a square tower and a pendant turret; in the left wall is a great stone emblazoned with the Uzerche arms.

▷ *Take Escalier-Notre-Dame on the right immediately beyond the Bécharie Gateway.*

Place des Vignerons

This little square, the Wine-Grower's Square, was formerly the fruit market. It is surrounded by old houses and the chapel of Notre-Dame, the oldest church in Uzerche. The covered La Perception passageway leads to a small terrace which affords a bird's-eye view of the Vézère and of part of the town.

Leave the **Tour du Prince Noir** (Black Prince's Tower) on your left and walk along rue St-Nicolas which brings you out onto place de la Libération. This square is dominated by the impressive mass of the church of St-Pierre.

Église St-Pierre★

This is an interesting Romanesque church, built in several phases: the chancel and north transept date from the 11C; the nave is from the 12C and was extended in the 13C. Fortified during the Hundred Years War, repaired in the 17C, the church was restored in the beginning of the 20C.

The 12C **bell tower** is Limousin in style. Three square tiers with paired windows and gables are surmounted by a fourth, octagonal in shape; this, in turn, is topped with a short roof covered in shingles which replaced the original stone pyramid roof.

To the south-west stands a massive **round tower**, erected as the defence point for the main door, built of rough-hewn stone with loopholes. Since restoration work on the church was undertaken last century, this tower is all that remains of the ancient defence system. The perimeter wall included 18 towers and five fortified gateways. Beneath the chancel, the 11C **crypt** (*access from the chevet outside--in the past, two stairways connected the crypt to the church*) is believed to be the oldest in the Limousin region; in the shape of a rotunda with three apsidal chapels supported by massive pillars. Traces on the wall and vaulting indicate that the ceiling was once coffered. The central room, with its single pier on a rectangular base, communicates with the ambulatory. The 14C tomb in the north chapel is of unknown origin.

The **nave** has broken-barrel vaulting and is flanked by narrow aisles. An octagonal dome rises above the transept crossing. In the chancel with its ambulatory and the side chapels, the **capitals** are ornamented with tracery, foliage and animals. Three of them have been converted into holy-water fonts; on one, monsters with lions' bodies and men's heads cavort.

Esplanade de La Lunade

From this esplanade, built on the site of the former monastic buildings, there is a **view** immediately below of the La Pomme district which rises in terraces along N 20, of the Vézère meander, and beyond, of the hills encircling the town.

Rue Pierre-Chalaud

It is lined with old houses adorned with Gothic and Renaissance doors and timbered houses. At the end of the street the **Château Tayac** (12C-14C) is a fine house with turrets and a door surmounted by a shield.

Centre Régional de Documentation sur l'Archéologie du Paysage

🕐*Open Jul-Aug, daily except Tue, 2.30-6.30pm; rest of the year by prior arrangement.* 🎫*No charge.* ☎ *05 55 73 26 07.*

Set up in the 17C **Hôtel du Sénéchal**, the regional centre documents recent archaeological research in the area, covering the period from the Iron Age to the late Middle Ages.

▶ *Return to place de la Libération.*

Walk along rue Jean-Gentet, where you will notice carved doorways, to the Bécharie Gateway and place Marie-Colein.

Door on Rue Pierre-Chalaud

E. Larribere/MICHELIN

Excursions

Masseret

16km/10mi N.

The village stands in a part of the Limousin countryside which is mostly woodland. In the centre of Masseret stands a modern tower with a viewing table as its top (104 steps). There is a beautiful circular **panorama**★: to the north can be seen the Ambazac hills, to the east the Millevaches plateau, the Monédières massif and on a clear day the mountains of Auvergne.

The Romanesque **church**, largely restored in the 16C, has a shrine dedicated to St Valérie dating from the 13C (*key available from the chemist's opposite the church*).

Église de St-Germain-les-Belles

11km/6.2mi N of Masseret.

This building dating from the 14C is a fine example of a fortified church. The façade and chevet are protected by machicolations. Inside, to the right of the chancel, a spiral staircase gives access to the look-out points high above the tall pointed vaulting, and the watch-path (*for guided tours, apply to the tourist office*).

Upper Vézère Valley

55km/34mi round-trip – allow 3hr

▷ *At the Turgot Bridge, take the D 3, the Eymoutiers road, which climbs steeply and goes through the Ste-Eulalie suburb.*

Belvédère

Travel 800m/0.5mi from the bridge and before a turning on the left you get a good overall **view**★★ of Uzerche perched on top of a rock and the Vézère running below. The church (St-Pierre) overlooks the many pinnacles atop the slate-covered turrets; below stand the many towers of Pontier Château.

▷ *Continue along the D 3 and turn right onto the D 26 shortly after Eyburie.*

Chamboulive

The countryside is a pleasant mixture of volcanic *puys*, hills and meadows, at an altitude of 434m/1 427ft. Inhabited as early as the Neolithic period, the region was prosperous in Gallo-Roman days.

The **church**, a Romanesque edifice renovated in the 15C, has a raised, deep belfry-porch, and its massive appearance is enhanced by the two storeys on the square tower, one Romanesque and the other Gothic.

▷ *Take the D 142 towards Uzerche and turn left onto the D 920 just before reaching Uzerche.*

Vigeois

An abbey was founded in the 6C; time and again it was ruined in wars until it was finally abolished in the wake of the French Revolution. The present **church** dates from the 12C, although it has been much restored. Note the interesting capitals near the transept and the historiated capitals decorating the apsidal chapels. ◷*Open Jun-Sep, 9am-7pm. Key available from the café opposite the church.*

A street leads down to the **old bridge**, also 12C, which runs a quiet course here. Nearby, **Pontcharal Lake** and the recreation centre is spacious and welcoming.

▷ *Drive N out of Vigeois along the D 7 towards Arnac-Pompadour then turn right beyond Jargassou Bridge. Follow C 7 then V 1 to Baby.*

Cascades de Bialet

▣*Picnic area.* A footpath starts at the wooden bridge across the stream; other wooden bridges crisscross the water which froths and tumbles its way down to the Vézère (*take care that children do not fall in*).

▷ *Continue on the minor road, which goes steeply down to Uzerche.*

Gorges De La Vézère★

67km/42mi round-trip – allow 4hr

Downstream from Uzerche, the Vézère goes through deep gorges; the railway line alone follows the river closely, yet there are some fine **views** from the Site de la Roche and from villages on both sides of the gorges.

▷ *Drive S out of Uzerche along the D 920 for 4km/2.5mi then turn right onto the D 3 to Vigeois, cross the Vézère and continue along the D 3. Shortly after Le Monteil turn left onto the D 9E to Estivaux.*

Belvédère de Comborn

The belvedere overlooks a meander of the Vézère and affords a view of the ruined **Château de Comborn**. Since 2001, the new owner has undertaken the restoration of the castle. The 18C section houses a restaurant (open Fri-Sun), but only a few vestiges remain of the 11C keep. Three vast cellars from the same period have also been preserved. ○⚬ *Open mid-Mar to mid-Nov, guided tour (45min), Sat-Sun, 2-6pm, Tue-Fri throughout the year by prior arrangement.* ○ *Closed Mon.* ⚬ *5€ (-12 years old: no charge).* ☎ *05 55 98 46 53.*

▷ *Continue along the D 9E3 to the end of the road and turn right onto the D 9.*

Site de la Roche★

A pretty little road leads to the edge of a precipice overlooking the Vézère gorges. To the right, a rocky trail under the chestnut trees leads to a **viewing table** (391m/1 283ft) which is well situated.

The view extends over the wooded **gorges du Saillant** in the foreground, and farther out to the village of St-Robert.

To the left, a path leads to the **panorama**, where there is another spectacular view over the gorges.

▷ *Return to the D 9.*

Allassac

The distinctive houses of this town are built in black schist and roofed with slate; some have red-sandstone corner pieces (rue L.-Boucharel).

The **church**, commemorating the beheading of John the Baptist, is also built of black schist, except for the lovely **southern door**★, where various colours of sandstone are set in contrast. The nearby **Caesar's Tower** (30m/98ft) is all that remains of the old medieval fortifications.

Before the First World War, the processing of slate for roofing brought prosperity to Allassac and Donzenac, as thatched roofs were replaced in the countryside all around. The last slate quarry closed in 1982.

▷ *Leave Allassac travelling NW on the D 134.*

Le Saillant

This hamlet is on a pleasant site at the mouth of the gorges. From the **old bridge** spanning the river, admire the Lasteyrie du Saillant manor, where the revolutionary orator Mirabeau (brother of the Marquis du Saillant) regularly came to visit. Do not miss the **six stained-glass windows**★ by Marc Chagall in the former castle chapel. Decorated between 1978 and 1982, they represent man's close links with nature. There are only four "Chagall chapels" in the world, including this one; there is another one in Kent (UK) and two in the USA.

▷ *Continue on the D 134 and turn right.*

Vertougit

This charming village is beautifully located – overlooking the **gorges de la Vézère** and just across from the Site de la Roche. It is a good place to stop and stretch your legs, admire the typical houses, the orchards and vineyards, or study the view from the viewing table.

▷ *Return to the D 134 and turn right to Voutezac.*

Voutezac

Built into the hillside, this agreeable village has a fortified church with a 15C square tower. At the corner of the street leading to Objat (wayside cross), there is an ox yoke surrounded by old farm tools.

▷ *Drive N along the D 3 to return to Uzerche via Vigeois.*

Château de VALENÇAY★★★

MICHELIN LOCAL MAP 323: F-4

Geographically, Valençay is part of the Berry region, but the château can be included with others of its kind which grace the Loire Valley, by virtue of the time of its construction as well as its enormous size.

▶ **Orient Yourself**: The town of Valencay and its castle are situated 42km/26km north of Châteauroux.

☺ **Don't Miss**: A tour inside the castle.

A Bit of History

A financier's château – Valençay was built c 1540 by Jacques d'Estampes, the owner of the castle then existing. He had married the daughter of a financier, who brought him a large dowry, and he wanted a residence worthy of his new fortune. The 12C castle was demolished and in its place rose the present sumptuous building.

Finance has often been involved in the history of Valençay; among its owners were several Farmers-General and even the famous **John Law**, whose dizzy banking career was an early and instructive example of inflationary practices.

Charles-Maurice de Talleyrand-Périgord, who had begun his career under Louis XVI as bishop of Autun, was foreign minister when he bought Valençay in 1803 at the request of Napoleon, who was seeking a place to receive important foreign visitors. Talleyrand managed his career so skilfully that he did not finally retire until 1834.

Visit

Château

ⓞ*Open Jul-Aug, 9.30am-7.30pm; end of Mar-Jun and Sep-1 Nov, 9.30am-6pm.* ⊜*8.50€ for admission to château and show (child: 4.50€).* ☎ *02 54 00 10 66. www.chateau-valencay.com*

The entrance pavilion is a huge building, designed like a keep only for show not defence, with many windows, harmless turrets and fancy machicolations. The steep roof is pierced with high dormer windows and surmounted by monumental chimneys.

Such architecture is also found in the Renaissance châteaux of the Loire Valley, but here we see the first signs of the Classical style: superimposed pilasters with Doric (ground floor), Ionic (first floor) and Corinthian (second floor) capitals.

The Classical style is even more evident in the huge corner towers: domes take the place of the pepper-pot roofs which were the rule on the banks of the Loire in the 16C.

West wing – The west wing was added in the 17C and altered in the 18C. At roof level the mansard windows alternate with bulls' eyes (round apertures). The tour of the ground floor includes the great Louis XVI vestibule; the gallery devoted to the

The majestic 16C château

B. Kaufmann/MICHELIN

Address Book

For coin categories, see the Legend at the back of the guide.

EATING OUT

Le Lion d'Or – *14 pl. de la Halle -* ☎ *02 54 00 00 87 -* 🕐 *closed Jan-Feb and Mon.* This former coaching inn is delightfully old-fashioned and ideally located across from the covered market. The dining room, decorated with woodwork in the style of the 1930s, is charming and in the summer the shaded terrace is a nice place to eat.

Auberge St-Fiacre – *36600 Veuil - 6km/3.6mi S of Valencay. Take the D 15, then a side road -* ☎ *02 54 40 32 78 -* 🕐 *closed 6-*

27 Jan, 1-14 Sep, Sun eve and Mon except public hols. This low 17C building in the middle of a flowery village has set up its terrace by a stream, beneath several horse chestnut trees. In chilly weather, the warmth of the country-style hearth and the dining room with its imposing beams is most hospitable.

LEISURE ACTIVITIES

Sound and Light Show – This nightly show, based around the theme of Capitaine Fracasse, a swashbuckling novel by Théophile Gautier, takes place in summer *(dates and times are available from the tourist office,* ☎ *02 54 00 04 42).*

Talleyrand-Périgord family; the Grand Salon and the Blue Salon which contain many works of art and pieces of Empire furniture, including the so-called Congress of Vienna table; and the apartments of the duchess of Dino.

On the first floor, the bedroom of Prince Talleyrand is followed by the room occupied by Ferdinand, the future king of Spain; the apartments of the duke of Dino and those of Madame de Bénévent (portrait of the princess by Elisabeth Vigée-Lebrun); the great gallery (with a *Diana* by Houdon) and the great staircase. Something of the spirit of the festivities organised by Talleyrand and his master chef, Marie-Antoine de Carême, still lingers in the great dining room and the kitchens beneath.

Park – Black swans, ducks and peacocks strut freely in the formal gardens near the château. Under the great trees in the park, deer, llamas, camels and kangaroos roam in vast enclosures.

Musée de l'Automobile du Centre

🕐♿*Open Jul-Aug, 10am-12.30pm and 1.30-7.30pm; Apr-Jun and Sep-early Nov, 10.30am-12.30pm and 2-6pm.* ✍*4€. Temporary exhibits Apr-Sep, by prior arrangement.* ☎ *02 54 00 07 74.*

The car museum, concealed in the park, contains the collection of the Guignard brothers, the grandsons of a coachbuilder from Vatan (Indre). There are over 60 vintage cars (the earliest dating from 1898), perfectly maintained in working order, including the 1908 Renault limousine used by Presidents Poincaré and Millerand; there are also road documents from the early days of motoring, old Michelin maps and guides from before 1914.

Lac de VASSIVIÈRE★★

MICHELIN LOCAL MAP 325: I-6 – LOCAL MAP SEE EYMOUTIERS

The lake covers 1 000ha/2 471 acres, behind the Vassivière Dam over the River Maulde. Set in dark green hills, it is the site of many regular sporting and cultural events (sailing, motorcycle endurance trials, Tour de France bicycle race, contemporary art exhibits and more).

The lakeside road (*route circumlacustre*) goes around the shoreline, offering beaches and coves for swimmers, fishing enthusiasts, sailors, and many footpaths for avid ramblers.

▶ **Orient Yourself**: The lake is situated approximately 11km/7mi northeast of Eymoutiers.

Don't Miss: A boat trip on the lake; the outdoor leisure activities on offer here; the Centre National d'Art et du Paysage (CNAP).

Also See: Aubusson; Eymoutiers.

Address Book

For coin ranges, see the Legend at the back of the guide.

WHERE TO STAY

Chambre d'hôte Villards - Bernard Blondel – *87470 Peyrat-le-Château - 2km/1.2mi from Peyrat-le-Château towards the Lac de Vassivière and then Villards - ☎ 05 55 69 21 36 - fermequestrevillards@wanadoo.fr - ⌾ - 5 rooms.* Comfortable, calm guestrooms have been installed in this old stone farm. A billiards room, the living room fireplace or the nearby Lac de Vassivière provide ample opportunity for relaxation and leisure. Meals may be taken on the terrace.

Hôtel La Caravelle – *Lac de Vassivière - 87470 Peyrat-le-Château - ☎ 05 55 69 40 97 - ⌾ closed 2-31 Jan - ▣ - 21 rooms.* Enjoy the view of the lake from your bedroom window. The breakfast room, living room and halls are adorned with reproductions of the famous Aubusson tapestries, Limoges enamels and works of art. The restaurant menu features regional cuisine prepared fresh.

SHOPPING

Ferme-Auberge Noëlle Digan - Lavergne – *7km/4.2mi NE of Peyrat-le-Château via the D 68 and D 51 - 23460 St-Martin-Château - ☎ 05 55 64 72 69 - pdigan@next.fr - ⌾ the shop is open all year round, 10am-9pm; the inn is open Jul-Aug by prior arrangement - ⌾ closed Nov-Mar.* This farm is devoted to raising a local breed of pig known as *cul noir*. The farmer is also a sculptor and his works are on display in the restaurant and for sale in the shop, along with local culinary specialities.

LEISURE ACTIVITIES

Base Nautique de Vauveix – *Vauveix - 23460 Royère-de-Vassivière - ☎ 05 55 30 57 11 - ⌾ open Jul-Aug, daily, 9am-noon and 2-6pm.* Sailing courses, boat and surfboard rentals.

Centre Équestre de Vassivière – *Masgrangeas - 23460 Royère-de-Vassivière - ☎ 05 55 64 72 12 / 06 88 23 84 79 - www.perso.club-internet.fr/stcev - ⌾ open daily.* This centre, a primary school for riding, offers outings ranging from trail rides to trips of several days (except in Jul-Aug). A children's hostel is also open during school holidays.

Vassivière-Club Tout Terrain – *Route d'Aubusson - 23460 Royère-de-Vassivière - ☎ 05 55 64 75 33 - vcttr@net-up.com - ⌾ open Mon-Fri, 8am-5pm - ⌾ closed on public hols.* This activity centre rents mountain bikes, quads, 4x4s, mini-motorcycles for children (Jul-Aug), and offers off-road vehicle excursions. Motorcycle races are also held here.

Ski Nautique Club Auchaise-Vassivière – *Digue d'Auchaise (between Auphelle and Royère-de-Vassivière) - 23460 Royère-de-Vassivière - ☎ 05 55 64 72 79 (in season) - ⌾ open Jun-Sep, daily, 10am-1pm and 3-7pm.* This large lake is a great place to water ski and this club can provide you with all the necessary equipment.

NIGHTLIFE

La Galère – *Broussas - 23340 Faux-la-Montagne - ☎ 05 55 67 98 07 - ⌾ open Jul-Aug, daily; off-season, Fri-Sat and eve preceding public hols.* La Galère is the most popular nightclub in the local area.

Visit

Île de Vassivière

⌾*Open all year. ☎ 0 810 19 23 87. Access: take the lakeside road S, towards Beaumont-du-Lac.*

▸ *The road goes around Vassivière Island and the smaller Île aux Serpents. After 4km/2mi, turn left towards Pierefitte and park the car in the parking area. Take the little train or cross the bridge on foot to reach the island. Boat trips are also available.*

Sheltered in the western part of the lake, Vassivière offers visitors the combined attraction of its natural site and of its works of art displayed around the island. The **views**★ from the bridge are wide open on the water and surrounding hills. The path from the bridge leads to the castle, once the home of Mme de Vassivière, who owned most of the land which was submerged when the lake was created to supply hydroelectric power. Now the tourist centre and temporary exhibits have taken the place of footmen and chambermaids. Beyond, stands the art museum, and the surrounding woodland is home to the sculpture park, botany trails, a deer park and a farm with animals.

Centre National d'Art et du Paysage (CNAP)★★

⌾*Open Apr-Sep, 11am-1pm and 2-7pm; Oct-Mar, daily except Mon, 2-6pm. ⌾ Closed 1 Jan and 25 Dec. ⌾ 3€. ☎ 05 55 69 27 27.*

Île de Vassivière

In 1991, a graceful new building (visible from the dam) rose up on the island in the middle of the lake, a centre for contemporary art which has since gained an international reputation.

The distinctive structure housing the collection was designed by the Italian architect Aldo Rossi, in cooperation with the French architect Xavier Fabre. The design inspires an image of a ship **(galerie)** flanked by a lighthouse **(phare)** 27m/89ft tall, and is well integrated in the landscape, pointing its prow up the hillside as though into a wave. The red brick, grey granite, and green paint on the metallic parts of the structure also bring it into harmony with the environment.

Inside the **lighthouse**, a spiral stair leads past a monumental sculpture to the viewing platform above. From here, the visitor can appreciate the length and breadth of the gallery (80×10m/262×33ft). Inside the long **gallery**, wooden beams on a high, keel-shaped ceiling again recall the nautical theme.

Contemporary artists, both French and foreign, are often invited to exhibit their works in the museum and the **sculpture park** (○ *open to visitors year-round; there is also a guided tour with the tour of the Centre d'Art Contemporain [see above]*). Along the path laid out for exploration of this outdoor extension of the museum are works by David Nash, Kimio Tsuchiya, Dominique Bailly and Jean-Pierre Uhlen. Beyond the artistic interest of the promenade, the woodland walk is enjoyable and offers views over the lake and forest. There is also a good view from the cafeteria on the ground floor of the museum.

Ruines de VENTADOUR★

MICHELIN LOCAL MAP 329: N-3

On a rocky spur high above the Luzège gorges, the ruins of the Château de Ventadour rise in an untamed natural site★.

▶ **Orient Yourself**: The castle ruins are located 7km/4.5mi southeast of Égletons.

▶ **Also See**: Gimel-les-Cascades; Meymac; Tulle.

Bernard de Ventadour

Ventadour was a literary hotbed in the 12C. Generations of lords and ladies composed poetry there. In this rarefied atmosphere, Bernard was born (1125), son of a castle servant. As a youth, he revealed an extraordinary talent for versifying, and became a tender and passionate bard of courtly love. The viscountess willingly lent her ear to the clever young man's ardent words. Indeed, her jealous husband had the handsome but humble bard sent packing, and thereafter kept a close eye on his lady.

Bernard de Ventadour was welcomed into the household of **Eleanor of Aquitaine**, duchess of Normandy, then married to Henry II Plantagenet. Eleanor, credited as an inspiration for the ideals of courtly love, liked Bernard's verses so well that when she became queen of England, she took him with her court to London. Later, Bernard followed her to Poitiers, and when the Queen was carried back to England as a prisoner of her husband, Bernard retired to the home of the count of Niort for the next 10 years. Drawn to the monastic life, the ageing poet returned to his homeland and the abbey at Dalon, near Hautefort Château (⚏ *see Château de HAUTEFORT*). There he met another famous troubadour, Bernard de Born, and passed away at the end of the century.

A Bit of History

The fortress – Its location and formidable defences made Ventadour seem impregnable. But the stronghold was vulnerable on one point – treason – and for 13 years was held by the English as the Hundred Years War raged. During the Renaissance period, the viscounts left the cold fortress for the cosier rooms of an elegant manor in Ussel (⚏ *see USSEL*). Speaking with pride of his castle, the duke of Ventadour told Louis XIV: "All the straw in the kingdom would not be enough to fill the moats of Ventadour."

Visit

Ruins

The ruins can be admired from the narrow road leading out of Moustier-Ventadour.

To reach the ruins, take the footpath, 30min round-trip. Restoration work in progress; beware of falling stones.

Two towers, high walls, old inner courtyards, vestiges of the main building and a barbican give an idea of what the medieval fortress must have been like. From the platform on the southern side, there is a dizzying **view** over ravines of the Luzège Valley.

Tour des Fossés

▶ *A tour of 7km/43mi starting from the base of the castle; continue turning to the right as you go along.*

Take the access road which turns into a narrow, but paved lane and dips sharply (⚏ hairpin curves) down into the *fossés* (natural moats) surrounding Ventadour Castle. Half way down, the road passes by the lowest part of the ruins, before leading to N 991. From that road, admire the picturesque **views**★ of the ruins and the bends in the River Luzège.

VIERZON

POPULATION 30 743

MICHELIN LOCAL MAP 323: I-3

Vierzon came to be in 1937, as four local administrative districts were joined (Vierzon-Ville, Village, Bourneuf, Forges). Its location is strategic, at the confluence of the River Yèvre and River Cher, the intersection of major routes, and the railway junction for the Paris-Toulouse and Nantes-Lyon lines; it is the gateway between the Champagne Berrichonne region and Sologne (whose forests begin just northwest of town).

▶ **Orient Yourself**: Vierzon is situated 39km/24mi northwest of Bourges and 58km/36mi northeast of Châteauroux.

🕐 **Organising Your Time**: Allow half a day to explore the Champagne-Berrichonne area.

Especially for Kids: The Maison de l'Eau and Hameau des Automates in Neuvy-sur-Barangeon.

👣 **Also See**: Bourges; Forêt d'Allogny; Reuilly-Quincy vineyards; Château de Valençay.

A Bit of History

Industrial heritage – The Comte d'Artois, brother of Louis XVI opened a forge in Vierzon in 1779, and in no time a number of industries began work, in particular ceramics and later, mechanical construction.

The first porcelain manufactory went into operation in 1816. At the turn of the 20C, there were a dozen such enterprises in town, making it second only to Limoges (it is still the biggest manufacturer of porcelain in Berry). The second field of production began in the mid-19C with the establishment of the Société Française de Matériel Agricole" (making farm machinery, today the company is called La Case-Poclain). The first mobile threshing machine in France was made there. Other companies included Brouhot (1860 – they went so far as to build cars) and Merlin (1879). This period is recalled by the iron architecture of the Grand Magasin de la Société Française, and by the presence of the canal, created in 1835 to link Vierzon to Montluçon. No traffic troubles its waters today, but strollers enjoy walking beneath the poplars on its banks.

Old Town

This pedestrian area has been artfully developed around the winding streets and old, half-timbered houses up against a slope watched over by a Gothic **belfry**, formerly the gate to the city.

Église Notre-Dame

🕐 ☀☀ *Open 9am-7pm. Guided tour available by prior arrangement,* ☎ *02 48 52 65 15.*

This church, built in the 12C, enlarged and renovated in the 15C (side aisles), is fronted by a belfry-porch and a basket-handled arch above the doorway. Inside, admire the restored barrel-vaulting and the Renaissance windows representing the Crucifixion (south wall of the chapel of Ste-Perpétue). The stone marked with a seal at the entrance to the chancel bears a long inscription in Gothic letters, noting the date of the church's foundation, 1409. In the transept, a painting by Jean Boucher depicts John the Baptist.

Square Lucien-Beaufrère

This garden, designed in 1929 in the Art Deco style, replaced an abbey whose remaining buildings now house the town hall offices. At the entrance, the 1935 **Auditorium wash-house** by Eugène Karcher is decorated with enamelled tiles; dating from the same period, the monument to fallen heroes is embellished with low-relief sculptures representing the trades practised in Vierzon. From the banks of the Yèvre there is a pretty view over the old town.

Excursions

Neuvy-sur-Barangeon

19km/11.8mi NW along the D 926.

Maison de l'Eau

🕐 *Open Jul-Aug, 10am-noon and 2-6pm (last entrance 1hr before closing); Jun and Sep, daily except Tue, 2-6pm; Apr-May and Oct, Sat-Sun and public hols, 2-6pm.* ☜4€ (5-14 years old: 2.50€). ☎ 02 48 51 66 65.

🧒 This 16C watermill, standing on the edge of a lake, presents the story of "water" through the seasons (animated scenes and audio guides): from spring rain falling on the Auvergne to frozen waterfalls in the Alps. There is also a section devoted to Neuvy and local millers and another one to the fauna and flora of the Sologne lakes.

Musée d'Histoire Militaire, Historimage

Along the road to Bourges, within the Fédération Maginot complex. 🕐 *Open Apr-Oct, daily except Mon, 9am-noon and 2-6pm.* ☜5€ (children: no charge). ☎ 02 48 52 64 63.

This museum, which illustrates the uniforms and equipment of French and foreign soldiers from the First World War to the present, stages an amazing show entitled "Le Carrousel de la Paix" involving many automata and special effects.

Le Hameau des Automates★

Opposite Historimage, along the D 944. Open Jul-Aug, 2.30-7pm; Easter to late-Jun and early-Sep to early-Nov, daily except Mon, 2.30-7pm. ☜10€ (children aged 5-12: 8€; under 5 years old: no charge). ☎ 02 48 51 63 00.

🧒 Two separate shows present the technical and artistic aspects of automata and the poetic charm of doves and pigeons. There are also reconstructions of Renaissance scenes and of an orchestra and a video presentation illustrating the making of automata.

Champagne Berrichonne

75km/46.5mi – allow 2hr

▶ *Leave Vierzon SE along the D 27 towards Quincy.*

Brinay

This village is tranquil on the banks of the Cher upstream from Vierzon. The Romanesque church is worth visiting for its 12C **frescoes**★.

▶ *Take the D 18E towards Méreau.*

Massay

The **church**, rebuilt between the 14C and the 16C, was once part of a Benedictine abbey founded in the 8C. The vestiges of the abbey include the chapter-house, parts of the dormitory (13C), cellars (12C) and the tithe barns. The 12C abbot's chapel (also known as St-Loup) is well preserved; it stood in the centre of the cloisters. The abbot's lodging dates from the 17C.

▶ *Leave the village travelling SW, towards Châteauroux.*

Vatan

Église St-Laurian – This restored church has retained a 16C chancel with windows from the same period, recounting the life of the saint. There are some interesting 8C paintings and sculpted door leaves dated 1498.

Musée du Cirque – This museum displays an interesting collection of posters, accessories, models and costumes connected with the circus world. ○*Open daily except Mon, 10am-noon and 2-6pm; Tue, 2-6pm.* ○*Closed 1 Jan, 1 May, 1 Nov and 25 Dec.* ◉*3.80€ (child: 1.50€).* ☎ *02 54 49 77 78. www.musee-du-cirque.com*

▶ *Take the D 922, N of town.*

St-Outrille

This village has an interesting **collegiate church**. Romanesque and Gothic styles are both present: the nave is 15C, the chancel, side chapels (except one) and the transept from the 12C. The east end – note the intertwining pattern on the pilasters of the blind vaulting – is surmounted by a curious twisted bell-tower covered with shingles. In the chancel, the capitals have a simple design of acanthus leaves, and sit atop slightly curved monolithic columns. The western doorway dates from the 14C.

Graçay

This medieval town, separated from St-Outrille by the River Fouzon, has kept its ramparts and a few old houses. The interesting **Musée de la Photo** retraces the history of photography. ○*Open Jun-Sep, daily except Mon, 10am-noon and 3-6pm; rest of the year, Sat-Sun and public hols, 10am-noon and 3-6pm by prior arrangement.* ○*Closed Jan and 25 Dec.* ◉*3€.* ☎ *02 48 51 41 80.*

▶ *Leave the village travelling E on the D 68.*

Nohant-en-Graçay

Inside the charming **Église St-Martin** *(Jun-Sep: 10am-6pm; the rest of the year: by appointment at the town hall,* ☎ *02 48 51 40 65),* the columns supporting the vaulting of the central tower bear remarkable 12C capitals. The unusual bell-tower with its spiral spire is similar to the one in St-Outrille.

▶ *Leave Nohant travelling N along the D 164.*

Genouilly

At the far end of town stands the **Église St-Symphorien**. This 12C edifice, with a handsome porch, has stained-glass windows made in 1536. The chancel is covered by a 13C vault, exceptional in Berry because it is in the *angevin* style typical of the region of Anjou. The slender columns support Romanesque capitals of acanthus leaves, interlacing patterns, foliated scrolls, faces and animals. On the capital of the pillar to the right, at the entrance to the chancel, there is an acrobat standing on his hands, accompanied by two imaginary animals who hold his feet. In the southern chapel, the mausoleum of the La Châtre family is from the turn of the 16C and 17C.

▶ *Return to Vierzon on the D 19 and D 90.*

INDEX

W – X

MAPS AND PLANS

Companion Publications

REGIONAL AND LOCAL MAPS

To make the most of your journey, travel with Michelin maps at a scale Regional maps nos 521, 525, 526, 519 and 522 and the new local maps, which are illustrated on the map of France below.

MAPS OF FRANCE

And remember to travel with the latest edition of the map of France no 721, which gives an overall view of the Dordogne-Berry-Limousin region, and the main access roads which connect it to the rest of France. The entire country is mapped at a 1:1 000 000 scale and clearly shows the main road network. Convenient Atlas formats (spiral, hard cover and mini) are also available.

INTERNET

Michelin is pleased to offer a route-planning service on the Internet: www.ViaMichelin.com. Choose the shortest route, a route without tolls, or the Michelin recommended route to your destination; you can also access information about hotels and restaurants from The Red Guide, and tourists sites from The Green Guide.

There are a number of useful maps and plans in the guide, listed in the table of contents.

Bon voyage!

Legend

Selected monuments and sights

Tour - Departure point

Catholic church

Protestant church, other temple

Synagogue - Mosque

Building

Statue, small building

Calvary, wayside cross

Fountain

Rampart - Tower - Gate

Château, castle, historic house

Ruins

Dam

Factory, power plant

Fort

Cave

Troglodyte dwelling

Prehistoric site

Viewing table

Viewpoint

Other place of interest

Special symbol

Fortified town (bastide): in southwest France, a new town built in the 13-14C and typified by a geometrical layout.

Sports and recreation

Racecourse

Skating rink

Outdoor, indoor swimming pool

Multiplex Cinema

Marina, sailing centre

Trail refuge hut

Cable cars, gondolas

Funicular, rack railway

Tourist train

Recreation area, park

Theme, amusement park

Wildlife park, zoo

Gardens, park, arboretum

Bird sanctuary, aviary

Walking tour, footpath

Of special interest to children

Abbreviations

A   Agricultural office (Chambre d'agriculture)

C   Chamber of Commerce (Chambre de commerce)

H   Town hall (Hôtel de ville)

J   Law courts (Palais de justice)

M   Museum (Musée)

P   Local authority offices (Préfecture, sous-préfecture)

POL.   Police station (Police)

🛡   Police station (Gendarmerie)

T   Theatre (Théâtre)

U   University (Université)

	Sight	Seaside resort	Winter sports resort	Spa
Highly recommended ★★★		🛆🛆🛆	❄❄❄	╪╪╪
Recommended ★★		🛆🛆	❄❄	╪╪
Interesting ★		🛆	❄	╪

Additional symbols

🄸		Tourist information
▬▬	▬▬	Motorway or other primary route
❶	❶	Junction: complete, limited
▭▭	▭▭	Pedestrian street
ɪ====ɪ	----	Unsuitable for traffic, street subject to restrictions
┉┉	----	Steps – Footpath
🚂	🚉	Train station – Auto-train station
🚌	🚌 S.N.C.F.	Coach (bus) station
•—•—•		Tram
Ⓜ		Metro, underground
🅿️ R		Park-and-Ride
♿		Access for the disabled
✉		Post office
☎		Telephone
▱		Covered market
⚔		Barracks
△		Drawbridge
℧		Quarry
✗		Mine
B	F	Car ferry (river or lake)
🚢		Ferry service: cars and passengers
⛴		Foot passengers only
③		Access route number common to Michelin maps and town plans
Bert (R.)...		Main shopping street
AZ B		Map co-ordinates

Hotels and restaurants

Hotels- price categories:

	Provinces	Large cities
🛏	<40 €	<60 €
🛏🛏	40 to 65 €	60 to 90 €
🛏🛏🛏	65 to 100 €	90 to 130 €
🛏🛏🛏🛏	>100 €	>130 €

Restaurants- price categories:

	Provinces	Large cities
🛏	<14 €	<16 €
🛏🛏	14 to 25 €	16 to 30 €
🛏🛏🛏	25 to 40 €	30 to 50 €
🛏🛏🛏🛏	>40 €	>50 €

20 rooms: *38.57/57.17 €*	Number of rooms: price for one person/ double room
⊏ *6.85 €*	Price of breakfast; when not given, it is included in the price of the room (i.e., for bed-and-breakfast)
120 sites: *12.18 €*	Number of camp sites and cost for 2 people with a car
12.18 € lunch- *16.74/38.05 €*	Restaurant: fixed-price menus served at lunch only – mini/maxi price fixed menu (lunch and dinner) or à la carte
rest. *16.74/38.05 €*	Lodging where meals are served mini/maxi price fixed menu or à la carte
meal 15.22 €	"Family style" meal
reserv	Reservation recommended
🚫	No credit cards accepted
🅿	Reserved parking for hotel patrons
🏊	Swimming Pool
▤	Air conditioning
🚭	Hotel: non-smoking rooms Restaurant: non-smoking section
♿	Rooms accessible to persons of reduced mobility

The prices correspond to the higher rates of the tourist season

NOTES